Ralph Waldo Emerson

Days of Encounter

Also by John McAleer

Unit Pride (with Billy Dickson)

Rex Stout: A Biography

Theodore Dreiser: A Biography

Theodore Dreiser's Notes on Life (with M. Tjader)

Artist and Citizen Thoreau

JOHN McALEER

Ralph Waldo Emerson
Days of Encounter

Little, Brown and Company
Boston   Toronto

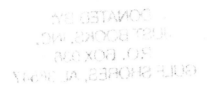

FIRST EDITION

Library of Congress Cataloging in Publication Data

McAleer, John J.
  Ralph Waldo Emerson : days of encounter.

  Bibliography : p. 713
  Includes index.
  1. Emerson, Ralph Waldo, 1803–1882 — Biography.
  2. Authors, American — 19th century — Biography.
  I. Title.
PS1631.M35   1984   814'.3   84-5777
  ISBN 0-316-55341-7

MV
Designed by Patricia Girvin Dunbar

Published simultaneously in Canada
by Little, Brown & Company (Canada) Limited

PRINTED IN THE UNITED STATES OF AMERICA

To the memory of
Mohandas Karamchand Gandhi,
who at Poona thirty-eight years ago
set me on my present course,
when he offered me a phrase from Emerson to live by :
''Speak the rude truth in all ways.''

Contents

List of Illustrations

Foreword

"EMERSON," said Stephen Whicher, "is a dangerous man to pigeon-hole." He was not exaggerating. Emerson has been called everything from a fraud and a lunatic to "*the* key figure in American literary history" and "the Buddha of the West." Those close to him said their age was "entertaining an angel unawares." But he continues to elude ready labeling.

Before he was eight Emerson lost his father. In the years immediately following he sometimes went supperless to bed and coatless in winter. By his own industry he paid most of his college fees. Tuberculosis afflicted him. Death took his exquisite young bride after only seventeen months of marriage. Doubts drove him from the ministry. His second wife was, during most of their forty-seven-year marriage, a neurasthenic invalid whose special needs called for infinite patience. His firstborn, his "morning star," died suddenly at five. To earn necessary income he lectured far and wide, braving sickness, floods, blizzards, near-Arctic cold, and, more often than not, a hostile press, to meet his commitments. He saw his home burn. He survived his seven brothers and sisters, most of whom died young, saw to the needs of a retarded brother, and escaped (though his foes said otherwise) a streak of madness that ran through his family. For a quarter of a century, during the very prime of his life, he withstood the scorn of the Harvard community till at last Harvard relented. Always, with a dignity that rivaled that of his forebear, Mary Perkins Bradbury, condemned to the gallows for witchcraft at Salem in 1692, he disdained to justify himself to his detractors.

Despite this constant downpour of vicissitudes, Oliver Wendell Holmes still thought it appropriate to say that Emerson had led a life devoid of incident, of nearly untroubled happiness. Surprisingly, Emerson would have agreed, believing that life compensated him adequately for the misfortunes that befell him.

Emerson has been charged with lacking a true vision of the reality of evil, with irresponsibly advocating self-reliant spontaneity at the expense of time-proven authority, with showing hostility to the reform of social and political abuses, with having no dramatic imagination, with failing to make allowances for the great passions. It is said that his thought lacked unity and coherence, that he made no contribution to the history of philosophy. These charges are valid only if Emerson was a man with a program, seeking acceptance as a systematic philosopher and reformer. He was not. His Concord was not Wittenberg but Winesburg. He saw men struggling individually to advance out of chaos. "I have taught one doctrine," he said, "namely, the infinitude of the private man." He sought to induce each man to follow his highest leading. No credulous optimist, he desired the progress of the species but did not see progress as the inevitable lot of mankind. Rejecting Darwin's mechanistic evolution, he believed that progress is dependent upon effort, its true basis being man's absorption, through the steady improvement of his moral character, into the Divine Source, the unifying force of the universe. Socialistic ideas of progress, taken up with such eagerness by men in the nineteenth century, were not for him. He cherished the poetry of individualism and sought to persuade men to be self-subsisting, thinking for themselves and acting from their own informed convictions. "Spoons and skimmers," he said, "you can make lie indistinguishably together — but vases and statues require each a pedestal for itself."

Nothing persuaded men more of the feasibility of Emerson's message than the example offered in his own conduct. John Jay Chapman concluded that his effectiveness came not from his philosophy but from his personal rectitude. Henry James the elder said: "There are scores of men of more advanced ideas than Mr. Emerson . . . but I know of none . . . whose nature exhibits half so clear and sheer a reconciliation of infinite and finite." James Russell Lowell pressed this conclusion to its outermost limits: "When one meets him [Emerson] the Fall of Adam seems a false report."

"I am," wrote Rutherford B. Hayes, after he left the White House, "far more content with whatever may come since I have read Emerson's calm, quiet, self-satisfied way of dealing with the deepest questions. . . . I will insist that the more we read of Emerson the better we like him; the wiser we will be; the better we will find ourselves, and by consequence (if anything is consequence), the happier." Britain's William Tyndall saw himself similarly indebted: "If anyone can be said to have given the impulse to my mind, it is Emerson; whatever I have done, the world owes to him." From Germany Herman Grimm wrote Emerson: "You write so that everyone reading your words must think that you had thought of him alone. The love which you have for all mankind is felt so strongly that one thinks it impossible that you should not have thought of single preferred persons, among whom the reader counts himself."

Emerson was not willing to believe that "a man comes into the world today with the field of truth monopolized and foreclosed." Men should be faithful to their own consciousness. That was the essence of his message. Even as institutionalized religion waned he saw man's need for faith continuing. At one of Bronson Alcott's "Conversations" in 1850, he observed: "We say our times have not religion, just as we have not sun when it rains; but the rain itself is a superlative effect of the sun. And so, while we depart from the forms once called religious, that very departure is the more religious." Man's need for faith, Emerson believed, could be met by persuading men of their responsibility to live in accordance with the universal or moral sentiment, seeking conformity with the Divine Source or Unity.

Emerson once wrote that Milton had "discharged the office of every great man, namely to raise the idea of Man in the minds of his contemporaries and of posterity." This office Emerson himself discharged with great success. His goal was not to win acceptance for his ideas but to convince mankind of its own inalienable worth. Expressing himself in terms that cooperated powerfully with his thought, Emerson uttered phrases that fixed themselves in the mind. His eloquence in affirming that in building character men could lift the state of mankind was the best of his gifts.

In "Works and Days" Emerson conjectures that in antiquity men called the Supreme Power of the Universe the Day — Dyaus, Deus, Zeus — because they saw the Day, as embodied in the sun, as "the Divine Power." He then asserts, "The days are ever divine . . . of the greatest capacity of anything that exists." He himself rejoiced in "the gifts" each new day brought and strove to endow with significance each day allotted to him. This life of Emerson is structured around those "days of encounter" which constituted for him spiritual, ethical, intellectual, ideological, emotional, or physical crises advancing the progress of the soul. We seek him in the intimacy of his domestic world, in the house, Bush, where, visitors said, it was "always morning," and strive to experience a sense of his extraordinary integrity, personal humanity, and goodness as it was communicated to those around him.

I have sought to accent Emerson's social background, the Boston milieu, the cloistered Renaissance occurring there in his lifetime, and his own role in initiating change and uplifting his age. This biography weighs the influence of Emerson's genetic and clerical heritage; his alienation from and later reconciliation with his father; his psychic vampirism; his struggle to bring his actions into harmony with his announced convictions; his impulse toward martyrdom.

Also explored here is the fluctuating state of Emerson's friendship with Thomas Carlyle; the perils of his intimacy with Margaret Fuller; his complex relations with Thoreau, Alcott, Hawthorne, Webster, and Charles Eliot. This biography undertakes to focus new attention on such neglected masterpieces as ''The Method of Nature''; to explore Emerson's stance on reform and his role as reformer; and to portray the man as seen and heard lecturing across America and shut up long hours alone in his study. Most especially, it explores Emerson's Grail quest for that complete universal man who, as Hawthorne hinted, was in Emerson himself most nearly embodied.

For fifty years after Emerson's death the light in his study at Bush was set glowing each night as though in anticipation of the master's return. For many the perceptions that illumine his pages attest that his rallying presence has never been withdrawn.

John McAleer
Mount Independence
Lexington, Massachusetts
30 January 1984

Chronology

1803	Born, 25 May, Boston, Mass.
1807	Death of brother John Clarke, 26 April.
1811	Death of father, William, 12 May.
1812–17	Attends Boston Latin School.
1817–21	Attends Harvard College.
1820	Begins keeping journals, January.
1821–25	Teaches "school for young ladies."
1822	Publishes first article, in *The Christian Disciple*.
1824	Writes "Good-bye, Proud World!"
1825	Admitted to middle class of Harvard Divinity School, 16 February.
1826	Approbated to preach as a Unitarian minister, 10 October.
	Preaches first sermon in Samuel Ripley's pulpit, Waltham, 15 October.
	Sails for South Carolina, seeking better health, 25 November.
1827	Sails from St. Augustine, 28 March. Meets Achille Murat.
1827–29	Serves as supply preacher.
1828	Mental breakdown of brother Edward.
1829	Ordained as junior pastor, Second Church of Boston, March.
	Marries Ellen Louisa Tucker, 30 September.

1831	Death of Ellen, 8 February.
1832	Resignation from Second Church accepted, 28 October.
	Sails for Europe, 25 December.
1833	Travels in Italy, France, England, and Scotland. Visits Landor, Coleridge, Carlyle, Wordsworth. Returns to America 9 October.
	Gives first lecture, "The Uses of Natural History," Masonic Temple, Boston, 5 November.
1834	Settles in Concord.
	Begins forty-year correspondence with Carlyle, 14 May.
	Death of brother Edward, in Puerto Rico, 1 October.
1835	Lecture series, "Biography," January–March.
	Meets Bronson Alcott.
	Purchases Coolidge house (later called Bush), Concord, July.
	Visits Harriet Martineau in Cambridge, 25 August.
	Delivers bicentennial address, Concord, 12 September.
	Marries Lydia (Lidian) Jackson, 14 September.
1835–36	Lecture series, "English Literature," November–January.
1836	Death of brother Charles, 9 May.
	Nature published, 9 September.
	Meets Margaret Fuller.
	Helps form Transcendental Club, September.
	First child, Waldo, born 30 October.
1836–37	Lecture series, "The Philosophy of History," December–March.
1837	Meets Henry David Thoreau.
	Writes "The Concord Hymn," July.
	Delivers "The American Scholar," Phi Beta Kappa Society oration, at Harvard, 31 August.
1838	Jones Very makes first visit to Concord, 4 April.
	Delivers "Divinity School Address," 15 July.
	Delivers "Literary Ethics," Dartmouth oration, 24 July.
1838–39	Lecture series, "Human Life," December–February.
1839	Daughter Ellen born 24 February.
1839–40	Lecture series, "The Present Age," December–February.
1840	Dedicates Follen Church, East Lexington, Mass., 15 January.

The Dial first published, July.

Declines to join Brook Farm community, 15 December.

1841   *Essays: First Series* published, 20 March.

Thoreau moves into Emerson home, 26 April, for two-year stay.

Delivers "The Method of Nature," Waterville (Colby) College, 11 August.

Death of step-grandfather, Ezra Ripley, 21 September.

Daughter Edith born 22 November.

1841–42   Lecture series, "The Times," December–January.

1842   Death of Waldo, 27 January.

Lectures in New York City; meets Henry James, March.

Assumes editorship of *The Dial*, July.

Visits Shaker community, Harvard, Mass., with Nathaniel Hawthorne, 27–28 September.

1843   Lecture series, "New England," Baltimore, New York City, Philadelphia, and Newark, January–March.

1844   Son Edward born 10 July.

Delivers address, "Emancipation in the British West Indies," 1 August.

Essays: Second Series, published 19 October.

1845–46   Lecture series, "Representative Men," December–January.

1846   *Poems* published, 25 December.

1847–48   Second trip to Europe, British lecture tour, 5 October–27 July.

Visits Carlyle, Martineau, Wordsworth.

1849   *Nature; Addresses and Lectures* published September.

Visited by Fredrika Bremer, 3 December.

1850   *Representative Men* published, 1 January.

Daniel Webster's "Seventh of March" address repudiated.

First western lecture tour, Cleveland and Cincinnati, May–June.

Death of Margaret Fuller Ossoli, 19 July.

1851   Speaks on the Fugitive Slave Law, 3 May.

1851–52   Lecture series, "The Conduct of Life," December–January.

1852   Edits *Memoirs of Margaret Fuller Ossoli.*

1852–53	Western lecture tour, December–January.
1853	Death of mother, Ruth Emerson, at eighty-five, at his home, 16 November.
1854	Lectures on poetry, Harvard Divinity School, 27 April.
1855	Engages in antislavery activities.
	Meets Walt Whitman in New York City, December.
1856	*English Traits* published, 6 August.
1857	Receives John Brown at Bush, March.
1859	Delivers Burns centenary address, 25 January.
	Death of brother Bulkeley, 27 May.
1860	*The Conduct of Life* published, 8 December.
1861	Mobbed at Tremont Temple by pro-slavery agitators, 24 January.
1862	Meets Abraham Lincoln, 1 February.
	Death of Thoreau, 6 May. Emerson gives funeral oration.
1863	Hails Emancipation Proclamation with "Boston Hymn," 1 January.
	Death of Mary Moody Emerson, 3 October.
1865	Daughter Edith marries William Hathaway Forbes.
1866	Given honorary LL.D., Harvard College.
1867	*May-Day and Other Pieces* published, 28 April.
	Elected Harvard Overseer.
1868	Death of brother William, 13 September.
1870	*Society and Solitude* published, March.
	Launches lecture series, "The Natural History of the Intellect," Harvard College, 26 April.
1871	Gives second Harvard lecture series.
	Visit to California; meets John Muir, April–May.
1872	Bush (Concord home) burns, 24 July.
1872–73	Travels to England, Europe, Egypt, 23 October–27 May.
	Farewell visit to Carlyle.
1874	*Parnassus* published.
	Son Edward marries Annie Keyes.
1875	Enlists editorial assistance of James Elliot Cabot.
	Discontinues regular journal entries.
	Letters and Social Aims published, December.

1876	Lectures at the University of Virginia, 28 June.
1879	Attends opening of the Concord School of Philosophy.
1881	Reads paper at Massachusetts Historical Society on the death of Carlyle, 10 February.
1882	Dies at Bush, 27 April. Buried at Sleepy Hollow.
1883–86	Emerson-Carlyle correspondence published.
1884	*Lectures and Biographical Sketches* published. *Miscellanies* published.
1892	Lidian Emerson dies at ninety, 13 November.
1893	*Natural History of the Intellect and Other Papers* published.
1909–10	*Journals,* edited by Edward Emerson and Waldo Emerson Forbes, published in ten volumes.

GENEALOGY

Peter Bulkeley = Jane Allen
(1583 – 1659)   (d. 1627)

Thomas Emerson = Elizabeth
(d. 1666)

Thomas Bradbury = Mary Perkins
(1611 – 1695)   (1617 – 1700)

Edward Bulkeley
(1614 – 1696)

Joseph (of Mendon) (1620 – 1680)
=
Elizabeth Bulkeley (1638 – 1693)

Caleb Moody = Judith Bradbury
(1637 – 1698)   (1638 – 1700)

Phineas Upham = Tamsen

Edward (of Newbury) = Rebecca Waldo
(1670 – 1743)   (1662 – 1752)

Samuel Moody (1676 – 1747)
=
Hannah Sewall (1677 – 1728)

Phineas Upham
=
Hannah Waite (d. 1789)

Joseph (of Malden) = Mary Moody
(1700 – 1767)   (b. 1702)

Daniel Bliss = Phebe Walker
(1714 – 1764)   (1713 – 1797)

Robert Haskins = Sarah Cook
(d. 1730)

William = Phebe Bliss
(1743 – 1776)   (1741 – 1825)

John Haskins = Hannah Upham
(1729 – 1814)   (1734 – 1819)

William (1769 – 1811)
=
Ruth Haskins (1768 – 1853)

Ralph Waldo = 1) Ellen Tucker (1811 – 1831)
(1803 – 1882)   2) Lydia Jackson (1802 – 1892)

Edward (1844 – 1930)
=
Annie Keyes (1847 – 1928)

Edith (1841 – 1929)
=
William Hathaway Forbes (1840 – 1897)

Waldo
(1836 – 1842)

Ellen
(1839 – 1909)

Ralph Waldo Emerson
Days of Encounter

I much prefer the company of ploughboys and tin-peddlers to the silken and perfumed amity which celebrates the days of encounter by a frivolous display, by rides in a curricle and dinners at the best taverns.

— Ralph Waldo Emerson, "Friendship"

Heaven walks among us ordinarily muffled in such triple or tenfold disguises that the wisest are received and no one suspects the days to be gods.

— Ralph Waldo Emerson to Margaret Fuller,
2 October 1840

There are no days in life so memorable as those
which vibrated to some stroke of the imagination.

1. A Universal Man

*A*s an unflinching advocate of self-reliance, Ralph Waldo
Emerson would have found it compromising to tell aspiring writers
how to write, even if he thought the effort worthwhile, which he did
not. A writer, he believed, had to make his own way. Thus, at fifty,
when a back-country lawyer in Michigan drew him aside to exclaim,
"Mr. Emerson, I see that you never learned to write from any book,"
he was as pleased as a struggling unknown would be. Despite his coy-
ness beginners often appealed to Emerson for guidelines. "There is no
way to learn to write except by writing," he told Charles Woodbury
at Williams College in 1865. "Whether one may dare leave all other
things behind, & write," he told Anna Katharine Green in 1868, was
not a decision that could be arrived at "by cold election." The writer
is driven to write: "If our thoughts come in such wealth & with such
heat that we have no choice, but must watch & obey & live for them,
the question is answered for us" — an answer as nearly transcendental as Emerson ever cared to get in such encounters. Fortified with
such insights, Anna Green a decade thence groaned and brought forth
a detective novel.[1]

Since Emerson saw his own approach to writing as a product of his
particular needs and aims, he never bothered to describe it to others.
Yet, just as his study and its contents are preserved, a mosaic of observations by himself and others preserves the man as he was occupied
in his creative hours and discloses the circumstances that made those
hours fruitful.

Emerson arose early and, from the period of the 1840's, when the gospel of cold-water bathing was proclaimed, took a cold bath in his bedchamber, in a big, hatlike, English tin tub. Of this practice he commented: "I begin to believe that the composition of water must be one part Hydrogen and three parts Conceit. Nothing so self-righteous as the morning bath . . . the pail of pleasure and pain, — Oh, if an enemy had done this!" He next got a fire going in the fireplace in his study, and then ate a simple breakfast — always, at least, a slice of apple pie made with a butter crust, and two cups of coffee. He then got to work, often as the hands of the clock marked the hour of six. For a short while in the 1840's — that decade of reform — he decided to try to get by on bread and water as his first meal of the day. He quit that practice when he found that it both preempted his thoughts and diminished his stamina.[2]

During his first years of residence in Concord Emerson sometimes took a woodland walk after breakfast. Later on, walking became the recreation of his afternoons. Such walks served a twofold purpose for him, one spiritual, the other physical. Nature spoke to him then most freely. And he believed the toughness of the shoe leather he wore out walking passed into the fiber of his being.

Sometimes, when there was a crux to resolve or an insight to be mastered, Emerson broke his morning work session with a stroll in the garden or, once he had established it, in his orchard. In autumn and in winter he kept pears ripening on the back of his bookshelves and, on occasion, might interrupt his work to reward himself with one. The selection was done with care since he believed there were only ten minutes in the life of a pear when it was perfect to eat.

Emerson's morning hours were sacred to him. Even when he had houseguests, customarily he did not emerge from his study till one o'clock, for the day's principal meal. Guests, Emma Lazarus being one, sometimes were dismayed to find that he would not thrust aside his regimen to pass the time with them. He held that we "must not let slip the gift of each new day." He wished he could work fourteen hours a day but knew he lacked the constitution for it. Often he worked two or three hours in the evening, but never past ten o'clock.[3]

Emerson had no desk in his study. A drum table in the middle of the room served some of the purposes of a desk, but when he wrote he sat in a rocking chair, writing on half sheets of paper that rested on a portfolio balanced on his knees. As he completed a page, he let it flutter to the floor. Sometimes he was found sitting amid a litter of pages, as was true when he wrote the poem "Voluntaries" before breakfast one morning while a guest of James T. and Annie Fields. He would arrange his pages while kneeling on the carpet. Alcott once discovered him lying on the floor, shifting his pages about, trying to arrive at some good order.

Writing for Emerson was not simply a joyous process of intercepting inspirations as they swarmed past. His son Edward wrote of him: "He said that if the scholar feels reproach when he reads the tale of the extreme toil and endurance of the Arctic explorer, he is not working as he should." Like most writers, Emerson had to contend with arid periods. Thus, on 14 December 1849 he acknowledged, "If I cease to task myself, I have no thoughts." Once, when the Harvard theologian Convers Francis conjectured in Emerson's presence that his lectures were the product of endless labors, he said, "Oh, no, I never write until I am driven to it by the time each week." But the preparations preliminary to writing went on all the time. Perversely, when a lecture was due, Emerson's muse set him to work on a poem. When a poem was needed, his mind ran to prose. "Every writer is a skater," he said, "and must go partly where he would, and partly where the skates carry him."[4]

Once Emerson gave a clue to the way his mind functioned when he spoke of his faculty for augmenting or supplementing stored facts over a period of time, apparently without conscious effort: "We read the same books a year, two years, ten years ago; we read the same books this month. Well that fact which struck us both, then, with equal force, I still contemplate. He has lost it. He & the world have only *this* fact. I have that *and* this."[5]

Much, Emerson believed, was accomplished by patience. When Margaret Fuller attested that " 'Tis best knocking in the nail overnight and clinching it next morning," Emerson commented, "I should give extension to this rule and say — Yes, drive the nail this week and clinch it the next, and drive it this year and clinch it the next." Considering the same argument from another vantage point, he said, "I can breathe at any time, but I can only whistle when the right pucker comes."[6]

Oliver Wendell Holmes said that Emerson "picked his way through his vocabulary . . . as a well-dressed woman crosses the muddy pavement to reach the opposite sidewalk." To John Albee it seemed that Emerson went "like a bird from one tree top to another." His essays, it was alleged, were begun at midpoint and then expanded in both directions without their author's knowing when he got either to the beginning or the end. Since it was his practice to cull from his journals striking thoughts that had come to him while walking, reading, or talking with others and then to blend these thoughts into a lecture, and later an essay, under a commodious "ragbag of a title," for example, "Human Culture," Emerson left himself vulnerable to the charge that he had produced "a beautiful square bag of duck shot held together by canvas," or "a chaos filled with shooting-stars," to quote the opinions of his friends Carlyle and Lowell. What his foes said need only be imagined.[7]

The condition of the end product was rendered still more esoteric by Emerson's practice of writing some of his lectures while on tour, of reducing the delivery time of a long lecture by skipping pages, of transferring pages from one lecture to another and pasting them up, and of excising from the final product every detail that might seem to be there merely to enliven or amuse, so that only "the most pregnant sentences and paragraphs" were retained. Remarking Emerson's "great compression and conciseness," Albee concluded that "Emerson mingles no water in his wine." In the essays he had undertaken "to distil the essence of libraries into a page; pages into a sentence; the sentence into a phrase; the phrase to a word." To "an impatience of the commonplace," Albee attributed Emerson's lack of cohesion, lack of logical sequence, and consequent obscurities.[8]

On occasion Emerson conceded that he was incapable of imposing a smooth progression on his material. Nowhere does he suggest that he had undertaken to replicate the experience of the sudden epiphanies that had come to him — brilliant moments of perception springing out of darkness — although, in fact, that is the impression his essays give. To Woodbury, Emerson did disclose that his method was not governed by caprice. "The most interesting writing," he said, "is that which does not quite satisfy the reader. Try and leave a little thinking for him; that will be better for both. . . . A little guessing does him no harm, so I would assist him with no connections."[9] Actually, he thought of diffuseness as the prevailing fault of the writing done in his day. What writers needed to cultivate, he believed, was "the science of omitting." Not only did he believe in omitting linking phrases, he deplored the use of a single superfluous word. He wanted his readers to realize that not a line he had written could be sacrificed, because he had left out every word he could spare.

Although Emerson was apt to be still working on his forthcoming lectures even as he was delivering the opening lectures of a new series, his work was not hastily prepared. When he was displeased with a lecture that he had taken twenty-one hours to write, he resolved to spend sixty hours on the next one. He took no shortcuts. He surrendered manuscripts to publishers only with great reluctance. Annie Fields said, when Emerson came to dinner one night in April 1865, "he brought what he then called some verses on spring to read to us, but when the reading was ended, he said they were far 'too fragmentary to satisfy him,' and quietly folded them up and carried them away again." Since Emerson kept all his rough drafts, the travail that attended his acts of creation is there for posterity to consider. Few writers have exercised greater care to do justice to their ideas. "Negligence in the author," he said, "is inexcusable. I know & will know no such thing as haste in composition."[10]

Emerson's study was plain and practical. A wind harp was his sole indulgence. Occasionally, when the pressure built, as he hurried to complete a lecture against a deadline, he would retreat with his notes to an inn or to the American House in Boston's North End, terminal point for the Concord stage. But he liked solitude in small infusions and soon returned to his study, alleging that he could write from no inkstand but his own.

Each night, until the final few days of his life, Emerson insisted on setting his study aright for the morning, fireplace cleared, every book and manuscript tucked away. An aura of order through the hours of darkness hung like a benediction over the quiet chamber to which, with the coming of a new day, he would return to leapfrog logic and, with incisive words, challenge anew mankind's complacency.

The stimulus Emerson sought in the world around him and in the people around him, as well as in books, is a serious aspect of his art. In an 1853 journal entry he suggested that when a civilization produces a representative or universal man "who knots up into himself the genius or idea of his nation" (he proposed Plato, Caesar, and Dante), that civilization has realized itself and thereafter withers away. From this fate he exempted only a Saxon society: "Saxondom is tough & many-headed, & does not so readily admit of absorption & being sucked and vampyrized by a Representative as fluider races." Whimsically, he reflected: "We ought rather to be thankful that our hero or poet does not hasten to be born in America, but still allows us others to live a little, & warm ourselves at the fire of the sun, for, when he comes, we others must pack our petty trunks, & begone." Although verbally Emerson may have put himself outside this company of vampires, perennial fascination with the subject suggests he was not sure he was not to be counted among them.[11]

Emerson concluded that other writers, in assimilating the ideas of those around them, had augmented their greatness. In his essay on Napoleon he recalled, "Mirabeau, with his overpowering personality, felt that these things which his presence inspired were as much his own as if he had said them, and that his adoption of them gave them weight." Emerson found it pertinent, moreover, that Goethe, cognizant of Mirabeau's adeptness at annexation, saw himself endowed with the same faculty. He quoted Goethe's words in corroboration: " 'My work is that of an aggregation of things taken from the whole of Nature, — it bears the name of Goethe. Such was Mirabeau: he had the genius . . . of observation; the genius of appropriation.' "[12]

Holmes said: "[Emerson] reading as he did . . . must have unconsciously appropriated a great number of thoughts from others." Elisabeth Luther Cary takes such debts into account in other terms: "It is not difficult to find in the first free flowing of Carlyle's genius certain general ideas, many of them directly imported from Germany, which are reproduced with the same frank appropriation in Emerson's early work, to be firmly knit into the fabric of his later thought." John Burroughs asserted: "Emerson . . . took what suited him, what he had use for at home. He was a provident bee exploring all fields for honey, and he could distill the nectar from the most unlikely sources." Emerson thought of his appropriations as what E. R. Marks characterizes as "creative assimilation." In his journal in 1832 he wrote: "What can we see, read, acquire, but ourselves?"[13]

Emerson drew sustenance from those he befriended — the young especially — as well as from the printed page. "The most attractive class of people," he said, "are . . . men of genius but not yet accredited; one gets the cheer of their light without paying too great a tax." Creative assimilation permitted Emerson to look upon those who stimulated his mind as a personal resource, quite as a merchant claims the profits of ships he has dispatched on trading missions.[14]

Discussing resources, Emerson, in 1836, used a curious analogy: "The world is the gymnasium on which the youth of the Universe are trained to strength & skill. When they have become masters of strength & skill, who cares what becomes of the masts & bars & ropes on which they strained their muscles."[15] He sometimes gave the impression that he thought friends were similarly expendable. Burroughs concluded: "When they had had their say, he was done with them. . . . The pearl in the oyster is what is wanted, and not the oyster." Burroughs insisted further: "Of the youth who is ripe for him he takes almost an unfair advantage."[16] The same thought troubled Woodbury. "No one meeting Emerson was ever the same again," he said. He explained:

> His natural force was so resistless and so imperceptible that it
> commanded men before they were aware. . . . Concord contained
> during Emerson's solstitial years a great light-house, shining
> far and wide, and showing many ships their goal, but covered with
> the shreds of wrecked barks and birds of all imaginable shapes —
> and some unimaginable — which had been attracted by its clear,
> cold, solitary flame. How many, just saved from the fire, but the
> wax of their wings forever melted, went hopping about the
> country with a bit of Emerson in their mouths, disseminating
> ordinariness and indistinctness.[17]

Some saw Thoreau among these wrecked barks and said that Emerson had ruined him. Thoreau's subsequent renown makes that an awkward thesis.

Yet the debts Emerson piled up to Carlyle, Coleridge, Thomas Clarkson, Sampson Reed, Samuel D. Robbins, and others, in the decade of the thirties, were substantial. Although Bronson Alcott, his vanity stroked by an apparent allusion to himself as the "Orphic poet," had, on a first reading of *Nature,* expressed only admiration for what Emerson had achieved, on reflection he thought he discovered there "several interesting similarities and even identities of thought" to materials of his own that he had lent to Emerson while he was writing *Nature* — two volumes of his journals and the manuscripts he entitled *Conversations* and *Psyche.*[18] Emerson acknowledged the parallels, but without dismay. He identified them as thoughts that he himself had independently entertained and had rejoiced to find had occurred to Alcott also. Of this phenomenon he said in "Self-Reliance":

> In every work of genius we recognize our own rejected
> thoughts; they come back to us with a certain alienated majesty.
> Great works of art have no more affecting lesson for us than this.
> They teach us to *abide by our spontaneous expression* with good
> humored inflexibility then most when the whole cry of voices is on
> the other side. Else tomorrow a stranger will say with masterly
> good sense precisely what we have thought and felt all the time,
> and we shall be forced to take with shame our own opinion from
> another.[19]

Pleased to escape that pitfall, Emerson was glad to take, without shame, those thoughts Alcott "echoed." Alcott's pleasure was less marked. Thereafter he suspected that Emerson appropriated other things he said. Judge Ebenezer Rockwood Hoar thought otherwise: "What is the difference between Emerson and Alcott? One is a seer, the other a seer-sucker."[20]

Franklin Sanborn saw both Thoreau and Ellery Channing as other resource figures in Emerson's cabinet of mortals. "Emerson's journal," he said, ". . . often owed some of its best suggestions, but never its best periods, to Channing, or to Thoreau's perceptive and creative imagination." Remarking on specific resemblances between Channing's "Spider" and Emerson's "Humble-bee," and between "Hymn of the Earth" and "Brahma," Frederick McGill says, "If in these cases Emerson ever recognized any debt, the fact is unrecorded."[21]

Like Nathaniel Hawthorne, who concluded that he required nothing of Emerson's philosophy, Margaret Fuller spun clear of Emerson's gravitational pull, but only after brushing dangerously close. To Emerson himself she described her peril in these terms: "I get, after a while, even INTOXICATED with your mind, and do not live enough in myself."[22]

In "Character" Emerson sought to dignify with a plausible explanation the strange, absorbing effect he had on others:

Higher natures overpower lower ones by affecting them with a
certain sleep. The faculties are locked up, and offer no resistance.
Perhaps that is the universal law. . . . How often has the influence
of a true master realized all the tales of magic! A river of
command seemed to run down from his eyes into all those who
beheld him, a torrent of strong sad light, like an Ohio or Danube,
which pervaded them with his thoughts and colored all events with
the hue of his mind.[23]

For all his earnestness here, the image Emerson conveys is of a veritable Saturn devouring his children. Yet, though the spectacle may be
overwhelming, it serves to remind us that Emerson saw life's successive encounters as stages on a spiritual journey marking the progress
of the soul. "Can I doubt," he asked, "that the facts & events & persons & personal relations that now appertain to me will perish . . .
utterly when the soul shall have exhausted their meaning & use?"[24]
   The wagon that Emerson hitched to a star accommodated but a single passenger. The isolation, the frigid, intergalactic remoteness of this
audacious journey is caught in an 1851 journal entry: "In some sort,
the end of life, is, that the man should take up the universe into himself, or, out of that quarry leave nothing unrepresented, and he is to
create himself."[25] Emerson once dreamed that the world was an apple
and that he, at the behest of an angel, devoured it. That act, however
awesome, was but a prelude to the ultimate act of vampirism — the
ingestion of the universe. Paradoxically, however, this action signifies
not a supreme act of selfishness but the ultimate renunciation of self,
the soul's absorption into the divine force that pervades the universe.
Like an unbroken line of saints and sages stretching backward through
time into the dim recesses of history, Emerson believed that the pursuit of this celestial love was the transcending goal before which all
other goals dwindled to nothingness. There was, he perceived, no greater
expression of love for his fellowman than to manifest in his own conduct of life an unwavering commitment to the pursuit of this ideal of
perfection. Only in the light of that fact can Emerson's steadfast commitment to his labors and persistent search for universal verities in
the beliefs and behavior of others, at the expense of personal attach-
ments, be fully comprehended.

> I must . . . postpone my visit . . . to a day when
> there shall be a better consent of stars.

2. Birth

*T*HE year was 1803 and in America the times were turning upward. The Supreme Court, showing the strength of democracy, had for the first time declared an act of Congress unconstitutional. Ohio had become the seventeenth state. Lewis and Clark were about to set out on their epoch-awakening overland expedition to the Pacific. In Massachusetts, the Middlesex Canal, which Thoreau would keep forever navigable in memory, had opened to traffic after a decade under construction. Boston's merchandise and the products of the Merrimack valley could now be exchanged with ease. In Boston, William Ellery Channing was called as pastor to the Federal Street Church. He would melt the glacier of Puritanism and increase the currents of grace. In the heavens, all the planets were aligned on one side of the sun — a syzygy — an astronomical event of such rarity it would not occur again for one hundred and seventy-nine years. To the credulous, anyone born under it was destined for greatness.

It was May. Nature was blooming. In London, on 25 May General William Earle Bulwer celebrated the birth of a third son, Edward, the future statesman and chronicler of the last days of Pompeii, who, undismayed by that city's fate, ultimately would tell Nathaniel Hawthorne that he wished someone would invent a new sin so that he could commit it.

In Boston, the Reverend William Emerson, pastor of Boston's First Church, on the night of 25 May set down in his diary a record of his round of activities. It was Election Day. He had heard Mr. Puffer's Election Sermon with approval. He had gone to a meeting of the Anthology Club at the home of Phineas Adams. And earlier in the day, as he was having dinner at Governor Caleb Strong's, Ruth Haskins Emerson, his wife, had given him a third son. This news had not disposed him to alter his agenda. "Mrs. E. well," he noted.[1] Evidently that sufficed. After all, Ruth had fifteen brothers and sisters. The new arrival was her fourth child. Surely there would be others. There were. Such oft-occurring matters need not be disruptive.

While William Emerson prized decisiveness, he knew he lacked true mastery of it. Yet he was able at once to enter in his diary his new son's name — Ralph Waldo, a name designed to gratify both his wife's family and his own. Ruth's brother Ralph, off now in the Orient, was a supercargo on one of the ships of a would-be merchant prince, George Williams Lyman, grandnephew of Colonel Timothy Pickering, lately secretary of state in President Adams's cabinet. These were stirring times for Boston's merchant princes, and every aspiring young man leaped at the chance to have a part in what was happening. Ralph, the youngest of John and Hannah Haskins's sixteen children, was born when his sister Ruth was eleven. On her had devolved much of the responsibility of raising him. When she married, he was seventeen. The China trade was prospering in 1803, and youthful supercargoes often came quickly into possession of great wealth. Many, however, never survived the hazards of the life. Their families had always to be prepared to learn that shipwreck or disease had claimed their loved ones. Neither the hope of a rich godfather nor the desire to keep Ralph's name alive in family annals need have been a factor, however, in William Emerson's decision to bestow Ralph's name on his new son. The bond of affection that existed between Ruth and her brother afforded reason enough. As surrogate father to the fatherless Emerson boys while they attended college, Ralph Haskins, in coming years, would confirm the strength of those ties.[2]

As for the name Waldo — Ralph Waldo Emerson's great-great-grandmother, wife of Deacon Edward Emerson, had been Rebecca Waldo. Edward and Rebecca both were from hardy stock. He outlived three wives; she outlived three husbands. Mary Moody Emerson, William's fire-spitting sister, who was keen on ancestry, thought Waldo a beautiful sound, a fact that heightens the probability that Emerson's tone deafness was genetic in origin. The legend that the Waldos were descended from Peter Waldo, founder of the Waldensians, is the far-fetched surmise of those who relish the notion that Emerson's role as dissenter also was genetic.

Milk Street, Carver Street, Chauncy Place at Summer — Franklin's birthplace, Poe's birthplace, Emerson's birthplace — a kite sent aloft at Chauncy Place could hover over Milk Street. From there to Carver Street a boy could roll, in ten minutes, a cask of Amontillado. Both

Franklin and Poe were born in near-hovels. Emerson's parsonage birthplace was a substantial manse. The street that ran past displayed rows of stately Lombardy poplars destined to topple like tenpins in the hurricane of 1815, but now sedate and composed. Not far from the tidewater and with a clear view of Bulfinch's copper-covered State House dome, the yellow clapboard manse stood, gable end to the street, in a neighborhood of bountiful gardens, expansive orchards, such as that of Judge William Prescott, just adjacent, celebrated for its St. Michael pears, and open pasture from which carried the sound of cow bells.[3] Its three acres held an orchard and an ample garden. "Situate at the *southerly* end of the Town of Boston" say the old records, but, actually, now in the heart of downtown Boston.[4] Emerson's memories of it would be Edenic. In later years, in Concord, it was an environment he would try to recreate.

In his journal on 26 May 1872, Emerson wrote: "Yesterday, my sixty-ninth birthday, I found myself on my rounds of errands in Summer Street, and, though close on the spot where I was born, was looking into a street with some bewilderment, and read on the sign 'Kingston Street' with surprise; finding in the granite blocks no hint of Nath. Goddard's pasture and long wooden fence, and so of my nearness to my native corner of Chauncy Place."[5] As alien as this scene was to him then, in a few months it would be more alien still, when a great fire laid waste the Boston heartland, taking with it every vestige that had remained of the environment in which Emerson had passed his childhood.

The history of the site of Emerson's birth discloses both ebbing and flowing phases of Boston's past. In the seventeenth century it had embodied the millenarian hopes of early settlers, Richard and Ann Hollingshead, come to the New World to prosper in the ways of the Lord. In 1680, the chronicles of the Hollingsheads told of a downward turn in fortunes. Aged paupers, they conveyed their property to the deacons of the First Church on condition that their needs be met for the remainder of their lives.[6] There the manse was built in 1710 and occupied by the pastor, Benjamin Wadsworth, until he was chosen president of Harvard in 1725 and moved to his family homestead in Cambridge.[7]

Wadsworth's successor at the First Church was Charles Chauncy, a progressive but firm man who, when he preached at the poorhouse, took for his text the words of Saint Paul, "If any will not work, neither shall he eat." He died at the Chauncy Place manse, as did his successor, the pleasant-spirited John Clarke. John Clarke caught nicely the spirit of the newer age in which Calvinism was giving way to Unitarianism in Boston, and Federalism was receding before the spirit of democracy.[8] Clarke's successor, William Emerson, Emerson's father, was writing a history of the First Church when overtaken by his final illness. He liked both Chauncy and Clarke well enough, on the basis of what he knew of them, to name a son after each.

The Chauncy Place manse was not William Emerson's last parsonage. It was pulled down in 1807. In November 1808 he took possession of a new parsonage, built facing the governor's mansion, a fact enhancing William's social prestige. On the site of the razed manse rose a new First Church, the fourth in the parish's history. That church stood sixty years before it, in turn, was torn down, in 1868, when the city of Boston bought the "Hollingshead lot" (which the deacons originally thought was not worth the price of drawing and recording the deed), for $58,000.[9] The sum would have surprised Richard and Ann Hollingshead. Greater still would have been their surprise had they known that their names would be kept in remembrance because their land became the site of the birthplace of the man who did most to overwhelm confidence in the beliefs that had brought them to America.

William Emerson, a dabbler in new things and new thought, had once deliberated cutting all denominational ties. It was left to his son Ralph Waldo, carrying within him submerged images of an idyllic world of orchards and gardens, to accomplish in America what Wordsworth had undertaken to do in England, to release religion from the confines of the churches and set it free in the world of Nature.

The genius of the day does not incline to a deed,
but to a beholding.

3. Parental Ties

*A*s one of the sixteen children born to her parents, Ruth Haskins saw a lot of regimentation in the course of her upbringing. Both
parents were devout and put a high value on character formation. Since
Ruth shared with her eight sisters a reputation for "eminent loveli-
ness of disposition," John and Hannah Upham Haskins may have been
on the right track.[1] Predictably, when Ruth, as the wife of William
Emerson, became a mother herself, she gave much thought to the formation of the character of her own children. In this endeavor she was
supported fully by her husband, yet, while Ruth was firm, severity
better describes William's approach to discipline. The difference is
accounted for by their own differences in makeup. Ruth had only to
follow her own natural inclinations to be a model of virtue. William
had to work at it. In fact, his diary shows that he often reproached
himself for indulging what he supposed was his frivolous side.[2] Since
William's known forebears were people "who wasted not their time in
idle play," he seems to have reproached himself for not measuring up
to their standards and to have resolved to spare his sons those defects
of character he had had to contend with in himself. William may even
have had a sense of urgency about this commitment. His health was
poor and indications were that the allotment of years given him to
watch over the welfare of his children would be sparse. Thus, through
their early years, the sons of William and Ruth saw their parents, first
and foremost, as agents of surveillance engaged in the dual tasks of
instilling in them an undeviating sense of right and wrong and disci-
plining them for study. Possibly William thought his own restive in-

15

clinations would never have asserted themselves if he himself had not, in his formative years, lacked a father's guidance. If so, occasional glimpses into the character of Ralph Waldo must have mystified him. Unlike his brothers, Ralph Waldo seemed inattentive to his studies and receptive to distractions.

Although his parents did not realize it, Emerson was receptive also to affection yet incapable of recognizing love in their responsible concern for his moral and mental well-being. Accordingly, when an incident occurred that made him conscious of his mother's affection for him, the realization both astonished and delighted him.

On some holiday, perhaps a day of parades and other festivities, he went off with his brother William and was gone till bedtime. He never imagined that his mother — that serene and earnest woman who each morning retired to her bedchamber for an hour of silent meditation and prayer — seemingly untouched by anxiety, would be anxious for his welfare. He was amazed, therefore, when, on their return, she cried out, with genuine feeling and thanksgiving, "My sons, I have been in an agony for you!" Emerson never gave a thought, even then, to the wretchedness he had caused her. What mattered, to the exclusion of all else, was that she cared for them, not as little vessels into which instruction could be poured, but as her sons. "I went to bed," he related years later, "in bliss at the interest she showed."[3] In such a household, obviously, intense affection was not usually shown or even meant to be inferred. Thus when the defenses were momentarily lowered and the true circumstances made evident, excitement was great. Since this happened rarely, Emerson learned more about guarding his emotions than about giving expression to them, a common deficiency in the Boston-bred.

As an adult, looking back on his boyhood, Emerson recalled it as "unpleasing."[4] Some readers believe that Emerson skipped boyhood altogether.[5] That view unfortunately was reinforced by the recollection of his lifelong friend William Furness, dredged up when Furness was in his ninth decade, that the only time he could ever recall Emerson playing as a normal child was when, in early boyhood, he romped on the floor with their mutual friend, Sam Bradford, and himself.

William Emerson, through deliberate effort, was exact in his manners and sternly methodical.[6] It was his strictness that Emerson would chiefly remember — most especially Father's forcing him into the salt sea to hasten the cure of a summer eczema. When Ralph was still a week short of his third birthday, William complained to a friend that "Ralph does not read very well yet."[7] In April 1810, when Ralph was six, William, absent from home, wrote to his wife enumerating his hopes for Ralph, whose failings seemed to be multiplying with his years. He looked for assurance that Ralph "regards his words, does not eat his dinner too fast, and is gradually resigning his impetuosity to younger boys."[8]

Like his father before him, William Emerson had a worldly bent that did not seem compatible with a vocation to the ministry. He had taught school for a few years after graduating from Harvard and became a minister chiefly to gratify his mother, after her hopes for him had been emphatically made known to him by his stepfather, Ezra Ripley, in loudly voiced prayers of petition. As a bachelor clergyman in the village of Harvard, a little way across the hills from his hometown of Concord, he had divided his time between devotional exercises and social recreation, rather preferring his bass viol, games of checkers, Gothic novels, and companionable glass of wine to the perusal of theological tomes and the preparation of sermons. He made frequent resolutions to put himself under iron discipline but soon found himself back playing checkers, singing, or watching with pleasure the young people dance at the local tavern. He also had an eye for fashion and took care, in his fine knee breeches and black silk stockings, that his legs were shown to good advantage. Fair-haired and blue-eyed, he was a handsome man and aware of that fact. To some, William Emerson, with his assertive carriage, elegant apparel, and gold-headed cane, was a Georgian fop. Maybe at times he thought so himself. Certainly in his diary he reproached himself often enough for lack of seriousness. But his gifts really were not those of the grave moralist. The parish duties he enjoyed most were the social visits, the hymn-singing, and the opportunities for eloquence that the pulpit afforded.

William's interest in Christianity was in its central ethics and not its personal or historical side. He had readily slipped away from the mild Calvinism that had been his heritage into the Unitarianism fast supplanting it in Boston and its environs. He daydreamed about starting a new church in Washington, D.C., where John Adams now was installed as president, which would require no statement of belief from anyone before admitting him to communion. At most this scheme was a passing fancy. In his *History of the First Church*, William, without qualms, upheld the orthodoxy of his eleven predecessors.

William's marriage to a wife who had been an Anglican, his duties as parent of a rapidly growing family (during the last fourteen years of his life he became the father of six sons and two daughters), his responsibilities as pastor of the First Church in Boston, which, in 1799, literally bought him away from his Harvard parish, were seen by him less as opportunities to deepen his spiritual perceptions than as prerequisites needed for establishing an environment hospitable to heightening both his own cultural awareness and that of the community he served. Boston, in 1790, had a population of 18,000. Over the next decade the number increased by 6,000, and between 1800 and 1810, the

decade that encompassed the full career of William Emerson as one of
the first men of Boston, it grew by another 9,000, to reach 33,000.
Thereafter the pace quickened. In every quarter Boston had come alive.

William Emerson was ideally situated to put his talents at the service of the burgeoning town. At forty-two he would be dead, but between thirty-two and forty-two he fulfilled himself more than many
men do in a lifetime of twice that duration. He was the pastor of
Boston's oldest and most prestigious church. All doors were open to
him, for then, as Ralph Waldo's Harvard classmate Josiah Quincy
later would note, ''On the topmost round of the social ladder stood the
clergy.''[9] And William was what his parish most needed — someone
in harmony with the spirit of the age and the needs of the emerging
nation. He replaced the old church edifice. He founded the Boston
Philosophical Society. He helped found the *Christian Monitor.* He helped
organize the Massachusetts Historical Society. He helped found the
Anthology Club, the principal activity of which was publication of a
journal, the *Monthly Anthology.* Members of the club met weekly for
dinner to discuss, over turtle soup, widgeon and teal, or woodcock, the
state of letters in particular, and afterward, over port and walnuts,
the state of letters in general. William served as editor of the journal,
the precursor of the influential *North American Review,* which his famous son would hold in contempt and be held in contempt by. He was
as well a founder of the library of the Anthology Club which, in 1807,
assimilated the Library of the Boston Association of Ministers to become the Athenaeum, the only library of substance in Boston accessible then, in any way, to the public and, ultimately, the world's finest
gentleman's library. Of this new library, which engaged also in the
promotion of literary and scientific studies, he was appointed one of
the five trustees.

There was more. William wrote for the *Palladium* and the *Polyanthos,* and other local publications, lectured to the Philosophical Society, the Society for the Promotion of the Study of Science, the Humane Society, the Agricultural Society, and the Singing Society. In
1808 he published *A Selection of Psalms and Hymns,* considered precocious for its time. He worked also on his history of his parish, published after his death. And to fill such idle hours as were left to him,
he was an Overseer of Harvard College, a member of the Boston School
Committee, chaplain of the state Senate, and chaplain of the Ancient
and Honorable Artillery Company.

William's greatest extravagance was neither his wardrobe nor his
larder, though it would be normal to think so because his tricornered
hat, gold-headed cane, elegant breeches, and the waiter in his sideboard, well provided with decanters of fine wines and spirits for such
regular callers as the governor and the members of the General Court,

must have devoured the chief part of his income. But the fact is, twenty-five percent of his income went for books. Unfortunately, only a stray volume or two of this library ever came into Emerson's hands in maturity, for it was one of the first things William's widow had to sell after his death, it being the sole legacy he left her, aside from six surviving children the worth of whom was not to be calculated in dollars.

When William Emerson complained that Ralph, approaching three, could not read well, he spoke perhaps in the character of a value-conscious Yankee. At two Ralph was already enrolled in a private school. Indeed, a letter written by Ruth to her sister, on 9 March 1806, reported: "William and Ralph now go again to Mrs. Whitwell's School," a statement that means they had been enrolled there previously, as well.[10] Mrs. Whitwell's was a Dame School and it was common then for Bostonians to begin their study of letters at such schools before they were three. Mrs. Whitwell was succeeded by Miss Nancy Dickson, who may have had more success with Emerson than her predecessor had. At least, in maturity, Emerson could remember spelling out at Miss Dickson's, on the red Mother Goose handkerchief of his schoolmate William Furness, the words printed there — "The House that Jack Built." Thus he collected his first "lustre" (his term for striking passages that caught his eye), and, quite characteristically, gathered it at random and not from a prescribed primer. Here, assuredly, was an interlude of happiness in Emerson's boyhood that he never forgot. In middle life Emerson said of Furness, then a Unitarian minister in Philadelphia: "He is the happiest companion. . . . The tie of school-fellow and playmate from the nursery onward is the true clanship and key that cannot be given to another."[11]

Ruth Emerson dressed her sons at first in yellow cotton, and, as they grew older, in blue nankeen trousers and jackets. Blue nankeen was a firm-textured, blue cotton cloth from China. It was common wear for children then, but few of them seem to have liked it. Oliver Wendell Holmes explains: "My recollection is that we did not think very highly of ourselves when we were in blue nankeen, — a dull-colored fabric, too nearly of the complexion of the slates on which we did our ciphering."[12] Compared with William Emerson's stunning attire or the cocked hat and gold lace of Sam's father, Sheriff Bradford, which awed Ralph, it perhaps was drab, but it is unlikely that the fact bothered him much. Plainness in dress was ever Emerson's preference, and blue nankeen can have been no worse than the black uniforms Harvard students were required to wear during Emerson's college years.[13]

With his busy round of activities, William Emerson had little time to remind his sons that they were Emersons, but his unmarried sister, Mary, who had handpicked his wife for him, took pains to make them conscious of their heritage and, more than that, that their heritage set them apart from ordinary mortals. They grew up convinced that they "had a peculiar proud carriage of the head, a hereditary trait."[14] Richard Garnett says of Emerson:

> Always among his schoolmates, he was never of them. There was a certain aloofness which never allowed them to consider him quite one of themselves. . . . This peculiar distinction he preserved through his life; without stiffness or churlishness, affectation or assumption, he always put and kept a distance between himself and others.[15]

Rebuked once in childhood for exhibiting superior airs, Emerson replied humbly, "I did not know it, sir."[16] His great-grandfather Joseph Emerson, as a boy, was advised that he walked in such a way as to suggest he thought his feet were too good to touch the ground. When Emerson's wife's sister, Lucy Brown, addressed the same remark to him as a grown man, he was much flattered.[17]

Rufus Dawes, his classmate at the Latin School, summoned up this remembrance:

> It is eight o'clock a.m.; and the thin gentleman in black, with a small jointed cane under his arm, his eyes deeply sunken in his head, has asked the spiritual-looking boy in blue nankeen, who seems to be about ten years old, to 'touch the bell'; — it was a privilege to do this; — and there he stands, that boy, whose image, more than any others, is still deeply stamped upon my mind, as I then saw him and loved him, I knew not why, and thought him so angelic and remarkable — . . . There is no indication of turbulence and disquiet about him; but with a happy combination of energy and gentleness, how truly is he father of the man![18]

Robert Gay, seeking an explanation for Emerson's personal authority, said: "The Emersons, whatever their dress and their simplicity of living, belonged to the Boston 'aristocracy.'"[19] Emerson had his own explanation: "I inherit from my sire a formality of manners and speech."[20] The Emersons carried an inner conviction that they were innately superior. After William's death, though they were stripped of material resources, their sense of predestined exclusivity sustained the illusion of social well-being and privilege.

By old-time Calvinistic standards, William Emerson was not severe in the moral and religious training he gave his children, yet, in maturity, Ralph Waldo, even in a mild adherence to it, displayed what seemed to the next generation like vestiges of orthodoxy, especially in his regard for the Sabbath observance. He often referred to its disappearance with regret. In the home of his childhood, the Sabbath began on Saturday night. Visits were not made or visitors received. Manual labor ceased. Such toys as there were were put away. Sunday was given over to churchgoing. Only in the evening, after a full twenty-four-hour observance, did the normal tempo of life resume.[21]

On ordinary days, at morning prayers, each member of the family, straight down the line to the most newly literate among them, read a passage he had chosen from Scripture. When Emerson was raising his own children, he insisted that respect for the Sabbath continue. He once startled his wife by calling a halt to a game of battledore and shuttlecock that she had sanctioned when rain on a Sunday afternoon had kept the children indoors.[22]

From time to time William Emerson had lost patience with certain members of his flock who, more than he was prone to do, advocated strict adherence to the traditional teachings of the church. Eventually his preference for literary over theological studies began to show. Yet, as befitted one nurtured on conservative Puritan staples, he was committed to the entrenched neoclassical standards and could not readily accept the contradictory manifestos of romanticism that exalted the emotions and were altering the character of literature, politics, and religion. When Emerson later scrutinized his father's theology, he concluded, perhaps incorrectly, that not a gulf but a modest fissure separated them. William was not a close student of theology nor did he aspire to be one. Apparently he found theological disputation tiresome. In these things his son would resemble him. But William showed not the slightest disposition to exalt intuition over intellect. He once told his son William: "It will grieve me excessively to have you a blockhead; but it will excessively delight me to have you a bright scholar."[23] In charting, after William's death, a program of disciplined studies for his sons, Mary Moody Emerson was shaping them in accordance with his plan, not with her own. William would no more have cared for the direction in which Ralph Waldo's thinking led him than Mary did.

"Men are," said Emerson, "what their mothers made them." Of himself this seems to have been true in a special sense. His cousin David Greene Haskins thought Emerson looked like his mother. Fredrika Bremer, the Swedish novelist, thought so, too. And when Arthur Hugh Clough saw her, he summed up his impressions in five words: "The original of Ralph Waldo."[24]

For some, Emerson's debt to his mother went beyond physical attributes or the impress of her training on his character. Bronson Alcott wrote in his diary in January 1850: "The best of Emerson's intellect comes out of its feminine traits and were he not as stimulating to me

as a woman and as racy, I should not care to see him and to know him
intimately nor often.'' Emerson himself was conscious of this an-
drogynous aspect of his nature. In early April 1842 he wrote in his
journal: ''Always there is this Woman as well as this Man in the mind;
Affection as well as Intellect.'' Lest we suppose he was speaking met-
aphorically, we need only consult a journal entry made the following
April: ''The finest people marry the two sexes in their own person.
Hermaphrodite is then the symbol of the finished soul.'' In September
1845 he said of William Lloyd Garrison, ''he lacks the feminine element which we find in men of genius.''[25]

Of Emerson, John Albee wrote in 1901, ''His manners — how shall
we speak justly of them! They were those of the finest woman one has
ever seen or heard.''[26] Despite his own gruff ways, or perhaps because
of them, Henry James, Sr., seemed comfortable only with an Emerson
whose feminine side was dominant. William Wynkoop concludes that
James discerned ''in Emerson . . . an 'angle of vision' on the feminine side of awareness, . . . a mode of perception . . . in which the
feminine predominated.''[27] In the sketch James did of Emerson shortly
after Emerson's death, published by William James in 1885, James
explored this theme further:

> I found in fact, before I had been with him a week, that the
> immense superiority I ascribed to him was altogether personal or
> practical — by no means intellectual; . . . that no other account
> was to be given of it in truth than that Emerson himself was
> an unsexed woman.[28]

Having chosen Ruth Haskins as a proper wife for William Emerson,
Mary Moody Emerson thought it fitting to enumerate the qualities she
had discerned in her: ''She is virtue's self. . . . In her look and manners is combined every thing which gives an idea of the whole assemblage of mild and amiable virtues. Added to this a natural good understanding and a uniform sense of propriety which characterises her
every action and enables her to make a proper estimate of every oc-
currence.''[29] Balanced against these virtues was a single quality that
Mary found lacking. Ruth was not pleasure-seeking, that is to say, not
fun-loving. Neither Ruth's life with William nor her life afterward
produced many calls on any fun-loving potential she might have had.
Her role in her husband's social life had been to see that the needs of
his guests were met. She made certain that her husband's home was
well maintained, that his meals were prepared, that his clothes were
kept in readiness (Ruth personally ironed William's lawn bands so
that they would never be less than perfect), that his children were
born and cared for. Hers was the usual lot of a minister's wife in those

years unless one was lucky enough, as her mother-in-law had been on her second try, to get a husband who danced attendance on her. Ruth got a husband who, despite his hemorrhaging lungs and the insidious tumor that finally cost him his life, kept up a whirlwind of activity until his last days. Together, they buried two children. Apart, she saw another four of them laid to rest. She had as well the worry of their illnesses and a never-relenting concern for the welfare of a son, Robert Bulkeley, who was retarded and periodically deranged. Since he could manage only the most simple tasks, his needs had always to be considered.

On his deathbed, William acknowledged that he had made no provision for the future welfare of his family, but owned that he was glad that that fact did not trouble him. "Our family, you know," he wrote to Mary, "have so long been in the habit of trusting Providence, that none of them ever seriously thought of providing a terrestrial maintenance for themselves and their households."[30] That was good thinking on his part. With a wife who was ever in harness and a sister who could join his wife in urging his children to scorn the comforts of life, which he himself had relished, he had nothing to worry about. Since Ruth was equal to the drudgery of running a succession of boarding-houses, and Mary equal to the task of putting the children through a spirited hymn-singing session when there was nothing in the house to eat, and Ralph and Edward were up to sharing one overcoat between them in winter, they would get on quite well. Still and all, any latent sense of fun in Ruth had no reason not to remain latent.

Ruth was almost twenty-eight when she married and going on forty-three when, only weeks apart, her last child was born and her husband died. Her husband's half-brother, the Reverend Samuel Ripley, said she was "as near heaven as she can be."[31] And her husband's eventual successor at the First Church, Nathaniel Frothingham, glossed that tribute for us: "Her mind and her character were of a superior order, and they set their stamp upon manners of peculiar softness and natural grace and quiet dignity. Her sensible and kindly speech was always as good as the best instruction; and her smile, though it was always ready, was a reward."[32] Mary Winslow, who, as William Emerson's ward, had lived with the Emersons in Ralph Waldo's boyhood, offers further the testimony of one who shared day-to-day existence with her, under the same roof: "I do not remember to have seen her impatient, or to have heard her express dissatisfaction at any time."[33] When, in old age, living in Emerson's home in Concord, Ruth fell out of bed one night and fractured her hip, she raised no alarm so as not to disturb the sleep of others.

Ruth was reputed to be "a good disciplinarian, firm and decided in the government of her children."[34] But kindness went hand in hand

with her firmness. A letter to her from Mary Moody Emerson urged
her to subdue at all costs the temperament of her daughter, Mary Caroline.[35] Since Mary Caroline was then but fourteen months old and so
sickly she would be in her grave by the time she was three, one shudders to think how a mother not endowed with Ruth's heroic serenity
and eminent good sense might have responded to this advice.

In William Emerson's time, in the dining room of the parsonage of
Boston's First Church, there hung above the sideboard a portrait of
his predecessor, John Clarke, who, felled in his pulpit by a stroke of
apoplexy, had died at forty-two. The likeness was of a man in a gown
of black silk and lawn bands, the requisite attire then for settled ministers. Clarke had merry eyes and a wide mouth for control of which
both amiability and joviality seemed to contend. His portliness suggested that he might have stood as a model for Jane Austen's Mr.
Norris, who, "plied with good things," had "popped off" just when
his benefice was wanted — struck down by apoplexy. William Emerson
had named his first son, born in the fall of 1799, just two weeks after
he had assumed his pastorate, John Clarke.

A portrait of Clarke's predecessor, Charles Chauncy, hung beside
Clarke's. Chauncy's stern look was faithful to the original. After this
man, William named his youngest son. Charles Chauncy Emerson never
cared for his name. Perhaps he remembered the portrait.

John Clarke Emerson may have liked the good-natured face that
gazed down upon the Emersons at mealtime, and may have relished
being the namesake of such a man. We shall never know because, at
seven, he lay dead in the adjacent parlor, with his three brothers looking on, William, who was six, Ralph, not quite four, and Edward, not
yet two. Ralph would remember nothing more of John Clarke than
this single fact — he had sat in the parlor with the family at the funeral. Yet John Clarke has made a contribution to our understanding
of Emerson. From letters that his mother wrote, stipulating the conditions of his upbringing, we are informed also about what Emerson's
boyhood was like.

John Clarke had had an older sister, Phebe. She died before he
reached his first birthday. Thus, for a season, until William was born,
he was the only child. He never lost this preciousness, even when, over
the four ensuing years, three brothers came to join him. At six, however, at the start of winter in 1805, John Clarke was sent to Waterford, Maine, as the temporary charge of the minister of that town,
Lincoln Ripley, and his wife. Lincoln Ripley was the brother of his
step-grandfather, Ezra Ripley. Lincoln's wife, Phebe, was John Clarke's
aunt, the sister of William Emerson. (She had married her stepfather's brother — Ezra, having been one of nineteen children, had them
in ample supply.) William's sister Rebecca also lived at Waterford.

She was married to John Clarke's uncle, Robert Haskins, one of his mother's younger brothers. Also living in Waterford at this time was Aunt Mary, the family matchmaker, who brought together not only Ruth and William, but Rebecca and Robert, and, later, Sarah Bradford and Samuel Ripley. Most likely she had arranged John Clarke's visit. She was a great arranger.

The probability is that John Clarke was sent to Maine because he was tubercular. Even then no one can have believed that a winter in Maine was a panacea for consumption. But in Boston, with three children under five and a direct role in keeping up her husband's social responsibilities — brother ministers came to dine on Thursdays; on Sundays the deacons and active parishioners were received — Ruth could not give John Clarke the attention his condition warranted. Her concern from afar, however, is evident in her surviving letters. To posterity some of her advice seems lamentable. In terms of what was believed and felt in that day, it stands as a model of good sense.

Beyond an incidental, if alarming, reference to John Clarke's diet — "You agree so exactly with us respecting a milk diet for children, that I shall not fear his having anything else, more than once a day meat or broth" — Ruth seemed more interested in building John Clarke's character than his constitution. Possibly she did not realize that John Clarke was as sick as he was because, at the end of her first letter to Phebe, she mentioned that the family had much to be thankful for, since the various illnesses that had visited them over the preceding year had proved fatal to no one. This she accepted as proof of God's goodness. Ruth's concern for John Clarke's moral well-being was explicit: "Suffer me to mention a few things. The first is, I wish him taught to practice agreeably the Golden Rule . . . and make him repeat, if you please, those four lines out of the Primer, 'Be you to others,' etc. I think he understands them." She then weighed his specific failings:

I have perceived sometimes in him a desire to evade prompt obedience. . . . It is very probable that I am myself wholly to blame for this appearance. He at times seems, through indolence, not disposed to help himself to many things which he is quite able to; for instance, if he finds any person inclined to wash and dress him, he will choose they should do it entirely, when, with very little help, he can do it wholly himself. . . . I much prefer he should wait on himself, and on others, too, in everything that he is equal to. I need not say, because I know you will not fail to inculcate on him respect to his superiors, love and amiable sweetness of deportment to his equals, and kindness and condescension to his inferiors, and to all animals and insects.[36]

This was sound advice if the character of a robust child was being formed, but hardly so when the child alluded to was in the grip of a terminal illness. Since her letters show that John Clarke seldom was out of her thoughts, Ruth cannot have seen the facts for what they were. "Oh, my sister," she wrote at the start of the separation, which lasted eleven months, "you cannot imagine, because you never experienced, what I now feel!" John Clarke's absence at Thanksgiving was noted with sorrow. By March Ruth was scheming to visit him in the summer. She would not rest easy, she said, if she did not see him. She made and sent him a suit of blue nankeen, together with "a few sugarplums." By April, although she announced she was sending him a gift box, she added, "I hope I shall hear he divides these things with his cousins and schoolmates." Responding to these directions, Phebe increased pressure on the boy. Ruth backed her up to the hilt: "However painful the task, we trust you will persevere in correcting everything you discover wrong in him. I am delighted with your resolution in withholding his books as you did, and also with the pains you took to make him humane and charitable." Nor had Ruth quite finished. "Give yourself no trouble in future," she added, "to inform us of the articles you cause him to give; but make him give of those things he values most, till he derives pleasure from bestowing."[37]

The standards Ruth upheld and the methods she advocated for attaining them seem to reflect William's theories of child-rearing more than her own. Under this regimen John Clarke seems to have been undergoing a slow martyrdom. If he accepted it with submissiveness, he was already the saint his mother hoped he would become.

When John Clarke came home in October, his arrival was unexpected. Ruth flew to the door to greet him. "He seemed happy," she wrote Phebe, "and met me with joy and a tremulous agitation." She thought that laudable. It fact it sounds ominous. He and little William leaped into each other's arms and hugged and kissed "for the space of two minutes."[38] John Clarke seemed like a man let out of prison after long years of confinement. So free a display of the emotions is nowhere else recorded in the annals of the Emerson family.

Ralph was not present when John Clarke arrived home. He was at Dame School. John Clarke thought Edward was Ralph. Only when Ralph arrived home and he kissed him was John Clarke convinced that Edward was Edward. Ralph himself was not demonstrative on this occasion. The cold nature he acknowledged already was asserting itself.

Conditioned to give away what he valued most, to please others, John Clarke did not have much fight left in him. We hear of him in this period dutifully repeating passages, to please his father, from "Addison, Shakespeare, Milton, Pope etc.," which suggests that the pressure on him to perform continued. "Notwithstanding the best advice that Boston affords, and the best attention we can give him," he failed rapidly.[39] With his father at his bedside comforting him with assurances that he had been a good boy and would go to heaven, John Clarke died of tuberculosis, five months after he arrived home from Maine, on 26 April 1807. The day following the seventy-fifth anniversary of that event, Ralph Waldo himself died. Had he been older when John Clarke died, psychology would say he succumbed to an anniversary illness engendered by survivor guilt or by remorse having its origin in subliminal longings that John Clarke should again depart so that he could resume the enhanced position in the family which he had occupied during John Clarke's absence in Maine. Apply that measure and Emerson's deathbed words, "Oh, that beautiful boy," allude not to his son Waldo, as commonly believed, but to his long-vanished brother John Clarke, of whom it was said "he developed very interesting traits of character" in his short lifetime. As for that, John Clarke had no choice.[40]

Whatever methods Ruth used to enforce discipline, she did not alienate her children. Uppermost in Emerson's thoughts when he was ready to establish himself in life was his desire to provide for Ruth a home and the comforts she had had to do without. During his first, brief marriage she was a member of his household and during the last eighteen years of her life she was with him in Concord. Her son William, a member of the New York judiciary, doted on her in equal measure. On her death Emerson was consoled that the closing phase of her life, as had been all its phases, was "so adorned by her own happy temper." To his friend Sam Ward he wrote: "She lived eighty-four years, yet not a day too long."[41]

A curious hint of the ties of affection that bound Emerson to his mother appears in such maternal metaphors as "The earth lies in the lap of an immense intelligence"; "that great nature in which we rest as the earth lies in the soft arms of the atmosphere"; "I have no hostility to nature, but a child's love to it. . . . I do not wish to fling stones at my beautiful mother"; and "I should lie down in the lap of earth as trustingly as ever on my bed." In the light of such passages Emerson's fondness for Raphael's madonnas is better understood.

In his own early years his mother found neither the occasion nor the inclination to show overt affection, and he came to acknowledge her love only when he recognized the sacrifices she made in his behalf. On attaining maturity Emerson came to cherish expressions of maternal love that affirmed active affection.

4. Mary Moody Emerson
A Vessel of Cumbersomeness

$\mathcal{O}$UR chief want in life," wrote Emerson in "Considerations," "is somebody who shall make us do what we can."[1] In Emerson's life Aunt Mary Moody Emerson was that spur. "She deserves," said Denton Snider, "to have her features chiseled and her bust set up in a prominent niche of her nephew's biography."[2] And so she does. Assessing her place in his life, Emerson concluded: "She must always occupy a saint's place in my household; and I have no hour of poetry or philosophy, since I knew these things, into which she does not enter as a genius."[3] Elizabeth Peabody once asked Emerson if he thought his education would have been affected much if his father had stayed on as pastor in rural Harvard. "Nature was there and books," Emerson replied. So he still would have had what was essential to him. "But how if your aunt Mary had not lived in your mother's Boston family, after your father's death, and concerned herself about your education?" Elizabeth persisted. "Ah," Emerson answered, "that would have been a loss! I could have better spared Greece and Rome."[4]

"Aunts of all kinds," said Goldsmith's Tony Lumpkin, "are damned bad things." Surely there were times when Emerson dwelt on that thought with Aunt Mary in mind. When she died, just short of her ninetieth year, on May Day 1863, Franklin Sanborn wrote of her: "She was thought to have the power of saying more disagreeable things in a half-hour than any person living. Reproof was her mission, she thought, and she fulfilled it unsparingly." Reading this, Emerson commented, "I see that he was well acquainted with Aunt Mary."[5] He himself found her "no easy flute" but "a bagpipe . . . from which

none but a native Highlandman could draw music.''[6] He spoke of her
bluntly, too: ''She could keep step with no human being but seemed
driven by some inner fury. Her rude speech and sometimes crude behavior sooner or later offended even those who recognized her great
worth.''[7] Emerson's brother William said she ''outraged all feeling
and propriety.'' Her sister-in-law Sarah Bradford Ripley, who described her as ''a friend who has had more power and influence over
me than any other being,'' also said that she was ''a person at war
with society as to all its decorums.''[8] Of herself Aunt Mary said, ''I
love to be a vessel of cumbersomeness to society.''[9] Emerson saw this.
He said: ''She is her own daily victim, unstable & whimsical & self
tormenting and so tormenting those about her, in the most extraordinary & painful degree. But all argument on the matter is wasted, &
her friends have only to keep as cool & as kindly as they can manage
it, towards this gifted but most unhappy woman.''[10]

In learning how to adapt to Aunt Mary's moods without forfeiting
self-control, Emerson acquired a valuable skill that, throughout life,
was a resource others esteemed. In his mother Emerson found a pattern for coping with Aunt Mary's outbursts. Aunt Mary herself remarked that Ruth never let herself be ruffled by family strife.

Emerson pictures Aunt Mary in a constant frenzy of activity: ''She
had the misfortune of spinning with a greater velocity than any of the
other tops. She would tear into the chaise and out of it, into the house
or out of it, into the conversation, into the thought, into the character
of the stranger.'' He sought to account for it: ''That field yonder did
not get such digging, ditching, filling & planting for any pay. A fanaticism lucky for the owner did it. . . . Neither can any account be
given of the fervid work in M[ary]. M[oody]. E[merson].'s manuscripts but the vehement religion which would not let her sleep nor sit,
but write, write, night & day, year after year.'' Aunt Mary's word for
herself was ''feverish,'' as in this instance: ''Had I prospered in life,
what a proud, excited being, even to feverishness, I might have been.
Loving to shine, flattered and flattering, anxious, and wrapped in others, frail and feverish as myself.''[11]

Aunt Mary was aware of her acrimonious nature and of the burden
it imposed on others. She saw herself as someone whose fate it was ''to
live to give pain rather than pleasure.'' But her compensating qualities mesmerized Emerson: ''Though we flout her and contradict her
and compassionate her whims, we all stand in awe of her penetration,
her indignant, eloquent conscience, her poetic and commanding reason.''[12]

Mary Moody Emerson's unusual upbringing had much to do with
her strange nature and peculiar genius. She was born in her father's
parsonage, the Old Manse, and was but eight months old when he held

her up to the window to watch the battle being fought at the North Bridge, only two hundred yards away, on the far side of his pasture. The next year, he went off to war as chaplain, leaving Mary with his mother in Malden because his wife, with a new infant and three older children to care for, had her hands full. At his death two months later, Mary's stay with her grandmother took on permanency. When her grandmother died, three years later, she was adopted by her father's childless sister, Ruth Sargent, and her husband, Nathan, who was amiable but shiftless. Sometimes she was put on watch for the sheriff, coming to arrest Nathan for nonpayment of debts. She also had the keep of another aunt who was mad. She did not have the companionship of other children and got only the bare rudiments of schooling. Ruth Sargent herself was testy and impractical. The best she could do for Mary was to keep her busy baking or carding wool. That was not enough for Mary. She read every book she could lay hold of, even a fragment of *Paradise Lost*, which she adored without knowing what it was.

Most of the books accessible to her were, of course, earnest expositions of Calvinist theology. She took it in wholeheartedly. God was omnipotent and man existed only to glorify Him. Human nature was totally depraved. This world, as decreed by the divine vengeance, was a vale of tears. Happiness was not to be found in this life but the next. Our duty here was to recognize our own worthlessness and that of all earthly things and to live in strict conformance with the dictates of the Bible.

To the unobserving Mary was probably just a child in the corner, because she never grew taller than four feet three inches, although she was quite perfectly formed. In an era when the average height of New England women was four feet nine and most men were only four or five inches taller, Mary's physical appearance was not a great oddity, but it did probably contribute to her unusual determination to bring herself to notice.

At seventeen Mary returned to the Manse to help her mother raise the three children born to her of her second husband, Ezra Ripley, the minister who, in 1778, had succeeded William Emerson as pastor at Concord. She stayed there eight years, but by now the independent traits that would make her difficult to get along with already were evident. They were characteristics that would show up in anyone forced to live far below his or her potential. Unfortunately, Mary's stepfather was no scholar and saw her theological and philosophical interests as presumptuous and unwholesome. Her testiness did not increase her chances of winning him over. Her brothers, however, found refreshing the difference she brought into the household. Her superior knowledge suggested a new day come to replace the old, a prospect exactly suited to adolescents at odds with a stepfather who, in Concord, epitomized authority. It can hardly have been a fluke that her brothers William and Samuel both let her select wives for them. She actually sought out Samuel's future wife, Sarah Alden Bradford, when Sarah was sixteen, and forced herself on her, without benefit of introduction. She had heard good reports of Sarah's bookish ways and devotion to an ailing mother and invaded her garret to find her. Sarah was aloof at first but finally was won over. Mary recognized in her a woman of true genius and would not be put off. That was fortunate for Ralph Waldo because Sarah also played a crucial role in his formation and, by her example, supplied the assurance that genius need not be either erratic or cantankerous.[13]

William Emerson's gratitude for being led by Mary to so suitable a wife should, of itself, have been reason enough for him to stay on amiable terms with her and it was, even though she was a constant goad to him — she was the not so still, not so small voice urging him to realize his whole potential. William was always glad to have Mary under his roof not merely because she made herself useful in a practical way but for the tone she set. There was no marking time with her. Things had to be moving forward. In October 1809 he wrote urging her to visit, assuring her that his sons needed her "healing attentions," not simply for "lame legs, wounded hands, and other calamities," but for their "minds and hearts." "I love you," he told her, ". . . your residence in my family until death or matrimony separates us is necessary to my happiness."[14]

In 1811, when William entered upon his final illness, he again petitioned Mary to join his household. She remained with the family for almost a year. Ruth wished to make the arrangement permanent.[15] But Mary's philosophical quest seemed to require a nomadic life-style. She found a pretext to be disagreeable and left. Soon afterward, she marked the first anniversary of William's death by writing Ruth a solemn Calvinistic letter in which William's failure to adhere strictly to the Scriptures was deplored and Ruth encouraged to concern herself with the spiritual welfare of her children to the exclusion of all else. It took much pleading before Ruth succeeded in getting her to rejoin the Emerson household the following January. Yet this time, as was to be her pattern hereafter, her stay was measured not in months but in weeks. Mary administered parenting to others as she administered medicines to herself — mixing assorted nostrums into one strong draught — so that an opportunity for convalescence between each treatment was much to be desired.

At thirty-seven, when Mary Moody Emerson first stepped into her brother's place as overseer of the education of his sons, she was spunky, positive, feisty, and galvanic. Elizabeth Hoar has left us further details — "a blue flash in her eyes like the gleam of steel — yellow hair, which, however, was cut close and covered up with a black band and a mob-cap."[16] Her complexion was a delicate pink and her skin smooth.

The mob-cap may have made its appearance in later years. The attire of those years, once seen, was unforgettable. At least from the time she was fifty, death had seemed to Mary a welcome state. "I pray to die," she wrote in July 1826. In preparation for her own death she made a flannel funeral shroud. But when death did not come for her, she decided that it was "a pity to let it lie idle." She began wearing it, then, an extraordinary sight — on horseback, riding sidesaddle to the Manse, clad in her white shroud, a scarlet shawl draping her shoulders. She wore out "a great many" shrouds, Emerson believed, before she got to the one that served as her grave clothes. "I wish you joy of the worm!" her friends had called to her gaily when they saw she was breaking in a new shroud. Even Waldo caught the contagion of it, promising to inscribe her gravestone, "Here lies the Angel of Death." Mary met these jests without perturbation. A woman with a trousseau of shrouds, who sleeps in a bed made to resemble a coffin, is not easily jarred. Nor would it have bothered her that when she did die and her body was borne to Sleepy Hollow on a misty day, dark under lowering clouds, there was merriment among the mourners when they concluded it was the sort of day she would have liked.[17]

Mary's essence was still undiminished when Thoreau described her in 1855:

> Miss Mary Emerson . . . the wittiest and most vivacious woman I know, certainly that woman among my acquaintance whom it is most profitable to meet, the least frivolous, who will most surely provoke to good conversation. She is . . . perseveringly interested to know what thoughtful people think. . . . She more surely than any other woman gives her companion occasion to utter his best thought. In spite of her own biases, she can entertain a large thought with hospitality. . . . In short, she is a genius, as woman seldom is, reminding you less often of her sex than any woman whom I know.[18]

Few could guess that Thoreau was talking about a woman eighty-one years old.

If, in speaking of Aunt Mary, Thoreau sounded like a male chauvinist, she herself supplied justification. Once, at a literary gathering, when some of the women present fell into conversation, she silenced them with a sharp rebuke — "Stop that chattering. I want to hear these men talk sense." Thoreau tells us that she thought "Men are more likely to have opinions of their own."[19]

Reflecting in his journal, in 1855, on the omniscience boys ascribe to their first mentors, Emerson owned that in boyhood he had assigned that attribute to Aunt Mary. ''Sir,'' Mary insisted, when queried concerning the prospects of her dead brother's children, ''they were born to be educated.'' And from that conviction she never wavered. She ''had an eye that went through & through you like a needle.'' He recalled further: ''Her wit was so fertile, and only used to strike, that she never used it for display, any more than a wasp would parade his sting.'' After her death he wrote: ''She gave high counsels. It was the privilege of certain boys to have this immeasurably high standard indicated to their childhood, a blessing which nothing else in education could supply.'' When offering guidance to his own children, Emerson would introduce them to some ''high counsel'' with the remark, ''As Aunt Mary used to say.'' Then would follow such adjurations as ''Lift your aims''; ''Scorn trifles''; ''Always do what you are afraid to do''; ''Sublimity of character must come from sublimity of motive.''[20]

By the perversity of fate, the key Aunt Mary had to give others would not cause doors to swing open for her. She told her journal, in a parable that might have been a dream:

> As a traveler enters some fine palace and finds all the doors closed, and he only allowed the use of some avenues and passages, so have I wandered from the cradle over the apartments of social affections, or the cabinets of natural or moral philosophy, the recesses of ancient and modern lore. All say — Forbear to enter the pales of the initiated by birth, wealth, talents, and patronage. I submit with delight, for it is the echo of a decree from above; and from the highway hedges where I get lodging; and from the rays which burst forth when the crowd are entering these noble saloons, whilst I stand in the doors, I get a pleasing vision which is an earnest of the interminable skies where the mansions are prepared for the poor.[21]

Psychotherapy could not have brought her to a better accounting of her dilemma.

From Aunt Mary, Emerson got more than high counsels and the will to persevere. Letters in which they wrestled with great issues flowed between them. To her he bared his private journals and she shared hers with him. The homely vigor Emerson sought in prose he first had from her, as when she wrote: ''I am emptied and peeled to carry some seed to the ignorant, which no idler wind can so well dispense.''[22] Emerson copied her letters into his journal as models of style. And sometimes he adapted her ideas and adopted her phrasing.

Though in due course dismayed by Emerson's theological heresies,

Aunt Mary took pride in his vivid prose style. If he had been more truly religious, she told him, he "could have written *Paradise Lost* — without the dull parts!"[23]

In 1836 would come the great, disruptive, dinnertime ruckus that brought an effective end to Aunt Mary's direct influence over her nephew. The details were never recorded, but the incident took place at Emerson's home in Concord, with Charles Emerson present. Mary had essayed some cruel sallies of wit, at whose expense we do not know. But an uproar followed and she vowed never to spend an hour in that house again, unless brought there on a litter. Considering further, she resolved that even in that condition she would refuse to enter. Generous invitations from both Emerson and his wife were afterward forthcoming, but, for many years, though letters continued to pass between Emerson and her and from time to time they met on neutral ground, she held literally to her vow. She was not ready to cast Emerson off wholly, of course. She admitted she could not rescind her "early admiration" of his "genius." She furthermore conceded that "two or three" of her jokes at the notorious dinner had been out of place.[24] But lurking behind this estrangement was her sorrowful resentment at Emerson's drift from orthodoxy. Although she had incited him to be daring in his youth, she had not foreseen the audacity of which he would prove to be capable.

On 4 May 1841, striving to heal the breach between them, Emerson was to write a remarkable letter to Aunt Mary. Nowhere else does he state so explicitly the contribution she made in helping him to complete his thoughts. He wrote:

> Some old letters which I have been reading with keen interest have brought your image before me yesterday & today with unusual vividness. I feel in every line I read of these prized MSS. the strictness of the tie that joins these two separated souls — yourself & me. . . . I feel as if only you & such as you (if such were), could challenge many things that now sleep & perhaps die in me. Yet why must we live so severed? Is it your pleasure? It is not mine. Is it that our wires were once predestined to exhibit opposite polarities when we met, with occasional explosion & angry scintillation. Undoubtedly I was always the offending party — I am in all my crises. . . . But can we not acquiesce — you as well as I — that all manner of private weaknesses & petulance should disfigure my little tablet, & yet we should meet where truly we are at one in our perception of one Law in our adoration of the Moral Sentiment and nearer earth in our cherished remembrance of those who made the hoop of our little broken circle?[25]

There followed an earnest appeal to her to come for an extended visit. She had been ill and Emerson, perhaps fearing they would part un- reconciled, seemed eager to be restored to her favor. But Mary, in a prompt reply, recalled the traumatic dinner-hour inbroglio and re- lented only to the extent that she invited Emerson to visit her.

In his pointed expression of need for her, Emerson seemed to be suggesting that he knew, at some level, that this estrangement was from someone to whom he bore a unique relationship — she who had been his surrogate father. It is striking, therefore, that as the time neared, in midsummer, when he would stage his reunion with Aunt Mary, he reviewed his memories of his father and subdued the latent feelings of hostility he had toward him, in effect, preparing himself to redefine his relationship with Mary, which he realized now could never be resumed on former terms. Curiously, even if William Emerson had lived until Ralph Waldo had attained his majority, he could not have been for him the role model his sister was, for those attributes of Aunt Mary's which Waldo adopted were the same ones which, without suc- cess, she had sought to instill in William. Where she failed with the father, she succeeded with the son.

Life then was calendared by moments & not by days,
threw itself into nervous knots or glittering hours.

---

5. A Boy's Ways

*M*Y recollections of early life are not very pleasant,'' Emerson told his journal on 27 March 1826.[1] Since he was then approaching twenty-three, the period he was referring to probably encompassed much more than early childhood, especially since, on this occasion, he was rebuking himself for not having done more with his life. Yet Emerson seems to have wanted to remember his boyhood years as bleak. There were low moments, to be sure. When he was two, he was stricken with an illness attributed to worms and withdrawn from Dame School. On another occasion, presumably that of a fire or threat of fire, he experienced the terror of being carried in the dark of night to a neighboring house. But no true disaster — a possible source of enduring traumas — appears to have attended this crisis.

Emerson was, it seems, accounted the least promising of the four normal brothers and may have been given a setback when Dr. Frothingham examined the shape of his head, which was small in size, and observed, ''If you are good, it is no thanks to you.''[2] Whatever the cause of Emerson's good behavior, the business of making him submit to the yoke of discipline began almost with the first day of his life. Perceiving him to be a thumb-sucker, his mother at once undertook to thwart him by attaching mittens to his nightdress.[3] When his son Waldo, not yet a day old, evidenced this same trait, Emerson relished his assertiveness.[4]

From time to time in boyhood, Emerson proved further that it was not his natural inclination to conform readily. Furness recalled that when they were at Rufus Webb's school together, seated side by side

on a single bench, Emerson sometimes picked his pockets.[5] Emerson's
son Edward says further: "From this school — I have heard his own
confession — he deliberately and continuously played truant, and enjoyed the stolen hours on the Common till such time as was needed for
'sorrow, dogging sin,' in the shape of bread-and-water confinement . . .
to run down its prey."[6] In that same period, when bored with lengthy
sermons at church, he had recourse to a mind game of his own de-
vising:

> I remember when a child in the pews on Sundays amusing
> myself with saying over common words as 'black,' 'white,' 'board,'
> &c twenty or thirty times, until the word lost all meaning &
> fixedness, & I began to doubt which was the right name for the
> thing, when I saw that neither had any natural relation, but all
> were arbitrary. It was a child's first lesson in Idealism.[7]

Emerson might have added that this was his first, tentative venture
into heresy and, while hardly world-shaking, sufficient to point him in
the direction of eschewing institutionalized religion in favor of personal intuition. Despite her vigilance, his mother was too idealistic
herself to catch the true implications of his mental flights. If Ralph,
on his return from services, was vague when she queried him about
the text of that day's homily, she was neither perplexed nor anxious.
She supposed that his want of specifics ascribed to a state of soul akin
to her own inner raptures.

Much of the time Emerson was thinking for himself, occasionally
with quaint results. One day he watched the efforts of a sawyer cutting up some portion of the twenty cords of wood the parish allowed
the Emersons for winter fuel. The task was still beyond the child's
strength, but finally he saw a way to be useful. "May I," he asked,
"do the grunting for you?"[8]

As Emerson grew older, the guidelines laid down for him for proper
conduct forced him to stifle natural preferences. On one such occasion,
he spent all of his pocket money on a sheet of gingerbread. He was
then stricken with such remorse that the vendor, who cannot have been
without knowledge of the merciless rigors of a conscience formed under New England Calvinism, allowed him to renegotiate the sale and
settle for half the sheet for half the sum.[9] On another occasion he laid
out six cents to rent a novel from a lending library and was so taken
aback by the tongue-lashing Aunt Mary gave him that he could not
bring himself to rent the companion volume to learn the outcome of
the story.[10]

For recreation in those early years, Emerson was expected to play
within the fenced grounds of the parsonage, with his brothers as play-

mates. Street games were ruled out, for these might bring him in contact with the Round-Pointers — rowdies from Windmill Point — or the equally pugnacious West Enders, with whom the Round-Pointers sometimes battled on the Common. Just once one of these ''rude boys'' bloodied his nose. Emerson claimed to regret that more such experiences did not come his way. Throughout his life, when roughnecks were around, Emerson was a voyeur, fascinated always with the vigor of their earthy language and regretful when his presence made them lapse into lackluster commonplaces. No matter how much he yearned to plunge into that other world, however, his training held.

Recalling the parsonage yard and the splendid abutting orchard of Judge Prescott, Emerson would, in maturity, write: ''It was separated by a brick wall from a garden and orchard southward, where pears grew; and I remember sitting on that wall and wishing for some of those pears.''[11] His covetousness, unlike that of the first parents, never progressed beyond the longing. It could have been this readily comprehended temptation Emerson was thinking about when he wrote ''Grace,'' expressing gratitude to God for having girded him about with ''Example, custom, fear'' to keep him from yielding to temptation. ''These scorned bondsmen,'' he owned, ''were my parapet. / I dare not peep over this parapet / To gauge with glance the roaring gulf below.''[12] If the woes of mankind began with a filched apple, we cannot suppose that in Emerson's eyes an infinite distance lay between a filched St. Michael's pear and that ''roaring gulf.''

A glimpse of Emerson in early boyhood is shared with us by Nathaniel P. Willis: ''We remember him perfectly, as a boy whom we used to see playing about Chauncey Place and Summer-street, — one of those pale little moral-sublimes with their shirt collars turned over, who are recognized by Boston schoolboys as having 'fathers that are Unitarians.' ''[13] Emerson himself elaborated on this very scene with a note of melancholy that suggests he relinquished the remembered circumstance reluctantly:

I was a little chubby boy trundling a hoop in Chauncy Place and spouting poetry from Scott & Campbell at the Latin School. But Time the little grey man . . . has taken that chubbiness & that hoop quite away (to be sure he has left the declamation & the poetry) and here left a long lean person threatening soon to be a little grey man, like himself.[14]

On the threshold of March in 1840, as winter gave signs of relenting, Emerson recalled for Margaret Fuller the days of his boyhood: ''I see plainly the old school-entry where . . . we spun tops and snapped marbles.''[15] The tops of his youth supplied Emerson a serviceable image. To him Aunt Mary was a whirling top. ''I often ask,'' he wrote Sam

Ward, "where shall I get the whip for my top . . . ?"[16] Progressing from hoops to tops to whirling atoms, on a whirling planet in a whirling universe, and the ascending spires of form of an evolving creation — his exultation at having a part in all this left him little time for lamentation over plans and hopes gone awry. This capacity for wonder, expectation, and delight gushed from the secret recesses of boyhood with a spontaneity it took him many years to acknowledge.

Boston Common, in Emerson's boyhood, offered young people many of the advantages of country life — sledding, foot races, marbles in season, and simple games of ball. "There was even a pond, where a beginner might try his first skates; and the salt water was close by, with wharves where he might catch flounders and tom-cod." The waterfront held further attractions: "When a boy I used to go to the wharves, and pick up shells out of the sand which vessels had brought as ballast, and also plenty of stones, gypsum, which I discovered would be luminous when I rubbed two bits together in a dark closet, to my great wonder." He went on:

> That, & the magnetising my penknife, till it would hold a needle; & the fact that blue and gambooge would make green in my pictures of mountains; & the charm of drawing vases by scrawling with ink heavy random lines, & then doubling the paper, so as to make another side symmetrical — what was chaos, becoming symmetrical; then hallooing to an echo at the pond, & getting wonderful replies. Still earlier, what silent wonder is waked in the boy by blowing bubbles from soap & water with a pipe.[17]

These pleasures were simple and cost nothing, or nearly so. Emerson does not appear to have missed out on too many of them.

In an 1837 journal passage Emerson acknowledged the universality of boyhood enjoyments: "I please myself with getting my nail box set in the snuggest corner of the barn chamber & well filled with nails & gimlet pincers, screw driver, & chisel. Herein I find an old joy of youth, of childhood which perhaps all domestic children share, — the cat-like love of garrets, barns, & corn chambers."[18]

Edward Emerson says: "Mr. Emerson always wished that, in his youth, he had been made to learn to dance and ride. Poverty, of course, forbade. He took pains that his son had these advantages."[19] Games and dancing, Emerson believed, did not add up to time wasted. In 1845 he wrote:

> The boy learns chess & whist & takes lessons in dancing; the watchful father observes that another has learned algebra & geometry, in the meantime. But the first boy has got much more

than those goodfornothing games with the games. He is absorbed for a month or two in whist & chess, but presently he will find them tedious & will learn in himself that when he rises from the game too long played he is vacant & forlorn, & despises himself. . . . These games, & especially dancing, are necessary as tickets of admission to the commonwealth of mankind, to a class of civilization.[20]

William Emerson, racked by the scourge of tuberculosis, had survived hemorrhaging lungs in 1807 but, by late 1810, he saw that something was rapidly taking his strength. Even as Ruth's abdomen swelled as she entered the final days of her eighth pregnancy, his body wasted. A dense, malignant tumor, mocking his wife's condition, grew in the pit of his stomach. Early in the new year he resigned some of his prized offices. His joy, in February, at the birth of a daughter, Mary Caroline, diminished with his realization that she would never know him. In mid-April his doctors compounded their incompetence by sending him on a pointless holiday to Portland, Maine, where he died twenty-seven days later, on 12 May. Resorting then to an autopsy, they finally diagnosed his illness.

Boston showed its grief by according William the full honors due a first citizen: much black crepe, the prayers, a funeral cortege so extensive its vanguard arrived at King's Chapel Burying Ground even as the last coaches were leaving the environs of the First Church. The Artillery Company marched before the hearse. William and Ralph, the latter still two weeks short of attaining his eighth birthday, walked behind it. And behind them followed other delegations on foot and fifty or sixty coaches. The grandeur of the spectacle was the one memory of the event Ralph retained in later years.

At the Burying Ground William's body was placed in the Cotton Tomb, so called because John Cotton, first pastor of the First Church, had been buried there in 1652. William's was the last body to be placed in this tomb.[21] Yet, even as it was sealed for a final time, there remained unwritten one further chapter to the Cotton and Emerson legends. Both men would live on in the descendants of William's son, Ralph Waldo, and his wife, Lidian Jackson, whose mother, Lucy Cotton, was a direct descendant of John Cotton.

On 19 May 1811, the Reverend William Bentley of Salem noted in his diary: "I have not yet seen the notice of the d[eath]. of Mr. Emerson. He was a pleasing speaker but more so at Harvard in his first charge than at Boston. He had the affections of his people in a great degree. He was not formed to admit the preference which younger men & new things can create."[22] Ralph Waldo was not privy to the contents of Bentley's diary, but sentiments he expressed many years later concerning his father do not contradict those of Bentley. Then he observed, in a letter to his brother William: "I have never heard any sentence or sentiment of his repeated by Mother or Aunt, and his printed or written papers, as far as I know, only show candor & taste, or I should almost say, docility, the principal merit possible to that early ignorant & transitional *Month-of-March,* in our *New England culture.*"[23]

By the reversal of expectations it entailed, William Emerson's death paradoxically lessened the ties of his children with their mother's family even as it brought them into closer alignment with his own. The First Church in some measure sponsored this result by making the Emerson family virtual wards of the parish during the two years immediately following William's death. At the same time, Ruth, influenced by the judgment of Aunt Mary, saw that her sons had an obligation to be continuators of the superior cultural tradition of the Emerson family rather than to follow the pattern of the Haskins family, which had emerged from obscurity only through John Haskins's industry. Such patronage as the Emerson boys might expect to attract certainly would come to them as the sons of William Emerson, not as the grandsons of a successful privateersman turned distiller, however respected John Haskins now was. Moreover, there were Emerson relatives able and ready to act for the children's interest — Ezra Ripley and his son, Samuel, both clergymen. John Haskins had been prosperous but was now elderly and his estate was to be portioned out among his numerous children, so that Ruth could not expect to receive from that quarter the income she would need to provide adequately for her family. Before William's death his family had enjoyed frequent holiday gatherings with their Haskins grandsire. Now, gradually, that custom waned. Religion itself may have been a factor. John was a devout Anglican and Ruth, in her heart, remained one. But, as Unitarians, her children were drawn by the natural affinities of William's family toward the Unitarian community. William's powerful friends, such as John Thornton Kirkland, newly installed as president of Harvard, would have wanted that. And, as events unfolded, Kirkland and others did open to Ralph and his brothers the way to those opportunities that would normally have been theirs had their father lived and prospered.

This is not to suggest that after William's death his children found their future assured. Largess for them was ten dollars a month sent anonymously by their kind and discreet friend Sheriff Samuel Bradford by way of Nathaniel Frothingham, now pastor of the First Church. Otherwise, to move toward their intended goals, enormous sacrifices were expected of them. Even Aunt Mary's help was governed by caprice. She came and went as her whims decreed. Ruth found the income she needed to maintain basic living standards while keeping her sons in college by running a succession of boardinghouses. She once specified these priorities for her children: "Their souls, their minds next, their bodies last."[24] Her sons accepted deprivations as their normal lot.

6. A Spartan Youth
The Laurels of Life

*D*EACON John White may have heard Ezra Ripley boast about Ralph Waldo's powers of declamation. Or perhaps the deacon merely took it for granted that the scion of a family that had held Concord spellbound with its oratorical gifts for three generations had inherited those gifts. Or perhaps the eleven-year-old boy, then in temporary residence in Concord because times in Boston were hard, relished being made much of. Whatever the explanation, whenever Ralph Emerson entered White's store, the clerk made him climb up on the sugar barrel and recite something for his customers. Edward Emerson surmised that on these occasions his father declaimed "Campbell's 'Glenara,' or the Kosciusko passage, or statelier verses from Milton."[1] That is not unlikely. At ninety-four, Mary Winslow, William Emerson's erstwhile ward, recalled that even as a boy Emerson had "a wonderful memory" and could spout part of the "Dialogue between Brutus and Cassius," and, in their entirety, "Franklin one night stopped at a public inn," and "You'd scarce expect one of my age."[2]

At eleven, Emerson was already at that stage which his uncle Samuel Ripley took note of when he asked him, "How is it, Ralph, that all the boys dislike you and quarrel with you, whilst the grown people are fond of you?"[3] Possibly Ralph Waldo's flair for rendering Virgil into fluent English heroics and striking off smooth Augustan couplets was the secret of his unpopularity with his peers. But his brothers, at least, acclaimed his skill. And so did his friend and first literary ally, William Furness. When they attended school together, Furness made drawings to illustrate an early Emersonian verse effort, "The History

of Fortus," which consisted of page upon page of octosyllabic couplets
recounting the deeds of a vigorous hero who must have been the alter
ego of his frail creator.[4] "Boy," his doctor told him, "you've got no
stamina."[5] True enough, he did lack stamina, but, nonetheless, he could
project it in a hero who slew twenty thousand warriors and, for good
measure, a brace of dragons.

Not only did Emerson not mind his barrel-top declamations, they
gave him a pleasing sense of accomplishment and may well have opened
his eyes to the gratification that came from holding an audience enthralled. After he became an illustrious man of letters, people fell silent when he entered the Concord store, as though his presence made
them self-conscious. He claimed that he regretted being shut out of
their camaraderie, but any veteran thespian could have told him that
what he really missed was being the active center of attention.

In the early years of the nineteenth century, nine was the age of
admittance to the Boston Public Latin School. Emerson entered as
soon as he was eligible. He was able, accordingly, to share in an interesting period of the school's history. To begin with, the old building
on School Street was torn down and he and his classmates were shifted
about town while a new building was being constructed on the site of
its predecessor. At the same time, he bore with the vagaries of a hard-
drinking, cane-wielding headmaster, William Biglow, who conducted
a reign of terror until his failings were given wide publicity by student unrest and he was replaced, in 1814, by an exemplary master,
Benjamin Apthorpe Gould.

At the Latin School the core curriculum was Latin and Greek. Supplementing this instruction during the hour before noon, Rufus Webb,
master of the nearby South Writing School, tutored a handful of boys
in writing and ciphering. Furness, who shared a bench with Emerson
at Webb's, would remember him bent over his paper, his tongue, signifying abstraction and concentration, fixed between his teeth or loll-
ing in cadence to his prose rhythms. A penchant fostered perhaps under the slack rule of Gould's predecessor, however, sometimes found
his concentration fastened elsewhere. More than twenty years later, he
boasted: "The four college years and the three years' course of Divinity have not yielded me so many grand facts as some idle books under
the bench at the Latin School."[6] Here, conceivably, was laid the foundation for his later championship of a more varied curriculum than
those he had known at the schools he had attended.

The occasions for rebellion and nonconformity that the Latin School
offered under William Biglow's irresponsible management may have
had more lasting consequences than anyone at that time realized. In
their sophomore year, Emerson's Harvard class, many of whom had
been classmates at the Latin School, staged an insurrection and Emerson dutifully supported it. At periodic intervals, for some years,

Emerson seems to have commemorated the Latin School insurgency with rebellions of his own. Emerging from a disciplined home in which acts of defiance were so deplored that the possibility of such behavior went unsuspected, Emerson found the pattern of resistance and protest that developed at the Latin School during his first year there itself an education. It awakened in him a sense of power he never afterward lost sight of.

On William Emerson's death, in addition to allowing his heirs to continue to live at the parsonage, the First Church generously granted Ruth his salary for six months and an annual stipend of $500 for seven years. Thus provided for, Ruth managed her household with some success until the summer of 1813, when she made preparations to move so that the new pastor, John Abbot, could take over his manse. But Abbot chose to come there for an interval as her boarder and then went abroad for his health. In October 1814, without again resuming his duties, he died. Ruth, meantime, had moved her family to her father's house on Rainsford's Lane. But that same October her father died also. Thereupon she undertook to conduct a boardinghouse on Beacon Hill.

The War of 1812 had brought hard times to Boston and a pall of menace. At one point the Latin School boys were sent with shovels to Noddle's Island to build defensive embankments. Emerson remembered the event as a kind of school holiday and could not be certain he had dug at all.[7] As the war deepened, prices soared — flour brought $17 a barrel — and Ruth, realizing she could not cope on her own, accepted, late in 1814, Ezra Ripley's offer to shelter her family in his Concord parsonage. That same year, Mary Caroline died of diphtheria. Ruth must have been glad to see the year end.

During this unstable period, when he was shunted from school to school, and home to home, while the economy turned topsy-turvy, and Aunt Mary came and went, and the threat of a British invasion loomed, Ralph Waldo found himself actually stimulated by events. He discovered that he had a flair for producing a poetical line and gave vent to his patriotic feeling by dwelling on Isaac Hull's defeat of the *Guerrière* and Oliver Hazard Perry's victory on Lake Erie. He resisted, however, Aunt Mary's suggestion that he memorialize James Lawrence's ill-fated contest with the British on the sea off Boston. His metier was singing of victories, not defeats. Even then, though the philosophy to sustain his outlook had not yet arrived, he was the poet of the positive. Yet he did confront unpleasant reality when he wrote verses on the death of John Haskins and, with touching sadness, led the household in prayer when Mary Caroline died — one of the first things to recommend him to the notice of Sarah Bradford, who was present on that occasion.

The kind of discipline that was maturing Emerson is indicated in a

letter he wrote to Aunt Mary in April 1813, describing to her, at her
request, a representative day in his life :

> Friday 9th I choose for the day of telling what I did. In the
> Morning I rose as I do commonly about 5 minutes before 6 then
> help *Wm* in making the fire after which I set the table for
> Prayers. I then call mamma about quarter after 6. We spell as we
> did before you went away. I confess I often feel an angry passion
> start in one corner of my heart when one of my Brothers get
> above me which I think sometimes they do by unfair means after
> which we eat our breakfast then I have from about quarter after 7
> till 8 to play or read. I think I am rather inclined to the former.
> I then go to school where I hope I can say I study more than I did
> a little while ago. I am in another book called Virgil. . . . After
> attending this school I go to Mr. Webb's private school where I
> write & cipher I go to this place at 11 and stay till one o'clock.
> After this, when I come home I eat my dinner & at 2 o'clock I
> resume my studies at the Latin School where I do the same except
> in studying grammar after I come home I do mamma her little
> errands if she has any then I bring in my wood to supply the
> break-fast room. I then have some time to play & eat my supper
> after that we say our hymns or chapters & then take our turns in
> reading Rollin as we did before you went. We retire to bed at
> different times I go a little after 8 & retire to my private devo-
> tions & then close my eyes in sleep & there ends the toils of the
> day.[8]

In the spring of 1814, Emerson first began to correspond with Sarah
Bradford. He was then eleven and she was twenty. At that time he
could make on her no claims of kinship. She was merely a friend of
Aunt Mary's. Another four years would pass before she entered the
family as the wife of the Reverend Samuel Ripley, who, as half-brother
of Emerson's father and Aunt Mary, had, on many occasions, stood in
place of a father to William's sons. At the outset, therefore, Sarah's
interest in Emerson was simply that of one precocious mind responding to another.
  When Sarah, evidently through her brother Gamaliel, an usher at
the Latin School and an admirer of Emerson's verse efforts, learned
that Emerson had begun a verse translation of Virgil's Fifth Bucolic,
she wrote him, in 1814 :

> My dear young friend, you love to trifle in rhyme a little now
> and then ; why will you not continue this versification of the Fifth
> Bucolic. You will answer two ends . . . improve in your Latin as

well as indulge a taste for poetry. Why can't you write me a letter
in Latin? But Greek is your favorite language; *Epistola in
lingua Graeca* would be still better. All the honor will be on my
part — to correspond with a young gentleman in Greek.[9]

She signed herself, "your affectionate friend, Sarah." As someone who
had little experience of openly acknowledged affection, Emerson leaped
to oblige, construing in pleasing hexameters another twenty-four lines
of Virgil. Thus Emerson came under the eye of his wisest, soberest
tutor.

Much has been made of the range and depth of Sarah Ripley's
learning. Recalling her at this stage, Emerson said: "At a time when
perhaps no other woman read Greek, she acquired the language with
ease, and read Plato, — adding soon the advantage of German Commentators." After Sarah's marriage, when Samuel brought boys into
their home to fit them for college, the task of giving advanced instruction in Greek and Latin fell to her. Emerson remarked after her death
in July 1867: "She became one of the best Greek scholars in the country, and continued in her latest years, the habit of reading Homer, the
tragedians, and Plato."[10] She has been deified as "a Greek goddess in
a Yankee wrapper, who washed the family clothes and scrubbed the
floors and translated Klopstock and taught Homer and Virgil and Aristotle in her husband's school."[11]

Emerson commended Sarah's realism as a teacher. "She leaves a
dunce to be a dunce . . . ," he said, "& believes that a loom which
turns out huckabuck can never be talked into making damask."[12] For
Sarah, Emerson versified his reflections on the virtues of Rollin's ancient history. His lessons and his reading were explored with enthusiasm in her letters, and in such a way as to cause him to feel that she
thought she was under obligation to him. Deftly she revised his translations, giving him a peerless opportunity to develop his responsiveness to the power of language. She also gave direction to his reading.

After Sarah's marriage to Uncle Samuel, when Emerson was a sophomore at Harvard, he wrote of her to his brother William: "The new
inhabitant [is] by far the finest woman I ever saw. . . . As to her
knowledge talk on what you will she can always give you a new idea —
ask her any philosophical question, she will always enlighten you by
her answer."[13] Assuming that what Sarah had to communicate was
exclusively the methods and insights of scholarship, Robert Gay thought
her influence best discerned in the careers of Emerson's brothers, William and Edward, rather than in his own career.[14] This estimate is
unjustly limiting.

Henry Lee, who was, with Emerson, an Overseer of Harvard at the
time of Sarah's death, and who remembered her as "the most learned,

brilliant and modest woman of 'Our First Century,' " said of her in an obituary notice: "Her faith in their intuitions and capabilities lifted them and shamed or encouraged them to efforts impossible under another instructor; for she did not merely impart instruction, she educated all the powers of mind and heart. . . . She seemed to have explored every region and to have intuitive ideas of every subject of interest."[15] The importance Lee assigns to Sarah's homage to intuition directs us to her influence on Emerson.

In an undated entry in his journal, written in 1844 or 1845, Emerson gave his impressions of Sarah: "She has quick senses and quick perceptions and ready sympathies which put her into just relations with all persons, and a tender sense of propriety which recommends her to persons of all conditions." She was the antithesis of the grubbing scholar: "She has not a profound mind, but . . . she is endowed with a certain restless & impatient temperament, which drives her to the pursuit of knowledge not so much for the value of the knowledge but for some rope to twist, some grist to her mill. For this reason it is almost indifferent to her what she studies." Emerson saw her alignment as transcendental: "She follows nature in many particulars of life where others obtrude their own will & theory. . . . She wishes to please & to live well with a few, but in the frankest, most universal & humane mode."[16]

The debts the Emerson brothers owed to Sarah's husband, Uncle Samuel, were beyond calculation. He gave them employment when they were students at Harvard. He supplied the means when ill health forced them to travel south. His home was ever open to them, his counsel ever available, his tongue came quickly to their defense. Yet only with Samuel's death in 1847 did Emerson take full cognizance of his obligations to him:

> I think often how serious is his loss to Mother. I remember him almost as long as I can remember her, and from my father's death in my early boyhood he has always been an important friend to her & her children. You know how generous he was to me & to my brothers in our youth at college & afterwards. He never ceased to be so, and he was the same friend to many others that he was to us. I am afraid we hardly thanked him.[17]

Thus Emerson wrote his wife, Lidian, from Manchester, England, when news of Samuel's death reached him. Samuel had died unexpectedly in his carriage at Concord, hurrying to welcome Thanksgiving guests — serving others till the very last.

Only in one way is Emerson's negligence to be accounted for. When he thought of the Ripley household, he thought of Sarah, who stood at

the center of her world for Samuel, too, as well as for Emerson. She
was one of the Fates that presided over Emerson's life and fortunes,
and Samuel was content to have it so.

The price of wood as much as the price of food may have driven
Ruth Emerson to seek haven in Concord for the winter of 1814–1815 —
the duration of their stay being bounded by the start of winter and
winter's breaking. They arrived in November; by 25 March Ruth was
back in Boston making things ready for their return. Ruth knew the
urban world best and saw there her best prospects for making her own
way. Perhaps, too, now that the Latin School had passed into capable
hands, she wanted the assurance that her sons would be prepared adequately for Harvard, where William was now enrolled.

There are no anecdotes suggesting that Emerson, whose prior acquaintance with Concord had been limited to summer holidays, felt, in
this interval, some mystic pull that told him his name would pass down
through history linked with Concord. Even Nature, in those bleak winter months, seems not to have spoken to him. A watershed moment
would have been compensation for years of hardship already endured,
and still to come. But there was none. Apart from his sugar-barrel
theatricals, the only reportable anecdote surviving from this Concord
sojourn concerns an awkward moment when Dr. Ripley made him shake
hands with two boys he had quarreled with. "What did you say to
them?" Aunt Mary wanted to know, later. He had said nothing, and
told her so. Aunt Mary was nonplussed. "You should have talked about
your thumbs or your toes," she expostulated, "only to say something!"[18]

The return to Boston began a two-year hopscotching about town.
The Emersons went first to Rainsford's Lane, where Ruth ran the house
for her unmarried sisters, then to Beacon Hill to care for the house
of the Daniel Parkers, absent in London. On the Parkers' return
they moved to an adjacent house, where Ruth kept boarders. There
were further moves — to Hancock Street, to Essex Street, still with
boarders.

The Parkers' house had been a favorite stopover. It was in the vital
center of town and had, to Aunt Mary's elation, a fine view of the Old
Granary Burying Ground, which Jean Stafford's Miss Pride later would
call "the jewel of the city." There Ruth had as boarder Lemuel Shaw,
one day to be Chief Justice of the Commonwealth and father-in-law
of Herman Melville. And there Emerson had but a handy distance to
go to drive the cow Ezra Ripley had given them around to the Haskins
paddock on Carver Street, adjacent to the house where Poe had been
born six years before.

These were lean years. Ralph and Edward, taking turns wearing

their sole overcoat, had to brave the taunts of schoolmates quick to
query, ''Whose turn to wear the coat today?'' Once Ralph was on his
way to buy shoes when the dollar for the purchase blew from his hand
to lodge in a drift of poplar leaves. Though a long and anxious search
ensued, it was never found. Once they went supperless when Edward
gave their supper loaf to the poor, and Sarah Bradford came by to
find Aunt Mary contriving to make do, in lieu of victuals, with tales
of heroism.

Handouts trickled into the house from concerned friends — sugar, a
cheese, muslin for a cap, a canister of tea, or a five-dollar bill, perhaps
surreptitiously tucked under the sugar bowl. This tactic of furtive giving Emerson himself adopted in later years when visiting the indigent
Alcotts. Sometimes the Emersons lacked firewood. Striving to keep warm,
Edward read Plato's dialogues while swaddled in a cloak, and, for
that reason, long associated Plato with the smell of wool. Yet Emerson
was not aggrieved by their poverty. Firkins suggests that the basis for
his doctrine of compensation was laid then.[19] For what was taken
something in equal measure was given. Edward Everett Hale offers
corroboration: ''I was standing with Mr. Emerson once at a college
exhibition, where a young man had easily taken the most brilliant honors. . . . I congratulated him, as I congratulated myself, on the success
of our young friend; and he said, 'Yes. . . . And now, if something
will fall out amiss — if he should be unpopular with his class, or if his
father should fail in business, or if some other misfortune can befall
him — all will be well.' ''[20]

In a passage in ''Domestic Life,'' Emerson created a scene evocative
of his own life in those struggling years:

> Who has not seen, and who can see unmoved, under a low roof,
> the eager, blushing boys discharging as they can their household
> chores, and hastening into the sitting-room to the study of to-
> morrow's merciless lesson . . . the warm sympathy with which
> they kindle each other in schoolyard or in barn or, wood-shed, with
> scraps of poetry or song, with phrases of the last oration or
> mimicry of the orator; the youthful criticism, on Sunday, of the
> sermons; the school declamation faithfully rehearsed at home . . .
> the first solitary joys of literary vanity, when the translation or
> the theme has been completed, sitting alone near the top of the
> house . . . the affectionate delight with which they greet the
> return of each one after the early separations which school or
> business require; the foresight with which, during such absences,
> they hive the honey which opportunity offers, for the ear and
> imagination of the others; and the unrestrained glee with which
> they disburden themselves of their early mental treasures when

the holidays bring them again together? What is the hoop that holds them stanch? It is the iron band of poverty, of necessity, of austerity, which, excluding them from the sensual enjoyments which make other boys too early old, has directed their activity into safe and right channels, and made them, despite themselves, reverers of the grand, the beautiful and the good.[21]

Emerson had reason to remember the satisfaction that came from study during this interval. Headmaster Gould thought well of him, and he repeated many times, at exhibition programs at the Latin School, the sugar-barrel triumphs of his Concord interlude. And he had the satisfaction of having Gamaliel Bradford cast a quatrain welcoming him to the hill of Apollo as a true poet.

In the summer of 1817, Emerson's immediate prospects looked uncertain. Benjamin Gould said he was ready for Harvard. The means to send him there were lacking, but William released some funds by meeting some of his own college expenses, teaching in Maine in the summer. The First Church assigned to Ralph the Penn annuity, which formerly had gone to William.[22] And their father's classmate and friend, John Thornton Kirkland, now president of Harvard, chose Emerson as his freshman messenger, which meant that he would be lodged at no cost.

To give a final flourish to this last summer in Boston, Emerson, in blue coat and white trousers, an artificial red and white rose in his lapel, stood on 2 July by the gunhouse on the Common, with other Latin School boys identically clad, as an honor guard for President Monroe as he rode past in a military parade that marked the occasion of his formal visit.

7. Harvard
In Merlin's Mirror

*E*MERSON'S Harvard classmates would remember him as someone whose courtly restraint discouraged intimacy. If he had come to Harvard beholden to no one, he might, on occasion, have been an instigator or shaper of opinion, as later he proved to be. He came instead laden with obligations. As the president's freshman messenger, announcing faculty decisions and summoning delinquent students, he was aligned with authority. The outright grants from the college and the First Church paid his board and much of his tuition, which at Harvard between 1807 and 1825 soared from twenty dollars a year to fifty-five. Total expenses for a student in average circumstances in this era approached $300 a year.[1] The luxury of displeasing those upon whom he was dependent was ruled out by courtesy and by sensible regard for his own prospects and those of his younger brothers, who expected, in their turn, to attend Harvard also. That Emerson actively weighed the advantages and disadvantages of asserting his independence at Harvard is improbable. From early childhood he had been taught to respect authority and to defer to those to whom he was under obligation.

Going back to Harvard's first graduating class, fifty-six of Emerson's forebears had graduated from Harvard. Although at least one of his mother's sisters, alarmed at Harvard's drift toward liberal Unitarianism, wanted him to go to Brown, where conservatism still held sway, Emerson did not share her apprehensions. He was certain Harvard could make him ''as good a minister'' as Brown could.[2]

Late in August 1817, Emerson had taken the Harvard entrance exams and passed unconditionally. He was fourteen. That was not remarkable. William had entered Harvard at thirteen and so had Emerson's future friend, Frederic Henry Hedge. At Harvard Emerson actually was challenged more by his financial obligations than by his studies. The First Church's Penn bequest paid only about thirty-three dollars yearly. He was given money from Harvard's Saltonstall Fund, too, but it was slow in coming. To acquit his remaining indebtedness, he had to depend on his own efforts, not only as messenger to President Kirkland and a waiter in Junior Commons, but as a teacher, on school holidays, at his Uncle Samuel's school in Waltham, and for three months, during the first semester of his freshman year, as private tutor to Samuel Kirkland Lothrop, the president's twelve-year-old nephew.

Years later, as a clergyman, Lothrop reconstituted his fourteen-year-old tutor as he recalled him:

> Nearly as tall as when he had reached maturity — a Saxon blonde, pale face, light hair, blue eyes. . . . He was a very peculiar person . . . with a wall of reserve about him which he would not let anybody penetrate; not caring much about sympathy, though receiving it not ungraciously; and while having nothing of self-assertion, being to a remarkable degree self-sustained, sufficient unto himself, and happy in his own thoughts, in his own soul.

Despite the reserve and self-sufficiency he attributed to Emerson, Lothrop saw him also as, in some ways, immature: "Too much of a boy himself, . . . he was little inclined to scold or lecture me, and more disposed to talk with me about men and things and to read to me pieces of his own poetry and prose composition."[3]

During the second semester of his freshman year, when he was not yet fifteen, Emerson began his Waltham teaching chores, having under his care fourteen pupils. More than twenty years later, in August 1841, he was to call up a vision of himself as he had been at Waltham in 1818:

> Robin went to the house of his uncle who was a clergyman to assist him in the care of his private scholars. The boys were nearly or quite as old as he, & they played together on the ice & in the field. One day the uncle was gone all day & the lady with whom they boarded called on Robin to say grace at dinner. Robin was at his wit's end; he laughed, he looked grave, he said something nobody knew what, & then laughed again, as if to indemnify himself with the boys for assuming one moment the cant of a man. And yet at home perhaps Robin had often said grace at dinner.[4]

Despite the exigencies that plagued him through college, Emerson took pride in the New England spirit that made his education possible,

applauding in ''Education'' the humor that enabled the poor man to
''put his hand into the pocket of the rich, and say, You shall educate
me, not as you will, but as I will: not alone in the elements, but, by
further provision, in the languages, in sciences, in the useful and in
elegant arts.''[5]

In 1817, when Emerson took occupancy of the room under the room
from which John Thornton Kirkland governed his domain, in that
building of which present-day Wadsworth House is a survival and amplification, Kirkland was seven years into a term that lasted till 1828.
As a liberal Unitarian minister, Kirkland trailed none of the filaments
of Calvinism that clung to many of his colleagues. A Johnsonian wit
and gentle manners linked him to the neoclassical tradition, while a
millenarian enthusiasm for an improved society made him both a sponsor
and an initiator of progressive cultural changes taking place in his
own day. Even when the War of 1812 produced an Embargo Act that
stunned the New England economy, Kirkland kept Harvard moving
on a forward course.

Despite his single status, Kirkland had a fatherly flair. His portly
build, amiable, boyish countenance, and habitual joviality offered reassurance to those who came under his jurisdiction. Not surprisingly,
although it was his custom to summon Emerson to his study with foot
signals, he did not stomp on the floor but confined himself to two light
taps. So little awed was he by the majesty of his office, he sometimes
eased the terrors of candidates for admission by breaking in on their
oral exams with a plate of pears.

Kirkland's father, likewise a clergyman, had evangelized the Oneida,
and Kirkland dealt with the untamed savages who came under his care
with equivalent tact and compassion. The students at Harvard in those
years were, for the most part, like Ralph Waldo himself, restive adolescents chafing at the restrictions they lived under and at a monoto-
nous academic regimen that heavily stressed memory work.

The interest Kirkland took in the four sons of his old friend William Emerson was exceptional even for a man who showed a caring
interest in all those who made up his community of scholars. Thus, at
a critical stage in his life and for the first time, Emerson became the
unofficial ward of a man who could provide a male role model and
stand in place of a father to him. To the extent possible for someone
with his manifold responsibilities, Kirkland lent himself to that cause.
The example he offered may have brought one unforeseen result. It
was his practice to quarry his sermons from disconnected notes, casting them in the epigrammatic style that Emerson subsequently found
so well suited to his own purposes.

We should not suppose that Kirkland functioned merely as a beacon
of benevolence irradiating, in a steadily advancing, never-relenting,

arc, the troubled visages of his charges. He did not tamper with the established curriculum. State funds made up part of Harvard's income, and the businessmen of Boston who ran the state government would not have tolerated any major curriculum revisions. In his quiet way, however, Kirkland set changes in motion. It is no coincidence that during Kirkland's presidency the Boston Renaissance began. Kirkland stood before the university community as an exemplar of industry and vision. He built Holworthy Hall, University Hall, and Divinity Hall. In the very year of Emerson's arrival, he founded the Law School. He landscaped the Yard, bringing an atmosphere of pleasantness to a hitherto bleak world that had offered the students the choice of seeing either an unbroken expanse of whortleberry swamps and wild pastureland or, in the other direction, a bare and blasted heath whose first obstruction in view, several miles distant, was the Boston State House atop the pinnacle of Beacon Hill. Yet he did not let his role as builder of a physical plant blind him to his responsibilities as an educator. He increased the number of professorships and course offerings. And he developed the college libraries.

When Emerson entered Harvard, he encountered a program of studies patterned on the English high school of the Renaissance era. Instruction was in the hands of drillmasters. In languages passages were assigned to be construed and declaimed. Much emphasis was placed on memory. Three of the professors who would influence him most were not at Harvard in 1817, Emerson's first year. Edward Everett and George Ticknor were studying in Germany. Edward Tyrrel Channing joined the faculty in 1819. Emerson studied Greek with Everett, but was especially dazzled by Everett's high-flown rhetoric, an infatuation that, under Channing's influence, he presently outgrew. Channing advocated a subdued delivery more consistent with a people living in a democratic society. In time Emerson would owe a comparable debt to Channing's brother, William Ellery Channing, which their nephew, Ellery, described later in these terms: "Dr. Channing first broke up the Johnsonian period into short sentences, and used simplicity for artifice. Emerson took this short style from Channing, but carried it farther; he wrote with much more point, and I think was never excelled, if equalled, in English."[6] Ticknor's French course led Emerson to Montaigne, whose prose was an endorsement of the principles of style Channing upheld.

Emerson's philosophy professors, Levi Frisbie and Levi Hedge, introduced him to the Edinburgh School of Scottish ethics. From this followed his acceptance of Richard Price's claims for the moral sense and his repudiation of John Locke's sensate philosophy. Thus, though neither Frisbie nor Hedge envisaged such a result, Emerson was stricken of his shackles and left free to pursue transcendentalism.

Frisbie was named Alford Professor of Natural Religion, Moral Philosophy, and Civil Polity the year Emerson arrived at Harvard and died, at thirty-nine, the year after Emerson graduated. His strength failing, his vision failing (a piratical kerchief sometimes bound his brow, cutting the flow of light to his aching eyes), Frisbie nonetheless met his responsibilities with a zeal that extended even to painstaking care given to the prose compositions of his students — a carryover from apprenticeship years as a Latin professor. His guidance, as well as that from Channing (to whom, in his senior year, Emerson submitted weekly themes), helped make Emerson aware of the folly of striving, as Everett did, after a brilliant effect. Commending Frisbie, on his death, as a man "of republican strength & elegant accomplishments," Emerson concluded, "Professor Frisbie will hardly be supplied by any man in the community."[7]

For making Harvard feel the gravitational pull of higher learning as it had taken shape in Germany, Emerson had Everett and Ticknor to thank. Under their influence formal lectures routed recitations. But he soon saw through Everett. Though Everett saved his floridity for pulpit and platform, and was urbane, fluent, even engrossing in the classroom, he was inexact in his scholarship and without ideas of his own. Ticknor, always thoroughly prepared, always intimately informed, a scholar in fact as well as in the image he projected, was the better man.

At Harvard Emerson associated mathematics with pure wretchedness. "Seldom, I suppose," he wrote in his journal, "was a more inapt learner of arithmetic."[8] Defensively, he told William that he did "not think it necessary to understand Mathematics & Greek thoroughly to be a good, useful, or even *great* man."[9] When Emerson turned from analytical to intuitive reasoning, he experienced no wrench of parting but rather a sense of glorious release.

As a sophomore, Emerson belatedly blended into the student body and had his first true experience of college discipline from a student's point of view. It was occasioned by the All Hallows food riot between freshmen and sophomores, which broke out at Sunday supper on 1 November 1818. In the history of Harvard in those years such incidents were not isolated. Andrew P. Peabody, a tutor at Harvard in the following decade, recalled: "Outrages involving not only large destruction of property, but peril of life — as, for instance, the blowing up of public rooms in inhabited buildings — were commonplace."[10] And William Hickling Prescott, the historian, owed his blindness to being struck in the eye with a hard crust, in 1812, during a riot in the Harvard Commons similar to the one in 1818.

Emerson's Greek professor, John Popkin, inordinately proud of his fine legs (still displayable in an age when knee breeches were worn), and receptive to the sobriquet of Doctor Pop (if the user were *his* student), was monitor when the riot erupted. He hurried to Kirkland, who came on the run to halt the melee. Then, in a display of firmness, a quality that did not come easy to him, Kirkland suspended as ringleaders the four sophomores most likely to have been responsible. Their classmates thereupon converged on the Rebellion Tree, an elm close to the Yard where, on the eve of the War of Independence, the Sons of Liberty had rallied their spirits. George Washington Adams, already on the road that would lead to alcoholism and suicide, whipped up their hurt vanity to an expression of further defiance. When Kirkland thereupon raised the number of suspensions, their classmates countered the move by voluntarily joining them in exile.

In this unanimous rebellion of the class of 1821, Emerson participated to the extent that self-respect required. He accompanied the others to the Rebellion Tree and with them broke off a twig while simultaneously vowing to oppose President Kirkland on the suspensions until he relented. Three weeks went by before tempers cooled and most of the students — though not all — were reinstated. About half the class petitioned for reconciliation within a week of the insurrection, however, and Emerson was probably among them since, in February, he was appointed a waiter at Commons, a post he would not have been eligible for had he fallen afoul of the administration. No other tree would play so Edenic a role in Emerson's future life as did the Rebellion Tree, but, in his "Divinity School Address," in the opening stanza of that lyrical statement of insurrection, he was to show that he could summon the whole world of Nature to his side when convinced his cause was right.[11]

At college Emerson's day began at five in the morning. When he had a paper to draft, he got up half an hour earlier. On such an occasion, in April 1819, he invited William to see him, from a distance, "in Merlin's mirror," at five in the morning, "standing at your old desk twisting & turning, endeavouring to collect thoughts or intelligence enough to fill the dreary blank of a page & a third more."[12]

For warmth in his room each student depended on a fire in an open fireplace, responsibility for which was his own, including the purchase of firewood. Most rooms also had a cannonball that, on bitter days, was heated red-hot and strategically placed on a metal support, wherever the heat it emitted could most benefit the room's occupant. In milder seasons cannonballs sometimes were rolled down the stairs in the middle of the night to startle the proctors awake.

Dr. Peabody's account of the furnishings of the rooms finds confirmation in other sources: "The feather bed . . . was regarded as a valuable chattel; but ten dollars would have been a fair auction price for all the other contents of an average room, which were a pine bedstead, washstand, table, and desk, a cheap rocking-chair and from two to four other chairs of the plainest fashion. I doubt whether any fellow student of mine owned a carpet.''[13]

In winter, obligatory morning prayers were held half an hour before sunrise, in the unheated chapel. During the ensuing hour and a half, recitations were heard in University Hall. A breakfast of coffee, hot rolls, and butter followed in the Commons. Classes met for lectures or more recitations between ten and twelve. The main meal of the day — plain fare such as baked beef and hard Indian pudding — was served at twelve-thirty.[14] In the afternoon further recitations followed, and evening prayers, at six. On these occasions, Emerson, like many of his classmates, brought secular reading with him to the chapel, Pascal's *Pensées* being a favorite, and, as an ethical work, judged by him to qualify as pious. Some years later, John Fiske was suspended from Harvard for perusing a secular work in chapel, but Pascal seems not to have put Emerson in jeopardy of any kind. He may even have benefited from his ideas on intuition, but certainly never looked into Pascal's work in pure mathematics, which would have terrified him.

The evening meal, after chapel, was as bleak as breakfast — tea ''and cold bread, of the consistency of wool.'' In those years Harvard had neither a gymnasium nor organized sports, a fact that helps account for the routinely occurring riots. Between the end of supper hour and eight o'clock, when the study bell rang and a monastic silence enveloped the college, students were free to indulge in such recreations as they could devise. In that interval song and merriment rocked this world of Academe. With the arrival of the great silence, studying was done by candlelight; the candles needed frequent attention and were, on that account, an impediment to concentration.[15]

The cornerstone for Gore Hall, a new library, was laid in 1813. The following summer 41,000 volumes were moved into the new building. During his freshman year Emerson drew out fourteen books from Gore, solid studies of philosophy and history.[16]

Although a blue Sabbath was observed at Harvard from eight o'clock on Saturday night until after evening prayers on Sunday, students were at liberty, on Saturday afternoons, to walk abroad. Most walked to Boston; Emerson usually did, to visit his mother. Sometimes, though, as with his friend of childhood days, John Lowell Gardner, he walked to ''Sweet Auburn's rolling gardens,'' the site which, in midcentury, became that Valhalla of distinguished Bostonians, Mount Auburn Cemetery.

A Harvard student who went to a theatrical performance in Boston was required to pay, if caught, a fine of ten dollars. The fine for going to a party in Boston was five dollars. Prohibitions against liquor, however, were not in force. Oliver Wendell Holmes says:

Wine was very freely drunk in those days, without fear and without reproach from the pulpit or the platform. I remember on the occasion of my having an ''Exhibition,'' that, with the consent of my parents, I laid in a considerable stock, and that my room was for several days the seat of continuous revelry. . . . It was still worse in my father's day, for when he went to college his mother equipped him with a Dutch liquor-case containing six large bottles filled with the various kinds of strong waters, probably brandy, rum, gin, whisky, doubtless enough to craze a whole class of young bacchanalians.[17]

Emerson was not averse to drinking wine on those occasions, not frequent, when he had the means to procure it, but he himself, he related, lacked the capacity to benefit by it, growing not convivial, as his fellows did, but ''graver with every glass.''[18]

During his junior year Emerson had for a roommate John Gaillard Keith Gourdin, one of the Southern gallants of the ranking social set at Harvard. In theory someone of Emerson's Spartan upbringing should have been ill at ease in Gourdin's company. Quite otherwise. Emerson approved of him.

Some allege that Emerson chose not to belong to the Porcellian Club or the Hasty Pudding Club because he did not find their interests compatible with his own. In fact, he could not afford to belong and, for that reason, probably was not asked. More to his liking, in any event, were the clubs he did join, the Conventicle and the Pythologian. He remembered the debates held, the papers read, the books read aloud and discussed, and was proud to tell William that membership in one of these clubs identified him as ''one of the fifteen smartest fellows.''[19] Yet the Pythologians forgathered for social as well as scholarly purposes, and Emerson remembered the Malaga wine that he drank in their company as the best he ever drank.

In January 1820 Emerson took a step that was of inestimable importance to his subsequent development as a writer. He began keeping a journal, a habit he held to for more than fifty years. The first move in this direction came in the previous month, when he began to keep a record of his reading. That record covers a period of five years and discloses interests predictably variegated. Of the playwrights he read Euripides, Aristophanes, Beaumont and Fletcher, Massinger, Baillie, Molière, Racine, and, especially, Shakespeare and Jonson. He read ten of Scott's novels, Smollett's *Peregrine Pickle*, and Fielding's *Tom Jones*. Otherwise novelists got slight notice. Poets fared scarcely better, mostly limited to Byron, Burns, and Boileau, though he did read some of Milton's prose, and his journal for the period shows ready knowledge of the poetry. As befitted a future essayist, Emerson's taste for expository prose at this stage of his life was considerable — More, Bacon, Johnson, Burke, Jeremy Taylor, Hume, Gibbon, Cook's *Voyages*, and, as well, lives of Cicero, Chaucer, John Knox, and Cotton Mather. He also read Voltaire, Montesquieu, and, of course, Montaigne. Apart from Cotton Mather and *The Federalist*, American authors seem to have held faint interest for this future advocate of the American scholar.

Looking back on his college years, Emerson once remarked: "In college, I used to echo a frequent ejaculation of my wise aunt's, 'Oh, blessed, blessed poverty!' when I saw young men of fine capabilities whose only and fatal disadvantage was wealth."[20] Aunt Mary did a good job of making blessings out of the deprivations that went with poverty. Unfortunately, as a result Emerson never was really able to enjoy then or later, without twinges of conscience, such pleasures as came his way. Sometimes, despite his conditioning, he had contrary moods to deal with. Not long before he finished college, he wrote of "feeling the humiliating sense of dependence & inferiority which like the goading, soul-sickening sense of extreme poverty, palsies effort."[21] While he was at Harvard, his mother was running a boardinghouse on Essex Street large enough to accommodate four families. It grieved him that she had to work so hard and do without so much so that her sons could be educated. In senior year when, as second-place winner in the Boylston Oratorical competition, he won thirty dollars, he wanted to buy her a shawl with it. It went instead to pay a baker's bill. He wrote to William, with obvious regret:

It appears to me the happiest earthly moment my sanguine hopes can picture, if it should ever arrive, to have a home comfortable & pleasant, to offer to mother; in some feeble way to repay her for the cares & woes & inconveniences she has so often been subject to on our account alone. . . . To be sure, after talking at this rate, I have done nothing myself — but then I've less faculty and age than most poor collegians. But when I am out of College I will (Deo Volente), study divinity & keep school at the same time, — try to be a minister & have a house.[22]

The idea apparently was to restore Ruth to her lost estate.

In a class of fifty-nine, Emerson stood thirtieth. To his younger brothers came the distinctions that had eluded him. He had had to make do with second prizes in the Bowdoin competition, in his junior and senior years, as well as placing second in the Boylston competition. Edward graduated as the first scholar in his class. Charles won first prize for his Bowdoin essay and was valedictorian when he graduated. "A chamber alone," Emerson at length concluded, "was the best thing I found at college."[23]

Build, therefore, your own world . . .

8. Commencement

*I*N 1821, Commencement Day at Harvard fell on 29 August. As was customary throughout that era, it was a state holiday. Banks were closed and businesses shut down. After all, the Commonwealth had a heavy investment in Harvard. As in the past, it contributed to Harvard's financial support, and it still drew on Harvard for its chief men of affairs in both public and private enterprises. Harvard reciprocated with elaborate receptions open to visitors who came to Cambridge and Boston in that season, capital advertising for both college and Commonwealth. The bill for these parties, which sometimes included dinner for five hundred people and more, usually was defrayed by the parents of wealthy seniors.[1] Although the mediocre son of a generous father was likely to be given one of the twenty-one parts assigned to the graduating seniors in the Commencement exercises, the burden of that possibility seems to have bruised the conscience of no one. That the government connived for it seemed sufficient justification.

As one of the impecunious students, Emerson was not one of those to whom the administration looked to underwrite a portion of the Commencement Day entertainment in 1821. Although his ranking in the class would have been even lower than it was had not some of his classmates had their grades lowered because of bad conduct, lack of interest among many of the eligible students in the parts offered elevated him to an active role in the exercises. As Class Poet, he read an original poem on Class Day, 17 July. At Commencement, in a Conference, also called a Colloquy, "On the Character of John Knox, William Penn, and John Wesley," he appeared as Knox, supporting his claims against those of the other two reformers. He cared little for either distinction.

Of Emerson's selection as Class Poet, Emerson's classmate Josiah Quincy (whose father, also Josiah Quincy, was soon to succeed Kirkland as president of Harvard, and sooner to be mayor of Boston), said: "Emerson accepted the duty of delivering the poem on Class Day, after seven others had been asked who positively refused. So it appears that, in the opinion of this critical class, the author of the 'Wood Notes' and the 'Humble Bee' ranked about eighth in poetical ability."[2]

Not much more luster attached to Emerson's participation in the Colloquy. These were parts usually assigned to the duller men. Emerson was, in fact, resentful that he had not been allowed to deliver an original poem at Commencement and met the obligation with scant enthusiasm. His friend Samuel Bradford related that he was "so disgusted that he would take no pains to commit to memory, and had to be greatly prompted before he had finished."[3] While certainly Emerson aspired to win renown as a poet, his dispirited performance as Knox may not wholly ascribe to the frustration he felt at not being able to come before the Commencement audience as a poet. Quincy's journal notations at the time indicate that Emerson's appearance as Class Poet likewise was without distinction: "Barnwell and Emerson performed our valedictory exercises before all the scholars and a number of ladies. They were rather poor and did but little honor to the class."[4] The poem was, in fact, inconsequential, the poet having limited himself to developing unexceptional arguments which must have been heard that year wherever commencements were held in America. Europe's sorry history was deplored and America's bright promise extolled. His alma mater was praised and his classmates urged to shed their frolic moods and confront the realization that "Life's motley pilgrimage must be begun."[5] Yet, even if Emerson had wrought a masterpiece, Quincy, who was consumed with his own importance, would not have said so. Earlier that morning Quincy had delivered a dissertation which, he said, "had the good fortune to please our college critics." Yet the day before, when Emerson delivered the dissertation on ethical philosophy for which he had won second prize in the Boylston competition, Quincy had dismissed it as "long and dry." Quincy also rejoiced in having edged out Emerson for first prize in this competition. In 1883, after Emerson was in his grave, and his fame assured, Quincy allowed himself to say with magnanimity: "I was of course much pleased with the award of this intelligent committee; and should have been still more gratified had they mentioned that the man who was to be the most original and influential writer born in America was my unsuccessful competitor."[6]

If the picture of events as they unfolded at Harvard's 181st Commencement hints of lurking unrest, then that is only as it should be. In Harvard annals the class of 1821 stands out as a restive one. For some while after the sophomore insurrection of 1818, this class had no assurance that it would be permitted a Commencement. The majority of the faculty wanted to cancel it and would have had not Kirkland overruled them.

During the last half of 1821 Emerson wrote nothing in his journal. But through the preceding fall and winter the entries often were tinged with anxiety and melancholy. He was concerned about his capacity to confront life and about his future prospects. At times he was physically ill. At other times he reproached himself for lack of moral stamina. On 25 October 1820, he wrote: "I find myself often idle, vagrant, stupid & hollow. This is somewhat appalling & if I do not discipline myself with diligent care, I shall suffer severely from remorse & the sense of inferiority hereafter. All around me are industrious & will be great, I am indolent & shall be insignificant."[7] In a counterproductive mood Emerson wrote: "I am in no haste to engage in the difficulties and tasks of the world, for whose danger and turmoil the independence is a small reward."[8] Nothing, for the moment, seemed quite as he wanted it.

Emerson's home situation at this time can scarcely have offered him much cheer either. His mother again had uprooted her household, moving this time from Franklin Place, where she had been only a year, to Federal Street, a bustling neighborhood where she could carry on her boardinghouse activities with greater convenience, and greater prospects of success while yet having room in the house for a school for young ladies that William had established. Rusk conjectures that Emerson did not find it pleasant to consider that "if Harvard friends came there, they were likely to find it filled with uncongenial people."[9] One member of that household, of course, was the feebleminded Bulkeley, now growing to maturity. At no time did Emerson show himself less than charitable in his attitude toward Bulkeley, but Bulkeley's behavior, sometimes boisterous and intrusive, made the matter of receiving guests a hazardous undertaking.

Commencement Day, for Josiah Quincy, was such a triumph as affluence assures. His father and brother came in a chaise from Boston to the old Congregational meeting house in Harvard Square where the ceremonies had been held now for a century. His mother and four sisters, all splendidly dressed, as befitted such an occasion, arrived in a carriage, and young Josiah himself, while the sexton was absent, personally sneaked them into the meeting house, securing for them the best seats. From their place of privilege the elegant Quincys beamed as Josiah delivered his oration.

Unlike the women of the Quincy family, Ruth Emerson did not seek the limelight on Commencement Day. For one thing, that would have been out of character. For another, she had but one good dress and it would not have counted for much in the swirl of splendor others provided. Actually, her major preoccupation that week had been the need to get Bulkeley out of the way, a feat she accomplished by taking him to Newton to stay with her sister Lydia Greenough. From past experience the family knew that if Bulkeley realized Commencement was in the offing he would want to attend. His loud voice and unruly ways could well spoil the day for Ralph.

For a Commencement dinner following the ceremonies, the Quincys had rented the large hall at Porter's. They made up a party of thirty, including Josiah's uncle, William Phillips, lieutenant governor of the Commonwealth. Soon they were joined by Governor Brooks and his aides, the sheriffs of Middlesex and Suffolk counties, the Governor's Council, President Kirkland, General Sumner, General Lyman, Colonel Pickering, and others.[10]

From Porter's the Quincy graduation party repaired to the president's house, where they were greeted by John Quincy Adams, another of Josiah's kinsmen, of course. With his sisters Quincy was soon off to the spacious Harrison Gray Otis mansion at 45 Beacon Street for a Commencement Day reception and cotillion. A grand supper was served, presided over by Mrs. Otis, Boston's foremost society hostess. Through the evening the elite — from Boston, Washington, New York, Philadelphia, and Virginia — mingled in the Otises' three brilliantly lighted drawing rooms. The party ran late into the night.[11]

Emerson's Commencement Day observances were of a different order. On 22 August he wrote to Sarah Ripley: "Commencement is a week from today, on the 29th — I shall not have a dinner and have not asked any body — for a conference [his Colloquy] is a stupid thing."[12] On Commencement Day itself, Emerson attended no parties but went home to Federal Street.

"Thus ends my college life," Quincy wrote at the end of his journal entry for that day. "I must now begin the world."[13] And so might Emerson have written — without Quincy's prospects but with a clearer head. In fact, he waited, choosing thirteen years later to end his first book, *Nature*, with a more ringing assertion: "Build, therefore, your own world."

On 12 July 1869, some forty-eight years out of college, Emerson wrote to Josiah Quincy, urging him to come to Concord on the fourteenth for a two o'clock dinner with several survivors of their class. "There is no business whatever," Emerson assured Quincy, "nothing but kind memories & congratulations, but these grow important in old age & to men far in the country. So I pray you to clothe yourself in your habitual serenity, & come & shine on us."[14] By then Emerson had built a world that would not topple.

9. Schoolmaster
The Fatal Entrance to Gehenna

*I*N those lively days of rising Boston a man who wanted to enter the ministry followed a certain pattern. Out of college at, say, eighteen, before beginning Divinity studies he needed time to consider, time to mature, and, more often than not, work that would bring him income. Usually that employment was schoolteaching. To pass from being instructed, to instructing the few, to instructing the many was a logical progression. Emerson's grandfather had followed it. His father had, too, and, more recently, his brother William. At Uncle Samuel's school in Waltham, readying private scholars for Harvard, Emerson had learned what would be required of him.

During his senior year at Harvard Emerson had gone out on a more ambitious assignment than Waltham provided. It was not a phase of his life that he cared to memorialize and his notice of it in his journal is stark and grim. He described what must have been a one-room, rural schoolhouse of a kind found in every village in that era and probably filled with farm boys whose huckabuck minds would never know the feel of damask. "My log-house on the mountains," he said, giving it the only identity he cared to give it. It is memorable only because, on 15 December 1820, he took a moment to describe the joy he felt when he burst out of its fetid confines:

> I claim & clasp a moment's respite from this irksome school to saunter in the fields of my own wayward thought. The afternoon was gloomy & preparing to snow, — dull, ugly weather. But when I came out from the hot, steaming, stoved, stinking, dirty a "b"-

spelling schoolroom, I almost soared & mounted the atmosphere at breathing the free, magnificent air, the noble breath of life. It was a delightful exhilaration, but it soon passed off.[1]

After graduation Emerson sought an ushership at the Latin School. When he failed to get it, he elected to assist William in conducting his school for young ladies. William's scholars were from Boston's first families, and he ran the school at a handsome profit. Nonetheless, to Aunt Mary, Emerson described his commitment as "the fatal entrance to Gehenna." With John Boynton Hill, a Harvard classmate, he was more graphic:

> To judge from my own happy feelings, I am fain to think that since Commencement, a hundred angry pens have been daily dashed into the sable flood to deplore & curse the destiny of those who *teach*. Poor, wretched, hungry, starving souls! How my heart bleeds for you! better tug at the oar, dig the mine, or saw wood; better sow hemp, or hang with it, than sow the seeds of instruction.[2]

Emerson was only eighteen when this lot fell to him. Moreover, as he put his case, he "had grown up without sisters, and, in my solitary and secluded way of living, had no acquaintance with girls." Edward, the year before, had taunted William, saying: "I was glad to hear that you had determined to commence school in Boston, and that you had such 'respectable' scholars. . . . Never did such a Narcissus appear in the character of a school-master before; therefore I hope the school will be full before people have time to find out how little you know." But William had taught school for a year in Kennebunk, Maine. He also had a knack for maintaining discipline, being able to "enforce a silence" with a mere tap of his pencil, a feat Waldo envied since it lay beyond his powers.[3]

Emerson is to be spoken of now as Waldo because he had decided, as his college days were ending, that he preferred to answer to that name. But a change of name did not at once turn him into a grave elder. His students terrified him and they knew it — scheming to make him blush (and blushes came easily to Emerson all his life), and, on occasion, pitting against him wills stronger than his own.

This interlude lasted three years, and Emerson, despite his self-proclaimed inadequacies, did well enough at it to take sole responsibility for the school at the start of the third year, when William went off to Göttingen to study theology. That did not prevent Emerson from giving his performance poor marks when, in 1865, his former students staged a reunion. He wrote:

Now I have two regrets in regard to the school. I was at the very time already writing every night, in my chamber, my first thoughts on morals and the beautiful laws of compensation and of individual genius, which to observe and illustrate have given sweetness to many years of my life. I am afraid no hint of this ever came into the school, where we clung to the safe and cold details of languages, geography, arithmetic, and chemistry. . . . If I could have had one hour of deep thought at that time, I could have engaged you in thoughts that would have given reality and depth and joy to the school, and raised all the details to the highest pleasure and nobleness.[4]

When he was out of college a year, Emerson took inventory and reported dismal results: ''I am a hopeless school-master, just entering upon years of trade, to which no distinct limit is placed; toiling through this miserable employment without even the poor satisfaction of discharging it well; for the good suspect me, and the geese dislike me.''[5] Part of his problem was that he wanted to be something more than even a good schoolteacher could be. He had vague dreams that he could not define. As time passed, they seemed to be losing what definition they had. It was not the goal of Divinity School that was slipping away. The money for that was coming in. He wanted something beyond that, or, possibly, instead of that. The goal refused to disclose itself.

Had Emerson's mountain-top school given asylum to a guru or had Emerson been able to inhale ''the free, magnificent air,'' with no obligation to enter ever again his rank schoolroom, he might have come sooner into that province which would sustain those ''castles in the air'' he saw collapsing about him. Strangely, the solution to his woes lay at hand. Even overlooked it would not be spurned, for, without full awareness of what was happening, Emerson, through the parlor school years, found himself pulled repeatedly and, as he saw it, against his true inclinations, into the world of Nature. It was Aunt Mary, that contradictory Calvinist who, for consistency's sake, should have shunned the sensate blandishments of Nature, who coaxed Emerson into giving Nature's bounty a try. Perhaps she was concerned about his health. Maybe she was further along in an appreciation of Wordsworth than she cared to admit to a nephew who, at that point, sneered at Wordsworth.

To placate Aunt Mary, Emerson put Nature to the test in the spring of 1822, walking thirty miles to Northborough with William. They put up at a farmhouse, near a pond, wandered in the adjacent woods, and sprawled in the grass in a clearing where they read from books they had brought with them. Nature, they surmised, if it was to yield any inspiration, would need some priming. Emerson also fished some on this lazy holiday. He came home believing he had given Nature a fair try. He reported the results to Aunt Mary:

> I thought I understood a little of that *intoxication,* which you have spoken of; but its tendency was directly opposed to the slightest effort of mind or body; it was a soft animal luxury, the combined result of the beauty which fed the eye; the exhilarating Paradise *air,* which fanned & dilated the sense; the novel melody, which warbled from the trees. Its first charm passed away rapidly. . . . Perhaps in the Autumn . . . and in a longer abode the mind might, as you term it, return upon itself; but for a year, without books it would become intolerable.[6]

Aunt Mary accounted for the disappointing results in her own way. "You should have gone alone," she told him.[7]

Emerson's rapprochement with Nature was closer at hand than either he or Aunt Mary realized. In May 1823 Ruth moved the family to the Canterbury section of Roxbury, a woody, undulating, rural stretch of farm country — "a picturesque wilderness of savin, barberry bushes, catbrier, and sumach" — at no great distance from the heart of Boston, where Waldo would continue to keep school, but rural enough, then and afterward, to be incorporated into Boston's Franklin Park.[8] Walking miles through the countryside to go and come as school required, and experiencing Nature on a day-to-day basis, took some of the city spirit out of Emerson. He was not consorting with Wordsworth yet, but Wordsworth's message, whether Emerson realized it or not, was infiltrating his world.

In a letter sent to Boynton Hill on 19 June 1823, Emerson related: "I teach, aye teach teach in town, in the morning, & then scamper out as fast as our cosset horse will bring us to snuff the winds & cross the wild blossoms & branches — of the green fields. I am seeking to put myself on a footing of old acquaintance with Nature, as a poet should." Canterbury turned things around:

> A pair of moonlight evenings have screwed up my esteem several pegs higher by supplying my brain with several bright fragments of thought, & making me dream that mind as well as body respired more freely here. And there is an excellence in Nature which familiarity never blunts the sense of — a serene superiority to man & his art in the thought of which man dwindles to pigmy proportions. In short, parti-colored Nature makes a man love his eyes.[9]

Recruited by Nature, Emerson, with a convert's zeal, was making his first attempt at enlisting another in her cause. He could not have guessed then that, as Nature's recruiter, his name someday would be coupled with Wordsworth's.[10]

In April 1824, "stretched beneath the pines" that enveloped Canterbury Lane and inspired its catachrestic name, Light Lane, Emerson wrote his first poem to attain popular distinction, "Good-bye, Proud World!" When Aunt Mary saw it, she must have felt like a justified sorceress — the poet was electing for the country over the city.

In the opening days of 1825, Emerson shut down his school. Teaching had paid his debts and left him enough to begin his Divinity studies at Harvard. He did not count it a success otherwise. "My scholars," he concluded, "are carefully instructed, my money is faithfully earned, but the instructor is little wiser. & the duties were never congenial with my disposition."[11] With this decision the Emersons moved in April 1825 to Cambridge from Canterbury, where they had stayed longer than they had stayed anywhere during the preceding decade. By then Emerson had already been two months in residence at Divinity Hall, adjusting, not too well, to being an urban dweller anew.

For all his resolutions, Emerson was not quite done with teaching. An eye ailment compelled him to lighten his program at the Divinity School. The next fall found him teaching in Chelmsford; the next spring, in Roxbury at Octagon Hall. Bronson Alcott was later to contend that an octagonal-shaped building had a salubrious effect on its occupants, but Octagon Hall had no spells to cast on Emerson.[12] Before three months were up he closed the school. Later in 1826, in Cambridge, at a house on Winthrop Square that his mother rented from Levi Hedge, he did his final teaching. Of the twenty students he had under his care for a single semester, several went on to become articulate gentlemen. They later assessed his qualifications as a teacher with a candor that would account for his abjuration of teaching had they been as forthright when he taught them.

Said Richard Henry Dana:

> A very pleasant instructor we had in Mr. E., although he had not system or discipline enough to insure regular and vigorous study. I have always considered it fortunate for us that we fell into the hands of more systematic and strict teachers, though not so popular with us, nor perhaps so elevated in their habits of thought as Mr. E.[13]

While Dana's scorn for transcendentalism predisposed him to cite Emerson's want of system, his criticism, nonetheless, had force. Emerson read Dana's *Two Years Before the Mast* (1840) and liked it, but took no credit for it. "He was my scholar once," he told William, "but he never learned this of me, more's the pity."[14]

Another of Emerson's students, Josiah G. Abbott, afterward a judge, had his reminiscences of Emerson relayed to posterity through Oliver Wendell Holmes:

> He was very grave, quiet, and very impressive in his appearance. There was something engaging, almost fascinating, about him; he was never harsh or severe, always perfectly self-controlled, never punished except with words, but exercised complete command over the boys. His old pupil recalls the stately, measured way in which, for some offense the little boy had committed, he turned on him, saying only these two words: "Oh sad!"[15]

John Holmes, Oliver's coruscating younger brother, likewise one of Emerson's charges in the Winthrop Square session, profiled him in these terms:

> Calm, as not doubting the virtue residing in his scepter. Rather stern in his very infrequent rebukes. Not inclined to win boys by a surface amiability, but kindly in explanation or advice. Every inch a king in his dominion. Looking back, he seems to me rather like a captive philosopher set to tending flocks; resigned to his destiny, but not amused with its incongruities.[16]

In 1821 Emerson had tutored Elizabeth Peabody in Greek, but was so shy their eyes never met. In fairness to Emerson, Elizabeth grew up to be one of the most formidable women of the age. Those who met her gaze ran the risk of being conscripted to serve her causes.

Taken in aggregate, these various accounts show surprising consistency — with one notable exception. No one judged Emerson as severely as Emerson himself. But if he was turning away from the schoolroom, he was also turning toward something:

> It is a peculiarity . . . of humor in me, my strong propensity for strolling. I deliberately shut up my books in a cloudy July noon, put on my old clothes and old hat and slink away to the whortleberry bushes and slip with the greatest satisfaction into a little cowpath where I am sure I can defy observation. This point gained I solace myself for hours with picking blueberries and other trash of the woods, far from fame, behind the birch-trees. I seldom enjoy hours as I do these. I remember them in winter; I expect them in spring.[17]

Thus wrote Emerson, not after prolonged association with Henry David Thoreau, whom he chastened for being content to be no more than "the captain of a huckleberry party," but only four years after he left Canterbury and nine years before his friendship with Thoreau began.

*I read with some joy of the auspicious signs of the
coming days, as they glimmer already through poetry
and art, through philosophy and science, through
church and state.*

10. Literary Awakening

*I*N 1824, on 19 April, the forty-ninth anniversary of the battle
fought on William Emerson's farm that began the American War of
Independence, Lord Byron, actively serving with a ready purse and a
ready hand the army waging a war for independence in Greece, died
at Missolonghi. Emerson's first written acknowledgment of that fact
came in a letter to Aunt Mary on 26 July. Boston, as did all the world,
mourned Byron's passing. There was a time when Emerson would have
mourned him, too, but not on the eve of entering the ministry, and
not, certainly, in a letter to Aunt Mary. Yet mingled with the litany
of phrases — "a man of dreadful history"; "blasphemer of heaven or
pander to sensuality"; "archangel ruined" — upbraiding Byron for
his atheism and "his sarcastic beastliness and coarse sneers," are passing acknowledgments of Byron's superior gifts. He had "left no brighter
genius behind him"; "the light of sublimer existence was on his cheek."
It was not easy to cease "the admiration of intellectual excellence though
depraved." His was "a spirit . . . finely touched." Thus "Men . . .
set no bounds to their expectation from Byron's creative genius. Wit,
argument, history, rhapsody, the extremes of good and ill — everything was to be expected from his extraordinary invention. He might
have added one more wonder to his life — its own redemption." Emerson relinquished the subject only after making one further ambivalent
statement. Better to "shake hands with Lucifer" than to pretend to
virtue while secretly loving sin. He managed to make a case for Byron
without giving Aunt Mary one good purchase from which to launch a
counterattack. To thwart such a woman was a feat Byron himself might
have commended.[1]

While Emerson was coming to an appreciation of Wordsworth by slow degrees, Byron had swept him off his feet during his sophomore year at Harvard. Concerning the third canto of *Childe Harold*, he had written to his brother Edward early in 1818: "[It] is the most beautiful poetry in my humble opinion that I ever read." In his journal he reported finding in Byron "a language for deep feeling and sublime thought." By 1823, however, assuming that tone of righteous wrath which he took to be the proper outlook of a minister in the making, he spoke of his erstwhile idol as "the profligate Byron," who, aligned with other skeptics, had "cast a malign light upon the earth." By 1824 he had perceived that Don Juan was "a breaker of all human & divine laws . . . ," while Byron himself had "laid hands on the everlasting foundation of human virtue," mocking "the first affections of the heart."[2]

In the final lecture of a ten-lecture series on English literature that Emerson gave in Boston in the winter of 1835–36, Byron was the first writer considered. Emerson's manuscript bears the title: "Byron, Scott, Stewart, Mackintosh, Coleridge: Modern aspects of letters." Byron was riding a new wave of popularity in Boston, but Emerson struck out for the opposite shore. "Men," he said, "begin to feel that his claims to a permanent popularity are more than dubious." Here, where he had to deal with an audience that did not judge Byron by Aunt Mary's criteria, he had to muster sound critical arguments to account for his exclusion of Byron from the company of the immortals. He began by conceding Byron's technical virtuosity: "His power of language and that peculiar gift of making it flexible to all the compass and variety of his emotion without ever marring the purity of his diction, is as remarkable in him as in any English writer since Dryden. No structure of verse seemed laborious to him." Yet Byron's knowledge and truth of sentiment were "very little," and "pride and selfishness" blunted his power of language. "Instead of marrying his Muse to Nature after the ordination of God, he sought to make words and emotions suffice alone, until our interest dies of a famine of meaning." Thus the fourth canto of *Childe Harold*, in its execution touched with genius, "ends in utter nonsense . . . from the poverty of thought."

Skirting a discussion of Byron's moral faults lest he be charged with bringing to bear on his subject a preacher's judgment, Emerson tasked him with an excess of "malevolent feelings." Byron had produced "volumes upon volumes of morbid emotional disgust." This fault seems a companion failing to the fatal note of "lamentation" that, in Emerson's opinion, made Shelley unreadable. In a final assessment, Emerson invited his auditors to believe that an affinity for Byron put them in the company of cutthroats: "How painful is it to feel on looking back at the writings of one who should have been a clear and beneficent genius to guide and cheer human nature the emotions which a gang of pirates and convicts suggest."[3]

Goethe had dismissed Byron's thinking as "childish." Thomas Carlyle gave impact to his first critical writings by pursuing that indictment to its obvious conclusion: "Shut your Byron; open your Goethe." Yet when Byron died, Carlyle wrote to Jane Welsh, his future wife:

> The news of his death came upon my heart like a mass of lead; thro' all my being, as if I had lost a Brother. Late so full of fire and generous passion and proud purposes; and now forever dumb. Poor Byron! and but a young man, still struggling amidst the perplexities and sorrows and aberrations of a mind not arrived at maturity, or settled in its proper place in life.[4]

Another striking phrase accounts for Carlyle's change of heart. Death had robbed us of "the noblest spirit in Europe." Taken in conjunction with his allusion to Byron's recent "proud purposes," it is evident that Byron's military posture as liberator had rehabilitated him in Carlyle's eyes. Neither then nor later would that fact have been crucial with Emerson. Thus, even before Emerson and Carlyle knew each other, the germ of Carlyle's theory of hero worship had begun to sprout. As time passed, his commitment to a belief in strong leadership would become central to his thinking. Meantime, Emerson, committed already to a belief in "the infinitude of the private man," was moving toward his theory of representative men. Therefore, in their contrasting attitudes toward Byron in the 1820's could be foretold the differences that, in the future, would pit Carlyle and Emerson against each other. In 1848, disillusioned with Carlyle after their second meeting, Emerson would, curiously, lump him with Byron, remarking in his notes, "In Carlyle as in Byron, one is more struck with the rhetoric than with the matter."[5]

In July 1846 Emerson unequivocally excluded Byron from the ranks of his representative men: "Byron is no poet: what did he know of the world and its Law & Lawgiver? What moment had he of that Mania which moulds history & man, & tough circumstances, — like wax? He had declamation; he had music, juvenile & superficial music."[6] Even as he redefined Aunt Mary's Calvinistic standards in terms of his own transcendental beliefs, his condemnation of Byron could still be seen as a result of his disapproval of Byron's alienation from virtue.

Emerson's last serious assessment of Byron comes in his preface to *Parnassus* (1874), a selection of his favorite poetry. Once again he expresses surprise at Byron's "rare skill for rhythm, unmatched facility of expression, a firm, ductile thread of gold." But Byron, he complains, has no "lofty aim," and "is starved for a purpose. . . . He revenges himself on society for its supposed distrust of him, by cursing it, and throwing himself on the side of its destroyers."[7] Yet thirty-three selections from Byron, totaling a thousand and twenty-five lines, appear in *Parnassus*. Only Shakespeare and Wordsworth received more notice.

Even as Emerson repudiated his attachment to the earthy Byron, he discovered, in the works of a writer of an earlier period, sanction for the use of earthier rhetoric than propriety countenanced. He had long sought authorization for writing plain, vigorous prose, but found it only in the early weeks of 1825, during his last days at Canterbury. The writer was Montaigne. The book was his *Essays*. And the impact these had on Emerson's style and literary practice superseded all others.

John Boynton Hill said Emerson introduced him to Montaigne while they still were undergraduates at Harvard. Emerson's real interest in Montaigne, however, developed later:

> A single odd volume of Cotton's translations of the Essays remained to me from my father's library, when a boy. It lay long neglected, until, after many years, when I was newly escaped from college, I read the book, and procured the remaining volumes. I remember the delight and wonder in which I lived with it. . . . Montaigne is the frankest and honestest of all writers. His French freedom runs into grossness; but he has anticipated all censure by the bounty of his own confessions. In his times . . . a certain nakedness of statement was permitted, which our manners . . . do not allow. . . . He will indulge himself with a little cursing and swearing; he will talk with sailors and gypsies.[8]

For playmates in boyhood Emerson had had chiefly the companionship of his four brothers. He could stare through the apertures in the parsonage fence, hoping to catch a glimpse of the rowdies he had been warned against, but that hardly requited his need to be involved in the world around him. Later he would say that books are good "only as far as a boy is ready for them. . . . Archery, cricket, gun and fishing-rod, horse and boat, are all educators, liberalizers; and so are dancing, dress, and street talk."[9]

As a young man Emerson decided that his deficiency in animal spirits was his "capital defect." All his life he felt himself a voyeur, peering through slats at those who were amply endowed with vital spirits. When he praised that fund of vitality in others, usually he sought a metaphor of boyhood to set it in a fitting context. He lauded "the masters of the playground and of the street, — boys who have the same liberal ticket of admission to all shops, factories, armories, town-meetings, caucuses, mobs, target-shooting, as flies have." Of health and what he called "wild power" Emerson owned, "I am much taken by it in boys, and sometimes in people not normal, nor educated, nor presentable, nor church-members — even in persons open to the suspicion of irregular and immoral living, in Bohemians, — as in more orderly examples." He allowed gypsies to camp on his idle acres and, like Montaigne, enjoyed talking with them. He said he found "the society of gypsies . . . more attractive than that of bishops."[10]

Rusk surmises that Emerson picked up from street boys the vocabulary he needed to realize his ambition to wield English "like a sharp stick among the rabble." He was open to such an influence but, at best, in those circumspect days, his indoctrination must have been partial. Indeed, during the Civil War, when Concord boys went off to camp, their senior officer asked the cadre not to swear in their presence because, being unaccustomed to such language, they were offended. Boston was not rural Concord, but it was, in Emerson's minority, the nucleus of a Puritan society and, as Henry James's Baroness Münster saw it in 1835, a haven for the innocent. For that reason, even Emerson's college years would not have found him making striking gains in attaining command of an earthy vocabulary. Once, at Harvard, two of Emerson's classmates gave him "an amusing account of a truckman who came to the college yard and bullied for an hour." Soberly he reported: "It was the richest swearing, the most aesthetic, fertilizing, — and they took notes." Without pleasure he reported that such language was not current with his associates: "Swearing has gone out of vogue on the earth, because, society which means discriminating persons, rejects unmeasured speech. Oaths never go out of fashion, but are always beautiful & thrilling; but the sham of them which is called profane swearing is rightly voted a bore. Sham damns we do not like." The common people made up the deficiency. He found satisfaction "in listening to the necessary speech of men about their work, when any unusual circumstance gives momentary importance to the dialogue. For blacksmiths and teamsters do not trip in their speech; it is a shower of bullets. It is Cambridge [Harvard] men who correct themselves and begin again at every half sentence."[11]

Emerson first came to appreciate fully the effectiveness of street talk when, in late 1832, he sailed on a three-week voyage to Europe on a fruit transport and, as one of five passengers, heard the sailors express themselves without restraint. "The college," he wrote, "is not so wise as the mechanic's shop, nor the quarter-deck as the forecastle." His sympathy with plain and graphic speech found endorsement, he believed, in Plato. "From mares and puppies; from pitchers and soupladles; from cooks and criers; the shops of potters, horse-doctors, butchers and fishmongers" Plato had drawn his illustrations, giving them a currency time had not made obsolescent. At the start of his ministry, endorsing a mode reminiscent of Puritan plain style, he told his congregation that "our Lord condescended to explain himself by allusions to every homely fact, and, if he addressed himself to the men of this age, would appeal to those arts and objects by which we are surrounded." Later he warned young preachers: "When there is any difference of level felt between the foot board of the pulpit & the floor of the parlor, you have not said that which you should say."[12]

In lectures given in 1835 Emerson would praise the earthiness of Michelangelo, Chaucer, Shakespeare, Bacon, Milton, and Jeremy Taylor, and commend Jonson, Herbert, and Herrick for their firm, simple sentences. Franklin's homely directness also had his approval, as did that of Davy Crockett and Abraham Lincoln.[13] In his early years as a speaker he was charged with wrapping a paucity of ideas in a panoply of rude verbiage. Even Bronson Alcott, who reverenced him, owned himself troubled by his "coarseness" of language until he hit upon the happy explanation that it supplied "a grounding and a symbolic quality of utmost value to one whose thought was prevailingly idealistic."[14] In a sense this was so. Emerson believed that truths from Nature often are embedded in aphorisms. Since aphorisms frequently are communicated through homely images and phrases and Emerson strove to convey his best thoughts in aphoristic form, he sought deliberately to cast them in the language of common life.

In 1850, when Montaigne was acknowledged by Emerson as one of his representative men, the phrase he used earlier to describe the language of truckmen and teamsters was now consigned to Montaigne himself because he saw that these men were continuators of the tradition Montaigne embodied: "The sincerity and marrow of the man reaches to his sentences. I know not anywhere the book that seems less written. It is the language of conversation transferred to a book. Cut these words and they would bleed; they are vascular and alive."[15]

In "Eloquence" Emerson asserted: "The speech of the man in the street is invariably strong. . . . You say, 'If he could only express himself'; but he does already, better than any one can for him. . . . The power of their speech is, that it is perfectly understood by all."[16] Perhaps it was such a passage as this that Walt Whitman had in mind when he said, "I was simmering, simmering, simmering and Emerson brought me to a boil."[17] Emerson did not anticipate the zestfulness of Whitman's response to his appeal but, grimacing, he accepted what he understood to be Whitman's true nature and a rhetoric evidently his by entitlement. He could say of Whitman what he had said of Montaigne, that he was "no effeminate parlour workman. . . . A gross, semisavage indecency debases his book . . . but the robustness of his sentiments, the generosity of his judgments, the downright truth without fear or favour, I do embrace with both arms."[18]

Whitman found a boon companion in a horse-car conductor. In farmers such as Edmund Hosmer, Emerson had his Yankee counterparts. In "Monadnoc" he alludes to the "fourscore or a hundred words" of "that hardy English root" that constitute the speaking vocabulary of New England farmers.[19] Even as Thoreau cultivated a hill-country woman, a riverboat man, the Wellfleet oysterman, and a teenaged cutlery peddler, Emerson upheld the merits of such men as Nathaniel Whiting, the unlettered mechanic of Marshfield, an eloquent idealist. With the simple and downright rested the hope of the future.

Visiting towns and cities where he was unknown, Emerson often suppressed letters of introduction, preferring to seek out lodgings where he could discourse freely with ordinary men.

Although in time Emerson, in some ways, grew conservative, the case he made at the outset of his career for "unmeasured speech" was not disputed by any of his later statements. "Art and Criticism" (1859) finds him holding firm:

> Montaigne must have the credit of giving to literature that which we listen for in barrooms, the low speech, — words and phrases that no scholar coined; street-cries and war-cries; words of the boatman, the farmer and the lord; that have neatness and necessity, through their use in the vocabulary of work and appetite, like the pebbles which the incessant attrition of the sea has rounded.[20]

Emerson had found that iridescent seashells gathered by the shore lost their beauty once their watery sheen evaporated. Stones were another matter. Their contours were a thing not of seeming but of substance. And so it was with words. Glittery words were ephemeral. Words that endured were those with strength and force.

11. Divinity Studies

*T*HE day was 25 March, in the calendar of the ancient church the feast of the Annunciation and for centuries observed in the Western world as New Year's Day, a proper time for affirmations and resolutions. In 1821, moreover, 25 March fell on the Sabbath, a day when men of faith seek to make themselves pleasing to God. The coming August, at eighteen, Waldo Emerson would graduate from Harvard. Time, then, that he came to a responsible decision about his future. Nor was that all. He wrote on that day:

> I am sick — if I should die what would become of me? We forget ourselves & our destinies in health, & the chief use of temporary sickness is to remind us of these concerns. I must improve my time better. I must prepare myself for the great profession I have purposed to undertake. I am to give my soul to God & withdraw from sin & the world the idle or vicious time & thoughts I have sacrificed to them; & let me consider this as a resolution by which I pledge myself to act in all variety of circumstances.[1]

An Emerson who made New Year's resolutions by the old calendar lived as well by the standards of an old New England that had not yet escaped the grim rule of Calvinism. Aunt Mary, who, it was said, wanted to see everyone except herself submissive to Calvinism, had done her work well. Only by the standards she had inculcated could Emerson brand himself a sinner and accuse himself of vicious behavior. He was right about one thing, however. Sickness had quickened his conscience. When health returned, his resolve to enter the ministry diminished in urgency. The usual reasons counseled postponement. Funds were lacking. Money was needed to keep Edward and Charles at Harvard, and for William, who was set to study for the ministry also. By teaching school Waldo could assume some of the burden his mother had borne so long. Furthermore, a few years hence he would have the maturity expected of someone called to God's service.

In the 1820's the Harvard Divinity School was in its first years. John Kirkland in 1816 had instituted a Society for the Promotion of Theological Education. This had led to the establishment of a modest three-man theological faculty, only one of whom was full-time, and the building of Divinity Hall. But the new institution, as "Harvard Divinity School," would not pass under direct university control until 1830, and would not grant degrees until 1870. It was, therefore, in Emerson's day, without established credentials. In Aunt Mary's eyes, accordingly, it was gravely suspect, inclined to new views that were rank heresy. If Waldo waited until he could afford to attend an ortho-dox Divinity School, he would, in her opinion, be far better off.

Three years later new circumstances prevailed. Emerson had taught school steadily since leaving college and was certain now that teaching was not his calling. Nevertheless, it had brought in enough income to enable him to pay his debts, contribute to the welfare of the family, and put aside money for his own future studies. He chose another Sabbath, 18 April 1824, to set forth his plans in his journal. He had long put first the needs of others, as Ruth had taught him to do. Now his topic was "Myself." He wrote: "I am beginning my professional studies. In a month I shall be *legally* a man. And I deliberately dedi-cate my time, my talents, & my hopes to the Church." That Emerson's decision should coincide with his twenty-first birthday was not a mat-ter of chance. Quiet planning had long been under way. Now, to affirm his awareness, he needed to take frank inventory of himself:

My reasoning faculty is proportionately weak. . . . Nor is it strange that with this confession I should choose theology, which is from everlasting to everlasting 'debateable ground.' For, the highest species of reasoning upon divine subjects is rather the fruit of a sort of moral imagination, than of the 'Reasoning Machines,' such as Locke.[2]

Even at this stage Emerson had taken his stand behind what he rec-ognized as "the moral sentiment," which later, as the intuitive fac-ulty, was to be the true bearer of transcendental enlightenment. Emer-son was lost to formal theological studies before he began them.

Fine preachers had appeared in Emerson's family in every generation — Samuel Moody, Joseph Emerson, Daniel Bliss, William Emerson the elder, and his son William, Emerson's own father. Emerson's
brothers and he rushed from place to place to drink in the eloquence
of Channing, Everett, and Webster. They lived in an age that set a
high premium on fine speaking. Charles and Edward won acclaim at
Harvard for their powers of oratory. Since Emerson's own voice was
beautiful, destiny, it seemed, had reserved a place for him in the pulpit. He reflected:

> In Divinity I hope to thrive. I inherit from my sire a formality
> of manner & speech, but I derive from him or his patriotic
> parent a passionate love for the strains of eloquence. . . . I am the
> believer . . . of brilliant promises, and can respect myself as the
> possessor of those powers which command the reason & passions of
> the multitude. The office of a clergyman is twofold: public
> preaching & private influence. Entire success in the first is the lot
> of the few, but this I am encouraged to expect.

Emerson ended his assessment, his confidence undiminished: "I cannot accurately estimate my chances of success, in my profession, & in
life. . . . My trust is that my profession shall be my regeneration."[3]

Writing to William, in Germany, on 20 May 1824, Emerson said, "I
have made some embryo motions in my divinity studies & shall be glad
of any useful hints."[4] William questioned only the timing. The school
he had founded was the cornerstone of their present prosperity. He
wondered if Waldo's plans to close it were not premature.

Emerson was then living near William Ellery Channing's church.
The "embryo motions" he mentioned referred to the appeal he had
made to Channing to get him started on his theological studies. Although Channing merely supplied him a reading list, Emerson was not
offended. He suspected that Channing was incapable of taking another's point of view or of opening his mind freely to anyone in private
conversation.[5]

Emerson took possession of room 14 on the lower floor of the new
Divinity Hall on 9 February 1825. The building had been erected on
land reclaimed from the Cambridge marshes. His room came cheap
because it was damp, a fact that soon exacted a cost not to be measured
in money.

The faculty, impressed with his private reading, admitted him to
the middle class. He had, for example, for several weeks been reading
a chapter of the Greek Testament every morning on arising. Channing's booklist also must have made a good talking point. That the
person who supervised the reading of the candidates was President

Kirkland must have helped matters, too. Emerson's self-appraisal, however, made the night before he returned to Harvard, was anything but self-congratulatory. "I have inverted my inquiries two or three times on myself, and have learned what a sinner & a saint I am. My cardinal vice of intellectual dissipation — sinful strolling from book to book, from care to idleness, is my cardinal vice still." This eclecticism, not too far inquired into, may have impressed Kirkland. But Emerson had no illusions about it. Not then, anyway. Later, when he realized that he profited from reading in that fashion, he proclaimed it a virtue. Stating that "Books are for the scholar's idle times," he read for lustres — passages that seemed to explode in his mind on impact. Once he had this warranty in hand, he became a consummate skimmer, transferring into his notebooks such observations and phrases as he judged to be of lasting value.[6]

A soberness beyond what the occasion mandated attaches to the last journal entry of Emerson's pre-professional life. "I have grown older," he wrote, "and have seen something of the vanity & something of the value of existence, have seen what shallow things men are & how independent of external circumstances may be the states of mind called good & ill."[7] This seems less the statement of someone about to confront life than the declaration of someone turning away from it. In fact, although he did not know it, Emerson was on the threshold of a life-threatening illness.

Had the curriculum of the theological school been fully articulated, Emerson would have had to withdraw soon after entering. Within a month his eyesight had failed him. Having been given permission by Andrews Norton, the nominal dean, he dropped into a passive role, neither reading the assigned texts nor reciting in class. Norton's later scorn for Emerson's transcendental dispensation — which seemed to make all books superfluous — may have stemmed from his certain knowledge that Emerson had made no formal study of theology.

Emerson's eye problems halted his journal-keeping for the remainder of the year. The last two entries were large and sprawling. The dampness at Divinity Hall induced rheumatism in one hip. He soon required a cane to walk. Then came a chest stricture, a cause for grave concern in a family already ravaged by tuberculosis. Conscious now that his body required the same notice he had been giving his soul, Emerson broke off his studies and removed to his Uncle Ladd's farm in nearby Newton, hoping that outdoor activities, including manual labor, would work a cure. And so it did, in some measure, though surgery was needed to restore his vision. The procedure went unrecorded but its effect was long-range. Emerson was almost fifty before he required glasses and in his mid-sixties before failing eyesight again posed problems for him.

To surmise that Emerson's triad of ailments was psychosomatically induced would be unreasonable. He was more apt to insist he was well when he was sick, than to insist he was sick when he was well. His younger brothers were grubbing students in a way that he could never be. But he did not reproach himself for lack of ambition. Later, when both Edward and Charles were dead, Emerson concluded that he had been spared because, unlike them, he had never taxed himself beyond his strength.

The months that immediately followed Emerson's departure from Divinity School provided him little of the leisure he may have thought he needed for convalescence. That he should have survived them offers not only proof of an unusual inner tenacity but a true forecast of his ability to accept the long series of sorrows and disappointments that would beset him through much of his lifetime. If lack of opportunity to worry about his own health was therapeutic, then, during that interval, he received such therapy in ample measure. First came Edward's tragedy. Doubly occupied, studying law in Daniel Webster's law office and teaching school in Roxbury, Edward, his strength failing rapidly, was diagnosed as tubercular. Plans were made to send him to the Mediterranean. He had been the one member of the family bringing in income. Waldo now received a couple of private pupils and agreed to conduct a school in Chelmsford, north of Boston, in the fall. His brother Bulkeley next required attention. As he passed into maturity, Bulkeley had become an emotional handful. Ruth could no longer cope with him, so Waldo took him along to Chelmsford. There, his condition worsened. Soon he was habitually deranged.

In the midst of this shambles of life, so far removed from the quiet regimen he had envisaged for himself as a divinity student, Waldo was given a further shock. In mid-October, William arrived home from Germany and announced that he was quitting the ministry for the law — plans that presently took him to New York. Since Charles was still an undergraduate at Harvard, the only one left to patch things together was Waldo himself. It is illustrative of his forward-reaching temperament that, even as he stood at the center of this maelstrom, the most harassed member of the family, the one person to whom everyone looked for support, he should have congratulated himself at not allowing his strength to be overburdened as Edward had done.

In short order Emerson arranged to board Bulkeley in Chelmsford, closed his school there, assumed control of Edward's forsaken school in Roxbury, looked to the support of his mother, and, at the same time, made an occasional appearance in Cambridge so as not quite to relinquish his place in the theological program.

William's exit from the ministry was not a blow to Emerson personally but, for his mother's sake, he was sorrowful. The world believed the Emersons owed society a preacher in every generation — or at least Aunt Mary did — and Ruth had done her best to uphold that tradition. By this time, on grounds of health alone, Emerson wondered if he himself was meant for the ministry, but the conviction that his mother must not be disappointed a second time was enough to keep him steady to his commitment. Ruth, eager to do her part, took a house in Cambridge, at Winthrop Square, not far from the Divinity School, so that Waldo was able both to attend classes and to teach that little band of intrepids that included Dana, Holmes, and Abbott.

In the fall of 1826, the momentum of duties that had carried Emerson along at last slackened, even though the duties did not. His weight loss was noticeable and the stricture in his chest became more insistent. Seeking an apt way to describe it, he spoke of it as "the mouse in my chest," an analogy that for vividness is as alarming today as when he first invoked it. Samuel Ripley had advanced Edward the money to go to Europe in search of better health. No less generous now, he was determined that Emerson must go south for the winter. Emerson acceded, promising to set out after he saw Edward, who was making preparations to return home, by every report having benefited much from his travels.

With this convalescent interlude also would come an opportunity for Emerson to weigh those influences which his recent reading had brought to bear on his thinking. A reading list he prepared for himself in the winter of 1825–26 includes works by Plato, Isocrates, Montaigne, Machiavelli, Cardinal de Retz, and Adam Smith. This list surely would not have been recommended by Andrews Norton. Yet it should not be cited as evidence that Emerson's interest in theological matters was slackening. In reality he had never looked forward to the required readings. All too typical was the attitude he had shown in a letter written to William, at Göttingen, on 20 November 1824: "Say particularly if German & Hebrew be worth reading for tho' I hate to study them cordially I yet will the moment I can count my gains."[8]

In the summer of 1826 Emerson made a discovery that not only gave him the justification he was looking for to explain his lack of true interest in theological disquisitions but opened his mind to Nature and literary creativity. He read Sampson Reed's newly published *Observations on the Growth of the Mind*. Reed was a Boston apothecary who had graduated from Harvard in 1819. At Emerson's commencement, in 1821, Reed had read a paper, "Genius," which Emerson had admired. But this scarcely prepared Emerson for *Growth of the Mind*. Although Reed did not disclose his sources, he had gone to Swedenborg for his most important ideas. That fact amazed Emerson when he later realized it. What struck him now were the ideas themselves. Hitherto he had viewed Nature as pagan and suspect. From Reed he learned that the poet, and, by extension, every man who sought the truth, must be receptive to his deepest intuitions and, in doing so, allow Nature to speak through him. Here, in a single, dazzling revelation, the hateful burden of analytical reasoning was dismissed forever.[9]

In Reed, Emerson found authorization to preach in the light of his own insights. It would sustain him through the years of his ministry and through the years that came after. Now he could spurn Locke with no sense of spurning reality. Its effect would be apparent in his writing from the time he began publishing. Thus, ten years later, on 12 September 1836, Bronson Alcott would write to Sophia Peabody: "Have you seen Mr. Emerson's *Nature?* If you have not, let me send you a copy. It is a divine poem on the External. . . . It reminds me more of Sampson Reed's *Growth of the Mind* than any other work."[10] Earlier in that summer of 1836, writing to William on 26 June, Emerson himself hinted at such a connection: "My little book is nearly done. Its title is *Nature.* Its contents will not exceed in bulk Sampson Reed's *Growth of the Mind.*"[11] Clarence Hotson would comment on the debt in these terms: "*Nature* . . . shows the influence of Reed, especially in its leading thought, the distinctly Swedenborgian doctrine of *correspondence,* the idea that Nature symbolizes the soul."[12]

From time to time, through the years, Emerson compiled lists of "My Men," men, living and dead, whom he esteemed as approaching his ideal of the complete universal man. Reed, in 1841, was on the list. On Emerson's final list, compiled thirty years later, Reed was still there. Reed himself showed no such fidelity. In 1838, for a new edition of *Growth of the Mind,* he wrote a preface in which he repudiated whatever the transcendentalists had once derived from him: "*Transcendentalism* is the parasite of sensualism; and when it shall have done its work, it will be found to be itself a worm, and the offspring of a worm."[13]

As early as 1 August 1826 Emerson had elected to stand for "approbation," that is, official sanction to preach. He wrote then to Aunt Mary: "In the fall, I propose to be *approbated.* . . . I do not now find in me any objections to this step." Emerson was not implying that he had emerged from a dark night of the soul to arrive at this decision. In candidates for the ministry humility decreed a period of soul-searching. To have never found objections might have implied slackness on the part of the deliberator. Later in this same letter, Emerson hinted that he might have considered his aversion to theological works an impediment to his vocation. His resolution of that difficulty, so close to Sampson Reed's words, affirms not only that he had read *Growth of the Mind* but that it may be credited with having dispelled any uneasiness he may have had about his want of sympathy with theological treatises. He said:

Much of what is subtle & mysterious in our intervals of mentality is more flattering and more favored than the ordinary

acquisitions in the general progress of the soul, — but what con-
gratulation ought to be heard in the earth from theist & patriot,
when God in these eminent instances of these our latter days
departs from the ancient inviolable sternness of an unrespecting
providence to harmonize the order of nature with the moral
exigencies of humanity.[14]

Both Uncle Samuel and his father, Ezra Ripley, were respected and
powerful members of the Middlesex Association of Congregational
Ministers, the agency that passed on a candidate's fitness for approbation. Emerson needed only their backing to win approval. As Ezra,
nearly thirty-five years before, had selected Emerson's father for the
ministry, now he was ready to set the feet of the son on the same road.
Given their basic temperaments, both Emerson's father and grandfather had been curious candidates for the ministry. Family expectations had misdirected them into that calling. This newest heir to the
sacerdotal life was even more displaced. In a few years he would venture into regions so alien to the orthodox that they would brand him
"the devil's henchman."

Although Samuel Ripley and his father did not find it necessary to
question Emerson narrowly on his beliefs at this time, his delicate health
seeming to them the paramount issue, they did judge him by his first
sermon — "Pray without Ceasing." Emerson wrote this sermon on 25
July 1826 and sent a copy of it to Aunt Mary. Mary Moody Emerson
never let anyone off easily. But Sampson Reed's influence, already
apparent, stirred Aunt Mary's legitimate concern. "Your reason is
God, your virtue is God," Emerson had written. And again he said
that Nature "helps the purposes of man." Emerson's "thinking Reed"
was no match for Aunt Mary's certain deposit of faith. She told him
flatly that his sermon lacked "unction and authority and allusion to a
venerable name." That was a shrewd thrust. The name of Jesus is
nowhere mentioned in the sermon and there are but single allusions to
"the Son of God" and "the Christian religion."[15] Already Aunt Mary
was taking alarm at the direction in which things were moving for the
young man who was to be the sole continuator of the ministerial tradition in the Emerson family. The Middlesex Association of Congregational Ministers, taking its cues no doubt from the candidate's kinsmen, had no such misgivings. Before this group, on 10 October 1826,
Emerson presented "Pray without Ceasing," and, detecting in it no
hint of unorthodoxy, the association granted him approbation. Emerson can only have found their confidence flattering, for he said later,
"If they had examined me strictly perhaps they would not have let
me preach at all."[16]

Five days later Emerson delivered the same sermon from Uncle

Samuel's Waltham pulpit to a dense throng of worshipers that included the whole of his family, not excepting Aunt Mary, who made a special trip down from Maine to be present. The fifteenth of October 1826 is a date worth recalling since, for the next fifty years, the sight of this man addressing an audience was to be, to countless thousands, an experience never to be forgotten. He would never again need to pack a hall with relatives to assure himself a favorable reception.

The day after Emerson preached at Waltham, he was in the stage-coach, returning from Waltham to Cambridge, when a fellow passenger, a farmer, spoke up. "Young man," he said, "you'll never preach a better sermon than that."[17] This pleased Emerson more than the man could have guessed because he had gotten the idea for the sermon from another farmer. The year before, when Emerson worked on Uncle Ladd's farm, a day laborer named Tarbox, whom he was haying with, remarked, "Men are always praying, and their prayers are answered." Emerson was intrigued, possibly because prayer — public prayer and petitionary prayer especially — was a matter to which he was giving an increasing amount of thought. When it came time to write a sermon, he wrote it around Tarbox's two thoughts, leading up to a significant ethical note — "Men should take heed, then, to pray for the right things."[18] Later Emerson would reduce the essence of the sermon to an epigram: "Be careful what you wish for because you most certainly will get it."

> The good soul nourishes me and unlocks new maga-
> zines of power and enjoyment in me every day.

12. Journey South

ON 12 November 1826 Emerson repeated his one and only sermon
before the congregation of Boston's First Church. Edward, who had
arrived home from Europe too late to hear him preach at Waltham,
was on hand to hear him this time. He was much restored and ready
to resume his law studies. Waldo, however, had not fared as well. His
health failing, he had come to the point where he could not keep up a
pretext of matriculating at the theological school. On 25 November,
two days after the reunited family celebrated Thanksgiving, he went
south on the *Clematis*, a ship of twenty-five sail, glorious even in the
age of sail.

At Charleston, finding that a Harvard friend was pastor there,
Emerson preached his never-ceasing sermon on ceaseless prayer.
Afterward his chest ached. As a further aggravation, Charleston was
colder in winter than he had anticipated. He moved on to St. Augustine on 10 January. The city having passed into American hands a
scant six years before, Spanish Catholic culture still predominated there
and there was no call for the services of a Unitarian preacher. Rather,
it was Emerson's turn to be instructed. At a meeting of the local Bible
society, which he attended at the Government House, discussions were
carried on against the background noises of a slave auction taking
place in the adjacent yard. ''Almost without changing our position we
might aid in sending the scriptures into Africa, or bid for 'four children without the mother who had been kidnapped therefrom.' ''[1] His
faith in the ability of institutionalized religion to assist the moral sentiment slipped another notch. More than ever he was convinced that

men must be guided by their intuitions rather than by an equivocating intellect. At the same time, the relaxed morals of St. Augustine's Catholics seemed to him more consistent than the severe morals of his Protestant brethren. They did not profess allegiance to a standard of lofty virtue while profiting from exceptions made to that standard. The amiability of the local priest, temporarily jailed for debt during the period of Emerson's stay, impressed him. Yet he had come to St. Augustine seeking not spiritual enlightenment but physical well-being, and all other concerns ultimately were pushed into the background by that overarching one. By late March, he was ten pounds heavier than when he arrived. At one hundred and forty-one and a half pounds, he was far from robust yet thankful even for that additional half pound. His recovery once launched, his body seemed to respond enthusiastically. Before he got back to Boston his weight soared to one hundred and fifty-two pounds, quite the most he had ever weighed.

As winter waned, Emerson started the journey northward, boarding at St. Augustine, on 28 March, the sloop *William*. One of his fellow passengers was Achille Murat, whose mother was Caroline, the sister of Napoleon Bonaparte. Murat's father, Marshal Joachim Murat, Napoleon's colorful and reliable cavalry leader, had been put on the throne of Naples by his imperial brother-in-law. The marshal had rallied to Napoleon's support following the escape from Elba. Captured at Waterloo, he was afterward shot by his subjects. Achille, who would have succeeded to the kingship of Naples had his father kept his throne, was not yet fourteen when Napoleon suffered his final defeat. On reaching his majority he settled in America and married Catherine Willis, Washington's grandniece. He now owned a plantation on the outskirts of Tallahassee.

From St. Augustine the *William* usually reached Charleston in two days; this voyage, however, took ten. Fifty miles out of St. Augustine a tempest blew the *William* off course. Subsequently the ship was becalmed for a week. This delay bothered some passengers, but not Emerson or Murat.

On 6 April 1827, when the *William* at last reached Charleston, Emerson made his meeting with Murat a topic of immediate report in his journal. His attestations of friendship for, and enthusiastic interest in, a man who was both a foreigner and a professed atheist seem remarkable.

I have connected myself by friendship to a man who with as ardent a love of truth as that which animates me, with a mind surpassing mine in the variety of its research, & sharpened & strengthened to an energy for *action* to which I have no pretension by advantages of birth & practical connexion with mankind

beyond almost all men in the world, — is, yet, that which I had
ever supposed only a creature of the imagination — a consistent
Atheist, — and a disbeliever in the existence, &, of course, in the
immortality of the soul. My faith in these points is strong & I
trust, as I live, indestructible. Meantime I love & honour this
intrepid doubter. His soul is noble, & his virtue . . . sublime.[2]

A letter Emerson wrote to William the next day supplements this
account. In a phrase that might have been culled from an epistle of
Saint Paul's he says, of "a direful passage," "We were becalmed,
tempest-tossed, and at last well nigh starved — but the beloved brother
bore it not only with equanimity, but pleasure." Here, however, he
parts company with Paul, because his solace and comfort was not Christ
but Murat: "My kind genius had sent me for my ship-mate Achille
Murat. . . . I blessed my stars for my fine companion and we talked
incessantly."[3]

Emerson was not ready to tell William that Murat was an atheist.
In Germany William had talked with Goethe. In Florida celebrities of
that stature were not to be found. But Murat was a good catch and, at
this stage, Emerson did not wish to diminish his coup in William's
eyes.

Writing to Aunt Mary on 10 April, Emerson expanded on his portrait of Murat. Yet no more did he speak of Murat's atheism in this
letter than he did when he wrote to William. Aunt Mary was not ready
for *that*. He told her ambiguously:

> There are some who take such a strong hold of my attention that
> I am fain to quit my stoic fur, and fairly go out of my circle and
> shake hands and converse with them. . . . Another time I will give
> you an account of one whom it was my good fortune to meet in
> East Florida, a man of splendid birth and proud advantages, but
> a humble disciple in the school of truth.[4]

Several factors went into Emerson's eager espousal of Murat. He
was flattered to have stirred the response of friendship in the bosom
of the prince royal of the Two Sicilies, a nephew of the most celebrated man of the century. Further, he was attracted to Murat's vigorous animal spirits, the lack of which he deplored in himself. In his
present puny state he would have been astonished to know that Murat
would be dead at forty-six and that he would survive him by thirty-
five years and leave a record of achievement so notable that men would
recall Napoléon Achille Murat, if at all, only because he had once made
a favorable impression on Emerson.

In Murat, Emerson found some of the attributes he admired in Montaigne — bold skepticism, candor, sincerity, as well as breadth of knowledge. Most cherished of the virtues he attributed to Murat was that Montaignean trait, a passion for truth. That Murat had not yet found the truth as Emerson then understood it did not dismay Emerson, though a letter he subsequently received from Murat discloses that Emerson had mounted an unprecedented defense of his faith in response to some of Murat's objections, and, to a degree, succeeded in opening his mind to the acceptability of Unitarian theology.

A letter written by Emerson to Murat in August 1827 has not been uncovered, but Murat acknowledged it in a lengthy reply sent on 3 September. Here we learn that Emerson was not mistaken in believing that Murat fully reciprocated his friendship. He had meant, Murat said, to explore further with Emerson the topics they had broached. Though illness had curtailed that hope, Emerson nonetheless had wrought a palpable change in his thinking. "I must tell you, however, candidly," he wrote, "that the state of my mind has been altered since our meeting. Your system has acquired as much in proberbility as mine has lost in certainty, both seem to me now nearly equally proberable." Murat went on to reveal that, on Emerson's recommendation, he had gone to Philadelphia from New Jersey, where he was staying, to hear William Furness preach. As a consequence, he looked with pleasure on the prospect of Unitarianism's taking hold in Florida. Murat promised that when he returned to Tallahassee in November, he would "be fully at leasure to engage myself . . . in any kind of polemical warfare which may lead to the mutual improvement of our minds."[5] This did not happen because both men found themselves, by then, heavily committed in other directions.

One dark secret attendant upon Emerson's encounter with Murat was entrusted by him neither to his journal nor his correspondents. Many years later he confided the story to Franklin Sanborn. While in Florida, he had played host to one or more fleas. He had supposed that fleas left unmolested persons of proper breeding and careful hygiene and had kept to himself the humiliating fact that he had become flea-bitten. Accordingly, it came as an immense relief to him when Prince Murat told him fleas were ubiquitous in the South and that he himself carried them. Since Murat's personal habits of hygiene were notoriously bad — he never bathed and kept a large woolly dog which he used as a spittoon — his assurances were of dubious value.[6] But Emerson did not know this. And that was all to the good. When he renewed his acquaintance with the problem of fleas while traveling in Italy in 1833, he endured the ordeal stoically.

Even the wonders of Europe did not expunge from Emerson's memory his happy encounter with Murat. On 22 September 1833, when he was on the broad Atlantic, sailing home from England, he wrote in his journal: "This time I have not drawn the golden lot of company, and yet far better than the last voyage. But that little one to Charleston from St. Augustine with Murat was worth all the rest."[7]

Late in November 1830, when his brother Edward was ill with tuberculosis and seeking a milder climate for the winter, Emerson recommended Magnolia, a community on the outskirts of Tallahassee, where accommodations could be had on attractive terms. At the same time he offered to advise Murat of his coming, confident that the Frenchman would look out for him. He did not know that, by then, Murat had left America and embarked on a series of adventures in Belgium and England. He returned to his Tallahassee plantation only after several years. It was there that he died in 1847 before his family's reemergence to a renown which he well might have added to had he lived. In 1830, visualizing Murat dwelling in contentment in his Florida domain, Emerson told William, "For myself I would pay a hundred dollars to live a little while with Murat."[8]

On his homeward journey Emerson preached in Charleston again and in Washington and found that the effort did not tax him. In Philadelphia, under the wing of Furness, he preached twice, the second time on "The Uses of Unhappiness," a sermon he had prepared before he left home, in the provident hope that he might have occasion to preach twice to the same congregation. As the last sermon he preached on his convalescent journey, he delivered "Pray without Ceasing," for the seventh time, to a New York City congregation, in June. Before this same congregation he also delivered his second sermon, bringing to a close what had proved to be a spectral anticipation of his later lecture tours. In all, during his seven months' absence, including a sermon he gave at St. Augustine, he had preached eight times. Delivery time for each of these sermons was less than half an hour. That this effort, at the outset, put a strain on Emerson's lungs speaks significantly of his frailty.

When Emerson first apprised Aunt Mary of his plans to seek approbation, he specified that he meant, at first, to preach only "at intervals." A "supply" minister was expected to preach twice on the Sabbath, at morning and at afternoon services. When Emerson did that, his lungs protested, especially at night when he was in bed. Nonetheless, on his return to Boston he found a substantial assignment awaiting him. Nathaniel Frothingham, the durable pastor of the First Church, wanted him to fill his pulpit for a few weeks. This meant, among other things, that he had to prepare additional sermons. Although he stumbled onto the scene with a nondescript sermon, hastily composed, in mid-June he was ready with a superior sermon on a Sampson Reed, Swedenborgian theme, "Compensation." This concept was to become a cornerstone belief of his new, inner-directed faith — "No man," he declared, "can enrich himself by doing wrong," because "a system of Compensations prevails by God's will amid all the dealings of men in common life."[9]

On 24 June, writing to William, Emerson owned that he was not sanguine about his future prospects in the ministry:

> I am all clay no iron. Meditate now & then total abdication of
> the profession on the score of ill health. . . . how to get my bread?
> Shall I commence author? Of prose or of verse? Alack of both
> the unwilling muse. Yet am I no whit the worse in appearance I
> believe than when in N.Y. but the lungs in their spiteful lobes sing
> Sexton & Sorrow whenever I only ask them to shout a sermon for
> me.[10]

Emerson may merely have been serving William notice that he was not able to assume, for long, the full burden of providing for the needs of his mother, Bulkeley, and Charles. William, now resettled in New York, was earning only three dollars a week in a law office and not able to help out at all. Even so, at the close of his letter, Emerson offered a hint that he meant to dispute his infirmities: "I have taken a room in Divinity Hall . . . and perhaps shall live there a little." The room he chose this time was remote from the marshy miasmas that had plagued him before.

When Frothingham returned to resume his pulpit, Emerson had only to choose among other bids awaiting him. Now, enlarging his commitment to Nature, he accepted an invitation to conduct a missionary tour through the western part of the state. It took him to Northampton, Greenfield, and Lenox, a challenge to which he responded too robustly at the outset because he walked most of the way to Northampton, a distance of more than a hundred miles. Even before he ascended a single Berkshire pulpit, his vitality was spent. Yet he was back at Concord scarcely long enough to gather up a change of linen from his mother, then living at the Manse as Dr. Ripley's housekeeper, before he went to New Bedford to begin an agreeable preaching relationship with Orville Dewey, pastor of the local Unitarian church, and a kinsman by marriage. This was a three-week commitment. After that, Emerson preached at his father's old church, at Harvard, Massachusetts; at Waltham, for Uncle Samuel; and next, at Watertown, for Convers Francis, who was married to Sarah Bradford Ripley's sister. Both Dewey and Francis had exceptional libraries of which Emerson, on these occasions, made excellent use so that, even while he could insist, "My eyes are not strong enough for me to be learned," he could return to the Divinity School with new insights.

Throughout the summer, Emerson sought to consolidate his physical gains by spending his weekdays at Concord, at the Manse, and putting into practice Sampson Reed's teachings, roaming field and woodland and communing with Nature.

Only in December did Emerson take firm possession of the room at Divinity Hall that he had contracted for six months earlier. Even then his name did not appear on the list of candidates and his attendance at lectures was spasmodic. As he could, he read. Three times in the ensuing months he declined pastorates, feeling unequal to the burden a full commitment would entail. Too many young ministers had died in the first years of their ministry for Emerson to have any illusions about receiving a miraculous burst of health to sustain him in his godly office. His brother Edward, he saw, was again taxing himself and faced with a new crisis. Through 1828 he spared himself in one way by doing little journal-keeping. Instead, the sermons he was adding to his stock became the repository of his newest perceptions.

When Emerson was at length ordained to the ministry, to assist Henry Ware, Jr., at Boston's Second Church, he described the day as his "execution day." So Nathaniel Hawthorne, entering into his thoroughly desired marriage with Sophia Peabody on 9 July 1842, said in a letter to his sister Louisa, "the execution took place yesterday."[11] From the lips of a young man embarking on a new venture, the connotations of the word "execution" all were joyous. Emerson did not take up his pastorate as though embarking upon his doom.

13. Ezra Ripley
An Old Semi-Savage

*I*N 1825 Phebe Ripley died in Concord, at the Manse that had been her home for fifty-six years, first as the wife of William Emerson and subsequently as the wife of his successor, Ezra Ripley. Of the eight children she had borne — five of them William's, three of them Ezra's — only Sarah, her daughter by Ezra, had stayed on with her, as companion and housekeeper. In 1826, however, Sarah died, and Ezra — at long last come into sole possession of the Manse — was struck with the realization that blood ties no longer linked the Emersons to his house. As titular grandfather to the sons of his stepson William Emerson, however, he had received them at the Manse for many years. He saw no reason why that situation should alter now. Accordingly, he spoke about it to Waldo: ''I wish you and your brothers to come to this house as you have always done. You will not like to be excluded; I shall not like to be neglected.''[1]

Emerson perhaps found this statement droll. The Manse, after all, had been built by William Emerson and had been the home of the Emersons for ten years before Ezra married Phebe. No matter that the original cost had been borne in large part by the parish with the object of seeing its minister well housed. No matter that Ezra's industry had maintained it for forty-six years. For William Emerson's heirs to be excluded from their ancestral home — that would be something indeed! That being their line of reasoning, when their mother succeeded to Sarah's role as Ezra's housekeeper, Waldo and his brothers found it easy to come and go from the old place with no real sense of conditions being altered.

In the spring of 1828 Waldo moved into the Manse for a stay of several weeks. When, in late May, he left to preach in New Hampshire, Edward, almost as his surrogate, supplanted him there. But the exchange was not quite an equal one. Edward was in a bad state, his mind taxed with excessive study, his lungs torn with consumption. When he was seized with fainting spells, Ruth sent a desperate appeal to Waldo, and he returned at once to help as he could. Late in June, without warning, Edward suddenly became a raving lunatic. In a letter to William sent on 3 July, Waldo described the situation:

> He has been now for one week thoroughly deranged & a great deal of the time violent so as to make it necessary to have two men in the room all the time. . . . His frenzy took all forms; sometimes he was very gay & bantered every body. . . . Afterward would come on a peevish or angry state & he would throw down every thing in the room & throw his clothes &c out of the window; then perhaps on being restrained wd. follow a paroxysm of perfect frenzy & he wd. roll & twist on the floor with his eyes shut for half an hour. — But what the need of relating this — there he lay — Edward the admired learned eloquent thriving boy — a maniac.[2]

He had to be admitted for a time to the McLean Asylum, where Bulkeley, compounding the family's grief, was already a patient.

Yet another lamentable aspect of Edward's tragic derangement was the hatred he showed, in this state, for Dr. Ripley. Amid his outcries, Ezra became the repeated object of his vituperations and denunciations. We are not told what form these accusations took. Possibly, because Ezra now, legally, was in exclusive possession of the parsonage, he branded him an interloper. If this is what he and his brothers thought, without the restraints that sanity imposed there was nothing to keep him from blurting it out. It was a fact, too, that none of the Emersons could quite forget that Ripley's heritage was not on a par with that of the Emersons. He was a simple man with sparse claims to learning. And it may be that in this crisis his limitations were shown to their worst advantage. Waldo may have had this very time in mind when he said of Ezra later: ''Out of his own ground he was not good for aught. To talk with the insane he was as mad as they.''[3]

Ezra, who was seventy-seven at the time of Edward's breakdown, had had to work on his father's farm at Woodstock, Connecticut, until he was twenty-one and came to Harvard as a freshman at that age. Piety rather than profundity led to his ordination at twenty-eight. Condescendingly, his classmates referred to him as ''Holy Ripley.'' It was after he succeeded to William Emerson's parish that he succeeded to his marriage bed as Phebe Bliss Emerson's second husband. He was still in his twenties. She was approaching forty.

Phebe seemed almost to be one of the perquisites that went with the office of minister in Concord, for William Emerson's predecessor had been her father, Daniel Bliss. Ministers came and went, Phebe stayed. If anyone can be singled out for infixing the idea that Ezra Ripley had risen above his station in succeeding to William Emerson's place in Concord, it is Phebe. She regarded herself as a great lady. Work was for others. She preferred to sit in her easy chair and hand down decrees governing the household. She kept William Emerson's letters in a little casket that rested on a high shelf behind her chair. At intervals she would take them down and weep over them, which put Ezra out of sorts when he would find her thus engaged. Even on the last night of her life she still was extolling William, dead then nearly fifty years, at Ezra's cost. "Don't call Dr. Ripley," she told her daughter Mary, with almost her last breath, "his boots squeak so. Mr. Emerson used to step so softly, his boots never squeaked."[4] Although Ezra waited on her hand and foot (squeaky boots and all), she never wearied of comparing her two husbands at his expense, and, as time passed, idealized William more and more. Her condescending attitude toward Ezra set the standards by which her Emerson descendants viewed him. She seems also to have provided a pattern that her grandson Waldo unwittingly followed in his dealings with his second wife. To be a second spouse in a family of idealists is not an enviable role.

William Emerson's house was set in twenty acres of land. When Ezra Ripley came there, his salary was five hundred dollars a year. With a large family to support and his farming skills as a resource, he fell naturally into the role of farmer-preacher, doing much of the farm work himself with no time left to cultivate a tradition of scholarship. Hawthorne, living at the Old Manse (he was the first to call it that), conjectured that Dr. Ripley, during his stay there, "had penned nearly three thousand discourses," but then, recollecting Ezra's predilection for extemporaneous preaching, conceded that he must be credited, too, for "the better, if not the greater, number that gushed living from his lips." He was impressed, also, that Ripley, in his old age and to the amusement of his neighbors, had set out a hundred apple trees. Though his grip on the gospel message diminished year by year, his hold on life did not. "The old minister," gloated Hawthorne, "before reaching his patriarchal age of ninety, ate the apples from this orchard during many years, and added silver and gold to his annual stipend, by disposing of the superfluity."[5] Ezra, in fact, remained on as minister at Concord for sixty-three years.

Short of stature, lean of build, attired still in smallclothes long after pantaloons had routed them, and wearing always a frock coat and stovepipe hat, by then a mark of eccentricity, Ezra Ripley was more and more a village character. Yet he knew human nature, his sermons dealt with practical matters that he was made mindful of on his parish

rounds, and he offered good counsel. None could rival him in public
spirit, and, so far as anyone could tell, when rain was needed, Dr.
Ripley, with his prayers, provided it. Once, when he prayed for rain
on Sunday and next day the rain came, Emerson remarked in his journal, with that derision which had become all but habitual with him
when Ripley was mentioned, "When I spoke of the speed with which
his prayers were answered, the good man looked modest."[6]

Emerson was never quite able to get Dr. Ripley's measure. He saw
that Ripley was no scholar: "He had no studies, no occupations, which
company could interrupt. His friends were his study." He was at times
uncouth. He could not "eat sponge cake without a ramrod." He was
naive: "Dr. R. says he has been eating an apple of which he sent the
graft to Waterford and he would give me a piece but that he has just
eat it up." He was credulous:

> One August afternoon, when I was in his hayfield helping him
> with his man to rake up his hay, I well remember his pleading,
> almost reproachful looks at the sky, when the thunder-gust was
> coming up to spoil his hay. He raked very fast, then looked at the
> cloud and said, 'We are in the Lord's hand; mind your rake,
> George! We are in the Lord's hand;' and seemed to say, 'You
> know me; this field is mine, — Dr. Ripley's, — thine own ser-
> vant!'[7]

He was old-fashioned and superstitious:

> He looked at every person and thing from the parochial point of
> view. I remember, when a boy, driving about Concord with him,
> and in passing each house he told the story of the family that
> lived in it; and especially he gave me anecdotes of the nine church
> members who had made a division in the church . . . and showed
> me how every one of the nine had come to bad fortune or to a bad
> end.[8]

Despite his conservatism, Dr. Ripley had found it increasingly difficult to reconcile the God of Calvinism, whose chief concern seemed
to be the castigation of mankind, with his own understanding of human nature. In time, at his behest, his parish dropped the whole of the
shorter catechism, passing, finally, into the Unitarian fold.

Moreover, in January 1829, when nearly eighty, Dr. Ripley took the
lead in launching the Concord Lyceum, the first successful town lyceum in America. Not only was it one of the few lyceums to survive
the Civil War and "probably," says Carl Bode in his definitive study
of the lyceum movement, "the most intellectual" of them all, it gave

Emerson on one hundred occasions an audience on which to try out new lecture materials.[9]

The embodiment in many ways of a world that, with Emerson's approval and incitement, was passing away, Ripley yet seemed responsive to men's needs. Thus, when Charles Chauncy Emerson died, in May 1836, Waldo found Ezra's remarks at church exactly fitting: "Grandfather," he wrote William on 15 May, "in the afternoon, called him by name in his own rugged style of Indian eloquence. 'This event seems to me,' he said, 'loud & piercing, like thunder & lightning. While many aged and burdensome are spared, this beloved youth is cut down in the morning.'"[10] Ultimately, Emerson justified Ezra's appeal by extending to him the merits of transcendentalism, espoused unawares. In his journal Emerson wrote of this, when at last he understood:

> These old semi-savages do from the solitude in which they live & their remoteness from artificial society & their inevitable daily comparing man with beast, village with wilderness, their inevitable acquaintance with the outward nature of man, & with his strict dependence on sun & rain & wind & frost; wood, worm, cow, & bird, get an education to the Homeric simplicity which all the libraries of the Reviews & the Commentators in Boston do not countervail.[11]

When Ripley died, in his ninety-first year, on 21 September 1841, his old meeting house was undergoing extensive alterations even to the point of being shifted around to face in the opposite direction, a fact that, to some of his parishioners, seemed theologically significant. Ezra had to be buried from the neighboring meeting house, across the brook. Though quick to grasp these events as symbolic of an era closing, Emerson, for the moment, dwelt on those aspects of Ripley which were compatible with Calvinism and not those which set him apart from that tradition:

> He has identified himself with the forms at least of the old church of the New England Puritans, his nature was eminently loyal, not in the least adventurous or democratical & his whole being leaned backward on the departed, so that he seemed one of the rear-guard of this great camp & army which have filled the world with fame & with him passes out of sight almost the last banner & guidon flag of a mighty epoch.

Emerson hastened to dissociate himself from that generation: "Great, grim, earnest men, I belong by natural affinity to other thoughts and schools than yours, but my affection hovers respectfully about your retiring footprints, your unpainted churches, strict platforms, & sad offices; the iron-gray deacon & the wearisome prayer rich with the diction of ages.'' He seemed reconciled to Ripley's passing: ''Now in his old age when all the antique Hebraism & customs are going to pieces, it is fit he too should depart, most fit that in the fall of laws a loyal man should die.''

For all that, a lurking sense of the other Ripley haunted Emerson's thoughts:

> No waste, & no stint, always open-handed; just & generous. My little boy, a week ago, carried him a peach in a calabash, but the calabash brought home two pears. I carried him melons in a basket, but the basket came home with apples. . . . He knew the value of a dollar as well as another man. Yet he always sold cheaper than any other man.

When Emerson came to the end of these first musings on Ezra's death, thoughts of Ezra's ties with Nature suddenly routed all formal detail about that death emblemizing the passing of the old faith. He declared: ''A man is but a little thing in the midst of these great objects of nature, the mountains, the clouds, and the cope of the horizon, & the globes of heaven, yet a man by moral quality may abolish all thoughts of magnitude and in his manners equal the majesty of the world.''[12]

In death Dr. Ripley appeared ''a handsome and noble spectacle.'' Emerson brought little Waldo with him to the parsonage to see him one last time. The five-year-old looked for a moment at the serene, motionless figure, and then proposed, ''Why don't they keep him for a statue?''[13] In a sense, Emerson heeded that appeal, preparing afterward a profile of this patriarch who always came down on the side of love when love and doctrinal certitude threatened to collide.

No one taught Emerson more about true charity than Dr. Ripley did, unless it was his son Samuel. But it was by Ezra that Samuel had been schooled in charity, so it was still to Ezra that the debt was owed.

14. Ellen Tucker
The Entireness of Love

*O*N a sliver of cardboard amid pressed leaves and flower petals in Ellen Tucker's album of poetry appear the words, "Waldo I love you Ellen."[1] To find this avowal there can surprise no one. A passage found in a journal Emerson kept in the summer of 1829 is another matter. Between a grave discourse on the office of a Christian minister and prosaic notations on the epic voyage of Columbus, a single line leaps out — "Oh, Ellen, I do dearly love you —."[2] Emerson was betrothed to Ellen Louisa Tucker and, in a few short weeks, would marry her. For someone who was convinced that the chord of affection did not vibrate within him, this declaration is not merely a curious intrusion, it is a glorious shudder passing down the wall of his aloofness and raising grave doubts about the soundness of its construction.

In his first year out of college, at eighteen, teaching young ladies when still he had never wooed one, Emerson was perhaps in terror of his emotions. It could be of this interlude that he wrote a few years later when he said:

> *Then eagerly I searched each circle round,*
> *I panted for my mate, but no mate found.*
> *I saw bright eyes, fair forms, complexions fine,*
> *But not a single soul that spoke to mine.*[3]

Discounting such plausible yearnings, he had on 13 May 1822 rebuked himself for his incapacity for affection: "I have not the kind affections of a pigeon. Ungenerous & selfish, cautious & cold. . . . There is not in the whole wide Universe of God . . . one being to whom I am attached with warm & entire devotion . . . and this I say at the most susceptible age of man. . . . It is a true picture of a barren & desolate soul.''[4]

At twenty Emerson still found no warmth in his nature. On 18 April 1824 he told of ''a signal defect of character which neutralizes in great part the just influences my talents ought to have . . . an absence of common *sympathies*. . . . Its bitter fruits are a sore uneasiness in the company of most men & women, a frigid fear of offending.'' Crothers argues that ''the chill was not in himself, but in the atmosphere that was about him.'' Emerson would not have agreed. ''What is called a warm heart, I have not,'' he said.[5]

On 28 September 1826 he reiterated his misgivings: ''I was born cold. My bodily habit is cold. I shiver in and out; don't heat to the good purposes called enthusiasm a quarter so quickly and kindly as my neighbors.'' And a significant new note is added: ''Yet, so depraved is self-conceit, that I sometimes imagined this very seed of wrath to be one of my gifts, though not graces.''[8] A more marked assertiveness is evident in a journal entry made at St. Augustine on 2 February 1827: ''I am cold and solitary, & lead a life comfortable to myself, & useless to others. Yet I believe myself to be a moral agent of an indestructible nature & designed to stand in sublime relations to God & to my fellow men.'' Coldness persists, yet is seen now as a possible asset! At the end of that same year he interpolated this phrase into his journal: ''I ought to apprise the reader that I am a bachelor & to the best of my belief have never been in love.'' To the foregoing, Emerson may have weighed adding the word ''before.'' We shall never know. Yet, whether he realized it or not, he had already met the great love of his life.[6]

In December 1827 Emerson had gone to Concord, New Hampshire, to minister there to the new Unitarian parish being organized by Colonel William Austin Kent, father of his Harvard classmate Edward Kent. He came for a three-week stay and preached at the courthouse. The day after Christmas, he was introduced to Edward's stepsister Ellen Tucker. Ellen's father, Bezaleel Tucker, owner of a Boston ropewalk, had died seven years before, when Ellen was nine. A widow of means, her mother then had married a widower of means, Colonel Kent, banker, tradesman, insurance executive. When President Monroe and, in due course, Lafayette and Daniel Webster visited Concord, they stayed with the Kents. But the scourge that smote Beza had smitten his family as well. Like her brother, sisters, and mother, Ellen was consumptive. Tuberculosis was, however, a terror the age lived with, and if Emerson was not instantly responsive to Ellen's pallid beauty when he first met her, her tender years rather than the state of her health governed his response. The attraction she had for him came on almost unawares. On this first visit to new Concord he recorded no formal mention of Ellen. The following May and June he came there again to preach. Since it was at this juncture that Edward's health gave way, Emerson had new cause to be aware of the transitory nature of human existence and of the need to seize on those moments of happiness that were offered, without insisting on perfection of conditions. Even if Ellen was "too lovely to live long," as he later declared, that ought not to keep them from cherishing together the time granted to them.

Only a subjective reading of Emerson's journal for the six ensuing months can isolate sentiments that reveal Emerson in love. With the coming of another December all need for guesswork ceases. Recruited again by Kent's parish, Emerson came bearing for Ellen a gift book inscribed with her initials. Such elegant books, a vogue then, put mawkish sentimentality within the reach of every rapturous lover. Even in love Emerson would have known its contents were insipid. The verse Ellen herself wrote was better than anything found in most gift books. That can hardly have mattered to her. She probably never took her eyes off the title long enough to examine the contents. The message was clear — *Forget me not.* And so was Ellen's response. On 17 December Emerson proposed and she accepted him. As always, all but speechless at times of great emotion, he noted tersely in his journal on 21 December: "I have now been four days engaged to Ellen Louisa Tucker."[7]

Emerson was human enough to be gratified that Ellen was an heiress but wholesome enough not to account that fact a part of her attractiveness. When they became engaged, the most that he himself had to offer was prospects, and he told her so. He had preached to advantage at Boston's Second Church and expected to be asked to affiliate with that parish — in fact, he was, the following month — as associate pastor, assisting the ailing Henry Ware. Ellen magnanimously interrupted, telling him, "I do not wish to hear of your prospects."[8] Thus both renounced the intrusion of material concerns in what seemed to them an alliance of their spiritual identities. Even when they spoke of their love in verse, earthly love was prized by them, it seemed, only as a step toward spiritual love.

Although Emerson already had thought about those circumstances which presently he would bring into balance in his doctrine of compensation — the belief that good and bad fortune are apportioned out to men in equal measure — when he wrote to Aunt Mary, early in the new year, touching on the "particular felicity" that had brought such joy into his present life, he found himself asking, "Will God make me a brilliant exception to the common order of his dealings, which equalizes destinies?'' What he alluded to as the ''straitened lines'' of his previous life, might, he intimated, have heralded this change of fortune, yet a gnawing apprehensiveness would not allow him to rest easy. He felt that his present joy overcompensated him for all that had gone before and thus could not hold.[9]

Behind Emerson's theorizing about equalized destinies, he must have entertained commonsense anxieties about Ellen's health. And so he should have. Before the end of the month Ellen was spitting blood again. For those thus afflicted the prevailing therapy prescribed jarring rides to induce expectoration. This therapy Emerson dutifully followed. Early in January Ellen and her family came to Boston to live. A ride to Concord and a return trip to Boston, the latter in wet weather, set her lungs hemorrhaging. In the spring she went back to New Hampshire but a visit from Emerson, in June, coincided with further hemorrhaging, produced, it was thought, by the excitement of his presence. The remedy for this was deemed to be horseback-riding, and Ellen soon was covering nine jouncing miles a day, no doubt with much jogging loose of the mucus clogging her lungs. In August, Emerson and she made a ten-day excursion to the White Mountains in a chaise, covering in all some two hundred miles over rough roads, with Mrs. Kent, whose lungs were as congested as Ellen's, following along in a covered carriage, simultaneously lending the betrothed couple the respectability that went with her presence and benefiting herself with many a desirable jounce.

To anyone with an eye for rapacity, an art alien to Emerson, who was ever a stranger to greed, it must seem inevitable that, at the close of this journey, he asked Ellen to make out a will in his favor. Surely he was prompted by nothing more than normal Yankee prudence. Both Ellen and her mother found this ''an ugly topic,'' but, all the same, capitulated. Emerson seems also to have urged Ellen to take out life insurance, with himself as beneficiary. It is a tribute to her affection for him, even in a practical Yankee society, that it survived intact these sensible recommendations, and equally a tribute to his ardor that, throughout these negotiations, he never gave her cause to doubt it. Ellen may not have wanted to think about his prospects, but he certainly was thinking about hers.

In early September, Emerson again had the Kents — Ellen and her mother and now her tubercular sister Margaret as well — off on a whirlwind romp over the cadaverous New England roads, to Worcester, Springfield, Hartford, Worcester again, and at last back to new Concord. On the fifteenth, to his friend Abel Adams, a trustee of the Second Church, he wrote: '' Ellen has borne all extremely well, & appears much stronger; & except a damp morning & one or two piecings out of our journey after dark — has ridden always in the chaise. . . .

We travel for air & jolting & these we have gotten.''[10] This positive kind of treatment, putting the burden of healing on Nature, wholly suited Emerson, who was never drawn to patent-medicine nostrums. The fact is, Ellen appears to have benefited from this strenuous therapy. To her doctor's surprise she was well enough to marry Emerson on 30 September at her stepfather's home in Concord. Her therapist, Waldo, however, limped to the ceremony on a cane, having come down with an inflamed knee. In October, when again he took up his duties at the Second Church, he had to sit while he preached. If Ellen wondered if she should have taken out a policy on him, she refrained from saying so.

The paradox of a restored Ellen married to an incapacitated Emerson did not long persist. When they took a house in Boston, on Chardon Street, Ruth Emerson moved in with them and relieved Ellen of the cares of housekeeping. Ellen went to church on Sunday in a carriage, a luxury that the affluent Parkmans, alone among her co-parishioners, enjoyed. But for Ellen it was no luxury. Under doctor's orders, with Emerson's hearty approval, her strength was being taxed to the utmost. *"Exercise — Exercise* is the command,'' she wrote to Mary Moody Emerson soon after her marriage, ''and I strictly obedient to all such, unless I can write walking or riding, must burden my friends with sleepy words or cease all intellectual exercise.''[11]

Correctly gauging that the Boston winter had taken a further toll of Ellen, in March Emerson set out with Margaret and her for Philadelphia, to intercept the advancing spring. They went by stage and ship, a tiring journey marked by many petty frustrations. By the time they arrived Ellen was weak and again spitting blood.

Emerson did not like Philadelphia and one day would say, ''If all the world was Philadelphia, suicide would be exceedingly common.'' But he relished being in Ellen's company and once, in fact, his friend William Furness came by their boardinghouse to find them ''walking with arms around each other, up & down their parlor.''[12] But Emerson had duties in Boston and was, moreover, restive away from his books. At Ellen's urging he left her with Margaret and went home, sending his accommodating mother back to Philadelphia to assist and support his fading bride. There were sermons to write, out of duty, and poems to write, out of love, and somehow Emerson got through the next fifty days until the Boston air was fragrant with spring blossoms and he could go south to take Ellen home again.

Remembering his salubrious Canterbury respite, Emerson had a house ready for Ellen in Brookline, with Ruth again as housekeeper. But the price of being in a rural setting was being four miles from his parish. That might have been bearable had not Ellen, in August, begun again to produce what Emerson, seeking to rout anxiety with rhetorical whimsy, referred to as "red wheezers." There seemed but one course to follow — he must take Ellen to a milder climate before another winter came. His brother Charles was less sanguine. "I doubt," he wrote William on 14 August, "whether there is any climate that will save Ellen."[13]

While Emerson prepared a new haven on Chardon Street, Ellen spent September with her family in New Hampshire. But now a tide of reversal that no doctrine of compensation could account for inundated Emerson's world. Bulkeley, passing into another violent phase, had to be readmitted to McLean. In New York, Edward's tuberculosis flared to new heights. Nothing, it seemed, but a retreat to Puerto Rico would save him. Emerson had no idea where the money for this would come from. Some measure of his desperation is evident in his appeal to William "to bundle him [Edward] up warm, & send him here immediately — for Mother and Ellen to nurse him."[14] Ellen was hardly ready for this, especially since her own mother and sister also were losing ground in their struggle against what Ellen spoke of as "the great enemy of our family."[15] But this burden, at least, was spared the Chardon Street household. Edward went to Puerto Rico. Wistfully, Ellen followed him there in her thoughts.

Boston fell into the grip of severe winter weather. In mid-January 1831 Emerson had to suspend morning worship because his parishioners could not wade through the deep snow to attend. Yet, through snowstorms and subzero temperatures, Ellen was sent forth on her daily salubrious rides. To Edward — pretending to pretend — she wrote proposing that in Puerto Rico he "pick out a pretty spot for Waldo & wife to live." Emerson now was firmly convinced he must go south with her "as soon as the snows melt." This he reported to Edward, who must have been thankful he had not crept into the charnel house on Chardon Street.[16]

On Wednesday, 2 February, Ellen was sent out on morning and afternoon rides. By Saturday she saw she was near death and both Emerson and his mother realized at last that nothing could be done to stay the course of events. Ellen's concern was not for herself but for those whom she would leave behind, especially her husband of seventeen months. No gift-book heroine ever met death with kinder solicitude, greater sweetness. On the sixth, a Sunday, Charles Follen and Nathaniel Frothingham preached for Emerson so that he would not have to leave Ellen's side. Charles Emerson had joined the vigil and that night, in a letter to Aunt Mary, recounted a scene that could have been culled from Irving's *Sketch Book,* prototype of all gift books:

> She spoke this afternoon very sweetly of her readiness to die. . . . She saw no reason why her friends should be distressed — it

was better she should go first, & prepare the way — She asked
Waldo, if he had strength, to read her a few verses of scripture —
and he read a portion of the XIV chapter of John — Waldo is
bowed down under the affliction, yet he says 'tis like seeing
an angel go to Heaven.[17]

Ezra Ripley prayed consoling prayers at her bedside on Monday
and afterward she took private leave of Charles, asking him "to cheer
up Waldo when she was gone, not to let him think too much of her."
Charles was awed. "She looks saint like," he said. A beautiful girl,
dying at nineteen, her face aglow with the hectic bloom induced by
the illness that ravaged her and the good will her faith engendered —
Ellen's radiance in those last hours cannot have been overstated either
by the brother who saw her as an angel or the brother who saw her as
a saint. A little after two on Tuesday morning, Ellen said she sensed
the end drawing near. She sought to know who was about her — mother,
sisters, husband — then bidding them be silent, prayed for all, kissed
them good-bye, and rapidly sank toward death, which came at nine
o'clock.[18]

So graceful was Ellen's leave-taking that she left those around her
not cast down but exalted. To Aunt Mary, that connoisseur of deathbed scenes, Emerson conveyed his first reactions in a letter written a
bare two hours later. Though dazed from lack of sleep, he had impressions to share with her that few were better qualified to appreciate:

My angel is gone to heaven this morning & I am alone in the
world & strangely happy. Her lungs shall no more be torn nor her
head scalded by her blood nor her whole life suffer from the
warfare between the force & delicacy of her soul & the weakness of
her frame. . . . I have never known a person in the world in
whose separate existence as a soul I could so readily & fully
believe & she is present with me now beaming joyfully upon me, in
her deliverance & the entireness of her love for your poor
nephew.[19]

Of Ellen's death Emerson wrote in his journal five days later: "Her
end was blessed. . . . She prayed that God would speedily release her
from her body & that she might not make this prayer to be rid of her
pains, 'but because thy favor is better than life.' . . . Never anyone
spake with greater simplicity or cheerfulness of dying." Emerson was
less tranquil about his own state of mind:

I shall go again among my friends with a tranquil countenance.
Again I shall be amused. . . . Shall I ever again be able to connect

the face of outward nature, the mists of the morn, the star of eve, the flowers, & all poetry, with the heart & life of an enchanting friend? No. There is one birth & one baptism & one first love & the affections cannot keep their youth any more than men.[20]

Emerson never prescinded from this view, which remained always a shadow over his second marriage. By compartmentalizing his grief in this way he gained in the short term but lost in the long, by closing the door forever on part of his emotional capability.

His way facilitated by Ellen's joyous reception of death and his own success in localizing finality, Emerson wore a look of benign acceptance sooner than anyone expected. Twelve days after Ellen's death he again stood in his pulpit, discoursing on a mourner's consolations with such detachment the occasional churchgoer would have had no hint that he spoke as a bridegroom lately bereaved. "By the spectacle of triumphant faith," he said, as one who had seen faith triumph over sorrow, "the dying chamber of youth where a thousand expectations are shattered may infuse more sweetness and joy into the soul than ever prosperity or praise could give."[21]

But prosperity was also in Emerson's thoughts and, in a letter to William, written on 24 May 1831, he reflected that he might soon be able to meet himself the whole of Bulkeley's expenses "without difficulty, especially as it seems that Ellen is to continue to benefit her husband whenever hereafter the estate shall be settled." Only his natural piety kept him from sounding sardonic when he added, "I please myself that Ellen's work of mercy is not done on earth, but she shall continue to help Edward & B. & Charles."[22]

While Emerson continued on good terms with the Kents and with Ellen's sister Margaret Tucker, her sister Paulina and her husband, Captain Nash, preferred that Ellen's posthumous works of mercy should benefit them rather than the Emersons. The estate was tied up in litigation, with Ellen's executor vowing that Emerson would never, in his lifetime, see a penny of her fortune.[23] By the time a first settlement was made, in the spring of 1834, when Emerson received in stock and cash $11,600, Margaret and Mrs. Kent had been vanquished by "the great enemy" and were in their graves, Margaret dying on 24 November 1832 and her mother on 28 February 1833. Not until July 1837 did Emerson receive the residue of Ellen's estate, $11,674.49. Prudently invested, the first sum brought him an annual income of $1,200. That did not constitute affluence unbounded, but Emerson long since had learned to live close to the dollar. As he saw it, Ellen had bequeathed him his freedom. He might not have quit his pulpit had he not thought so.

As his optimism had lasted through two years of jolting rides with

Ellen, the good cheer her legacy invoked ran in tandem with his grief. In June 1831 he declined, with dignity, an invitation to deliver the Phi Beta Kappa poem at the Harvard Commencement, explaining, ''I have not at present any spirit for a work of that kind, which must not be a dirge.''[24]

Ellen was buried in her father's tomb at a cemetery close by the Roxbury Latin School. For several months Emerson walked out daily to visit the grave, even in foul weather.[25] On 29 March 1832 he made a one-sentence entry in his journal: ''I visited Ellen's tomb & opened the coffin.''[26] In 1857, when the body of Waldo, his firstborn, was transferred from the Ripley tomb at Concord's Hillside Burying Ground to Sleepy Hollow, Emerson opened his coffin and looked at his remains as well. Waldo had then been dead fifteen years. There was a family precedent for this morbid postmortem inspection. Emerson's father, by his own labor, exhumed his father, eighteen years after his death, to look upon his face. Emerson spoke thereafter neither of his reasons for viewing Ellen's entombed corpse, thirteen months after her death, nor did he disclose the substance of such reflections as the intrusion occasioned. Clearly, he was not so dismayed as to be discouraged from hazarding the same experiment again a quarter of a century later. But his visits to the gravesite ceased. At some later time he may have confided to Lidian, his second wife, his state of mind then, because, after his own death, Lidian, though nearly eighty, for a time walked two miles daily to visit his grave, then ceased to go, declaring she did not believe he was there and that it was a mistake to associate the grave with her thoughts of him.

In a striking passage found in his journal for 4 March 1838, Emerson reviewed his relationship with Ellen and his brothers and charged himself with shallowness:

Last night a remembering & remembering talk with Lidian. I went back to the first smile of Ellen on the door stone at Concord. I went back to all that delicious relation to feel as ever how many shades, how much reproach. Strange it is that I can go back to no part of youth, no past relation without shrinking & shrinking. Not Ellen, not Edward, not Charles. Infinite compunctions embitter each of those dear names & all who surrounded them. Ah could I have felt in the presence of the first, as now I feel my own power & hope, . . . I might haply have made her days longer & certainly sweeter & at least have recalled her seraph smile without a pang. I console myself with the thought that if Ellen, if Edward, if Charles could have read my entire heart they should have seen nothing but rectitude of purpose & generosity conquering the superficial coldness & prudence. . . . They never needed to shrink at any remembrance; & I — at so many passages that look to me now as if I [had] been blind & mad. . . . This is the thorn in the flesh.[27]

While such remorse in another might point to some major transgression, Emerson's self-reproach, it is reasonable to suppose, arose entirely from his failure to be open in his affections. Yet what are we to make of these dark lines written by Ellen?

> *I will not stay on earth Waldo*
> *Unless thy love is mine. . . .*
>
> *Sweeter the green sod for my bones*
> *The black earth for my head*
> *The wind, than thy cold altered tones*
> *Whence all of love had fled.*[28]

When, on 24 February 1839, Emerson's second wife gave birth to their first daughter, Emerson expected to name her Lidian. The day following he wrote in his journal: "Lidian, who magnanimously makes my gods her gods, calls the babe Ellen. I can hardly ask more for thee, my babe, than that name implies. Be that vision & remain with us, & after us."[29] Possibly Lidian thought the new Ellen might exorcise the ghost of the old one, giving her access to the place in her husband's heart that was rightfully hers. If so, her strategy failed.

From the outset of his courtship of Lydia (presently Lidian) Jackson, Emerson seemed to assume that a second marriage was not a divine calling but a human convenience. He reported to William: "I announce my engagement in a very different feeling from that with which I entered my first connection. This is a very sober joy."[30] He then went on to enumerate Lidian's fine points much as though he was discussing the attributes of a prize ewe at an agricultural fair. Seven weeks after he became engaged he could still revert, in his journal, to his one first love: "I loved Ellen, & love her with an affection that would ask nothing but its indulgence to make me blessed." A scant two months after he married Lidian, he had new confidences for his journal: "The charming beauty which a few years ago shed on me its tender & immortal light. She needed not a historical name [Lidian was descended from John Cotton] nor earthly rank or wealth. She was complete in her own perfections."[31]

After four years, with daughter Ellen to dandle on his knee, Emerson thought still of the other Ellen: "She was like a tree in flower . . . and she taught the eye that beheld her, why Beauty was ever painted with loves & graces attending her steps."[32] Lidian could not compare with this idealization. In fact, an Ellen risen from the tomb, coming radiant from the land of the blessed, could not have measured up to this rapturous reincarnation.

Seven years into his second marriage, Emerson published in *The Dial* (which he himself edited) some of the love poems exchanged between Ellen and himself. Later, in his first volume of published verse, other love poems to Ellen would appear. None to Lidian was published because he wrote none. Now he rejoiced in those "bright revelations" made to him of woman's "best nature." Lidian, evidently, was singularly lacking in such revelations since the one source he credited was "The angel who walked with me in younger days."[33]

Had Ellen's legacy subsidized Emerson's postministerial career, consciousness of his debt to her might have required the reparation of expressions of loyalty constantly reiterated. In fact, it did no more than cushion him from the extremes of poverty. To provide for his family, he had to exert himself and to learn to stretch his means to cover essentials. Lidian, therefore, did not have to live with the specter of an Ellen who put the food on her table and the clothes on her back. At the outset of their marriage, in fact, Emerson surprised her with the news that they would have to live frugally. The death of her own father and the theft of a portion of her inheritance had forced on her a diminished life-style which she little relished. She supposed marriage would restore her to her former bountiful estate. To find herself under the necessity of making patchwork of bits of carpet to keep her floors covered, and instructing seamstresses to refashion the remnants of her once fine wardrobe into garments for her children, was not what Lidian had anticipated. She met the challenge, but it took its toll. The modest prosperity that devolved to them from Ellen's legacy cannot have weighed much in her thoughts as she coped, day to day, to keep up for her family the semblance of comfort.

In 1848, when Emerson was in England, he wrote two letters to Lidian in response to letters from her in which she sought to draw from him a firm declaration of affection. Her letters are not extant but his replies make explicit their context. He wrote first:

> Ah, you still ask me for that unwritten letter always due, it seems, always unwritten, from year to year, by me to you, dear Lidian. . . . It must content you for the time, that I truly acknowledge a poverty of nature, & have really no proud defence at all to set up, but ill-health, puniness, and Stygian limitations. . . . Besides am I not, O best Lidian, a most foolish affectionate goodman & papa, . . . when I am once in Concord? . . . Well I will come again shortly and behave the best I can   Only I foresee plainly that the trick of solitariness never never can leave me.[34]

This letter cannot have satisfied Lidian. Here we see Emerson falling back on his old bachelor pose of pleading an insufficiency of warmth in his nature but this time offering in lieu of it the consolation that he is a dutiful householder and doting father. That was not what Lidian wanted to hear.

In Emerson's absence, Lidian, perhaps hoping to find the elusive key to his heart, had been reading Ellen's letters to him. He had never kept these out of her reach and can only have been gratified that she took pleasure in them. Like his grandmother Phebe Ripley, he made no secret of the pleasure he himself took in rereading the letters of a departed spouse. Apparently Lidian alleged unstinting admiration for them. As a stratagem, if that is what it was, this worked no better than had naming a daughter Ellen. Emerson naively assured her that the letters "deserved all you have said. For they came out of a heart which nature & destiny conspired to keep as inviolate." He should have stopped there but did not. "I am deeply gratified by your pleasure & sympathy in them," he went on. ". . . But you should have seen Ellen. When she left this world, I valued everybody who had seen her, and disliked to meet those who had not."[35] This much ground he now yielded — despite the fault of her not having known Ellen, Lidian was given leave to join the chorus of her admirers. Evidently to merit entitlement to this status, Lidian presently recalled that she once attended a riding school in which Ellen was enrolled so that, therefore, she *had* seen her! That Emerson was as deficient in affection as he thought he was admits of some doubt but that he was tactless in consigning it admits of none. Henry Pommer states the problem exactly: "It is not that Emerson failed to love Lidian, but that he never stopped loving Ellen more."[36] Some women would have been content to settle for that. Lidian was a curious woman and, in time, would grow more curious, but she was never so strange as not to mind being second in her husband's preference.

Even as Emerson sought to define his relationship with Lidian, he weighed his capacity to relate to his fellowman and concluded he had been holding himself in reserve for some superior relationship that had not yet offered. On 6 May 1837 he wrote:

Sad is this continual postponement of life. I refuse sympathy & intimacy with people as if in view of some better sympathy & intimacy to come. But whence & when? . . . Scarcely can I say that I see any new men or women approaching me; I am too old to regard fashion; too old to expect patronage of any greater or more powerful. Let me suck the sweetness of those affections & consuetudes that grow near me, — that the Divine Providence offers me. . . . I was made a hermit & am content with my lot.[37]

That same year Emerson speculated:

> I approach some Carlyle, with desire & joy . . . with an expectation of some total embrace & oneness with a noble mind & learn at last that it is only so feeble & remote & hiant action as reading a Mirabeau or a Diderot paper. . . . More we shall not be to each other. Baulked soul! . . . Every man is an infinitely repellent orb, & holds his individual being on that condition.[38]

Bronson Alcott, worshipful of Emerson though he was, sensed that Emerson held him off. He commented: "One subtraction from the pleasure the reading of his books — shall I say his conversation? gives me, his pains to be impersonal or discrete."[39] He knew something was amiss in their relations.

On 11 June 1839, after recopying "Love," a lecture delivered the foregoing December, Emerson wrote:

> I see well its inadequateness. I am cold because I am hot, — cold at the surface only as a sort of guard & compensation for the fluid tenderness of the core, — have much more experience than I have written there, more than I will, more than I can write. In silence we must wrap much of our life, because it is too fine for speech, because also we cannot explain it to others, and because somewhat we cannot yet understand. . . . A better & holier society will mend this selfish cowardice and we shall have brave ties of affection not petrified by law . . . brave as I have said because innocent and religiously abstinent from the connubial endearments, being a higher league on a purely spiritual basis.[40]

In "Love" Emerson sought to deal with the charge brought against him that his was a nature without warmth. "The delicious fancies of youth," he said, "reject the least savor of a mature philosophy, as chilling with age and pedantry their purple bloom. And therefore I know I incur the imputation of unnecessary hardness and stoicism from those who compose the Court and Parliament of Love." He continued:

> I have been told that in some public discourses of mine my reverence for the intellect has made me unjustly cold to the personal relations. But now I almost shrink at the remembrance of such disparaging words. . . . The coldest philosopher cannot recount the debt of the young soul wandering here in nature to the power of love, without being tempted to unsay, as treasonable to nature, aught derogatory to the social instincts.[41]

Thus acknowledging the climate in which he was writing, Emerson undertook to show that sexual love, as the first phase of love, is meant to be sublimated in a love of virtue that overwhelms the physical. This would be the theme also of his long poem "Initial, Daemonic and Celestial Love," first published in 1846. John Jay Chapman, who saw this argument as repackaged Puritanism, on that account declared: "If an inhabitant of another planet should visit earth, he would receive, on the whole, a truer notion of human life by attending an Italian opera than he would by reading Emerson's volumes. He would learn from the Italian opera that there were two sexes."[42]

Although his friendship with Margaret Fuller, who openly campaigned to dispel his coldness, was already well advanced by 1839, in that year Emerson would still mount in his journal, in abstract terms, a defense of his aloofness:

> Some people are born public souls, and live with all their doors open to the street. Close beside them we find in contrast the lonely man, with all his doors shut, reticent, thoughtful, shrinking from crowds, afraid to take hold of hands . . . and, though loving his race, discovering at last that he has no proper sympathy with persons, but only with genius and aims. He is solitary because he has society in his thought, and, when people come in, they drive away his society and isolate him. We would all be public men, if we could afford it; I am wholly private; such is the poverty of my constitution.[43]

On 14 November 1839 Emerson noted that Margaret Fuller, alluding to his next lecture series, set for December, had written to say that "she waits for the Lectures seeing well after much intercourse that the best of me is there." He conceded her point and noted as well that another's remark repeated to him "that I 'always seemed to be on stilts' " was apt. He then went on severely:

> Most of the persons whom I see in my own house I see across a gulf. I cannot go to them nor they come to me. Nothing can exceed the frigidity & labor of my speech with such. You might turn a yoke of oxen between every pair of words; and the behavior is as awkward & proud. I see the ludicrousness of the plight as well as they. But having never found any remedy I am very patient with this folly or shame, . . . in the belief that this privation has certain rich compensations inasmuch as it makes my solitude dearer & the impersonal God is shed abroad in my heart more richly & more lowly welcome for this porcupine impossibility of contact with men.[44]

Even as Emerson observed the paces of an intricate gavotte with Margaret, he continued to ponder the impact of what he judged to be his austere nature on others. To Lidian he wrote from Nantasket on 8 July 1841: "Dear love to Mother & to the children two — even the icy become affectionate at a distance from home, and I who am, as you know, all wax, begin to melt at thirty miles."[45] Still seeking a philosophical basis for the position he occupied, he ended his essay "Compensation," written that same year, thus:

> The death of a dear friend, wife, brother, lover, which seemed
> nothing but privation, somewhat later assumes the aspect of a
> guide or genius; for it commonly operates revolutions in our way
> of life, terminates an epoch of infancy or of youth which was
> waiting to be closed, breaks up a wonted occupation, or a house-
> hold, or style of living, and allows the formation of new ones more
> friendly to the growth of character.[46]

Margaret Fuller, then, was but one of Emerson's stepping-stones to higher union.

Lidian, as well as Margaret, must have found this idealism trying, and more so since she was most intimately affected by it and understood it less. Emerson implies as much when he says:

> I would have them [my friends] where I can get them, but I
> seldom use them. . . . Though I prize my friends I cannot afford
> to talk with them and study their visions lest I lose my own. It
> would indeed give a certain household joy to quit this lofty
> seeking . . . & come down into warm sympathies with you but then
> I know well I shall mourn always the vanishing of my Mighty
> Gods.[47]

By 1844 Emerson had placed himself at a grander remove from others, having ascended a few rungs higher toward a state of spiritual self-sufficiency:

> There are moods in which we court suffering, in the hope that
> here at least we shall find reality, sharp peaks and edges of truth.
> But it turns out to be scene-painting and counterfeit. The only
> thing grief has taught me is to know how shallow it is. That, like
> all the rest, plays about the surface, and never introduces me into
> the reality, for contact with which we would even pay the costly
> price of sons and lovers. . . . An innavigable sea washes with
> silent waves between us and the things we aim at and converse
> with. Grief too will make us idealists. In the death of my son, now

more than two years ago, I seem to have lost a beautiful estate, —
no more. I cannot get it nearer to me.[48]

In June 1845 Emerson wrote: ''Even for those whom I really love
I have not animal spirits.''[49] What once he would have meant as a
lament now was becoming a boast.

Writing to Gisela von Arnim, daughter of Goethe's Bettina, on 10
July 1859, he sought, without success, to recruit a correspondent who
might aspire to generate the affections of genius. He told her: ''If you
will write such another letter as you have written, perhaps all my ice
will go, and I shall suddenly grow genial and affable.''[50] The years
were working a change in him. No letter Margaret Fuller wrote to him
had been able to elicit such a response. Neither Margaret nor any of
his Brahmin contemporaries ever expected that ice to break. Thus
Holmes would write of him, after his death: ''What man was he who
would lay his hand familiarly upon his shoulder and call him Waldo?''[51]

Every day, every act betrays the ill-concealed deity.

15. Theological Doubts

*L*ATE in May 1832 Emerson gathered some of the prominent members of the Second Church at his house on Chardon Street so that he might expound to them some new thoughts he had about the Lord's Supper. To those assembled he explained that scruples about this ordinance lately had begun to trouble him. He found it unreasonable to believe that Jesus meant it to be kept for all time. If required of him, he granted, he could tolerate it as a commemorative act, but he wished to forgo the actual use of bread and wine at the reenactments and to drop the claim that Jesus had enjoined the rite on all Christians for good and always.

Emerson's disclosures must have come to his parishioners as a painful surprise. Hitherto he had seemed well disposed to the observance. In March 1829, preaching on the Christian minister, he had deplored the common view that it was "a melancholy memorial." In a later sermon, "A Feast of Remembrance," he remarked that in the primitive church, "All who named the Lord's name partook of his supper." From that fact he could then educe but one conclusion — "And so should all now."[1]

A committee was formed by his parishioners to consider how to deal with Emerson's desire. On Saturday, 2 June, looking back on the reaction his views had stirred, Emerson saw concluding "a week of moral excitement." But there was more to his protest than the committee could possibly imagine. Privately he was calling into question not merely the Lord's Supper but the ministry he belonged to and the faith that it served. "I have sometimes thought," he wrote in that same journal entry, "that in order to be a good minister, it was necessary to leave the ministry. The profession is antiquated. In an altered age, we worship in the dead forms of our forefathers. Were not a Socratic paganism better than an effete, superannuated Christianity?"[2]

Emerson's strictures on his calling were not something he had rushed to adopt once he had taken his first bold step. The basic argument had already taken shape in his mind the previous January. On the tenth he observed:

> It is the best part of the man, I sometimes think, that revolts most against his being a minister. . . . How much power he sacrifices by conforming himself to say & do in other folks' time instead of in his own! The difficulty is that we do not make a world of our own, but fall into institutions already made . . . and this accommodation is . . . a loss of so much integrity and . . . of so much power.[3]

Yet, he could not sever his bonds then. For men to turn their backs on "approved forms and accepted institutions," to follow their own fancies, could lead only to anarchy. Evidently, between January and June something remarkable had happened to cause Emerson to make the chaos-provoking move. We can have no certitude about what did jog his mind during that period, but two events of which we are aware at least seem capable of altering his direction, especially if they are seen as reinforcing one another. In March 1832 he had opened Ellen's coffin and gazed on the corruption which a year in the grave had visited on her. The following month news came that on 22 March Goethe had died. Emerson was sufficiently smitten that he thrice alluded to the fact in his journal, the third time asserting that though an irreplaceable man like Goethe had died and he himself was in failing health, truth remained inviolate.[4] From Goethe, William Emerson had received the charge to stay in the ministry. But William had rejected that charge while Waldo, like a relay runner, had continued on in his place. The realization that human existence is fleeting but truth survives may have released him now from the bewitchment that had held him on the narrow path of duty. He must no longer accommodate the wishes of the dead but move in the direction in which truth beckoned him.

Emerson was not the first of his family to weigh seriously the issue of the Lord's Supper. That distinction belonged to the Reverend Joshua Moody, his great-great-granduncle. Joshua, who graduated from Harvard in 1653, organized the First Church in Portsmouth, New Hampshire. In 1683 he was put on trial and sentenced to prison for refusing to heed the orders of the Anglican governor, Cranfield, to administer

the Lord's Supper in accordance with the form decreed in the Book
of Common Prayer. He sought haven in Boston, where he was elected
president of Harvard in 1684, but declined to serve. (It was in his
place that Increase Mather was elevated to that office.) Joshua accepted instead the pastorate of Boston's First Church, future parish
of his great-grandnephew, William Emerson. When he died, in 1697,
he was once again pastor at Portsmouth, the Glorious Revolution having routed his high-church foes. Waldo knew that Joshua had made
himself a figure of controversy over the issue of the Lord's Supper;
the facts were given in William Emerson's history of the First Church.[5]
In his own time, William Emerson himself was uneasy about this rite
and had nebulous thoughts about liberalizing it. And just two years
into the past, in September 1830, young William had scandalized Ezra
Ripley by contending that the rite was not obligatory.

Moncure Conway thought it possible that Emerson had actively considered the subject as early as 1827, when his Quaker friend Mary
Rotch of New Bedford had protested the rite by exiting beforehand.[6]
That seems doubtful. As late as the summer of 1829 he spoke of a
Christian minister as one who got "strength of virtue & light & love,"
as one chosen "to come bearing in his hand the immortal Word . . .
to commemorate the breaking of the body that was broken for us &
the blood of the great sacrifice."[7] His authorized biographer, James
Elliot Cabot, surmises that his real quarrel was not with this specific
observance but with "the authority on which all doctrines and observances rest."[8] Rusk concurs, supposing that Emerson chose the Lord's
Supper because it was a long-standing subject of disputation and, as
a public ceremony rather than an abstract idea, a concrete issue that
his parishioners could readily grasp.[9]

Emerson may have recalled that Jonathan Edwards crossed his spiritual Rubicon when he made the Lord's Supper an issue at his Northampton parish in 1750. Edwards, far from questioning its obligatory
standing, had insisted that it be administered only to those "who could
give evidence of a true conversion." Paradoxically, then, while their
positions on this issue were antipodal, both were dissatisfied with the
perfunctory, rote way in which the sacrament had come to be administered in later times.

A committee of seven weighed Emerson's disclosure that "he could
no longer administer the Lord's Supper as a divinely appointed, sacred ordinance . . . that he could henceforth conduct the service only
as a memorial service, without attributing to it any deeper significance."[10] None of the committee members was ill disposed toward him;
three of them, George A. Sampson, Dr. John Ware, and George Barrel
Emerson, his cousin, were close friends. Nonetheless, they declined to
sanction the change Emerson wanted and, as spring passed into sum-

mer, the parish voted to back their judgment. They hoped Emerson could accept that fact because they were not anxious to see him depart.[11]

In view of Emerson's state of mind, the parish, in terms of its needs, had acted wisely. This was but the first of many steps Emerson would take to free himself from conforming usage and, ultimately, from formal adherence to Christianity itself. Two years later, when a Unitarian parish in New Bedford offered to accommodate itself to Emerson's wishes on the Lord's Supper issue, he declined because he wanted now to dispense as well with public prayer.[12] Had this point been granted, another would have risen to succeed it.

Two choices confronted Emerson. He could conform or he could resign. While his next step seemed clear, he had more than his conscience to satisfy. If he resigned his office, his resignation from the ministry should logically follow. Fortunately a period of reprieve intervened that enabled him to review his position without haste. Repairs had to be made on the Second Church and it closed its doors for six weeks.

On 22 June, the day after the parish announced the results of its deliberations, Emerson set out for Waterford, Maine, in the company of his brother Charles. Aunt Mary was there and he wanted to extend to her the courtesy of reviewing his situation with her. That he thought she might be able to convince him to alter his opinion is unlikely, because he had already begun to gather the materials he needed to make a formal statement of his position, something which, remarkably, he could not have done when he confronted the parish with his scruples. On 11 June he borrowed from the Boston Athenaeum Thomas Clarkson's *Portraiture of Quakerism*, from which he took the arguments that make up two-thirds of the sermon on the Lord's Supper he would deliver to his parish the following September as his last message to them. Among Emerson's works this sermon is recognized as outstanding for its "consecutive logical reasoning" and concise phrasing. Actual credit must go to Clarkson, whose arguments Emerson skillfully condensed. While he changed the sequence of some minor details and dispensed with Clarkson's frequent repetitions, that was about as much as he could manage since anxiety over the decision he was facing brought on a siege of dysentery that would, over the ensuing months, reduce him to a state of near-invalidism.[13] To supplement Clarkson, Emerson also brought with him on his journey north William Sewal's *History of the Quakers* and Henry Tuke's *Memoirs of the Life of Fox*. Without question his apostasy was being carried out under Quaker auspices. That Quakers shunned binding beliefs appealed to him. Perhaps that is why he later told his cousin David Greene Haskins, an Episcopal clergyman, "I am more of a Quaker than anything else."[14]

At the start of his sermon, Emerson offered a broad hint about his sources, saying, "It is now near two hundred years since the Society of Quakers denied the authority of the rite altogether, and gave good reasons for disusing it."[15] No one followed up the hint. Even when Octavius B. Frothingham published the entire sermon in *Transcendentalism in New England* in 1876 — making it for many years the only Emerson sermon to be in print — no inquiry into Emerson's Quaker sources was undertaken.[16]

Aunt Mary stood no real chance of persuading Emerson to remain in his pastorate, but he gave her a week to pummel him with arguments and appeals before he retreated, with Charles, to Conway, New Hampshire. Aunt Mary actually seems to have won more ground from Charles than Waldo. In May, Charles, assessing Emerson's state, concluded, "He suffers like most ministers from being too much sheltered & treading too uniform a track — there is danger of growing exclusive & fastidious & losing some faculties of action."[17] On 6 July, however, he wrote William from Conway, "I hope his own mind will be brought to the persuasion that it is his duty to stay where he is & preach & pray as he has done & administer the ordinance as nearly as he conscientiously can, in accordance with the faith & wishes of his pious parishioners."[18] Doubtless still nurturing this hope, Charles went on to Boston, leaving Waldo at Conway, settled in as a boarder with a private family where he could think and work without distraction. By the fourteenth he had moved on, putting up at the Ethan Allen Crawford House at Crawford Notch. "How hard to command the soul, or to solicit the soul," he wrote in his journal that day. And he reflected further: "The good of going into the mountains is that life is reconsidered."[19] The next day he recorded a long and earnest reassessment of his position that found him at times skirting capitulation but, at length, holding firm:

> The hour of decision. . . . Do not destroy what is good and
> useful in a high degree rather than comply with what is hurtful in
> a small degree. The Communicant celebrates on a foundation
> either of authority or of tradition an ordinance which has been the
> occasion to thousands . . . of contrition, of gratitude, of prayer,
> of faith, of love & of holy living. . . . God forbid it be in my
> heart — to interrupt any occasion thus blessed of God's influences
> upon the human mind. I will not, because we may not all think
> alike of the means, fight so strenuously against the means, as
> to miss of the end which we all value alike. . . . But this ordinance
> is esteemed the most sacred of religious institutions, & I cannot go
> habitually to an institution which they esteem holiest with indifference & dislike.[20]

Emerson may have chosen the Lord's Supper ordinance as his test issue because it was a recognized topic of controversy and lent itself to arguments readily grasped. And he may have gone to the White Mountains resolved to draw up a statement that allowed for no turning back. But he was too just a man to follow a predetermined course while blocking his ears to the appeals of others. When he made his final decision, he was convinced he was leaving his parish so that he could live with his conscience and not because he had contrived an excuse to separate himself from a calling for which his enthusiasm had waned. Nor should we be beguiled by Conway's efforts to make a fanciful linkage between Emerson's action and the calling of his earliest American Emerson forebear, Thomas Emerson of Ipswich: "Thus the descendant of Thomas Emerson, baker, did not seek to feed the hunger of his villagers with tidings of heavenly bread harvested in ancient times and far lands. . . . He lived and labored as in the living garden of a living God, and gave of its fruits to all whom he met."[21]

His resolve once taken, Emerson was ready to push himself toward new goals. Impelled by nervous energy, he climbed Mount Washington, attaining the summit in four hours and fifteen minutes, though inexperienced climbers, such as he was, customarily took six. Dispirited and anxious for his health, he broke off his holiday and returned to Boston.

When, at the start of August, the Second Church reopened, Emerson was physically unready to confront his congregation even to conduct regular services, much less set before the faithful a final, ringing affirmation of his beliefs. Other ministers covered for him until his ailment abated and strength returned. Finally his sermon on the Lord's Supper was announced for 9 September and he delivered it to a thronged church. While Mary C. Turpie and Frederick B. Tolles point out that Emerson took courage from the parallel he found between his ordeal and that which George Fox, the founder of Quakerism, endured, and Emerson's own journal upholds this supposition, beyond question Clarkson provided the logic of his stand. To placate the deacons and the diehards, he even reviewed Clarkson's formal exegesis — he knew they would be satisfied with nothing less. A Quaker would have realized where his arguments came from, but no Quakers were in his congregation, not even a Hicksite, though in New Bedford they had been taken into the congregation of his Unitarian kinsman Orville Dewey. To allow his listeners to believe the position he outlined was based on his own original research was not without advantages. Possibly it could win them over. Emerson's misgivings at making the break his position seemed to require were so substantial that he could not resist giving himself that much of a purchase. Thus "The Lord's Supper," the most important sermon Emerson ever gave — the sermon that altered the direction of his life — was also the most derivative. Yet the conclusion was distinctly his own and all the more striking because it departed radically from the dispassionate tone Clarkson's material prescribed. He came back strongly to the resolution recorded in his journal nearly two months earlier. "It is my desire, in the office of a Christian minister, to do nothing which I cannot do with my whole heart." Where then did that leave him? He explained that he had no wish to undermine the beliefs of others and had made this presentation of his views solely because the circumstances of his office required it. "That is the end of my opposition," he said, "that I am not interested in it. I am content that it stand to the end of the world, if it please men and please Heaven, and I shall rejoice in all the good it produces."[22]

To these words some of Emerson's auditors must have reacted as Barrett Wendell later would: "It is doubtful whether the whole literature of heresy contains two phrases which to any mind still affected by traditional Christian faith must seem more saturated with serene insolence." Others, maybe the majority, would have accepted O. W. Firkins's verdict when he designated them "Words of unequalled loftiness and benignity, but their withdrawnness, their sequestration, is unequivocal." Few could have let them slip past unremarked.[23]

Matters, Emerson knew, could not rest there. Since the parish wished the Lord's Supper to be administered in accordance with past practice, his duty was clear. "I am about to resign into your hands," he told them, "that office which you have confided to me." He made one further point, however, often misunderstood by posterity. He was resigning his pastorate merely, not his ministry. Quite otherwise, he insisted: "I am consoled by the hope that no time and no change can deprive me of the satisfaction of pursuing and exercising its highest functions."[24] Thus Emerson's periodic appearances in the pulpit throughout the remaining years of the decade, and occasional officiating at weddings, as, for example, that of Sam Staples in 1839, cannot be regarded, as they sometimes are, as evidence that Emerson was beset by wavering moods.

The most durable part of Emerson's sermon, in terms of his own beliefs as subsequently he enunciated them and lived by them, was his statement of his understanding of what it meant to be a Christian. Here he defines Christianity in terms liberal enough to accommodate his own faith as it presently unfolded:

> If I understand the distinction of Christianity, the reason why it is to be preferred over all other systems and is divine is this, that it is a moral system; that it presents men with truths which are their own reason, and enjoins practices that are their own justification. . . . I am not engaged to Christianity by decent forms, or saving ordinances. . . . What I revere and obey in it is

its reality, its boundless charity, its deep interior life, the rest it
gives to the mind, the echo it returns to my thoughts, the perfect
accord it makes with my reason through all its representation of
God and His Providence; and the persuasion and courage that
come out thence to lead me upward and onward. Freedom is the
essence of this faith. It has for its object simply to make men good
and wise.[25]

Charles Feidelson contends: "The theme of the sermon on the Lord's
Supper is the fossilization to which every form is subject when it de-
generates from a creative force into a static sign."[26] Certainly Emerson had rallied to the side of self-reliant individualism.

The tone of Emerson's sermon was, in its mildness, a reminder to
his parishioners that the dilemma he offered them could not be lightly
resolved. Under ordinary circumstances a parish whose minister declined to bless and distribute the bread and wine once a month would
not have debated his resignation; they would have insisted on it. But
Emerson was popular with the members of his flock and the choice he
offered them threw them into dismay. One episode brought home to
him, as nothing else did, the distress he had occasioned. A lady in his
parish was accustomed to seek him out during the week to discuss with
him the previous Sunday's sermon. When she did not come to him
after he preached on the Lord's Supper, he took the initiative and
asked her what she thought of it. In response, she shook her head
mournfully and intoned the words of the Magdalen: "Ye have taken
away my Lord, and I know not where ye have laid Him." Had Emerson been glib he might have seen this as an opportunity to remind the
woman that Mary Magdalene soon learned her sorrow was misplaced
and her apparent loss was mankind's gain, but to him such a retort
would have seemed casuistry. Quite otherwise, he fell in with her mood,
and, recalling the incident in after years, said, "That was one of the
most touching comments on my decision."[27]

The parish came to no quick determination on the matter. Indeed,
in the opinion of Charles, who wrote on 18 September to tell William
how things stood, two-thirds of the congregation were behind Emerson. But the matter was not to be decided along democratic lines. The
decision rested with a committee made up of the true proprietors of
the parish, the men who funded it. These men liked Emerson personally, but theologically they were not precocious.

Toward the end of the month, Emerson, still seeking an effective
panacea for his dysentery, slipped away with his mother for a few
days' rest to Hopkinton, Massachusetts, in the next century a town
that would come to international fame as the starting point of the
Boston Marathon. While for Emerson, who saw himself nearing the

finish line, that fact would have seemed ironic, without his full realization the period of waiting he had entered into was much more a time of beginnings than endings. With his departure from the Second Church unsuspected vistas of opportunity would open up to him.

The night before the final decision was made Emerson passed some time with a fellow clergyman. His situation was not their topic. Only when he arose to leave did he allude to it, saying then, "This is probably the last time we shall meet as brethren in the same calling."[28] He realized, then, that with this break his vocation was doomed.

On 21 October, with matters still pending, Emerson preached again at the Second Church, his topic "The Genuine Man," his theme the man who puts under scrutiny each opinion and practice society tolerates and, not bowing to outside pressure, decides for himself whether or not he will abide by it. To the deliberating committee this was a clear signal that Emerson was not in a compromising mood. When time came for the final vote, some of those eligible to vote stayed home, able neither to support Emerson nor to condemn him. The vote was close, thirty-four to twenty-five. Emerson's resignation was accepted. By a margin of ten votes, with fifty people voting, it was decided that he should be paid through the end of the calendar year. It was then 28 October.

Still racked by dysentery, Emerson looked poorly enough at the end of this ordeal for his deliberations on what to do next with his life to seem almost irrelevant. His immediate task, it seemed, was to preserve his life. To this end, Dr. John Ware, one of his supporters through the parish deliberations, urged a sea voyage. Emerson fell in with the suggestion and chose Italy as his destination. To facilitate that move the Second Church paid him his salary in full on 21 December, four days before he was to sail on a fruit packet belonging to one of his parishioners. The day following he sent to the parish a farewell letter, elegantly printed on white silk.[29] Still mourning their strayed shepherd, the parish had three hundred copies printed so that each parishioner could have a remembrance of the man so many esteemed.

Not everyone took the news of Emerson's resignation as amiably as those who took his welfare and farewell to heart. Cabot speaks of "loud whispers of mental derangement." John Jay Chapman says that his grandmother, Maria Weston Chapman, first became aware of Emerson when a neighbor said, "Oh, have you heard? The new minister of the Second Church has gone mad." Even Ezra Ripley thought his behavior best explained in such terms. By contrast, the opinion of Bishop Huntington, as reported many years later by Moncure Conway, oozes with Christian kindness: "To a degree Mr. Emerson's aberrations in religious thought were due to his ineptitude for thinking consecutively and logically on any abstract subject."[30]

After Emerson was on his way to Europe, Aunt Mary, in her own distinctive fashion, reviewed the subject in a letter to Charles:

> It is far sader than the translation of a soul by death of the body to lose Waldo as I have lost him. . . . You talk of his being a '*reformer*'. . . . A reformer! and beginn at the wrong end? annuling a simple rite w'h has bound the followers of Jesus together for ages & announced his resurrection! A reformer — who on earth with his genius is less able to cope with opposition? Who with his good sense less *force* of mind — and while it invents new universes is lost in the surrounding halo? . . . No, he never loved his holy offices — and it is well he has left them.[31]

Here lingers an echo of the arguments she had used in a futile effort to turn Emerson from his purpose. More than that, here is a wealth of speculation on Emerson provided by someone who had had him under the closest scrutiny during much of his lifetime. No one would have profited more than Emerson himself from these observations. Most intriguing of all was Aunt Mary's vision of Waldo lost in the surrounding halo of a universe called into existence by his imagination. Clearly, she was on to something.

Rusk says that Emerson "later remembered with disgust" his Lord's Supper sermon;[32] he thought that overmuch was made of it. In 1843, while visiting Philadelphia, he was introduced to the antislavery campaigner Lucretia Mott, and was disgruntled to learn "that her interest in me respected my rejection of an ordinance sometime somewhere." "I was challenged," he reported, "on the subject of the Lord's Supper, and with great slowness & pain was forced to recollect the grounds of my dissent in that particular. You may be sure I was very tardy with my texts." Even had he compounded his own arguments, he could hardly be faulted for not recalling the particulars a decade later. But recollecting these grounds may have been painful to him for another reason. When his friend Cyrus Bartol weighed leaving the ministry, Emerson discouraged him, recalling for Bartol's benefit "his own pain in the rupture of the pastoral tie."[33]

Years after the event Bartol inquired about the sermon, and Emerson made him a gift of the original manuscript, accompanying it with a few remarks:

> I have explored the old nooks, & am resolved to smother you with a share of the same dust which I encountered: so I send you the *ipsissima verba* to which you refer, — all yellow, — and infirm as old, I dare say, without daring to look. If you have courage, you can read the sermon; but, I doubt, a page of it will suffice. As you

hint, it was a sad matter to me, who have quite too much sympathy to be a right reformer.[34]

Nothing else Emerson wrote was repudiated by him with even a hint of the vehemence he shows here. That fact must ever intrigue us.

> Each philosopher, each bard, each actor has only
> done for me, as by a delegate, what one day I can do
> for myself.

16. Samuel Taylor Coleridge

*A*LTHOUGH Emerson's health sent him to Europe on Christmas Day, 1832, aboard the brig *Jasper,* when he got there he needed a reason acceptable to his Puritan conscience to justify his peregrinations. Perhaps that was when he decided he had come in search of a guiding light.

During the ensuing seven months before he crossed the Channel to England, Emerson saw much that gave him pause. In Sicily, beset by mercurial moods, he one day felt drawn to retire among the Capuchins, on another to pass the remainder of his life as a fisherman casting his nets into the sea. Arriving on the Italian peninsula, he peered through sulfurous vapors into Mount Vesuvius, inspected the excavations at Pompeii, crossed the treacherous Pontine marshes at night, and, in Rome, put up in the Piazza di Spagna, where, just a dozen years before, Keats had died. At the Vatican he followed the Holy Week services, mingled in a throng that contained another ruminative cleric, John Henry Newman, and knelt to receive with reverence the pope's Easter blessing. Curiously at odds with a Calvinistic heritage that abjured the sensate, he quit St. Peter's only with reluctance.

In Florence the liberated Emerson sighed over the beauty of the Medici Venus, and in Venice over the wonder of St. Mark's bathed in the light of a full moon. He saw da Vinci's *Last Supper* in Milan and there made a pilgrimage to the tomb of Saint Charles Borromeo, whom he had come to admire. In Lausanne he went readily to see Gibbon's house but unreadily to see at Ferney the château of Voltaire, whom he despised. In Paris, where he checked into a pension for a month, with cosmopolitan impartiality he toured the morgue, spoke to Lafayette at a Fourth of July fête, heard lectures at the Sorbonne, read in the public reading rooms, and, at the Jardin des Plantes, experienced a minor epiphany when he beheld an organized collection of specimens which suggested to him that there is "an occult relation between the very scorpions and man."[1]

But physical phenomena, the ruins of ancient civilizations, and works of genius were no substitute for the human contact Emerson was seeking. Truly what he was questing was a guru. Having several candidates under consideration, he sought them out, one after another. In Florence, he had visited Walter Savage Landor and found that he did not answer that purpose. In London, in August 1833, he went in pursuit of the next candidate, his search taking him to Highgate Hill, a little beyond London's swirling vortex, a little above its turbulence and spume. The object of his quest was Samuel Taylor Coleridge, who for the past sixteen years had made his home at Number 3, Highgate, with Dr. James Gillman. Emerson did not know this. In fact, he was a complete innocent about this whole visit. He did not know that Coleridge, now nearly sixty-one, had been broken in health for twenty years and would long since have succumbed to opium addiction had not Gillman taken him under his own roof, weaned him from his vice in agreeable surroundings, and, to the limited extent that was possible, effected his rehabilitation. In all his years with Gillman, Coleridge had lived as a shut-in, rarely leaving the house.

Emerson was unaware, also, that Monday was not the proper day to call on Coleridge, that he received callers — ordinarily friends of long-standing — only on Thursdays. Neither did he realize that Coleridge's regimen was such that he did not rise before noon. And he came confidently to call without a letter of introduction, having been assured by someone that eminent men were tolerant of such intrusions. Evidently he did not realize either that Coleridge counted his Unitarian phase as one of the follies of his youth and had reembraced with ardor the Church of England, which had counted among its clergy his father and three brothers and would have supplied him his calling too had not Unitarianism turned him from that purpose. Quite likely Coleridge now ascribed his manifold woes to the theological caprices he had formerly indulged. Finally, Emerson either did not know that Coleridge's visitors were expected to limit their stay to half an hour, so as not to tire the shattered recluse, or, relishing his opportunity, ceased to be mindful of that fact before the half hour had stretched into an hour.

For Emerson the visit was an occasion of constant surprises. He had had to ask around before he found someone who correctly surmised whom he was looking for. Since Coleridge was rarely to be seen, few people in Highgate were aware of his presence among them. At last a porter conjectured that it was the "elderly gentleman with white hair" that Emerson wanted and led him to Gillman's house. This description of Coleridge can only have surprised Emerson because when Coleridge did receive him he was confronted by "a short thick old man with bright blue eyes, black suit & cane," who was "any thing but what I had imagined."[2] The vital substance of Coleridge's writings had prepared Emerson for someone whose manner and spirits were akin to his thought. Thus we must remember that Emerson's account of his visit to Coleridge is inevitably tinctured by Coleridge's failure to measure up to the impossible expectations of a young man who thought he was going to behold a veritable demigod.

Emerson's first try at seeing Coleridge met with a rebuff. He sent up a note asking leave to pay his respects. Coleridge, through a servant, sent down word that he was still in bed but would see the visitor if he called again after noon. Emerson appointed the hour of one for his return. He did well if he used the intervening time to have a cup of tea, because Coleridge offered him none.

Carlyle said that Coleridge, in those later years, treated visitors as if they were empty buckets put before him so that he might pump into them a flood of utterance. This was done without thought as to homogeneity of content, and, indeed, without much consciousness of the discomfiture it inflicted on his visitors. It was more or less automatic, a way for Coleridge to exhibit himself to people who surely had come not to impress him but to be impressed. He allowed no real opportunity for conversation. One listened and, if willing to be rude, interrupted occasionally, though with no hope of altering the direction of his remarks. The alternative was to listen in silence. Conceivably, Coleridge wanted it that way. To enter into an exchange of remarks would be to compel himself to explore new avenues of thought or possibly to enter into disputation. As Emerson afterward summed up the encounter: "The visit was rather a spectacle than a conversation, of no use beyond the satisfaction of my curiosity."[3]

Having determined that his visitor was from Boston, Coleridge first sought to ascertain if Emerson knew Washington Allston. Allston, "the American Titian," had formed an enduring friendship with Coleridge when the two met in Rome in 1804, and Coleridge often received Allston at Highgate as his guest. A South Carolinian by birth, Allston had graduated from Harvard in 1800, and had married, in turn, a Channing and a Dana. Boston was now his home. Emerson had but to own a knowledge of Allston for Coleridge to discourse on his merits at length. This led naturally to the Channings. Coleridge had loathed the first Mrs. Allston but commended her kinsman William Ellery Channing, whom he had met when Channing visited England in 1822. While he liked Channing personally, he deplored his espousal of Unitarianism as "an unspeakable misfortune." Without surcease Coleridge broadened that topic to "burst into a long & indignant declamation upon the folly & ignorance of Unitarianism[,] its high unreasonableness."[4] As he spoke he seized up from a table close by, in a gesture that Emerson was sure he had set the stage for beforehand, a book by Bishop Daniel Waterland, on the flyleaves of which Coleridge had written several pages of notes. Waterland had been a spirited defender of Trinitarianism in the eighteenth century, and this fact provided such justification as Coleridge needed to bring his notes into his current disquisition on the shortcomings of Unitarianism. The exertion this effort had required of him brought Coleridge to a first pause. Here Emerson's Boston-bred sense of fair play asserted itself : "I remarked to him that it would be cowardly in me, after this, not to inform him that I was an Unitarian." To this disclosure Emerson tactfully appended an assurance that he was, nonetheless, "much interested in his explanations."

When a second chance came to speak, Emerson further "insisted that many Unitarians read Mr. Coleridge's books with pleasure & profit who did not subscribe to his theology." But Coleridge was not to be turned from his purpose by any amount of compliments. When Emerson confessed his Unitarian adherence, Coleridge, unwilling to acknowledge that he had committed a faux pas, assimilated the information with the observation, "Yes, I supposed so," and continued to speak in the same vein he had been speaking in.[5] Coleridge found it hard to credit that, after centuries of acceptance, Saint Paul's doctrine of the Trinity should be challenged. It was lamentable that Channing "should embrace such views." Channing, he suspected, "loved Christianity for . . . the good in it & not the true." Then came his summary indictment : "He knew all this about Unitarianism perfectly well because he had once been an Unitarian & knew what quackery it was." He went on to affirm that if Emerson pitted his views against his own, "his would be the hotter side of the fagot."[6]

Perhaps the pause that came now was meant to let Emerson know that his allotted half hour was up. If that was so, then Emerson failed to take the hint. He asked instead if a passage in the third volume of *The Friend* was a verbatim quotation. Coleridge admitted to having "filtered it," explaining that the man who wrote it "was a chaos of truths, but lacked the knowledge that God was a God of Order."[7] With that his theme, Coleridge gravitated to a comparison of Malta and Sicily, which Emerson had, at some point, managed to mention as stops on his current travels. Speaking chauvinistically, Coleridge asserted that "the force of law & mind" prevailed in Malta whereas everything in Sicily, done by the government, was contrary to common sense. With so much stress on law and order, one surmises that Coleridge, had he survived to read Emerson's *Essays,* would have found them unsatisfactory. Emerson cannot have foreseen this difficulty, however, because when he assessed the visit in his journal, he concluded: "Much of the discourse was like so many printed paragraphs in his book, perhaps the same; not to be easily followed."[8] He repeated the phrase, word for word, when he retold the story of his visit in *English Traits* in 1856, finding it as valid then as when he first wrote it.

Emerson must have furnished enough direction to his conversation with Coleridge to have kept his host on the topics of theology and philosophy, as he preferred, because it was only as he arose to depart that Coleridge said to him: "I do not know whether you care about poetry but I will mention some verses I lately made upon my baptismal anniversary." Thereupon, "with great emphasis," he recited "ten or twelve lines that were very interesting," standing as he declaimed them.[9] That Coleridge should have suggested that Emerson's interest might lie elsewhere indicates that the encounter may not have been quite the blank rhetorical exercise for Coleridge that Emerson seemed to think it was. Emerson had no interest at all in Coleridge's poetry. The only one of Coleridge's poems which he knew was "The Rime of the Ancient Mariner," which he deplored as "a modern antique" and advised young poets not to emulate.

As Emerson was leaving, Coleridge took him into an adjacent room to see an Allston painting that a veteran picture-dealer, passing through the same parlor, had taken to be a Titian or Paolo Veronese original. His cravat and neat black attire smudged with snuff, which he had taken with a liberal hand off and on during the visit (maybe that is when his pauses came), Coleridge, in taking leave of Emerson, implored him to call on Allston when he got back to Boston, to convey his regards to him. Emerson may have gone beyond that. One of Allston's celebrated paintings, *Uriel in the Sun,* perhaps first awakened Emerson's interest in that archangel whose identity he, a few years later, usurped.[10]

Considering that Emerson had gone to Highgate Hill unheralded, on the wrong day, rousted Coleridge out of bed, and hustled him into his black suit, while he was still so rheumy he had repeatedly to take snuff to clear his head, and then overstayed his welcome, he truly was not treated badly by Coleridge. For an ailing man of naturally irascible moods, who would go to his grave not many months in the future, Coleridge had received his unknown guest with an amiability that bordered on affection.

A young man who calls on a world-renowned writer and is given an hour of his time, with the writer performing for the full hour, has fared well. Emerson had not gone to Highgate to hear himself talk. Nor could he suppose that he had anything of substance to impart to Coleridge. What questions could he have had to ask, then? Only in *English Traits* does he complain that he found Coleridge "old and preoccupied," unable to "bend to a new companion and think with him."[11] This objection never occurred to him twenty-three years earlier, when he first told of the visit in his journal. Carlyle, at thirty-seven vital, perky, and lonely, could be an instant friend to him. But by what reasonable expectation could Emerson think that Coleridge, at sixty, battered by life, infirm and failing, snug in the world he had withdrawn into, and beyond ambitions and expectations, could slip into a role of comradeship with him? He had reason to congratulate himself that Coleridge had not turned him back at the threshold.

17. Thomas Carlyle
A Window Flung Open to the Azure

*T*HE moors of Dunscore were dense in their heathery bloom, and bees, as always in late August, made the air vibrate through the long, daylight hours as they gathered the thick honey into their hives. At Craigenputtock (in Gaelic "Hill of the Hawk"), from the white-washed moorland farmhouse that Jane, his wife, had inherited from her father, Thomas Carlyle sometimes would walk out over the rude and forsaken hills of Nithsdale to where he might gaze off at Criffel, trussed in the green shackles of summer, or look down into the serene visage of Wordsworth's Lake Country washed clean by the morning mists. Because their means were sparse, five years before, Carlyle and Jane, then less than two years married, had gone to the remote farm to live. There Carlyle had kept busy writing articles and a book, *Sartor Resartus* (now beginning to appear in serialization), reviewing, translating (*Wilhelm Meister*), and deepening his hold on German literature where, he had been told by a friend, a decade past, he would find what he was seeking.

Dumfries, the nearest city, was sixteen miles away. Within seven miles, Carlyle complained, there was no one to speak to. Even the minister of Dunscore kirk shunned them when once he came to realize that the Carlyles were not people of conventional religious faith. But life on the Dunscore moors was not the bleak exile Carlyle would have had others believe it was. Craigenputtock lay across the burn, the dwelling a stone house of two stories, larger than most farmhouses, with good windows set in its thick walls, and a study for the master into which sunlight poured during the day — at night a room soon made cosy with a roaring fire. In a cottage by the yard lived Carlyle's man-of-all-work, his brother Alick, whose presence dispensed Carlyle from the need of performing farm chores. Life here was better than ever it had been for Carlyle, having grown up at Ecclefechan as one of seven children of a stonemason. But he had seen London. He thought he would find his fortune there. And that is where he longed to be. Thus, on 24 August 1833, a flood of melancholy would inundate his journal: "I am left here the solitariest stranded, most helpless creature that I have been for many years. . . . The idea of the universe struggles dark and painful in me, which I must deliver out of me or be wretched."[1]

Before that week was out a visitor, who came and passed a day and a night at Craigenputtock, would say of Carlyle in a letter to a friend: "I am afraid he finds his entire solitude tedious; but I could not help congratulating him upon his treasure in his wife & I hope they will not leave the moors, 'tis so much better for a man of letters to nurse himself in seclusion than to be filed down to the common level by the compliances & imitations of city society."[2] The visitor had passed much of his life in an urban world but now had begun to reject many of its values. Though he urged the Carlyles to stay where they were, his appeal was to no avail. The following spring they removed to London, and there they made their home thenceforth. For his part, the visitor, won over by his own argument, subsequently forsook the city for the country, where he would live till the end of his days. Before he withdrew he wrote his name in Carlyle's journal, at Carlyle's request, in the space immediately following the Scotsman's jeremiad — no adjuration, no hopeful bromide, just the words — Ralph Waldo Emerson.

As early as 1827, Emerson had encountered Carlyle's articles on German literature, appearing anonymously in the *Edinburgh Review*. As late as May 1832 he would commend a piece by Carlyle without knowing the author's identity. "I am cheered and instructed," he told his journal, "by this paper on 'Corn Law Rhymes', in the *Edinburgh*, by my Germanic new-light whoever he may be." In October he learned that this "new-light" was Thomas Carlyle. This man seemed to Emerson his natural affinity, for he spoke of the dawning of an age of "new Spirituality and Belief; in the midst of old Doubt and Denial, as it were, a new revelation of Nature, and the Freedom and Infinitude of Man, wherein Reverence is again rendered compatible with Knowledge, and Art and Religion are one."[3]

When Emerson went to Europe, it was in the back of his mind to see Thomas Carlyle and pay him his respects. In Rome, prospects for that happening emerged when Gustave, the nephew of Baron d'Eichthal, a French peer and member of a prominent Jewish banking family, gave him a letter to John Stuart Mill, in London, asking Mill to arrange for Emerson to meet Carlyle. The baron was a personal friend of Carlyle's.

In Edinburgh Emerson learned that Carlyle had withdrawn to the remote farm in the Nithsdale hills. Emerson pressed on. When at Dumfries he learned that there was no regular conveyance that would take him into the hill country, he recruited a driver with an old rusty gig to carry him the final distance. The day was Sunday, 25 August. In Emerson's native Massachusetts Sunday travel was frowned upon and those who undertook it for no sufficient purpose were sometimes forcibly detained. In Scotland, men, Covenanters and all, were more reasonable. And so Emerson was off, sallying over Buccleuch Bridge, trundled past disciplined red sandstone walls that checkered the lowlands beyond Dumfries, past irregular walls of granite boulders in the climbing Dunscore countryside — past tufts of yellow gorse, hedgerows, stunted elms and hawthorns, spruce clumps, at last to a gap, on the ridge beyond which lay his goal.

Emerson's gig pulled up before the farmhouse on Craigenputtock Hill in the early afternoon, while the Carlyles were at their noonday meal. In London, introducing himself with the d'Eichthal letter, Emerson had asked Mill to advise Carlyle of his coming. Mill had obliged, though in lackluster terms. Carlyle quickly found the visitor much more to his liking than Mill had thought possible.

Carlyle needed homage to lift his spirits. Flattered that Emerson had gone to such trouble to see him, he furloughed the gig till the morrow at the same hour, and told Emerson he must stay the night. He, moreover, was eager for conversation and the worshipful young American, whose knowledge of his writings was at once apparent, offered him the prospect of splendid comradeship, an expectation in which he was not disappointed. Each man later wrote an account of the visit, and these are valuable both for insights they give us into the start of what would develop into a lifelong friendship between two of the most important literary men of the nineteenth century, and for the look they give us into Carlyle's life at Craigenputtock, which otherwise would be undocumented.

To Alexander Ireland, a Scotsman who had befriended him and helped him fix on Carlyle's whereabouts, Emerson wrote, on 30 August, of his visit:

He [Carlyle] is the most simple frank amiable person — I
became acquainted with him at once, we walked over several miles
of hills & talked upon all the great questions that interest us
most. The comfort of meeting a man of genius is that he speaks
sincerely that he feels himself to be so rich that he is above
the meanness of pretending of knowledge which he h[as] not &

Carlyle does not pretend to have solved the great problems
but rather to be an observer of their solution as it goes forward in
the world.

Hereupon Emerson skimmed lightly over some of the other topics that
had made up his conversation with Carlyle, such as religious truth and
eminent men, choosing not to go into detail as he would when he recounted the visit in *English Traits*. At that stage, he looked upon it as
a private revelation to be confined within his own bosom. Emerson told
Ireland, "He talks finely, seems to love the broad Scotch, & I loved
him very much, at once."[5] To his journal Emerson made a freer confidence: "A white day in my years. I found the youth I sought in
Scotland & good & wise & pleasant he seems to me. . . . I never saw
more amiableness than is in his countenance."[4]

On his return to America, importuned by James Freeman Clarke,
then in Louisville, Kentucky, for news of Carlyle, Emerson was even
more chary of details than he had been when writing to Ireland. Carlyle, he said, was cheered to learn that "young men unknown to him"
read his papers in America.[5] Emerson suggested that Clarke go to
Scotland himself and seek out the behemoth at Craigenputtock, telling
him, in effect, "The message I received from the oracle was for my
ears only. If you want to learn what I learned then you must endure
the pangs I endured." Clarke, who ultimately as a professor at the
Harvard Divinity School pioneered the study of comparative religions, cannot have been offended by Emerson's wariness. As editor of
The Western Messenger (1836–1839), he published Emerson's first
printed poems. He remained Emerson's lifelong friend and preached
at his funeral.

When countless letters, written over more than a score of years, had
passed between Carlyle and Emerson, and further personal encounters
had taken place, during Emerson's second visit to England, in 1847–
1848, Emerson at last published his detailed account of his whirlwind
visit to Craigenputtock. The passage of time and their own augmented
reputations inevitably exalted the substance of Emerson's account. The
vehicle that brought Emerson to Craigenputtock, which Carlyle had
described as "an old rusty gig," now became, in Cinderella fashion,
"a private carriage." The isolated farmhouse where Carlyle endured
tedious solitude now became the place "where the lonely scholar nour-
ished his mighty heart." Carlyle had talked that day, said Emerson,
of immortality and "of the subtle links that bind ages together, and
saw how every event affects all the future." As they sat resting on
one of Nithsdale's slopes, Wordsworth's country stretching to the horizon below them, Carlyle, his "cliff-like brow" yet another crag in
this environment, telescoped the centuries into the present moment:

"Christ died on the tree: that built Dunscore kirk yonder; that brought you and me together. Time has only a relative existence."[6]

In *English Traits*, Emerson does not repeat what he told Clarke, that when Carlyle spoke of his plans for forsaking the farm for the city he had sought to dissuade him. Time and again Emerson would seek in vain to persuade Carlyle to come to America to settle in Concord. It never occurred to him that it was not America that Carlyle was afraid of, but Concord. To James T. Fields, however, Carlyle eventually admitted that he thought Concord would be a morbidly dull place to live.[7] Had Emerson made Boston his seat and sought to lure Carlyle there, possibly Carlyle would have come. Yet if, in those circumstances, he had, he would have found a lesser Emerson. To be as he was, Emerson needed the environment Concord offered. Paradoxically, it was not Carlyle that Craigenputtock nurtured, but Emerson. Emerson left there convinced that rural seclusion best served the needs of a man of letters. Thus there was, from the outset, a divergency of viewpoint separating the two men which Emerson, at least, discounted because Carlyle, after all, was then living the way Emerson wanted to live. Yet, in this fact a canny observer might have discerned the opening fissure of the gulf that gradually widened between them, sundering them as thinkers if not as friends. O. W. Firkins says of the Craigenputtock encounter: "They separated before the inevitable dissonance had time to emerge."[8] That is true, and because it is their friendship was free to develop as it did. But, discernible or not, the dissonances that ultimately appeared reverberated back to Craigenputtock. Cabot reminds us that even at the time of this first meeting, despite the things they had in common — careers in the ministry renounced, institutionalized Christianity renounced, their philosophical idealism, their belief that the reformation of society begins with the reformation of the individual — their leading ideas were antipodal: "Had they been required respectively to define by a single trait the farthest reach of folly in a theory of conduct, Carlyle would have selected the notion that mankind need only to be set free and led to think and act for themselves, and Emerson the doctrine that they need only to be well governed."[9] Emerson, though he kept his own counsel while with Carlyle, did disclose to Ireland a few days later that he had not been swept out to sea by the heady atmosphere that prevailed in Carlyle's company. "My own feeling," he said, "was that I had met with men of far less power who had got greater insight into religious truth."[10]

For Emerson, when he wrote *English Traits*, the differences in lifestyle that separated Carlyle and himself were a matter past recall. He capitulated gracefully or so he made it appear: "He was already turning his eyes toward London with a scholar's appreciation. London is the heart of the world, he said, wonderful only from the mass of human beings. He liked the huge machine. Each keeps its own round.''[11] Emerson must have winced as he wrote that. But he knew Carlyle better then than he had known him in August 1833. His later assessment of Carlyle is not truly a part of what he thought and felt while sojourning with him at Craigenputtock or in the days that came immediately after. The Carlyle from whom he took direction was the Carlyle he met then, not the Carlyle he came to know later. And what was true for Emerson was true also for Carlyle. His first impressions of Emerson are something he recurred to again and again through the years, guarding them as a sacred trust that later inklings of disillusionment could not violate.

Early in their correspondence, Emerson, harkening to Carlyle's request that he appraise him of his present activities, grandly replied, ''Account me 'a drop in the ocean seeking another drop,' or God-ward, striving to keep so true a sphericity as to receive the due ray from every point of the concave heaven.''[12] Emily Dickinson, meeting Colonel Higginson's queries, would not define herself in more elusive terms. Emerson was taking no chances. He understood that Carlyle, at Craigenputtock, had shared the ensorcellment he had experienced, and he was not ready to resume mere mortal form in his presence. Some years later, indeed, when Emerson, at Carlyle's insistence, sent him a daguerreotype of himself, Carlyle deplored it as a likeness of a corpse, so strongly had he built up an image of an idealized Emerson.

Twenty-five hours after his arrival at Craigenputtock, his gig returned to bear Emerson back to Dumfries in time to catch the night coach to England. Two days after his departure, Carlyle wrote to his mother to tell her of ''three little happinesses'' that had befallen them. A man had tuned their piano. A sportsman had paid them five pounds for the right to hunt on their land. And, ''Our third happiness was the arrival of a certain young unknown friend, named Emerson, from Boston, in the United States, who turned aside so far from his British, French, and Italian travels to see me here!'' What mother would not be pleased to know that a citizen of the world had beaten a path to her son's door? — especially the visitor Carlyle went on to describe: ''He seemed to be one of the most lovable creatures in himself we had ever looked on. He stayed till next day with us, and talked and heard talk to his heart's content, and left us all really sad to part with him.''[13]

Dutifully Carlyle reported to Mill, on ''Emerson, your Presentee,'' in this cordial estimate: ''A most gentle, recommendable, amiable, wholehearted man. . . . A good 'Socinian' understanding, the clearest heart; above all, what I loved in the man was his health, his unity with himself; all people and all things seemed to find their quite peaceable adjustment with him, . . . a spontaneous-looking, peaceable, even humble one.''[14] For the first time Emerson's worth had been certified by a discriminating judge outside the community that accorded him respect as a hereditary right. Mill, for his part, was surprised, replying to Carlyle, ''I should have thought *he* was about the last person who would have interested you.''[15]

To Richard Milnes, Carlyle wrote of Emerson's visit: ''We kept him one night, and then he left us. I saw him go up the hill; I didn't go with him to see him descend. I preferred to watch him mount and vanish like an angel.'' Jane's recollections appeared to parallel those of her husband. In a postscript to one of his letters to Emerson, she wrote: ''I should never forget the visitor, who years ago in the Desart, descend[ed] on us, out of the clouds as it were, and made one day there look like enchantment for us, and left me weeping that it was only *one* day.''[16] All was not quite as it seemed, however. Writing on 23 November 1833 to Henry Inglis, Jane alluded, with mild disdain, to Emerson's visit saying, among other things, that while they were ''thankful to Providence for the windfall of a stray American,'' she was amused that Emerson had expected to find Carlyle a veritable ogre.[17]

Emerson's visit to Craigenputtock was Carlyle's topic in 1866, the evening after he addressed the University of Edinburgh as its newly installed Lord Rector, a few days before Jane's sudden death. On that occasion he told Moncure Conway: ''I did not then adequately recognize Emerson's genius; but she and I thought him a beautiful transparent soul, and he was always a very pleasant object to us in the distance. Now and then a letter still comes from him, and amid the smoke and mist of the world it is always as a window flung open to the azure.''[18] This passage recalls Carlyle's first letter to Emerson, in which he saluted his ''supernal character . . . so pure and still, with intent so charitable; and then vanishing too so soon into the azure Inane, as an Apparition should!''[19]

From 30 August to 4 September 1833 Emerson waited at Liverpool for autumn tempests to abate so that he could sail for America. During that interval he lodged at the Star and Garter on Paradise Street, where he told his journal, ''Ah me Mr Thomas Carlyle, I would give a gold pound for your wise company this gloomy eve.''[20] It was predictable that he should have cherished the affectionate welcome he received at Craigenputtock. He was disposed to be pleased and even a civil welcome probably would have gratified him. What is striking and gives posterity much to ponder is the impression this complete unknown made on the Carlyles. How often does an admirer find an admirer in the celebrity he has come to pay homage to? In the reception Emerson received from the Carlyles there is a clear prophecy of the effect he would have on his later audiences. In him the Carlyles had found "an angel," "an Apparition," "a beautiful transparent soul," a being "descended out of the clouds," "one of the most lovable creatures in himself we had ever looked on." Who, considering the unanimity of these images, would not, had he been in residence in that moorland farmhouse, have sent away "the old rusty gig" and welcomed this unknown guest? The wonder is that the Carlyles let him leave at all.

> I would rather have a perfect recollection of all I
> have thought and felt in a day or a week of high
> activity than read all the books that have
> been published in a century.

18. William Wordsworth

*W*HEN, from the hill country where he had found Carlyle, Emerson had looked down into England and saw spread before him the region that Wordsworth with his pen had made his own, he had no need to contemplate it as a far-off dream because he meant to visit Wordsworth next. He moved with dispatch, arriving at Ambleside on 27 August, and, on the morning of the next day, went forth from there to Rydal Mount, where Wordsworth, dwelling in rural isolation, had found the inspiration that made him the most acclaimed poet of his time.

As had been his way with Coleridge, Emerson thought an avowal that he had come to pay his respects constituted introduction enough. Nor was he mistaken in his assumption. On his arrival, Wordsworth's daughters promptly summoned their father in from his garden. Wordsworth, just back from Scotland, where he had visited Staffa, had been composing the last of a sequence of four sonnets on Fingal's Cave when the interruption came. With no animosity he made incidental mention of this fact. With no remorse Emerson accepted passively the news that he had checked the creative flow. He was struck, however, by Wordsworth's appearance.

Wordsworth was plain, white-thatched, and, to a young man's eyes, elderly at sixty-three. He had lately had a fall but with no worse results than a broken tooth. In fact, he was sufficiently fit to take Emerson on a tour of his garden and to walk most of a mile with him. The one striking thing about Wordsworth's appearance was a pair of green goggles that he wore. To Emerson they were "disfiguring." Only as an afterthought did Wordsworth explain that they were necessary because his eyes were much inflamed. This, he emphasized, was not a hardship for him as a writer. He could not read at the moment but since it was his custom to compose and carry in his head hundreds of lines of poetry before he wrote them down, he had not had to curtail his writing activities.

As had Coleridge, Wordsworth did much of the talking. Although Emerson did not agree always with his views, in reporting them he gave no sense of having felt browbeaten. "His egotism," he insisted, "was not at all displeasing, obtrusive, as I had heard." Moreover, "Off his own beat, his opinions were of no value."[1] "He made," Emerson decided, "the impression of a narrow and very English mind; of one who paid for his rare elevation by general tameness and conformity."[2] In retrospect, at least, this fact did not surprise Emerson. When he came to his final assessment of the visit, nearly a quarter of a century later, he said: "It is not very rare to find persons loving sympathy and ease, who expiate their departure from the common in one direction, by their conformity to every other."[3] In Emerson's own case, in later years, his blameless personal life was cited by his admirers as evidence of his basic soundness and, therefore, a reason for giving serious consideration to those of his views which marked a "departure from the common." If Emerson thought this argument might be applied with good effect to Wordsworth, he did not say so, possibly because Wordsworth's thinking on many issues proclaimed a conservatism that Emerson at no time in his adult life would have found palatable. Emerson's essential tolerance of the man he found at Rydal Mount ascribes to the conclusion he had come to, by slow and painful degrees, that Wordsworth was the great poet of the age.

Wordsworth's garden was more than a garden, of course, for through it ran the gravel path the poet trod as he drew from the recesses of his brain line upon line of poetry. To be ushered to this hallowed spot by Wordsworth himself was an unmistakable compliment. Now nothing would do but that he must show Emerson what his most recent pacing had yielded. He had spoken of the sonnets he had written on Fingal's Cave. "If you are interested in my verses," he commented, "perhaps you will like to hear these lines," meaning the three sonnets already completed.[4] Emerson had not foreseen this offer, the more remarkable because Wordsworth had said nothing to lead up to it, but the troubadour's tune was all the more precious for being freely bestowed, and Emerson assured Wordsworth he would welcome such a recital.

As Emerson's visit to Coleridge was ending, that poet had declared that he would recite some lines recently composed and then had done just that. This had seemed almost a stage feat, the popular performer gratifying his public with a declamation piece on his last recall. Wordsworth seems to have mustered his energies for his recitation with quaint assurance so that he appeared less a veteran thespian than a stalwart scholar. ''He recollected himself for a few moments,'' said Emerson, ''and then stood forth and repeated, one after the other, the three entire sonnets with great animation.''[5] Thinking back upon this experience when he was writing *English Traits*, Emerson interpolated reflections he had not hinted at in the journal entry contemporary with the event:

> This recitation was so unlooked for and surprising, — he, the old Wordsworth, standing apart, and reciting to me in a garden-walk, like a school-boy declaiming, — that I at first was near to laugh; but recollecting myself, that I had come thus far to see a poet and he was chanting poems to me, I saw that he was right and I was wrong, and gladly gave myself up to hear.[6]

Later critics, dismissing Emerson's self-reproach as merely a pretext resorted to so that he might indulge himself in casting Wordsworth in the ludicrous role of schoolboy, suggest that Emerson is superimposing on the incident an analogy that never entered his thoughts when, as an audience of one, he paused with Wordsworth on his trotting track so that the bard might grant him the privilege of being the first to hear the Staffa sonnets. That is not true. The kernel of the idea appears in the original journal entry, as something of a postscript: ''The poet is always young and this old man took the same attitudes that he probably had at 17 — whilst he recollected the sonnet he would recite.''[7] Emerson was not accustomed to mounting improvisations on his memories. What he was recording here, in reality, was not a poet's presumption but his own abasement. For his analogy he did not need to go beyond his own experience. He may have been thinking of those times when, as a child, he was set to work ''spouting poetry'' at Deacon White's store and at the Latin School.[8] That he found such enforced exhibitionism embarrassing is clear from his allusions, elsewhere, to such performances as gaudy spectacles. Once, when his cousin David Haskins asked him, as they were walking on Boston's crowded State Street, to what Carlyle's affected style might be attributed, Emerson had replied:

> I presume that Mr. Carlyle desires to secure attention. If I had something of great importance to say to the crowd that now jostles us, I am sure I should be at my wits' end to get a hearing. But suppose I should plant a hogshead over there against Scollay's building, and should mount upon it with ribbons of all the bright

colors streaming from my hat, and arms, and button-holes, do you not think I should be sure of an audience?[9]

Emerson, thus attired, declaiming from a hogshead in Scollay Square — now there is a spectacle worthy of the inventiveness of Dickens. Wordsworth, an *Alice in Wonderland* figure, entrenched behind his macabre green goggles, the white hair that betokened his years beckoning in the breezes, may well have seemed to Emerson a caricature of the very lad he himself once had been, or of the schoolboy Wordsworth himself had once been, reciting, with shining morning face, lessons learned by rote for an earnest master.

Coleridge, as poet, critic, philosopher, polemicist, and theologian, came before the world in many guises. Emerson had been indifferent to Coleridge's status as a poet and, on that account, cannot be reproached for making only incidental reference to it. But the footsteps that had taken him to Rydal Mount had taken him on a pilgrimage to a poet. Throughout his visit he had shown a receptiveness and indulgence that Wordsworth's simple and obliging manner do not wholly explain. Near the close of his account of the visit Emerson offered an explanation for his behavior. If Wordsworth's ego had not asserted itself offensively, "To be sure it met no rock. I spoke as I felt with great respect of his genius."[10]

In 1855, on 16 January, Emerson's young friend Franklin Sanborn, then a student at Harvard, called on Longfellow unannounced and, at the end of an hour, stood up to go. Longfellow urged him to stay. To this Sanborn replied, "Young men are apt to receive more pleasure from their visits than they give." That brought a confession from Longfellow. On his first visit to Germany, in 1829, he had longed to go to Weimar to see Goethe but had not gone. "I thought," he said, "I should have nothing to say to him, and so I did not go." Thereafter he had regretted his diffidence. In retrospect, he concluded that it was much better to be daring in such matters. Bearing a letter of introduction to Emerson, Longfellow, accordingly, once sought him out on board a ship they both were traveling on. He found Emerson "sitting inside a coil of rope, with his hat pulled over his eyes." If ever a man seemed unapproachable then, surely, in these circumstances, it was Emerson. Nonetheless, this time Longfellow persevered and Emerson received him cordially. Moreover, he got from him a letter of introduction to Carlyle to make use of on an impending visit to England. Thus was Longfellow launched as a celebrity seeker.[11] Emerson himself attained early mastery of this process. No matter how much of an imposition such visitations were, the intimate record he kept of them tells us he did well to persevere.

Although Wordsworth, at sixty-three, was, unlike Coleridge, fit and industrious (he would see eighty), like Coleridge he had a compulsive need to direct at his visitor an unceasing flow of chatter. He was perched, through the whole of Emerson's visit, on an illusory sugar barrel. Indoctrination does not seem to have been his principal aim, but a sharing of ideas. Too often approached as an oracle, perhaps he wanted to show that his intuitions brought him to reasonable conclusions. By way of contrast he saw society menaced ''by a superficial tuition out of all proportion to its being restrained by moral Culture.'' This he saw as notably the state of affairs in America where he feared money and politics were the chief concern of a people who lacked an upper class ''to give a tone of honor to the community.'' Emerson was startled to hear him say that the remedy was a civil war in America to teach her citizens the ''necessity of knitting the social ties stronger.''[12]

While unprepared to do battle with Wordsworth on social issues, when the topic turned to letters, a subject within the range of competency of them both, Emerson did dissent and found Wordsworth, unlike the other illuminati he had visited, receptive to his demurs or, at least, not impervious to them. Wordsworth thought Carlyle wrote obscurely. Emerson let that go by. Wordsworth thought Carlyle ''was clever & deep but that he defied the sympathies of everybody.'' Emerson let that go by, too. Nor did he object when Wordsworth said that, while Coleridge ''wrote more clearly'' than Carlyle, he wished he ''would write more to be understood.'' When he said, however, that he thought Carlyle was insane part of the time, Emerson sprang to Carlyle's defense. More surprisingly, when Wordsworth abused Goethe's *Wilhelm Meister* ''with might & main,'' Emerson urged its merits on him. Having encountered in the first part ''all manner of fornication,'' Wordsworth (who as a young man had sired a child out of wedlock) had shown his indignation by flinging the book across the room. On Emerson's recommendation he agreed to give the book a further trial.[13] Since Emerson never shone as a persuader in disputation, we are left to conclude that during this conversation, as the record suggests, Wordsworth had offered his strictures in mild tones.

The talk turned now to Wordsworth's poetry. Wordsworth confided that, of his own poems, he preferred those ''which touched the affections.'' The didactic poems, which dealt with social issues, would not, he surmised, survive the issues that had occasioned them. He saw them as peripheral to his true interests. Hence his tractability.

Urged by Emerson to publish the poems he had lately written, a serene Wordsworth told him that ''he never was in haste to publish[,] partly because he altered his poetry much & every alteration is ungraciously received but what he wrote would be printed whether he lived or died.''[14] As a poet, Emerson would follow this same pattern.

On the return walk to Ambleside, Wordsworth was Emerson's companion much of the way, pausing now and again, in the midst of his talking, to underscore with an emphatic silence some word or bit of verse. At length, "with great kindness," he took leave of his Boston visitor and struck out across the fields to return to Rydal Mount.

In 1841 Wordsworth wrote briskly to a friend:

> Do you know Miss [Elizabeth] Peabody of Boston? She has just sent me, with the highest eulogy, certain essays of Mr. Emerson. Our Carlyle and he appear to be what the French used to call *esprits forts,* though the French idols showed their spirit after a somewhat different fashion. Our two present Philosophes, who have taken a language which they suppose to be English for their vehicle, are verily "par nobile fratrum," and it is a pity that the weakness of our age has not left them exclusively to this appropriate reward — mutual admiration. Where is the thing which now passes for philosophy at Boston to stop?[15]

Townsend Scudder thinks it doubtful that Wordsworth realized Emerson the essayist and the man from Boston who had visited him eight years before were one and the same. Yet perhaps he did. Eleven years separated William Ellery Channing's visit, in 1822, from Emerson's, yet Wordsworth recalled him so well he was able to place his hand on the very chair Channing had sat in as he told Emerson of that encounter. The parallel he drew between Carlyle and Emerson suggests that a memory of Emerson's stout defense of Carlyle lurked still in his mind, although by then others were remarking on affinities linking the Scotsman and his Yankee champion. Also, to suppose that Emerson could visit Carlyle and Wordsworth in the same week and so impress Carlyle that the memory of that visit never dimmed and yet so little impress Wordsworth that the passage of a few years effaced all memory of the visit tries our credulity. Yet that could be so. Carlyle, at that time a virtual unknown, attracted no visitors. An unceasing stream of visitors sought out Wordsworth, already a literary landmark, at Rydal Mount. Indeed, he was concerned that they would leave his cupboard bare until Harriet Martineau told him to offer them nothing. And thus he treated Emerson, perhaps counting him merely as one among the multitudes of those who made him an object of pilgrimage.

Fifteen years after the first meeting, Emerson visited Wordsworth a second time. In recounting the visit, he said nothing to indicate that Wordsworth, either by utterance or implication, was aware that they were not meeting for the first time. The plain truth is that Wordsworth had forgotten not only the chair Emerson had sat in, he had forgotten the sitter, too. But a man who has just completed his eleventh septenniad has his privileges and, for Wordsworth, one of those must have been the right to forget a man whose ideas seemed so alien to his own.

The day of facts is a rock of diamonds . . . a fact is
an Epiphany of God.

19. Glimpses of the Universal

*E*MERSON had not gone to Europe an empty vessel into which men of perception were invited to pour their ideas. His mind, already seething with awareness, sought from them only the stimulus that comes from an exchange of ideas among men in many ways operating on the same high mental plane. That watershed moment in Emerson's life when he came home from Europe, his mind vastly awakened and ready to carry him forward toward the major goals he had conceived of as his, gives us occasion to examine some of those seminal episodes in his intellectual history that made inevitable his ultimate accomplishments.

In his senior year at Harvard, in Levi Frisbie's class, Emerson had encountered the Scottish realists, most particularly Dugald Stewart, and read that man had an intuitive moral faculty which enabled him to distinguish between right and wrong. This sense, the Scots said, supplemented man's analytical powers, which John Locke had described. Emerson's professors agreed with the Scottish school; among his texts, however, he found another writer concerning whom they had reservations but with whom he found himself in greater sympathy — Richard Price, an English Unitarian and the author of *A Review of the Principal Questions and Difficulties in Morals*. On 14 March 1821 Emerson noted in his journal that Price believed ''right & wrong are not determined by any reasoning or deduction but by an ultimate perception of the human mind.''[1] That Emerson found the idea breathtaking is suggested by the modification he made of Price's wording. Price had not said ''an ultimate perception'' but ''some immediate power of perception.'' Thus, as Price saw it, the moral sense asserted itself not gradually, while being sustained by the intellect, but spontaneously and unassisted. Unlike the Scottish realists, Price made a clean break with Locke.

By the following year, Emerson spoke of this powerful faculty, which Price had identified, as the moral sense or moral sentiment and in terms which showed that the idea intrigued him, as in fact it did since it became for him a creed he held to throughout his lifetime. He wrote:

> Moral Sense; a rule coextensive and coeval with Mind. It derives its existence from the eternal character of the Deity . . . and seems of itself to imply and therefore to prove his Existence. . . . whence comes this strong universal feeling that approves or abhors actions? Manifestly not from *matter*, which is altogether unmoved by it and the connection of which with it is a thing absurd — but from a *Mind*, of which it is the essence. That Mind is God.
>
> This Sentiment which we bear within us, is so subtle and unearthly in its nature, so entirely distinct from all sense and matter, and thence so difficult to be examined, and withal so decisive and invariable in its dictates — that it clearly partakes of another world than this and looks forward to it in the end. . . .
>
> This Sentiment differs from the affections of the heart and from the faculties of the mind. The affections are undiscriminating and capricious. The Moral Sense is not.[2]

Conceivably Price's theory had been made palatable to Emerson before this time by William Ellery Channing, whose sermons he often heard. Channing too owned a debt to Price: ''I read Price when I was in college. Price saved me from Locke's Philosophy. . . . His book, probably, moulded my philosophy into the form it has always retained, and opened my mind into the *transcendental depth*.''[3] Emerson could have made this same statement.

Convinced that rationalism and empiricism were spiritually limiting, Emerson came to believe that ''The moral law lies at the center of nature and radiates to the circumference.'' It ranges throughout the universe of matter. Man's intuitive insight into moral law Emerson identified, over the years, under various titles — the moral sense, the moral sentiment (Adam Smith's *The Theory of Moral Sentiments* [1759] was in his library), universal sentiment, and Reason. The source of the moral sense was ''the Supreme Spirit,'' ''the superincumbent Spirit,'' or ''the Over-Soul,'' dwelling in all men and women. Ultimately Emerson was to define Christ's role as that of a man who sought to teach other men that all men in common were, through the moral sentiment, sharers in God's divinity. The rites of Christianity, therefore, were superfluous. In his journal on 5 March 1838 Emerson expounded on this point: "You can never come to any peace or power until you put your whole reliance in the moral constitution of man & not at all in a historical Christianity. . . . Christ preaches the greatness of Man, but we hear only the greatness of Christ."[4] The value of Christianity, Emerson decided, rested in its ethical content. Ultimately everything came down to one simple truth — a man who lives in deepest harmony with the impulses of his own moral being is, as a consequence, truly good.

Concluding that the world of matter confirmed the moral sense, Emerson produced a doctrine of correspondence to attest to it. "The laws of moral nature," he said, "answer to those of matter as face to face in a glass." And again: "The axioms of physics translate the laws of ethics." Yet again: "Things are saturated with the moral law. There is no escape from it. Violets and grass preach it; rain and snow, wind and tides, every change, every cause in Nature is nothing but a disguised missionary."[5] In 1838 he would tell his Divinity School audience: "I look for the new Teacher, that shall follow so far those shining laws, that he shall see them come full circle; . . . shall see the world to be the mirror of the soul; . . . and shall show that the Ought, that Duty, is one thing with Science, with Beauty, and with Joy."[6] The Free Religious Association would be told in 1869: "The first simple foundation of my belief is that the Author of nature has not left himself without a witness in any sane mind: that the moral sentiment speaks to every man the law after which the Universe was made."[7] That all men were not receptive to the moral sentiment, even so, was obvious to him:

> The illusion that strikes me as the masterpiece in that ring of
> illusions which our life is, is the timidity with which we assert our
> moral sentiment. We are made of it, the world is built by it, things
> endure as they share it; all beauty, all health, all intelligence
> exist by it; yet we shrink to speak of it or range ourselves by its
> side. . . . The courts snatch any precedent at any vicious form of
> law to rule it out; legislatures listen with appetite to declamations
> against it and vote it down.[8]

By no means, however, did Emerson despair. In "Fate" he would insist: "The moral sense is alone omnipotent."[9]

Not until 1834 did Emerson accept the word "Reason" as another term to describe the "immediate power of perception" that Price had identified. Then, in Coleridge's *Aids to Reflection*, he came upon the distinction between Understanding and Reason that Coleridge supposed described the conclusion Immanuel Kant had reached. To his brother Edward, on 31 May 1834, he summed it up in these terms:

Reason is the highest faculty of the soul — what we mean often
by the soul itself; it never *reasons,* never proves, it simply per-
ceives; it is vision. The Understanding toils all the time, compares,
contrives, adds, argues . . . dwelling in the present the expedient
the customary. . . . The thoughts of youth, & "first thoughts," are
the revelations of Reason. [*sic*] the love of the beautiful & of
Goodness as the highest beauty the belief in the absolute &
universal superiority of the Right & the True But understanding
. . . contradicts evermore these affirmations of Reason & points at
Custom & Interest and persuades one man that the declarations
of Reason are false & another that they are at least impracticable.
Yet by & by after having denied our Master we come back to see
at the end of years or of life that he was the Truth.[10]

Coleridge had put it succinctly: "Reason is the power of universal
and necessary convictions, the Source and Substance of Truth above
sense, and having their evidence in themselves." Here were Price's
views sanctioned in a new philosophical vocabulary. Confidently,
Emerson would proclaim in "Literary Ethics": "The vision of genius
comes by renouncing the too officious activity of the understanding,
and giving leave and amplest privilege to the spontaneous sentiment."[11]
Actually, though Emerson knew it neither then nor later, Coleridge,
in his eagerness to find moral guidelines to uphold Christian ethics as
scriptural authority was being breached by rationalist assaults, had
misread Kant. C. E. Vaughan says Kant assigned to Reason no more
than "a 'regulative' or suggestive function in the ordering of knowledge," and conceded to Understanding "sole title to the discovery of
truth." Kant's own scornful summation of intuitionalism confirms
Vaughan's assessment:

A so-called philosophy is now advertised in which, in order to
possess all philosophical wisdom, one . . . has only to listen to and
enjoy the oracle that speaks within oneself. It is announced that
those who follow this philosophy . . . are able by a single penetrating glance into their own inwards to accomplish all that others
can achieve by the utmost industry. . . . The philosopher of
intuition . . . discovers his own nature, not by the herculean labor
of self-knowledge built up patiently from the foundation, but by
a sort of self-apotheosis which enables him to soar above all this
vulgar task-work.[12]

Elsewhere Kant would say: "As to moral faculty, this supposed special sense, the appeal to it is indeed superficial when those who cannot
think believe that feeling will help them out, even in what concerns

general laws.''[13] Had they but realized it, Emerson's adversaries to refute him needed only to invoke the name of Kant, whom, even in his essay ''The Over-Soul,'' Emerson identified as a proponent of the intuitionist school.

Those powers of spontaneous or transcendental awareness that Emerson believed were accessible to himself and to all mankind can be accounted for in a natural way.

Woman, because of the obligations entrusted to her by Nature and by custom and tradition, has a responsiveness to nonverbal gestures far surpassing man's ability to read the same signs. As spouse, woman in her traditional role has prided herself on anticipating the needs and predilections of her mate. As mother, she is alert to detect in her offspring evidence of discomfiture, illness, or behavior that could signal physical, mental, or moral dangers. The limits of her physical strength have compelled her reliance on her own perceptiveness to ward off threats of every gradation. What in the past has been heralded as woman's superior intuition now is spoken of as her superior ability to interpret nonverbal gestures. While epochs of conditioning have given women an enormous lead in this accomplishment, men are able also to cultivate it, either by conscious effort or unconsciously when, in early life, a woman's influence is paramount in their upbringing. A male child raised by caring women has unusual opportunities to see this power displayed. If observant and reflective, he can gain mastery of it. Emerson had such opportunities and was responsive to them to an exceptional degree.

Ruth, Emerson's mother, was a quiet woman, demonstrative not by explicit actions but only by implication. To be understood she had to be read closely. It was worth the effort. That she came from a large family in which the wants of others had naturally to be considered and in her marriage had the care of three terminally ill children, a retarded son, and several gifted children, as well as a husband who suffered a prolonged and fatal illness, gave her an exceptional opportunity to cultivate to its fullest potential her capacity for responding to the nonverbal gestures of others. Everything we know about her assures us that she did not shirk this role. Consider further that Emerson's father, during his short lifetime, was more often than not absent from home. Even in that interval when he enjoyed good health, the rearing of his children fell largely to his wife. When Ralph Waldo was two, he was enrolled at a Dame School and was introduced to the rudiments of reading by two women. This instruction was reinforced by further guidance received from Aunt Mary, Sarah Bradford, and numerous Haskins aunts. Not by chance did Emerson, in marking his attentiveness to the world around him, speak of possessing ''womanly eyes.'' Denton Snider says Emerson and his brothers ''grew up wholly under the hands of brave women, though with some external assistance from good men.'' Conway, reviewing in more dramatic terms the circumstances of Emerson's upbringing, ranges his mother, Aunt Mary, and Sarah Bradford around him as the ''Three Fates.''[14]

To women Emerson readily assigned a greater degree of awareness of things than men possess. Not recognizing, however, that this lay in their keener responsiveness to nonverbal gestures, he acknowledged their superiority in transcendental terms: ''The truth is in the air, and the most impressionable brain will announce it first, but all will announce it a few minutes later. So women, as most susceptible, are the best index of the coming hour.''[15] From Emerson, his son Edward had the story of Mrs. Bemis, a simple Concord woman who would not miss a lecture by Emerson, though she ''understood no word,'' because she ''got the lesson from the tone and attitude of the man.''[16] Emerson never realized that the process was exactly as here described.

Writing ''The Comic,'' Emerson began with a striking passage:

> I find few books so entertaining as the wistful human history written out in the faces of any collection of men at church or courthouse. The silent assembly thus talks very loud. . . . The doctor's head is a fragrant gallipot of virtues. The carpenter still measures feet and inches with his eye, and the licensed landlord mixes liquors in motionless pantomime. What good bargains glimmer on the merchant's aspect! . . . You shall see eyes set too near, and limited faces, faces of one make and invariable character. How the busy fancy inquires into their biography and relations! . . . In the silentest meeting, the eye reads the plain prose of life, timidity, caution, appetite, ignorance.[17]

In the nineteenth century, phrenology, as a forerunner of rational psychology, drew the attention of many serious-minded people, for example, the philosopher John Fiske, who yearned for some way to classify people. Emerson remarked this enthusiasm.[18] In 1832, the co-founder of phrenology, Johann Kaspar Spurzheim, lectured in Boston, gaining receipts of $3,000. While Spurzheim died in Boston of typhus before he could spend his profits, Emerson never was reconciled to his success. In one of many disparaging comments he made about him, he said in 1835, in a letter to Elizabeth Peabody: ''I had rather not understand in God's world than understand thro' and thro' in . . . Spurzheim's.''[19] In November 1834 Emerson sent Carlyle an article by Frederic Henry Hedge, published in *The Christian Examiner,* in which Hedge excoriated phrenology. Yet Emerson kept a good opinion of his Harvard classmate George Henry Calvert, who wrote the first American book on phrenology, and had two books on the subject in his library. Seemingly he hoped some useful science would evolve from phrenology. In 1842 he wrote: ''When shall we have a grammar of phrenology that shall indicate the signs of probity, of sanity in any face? We know them, but know them not.''[20] Cesare Lombroso's work came too late for Emerson to know about it, otherwise, surely, he would have considered it.

In *The Conduct of Life* Emerson would make his most revealing comments on his understanding of body language:

> The soul which animates nature is not less significantly pub-
> lished in the figure, movement and gesture of animated bodies,
> than in its last vehicle of articulate speech. . . . Nature tells every
> secret once. Yes, but in man she tells it all the time, by form,
> attitude, gesture, mien, face and parts of the face, and by the
> whole action of the machine. . . . The whole economy of nature is
> bent on expression. The tell-tale body is all tongues. . . . The
> face and eyes reveal what the spirit is doing . . . what aims it has.

What the eyes disclosed Emerson found particularly significant: ''The eyes of men converse as much as their tongues. . . . You can read in the eyes of your companion whether your argument hits him, though his tongue will not confess it.''[21]

Early in January 1835 Emerson, mindful surely of the mutual attraction that lately had sprung up between him and Lydia Jackson, wrote: ''There are some occult facts in human nature that are natural magic. The chief of these is the glance. . . . The mysterious communication that is established across a house between two entire strangers, by this means, moves all the springs of wonder.''[22] On a less dramatic plane he would remark that he could enter a shop and, without verbal exchange between the clerk and himself, communicate his wants successfully.

Emerson was struck by how much even simple people silently reveal themselves. He wrote in 1837:

> I see with awe the attributes of the farmers and villagers whom
> you despise. A man saluted me today in a manner which at once
> stamped him for a theist, a self-respecting gentleman, a lover
> of truth and virtue. . . . How expressive is form! I see by night
> the shadow of a poor woman against a window curtain that
> instantly tells a story of so much meekness, affection and labor as
> almost to draw tears.[23]

He made this his theme again, in 1841:

I frequently find the best part of my ride in the Concord coach
from my house to Winthrop Place to be in . . . the North End
of Boston. The dishabille of both men & women, their unrestrained
attitudes & manners make pictures greatly more interesting than
the clean shaved & silk robed procession in Washington & Tremont
streets. . . . No citizen, or citizen's wife, no soul, is without organ.
Each soul is a soul or an individual in virtue of its having, or I
may say being a power to translate the universe into some particular language of its own . . . into something great, human, &
adequate.[24]

Commenting once on his alleged tone deafness, Emerson said, "I
think sometimes that my lack of musical ear is made good to me through
my eyes: that which others hear, I *see*."[25]

At the close of "The American Scholar" address Emerson would
set down his philosophical understanding of what it meant for him to
seek in the particular world around him glimpses of the universal:

I embrace the common, I explore and sit at the feet of the familiar, the low. Give me insight into to-day, and you may have the
antique and future worlds. What would we really know the
meaning of ? The meal in the firkin; the milk in the pan; . . . the
glance of the eye; the form and gait of the body; — show me the
ultimate reason of these matters; — show me the sublime presence
of the highest spiritual cause lurking, as always it does lurk, in
these suburbs and extremities of nature; let me see every trifle
bristling with the polarity that ranges it instantly on an eternal
law; . . . and the world lies no longer a dull miscellany and
lumber room, but has form and order; there is no trifle; there is
no puzzle; but one design unites and animates the farthest pinnacle and the lowest trench.[26]

To perceive through the instrument of the body was, for Emerson,
not enough; he had to know through the powers of the soul.

Let him find his superiority in not wishing superiority;
find the riches of love which possesses that which
it adores; the riches of poverty; the height of
lowliness; the immensity of today; and, in the
passing hour, the age of ages.

20. The Poet-Philosopher

*A*s early as June 1826 Emerson was expressing interest in the
ideal of the representative man. In a letter to Aunt Mary, he spoke of
the opinion, lately advanced by Edward Everett, that "geniuses are
the organs, mouthpieces of their age; do not speak their own words,
nor think their own thoughts."[1] He found the idea unpalatable yet
conceded that it was probably true.

While this idea was new to Emerson, it cannot have been new to
Everett because basically it was a restatement of Hegel's view that the
great man is an expression of the spirit of an era or a people. Everett
would have encountered it during his years of study in Germany, if
not in Hegel's own work, then in the writings of the French Eclectic
Victor Cousin. Cousin, in his *Introduction to the History of Philosophy* (1829), repeatedly uses the word *representant* to describe men
who typify their epoch. Cousin's book came into Emerson's hands in
1831, and he read it eagerly then and a second time when it became
available in translation, in 1832. In 1833, when he visited Wordsworth,
he told him that everybody in Boston was reading Cousin. Although
Emerson consulted Cousin's translation of Plato and owed to Cousin's
treatment of the Bhagavad Gita his first appreciation of Hindu philosophy, these obligations do not compare with the debt he owed Cousin
for the concept of the representative man, for this concept added another dimension to his most cherished ideal — the actualization of the
complete universal man.

Emerson subscribed to the Neoplatonic concept that the soul contains all knowledge. His idea of the complete universal man was some-

one whose mental and spiritual powers were so awakened he was able to utilize fully the potentials of the soul. He saw the true poet as one who "stands among partial men for the complete man." He described him as "the man without impediment, who sees and handles that which others dream of, traverses the whole scale of experience, and is representative of man, in virtue of being the largest power to receive and impart."[2] Emerson knew that he was describing an ideal that existed only in the abstract, yet he believed the true poet approximated it more closely than other men. That is as much as he would claim. "We have yet," he acknowledged, "no man who has leaned entirely upon his character."[3]

For Emerson the goal of actualizing the ideal of the complete universal man was a kind of Grail quest. He offered Kant's definition of moral conduct as a context within which to cultivate such completeness: "Act always so that the immediate motive of thy will may become a universal rule for all intelligent beings."[4] The duty of life for all men was to find out the law and obey it. Growth toward perfection called for unflagging zeal. "Act naturally," Emerson said, "act from within, not once or twice, but from month to month, without misgiving, without deviation, from year to year, & you shall reap the costly advantages of moral accomplishments."[5] This task was each man's responsibility.

Twenty-five years after he published *Nature* in 1836, Emerson counted it a virtue that he had not recruited a single disciple. That was, he said, in keeping with his goal of bringing men not to him but to themselves. His conviction that the pursuit of perfection was to be undertaken in isolation accounts, in part, for his remoteness in his relations with others. He explained: "Duties are as much impediments to greatness, as cares. If a man set out to be rich, he cannot follow his genius; neither can he any more, if he wishes to be an estimable son, brother, husband, nephew, & cousin."[6] The omission of the category of father may be significant. Had he had the chance to be a father to his lost son, Waldo, Emerson might well have suspended his personal quest for self-perfection. In a letter to Carlyle, written when Waldo died, he said as much: "How often I have pleased myself that one day I should send to you this Morningstar of mine, & stay at home gladly behind such a representative."[7]

Townsend Scudder surmised that Emerson spoke and wrote for effect, with "fame standing before him as a dazzling award." Thus it was as "the accomplished scholar," not "the perfect man," that he hoped to realize himself.[8] Stephen Whicher took a like view, charging that Emerson had pursued "the dream of greatness."[9] Phrases that Emerson wrote at twenty-two might seem to support this thesis — "Shall I embroil my short life with a vain desire of perpetuating its memory when I am dead & gone in this dirty planet?'' and ''I confess the foolish ambition to be valued.''[10] But in this period he was preparing himself for the ministry and carrying on the appropriate rites of passage exercises in self-evaluation that commonly led to self-recrimination and anxieties about worthiness of motives. At twenty, it should be recalled, he also wrote: ''I would learn to love Virtue for her own sake. . . . I would sacrifice inclination to the interest of mind & soul. . . . Every wise man aims at an entire conquest of himself.''[11] Emerson knew ambition. In fact he called ambition ''the leprosy of the Emersons'' and thought it killed his younger brothers. Yet evidence is strong that he strove to be, himself, the complete universal man whom he sought. Thoreau said of Emerson that there was ''More of the divine realized in him than in any.''[12] Snider concluded: ''Emerson relives the lives of heroes, traces in their deeds his own very soul, discerning and identifying both in them and in himself the Standard Man, the Universal Person who individuates his oneness into the Many.''[13] Elisabeth Luther Cary insisted: ''Emerson himself represented most of the essential qualities for which he sought human types, 'for the secrets of life are not shown except to sympathy and likeness.' ''[14] Alluding to a passage Emerson wrote in 1846 in which he said, ''We shall one day talk with the central man and see again in the varying play of his features all the features which have characterized our darlings, & stamped themselves in fire on the heart,'' Joel Porte says: ''This great inclusive figure, chasing his own incarnations down through the years, whom Emerson one day expects to meet and talk to, is in fact the very self he has always been talking to.''[15] Perhaps Hawthorne was the first to recognize this fact when he wrote ''The Great Stone Face'' with a protagonist who long sought a man of destiny, only to find that he himself was that man. Many took his protagonist to be Emerson.

Emerson's disavowal of the role of active reformer is best understood in the context of his pursuit of perfection. Sherman Paul says: ''Loyal to his own gifts, he let others carry on the work of reform; and for himself he stuck to the primary duty on which he felt he had been called — the duty of perceiving and reporting truth.'' He continues: ''Early in his relations with Emerson, Thoreau recognized that . . . the task he set himself — 'to realize a divine life' — was a higher and more arduous one than that of reform. Indeed, it was the supreme reform, the reform of man and not his exterior life.'' Paul concludes: ''Emerson created a new calling with its own rewards: the poet who, in harmonizing with nature, realized a divine life. Success was therefore identical with self-realization, with the 'more intense life.' ''[16]

To pick among Emerson's readings in Plato, Neoplatonism, German Idealism, French Eclecticism, the Sanskrit scriptures, or the Persian poets, and then identify one of them to the exclusion of the others as the chief source of his ideas, does justice neither to his thought nor his method. He did not aspire to be the heir of any one philosophical tradition and, even had he wanted to be so regarded, he realized that he had studied none with sufficient thoroughness to merit that status. He never pretended to be a systematic philosopher. "I need hardly say," he owned in 1839, "to anyone acquainted with my thoughts, that I have no System."[17]

By strict accounting Emerson was an eclectic reader. He skimmed books, sometimes reading them from back to front, interested only in "lustres." Such a program was given feasibility by his Neoplatonic faith in the underlying unity of all things. "The mind," he explained, "is urged to ask for one cause of many effects. . . . All philosophy, of East and West, has the same centripetence."[18]

In Emerson's opinion, Plato stood first among philosophers: "Plato is philosophy, and philosophy, Plato." To one who believed this, there could be no problem in believing also that "Out of Plato come all things that are still written and debated among men of thought."[19] Yet, much as he reverenced Plato the philosopher, it was in Plato the man that Emerson sought and found a role model. Plato was his true poet, his complete universal man, his central man, plus-man, or, at least, the man who most fully approached that status. This is what Holmes meant when he said, "Plato comes nearest to being his idol, Shakespeare next."[20] Lewis Mumford held that "Emerson's Platonism was not a matter simply of following Plato: it was a matter of living like Plato, and achieving a similar mode of thought."[21]

Because Emerson developed no rigorous philosophy, he has been dismissed as a poet who mistakenly strayed into the realm of the philosophers. But he is too broad-ranging to submit to narrow categorization. In Plato he saw both poetry and truth: "A philosopher must be more than a philosopher. Plato is clothed with the powers of a poet."[22] In this context he had no difficulty reconciling his own role as poet-philosopher.

Emerson's thinking was shaped by several important Platonic ideas. Plato's idealistic vision of Nature, the precedence he gives to mind over matter, his arguments for the union of opposites, his theory of universals, all find expression in Emerson's writings. In the *Theaetetus* Plato postulated the theory that knowledge is neither sense perception, which alters constantly, nor true judgment. For Plato, true knowledge had to be knowledge of the universal because the universal is not subject to the flux of the sensual world, but is abiding. Plato did not deny the physical world or even give separate existence to the universals; such ideas had to await the coming of the Neoplatonists. But Plato did give his universals a corresponding reference in the real world of sense perceptions. The Platonic discussion of universals and particulars is frequently Emerson's topic.

When Emerson went directly to Plato, the Neoplatonic influence pursued him because the translation he chiefly relied on was that of Thomas Taylor, another Neoplatonist. As a result, the "light from Plato is somewhat refracted."[23] The notions of overarching Unity, of a God-like One, of mysticism, which engrossed him, do not exist in Plato but only in Neoplatonic interpretations of his work. Their influence on Emerson's essay on Plato is marked.

Emerson was led to Neoplatonism through the Cambridge Platonist Ralph Cudworth, whose *True Intellectual System of the Universe* (1678) he first read while at Harvard. Vivian Hopkins contends that Cudworth formed the mold for Emerson's apprehension of Neoplatonic thought. Cudworth's book was one of three volumes he counseled the Dartmouth College library to purchase, in the summer of 1838. From Aristotle and Plotinus (the latter the foremost Neoplatonist, although Emerson did not mention him in his journal before 1830), Cudworth gathered insights that led him to speak of "an energetic principle which imposes God's commands upon matter." He insisted, also, that Spirit controlled Nature. These ideas, of course, had a major impact on Emerson's thinking.[24]

The influence of Plotinus on Emerson's thought is preeminent. The schematic elaborated in "The Over-Soul" is Plotinian.[25] Neither writer stresses the role of evil in the world. Both conceptualize a transcendental One that is simultaneously immanent; the One being merely the other side of human consciousness, since it infuses not only itself and Nature, but man as well. According to both Plotinus and Emerson, man, being of the same One, is able to behold the One — if only he can attune himself to it. Of first importance is the similarity between Plotinus's One and Emerson's Over-Soul.[26]

The concept of the World-Soul, or Over-Soul, is the most metaphysical of Emerson's ideas, and, consequently, seen by some as farfetched and difficult to accept. While the term is Emerson's own, the Over-Soul is much like the "all encompassing One" of Plotinus in that it incorporates and infuses both man and what usually is referred to as "God." Man participates in God because the Over-Soul infuses man. In "The Over-Soul," Emerson says: "I am constrained every moment to acknowledge a higher origin for events than the will I call mine." Thereupon he undertakes to describe "that Unity, that Over-Soul, within which every man's particular being is contained and made one with all other." Emerson's debt to Plotinus is evident when he writes that "within man is the soul of the whole; the wise silence; the universal beauty, to which every part and particle is equally related; the eternal ONE."[27]

"Ineffable," Emerson said, "is the union of man and God in every act of the soul." By thus linking man and God so intimately, Emerson committed himself to an awkward stance on evil. Since the Over-Soul is the compelling force in reality, and since, by definition, the Over-Soul is good, then by necessity the world is moral, and evil does not partake of reality.[28] This conclusion Emerson pursued in "Compensation" and was widely disdained for it — in his own day by Carlyle and, afterward, by countless critics in the heyday of realism and naturalism, and beyond.

The similarities of the concept of the Over-Soul to Neoplatonism are obvious — the idea of an overarching Unity, or One, that infuses man, and God, and Nature. Emerson, however, did not distinguish his Over-Soul as a trinity, as Plotinus did. There was no need for that. His One (or Unity), man and Nature, already corresponded to Plotinus's One, Spirit, and Soul, in that sequence. The commendableness of Emerson's Over-Soul — for him and for those who scrutinize the concept closely — is that it fits not only his Neoplatonic scheme, but also the Idealist scheme, the Oriental scheme, and the scheme of the transcendentalists. All the transcendentalists inclined to a conception of a universal Oneness or Spirit that approximated Emerson's.

W. T. Harris has suggested the Bhagavad Gita as the source of Emerson's concept of the Over-Soul, since in the Gita the Supreme Spirit is spoken of as "Adhyatma (*Adhi* meaning *above* and *atma*, the soul, not the soul that presides over all, but that which is above the soul itself)."[29] But since Emerson first read the Gita only after he had written "The Over-Soul," it could not have been his source. Even less valid is Robert Detweiler's contention that, inasmuch as Emerson used the term only twice in his essays, the Over-Soul is mistakenly assumed to be at the center of his thought.[30] Regardless of what name Emerson assigned to it, the concept is prevalent in his works from the earliest to the latest. It is found in *Nature,* in *The Conduct of Life,* and in all the works intervening.

"There is one mind common to all individual men," Emerson wrote in "History." "Speak your latent conviction, and it shall be the universal sense ; for the inmost in due time becomes the outmost," he said in "Self-Reliance." And there, too, he alludes to "that divine idea which each of us represents."[31] The One is central to Plotinus. Brahma is central to Hinduism. To Emerson, the Over-Soul is central.

That Emerson acquired much of his knowledge of German Idealism at second hand and made an eclectic use of it was perhaps inevitable. He was not a linguist and, when the choice offered, preferred to read translations. Soon after he became acquainted with Frederic Henry Hedge in 1828, Hedge, who had studied in Germany, sought to interest him in German literature. Hedge related : "He laughingly said that as he was entirely ignorant of the subject, he should assume that it was not worth knowing." Since Hedge was later described as "the worst teacher of German that ever lived," Emerson may have escaped a permanent aversion to German scholarship by declining Hedge's offer of assistance. Sometime later, when Emerson did study German, it was to please Carlyle, who insisted that he read Goethe in the original. His reading knowledge of German ultimately was adequate, but he never learned to speak or write it.[32]

Several members of the Transcendental Club (called at first Hedge's Club), formed in 1836, were good German scholars — Convers Francis, George Ripley, Orestes Brownson, Margaret Fuller, John Sullivan Dwight, and Theodore Parker. Thoreau also learned German, after receiving instruction from Brownson. When Emerson needed help with his German, he could turn to one of these friends, and, presumably, also to Charles Follen. But, in its early stages, Convers Francis, more than anyone else, nurtured Emerson's interest in the German philosophers.

Emerson confronted German Idealism not as a systematic philosopher but rather as one standing on that middle ground between philosophy and literature which Coleridge and Carlyle occupied. His introduction to it came from the writings of Dugald Stewart. That could have been disastrous because Stewart's misunderstanding of Kant came close to being total. But when Emerson went on to read Coleridge and Carlyle, he found this out for himself. Subjective colorings mar their presentation of Kant's critical philosophy, yet through them both (especially Carlyle, whose version of German philosophy, though less reliable, was more literary and therefore more pleasing to him), Emerson was made receptive to the speculations of the Idealists who followed in Kant's wake.

Three philosophers dominate the school of German Idealism — Johann Gottlieb Fichte, Friedrich Wilhelm Joseph von Schelling, and Georg Wilhelm Friedrich Hegel. All three — as was true also of Coleridge, Carlyle, and Emerson — pursued theological studies before embracing Idealism, a factor that explains, in part, their lofty goals. Of the three, Hegel, though foremost among them, is in Emerson's development less significant than Fichte and Schelling. Yet even their influence was not overwhelming. Fichte's idea that God and the external world are only the soul projecting itself had obvious appeal, but his skepticism and subjectivity did not. Emerson was intrigued, as Coleridge and Cousin had been before him, by Schelling's philosophy of Nature but presently alienated by his severe, mathematical logic, to the point of acknowledging that he could neither read him nor take an interest in what he was told about him. Until the mid-1840's he had little knowledge of Hegel and saw no need to acquire more.[33]

While Kant, strictly speaking, was not an Idealist at all, he holds an important place among the mélange of influences acting on Emerson during his most innovative and creative years. The roots of the German Idealists are implanted in Kant's philosophy, even though one of Kant's chief goals had been to attack the entrenchments of the metaphysicians, including Idealists, who preceded him. Because Kant posited the unknowable thing-in-itself, as opposed to the world of knowable phenomena, the Idealists who came *after* Kant saw themselves as his heirs. Kant also posited the distinction, vital to both Coleridge and Emerson, between Understanding and Reason. He is important, too, because he proclaimed the veracity of consciousness, even though he contended that there is, beneath consciousness, an unknowable, transcendental ego that synthesizes its various operations. As a final distinction, Kant was the first to use the word "transcendental" — a term emanating from his notions of the transcendental ego and the transcendental object.

Kant contended that neither rational thought alone, nor experience alone, is able to provide us with knowledge of the world. He believed perceptions must be ordered around an a priori conception of space and time. He held that we cannot know whether or not there are things-in-themselves, and that what we do know is due to the synthesizing operation of our minds. This operation, however, is not carried out by the "self" of which we are aware, but by a self about which we can know nothing, a transcendental ego behind it that is not an object of our consciousness.

Unable to accept the impasse created by Kant's notion that ultimate reality, the thing-in-itself, is unknowable, the Idealists asserted that all things are to be regarded as products of thought. To escape the charge of solipsism, they went behind the thinking subject to posit a greater intelligence, one that embraced both subject and object, while simultaneously transcending the subject-object distinction. By making reality the process by which absolute thought or reason clothes itself in visibility, the Idealists made reality intelligible — intelligible to the human mind, which they held to be absolute thought reflecting on itself.

For the Idealists, then, reality — the world and history — is the self-expression of infinite thought or reason. Reflection of the kind Emerson especially prized — so-called spontaneous perception — is, for the Idealist, the self-awareness or self-consciousness of absolute reason transmitted through the mind.

The cardinal concepts of German Idealism find ample expression in Emerson's work. The Kantian distinction between Reason and Understanding is there, and all that follows — the notion that ideas are the ultimate reality; the concept of an absolute reason or spirit that pervades both subject and object, mind and matter, yet transcends both; the conception of that reality as an expression of that ultimate principle; and the capacity of the mind to know this reality intimately and thoroughly, since reality is a manifestation of reason, and reflection nothing other than self-awareness, in and by the mind, of this ultimate reason.

In May 1834 Emerson had explained to his brother Edward how Reason and Understanding differ from one another. A year later, he has passed far beyond that tentative description, telling his journal: "Our compound nature differences us from God, but our Reason is not to be distinguished from the divine Essence."[34] Here he is supplementing Kant's distinction between Reason and Understanding as he has received it from Coleridge. Understanding is seen as a limiting faculty. But Reason, as perceived through a fusion of Platonism and German Idealism, is seen to express the Divine Essence. Emerson now was occupying ground well above the position Kant had thought to occupy. Moreover, although it remained to be announced, he had formulated the basis for his concept of the Over-Soul.

Emerson saw men caught up in a force of boundless power. In his journal in June 1835 he wrote: "Reason is the superior principle. Its attributes are Eternity & Intuition. We belong to it, not it to us."[35] He saw the function of Reason as integrative. Observing the many, it composes them into one. It prophesies as well: "The Understanding listening to Reason, on one side, which saith *It is,* & to the senses on the other side, which say *It is not,* takes middle ground & declares *It will be.* Heaven is the projection of the Ideas of Reason on the plane of the Understanding."[36]

Emerson saw Understanding as subordinate to Reason because it substitutes "seeming" for "being." He explained: "The Understanding is the executive faculty, the hand of the mind. It mediates between the soul & inert matter. It works in time & space, & therefore successively. It divides, compares. . . . It commands the material world, yet often for the pleasure of the senses."[37] It serves the mind, but it cannot be the mind. It cannot create.

Reason supplants what is lacking in Understanding and can be possessed only by those who have integrated a vision of the external world with a comprehensive understanding of Nature. Emerson argued that empirical knowledge did not lead to truth: "Translate, collate, distil all the systems, it steads you nothing, for truth will not be compelled in any mechanical manner."[38] In *Nature,* he says: "The best read naturalist . . . will see . . . that it [truth] is not to be learned by any addition or subtraction or other comparison of known quantities, but is arrived at by untaught sallies of the spirit, by a continual self-recovery, and by entire humility."[39] The moment of illumination springs not from Understanding but from Reason.

In the opening section of *Nature,* Emerson says: "We must trust the perfection of the creation so far, as to believe that whatever curiosity the order of things has awakened in our minds, the order of things can satisfy. Every man's condition is a solution in hieroglyphic to those inquiries he would put."[40] The identity of mind and matter through spirit sanctions man's trust: "This relation between the mind and matter is not fancied by some poet, but stands in the will of God, and so is free to be known by all men."[41] He clarified: "The world proceeds from the same spirit as the body of man."[42] Yet man's awareness of this truth and consequent ability to act in harmony with it, can be lost if he fails to be one with Nature. In these circumstances "we are as much strangers in nature as we are aliens from God."[43]

To grasp the unity of the universe we must rely on Reason: "Reason transfers all these lessons into its own world of thought, by perceiving the analogy that marries Matter and Mind."[44]

Though in his first series of *Essays* Emerson was to shift his attention from Reason to man's ability to know the world and to the ultimate principle which allows it, in doing so he gave even further expression to Idealist principles. The identity of each man with this universal force, he declared, is absolute and complete: "Who hath access to this universal mind is a party to all that is or can be done."[45] Even more specifically, he said: "Of the universal mind each individual man is one more incarnation."[46] Emerson's term for this universal mind is "the Over-Soul" — "that Unity, that Over-Soul, within which every man's particular being is contained and made one with all other."[47] By the time he came to write this, Emerson knew that in Hindu thought Atman and Brahman existed in the same principle of being, thus reaffirming the conception of the German Idealists that the universe is pervaded by one all-comprehensive reality, be it variously designated Reason, Absolute Spirit, or Idea.

The German Idealists had sought to escape the Kantian impasse of unknowable things in themselves by contending that only ideas matter, and by equating the rational with the real. By identifying man's mind with the universal mind, Emerson attested that he stood with them in believing that the world is knowable. He insisted: "With each divine impulse the mind rends the thin rinds of the visible and finite, and comes out into eternity, and inspires and expires its air."[48] And again: "The soul is the perceiver and revealer of truth. . . . We know truth when we see it, from opinion, as we know when we are awake that we are awake."[49] Emerson later designated this "Revelation" as a form of communication accomplished by "an influx of the Divine mind into our mind."[50]

Emerson's championship of self-reliant individualism was an inevitable consequence of his espousal of German Idealism. If our deepest thoughts share the same Reason with the world, if each mind is part of that Reason, and if ideas alone are real, then we have every reason to trust our own thoughts: "To believe your own thought, to believe that what is true for you in your private heart is true for all men, — that is genius."[51]

While Emerson never thought of himself as a mystic and would have discouraged others from identifying him as one, at various times he has been so characterized. The reason is apparent. In their transcendental themes and idiom, in their power fueled by intense inspiration, his essays and poems indicate that the author exists on a plane of awareness far above the ordinary world other men know. Yet, by most criteria, including his own, Emerson does not qualify as a mystic. In fact, in "The Poet" he rejects mysticism on the grounds that it "consists in the mistake of an accidental and individual symbol for a universal one."[52] Holmes sided with Emerson, not necessarily in his estimate of mysticism but in his refusal to answer to the name of mystic. "Too much," Holmes said, "has been made of Emerson's mysticism. He was an intellectual rather than an emotional mystic, and withal a cautious one. He never let go the string of his balloon. He never threw over all his ballast of common sense so as to rise above an atmosphere in which a rational being could breathe."[53]

In determining Emerson's actual status much depends upon our definition of the word "mystic." If an inquiring soul, a reflective yet expansive mind, and a hunger for wisdom make up the essentials of mysticism, then many people who shun the status of mystic deserve to be counted in that company. Yet Emerson, we know, thought that even the title "the sage of Concord," sometimes applied to him, accorded him a distinction he did not merit.

To the extent that they strove to grasp the world in its totality, in its unity amid all the particulars, many of the transcendentalists ranked as agents of mysticism. And none among them more than Emerson made unity an organizing principle of thought.[54] Yet much separates the individual who pursues theological inquiry, no matter how intently, and that individual who passes his life in rapt meditative silence or recurrent bouts of ecstasy. Emerson, whose expansive mind constantly sought validation of truth in the world, could be no one's devotee for long. He sought out other philosophies and religions, hoping to find perceptions that would validate his *own* thoughts. He was not intoxicated with God nor was he subject to mystical experiences.[55] Nonetheless, when it suited his own intuitional philosophy, Emerson did adopt the terms of mysticism.[56] That fact alone can account for the desire of some critics to extend the perimeters of mysticism to embrace him. A celebrated passage in *Nature* often is cited as evidence that Emerson, at times, experienced moments of mystical ecstasy:

Crossing a bare common, in snow puddles, at twilight, under a clouded sky, without having in my thoughts any occurrences of special good fortune, I have enjoyed a perfect exhilaration. I am glad to the brink of fear. . . . Standing on the bare ground, — my head bathed by the blithe air, and uplifted into infinite space, — all mean egotism vanishes. I become a transparent eyeball; I am nothing; I see all; the currents of the Universal Being circulate through me; I am part or particle of God.[57]

Refusing to be overwhelmed by the state of spiritual exaltation that Emerson seemed to be reporting in this passage, Holmes said: ''Emerson's calm temperament never allowed it to reach the condition he sometimes refers to, — that of ecstasy. The passage in *Nature* where he says 'I become a transparent eyeball' is about as near as he ever came.'' In fact, this passage is a reworking of a passage entered earlier in his journal.[58] There he had merely reported the exercise of a divine faculty. Only in the reworking did he raise himself to the dignity of being a particle of God. This passage is therefore better cited as an illustration not of Emerson's mystical bent but of his poetic imagination.

That Emerson skirted the mystical state and may, at one time, have even been desirous of experiencing it cannot be disputed. At twenty, as he prepared to begin his Divinity studies, he remarked in his journal: ''The highest species of reasoning upon divine subjects is rather the fruit of a sort of moral imagination, than of the 'Reasoning Machines,' such as Locke & Clarke & David Hume.''[59] Addressing his brother Edward, he wrote in February 1827, ''Much of what we learn, and to the highest purposes, of life is caught in moments, and rather by a sublime instinct than by modes which can be explained in detail.''[60] Here he seems to be describing what mystics identify as the ''ecstatic moment.'' He would elaborate further:

We do not determine what we will think. We only open our senses, clear away as we can all obstruction from the fact, and suffer the intellect to see. We have little control over our thoughts. We are the prisoners of ideas. They catch us up for moments into their heaven and so fully engage us that we take no thought for the morrow. . . . By and by we fall out of that rapture, bethink us where we have been, what we have seen, and repeat as truly as we can what we have beheld. . . . We carry away in the ineffaceable memory the result, and all men and all the ages confirm it. It is called truth.[61]

In ''The Over-Soul'' he wrote:

I am born into the great, the universal mind. I, the imperfect, adore my own Perfect. I am somehow receptive of the great soul,

and thereby I do overlook the sun and the stars, and feel them
to be the fair accidents and effects which change and pass. More
and more the surges of everlasting nature enter into me. . . .
So come I to live in thoughts and act with energies which are
immortal.[62]

Emerson might announce such experiences but he does not fully report them, which leaves their mystical origins in doubt. Most usually,
what he reports is a poetic perception — again, quite distinct from an
ecstatic moment. Bliss Perry placed Emerson in that category that
William James called "healthy-minded" mystics, but Harold Bloom,
less indulgent, concluded: "Mysticism, according to one famous definition, has not the patience to wait for God's revelation of Himself.
Emersonianism has not the patience to wait for mysticism."[63] Emerson's receptiveness was noteworthy but it was the receptiveness not of
a mystic but a poet. Relevant to that point, Quinn notes that Emerson's "acquaintance with mystical literature gave him a number of
metaphors, but it did not, nor conceivably could it, give him mysticism."[64] The eyeball metaphor, incidentally, was taken over from Plotinus.

Emerson's ambivalence toward Jakob Boehme and Emanuel Swedenborg (whose status as mystics is not disputed) shows how he found
it hard to relate to the vague particulars of mysticism even while he
sympathized with the direction in which it moved. He wrote of Boehme,
in 1844: "His excellence is in his comprehensiveness, not like Plato in
his precision. His propositions are vague, inadequate, & straining. It
is his aim that is great."[65] Boehme, like Plotinus, developed a tripar-
tite metaphysics. Through direct religious experience he concluded that
God was the undifferentiated absolute of being, and that it had a will
toward self-intuition responsible for what he designated the "eternal
regeneration of the Trinity." This calls attention to a major difference between Boehme and Emerson. Boehme stayed in the realm of
religion. Emerson moved into the secular. Both contended that mystical experience is attainable, but "Emerson came to mysticism for the
insight it afforded into the governance of human life [while] Boehme
was so ensnared by the ecstasy of direct communication with God that
he looked to it as a harbinger of salvation in the next world."[66]

Between 1835 and 1849, as a natural consequence of his philosophical inquiries, Emerson worked on material that was published in the
last days of December 1849 as *Representative Men*. His six subjects
were a philosopher, a mystic, a skeptic, a poet, a man of the world,
and a writer — Plato, Swedenborg, Montaigne, Shakespeare, Napoleon, and Goethe. Emerson saw it as the function of great men to teach
and inspire others to greatness by their receptivity to the universal

mind. While none reaches the highest unity, their respective gifts combine to illustrate the unity of the human mind — "the genius of humanity."

Emerson believed that each great man realizes in himself some of the godlike potentials inherent in all men. Plato attempted a theory of the universe. Montaigne acknowledged the supremacy of the moral sentiment. Swedenborg saw the universality of every natural law and its correspondence to spiritual law. Three of Emerson's representative men fell short of such greatness. Goethe did not submit himself to the moral sentiment. Napoleon divorced intellect from conscience. Shakespeare was deficient in spiritual intuition. So Emerson concluded. He knew of no one man who was that essence men are seeking, but each great man makes a contribution by letting in the element of Reason. Great men thus "are a collyrium to clear our eyes from egotism." In their respective gifts they affirm the reality of the unity of the human mind that man seeks. *Representative Men* stands as Emerson's most inclusive effort to apply his general ideas. There he undertakes to distill out of great reputations the essence of the complete universal man, the goal toward which all his explorations converged.

We live day by day under the illusions that it is the
fact or event that imports, whilst really it is not that
which signifies but the use we put it to, or what we
think of it.

21. Father Taylor : The Sailors' Poet

*J*UST after New Year's in 1835, during a three-day visit to Boston, Emerson, weary of listening to country preaching, made
his Sunday memorable by going to the Swedenborg Chapel in the
morning and the Seaman's Bethel in the afternoon. The preacher he
heard in the morning, to his surprise, hewed to tradition. But at the
Bethel the preaching was wild and glorious and that did not surprise
him because the sailor-preacher, his friend Father Edward Taylor, was
in the pulpit. Taylor was an original who would in time catch the
attention of Dickens, Melville, and Whitman, enough so to get into
Dickens's *American Notes,* to scale Melville's pulpit as Father Mapple
in *Moby Dick,* and to disclose to Whitman rhetorical horizons un-
dreamed of. "When Father Taylor preach'd or pray'd," Whitman said,
"the rhetoric and art, the mere words (which usually play such a big
part), seem'd altogether to disappear, and the *live feeling* advanced
upon you and seiz'd you with a power before unknown." In 1860,
when Whitman attended several of Father Taylor's services, Taylor
was already sixty-seven years old, but Whitman, without hesitation,
declared him to be the only "essentially perfect orator" he had ever
heard, not excepting Webster.[1] No matter. Webster, too, in his day,
had professed admiration for Taylor's preaching.

Like Whitman, Edward Taylor was self-taught. Orphaned and
homeless at seven, he had gone to sea as a cabin boy. Ten years later a
Methodist preacher kindled his spirit. Taken captive by the British
during the War of 1812, he preached to his fellow prisoners at their
request. On his release he learned to read and began a fifty-year min-

istry to Boston's maritime community that ended only with his death in 1871. Taylor's Bethel, like Emerson's former parish, Boston's Second Church, was in the North End. During the days of his pastorate at the Second Church, Emerson had sometimes preached at the Bethel and, to the consternation of the orthodox, actively supported Taylor's endeavor. When Emerson further confounded them by resigning his pulpit, Taylor tweaked the Unitarians. "What is to become of your heretic Emerson?" he asked. "I don't know where he will go when he dies. He is hardly good enough to be accepted in Heaven, and yet (the dear creature), Satan wouldn't know what to do with him."[2]

Writing to Charles on 19 January 1832, Emerson remarked that Taylor, making an appeal for funds for the Port Society from Channing's pulpit, had carried the day. "Glad was I," he said, "to have ye Dr hear somebody as good as himself do what he could not do."[3]

During the year that followed his return from Europe, Emerson had poured his restive energy into several undertakings. As a supply minister, he had preached in a variety of pulpits but chiefly in Boston and New Bedford. More to his liking, he had appeared before Boston audiences as a lecturer, speaking on such dissimilar topics as "The Uses of Natural History," Italy, great men, and poetry. Now, for the first time in his life he could afford to shy away from commitments. The courts had determined that the whole of Ellen's share of her father's estate should pass to him as surviving spouse. In October 1834, making up his mind to say and write only what uniquely expressed himself, he moved to Concord, half-resolved to settle there with his mother.

During this restraint-free year Emerson's spiritual posture reflected his new-found independence. At New Bedford he strengthened his ties with several Quakers, particularly Mary Rotch, a kind of Quaker Aunt Mary. Their individual spiritual autonomy seemed attractive to him. From what he could learn of the Swedenborgians he found them also spiritually alive, enough so that it was even rumored that he had affiliated with them. But he no more thought of joining them than he had of allying himself with Father Taylor. These were interests he needed, however, to reassure himself that there were viable alternatives to the inert forms of worship his new Concord neighbors complacently espoused. Charles was similarly smitten. We find Emerson, in November 1836, writing at the end of a long note on Father Taylor: "Do not forget Charles's love of him who said if he were in town he would go & record all his fine sayings."[4]

Taylor, for his part, frowned on orthodox Calvinism. Once he remarked to a man who clung to the old, dour views, "Oh, I see! your *God* is my *Devil!*"[5] On another occasion he addressed a man of similar convictions: "You tell me a great deal of what the devil does, and what power he has; when did you hear from Christ last?"[6] Taylor, however, made no pretext of extending the cloak of his faith wide enough to encompass transcendentalism. Once, after hearing a lecture on the subject, he observed, "It would take as many sermons like that to convert a human soul as it would quarts of skimmed milk to make a man drunk."[7] And he may well have approved of the quip of his clever daughter, who accompanied him on one of his visits to Brook Farm: "Transcendentalists are those who dive into the infinite, soar into the illimitable, and never pay cash!"[8] Still, on several occasions, he spoke out for Emerson, whom he acknowledged to be more like Christ than any other man he had known. When one of his own coreligionists cautioned him about fraternizing with Emerson since Emerson was headed for hell, Taylor answered, "It does look so, but I am sure if Emerson goes there he will so change the climate that emigration will set that way."[9]

To John Andrew, governor of Massachusetts during the Civil War, and one of his solid admirers, Taylor offered this candid yet inoffensive assessment of Emerson, saying, with beguiling honesty, what others believed but were reluctant to say so forthrightly: "Mr. Emerson is one of the sweetest creatures God ever made; there is a screw loose somewhere in the machinery, yet I cannot tell where it is, for I never heard it jar. . . . But still he knows no more of the religion of the New Testament than Balaam's ass did of the principles of the Hebrew grammar."[10]

In an assessment of Taylor, made after visiting the Bethel in January 1835, the first of several assessments he would make of Taylor over the next five years, Emerson said:

> This Poet of the Sailor & of Ann Street — fusing all the rude hearts of his auditory with the heat of his own love & making the abstractions of philosophers accessible & effectual to them also . . . is a work of the same hand that made Demosthenes & Shakespear & Burns & is guided by instincts diviner than rules. . . . He is a living man & explains at once what Whitefield & Fox & Father Moody were to their audiences, by the total infusion of his own soul into his assembly, & consequent absolute dominion over them. How puny, how cowardly, other preachers look by the side of this preaching.[11]

Clearly, Emerson reciprocated Taylor's affection for him. Indeed, here it is set forth without stint, for, unlike Taylor himself, Emerson made no attempt to look at the man and his ideas separately. For Taylor, it was heroic that he could love Emerson even while he found unacceptable the theological views Emerson espoused. Much to his credit, given his narrow indoctrination, he saw that it was the man that mattered. Emerson, at this stage, is less to be credited for not deploring Taylor's want of theological sophistication, the predictable result of his haphazard education. He suspected that Taylor illustrated the power of the moral sentiment to guide man aright.

The year 1835 saw further contacts between Taylor and Emerson. On 26 April Emerson preached for Taylor at the Bethel.[12] At the end of August, just two weeks before Emerson married for a second time, Taylor visited Emerson and the Ripleys at the Manse. Dr. Ripley showed him the battlefield and Taylor told him: "You must write on the monument, 'Here is the place where the Yankees made the British show the back seam of their stockings.' "[13] Emerson, busy then preparing an oration to mark the bicentennial of Concord's founding, found Taylor predictably droll.

On 28 November 1836, Emerson made Taylor the subject of another long journal entry. That they had met lately is evident:

Edward Taylor is a noble work of the divine cunning who suggests the wealth of Nature. If he were not so strong, I should call him lovely. What cheerfulness in his genius, & what consciousness of strength. "My voice is thunder," he said in telling us how well he was. and what teeth & eyes & brow and aspect. . . . His vision poetic & pathetic, sight of love, is unequalled.[14]

Emerson was awed that Taylor could transform the ragbag derelicts who came to him "into sons of light and hope."

What Emerson had implied earlier he now insisted on, that Taylor was guided by spontaneous intuitions:

A creature of instinct, his colors are all opaline and doves'-neck-lustres & can only be seen at a distance. Examine them & they disappear. . . . So with Taylor's muse. It is a panorama of images from all nature & art, whereon the sun & stars shine but go up to it & nothing is there. His instinct, unconscious instinct is the nucleus or point of view.[15]

The following year, on 14 March, Taylor came to Concord, as Emerson's houseguest, to lecture on temperance at Dr. Ripley's church. Emerson relished this chance to assess him at close hand, as orator, minister, and private individual. Initially Emerson seems almost to be describing himself as he appeared on the lecture platform to his own admirers. Assuredly his style, as it evolved, incorporated modifications of Taylor's style. He wrote:

> A wonderful man; I had almost said, a perfect orator. The utter
> want & loss of all method . . . the bright chaos come again of his
> bewildering oratory, certainly bereaves it of power but what splen-
> dor! what sweetness! what richness what depth! what cheer! How
> he conciliates, how he humanizes! how he exhilarates & ennobles!
> Beautiful philanthropist! godly poet! the Shakespeare of the sailor
> & the poor.

Emerson conceded his admiration for Taylor's style as a man: "He is
a very charming object to me. I delight in his great personality, the
way & sweep of the man which like a frigate's way takes up for the
time the centre of the ocean." The man who in boyhood played word
games in church to keep from falling asleep was appreciative of the
alternative Taylor offered: "The wonderful & laughing life of his illustration keeps us broad awake. A string of rockets all night."[16] The
image all but anticipates Lowell's later description of an Emerson lecture as "a chaos full of shooting-stars."

Emerson next mentioned being with Taylor in an account of a meeting of the Transcendental Club at the house of Cyrus Bartol, on 27
May 1840, when Taylor, as an invited guest, addressed the group for
half an hour. Although among the club members none knew Taylor as
well as Emerson did, Taylor's fame, lately enhanced by Harriet Martineau's warm praise of him in *Retrospect of Western Travel*, already
was assured, so no one could have failed to realize that he was in for
a remarkable encounter. The results gratified Emerson: "At Bartol's
our Club was enriched by Edward Taylor's presence. . . . How willingly every man is willing to be nothing in his presence, to share this
surprising emanation & be steeped & ennobled by the new wine of this
eloquence."[17]

Taylor did not come among them to preach a transcendental message, but the message Emerson got was one that reinforced his own
faith in self-reliance: "Instantly you behold that a man is a Mover, —
to the extent of his being a Power, and in contrast with the efficiency
thus suggested, our actual life & society appears a dormitory. We are
taught that earnest impassioned action is most our own & invited to
try the deeps of love & wisdom, — we who have been players & pa-
raders so long." Thus Emerson is seen imbibing, at the outset of his
public career, the lesson of self-reliance from another. In Taylor
Emerson found, as well, reinforcement for his own goodness and sincerity: "I think I am most struck with the *beauty* of his nature. This
hardfeatured, scarred, & wrinkled Methodist whose face is a system of
cordage becomes whilst he talks a gentle, a lovely creature."[18] Dickens, without insisting on so total a transfiguration, acknowledged, two
years later, a similar impression: "He looked a weather-beaten, hard-

featured man. . . . Yet the general character of his countenance was pleasant and agreeable.'' Dickens was struck by Taylor's imagery, which he found ''often remarkably good,'' but saw that he owed his unique rapport with his congregation not to that but to his remarkable sublimation of self : ''He studied their sympathies and understandings much more than the display of his own powers.''[19]

In a celebrated passage in his ''Divinity School Address,'' alluding to Dr. Ripley's assistant, Barzillai Frost, Emerson had said that while sitting in the church listening to him, he had watched the snow falling outside and had been better able to relate to its animation than to Frost's rigidity. Boredom rather than dissent caused him to stop going to church in Concord during that period. His elation can be well imagined, therefore, when he wrote, on 23 June 1845 : ''It was a pleasure yesterday to hear Father Taylor preach all day in our country church.''[20] With this observation he began his longest and most scrutinizing assessment of Taylor as man and preacher. It would also be his last. Taylor's ministry still had another twenty-five years to run, but Emerson had come to believe that he had ''got to the bottom of him,'' and, accordingly, let other interests preempt his attention.

Emerson was impressed by the kind of congregation Taylor drew at Concord. Ministers from the surrounding area flocked to hear him, of course ; Thoreau, Horace Mann, Ellery Channing, Samuel Hoar, Edmund Hosmer, and those erstwhile Brook Farmers, Almira Barlow, Minot Pratt, George Curtis, and his brother Burrill, were there, too. ''Nobody but Webster,'' said Emerson, ''ever assembles the same extremes.''[21]

Repelled by the rich and privileged congregation that Channing preached to at the Federal Street Church, Horace Mann often had gone to the Bethel to hear Taylor. He cherished Taylor's disarming candor and simplicity — ''Oh Lord, deliver us from bad rum and bigotry'' — and once took up a collection to send Taylor on a holiday.[22]

Unfortunately, the Hawthornes were no longer living in Concord when Taylor made his visit. Otherwise Sophia, who admired Taylor and in the past had urged Hawthorne, to no avail, to hear Taylor preach, might finally have had her way. Hawthorne had dodged artfully to avoid this personage to whom others — even Longfellow often went to Boston on Sunday to hear Taylor — had capitulated en masse. On 15 March 1840, Hawthorne wrote Sophia :

> Most absolute little Sophie, didst thou expressly command me to go to Father Taylor's church this very Sabbath ? Now, it would not be an auspicious day for me to hear the aforesaid Son of Thunder. . . . I feel somewhat afraid to hear this divine Father Taylor, lest my sympathy with your admiration of him be colder

and feebler than you look for. . . . Will you promise not to be troubled, should I be unable to appreciate the excellence of Father Taylor? Promise me this, and at some auspicious hour, which I trust will soon arrive, Father Taylor shall have an opportunity to make music with my soul.[23]

The fact that a particular resonance was looked for was enough to make Hawthorne respond in a different register.

Just prior to Taylor's visit to the Transcendental Club, Emerson had written in his journal: "I went to the circus. . . . One horse brought a basket in his teeth, picked up a cap, & selected a card out of four. All wonder comes of showing an effect at two or three removes from the cause. Show us the two or three steps by which the horse was brought to fetch the basket, and the wonder would cease." At Bartol's house Emerson made a resolute effort to discover the two or three steps that resulted in the wonder that was Edward Taylor. Possibly as Taylor's chief advocate in Concord (Taylor was, after all, a Methodist, not a Unitarian), he may even have felt himself to be something of an impresario exhibiting a prize performer. On that account, allusions to Taylor's presentation as "a perfect Punch & Judy affair," and to him as "a minstrel; all the rest is costume" — may have suggested themselves naturally to Emerson as the appropriate idiom in which to describe what he saw and heard. Dickens, of course, grasped this aspect of Father Taylor full well and gave over a page to describing him strutting upon his pulpit as upon a stage, with Bible as prop and a "painted drapery of a lively and somewhat theatrical appearance" hanging behind him as a backdrop.[24]

Emerson was not dissatisfied with or disillusioned in Taylor. Not for a minute did he categorize his antics as mere theatrics. He continued to believe that Taylor did not contrive his effects. Taylor's success rested with his "sympathetic communication with his auditory." Here was the key to understanding his appeal: "This free happy expression of himself & of the deeps of human nature, of the happier sunny facts of life, of things connected & lying amassed & grouped in healthy nature, that is his power and his teacher." He conveyed "a wisdom not his own." The person himself was laudable: "How joyfully & manly he spreads himself abroad. . . . He is perfectly sure in his generous humanity. He rolls the world into a ball & tosses it from hand to hand." Sincerity made Taylor's methods creditable. Put under analysis they were, of themselves, almost absurd:

> The preaching quite accidental & ludicrously copied & carica-
> tured from the old style, as he found it in some Connecticut tubs.
> . . . The slips & gulfs of his logic would involve him in irreparable

ridicule if it were not for the inexhaustible wit by which he dazzles & conciliates. . . . Everything is accidental to him! his place, his education, his church, his seamen, his whole system of religion a mere confused rigmarole of refuse & leavings of former generations — all has a grinning absurdity. . . . He is incapable of thought; he cannot analyze or discriminate; he is a singing dancing drunkard of his wit. . . . Not the smallest dependence is to be put on his statement of facts.

All this was tolerable because there was no duplicity in it. Such a man was superior in terms of the part he had to play. Still, he did not stand in the first order of genius.[25]

No one else seemed to incite Emerson to use exclamation points as Father Taylor did. Taylor overwhelmed him — yet not to the extent that he could not grasp that Taylor's untutored genius had limitations. Transcendentalism required some direction from Understanding, evidently, as well as from Reason. Emerson even surmised that Taylor would be more content among barroom revelers than among those who stood in judgment over them, but, on that account, loved him only the more.

In May 1846 Emerson, seething over Alcott's failure at Fruitlands, commented: ''Alcott & Edward Taylor resemble each other in the incredibility of their statement of facts. One is the fool of his idea, the other of his fancy.''[26] Emerson was not quite so far distant from the rational world as his detractors supposed him to be.

22. Ancestry
The Gate of Gifts

F AMILY pride," said George Woodberry, "was an important trait
of old New England. . . . The Emersons had it . . . they were educated to be Emersons."[1] Although when Emerson was gathering materials for the historical address he gave at Concord in September 1835,
to mark the town's bicentennial, he had to delve into old records to
convince himself that he was descended from a founder of the town,
Peter Bulkeley, he had already heard much about his forebears from
Aunt Mary. As he related: "The kind Aunt whose cares instructed
my youth . . . told me oft the virtues of her & mine ancestors. They
have been clergymen for many generations, & the piety of all & the
eloquence of many is yet praised in the Churches. But the dead sleep
in their moonless night; my business is with the living." And he elsewhere noted: "When I talk with a genealogist, I seem to sit up with a
corpse." Since he professed to believe that it is the nature of genius
"to spring, like the rainbow daughter of wonder, from the invisible,
to abolish the past and refuse all history," a view consistent with his
commitment to a belief in spontaneous wisdom and self-sufficiency, he
may well have had no natural disposition to dwell on his forebears.
Even Aunt Mary remembered that when she took him, as a small boy,
to Malden, to visit the grave of his great-grandfather Joseph Emerson,
he had, with boyish heedlessness, skipped around among the graves.[2]

But Aunt Mary did her work well. Skip as Emerson might through
the world of the living, his thoughts often drew him back to the moonless night of the dead. "How shall a man escape from his ancestor,"
he asked, "or draw off from his veins the black drop which he drew
from his father's or his mother's life?" Did Hawthorne ever speak of

the weight of the past in grimmer terms? In a certain mood Emerson saw genes as decisive: "Men are what their mothers made them. . . . When each comes forth from his mother's womb, the gate of gifts closes behind him. . . . So he has but one future and that is already predetermined in his lobes. . . . All the privilege and all the legislation of the world cannot meddle or help to make a poet or a prince out of him."[3]

Coming from a class which, over the course of two centuries, had put its stamp on the world he lived in, and living in an age when an influx of newcomers accentuated the need for that class to hold together to preserve its identity, Emerson, despite his declared scorn for the past, inevitably found himself taking shelter behind his heritage, embracing predestination in its new guise of hereditary determinism leniently modified by ameliorative evolution. He reflected: "A man finds room in the few square inches of the face for the traits of all his ancestors." He spoke further, of "the seven or eight of us rolled up in each man's skin, — seven or eight ancestors at least," whom a man feels and represents, and who "constitute that variety of notes for that new piece of music which his life is." Yet he allowed for the implantation of additional characteristics: "They may become fixed and permanent in any stock, by painting and repainting them on every individual, until at last Nature adopts them and bakes them in her porcelain."[4]

Henry James saw Emerson himself as illustrative of this theory:

It is impossible to imagine a spirit better prepared in advance to be exactly what it was — better educated for its office in its faraway unconscious beginnings. There is an inner satisfaction in seeing . . . such a proof that when life wishes to produce something exquisite in quality she takes her measure many years in advance. A conscience like Emerson's could not have been turned off, as it were, from one generation to another: a succession of attempts, a long process of refining, was required. . . . His reader envies him this transmitted unity. . . . It must have been a kind of luxury to be — that is, to feel — so homogeneous.[5]

John Burroughs reached the same conclusion. "There is a quality in him . . . a chivalry in the blood, that dates back, and has been refined and transmitted many times."[6]

THE MOODYS

In Emerson's forebears, Nathaniel Hawthorne found a cornucopia for the writer. In *Mosses from an Old Manse* he dealt, in turn, with Daniel Bliss, William Emerson, and Ezra Ripley, Emerson's great-grandfather, grandfather, and titular grandfather respectively. To write "The Minister's Black Veil," he went back to one of Emerson's great-granduncles, Joseph Moody of York, Maine, for his subject. Joseph's sister Mary, married to Joseph Emerson of Malden, was Ralph Waldo Emerson's great-grandmother. Her father, the Reverend Samuel Moody, was a renowned eccentric, "exceedingly irritable and sometimes almost outrageous." When Samuel was sixteen, in 1692, his maternal grandmother, Mary Perkins Bradbury, was brought to trial as a witch. Not disposed by temperament to speak in her own defense, Mary, much as her descendant Ralph Waldo Emerson would do when set upon by his critics, let her family and friends plead her cause. She was found guilty and condemned to be executed. Thereupon her supporters connived her escape from jail and concealed her until the witch-hunting hysteria subsided. She alone among those sentenced to death escaped the gallows in this fashion.[7] Tradition holds that the odd streak came into the Moody family with Mary.

Samuel Moody was one of the preachers who aligned themselves with the Great Awakening. His fiery vehemence led to his being compared in his own time to George Whitefield, the foremost evangelical of the day. At the siege of Louisburg in 1745, though almost seventy, Samuel won distinction as preacher, fighter, and iconoclast. He was a blustery personage who never hesitated to haul a derelict parishioner out of a tavern or a decamping one back into the meeting house, howling at him, "Come back, you graceless sinner, come back!" He was steadfast, missing only two Sabbaths in forty-five years, and solicitous of the needy to the point where once he gave away his wife's only pair of shoes. His spouse, Hannah, had been one of the Sewalls, hardy exemplars of Puritanism, the niece of Judge Samuel Sewall. Thus Emerson could count among his forebears both a judge who sentenced witches to the gallows, at Salem in 1692, and, as well, one of the witches so condemned. Even Hawthorne, whose great-grandfather, John Hathorne, sat in judgment on Mary Bradbury, could not claim that double distinction.

William Moody, saddler and farrier, the grandfather of Samuel Moody, was said to have been the first man to shoe an ox. He migrated to Massachusetts from Ipswich, England, in 1633. Samuel's father was Caleb, William's third son, a sergeant-at-arms. His wife, Judith Bradbury, was the daughter of Captain Thomas Bradbury, who came to America as agent to his brother-in-law Sir Ferdinando Gorges, "the father of English colonization in America," the man who procured the Plymouth Company its charter.

Emerson's Moody heritage doubtless was in the minds of some who saw in every independent stand that he took new proof of his derangement. In such circumstances it was easy to overlook the streak of genius that also came with the Moody strain.

THE HASKINSES

Through his mother, Emerson was also a Haskins. Though in the Haskins line no procession of ministers wended its way back into the murky recesses of history, the Haskins heritage made a contribution to shaping the man Ralph Waldo Emerson became.

Of the five Emerson brothers who lived to maturity, Waldo was said to resemble his mother most. According to Daniel Chester French, Emerson's face, viewed from the left, was that of a businessman. That the Emerson genes could have bestowed a businessman profile is improbable right to the brink of absurdity. Joseph Emerson of Malden, Emerson's great-grandfather, had even prayed that none of his descendants would know prosperity. God seems to have answered his prayers even unto Waldo's generation because, however much Waldo looked like a businessman, he had a sorry head for figures and felt unclean when he had to dispute money matters with others. Grandfather Haskins, on the other hand, had parlayed a barrel-making business into a prosperous career as a distiller. That was a dollars-and-cents accomplishment. But much more than a talent for success in the marketplace came with Emerson's Haskins ties.

Not until John Haskins began to make his way in the world was the name Haskins of any consequence in Boston. The road had not been easy. John's father, a cooper, came to Boston — either from England or Virginia, no one could recall — in the early years of the eighteenth century. At sixteen months John had been stricken with smallpox. His death assumed, his body was placed with that of his father, who had succumbed to the same illness in the same hour. But air from an open window revived him. An only child, he stayed with his mother till he was eighteen, when she married another cooper. He then ran off to sea, something he had been longing to do. As a crewman aboard a privateer, he was twice captured, first by the Spaniards, then by the French, who were at war with England. Rescued by an American ship, he arrived home, purged of his hankering for the sea. He went peacefully to work for his stepfather, Tom Hake, who liked him well enough to leave him his business when he died in 1755. A fling as a privateersman was not uncommon for an adventurous youth in those days; both Hawthorne and Thoreau had grandfathers who took a turn at it. The experience ushered John Haskins into a robust manhood. He emerged from his maritime interlude a man of above-average height, build, and physical strength, with a marked military carriage, a welcome supplement to the Emerson genes. The Emersons, mostly scholarly shut-ins, were noted for their puny physiques.

In 1752, when he was twenty-three, John married Hannah Upham of Malden. The officiating minister was Joseph Emerson, who was not destined to know that, forty-four years thence, a daughter born of this marriage would marry his grandson William and produce an heir who would keep the Emerson name in permanent remembrance.[8]

John Haskins was not marrying into money, as is the wont of ambitious young men eager to accelerate attainment of their material goals. He even paid for Hannah's wedding dress. But he can never have regretted his bargain, since Hannah was a wife almost ideally suited to him.

Hannah's history was similar to John's. When she was four, a pernicious throat infection, probably diphtheria, killed her father and her three siblings and brought her to the point of death. As an only child, providentially spared, she was schooled in her upbringing to be virtuous and devout. Accounts of her calm and happy temperament and amiable disposition tally so exactly with those descriptions that have come down to us of her daughter Ruth, Emerson's mother, and Ruth's eight sisters that we must surmise that her virtues were not exaggerated and that her children learned from them. Tradition also assigns Hannah "well balanced powers of mind." When death sundered a marriage that lasted nearly sixty-three years, her son Ralph noted in his journal: "No couple ever lived more happily together during their married life." That could not always have been easy because Hannah bore John sixteen children, of whom Ruth was the tenth.

The Uphams were the kind of family Joseph Emerson could relate to — pious, sensible, unpretentious. They were also a family that had come to distinction in former times, thus giving Ruth Haskins a social heritage comparable to that enjoyed by the Emersons. Hannah was descended from a much-respected *Mayflower* Pilgrim, John Howland; from Captain John Waite, Speaker of the House of Deputies; and from a Colonial hero, Lieutenant Phineas Upham, slain in the great swamp fight with the Narragansetts. She also was a collateral descendant of both the first and fourth presidents of Harvard, Henry Dunster and Urian Oakes.[9]

Given such antecedents, it is not surprising that, added to her other qualities, Hannah Haskins was tenacious. Like her husband, she had been raised a Congregationalist. But John's father had been an Anglican, and soon after his marriage John affiliated with King's Chapel, then still under the jurisdiction of the Church of England. Hannah held fast to her established mode of worship. If this split in their theological preferences was a bone of contention between them, it was not a much-worried bone. "There are many ways to Heaven," John said, "but the Episcopal church is the turnpike road." That was about as intimidating as he ever got — scarcely grounds for open strife.

John Haskins let his children decide for themselves which church they would attend. From the mansion John built on Rainsford's Lane, the family would set out together for the Sabbath services. John was a notable spectacle, cocked hat on his head, red cloak sweeping behind, marching along the street with his army of children trooping after him. Until the end of his days, perhaps as a way of asserting his Royalist leanings, John dressed thus in the fashion of pre-Revolutionary times. At the corner of Winter and Marlborough (the future Washington Street), Hannah swerved off to the New South with her contingent while John struck onward to Trinity with his, gratified that all the children had at least experienced Anglican baptism.

Ruth elected to follow her father's faith, yet unlike her mother, she adopted her husband's religion. She continued to read the Book of Common Prayer, however, and her son Waldo never doubted that, in her heart, she stayed an Anglican. Emerson on several occasions owned that he was stirred by the poetic appeal of Roman Catholic services, even to the point of saying that if a Catholic cathedral stood in Concord he would probably frequent it. The sensate spirit of his cockatoo grandfather evidently slumbered in his nature.

That pageantry was not the chief appeal Anglicanism had for John Haskins is evident in the fierce rearguard action he staged when King's Chapel shifted to a Unitarian posture and adapted the Book of Common Prayer accordingly. On that occasion John prepared a sixteen-page document in which he argued strenuously in support of the Trinitarian position and against adoption of the changes, which, even so, won by a vote of twenty yeas to seven nays.[10]

Somewhere along in midlife John Haskins had made a career change and left the trade of cooper to become a distiller. This new career brought increased prosperity with it, and an elevated life-style. To keep himself humble, however, John made it his practice to have two or three paupers in to dine with him once a year.

John did not find it patronizing that Boston spoke of him as "Honest John," and, indeed, could not ascribe that soubriquet exclusively to business dealings. He was sought out for his advice, and once, though rather against his inclinations, dug a hole in his cellar and hid there for a friend, who said he trusted him sooner than he would a bank, a large sum of money over which he placed a hogshead filled with water. His common sense was accompanied by a pithy wisdom of homely aphoristic substance, which often passed into common currency, another quality his celebrated grandson was to share with him.

Ralph Waldo was eleven when John Haskins died at eighty-six. By then William Emerson was almost four years dead. Ralph was but one of forty-six grandchildren John left behind, but he cared enough to mark "the calm exit of the aged saint" with a verse tribute.[11] It held mostly to the conventional pietism of the day but conveyed the impression that Emerson was fond of his grandsire. Much later, he would remember telling John that he was enrolled in school and receiving, in return, a pat on the head and an encouraging, "That's clever. That's clever," a scene which suggests almost a parody of old age but one that Emerson recalled with satisfaction.[12]

John Haskins did not forget what it was like to be a child. David Haskins, another grandson who went into the church — as an Episcopal minister — recorded that once, while the family was gathered at dinner, a fire broke out in a neighboring building. John's sons sprang from their chairs in excitement. John stayed them with his hand for the grace with which he concluded meals. "The Lord be praised for all his mercies," he said, lids lowered in solemn benediction. Then they fluttered open. "Now, boys, run!"[13] he urged.

The remains of John Haskins and those of Hannah, who survived him by five years, dying also at eighty-six, were buried in the family tomb beneath Trinity Church.[14] The last of John's daughters died in 1854, at Rainsford's Lane. Thereupon the house was sold. In 1862 it was razed and a school built upon the site.

THE BULKELEYS

In contrast to the Haskins lineage Emerson found in the records of his Bulkeley progenitors much mainline history and a scheme of events that made him seem, in some particulars, a true continuator of Bulkeley traditions.

In 1634, Peter Bulkeley, the rector of Odell in Bedfordshire, was silenced when he acknowledged to Archbishop Laud's vicar general that he neither made the sign of the cross in baptism nor wore a surplice when he preached. These were calculated gestures attesting sympathy with Puritan reforms and Bulkeley knew that in pursuing them he was casting his lot openly with the rebel party. But Peter, a stern man who asked much of himself as well as of his parishioners, probably already looked to his next move even before he invited the consequences of his apostasy. He was no obscure personage. The Bulkeleys were descended from that noble Cheshire family which traced back to Robert Bulkeley, one of the barons who compelled King John to put his name to the Magna Carta. Peter had been a Fellow at St. John's College, Cambridge, and succeeded to his father's parish in 1620 after assisting him for ten years. His first wife was Jane Alleyn, daughter of a baronet and aunt of Oliver St. John, who was to become King Charles's solicitor general and, subsequent to that, chief justice of the Common Pleas. One of his descendants was the brilliant Henry St. John, Viscount Bolingbroke, secretary of state under Queen Anne and man of letters, a fact that gives Ralph Waldo Emerson blood ties with an illustrious figure in English literature.

Peter Bulkeley's second wife, Grace Chetwood, also was the daughter of a baronet, Sir Richard Chetwood. By Jane, Peter had nine sons and two daughters. To this number Grace added another four children. Peter had land and means to go with his heritage and his needs. Some of his sons followed in the family tradition. Edward, for example, went to Cambridge and afterward took Holy Orders. He seems, however, to have supported his father in his nonconformist views, arriving in Boston to view prospects there in 1634, a year before Peter himself arrived. Peter made proper use of that year, having quietly sold off his possessions. He thus had some six thousand pounds to take with him to America, a fortune which gave assurances of security to the wide-eyed brood that accompanied him.[15]

Peter came to America not solely to pursue religious freedom. With his heritage, his wealth, and his ready-made following of family, he was domain-minded and soon set his eyes on a wilderness site — a six-mile tract bordering the Musketaquid River, west of Boston, set apart by the Great and General Court in the year of Peter's arrival. There he came with his family, and eleven other families, to be co-founder, along with John Jones, another Cambridge man, of the town they called Concord, a name signifying the peace they expected to find in the wilderness. On 6 April 1637 both men were ordained as ministers of the new parish — the colony's twelfth church — Jones as pastor, Bulkeley, who had brought with him his scholar's library, as teacher. No representatives of the Boston church attended the ordination nor did the governor. As preachers, Jones and Bulkeley were adjudged hairsplitters. Peter was, in fact, a severe man, even by Puritan standards, an autocrat who out-rounded other Roundheads with his close-cropped hair and plain dress, and rebuked them with his exactness of conscience and incessant catechizing. The local Indians caught his mode when they characterized him, without conscious malice, as "the Big Pray."[16] But Peter, at Concord, saw to his temporal as well as his eternal needs. This first inland settlement on the northeastern seaboard was funded chiefly with his money. Accordingly he reserved for himself the gristmill rights in that area foreseeably the center of the town, and saw to it, after a meeting house was built, that the first house built was for his occupancy. The other settlers, meantime, had to make do with earthen shelters dug into the ridge that ran along the edge of the settlement.[17]

Bulkeley's firmness was attested to in the early days of his arrival in the colony when he served as co-moderator, with Thomas Hooker (founder of Connecticut), of the synod appointed to rule on the teachings of Anne Hutchinson. Her insistence on the real presence of the Holy Spirit in true believers was a doctrine much more audacious then than it would be when reintroduced by Ralph Waldo Emerson two hundred years later. Since Hutchinson's teachings would set men free not merely from all rites and formulas but from Holy Writ itself, she had to be quashed if the Bible Commonwealth was to endure. Bulkeley's synod banished the heretic and her followers to Rhode Island. Anne and a number of her followers later were slaughtered in the forest by Indians, which, to those who condemned her, seemed a handsome vindication of their judgment.

In 1646, Bulkeley published a collection of his sermons, *The Gospel-covenant; or the Covenant of Grace Opened,* in which he affirmed his belief in unconditional election. Of more interest is Peter's description of Concord as a place ''at the end of the earth,'' or otherwise as ''a solitary desart place.''[18] An estate in New England was not an estate in Bedfordshire and Bulkeley had come to know the difference. For Puritans, Bulkeley's book was absorbing reading. Published in London, it had a second edition. In the next century, after reading it, Ezra Stiles, president of Yale, designated its author as ''one of the three or four most valuable ministers in the early days of the colony.''[19]

In 1644, John Jones, falling out with Bulkeley, abandoned Concord to him and departed for Fairfield, Connecticut, with one-seventh of the town's population. With him went two of Bulkeley's sons, Daniel, who was land-hungry, and Thomas, recently married to Jones's daughter, Sarah. Concord, in those early times, appears to have had some difficulty in living up to its name. Bulkeley was ten years older than Jones. He was rich. Jones was poor. And, because of his aristocratic connections, in matters of difference Bulkeley was deferred to by the Boston authorities. Jones withdrew to Connecticut to make a fresh start in a place where the odds would be more in his favor.[20] A ''solitary desart place'' did not guarantee that men would be saints.

As minister and as autocrat, Peter Bulkeley reigned over Concord until his death in 1659, when, his wishes for a dynasty being fulfilled, his son Edward, then forty-five, succeeded him. Peter's estate by then had shrunk to thirteen hundred pounds but he had still made his mark on the colony. His son John was in Harvard's first graduating class. In 1645 John deeded Harvard an acre and a half of land that today includes that portion of the Harvard Yard where stand the Widener and Houghton libraries and Wigglesworth Hall.[21] Peter himself, prior to his death, gave Harvard much of his valuable library. Edward had no need of it. He was not the scholar his father was. In fact, in 1668, John Hoar of Concord was fined ten pounds for regaling topers at a local tavern with the observation that Edward's blessing, given on dismissing the meeting-house assembly, came to no more than ''vain babbling.''[22] Life in the wilderness was not designed to perpetuate the august heritage that was Peter Bulkeley's pride. After a few generations his descendants in Concord signed their names with *X*'s. His theological integrity was no better maintained. Edward's son Peter fell under censure in 1685 for toadying to the Anglican Governor Andros, as a member of his Council.

When Ralph Waldo Emerson settled in Concord in 1835, exactly two hundred years after Peter Bulkeley's arrival in America, he must have grimaced to realize he was sprung from the loins of the man who had sent off to her death in the wilderness "the sainted Anne Hutchinson," the true precursor of New England transcendentalism. But Aunt Mary knew her facts. Reverend Joseph Emerson of Mendon, grandfather of Ralph Waldo's great-grandfather Joseph, had taken for his second wife Elizabeth Bulkeley, daughter of "vain babbling" Edward. Ralph Waldo was descended from their son Edward.[23] With this marriage there came into the Emerson line a surge of energy not apparent before.

Could I only have begun with the same fire which I had on the last day, I should have done something.

23. The Action at the North Bridge

*I*N 1843, shortly after he moved into Concord's Old Manse with his bride, Nathaniel Hawthorne made an inventory of the garret and found there, in "the Saint's Chamber," so called because it had served as an oratory and study for clergy who had lived in the Manse in times past, "a tattered and shrivelled roll of canvass."[1] It proved to be a portrait of a clergyman, wig, band, gown, and Bible attesting his position in the eighteenth-century world he had inhabited, his stern eye vouching for an intimidating authority that, in Hawthorne's day, aspiring clergymen sensibly disavowed. Not reconciled to denying Gothic attributes to this personage, Hawthorne wondered if he was now face to face with the ghost who haunted the Manse. Although he realized the subject of the portrait was the Reverend Daniel Bliss, great-grandfather of Ralph Waldo Emerson, that knowledge did not disconcert him. Bliss had been a man of controversy in his time, and even his grandson William, Ralph Waldo's father, had scoffed at him as a would-be revivalist whose aspirations had exceeded his attainments.

THE BLISSES

Of the one hundred and seventy-nine years during which Emerson's kinsmen ministered to the people of Concord, Bliss's allotment had been twenty-six years. He first mounted his pulpit in 1738, and held it until 1764, when, at fifty, he died.

Bliss had come to Concord from Yale, a crusading evangelist re-

sponsive to that spiritual crusade then bringing to New England a
new birth of faith — the Great Awakening. In 1741 he brought George
Whitefield, the most spectacular evangelist of his era, to Concord for
a service so enthusiastically anticipated it had to be scheduled as an
outdoor event to accommodate all those who wanted to attend. When
he ended his sermon, Whitefield turned to the rapt Daniel Bliss, and
pronounced him "a child of God." That night, Whitefield reported
later, "Brother Bliss broke into floods of tears and we had a sweet
refreshing in our way to the heavenly Canaan."[2]

Bliss's predecessor, John Whiting, had been deposed for neglecting
his duties and, while village wags declared that they were "transported to bliss" by the change, Daniel's enthusiasm was not unanimously approved of. In fact, a third of the congregation withdrew to
form a second church under Whiting's leadership, while Bliss, rebuked by a council of elders culled from fourteen churches, was made
to promise to stop stirring things up in other towns and to avoid
preaching as his impulses dictated. Indeed, though his great-grandson
would have deplored his overwrought style of preaching, its substance
seems an interesting anticipation of Emerson's own controversial endorsement of the moral sentiment as the true guide to faith.[3]

The schism in Bliss's parish ended, thirteen years into his pastorate,
only after the death of Whiting. The last stage of that pastorate was,
for Bliss, a personal triumph. Whitefield came again and preached on
Sunday, 11 March 1764. His sermon was given in the afternoon. Daniel had preached that morning. The general feeling was that Daniel
outdid the visitor. Whitefield thought so, too. "If I studied my whole
life," he said, "I could not have produced such a sermon."[4] Perhaps
he was being magnanimous. Already terminally ill, Bliss would be dead
in a few weeks. That sermon was his last.

Bliss left a wife and seven children. Phebe, eldest of his three
daughters, as the wife of William Emerson, her father's successor, was,
of course, Ralph Waldo's grandmother. Another sister married Isaac
Hoar, giving the Emersons blood ties with the Hoar family, to which
Ralph Waldo also would be bound by great affection.

Daniel Bliss, Jr., who had been on the staff of the Tory governor,
Thomas Hutchinson, gave aid to the British on the eve of the Revolution, supplying information concerning the collection of arms at Concord. William Emerson complained darkly, "Verily our enemies are
of our own household."[5] William was prone to dramatize things but,
in this instance, had spoken the truth. Soon after the battle of Concord, Daniel took flight. There was no future reconciliation.

Phebe Walker Bliss, wife of Pastor Bliss, was reputed to be a marvel
of faith who "never fell before affliction." Even as her husband lay
dead in her house, she attended church services as usual. On that ac-

count Phebe, her daughter and namesake, tasked her with lack of feeling only to perceive that her mother was not accessible to her censure but "rapt in another world."[6] When Ralph Waldo's sister, Mary Caroline, died in 1814, Ralph, then eleven, conducted family worship with grave and sweet composure, to some an indication of specific debts to his Bliss heritage.

"Yet not for all his faith can see / Would I that cowlèd churchman be," wrote Emerson in the opening stanza of "The Problem." With equal vehemence, no doubt, he would have insisted that he had no wish to be the bewigged, begowned, stern cleric whose likeness Nathaniel Hawthorne found rolled and shriveled in the Saint's Chamber at the Old Manse. Apparently even Bliss's daughter Phebe, who, for nearly sixty years had called the Manse home, had not seen fit to preserve and exhibit this icon. Yet Daniel Bliss's theological insurrection at Concord and his eventual triumph there were an early enactment of the larger role his descendant would assume while not a village merely but the whole world looked on.[7]

THE EMERSONS

Emerson's preparation for writing, in 1835, his bicentennial address on the founding of Concord, an event that conveniently came in the same year in which the sixtieth anniversary of the Concord fight was being observed, gave him a new perspective on his ancestors. It also gave him an enigmatic tradition to ponder, in reaction to which his own integrity was deepened.

In 1827, Ezra Ripley, then seventy-six, had published *A History of the Fight at Concord.* He had been provoked to write his book by a pamphlet, *The History of the Battle of Lexington,* written by a Major Phinney, which alleged that Lexington, not Concord, offered the British the first armed resistance on 19 April 1775, to begin the War of Independence.[8] Now, at eighty-four, the resolute Ripley took Emerson around town so that he might speak personally with a few ancients who were actual survivors of the battle. Emerson was dismayed at Dr. Ripley's methods of interrogation:

It is affecting to see the old man T[haddeus] Blood's memory taxed for facts occurring 60 years ago at Concord fight. "It is hard to bring them up," he says, "the truth never will be known." The Doctor like a keen hunter unrelenting follows him up & down barricading him with questions. Yet cares little for the facts the man can tell, but much for the confirmation of the printed History.[9]

Ripley's persistence was meant to call forth from Blood an account of heroism. So far as Emerson could determine, Blood's impression plainly was that there was no great courage exhibited, except by a few.[10]

According to Emerson family lore, William Emerson, Emerson's grandfather, had been a glorious patriot. He had played a leading role in the battle of Concord, as was appropriate since it was fought on the margin of his farm, and afterward had gone off to Fort Ticonderoga as an army chaplain, only to die a short while later of cholera or typhoid. Curiously, however, he was dead fifty years before the town of Concord, whose pastor he had been, saw fit to pay his memory tribute. That was in 1826. Thus even his widow, who died in 1825, having survived her husband for forty-nine years, did not live to see his name exalted in Concord. The eventual memorial was a monument erected in the Hill Burying Ground. The inscription on it read: "Enthusiastic, eloquent, affectionate and pious / He loved his family, his people, his God, / and his country. / And the last he yielded / The cheerful sacrifice / of his life." It says nothing to link him to the battle of Concord, nor did the spurned epitaph proposed at that time by his daughter, Mary Moody Emerson, although it claimed, imprecisely, that he "died 1776, in the Army where he was appointed Chaplain."[11]

Emerson himself, in reporting William's role in the Revolution, propounded a modest statement:

> He felt so deeply the cause of the Colonies that he made it the subject of his preaching and prayers and is said to have inspired many of his people with his own enthusiasm. I have found . . . an almanack of April, 1775 in which at the close of the month he writes, "This month remarkable for the greatest events of the present age."[12]

To this disclosure Emerson added a qualifying observation: "He at least saw the important consequences of the 19th," quite as though William had missed out altogether on some other aspect of the event. Emerson had good grounds for implying such a possibility.

William Emerson was the twelfth child in a family of thirteen. His father, Joseph Emerson of Malden, pursued his ministerial calling with relentless dedication and expected his sons, three of whom became ministers, to be as scholarly as he was. In evidence of this fact Mary Moody Emerson offered this anecdote: "When William was cocking hay one afternoon his father looked out the window and called, 'Billy! Billy! that is a waste of your precious time. Go back to your books!' but his mother said, 'No, it does him good to work a little, he has books enough.'"[13] Aunt Mary's conclusion was: "If it had not been for my grandmother, my father [William] would have been killed, perhaps by confinement, for his father thought he ought never to leave his lessons."[14]

When William arrived at Harvard, he broke loose. On one occasion he was fined ten shillings for throwing bricks, sticks, ashes, and such in at the door of the Hebrew School.[15] An entry made in the diary of Joseph Lee of Concord, on the day William was ordained minister of Concord, 1 January 1766, suggests that William's transgressions at Harvard brought him an unwelcome reputation. From a neighboring clergyman, Mr. Clark of Lexington, Lee heard: "I know that there is a young Emerson has been at College but have not heard that he has ever thought of preaching, for he is a wild chap." Lee talked with Emerson himself and recorded that William allowed "that he had fooled away his time and that he was very much to blame and ought to go back to College and study divinity for two years before he undertook to supply a pulpit in any place." So far as Lee could make out, the best that could be said for this onetime rapscallion was that "Billy Emerson was a converted man."[16]

Lee was not the only man to question William's fitness for the office he assumed. In his own diary that day, William, without amplification, noted: "In ye Morning read a Confession of Faith, to ye satisfaction of ye whole Council, excepting Mr. Sherman of Bedford who saw reasons best known to himself, to make further interrogations, to ye great Disturbance of ye Council."[17] Nathaniel Sherman, the minister at adjacent Bedford (a part of Concord till 1729), was the brother of Roger Sherman, a signer of the Declaration of Independence, who numbered among his grandchildren Ralph Waldo Emerson's cherished friends Elizabeth, Ebenezer Rockwood, and George Frisbee Hoar.

In fairness to William, he was then about to marry Phebe, daughter of his predecessor, Daniel Bliss. The ill will that arose from the doctrinal controversy that had occurred during Bliss's pastorate was not yet wholly dissipated. William's alliance with the Bliss family made him heir to that ill will. Even after he was settled as pastor, it hung on. Three years afterward, Lee, petitioning for his removal, stated: "I complain of the Rev'd. Pastor many Imprudences, gross Blunders to say no worse and of his Breach of Promise by all which I apprehend he has rendered himself unworthy of the Sacred Character of a Minister of Jesus Christ."[18] Since by then William had married, sired two children, and begun building, with generous help from the parish, his three-story manse by the North Bridge, one can only assume that Lee's objections to him concerned not frivolous behavior but the conduct of his office. Shattuck speaks of William's "facetious" conversation, his "evangelical" doctrine, "fervency of spirit," and "ardent zeal." For the rigidly orthodox provocation enough could be found here. Yet William was pledged firmly to the short catechism and readily joined his parishioners in affirming anew his faith in the Covenant of Grace. To all but the most exacting he should have seemed resolutely orthodox.[19]

The ten years of William's pastorate led up to and into the War of Independence. Much of his fervency and zeal he channeled into that cause. In January 1775, after hearing him preach as chaplain of the Provincial Congress, sixty men enlisted in the Minutemen. On 13 March he preached to good effect at a general review of the militia companies of Concord, Lincoln, and Acton. On that occasion William's auditors heard him declare:

> The Man who enters the Lists without a thought of his Duty
> and with no other view but to make a pompous Appearance, that
> he have an Opportunity to look big, and to stalk proudly in
> Armor, will doubtless act the cowardly Part when he sees the
> Enemy approaching, and Danger and Death flying thick around
> him. These add not to the Safety or Defense of a people but may
> be the unhappy Cause of intimidating the Spirits of other Men,
> and making them quit their Posts, to their unspeakable Shame and
> everlasting Infamy![20]

William seems to have taken the true measure of such personages. Thus is his own behavior on the day of the Concord battle all the more inexplicable. On that day, as the British drew near Concord, the Minutemen and the alarm companies were formed into squads on the village Common. There, William, musket in hand, cartouche box slung from his shoulder, strutted back and forth in front of them, calling out, "Let us stand our ground! If we die, let us die here!" Even as he rallied the squads, he had an encouraging word for the individual soldier, too. Sensing the apprehensions of young Harry Gould, he tossed him a bracing word as he passed along the line. "Stand your ground, Harry! Your cause is just, and God will bless you."[21]

For the Minutemen to have acted on Emerson's impetuous advice would have been foolhardy. Neither in numbers nor in weaponry nor in discipline were they the match of the advancing British. Fortunately, Emerson was overruled by the common sense of Colonel Eleazer Brooks of Lincoln, a man of experience and good judgment, who, mindful that they had been formed as a defensive force only, counseled the men *not* to stand their ground but to withdraw toward the bridge spanning the Concord River, a mile north of the Common.[22] The realization that Brooks was right or the more startling realization that, if a battle was going to take place it was going to happen on his own farm beside which the approach to the bridge lay, may have given William Emerson a change of heart. Whatever the reason, as the colonists withdrew and the rising sound of British drums and fifes attested their approach, William dropped out of the ranks and hurried into his manse. After all, as a clergyman he was not expected to fire a weapon. And who could have foreseen that weapons might be fired within range of his wife and four babes? Furthermore, someone had come to tell him that his wife had fainted from fright when their black field hand, ax in hand, had rushed into her room exclaiming, ''The Red Coats have come!''[23]

Phebe's granddaughter, Sarah Ripley Ansley, no kin of William's, protested vehemently, in later years, when Concord scoffers said that William cowered in his house while the battle was under way. She had always heard, she insisted, that William was outside the whole time. Another granddaughter, a daughter of Samuel Ripley (likewise no kin of William's), was even more certain of William's whereabouts: ''My Father said that his mother sat at the window all day long on the 19th of April, wondering where her husband was. . . . She said that he was out cheering on his parishioners and exhorting them, but could not fight because he was a minister.''[24] The next generation of Ripleys was even more sure of things. As the memories of the veterans faded, the memories of the coming generations sharpened. At ninety, Phebe Ripley Chamberlin wrote:

> It is a great mistake that our grandfather [thus she annexed William as her blood kin] remained in the house. Grandmamma told me herself that she felt hurt because he did not stay more with her, and once when he was feeding the women and children with bread and cheese she knocked on the window and said to him that she thought she needed him as much as the others. . . . Then again Grandmamma said that she sat by the window and saw the battle at the bridge, and Grandfather was surely with them there for he had been holding back our men from firing. . . . I do think it is too bad that anyone should get up a story that our Grandfather was wanting in courage or loyalty.[25]

Three weeks after the battle, W. Gordon, a minister from Roxbury, visited Concord and talked with William and came away believing that William ''went near enough to see it and was nearer the Regulars than the killed.'' Yet, somewhat ambiguously, he added: ''He [William] was very uneasy till he found that the fire was returned, and continued till the Regulars were driven off.''[26] At that stage, William could again have taken refuge in his house.

When Nathaniel Hawthorne wrote of the Old Manse, it never occurred to him that William Emerson may have gone out into the thick of the battle. Writing in the study, the windows of which best commanded a view of the battle site, Hawthorne said, repeating what he had been told:

It was at this window that the clergyman, who then dwelt in the Manse, stood watching the outbreak of a long and deadly struggle between two nations; he saw the irregular array of his parishioners on the farther side of the river, and the glittering line of the British, on the hither bank. He awaited, in an agony of suspense, the rattle of the musketry. It came — and there needed but a gentle wind to sweep the battle-smoke around this quiet house.[27]

Certainly, no one had more opportunity than Dr. Ripley did to hear from Phebe's own lips a true account of what occurred. She was his wife for forty-five years and was never reluctant to enumerate to him the many virtues of his predecessor. It was the thoughtful and dutiful Ripley who successfully urged that the town erect the monument in William's memory. And if the inscription he wrote for it placed foremost William's enthusiasm and eloquence yet said nothing about heroism, then this must be as it was reported to him. It was Ripley who wrote a history of the battle, making out the best case he could for Concord men. That he knew otherwise, yet wrote as he did about William Emerson on that celebrated day, is unthinkable. His account of William's conduct must be accepted as an accurate transcript of the account given him by the woman who was William's wife on that day and Mrs. Ezra Ripley during most of the fifty years that followed. It was Ripley, too, who, on his own initiative deeded over a piece of his land — land that had once been William's — to assure that the site of the battle would be properly preserved and venerated. Yet, in his history of the battle Ripley unequivocally says, when mentioning the British force that came to the bridge: "Their conduct was observed by the Rev. Mr. Emerson and his family, who had witnessed the whole tragical scene from the windows of his house near the battleground."[28]

Possibly Phebe Bliss Emerson did sit at her window throughout the day, wondering where her husband had gone, but during most of that time she most assuredly was not watching a raging battle in progress. The encounter at the North Bridge took place between nine-thirty and ten in the morning. The main British force had remained back in the center of town. The men sent to the North Bridge were but a token unit. They fired on the Minutemen what was meant to be a warning round and the Minutemen returned their fire. Only then did the British, who numbered eighty or ninety troopers, realize they were up against the main body of the foe, a militia approaching four hundred and fifty men. They at once broke off the fight and began their retreat. The actual exchange of fire had lasted only a few moments.[29] And the Minutemen did not take off in pursuit of the retreating enemy since they were not eager to confront the main British force or to provoke them into setting the town ablaze. Only later, as the British, who were two divisions in strength, began to retreat, did the Minutemen pluck up their courage and begin their harassing action.

When Emerson was preparing his bicentennial address, he found, in a trunk in the Manse, William Emerson's own diary, in which he gave his account of the battle. Nowhere in this account does William speak of his own actions. It is written in such a way that no reader could guess that he himself had proposed that the Minutemen and alarm companies should make a stand in the town. Nor could any reader guess from William's account that he had not personally crossed the North Bridge with his parishioners to the ground where they made their stand. His "we" — "We retreated over the bridge"; "We received the fire of the enemy" — appears to include himself, when actually it refers to the armed patriots as a body.[30] Amelia Emerson writes:

> Many others have told further incidents of the fight. Strangely enough, those of the family who watched from the windows of the Manse apparently left no written detailed accounts of this, the most exciting day of their lives. William Emerson must have felt the full shock, surrounded as he was by his people, his small children crowding around, his anxious wife, and the British at his doorstep.[31]

To Ralph Waldo Emerson the reason why William's widow and the older children chose not to prepare eyewitness accounts of the battle was apparent. It was better to entrust memory of William's role to the ambivalent account he himself had prepared. (On the battle action, incidentally, he expended fewer than fifty words.)

After the Concord fight William Emerson passed a busy year, agitating repeatedly in neighboring towns to enlist support for the Sons of Liberty and encouraging the men in Cambridge being brought together to form the Continental Army. And, in what may be his truest claim to fame, when the army found it necessary to requisition the Harvard buildings as barracks, he successfully petitioned Harvard College to relocate in Concord.[32] This move, incidentally, brought Ezra Ripley, then a student at Harvard, to Concord. Thus, unawares, William found for Concord its future minister and, for his wife, her future husband.

To the British commander, General Gage, William Emerson was described as "A very bad subject of His Majesty."[33] Dislike of Emerson was not limited to the enemy, however. Caleb Gannett, a minister then serving as Purveyor for Harvard, deplored Emerson's commemorative sermon given at Concord on the first anniversary of the battle:

Mr. Emerson held an Exercise in ye Meeting House, P.M. being the Anniversary of the Concord Fight which was in mode like a Sunday's Exercise, except instead of a Sermón he attempted, as I suppose, an Oration consisting of an account of the Behavior of the Troops when here, and some general Observations to include Gratitude to Heaven — a flat, insipid thing, to say no more & performed in a miserable manner.[34]

William Emerson's oration, which is silent about his own role in the Concord battle, has been preserved. On the basis of its rhetorical content, it can scarcely have been more pleasing to his grandson Waldo than it was to the Reverend Mr. Gannett.

Although William's service as a chaplain to the Revolution was crowded into a brief span, it was long enough to bring him face to face, once more, with uncomfortable reality. The Concord Company set out for Fort Ticonderoga on about 12 August 1776. William, whose wife had given birth to their fifth child, Rebecca, on 3 August, set out after them on 16 August, putting up along the way at the homes of fellow ministers, deeming that more agreeable than such comforts as the military could offer.

No battle action was imminent at Fort Ticonderoga. The enemy was one hundred and thirty miles away. That was just as well. No rules of sanitation were in force at the fort, and disease had spread throughout the whole encampment with a resultant collapse of morale. As chaplain, William had access to the choicest cuts of contaminated meats and, by his own account, partook of them with avidity. He soon fell ill, but even before that happened, he wanted to be quit of the military. Of these circumstances Ralph Waldo wrote in 1835:

He was bitterly disappointed in finding that the best men at home became the worst in the camp, vied with each other in profanity, drunkenness & every vice, & degenerated as fast as the days succeeded each other & instead of much influence he found he had none. This so affected him that when he became sick with the prevalent distemper he insisted on taking a dismission not a furlough, & as he died on his return his family lost, it is said, a major's pension.[35]

By mid-September, William had procured his release and set out for home. He got as far as Gookin's Falls on Otter Creek, on the outskirts of Rutland, Vermont, when once again he had to seek a fellow minister's hospitality. A letter to his wife shows that he had a clear grasp of his own prospects though a somewhat idyllic one of hers: "Don't distrust God's making Provision for You. . . . I desire to leave You in

the Hands of a Covenant keeping God, and whether he sees fit to restore me to Health or not, I am willing to leave the Matter with him
who, does all Things well.''[36] Since Phebe did have much the same life
that she would have had had William lived, posterity has no cause to
begrudge him the consolations his faith gave him as his life neared its
end.

After William's death on 20 October 1776, his benefactor, Reverend
Benajah Roots, wrote that very day a consoling letter to William's
parish, saying all the appropriate things they would want to hear about
their late pastor's fortitude, composure, and resignation during his
last illness, and assuring them, in the stereotyped phrases common in
that day at places even more sophisticated than Otter Creek, that now
that William has taken ''his flight from this world of sin and sorrow
to the realms of light and regions of eternal day,'' he has ''Doubtless
. . . joined the glorious throng of Angels and is tuning harp with them
in the praise of the great Redeemer.''[37]

Roots buried William in the grave next to the one he himself would
occupy. Fifteen years later, Emerson's father, William, who was only
seven when his father resigned him to the care of Providence, went to
Otter Creek and dug up both ministers. Since he had no plans to return William's body to Concord, what he expected to gain from this
undertaking remains a mystery. His one observation concerning his
father's corpse was that he ''found the hair much grown.'' He shov-
eled the earth back and went away without leaving any record of the
gravesite, which was, most likely, in what is now the Pleasant Street
Cemetery in West Rutland.[38]

Emerson seems always to have held suspect loud displays of patriotic enthusiasm. On 10 December 1824 he wrote: ''When a whole
nation is roaring Patriotism at the top of its voice I am fain to explore
the cleanness of its hands & purity of its heart. I have generally found
the gravest & most useful citizens are not the easiest provoked to swell
the noise.''[39]

As Emerson made ready to begin his Divinity studies, he dropped a
hint, not untinged with irony, that he did not mean to take either his
father or his grandfather as his pattern. ''I inherit,'' he wrote, ''from
my sire . . . or his patriotic parent a passionate love for the strains of
eloquence. . . . What we ardently love we learn to imitate.'' He continued pointedly, however: ''The most prodigious genius, a seraph's
eloquence, will shamefully defeat its own end if it has not first won
the heart of the defender to the cause he defends.''[40] Long afterward
he would gloss this remark: ''Patriotism and truth require more than
fair words.''[41] Emerson loathed any inconsistency between what a man
preached and what he practiced and rigidly accepted the consequences
of his own actions, never flinching from any repercussions they brought.

''Always do what you are afraid to do,'' Aunt Mary had counseled him. In accepting that advice and acting on it, he had added a corollary: ''And once it is done do not relent in your courage.''[42]

The great moments of Emerson's life always would turn on his scrupulous adherence to this standard of conduct. Whether or not he believed that William came unfairly by his reputation for deeds of heroism, he acted always with painstaking scrupulosity to see to it that his own declared principles were carried into effect with a zeal no less eloquent than the rhetoric with which they had been proclaimed. That a legend of heroism in his family should, upon investigation, fade into insignificance bruised Emerson's psyche. His consequent determination that his own integrity should stand up to every assault, be it physical, psychological, or moral, gave rapture to his convictions and strength to his deeds.

24. Lidian
The Second Connection

$\mathcal{O}$ N 12 September 1835, Concord celebrated the two hundredth anniversary of its settling and Emerson, as the principal speaker of the day, delivered the oration he had had in preparation for many weeks. He was on the eve of his second marriage and this research probably helped convince him that Concord had claims on him that took precedence over the desire of his bride-to-be, Lydia Jackson, to live in her native Plymouth.

The previous January Emerson had written a proposal of marriage to Lydia, a woman to whom, hitherto, he had never conveyed, by any spoken or written word, even a hint of his affection. Despite that, in their restrained encounters they had conceived an affinity for each other. Emerson knew that he wanted her. Lydia knew she wanted him. Psychologically, actually, Lydia had been readying herself for this marriage for some time. She enjoyed her family and friends and her life at Plymouth, but she believed marriage a more blessed state than the single state, an outlook strengthened, no doubt, by her reading of Swedenborg, who looked upon the single state as pernicious. Lydia was older than Emerson by eight months and her hair was already touched with gray. At thirty-three she knew her prospects were fast diminishing. Quite apart from that, from an unlooked-for source she got helpful hints that Emerson was the man she was fated to marry. Emerson's courtship, as she saw it, took place on a spectral plane about which he knew nothing till after they were married.

In 1834, while visiting her sister, Lucy Brown, in Boston, Lydia, at a Sunday afternoon service at the Twelfth Congregational Church on

Chambers Street, caught her first glimpse of Emerson. He was supplying the pulpit for the pastor, Dr. Barrett. Her seat was beside the
pulpit, and her first impression of Emerson, seen from that angle, was
that he had an incredibly long neck, an illusion enhanced by his narrow, sloping shoulders. But, when he began to speak, his sermon so
absorbed her that she sat in an all but catatonic state of immobility,
which she became aware of only when the sermon ended and she felt
the strain of her rigidity. Reputedly, after this service Lydia told a
friend, "That man is certainly my predestined husband."[1]

The next time Lydia saw Emerson was on Chambers Street. The day
was a Sunday and he walked ahead of her, the wind whipping the
folds of his clerical gown. She was as enticed by this as Robert Herrick
was by the liquefaction of Julia's clothes. Before the year was out,
Emerson came twice to Plymouth to preach at the old First Church
for the pastor, Dr. James Kendall, leader of the local intelligentsia, a
visit arranged for by George Partridge Bradford, Sarah Ripley's
brother, who stood in relation to Emerson as a kind of step-uncle. In
those years Lydia was teaching Sunday school, and intimates who knew
her thinking, hearing Emerson, were struck by the unanimity of their
views. His second sermon so moved her that she slipped away after the
service before anyone could accost her and dispel her state of exaltation. At home, in her room, she could hug her mood to herself in utter
bliss. Lydia relished such moments. After her engagement to Emerson
she regularly got two letters a week from him and these she always
opened in her room and read over and over before sharing the contents
with the appreciative Lucy. That she needed this isolation at such times
was well understood by the members of her household, and her exclu-
siveness was respected. During the first decade of their marriage she
dealt with all her letters from Emerson in the same way; she would
lock herself in to read them, ashamed because she knew that Ruth
Emerson, who lived eighteen years under the same roof with them,
was eager to know what her son had written.

Lydia's first apparition happened at home, in the Winslow house,
the Plymouth mansion built in 1745 by Edward Winslow, the Tory
great-grandson of Governor Edward Winslow, and, since 1782, in the
hands of the Jacksons. Lydia's fine room looked toward the sea, near
enough for the site of Plymouth Rock to be in plain view. The wain-
scoting and mantelpieces throughout the house were said to have been
made in England, as was the exquisitely carved staircase. One day,
Lydia was ascending this staircase when she beheld a vision of herself,
in bridal attire, descending these same stairs in the company of Emerson, who was dressed as a bridegroom. Since the whole of her personal
acquaintance with Emerson up to this time consisted of having taken
tea with him, once or twice, at the home of mutual friends, the Rus-

sells, with whom Emerson stayed when in Plymouth, she did not know how to account for the intimacy of this vision. Her reaction on taking in this apparition of herself with Emerson bound and delivered into her hands, was to exclaim aloud, "I have not deserved this!"[2] She tried then to forget that it had happened.

Had Lydia known it, her situation somewhat paralleled that of Ellen Louisa Tucker, Emerson's first wife, as it had developed in their brief period of courtship. Like Ellen, she was the daughter of a deceased merchant. Like Ellen, she was tubercular. Like Ellen, she had encountered Emerson when he came to her town to preach. And, like Ellen, she first met Emerson on an almost formal basis, with no clear indicators that the bolt of love had struck. Emerson's adeptness at communicating through nonverbal gestures, always acute, seems never to have been more keen than when he was in love. With Lydia, this phase of his relationship with her, unbeknownst to her, seems to have spanned the whole of their period of courtship.

On a Sunday night, 25 January 1835, the feast day commemorating Saint Paul's conversion on beholding a vision of Christ, Lydia had a second vision. There was Emerson's face close to hers, beautiful to behold, which was no great wonder since she had already come to believe him "an angelic being." The vision stayed only for a moment before it vanished. After that no further visions were called for because the man himself was hers. His letter proposing marriage came the next day. She was certain always that his face had appeared to her at the very time he was penning his letter.[3] Had Lydia made her home in Salem instead of Plymouth, the possibility of witchcraft would have to be considered.

If the intensity of Emerson's thoughts as he wrote his letter did project an image of himself before Lydia's receptive eyes, we should not find that fact past belief. While much of the letter seeks to assure her that he finds her thinking so compatible to his own that there can be no question but that they suit one another, in its opening statements the letter contains thoughts unexpected in a proposal of marriage, especially from a widower as yet unreconciled to the loss of his first love.

"I obey my highest impulses in declaring to you the feeling of deep and tender respect with which you have inspired me," Emerson said. "I am rejoiced in my Reason as well as in my Understanding by finding an earnest and noble mind whose presence quickens in mine all that is good and shames and repels from me my own weakness."[4] In addressing someone made receptive to him by a spectral manifestation Emerson could not have begun better. Lydia would have been informed of the Coleridgian distinction between Reason and Understanding and would know that the impulses Emerson spoke of were promptings from the divine spirit within. A proposal formulated under such conditions could only be regarded as conceived under super-natural auspices. As such, its emissary might well be a vision of the ecstatic face of the petitioner.

From this portentous beginning, Emerson went on at once to let Lydia know that what he had to offer was not secondhand love given previously to another but something new and distinct. Simultaneously, he undertook to exonerate himself from the guilt that could come from betraying the memory of Ellen, and to offer Lydia a love he had no prior experience of, on a plane that their mutual grasp of ''everlasting principles,'' as disseminated by the moral sentiment, had made acces-sible to them. He explained: ''The strict limits of the intercourse I have enjoyed, have certainly not permitted the manifestation of that tenderness which is the first sentiment in the common kindness be-tween man and woman. But I am not less in love, after a new and higher way.'' Well might Lydia lock herself up with a letter that con-tained such sentences. Was Emerson merely referring to what had pre-viously passed between them? Or was he seeking in the alliance now desired a love that would carry them both to the highest spiritual plane? Or, incredible as it might seem, was he implying that his first marriage had never been consummated?

The reception of such a letter from a man whose very handwriting was unfamiliar to her, so that the surprise on reading it was total, gave Lydia a heady experience that she could never forget, especially since, hitherto, she had not faced the reality of her love for Emerson and, to the extent that she suspected it, never imagined that the attraction she felt Emerson would not only experience also but openly acknowledge. With bold purpose, which of itself attested to his superior harnessing of his intuitive powers, Emerson had dispensed with a tiresome inter-lude of maneuvering and brought the matter to the point of resolution.

Displaying an eagerness he seldom rose to, Emerson asked, ''Can I resist the impulse to beseech you to love me?'' He disclosed, too, that he had put pen to paper the instant he decided that he wanted her to be his wife. ''I had,'' he said, ''no leave to wait a day after my mind was made up.'' This phrase, at least, suggests that he weighed the mer-its of the move as any ordinary mortal might and had not been im-pelled by a divine impulse. Possibly it reveals not a retreat from the high terms in which he had framed his proposal but simply a break-down in rhetoric, betraying his state of excitement. Yet he did so far recollect himself as to suggest that Lydia appoint a time for him to come to Plymouth so that they might explore together and dispatch such problems as might seem obstacles to their union. At least he did not have to talk wills and insurance policies. Lydia's tuberculosis was arrested.

A curious interview followed. On Lydia's summons, Emerson came

at once, and, her eyes shut all the while, as though to avoid looking
into what she described as "the two blue flames" of her suitor's eyes,
she quizzed him closely, quite as she did her Sunday school students.
Emerson, afterward, drolly designated the encounter as "that catechism with closed eyes." Lydia explained that she fitted well into her
present pattern of life and would forsake it only if she was certain he
loved her and needed her enough to warrant the exchange. The occasion was not for her, however, a mere bartering session for advantageous terms. On receiving the proposal, she had wondered, after the
first shock had passed, how Emerson could "condescend to her."[5] She
wondered if she was deserving of him. She told him that housekeeping
did not stand high in her accomplishments and that she would not
shine in that role. Her inquisition was thorough but not petty. Proto-
col required that the small print be gone over. Yet, since they wanted
each other, none of the difficulties they discussed seemed of real consequence. When Lydia opened her eyes at last, it was to look upon the
man whose proposal of marriage she now had accepted.

Emerson had undertaken to procure himself a wife with about the
same matter-of-factness he was to show later in the year when it came
time to gather information for his bicentennial address. He let William know that his attachment for Lydia in no way approached the
intensity of his first love.[6] Lydia also was apprised of this fact. A
special part of him was forever Ellen's. Lydia would have to accept
that. She did, making no fuss about it, for they were living in times
when love's idyll more often than not was shattered by death's sudden
advent, leaving behind a chastened survivor who felt his or her world
never could be whole again.

Sam Staples, who in ten years' time would be Concord's jailer and
enter history when he jailed Thoreau for nonpayment of taxes, was
but a stable boy in 1835, and it was he who delivered to the Manse, on
the afternoon of Sunday, 13 September, the horse and chaise Emerson
would need to drive the sixty miles to Plymouth to bind himself to
Lydia with bonds far surer than any Staples later would command.
While the day was still bright, Emerson set off with someone's small
daughter who was to be his traveling companion as far as Boston. It
was then he noticed that the stable owner, caught up in the festive
mood of bicentennial events, had festooned the horse in new reins of
bright yellow webbing. "Why, child," Emerson exclaimed to his companion when he noticed them, "the Pilgrims of old Plymouth will think
we have stopped by the wayside and gathered golden-rods to weave
the reins with."[7] It was the season for goldenrod. He was jesting with
the child, of course, when he offered this explanation for getting rid
of his aureate reins. The truth was, they outraged his sense of circum-
spectness. Before leaving town, he paused at the stable to have them

changed, riding off this time with an inconspicuous green pair. If along the country ways, as he passed, spears of bright goldenrod bristled their insurgency at the sight of those somber green reins, it would not have mattered to Emerson. "Too much parade," he had afterward observed, when his bride put up white dimity window curtains, with matching fringe, on the four windows of their bedchamber, and she had had to take them down again. With her false curls she fared better. "Secrets of the toilette, secrets of the toilette! Best kept out of sight," Emerson chanted when he espied them on her dresser. But these, at least, he tolerated. After all, as his wife persuasively argued, "It is better taste to ornament the hair with hair, than with ribbon or flowers."[8]

Emerson spent Sunday night in Boston, then, next day, set off in storm and gale for Plymouth. The tarnished goldenrod must have drooped now, no longer in contention with the sobriety of the man with the green reins. As someone who was always thankful when bad weather "assisted his own retirement,"[9] Emerson would have seen this as his kind of day. He may even have paused somewhere on the road to indulge in last moments of introspection. He was expected at noon. He appeared at four. And no spectral Emerson came to help Lydia bridge the interval while she awaited the arrival of the man himself.

Daughter of a seafaring family, in a sailors' town, and like all good mariners a reader of omens, Lydia — henceforth called Lidian by her husband because he thought of her as "my Lydian Queen" and because he had an ear for rhythms, not of the sea but of prose — thought it a favorable augury when the skies cleared soon after Emerson's arrival.[10]

The thirty-two weeks that had gone by since they had announced their engagement had been filled with incidents and planning relating to their future even though Emerson had had to give the major portion of his time to preparing and delivering lectures, including, finally, his Concord address, which took an hour and forty-five minutes to deliver, vastly longer than the brief battle that sixty years earlier had made Concord famous. Over those weeks they had had, if not battles, then a series of skirmishes to fight, and from these Emerson had emerged the victor, setting the pattern that would keep Lidian in a defensive posture throughout the years of a marriage supposedly founded not on superficial sensuous attachment but on a solid union of mental sympathies and spiritual goals.

First came the dispute over where they should live — the first coastal town or the first inland town — Plymouth or Concord. Both had unassailable claims to respectability and, by tradition and sentiment, Lidian was linked to Plymouth by ties even stronger than those that bound Emerson to Concord. Though through her mother (who, like her father, died in 1818) she was descended from John Cotton, the seventeenth-century Boston divine, she was descended also from Josiah Winslow, brother of Governor Winslow, who arrived in Plymouth on the *White Angel* in 1631.[11] Her family had been permanently in Plymouth since that time. While Emerson had only lately realized that Concord had strong claims on him, he now could be adamant on the subject, writing to Lidian on 1 February:

> Under this morning's severe but beautiful light I thought dear friend that hardly should I get away from Concord. I must win you to love it. I am born a poet, of a low class without doubt yet a poet. That is my nature & vocation. . . . A sunset, a forest, a snow storm, a certain river-view, are more to me than many friends & do ordinarily divide my day with books. Wherever I go therefore I guard & study my rambling propensities with a care that is ridiculous to people, but to me is the care of my high calling. Now Concord is only one of a hundred towns in which I could find these necessary objects but Plymouth I fear is not one.[12]

A follow-up letter took a more insistent tone: "For me to go to Plymouth would be to cripple me of some important resources & not so far as I see to do any work I cannot do here."[13] Her capitulation predictably followed. For good measure, however, Emerson told her that there were people in Concord who needed the benefit of her spiritual insight. In point of fact, Charles Emerson was planning to marry Elizabeth Hoar and settle in Concord as a member of her father's law office and that, as Emerson later admitted to Lidian, was the strongest inducement he had for remaining there.

When Emerson married Ellen Tucker, he was unknown and only his family took an interest in his choice. His betrothal to Lidian intrigued many, for he had become a man to watch. The intellectual women of Boston assessed Lidian almost in relays. Elizabeth Peabody spent some time with her and, with a canniness that did her credit, found her "*unaffected* but *peculiar.*" Sarah Freeman Clarke found her "almost the equal of Emerson," and "a searing transcendentalist." Lydia Maria Child reported that Emerson was about to marry a Swedenborgian.[14] Sifting the rumors that came to her, Margaret Fuller, who had not yet met Emerson, concluded that he had chosen a wife who would make him happy. None of the appraisers, including Charles Emerson, accounted Lidian beautiful.

If Emerson's public was won over readily, his family took more convincing. Collectively they seemed to approve. Individually they had reservations. With his legacy from Ellen and his rising prospects, Emerson was now a catch. While Lidian was an heiress, also, in a modest way, her legacy came with strings attached to it. She felt an obligation toward her sister, Lucy, who, having been abandoned by her husband, Charles Brown, and left with two small children to support, was in narrow circumstances. Brown, in fact, had fled the country after plundering not only Lucy's inheritance but Lidian's as well, leaving the resources of both sisters much diminished. Magnanimously, Emerson agreed that the six hundred dollars that Lidian's decimated inheritance brought in annually should be assigned to Lucy. Lidian, then, unlike Ellen Tucker, was coming to Emerson without a dowry. Added to that, when she visited the Emersons in Concord, she struck them as high and mighty. Ruth Emerson professed to like her but sized up the match as "a Petruchio sort of affair." Emerson, when he invited Lidian to visit his mother at the Manse, had said affably, "You should come here & on the Battle-Ground stand the fire of her [Ruth's] catechism."[15] In saying that Emerson came closer to the facts than he realized. But if Ruth thought her son faced the task of subduing his new wife, she misjudged Lidian. She was in awe of Emerson and submissive to his will. On one point only she would not yield. Against his wishes she would call him only Mr. Emerson. All their married life she acknowledged him in public and private under no other appellation. Emerson's sober demeanor did not help matters. Even his mother, after his ordination, never again addressed him by name but as "my son."

Ultimately, Aunt Mary designated herself devil's advocate for the family. She visited Plymouth and did her best to make herself disagreeable to Lidian's relatives, partly because she liked to stir things up, partly to put matters to the test. Lidian's peculiarity standing her in good stead, she even believed that in Aunt Mary she had found "a congenial soul" with whom she had had "high and sweet communion."[16] Not at all. Emerson, possibly intervening because he knew the mischief Mary was capable of, had come to fetch her after a stay of two days. Mary confessed later to Lidian: "I spent the whole time we were riding to Concord in trying to make Waldo give you up, and ran you down in every way I could. I cannot bear to lose my nephews and did the same when Charles was engaged to Elizabeth." Aunt Mary accomplished more than she realized. Emerson's next letter to Lidian accused her of valuing herself too high and of presuming herself qualified to sit in judgment on others. Lidian was shattered. Yet she did not lose control. She discovered that Aunt Mary had unsettled Emerson by twisting some of her remarks out of context.[17] Had Lidian's brother, Dr. Charles Jackson, alleged discoverer of ether anesthesiology, made his find in that hour, Lidian might have been tempted to suggest that he put Aunt Mary under for a long stay.

Early in July, Emerson bought the seven-year-old Coolidge house, across from Revolutionary Ridge on the Lexington Road. It was large enough to accommodate his mother as well as Lidian and himself, but he proposed to add rooms so that Charles and Elizabeth could live there too. As the day of the wedding neared, Ruth and Charles helped set the house in order. Lidian contributed much of the furniture, chiefly household furnishings that Lucy sold to her for a thousand dollars. Lidian was to take occupancy of Coolidge Castle, as Emerson at first called it, sight unseen, for custom frowned on a bride's seeing her home before marriage. At least Lidian did not have to begin house-keeping under Ruth's experienced eye. When the bridal couple got home, Ruth would be in New York visiting William, a prudent mea-sure if the main bout between Katherine and Petruchio was in the offing.

There must have been a supper at the Winslow house after Emer-son's arrival but Lidian remembered only that Emerson and she talked in the parlor, from four o'clock on, so engrossed that the clock struck seven before Lidian realized she should long since have dressed for the ceremony, set for seven-thirty. George Bradford arrived to attend Emerson, and Dr. Kendall to marry them, and an assortment of Lidi-an's aunts, uncles, cousins, and friends to celebrate. Still Lidian did not come downstairs. Emerson at last went up to fetch her. They met on the landing, bride and bridegroom, and came down together and all at once Lidian realized that this was as it had been in the vision she had had the prior year.

Dr. Le Baron Russell (who later, with Emerson's connivance, would arrange for publication of Carlyle's *Sartor Resartus*) and his sister stood up for the couple. They became husband and wife, standing be-fore a fireplace adorned with Bible tiles. This must have suited Lidian, who never made a move without recourse to *Sortes Biblicae* and rarely failed to open the Bible to the thought she needed.[18]

Next morning, in the rented chaise, the bridal couple set out for Concord, whence they arrived at five or six in the afternoon. Whether the day was bright or dull no one remembered to note. Although Li-dian preferred dull days, chances are that she would have liked gol-denrod reins for the horse that drew her wedding coach, but she had no say. For Emerson the grand passion had come and gone. He was looking now toward a life where drama was enacted only in the soul — his, that is, not Lidian's.

Emerson paid $3,500 for Coolidge Castle, for which sum he got an Early Federal house with "the only good cellar that had then been built in Concord," a barn, and "two acres six rods of land." Although it stood "in low land . . . on the skirt of the village," the soil was well drained and the mile-long southward slope of opposite tableland gave the spot milder weather in winter than much of the rest of Concord experienced.[19] Though much has been made of the advantage the scholar had in not being located in the thick of the village, the Emersons were not isolated from others. Their house lay along the main stagecoach route, and the East Primary School stood just fifty paces from Emerson's study. During both the morning and afternoon recesses the shrill voices of young children playing in the road before his gate carried readily to his ears. And across the stream that ran behind his house stood the haven for the town poor, from which, frequently, were heard the appalling screams of Nancy Barron, a long-detained madwoman.[20]

The principal lack of the property was landscaping. In 1842, Emerson wrote: "I retreat & hide. . . . When I bought a house, the first thing I did was to plant trees, I could not conceal myself enough." Early in November 1836, a few days after his son Waldo was born, he went to the woods and dug up "six hemlock trees to plant in my yard, which may grow whilst my boy is sleeping." The next year, Uncle Samuel made him a gift of thirty-one pine and chestnut trees. This was the origin of the nine chestnut trees that later dominated his front yard and brought children to his door in September to ask if they might gather the gleaming mahogany chestnuts that had burst from their burrs. Today one chestnut tree stands there still.[21]

On 10 May 1838, Emerson wrote to Carlyle: "A week ago I set out on the west side of my house 40 young pine trees." Later he would report, with elation: "To the balsam, fir-tree by my study window come the ground squirrel, oriole, cedar-bird, common gross-bill, yellow-bird, goldfinch, cat bird, parti-colored warbler, and robin."[22]

As the tree-planting increased, so did Emerson's acreage, till soon the original two acres grew to nine. By the spring of 1847, Emerson had enough land to set out one hundred and twenty-eight fruit trees, chiefly pear and apple, but a few plum also.

On 6 April 1841, Emerson made an entry in his journal which suggested that his admiration for his home had a few qualifications:

> I am sometimes discontented with my house, because it lies on a
> dusty road with its sills and cellar almost in the water of the
> meadow. But when I creep out of it into the night or the morning
> and see what majestic and what tender beauties daily wrap me
> in their bosom, how near to me is every transcendent secret of
> Nature's love and religion, I see how indifferent it is where I eat
> and sleep.[23]

By September 1862 the compensations of Nature seem to have won out entirely: "When I bought my farm, I did not know what a bargain I had in the bluebirds, & bobolinks, & thrushes; as little did I know what sublime mornings sunsets I was buying." Two years later Emerson spoke of an ideal that his house met: "My idea of a home is a house in which each member of the family can on the instant kindle a fire in his or her private room. Otherwise their society is compulsory and wasteful to the individual."[24]

After some years, the Emersons, among themselves, referred to their house as "Bush," the name still used to designate it by their descendants in the present day.[25] In "Good-bye, Proud World!", written in the tranquil haven of Canterbury, Emerson had said:

> *O, when I am safe in my sylvan home,*
> *I tread on the pride of Greece and Rome;*
> *And when I am stretched beneath the pines,*
> *Where the evening star so holy shines,*
> *I laugh at the lore and the pride of man,*
> *At the sophist schools and the learned clan;*
> *For what are they all, in their high conceit,*
> *When man in the bush with God may meet?*[26]

The house Emerson brought Lidian to, where they would live together for the next forty-seven years, became that sylvan home where he confronted the life of the spirit, truly meriting the name of Bush.

While Lidian relinquished Plymouth, Plymouth never relinquished Lidian. Her daughter Ellen would write of her after her death:

> In her fifty-seven years of life in Concord she had never taken root there, she was always a sojourner, her home was Plymouth, a never-dying flame of love for Plymouth burned in her heart and burst forth in praises of its people. . . . She cared for some people in Concord, and always expected . . . to go herself to every town-occasion. Yet they were not something of which she was a part. She only came. . . . But of every movement of Plymouth, though only heard-of she felt herself a part. This was not willful, it was hardly conscious, purely natural.[27]

Aunt Mary sensed this long before others perceived it. "You know dear," she said to Lidian once, "that we think you are among us, but not of us."[28]

Through the years, as often as she could escape Concord, Lidian fled to Plymouth. Had she felt needed enough, however, she might not have seen herself as an exile. Not long after Waldo's birth, Emerson had begun to speak of Lidian as "mine Asia." Carpenter sees this term as a synonym for the female principle. Rusk relates it to Lidian's conservatism. Yet Emerson first used it in writing, on 8 January 1837, when Lidian interrupted him just as he began a journal entry. He disclosed: "I had come no farther in my query than this when mine Asia came in & wrote her name, her son's & her husband's, to warm my cold page." In this context it seems that he was using the word "Asia" in the same sense he used it later in his "Plato," where he defines "the Asia in his [Plato's] mind" as "the ocean of love and power, before form, before will, before knowledge, the Same, the Good, the One." In this context "mine Asia" identifies Lidian as the companion not of his intellect but of his heart. Thus, even as Emerson embraced her, he excluded Lidian from a part of his life. She was not to be the sharer in his ideas she had expected to be. This fact, too, was a source of her chronic state of unhappiness.[29]

Lidian's unrelenting sense of exile was, in itself, enough to account for the moods of melancholy that often took hold of her and for the illnesses she seldom was free of. Emerson's journals chronicle a loose history of these ailments and anxieties. In the early years of their marriage he may have assigned Lidian's complaints to the normal complications of childbearing. He did not consider the possibility that she felt she was competing for his attention against his work, his family, and his memories of Ellen. Shortly before the birth of her first daughter, in February 1839, Lidian told Emerson that she had dreamed the night before that she was with him in heaven and they had conferred with Ellen, who surrendered him to her and withdrew. "None but the noble dream such dreams," Emerson told her, yet with no thought of surrendering Ellen. Quite otherwise, he could write in his journal that he had had a "remembering talk with Lidian" about Ellen, which brought back "all that delicious relation." He also invited Lidian to read Ellen's treasured letters. If Lidian was not to hold Emerson's attention one way, she would have to get it by another.[30]

An 1837 account finds Emerson discussing Lidian's ailments as a predictable phenomenon:

> Lidian remembers the religious terrors of her childhood, when *Young* [i.e., his *Night Thoughts*], tinged her day & night thoughts, and the doubts of *Cowper* were her own; when every lightning seemed the beginning of conflagration, & every noise in the street the crack of doom. . . . These spiritual crises no doubt are periods of as certain occurrence in some form of agitation to every mind as dentition or puberty. Lidian was at that time alarmed by the lines on the gravestones.[31]

In 1843, her spirit lacerated by the death of her son Waldo the previous year, Lidian revealed the fuller depths of her melancholy. In his journal Emerson set down her words—"Dear husband, I wish I had never been born. I do not see how God can compensate me for the sorrow of existence.'' Additional words inscribed over these are illegible. An attempt was made to make the whole illegible by heavy inking out.[32]

The record continues. To William, Emerson wrote in June 1843: ''Lidian remains still quite a wreck of dyspepsia & debility and it is high time for her to get a great deal better.'' To Margaret Fuller he wrote on 27 November 1843: ''Lidian would most gladly have attended your class last Thursday, but she has been quite ill with cold, debility & other ails to which her flesh is much too much heir to.'' In April 1844 he told William that their mother was lonely because he was busy with his tasks and ''Lidian's feeble health & mind preoccupied with household cares.'' September 11, 1846, found him dealing with a melancholy letter Lidian had written him from Plymouth: ''I am sorry to see a little stroke of black in the end of your picture, as I thought Plymouth air & freedom & friends would scatter every cloud for three weeks at least.'' In 1848, while Emerson was in England, Lidian spent much of the winter in bed, the doctor coming daily. Her chest of select homeopathic remedies and a selection of four or five medical books that she diligently consulted for forty years were her chief solace. She spoke of her dependency on the ''poppy.''[33]

On 11 April 1850, Emerson wrote to Margaret Fuller: ''Lidian is never well, but perhaps not much more invalid than you knew her.'' To her brother's wife, Susan Jackson, he wrote on 22 November 1853, ''Lidian . . . is not very well today, but means to be well tomorrow.'' This facetious thrust now came regularly into Emerson's reports on Lidian's condition. He loathed illness and supposed that illness was her recreation. To Emily Drury he wrote on 18 June 1854: ''My poor broken-to-pieces wife made it impossible what else would have been a happiness, to ask you to come to us; & we have had lately no public house.'' To his sister-in-law, Susan Emerson, he wrote on 15 May 1855: ''Lidian has withdrawn into silence, immediately after dinner.'' And so the pattern went down through the years.[34]

Ellen would say of Lidian in her last decade:

It was one of the marks of age that Mother no longer remembered that she *always* felt sick in the morning. So every morning she now thought she had been taken with a serious illness. After her breakfast she felt better, and then she did not remember that she had been alarmed. In the afternoon she felt well and was full of love for her own dear town and all its inhabitants.[35]

The Waldo of the next generation, the son of Emerson's younger daughter, Edith Emerson Forbes, noted in his journal in March 1909:

Mother told me a few days ago of how Aunt Ellen used to take care of Grandmother Emerson. Grandmother had been given morphine by a doctor who let her have the bottle herself and take it when she went to bed. Grandmother's memory began to fail, and she would think she had not taken the medicine and take it a second time. Aunt Ellen therefore took the custody of the bottle; and this hurt Grandmamma's feelings; but she would come occasionally and ask for the medicine when she had already had it, thinking she had not. This was one of Aunt Ellen's difficulties.[36]

From *The Life of Lidian Jackson Emerson,* Ellen's memoir of her mother, written after Lidian's death but not published until 1980, more than seventy years after Ellen's death, we have our most intimate account of the curious lady to whom Emerson was married for nearly fifty years. From Ellen we learn that, from forty to seventy, "sadness was the ground color of her life." She was, as well, morbidly sensitive. "Her poor mind was all worn to deep and hopeless ruts," by perpetual contemplation of slights real and fancied — "the dungeon in which she suffered for so many years." Unable to cry, she might be found, "violently pacing her room, looking wild, and wringing her hands." A vase an inch out of alignment was a torment. If from her bed she saw a large book resting on a smaller one, she would arise and reverse their order so that the smaller book could rest comfortably.

Lidian's compassion for animals was immense. As a girl she suffered agonies when her aunt refused to feed two stray cats in winter and "used to wish I had never been born," she said, when telling her children of the incident. In winter she wound wool on the hens' roosts to keep their feet warm and, in summer, had Thoreau make them booties of morocco leather so that they could run free in the yard without scratching up plants. Once, when newspapers were stuffed into the fireplace to block the emergence of a rat that had taken haven there, Lidian tucked a doughnut in among them lest, during the night, the rat should feel hungry.

Within limits Lidian's garden became her refuge. She stocked it with plants brought from Plymouth. Bright light repelled her. "The sun, my enemy," she lamented, when out of doors. Emerson's glorious walks were not for her. If ever they took a walk together, no record of the event survives. When she visited Plymouth, she must have avoided the beach because the glare of sunlight on the water and the sand brought on the urge to self-destruction. Her inner clocks appear to have been out of synchronization. In her bedchamber she kept the shutters closed to screen out the light. And her inclination was to shut out people, too. When guests were in the house she might keep to her room. Some of them professed to be put off by her "far-away" manners. For her part, she felt that, too often, they treated her as though she were Emerson's housekeeper. "Mother dreads company" became a household byword. Occasionally she would exert herself and invite guests and relate to them well.[37]

Much of Lidian's mystical bent did not surive her marriage. She retreated into what passed for Christian orthodoxy among the Unitarians of her day. Her unorthodoxy showed itself only in occasional whimsical remarks of which Emerson kept some record. Most of these remarks belonged to the early years of their marriage. In July 1841 Emerson related that "Lidian says that the only sin which people never forgive in each other is a difference of opinion." In April 1842 he wrote: "Queenie [another of his pet names for Lidian] says, 'Save me from magnificent souls. I like a small common sized one.'" She also said she thought it was sinful to go to church on Sunday, though habitually she went. Emerson observed with approval that she had a talent for swearing, though the closest he came to recording an episode of her earthiness is when he wrote: "Queenie looks at Edie kicking up both feet in the air, and thinks that Edie says 'the world was made on purpose to carry round the little baby; and the world goes round the sun only to bring titty-time.'" Edith's clocks evidently were better regulated than her mother's.[38]

At times Lidian must have acquitted herself well as a conversationalist, unless, of course, her strange observations passed for brilliancy. When James and Annie Fields had dinner with the Emersons on 8 January 1864, Annie, reporting the event at second hand, said:

> Mrs. E. looked deadly pale, but her wit coruscated marvellously; even Mr. Emerson grew silent to listen. She said a committee of three, of which she was one, had been formed to pronounce upon certain essays (unpublished) of Mr. Emerson, which they thought should be printed now. She thought some of them finer than any of his published essays. He laughed a great deal at the fun she *poked* at the earlier efforts.[39]

That Lidian, when her mood was elevated, used the occasion to chide her husband can be counted amusing — only if that was not the pattern such moods habitually followed.

Lidian's beautiful carriage and walk were much commended and she retained these attributes by walking around her room daily with a book on her head.[40] She was slight of build. Her habitual attire was a black skirt of silk or cashmere and a black velvet blouse. At an Emerson garden party, Sophia Hawthorne once described her as looking "like a lady abbess in her black silk with a white winged head dress."[41] Her hair, never cut in her lifetime, was always covered at home by a white illusion cap, tied under her chin with baby blue ribbon. Her complexion, which the sun never touched, was unusually fine and fair, unwrinkled even at ninety.[42]

Emerson, having served a valuable apprenticeship catering to the whims of Aunt Mary, coped with Lidian's eccentricities by treating her as a *lusus naturae*. "I don't think any family before ever has contained so curious, and interesting a character as she is," Ellen said, reflecting the level of response Emerson arrived at. Lidian's sudden scream at table when a spoon fell became a family joke. The same was true of her encounters with furniture left in her path. After one such episode, Ellen wrote: "This morning at breakfast Father and I laughed to recall the scene and Father pitied the 'various calamities that mark her course from day to day.'" "She loves a good delivering scream," Emerson owned cosily. Accounting for Lidian's penchant for experiencing undue stress at trifles, Emerson said, "The arrows of Fate stuck fast in Lydia."[43]

Asked to describe Lidian, Emerson limned this likeness: "A tall thin lady, dressed in black, with a white face and her eyes fixed on the distant future." He might have been describing a corpse.[44]

Of her life with Emerson, Lidian told Ellen, "I have been a good wife to your father in one way. He has never gone to his drawer at any time without finding there what he wanted."[45] Many men have had to settle for less. Once, in fact, while on a lecture tour, Emerson found that the shirts Lidian had packed for him had been measured wrong. The collars were too small. If the displeasure he reported then was a fair sample of Emerson in a combustible state, Lidian's attentiveness was not mere dutifulness, it illustrated the instinct for self-preservation.

As a meal-planner, Lidian was not at her most efficient. Emerson was oblivious to what he ate so that fact did not matter to him personally. In 1847, when Thoreau raised for him a bountiful crop of buckwheat on the tract of land across from his house — the so-called heater piece — Lidian made a buckwheat pudding from it that Emerson said tasted "like the roof of a house." But that objection was not typical. It took his mother to notice that Lidian had served twenty consecutive legs of lamb without realizing she was not varying the menu.[46]

Edith, assessing Ellen's memoir of Lidian, dissented. "I think," she said, "the picture of Mother's sorrow is too dark & decided. No doubt she felt so in her dark hours & when fatigue — or dyspepsia or some wound to her over-sensitive spirit oppressed her. But she was of too hopeful and healthy a mind naturally to be always sad — She was able to enjoy a great deal."[47] As for that, Edith was not living at Bush during the last twenty-seven years of her mother's life. Ellen was.

Only a week after he became engaged to Lidian, Emerson had lectured in Boston on Milton. Commenting on Milton's *Doctrine and Discipline of Divorce,* he observed:

It is to be regarded as a poem on one of the griefs of man's condition, namely, unfit marriage. And as many poems have been written upon unfit society . . . yet have not been proceeded against . . . so should this receive that charity, which an angelic soul, suffering more keenly than others from the unavoidable evils of human life, is entitled to.[48]

In 1840 we find him reporting ''a droll dream'' in which he assisted at a debate on the Institution of Marriage and heard raised ''grave & alarming objections'' to marriage that ended when a protester turned a fire hose on the audience and specifically on Emerson himself. He concluded, ''I woke up relieved to find myself quite dry, and well convinced that the Institution of Marriage was safe for tonight.''[49] Aside from its Freudian implications, this does not sound like the dream of a man who has made a ''fit marriage.'' The following year, he told his journal:

I think . . . the writer ought not to be married; ought not to have a family. I think the Roman Catholic church with its celibate clergy & its monastic cells was right. If he must marry, perhaps he should be regarded happiest who has a shrew for a wife, a sharp-tongued notable dame who can & will assume the total economy of the house, and, having some sense that her philosopher is best in his study suffers him not to intermeddle with her thrift.[50]

Happiness, after all, is not the assured lot of a victorious Petruchio.

Lidian would elicit from Emerson in 1848, while he was in Europe, a curious letter in which he acknowledged his inadequacies as a husband and, perhaps, sexual partner. But in January 1850 he reported philosophical insights that suggest he had found a status for marriage which now made the state a desirable one: ''Love is temporary & ends with marriage. Marriage is the perfection which love aimed at, ignorant of what it sought. Marriage is a good known only to the parties. A relation of perfect understanding, aid, contentment, possession of themselves & of the world, — which dwarfs love to green fruit.''[51] Having come to this wisdom, Emerson went on with his life.

Ironically, as Emerson's world darkened in his last decade, Lidian became a social being, playing whist with the Alcotts and adjusting her sleeping habits so that she could attend local lectures and social events. Perhaps the change came because, at last, they had ample means, and her long, stifling years of having to make do with narrow means were at an end, or because Emerson, enfeebled, had passed from a position of dominance to one of dependency.

*The day is always his who works in it with serenity
and great aims.*

25. Harriet Martineau

*O*N 25 August 1835, on the second anniversary of his visit to Carlyle, just after he bought Bush and just before he married Lidian, Emerson paid a courtesy call, at the Cambridge home of Professor John Farrar, on Harriet Martineau, a pioneer British feminist, then on an extended American lecture tour. A short while before, Harriet Martineau had almost been mobbed in Boston by people hostile to her outspoken advocacy of the abolitionist movement. A nasty incident was averted only by the timely intervention of Charles Emerson. In her *Retrospect of Western Travel* (1838), she retold the story: "At the time of the hubbub against me in Boston, Charles Emerson stood alone in a large company in defence of the right of free thought and speech, and declared that he had rather see Boston in ashes than that I, or anybody, should be debarred in any way from perfectly free speech."[1] Emerson's call endorsed Charles's stand. It signified neither his endorsement of Harriet herself nor the cause she served but merely his concurrence with his brother's stated conviction that she should be allowed the right to speak her mind.

On his visit Emerson found Harriet "a pleasant, unpretending lady whom it would be agreeable to talk with when tired and at ease." The occasion of his visit did not show her to such advantage. "She is too weary of society to shine," Emerson said, "if ever she does." At the same time, "by her facile admiration of books & friends," she also, in Emerson's opinion, exposed "her speedy limits."[2] One of the friends she seems to have presented to him that day — Emerson was never sure about this — was Margaret Fuller. If so, Harriet, with her facile words, blurred her image. Ordinarily, considering these circumstances, Emerson's acquaintance with Harriet might have gone no further, yet, before year's end, he invited her to visit him at Concord. Harriet took this to mean that he was serving public notice that she was under his protection.[3] It is doubtful that Emerson had any such thing in mind. What is probable is that he wanted to know her better. He had, in fact, been curious about her for some time. In August 1833 he had seen her in London.[4] The following month, while in Liverpool making ready to sail for America, he had heard her brother, James Martineau, a Unitarian divine destined to be a philosopher of renown, preach at the Paradise Street Chapel, where he was pastor. In April 1835, he reported to Carlyle that she had lately been the houseguest of his friend William Furness in Philadelphia.[5] He had his eye on her, and had no crisis come while she was visiting Boston, it is still likely he would have extended hospitality to her. Charles, indeed, had invited her to Concord on 12 September, on the eve of Waldo's commemorative address, but her already formulated plans to visit the White Mountains with the novelist Catharine Maria Sedgwick kept her from coming.[6] Cabot believed the visit came later that year, but Ellen Emerson, in her life of her mother, states otherwise: "In January [1836] Miss Harriet Martineau with her companion [Eliza Farrar] came to stay for a few days. This visit gave Mother great pleasure. Miss M. was very deaf but they had good talk together nevertheless."[7] By then Lidian had had some success in furnishing the house and Charles had come to live there, circumstances that would have added to the pleasure of the visit for Harriet. When Charles died in May, Harriet wrote to Emerson at once, from Stockbridge, Massachusetts, with expressions of sympathy. Emerson's reply, which begins "My dear friend," is as to someone who had come to know them both well.[8]

Harriet sailed for England in July, with Mrs. Farrar. Beforehand, she arranged for the Emersons to receive Margaret Fuller for a visit. Margaret had planned to accompany the two women to Europe, but her father's sudden death from cholera late in 1835 had made that impossible. Harriet thought the visit would be good for her in this trying time, and good for Emerson too. She saw also that an encounter, already long overdue, between these two remarkable people could have far-reaching consequences. Never was Emerson's hospitality better repaid.

In 1837, Harriet's two-volume work, *Society in America,* was published. Emerson began reading it at once and came away with a higher opinion of her mind than he had had before: "I honored the courage and rectitude of the woman. . . . The respect for principles is the genius of the book & teaches a noble lesson through every page. I will thank those who teach me not to be easily depressed."[9] There is a paradox here, surely, for Emerson to others seemed immune to depression while Harriet, throughout her lifetime, was notoriously vulnerable to it.

The following year, Carlyle, whose friendship with Harriet did not begin until after her return to England and may have been precipitated by Emerson's intervention (through Furness she first became acquainted with *Sartor Resartus*), wrote in March to tell Emerson: "Miss Martineau has given you a luminous section in her *new* Book about America [*Retrospect of Western Travel*]; you are one of the American 'Originals,' — the good Harriet!"[10] Carlyle did not foresee the embarrassment Emerson would report in his next letter, sent on 10 May, after he had seen Harriet's "luminous" tribute:

> Meaning to do me a signal kindness (& a kindness quite out of all measure of justice) she does me a great annoyance, — to take away from me my privacy & thrust me before my time (if ever there be a time) into the arena of the gladiators, to be stared at. I was ashamed to read, & am ashamed to remember. Yet, as you see her, I would not be wanting in gratitude to a gifted & generous lady who so liberally transfigures our demerits. So you shall tell her, if you please, that I read all her book with pleasure but that part.[11]

When Sophia Peabody read this account, she wrote to her sister Elizabeth in terms that might explain Emerson's blushes: "I admire her picture of Mr. Emerson. I think that Mr. Emerson is the greatest man that ever lived. *As a whole* he is satisfactory. Everything has its due with him. In all relations he is noble. He is a unit. His uncommon powers seem used for right purposes. . . . He is indeed a 'Supernal Vision.' "[12]

Emerson's pique, which was genuine enough, was aggravated, moreover, by the scornful verdict Harriet had rendered, in the second volume of *Society in America,* on Bronson Alcott's Temple School. Harriet had visited the school in the company of Richard Henry Dana. Her endorsement of Alcott's methods had been anticipated. Although Margaret Fuller rebuked her in terms that brought a permanent cooling of their friendship, Harriet's remarks sealed the school's doom. When Emerson wrote to Carlyle deploring Harriet's effusive accolade, the Temple School was in its death throes. He could scarcely beam even as Abba Alcott was saying of Harriet: "She took the bread from the mouths of my family."[13] Yet, unwittingly, Harriet did Alcott a good turn (even though it brought further misfortune in its wake) when she passed along the two books that told of his work — the *Record of a School* and *Conversations with Children on the Gospels* — to

James Pierrepont Greaves, the educational reformer. Greaves, enthralled, founded Alcott House and extended the invitation that brought Alcott to England and set in motion that chain of events which resulted in the Fruitlands experiment.[14]

Harriet meant well. Something remarkable, she realized, was happening in Boston. "I certainly am not aware," she said, "of so large a number of peculiarly interesting and valuable persons, living in any near neighborhood, anywhere else but in London." Emerson she singled out as the central figure in this exceptional gathering:

> There is a remarkable man in the United States without knowing whom it is not too much to say that the United States cannot be fully known. I mean by this, not only that he has powers and worth which constitute him an element in the estimate to be formed of his country, but that his intellect and his character are the opposite of those which the influences of his country and his time are supposed almost necessarily to form. I speak of Mr. Emerson.

Emerson never was comfortable with superlatives; but to have it said of you that you are laudable because you are immune to the deleterious agencies permeating the environment which you inhabit is to invite immediately your repudiation by those with whom you share that environment. Harriet had more to say:

> He is yet in the prime of life. Great things are expected from him; and great things, it seems he cannot but do if he have life and health to prosecute his course. He is a thinker and a scholar. . . .
> The thinker is ever present to the duty, and the scholar to the active business, of the hour; and his home is the scene of his greatest acts. . . . He is known at every house along the road he travels to and from home by the words he has dropped and the deeds he has done. The little boy who carries wood for his household has been enlightened by him, and his most transient guests owe to him their experience of what the highest grace of domestic manners may be. . . . I could give anecdotes; but I have been his guest, and I restrain myself.[15]

Harriet had been an observant guest. Though Emerson had been settled in his house less than four months when she came on her visit, she caught a sense of his life-style and of his place in the Concord community that would hold true for the next forty-six years.

As a reformer herself, Harriet ruthlessly annexed Emerson as a reformer, engendering the deed in the desire: "He is ready at every call of action. . . . He has ever ready his verdict for the right and his right hand for its champions. . . . He is ever present with their principles, declaring himself, and taking his stand, while appearing to be incapable of contempt of persons." After this laudation of his intellect and character, Harriet could not desist without good words for the person. Her periodic infatuations with men who inspired her suggests that these concluding remarks may originate in an emotional attachment she formed for him, no less genuine for being unrealizable: "Earnest as is the tone of his mind, and placidly strenuous as is his life, an exquisite sense of humor pervades his intercourse. A quiet gayety breathes out of his conversation; and his observation, as keen as it is benevolent, furnishes him with perpetual material for the exercise of his humor." Here was an aspect of Emerson often picked up by his lecture audiences but excluded from his essays by his own choice. That it communicated itself to a visitor is reassuring. But Emerson's sense of humor was Yankee and his visitor British — at this level, restraint spoke to restraint, even if it was Harriet's want of restraint on a social issue that gave spirit to their Boston encounters.

Harriet found herself hard pressed to settle on Emerson's salient trait, but she was a determined woman and soon settled on one compatible with her own preferences:

> If, out of such a harmony, one leading quality is to be distinguished, it is in him modest independence. A more entire and modest independence I am not aware of having ever witnessed, though in America I saw two or three approaches to it. It is an independence equally of thought, of speech, of demeanor, of occupation, and of objects of life, yet without a trace of contempt in its temper, or of encroachment in its action.[16]

This is a rather good description of Harriet's brother, James. As time passed, James, who died at ninety-five, came more and more to sound like Emerson. Harriet may have been the first to perceive the parallel.

26. Charles Emerson
The Sky Is Less Grand

*I*N late April 1836 Emerson interrupted a series of six lectures, "English Biography and Literature," which he was giving in Salem, to accompany his brother Charles to Staten Island. A severe cold Charles had come down with in March had been succeeded by symptoms of active tuberculosis. William had just moved into his new house on Staten Island and his mother was there visiting him. Although Charles was too ill to go to New York alone, everyone thought the change would benefit him, so he went. Emerson himself came back directly and gave the last four Salem lectures during the first week of May, intending, once the series was ended, to return to New York to oversee Charles's convalescence. It was essential, he told Lidian, that Charles "be kept in the air & in motion," otherwise he might "easily lose the power of going abroad & with it the chance of restoration."[1] Despite the sad outcome of Ellen's illness, Emerson still believed that activities which induced the tubercular to free their lungs of its mucus content held out the best promise of recovery. This was the regimen that was followed. Although William showed enough anxiety in a letter written on 7 May to cause Emerson, accompanied by Elizabeth Hoar, who was to be married to Charles in September, to set out for Staten Island on the morning of 10 May, Charles was induced to go for a ride with his mother on the afternoon of the preceding day. When he came into the house on his return, he walked unsupported but then sank wearily to the stairs and lost consciousness. After a few moments he died. Thus, though they did not realize it, even before Emerson and Elizabeth left for Staten Island to comfort Charles, Charles was past comforting.

Hitherto Emerson had experienced no other shock comparable to what he felt now at this loss. His grief when Ellen died had been vast, but he had foreseen that event and was prepared for it. Edward's death, which occurred in Puerto Rico on 1 October 1834, was also something he was prepared to accept. Soon afterward, he wrote to Carlyle:

> I had quite recently received the news of the death of a brother in the island of Porto Rico, whose loss to me will be a life-long sorrow. As he passes out of sight, come to me visible as well as spiritual tokens of a fraternal friendliness which by its own law, transcends the tedious barriers of Custom & nation, & opens its way to the heart. This is a true consolation and I thanked my jealous Δείμων for the godsend so significantly timed.[2]

Under the heading of compensation this loss seemed supportable.

Even Lidian must have been surprised at the magnitude of her husband's grief as he told her of his feelings in a letter written on 11 May, the day of Charles's funeral.

> I can never bring you back my noble friend who was my ornament my wisdom & my pride. . . . I should not have known how to forgive you an ignorance of him, had he been out of your sight. . . . You must be content henceforth with only a piece of your husband; for the best of his strength lay in the soul with which he must no more on earth take counsel.[3]

A family friend, Robert Cassie Waterston, who accompanied Emerson to the cemetery, wrote afterward to Elizabeth Peabody that Charles's death had brought Emerson to the brink of hysteria. As he turned away from the grave, his pent-up feelings had given way in an incongruous laugh and he had cried out, ''Dear boy!''[4]

Home again in Concord five days after Charles's funeral, Emerson made his journal his confidant:

> Beautiful without any parallel in my experience of young men, was his life. . . . Now commences a new and gloomy epoch of my life. . . . Who can ever supply his place to me? None. . . . The eye is closed that was to see nature for me, and give me leave to see. . . . I used to say that I had no leave to see things till he pointed them out, and afterwards I never ceased to see them.[5]

By September Emerson could write of his loss to Carlyle with some restoration of calm, but his sorrow and sense of loss still were intense:

"I have lost out of this world my brother Charles . . . the friend and companion of many years. . . . I have put so much dependence on his gifts that we made but one man together; for I needed never to do what he could do by noble nature much better than I."[6] If Emerson believed this literally, that belief may go far to explain his later annexations of the personalities and talents of others.

In the weeks and months following, though Emerson had believed life for him had come to a premature halt, he had had responsibilities to meet and had resumed the business of living. Even as Lidian and he awaited the birth of their first child — a son, Waldo, born on 30 October — he completed his first book, *Nature*, in August and edited *Sartor Resartus* for publication. He also scrutinized Charles's literary remains, supposing he would cull from them, for publication, materials that would perpetuate his memory. Instead, he found that Charles's "scorn of written composition" was bona fide — "He was born an orator, not a writer. His written pages do him no justice." There was an "immense disparity between his power of conversation and his blotted paper."[7] And so it would be with many others for whom Emerson at first had great hopes — Alcott, Fuller, Channing, Very, Cranch. This crucial lack never ceased to baffle him.

Although Emerson overestimated his dependency on Charles, he was not alone in believing that the world had suffered a great loss. The youngest of the Emersons, Charles, from his earliest years, had seemed marked for distinction. As Junior Sophister at Harvard he had won the Boylston Prize in rhetoric. In a brilliant class he stood in the first rank. Trim, lithe, his eyes as renowned for their blueness as Waldo's were, his face effulgent with a burning through of soul, he could escape notice nowhere. When a question was raised about the feasibility of Charles's setting up practice in Concord, Daniel Webster had exclaimed: "Let him settle anywhere! . . . Let him settle in the back woods of Maine if he chooses; the clients will throng after him."[8]

At Salem, Sophia Peabody was stricken even on hearing the news of his illness. To her sister Elizabeth she wrote, "I can think of nothing now but Charles Emerson. A sudden gloom seems to overshadow me."[9] To comfort Elizabeth Hoar, Sophia soon occupied herself by making for her a medallion relief of Charles.

To those who gathered for Charles's memorial service at Concord, Dr. Ripley intimated that he would gladly have gone in Charles's stead. Oliver Wendell Holmes, one of Charles's Harvard classmates, commemorated him in a verse tribute, "Poetry; A Metrical Essay":

> *Thou, calm, chaste scholar! I can see thee now,*
> *The first young laurels on thy pallid brow,*
> *O'er thy slight figure floating lightly down*

In graceful folds the academic gown.
On thy curled lip the classic lines, that taught
How nice the mind that sculptured them with thought.
And triumph glistening in the clear blue eyes,
Too bright to live, — but oh, too fair to die![10]

Although Holmes wrote these lines in 1836, in the heat of his emotions, nearly fifty years later, in his biography of Waldo, he still would remember Charles as "the most angelic adolescent my eyes ever beheld." To William Ellery Channing, also, Charles Emerson's death was tragic. "I think," he said, "Massachusetts could not have met a greater loss, than that young man."[11]

During the short interval he was established in Concord, Charles had won wide acceptance. His lecture, "The Life and Death of Socrates," given to the Concord Lyceum in the first year of its existence, was so well received some Concordians disputed the wisdom of the town committee's selection of Waldo instead of Charles to give the bicentennial address. He also taught a class in Dr. Ripley's newly instituted Sabbath School and was popular with his charges. Judge John S. Keyes, who had been one of his pupils, recalled long after that the hour in Charles Emerson's Sunday School class was "the one bright spot in the desperate New England Sabbath of those days."[12]

Out of character with the panegyrics that accumulated around Charles's name is a curious entry in Thoreau's journal, in the summer of 1851. That it was suppressed by Thoreau's editors in the 1906 edition of his journals need not surprise us. Thoreau, who had been touring the environs of Daniel Webster's far-flung Marshfield estate, wrote:

> Took refuge from the rain at a Mr. Stetsons in Duxbury — told me an anecdote which he heard Charles Emerson tell of meeting Webster at a splendid house of ill fame in Washington where he [Charles] had gone unwittingly to call on a lady whose acquaintance he had formed on the stage. Mr. Webster coming into the room unexpectedly — & patting him on the shoulder remarks "This is no place for young men like you."[13]

Even by implication Thoreau does not dispute Charles's alleged explanation for his presence in a bordello. Presumably had he gone there for the usual reasons he would not have told the story. But, then, we do not know to what extent he regarded Stetson as a confidant or how creditable a source Stetson himself was. Possibly the encounter was someone else's and Stetson assigned it to Emerson because Thoreau, as a friend of the Emersons, could be expected to respond to the story with heightened interest. Leonard Neufeldt assumes the story was suppressed in 1906 out of deference to Webster's reputation. Yet the desire not to blemish Charles Emerson's immaculate reputation or embarrass the Emerson and Hoar families would have been paramount with Thoreau's editors. After all, Charles had been associated in law practice with Samuel Hoar and engaged to marry his daughter Elizabeth. To make Charles's visit to a whorehouse known could only have led to broad and vulgar jokes about his betrothal to a Hoar.

Of Charles, Moncure Conway said, "He did not die but was caught up into the spirit of the brother who mourned him so profoundly." This tribute might cause us to think Emerson owed something to Charles's thinking. But such of his papers as survive show that his mind was unexceptional. The fact is, even as Edward and Charles were being lauded for their successes, Edward had insisted that the hopes of the family rode with Waldo. Even Holmes, despite his admiration for Charles, did not hesitate to accord to Waldo the position of eminence: "Being about seven years younger than Waldo, he [Charles] must have received much of his intellectual and moral guidance at his elder brother's hands." E. P. Whipple was still more pointed in the conclusion he came to:

> At the time he [Waldo] acquired notoriety but had not yet achieved fame, it was confidently asserted in all Boston circles that his brother Charles . . . was greatly his superior in ability, and would, had he not died early, have entirely eclipsed Ralph; Emerson himself, the most generous and loving of brothers, always inclined to this opinion. But there is not an atom of evidence that Charles, had he lived, would have produced works which would be read by a choice company of thinkers and scholars all over the world.[14]

George Stillman Hillard, Charles Emerson's principal rival in the class of 1828 at Harvard, commended Charles because he could take a simple line of Latin that could be rendered straightforwardly as "The whole house was on fire," and so swathe it in fustian that it read rather "The entire edifice was wrapped in flames."[15] Some later phrases that Emerson salvaged from among Charles's literary detritus for inclusion in *The Dial* are enough like this passage to recall Huck Finn's dreary encounter with the literary remains of Emmeline Grangerford. Consider: "For Bible and psalmbook, I had the grand page of nature, and many a holy verse I read from off the brown sward and the trees." Or again: "I bestride my poney [sic], and we brush with hasty step the dews away."[16] Such lines would bring blushes to Richard Jefferies.

Six months before Charles died Emerson quoted him as saying, "the nap is worn off the world.''[17] The truth is, Charles had a shorter trajectory than Waldo and, even before the onset of the illness that killed him, his spirits flagged and enthusiasm gave way to melancholy. He neither sounded nor acted like a young bridegroom on his way to the altar. Perhaps his vital powers failed him. But possibly his strength failed only after his interest failed. We have Emerson himself for our authority that Charles wanted to exit life quickly when his time came. Had he lived it seems improbable that he would have fulfilled the expectations others had for him.

At the conclusion of the opening section of *Nature*, published four months after Charles's death and written, in part, in that interval, Emerson says, in what Holmes believed to be an allusion to that specific bereavement: ''Then, there is a kind of contempt of the landscape felt by him who has just lost by death a dear friend. The sky is less grand as it shuts down over less worth in the population.'' ''This,'' said Holmes, ''was the first effect of the loss; but after a time he recognizes a superintending power which orders events for us in wisdom which we could not see at first.'' To illustrate, he called attention to a later passage in *Nature*, in ''Discipline,'' where Emerson says that when a friend has done his part in communicating wisdom to us ''it is a sign to us that his office is closing, and he is commonly withdrawn from our sight in a short time.''[18]

When Emerson's son was born in October 1836, Elizabeth Hoar wanted him to be named Charles.[19] Emerson declined. When a second son was born, eight years later, Emerson named him Edward. His brother Edward's life, Emerson remembered, had been ''a tragedy of poverty and sickness tearing genius.'' Charles's life had been ''healthy and human.'' It stood as a completed chapter, commemorated in itself, requiring no further memorial. In no sense was Emerson's own life a memorial to Charles. Only his detractors would argue so.

27. *Nature*

*N*ATHANIEL Hawthorne believed that Emerson, with begrimed prints of his Puritan forebears looking on, wrote *Nature* in the soot-blackened, second-floor room in the Old Manse from which William Emerson and his family had viewed the battle of Concord sixty years before. In fact, almost certainly Emerson wrote most of it in his own study at Bush. That does not mean, however, that the book had not begun to take shape earlier. We know, for example, that in June 1829, with "Summer" as his topic, Emerson had preached on Nature under four headings that anticipated the first four headings — "Commodity," "Beauty," "Language," and "Discipline" — of the book published seven years later. These represent the classes into which Nature's uses and values can be put, how Nature affects the soul. In *Nature*, under three additional headings, he would explore the operation of man's spirit upon Nature. In 1833 the matter again concerned him. Sailing past the coast of Ireland on 6 September, homeward bound after his travels in Europe, he wrote in his journal: "I like my book about nature & wish I knew where & how I ought to live. God will show me."[1] Either he had already formulated the plan of the book or actually had begun to write it.

In 1836 Charles's death made Emerson acutely conscious of the fleeting character of human existence and stirred in him a compulsion to get on with the work he hoped to accomplish in life. He gave expression to this mandate by resuming work on *Nature*. As early as 28 June he could report substantial results. Writing to William, he said: "My little book is nearly done. It's title is 'Nature.' . . . My design is to follow it by & by with another essay, 'Spirit'; and the two shall make a decent volume." He was still at work on it on 2 August, for on that date Alcott mentioned it in his journal: "Mr. Waldo Emerson . . . is now writing a work, of a high intellectual character, which he calls *Nature.*" Nor was he done on 8 August, for then he wrote William: "The book of Nature still lies on the table. There is, as always, one crack in it not easy to be soldered or welded, but if this week I should be left alone after the probate affair [of Charles's will] I may finish it."[2]

Scholars never have wearied of trying to expose the crack Emerson was referring to and count it a coup to focus attention on an aspect that others have overlooked. Emerson, for example, had trouble reconciling his belief in an ultimately perfect organic unity, which must necessarily be static, and his belief in a continually changing dynamic diversity which, because it continues to change, cannot be either perfect or unified.[3] Since few philosophical problems are fissure-free, no one can isolate with certainty the crack Emerson meant. Inasmuch as he announced the problem as he was coming to the close of his labors, it is reasonable to conjecture that he saw his problem as being the difficulty he encountered in trying to reconcile mind and matter. He left it unresolved. He could not say whether mind existed independent of matter. Since this is one of the irreconcilables that have thwarted philosophers throughout history, he can hardly be held to account for having let his book pass into print without effecting the fusion he sought for.

Nature was published on 9 September 1836. The printer charged a hundred dollars to print a thousand copies and this expense Emerson himself met in full. The resultant book was a slim blue volume of ninety-four pages. It bore no author's name yet its authorship was no secret since Emerson gave copies to many of his friends and these made up the majority of those who took any interest in the book at all.

Nature has been called "quintessential Emerson," and that describes it fairly. Yet few people came to know Emerson's ideas through this book. Most came to an awareness of them as he expounded them, bit by bit, in simpler language and with greater clarity, in his subsequent lectures and essays. Even among those allied to him in thought, *Nature,* on its appearance, came in only for a divided share of attention because two other treatises expounding the transcendental outlook were published about the same time and, on account of their greater clarity and explicitness, received fuller discussion. These were Orestes Brownson's *New Views of Christianity, Society, and the Church,* and George Ripley's *Discourses on the Philosophy of Religion.* Historically speaking, *Nature* had neither the impact it ought to have had nor the impact it was said to have had.

What Emerson did in *Nature* was to explore tentatively the essence of most of those ideas eventually characterized as Emersonian. It is what Carlyle called Emerson's Ground-Plan.

Making self-reliance his cause from the outset, Emerson begins by deploring a retrospective age that "builds the sepulchres of the fathers." He wants men in the present day to behold "God and nature face to face," rather than to know them merely through traditions passed down to them. "Why," he asks, "Should not we also enjoy an original relation to the universe?"

Considering first the broad topic of Nature itself, Emerson finds it regrettable that few adults have more than a skimming acquaintance with nature. Invoking, as Wordsworth earlier had done, the Platonic doctrine of preexistence, he declares that an authentic lover of Nature retains "the spirit of infancy even into the era of manhood." Then, in the much-cited "bare common" passage, he discloses that he has experienced that preexistent soul-state which opens one to those intuitions attesting intercourse with the universal mind.

Under the heading "Commodity," Emerson calls attention to the benefactions our senses and persons owe to Nature. Under his next heading, "Beauty," he examines three types — physical beauty, which is perceived in natural forms; spiritual, "the mark God sets upon virtue"; and intellectual, order in Nature as recognized by the intellect. In its highest sense Beauty expresses the final cause of the universe. Truth and goodness express "the same All."

Under "Language" we learn that every word originated in some physical appearance, which is, in turn, a symbol of some spiritual fact. As a corollary to this, Emerson emphasizes a belief he had been long partial to and which helps explain his undeviating commitment to and eventual consummate mastery of epigrammatic form: "the proverbs of nations consist usually of a natural fact, selected as a picture or parable of a moral truth." Into this division of *Nature* Emerson introduces a succinct passage, fundamental to his thought and virtually a distillation of the central thesis of his book — and thus a parable of the truth he means to convey:

> Throw a stone into the stream, and the circles that propagate themselves are the beautiful type of all influence. Man is conscious of a universal soul within or behind his individual life, wherein, as in a firmament, the natures of Justice, Truth, Love, Freedom, arise and shine. This universal soul he calls Reason: it is not mine or thine or his, but we are its; we are its property and men. And the blue sky in which the private earth is buried, the sky with its eternal calm, and full of everlasting orbs, is the type of Reason. That which intellectually considered we call Reason, considered in

relation to nature, we call Spirit. Spirit is the Creator. Spirit
hath life in itself. And man in all ages and countries embodies it
in his language as the FATHER.[4]

"Discipline" is Emerson's next category. Here we learn that all
elements in Nature are educative, leading the Understanding and Reason to moral awareness.

In "Idealism," where presumably his imperfectly welded crack awaits
the detection of the close observer, he acknowledges that while the absolute existence of matter seems irrefutable to the Understanding,
Reason "tends to relax this despotism of the senses, which binds us to
nature as if we were a part of it, and shows us nature aloof, and, as it
were, afloat." Yet he finds that the poetic imagination and philosophical ideas range through matter, altering it and even dissolving it. Ideas
can exist apart from matter and outlast it. Moreover, "Intellectual
science has been observed to beget invariably a doubt of the existence
of matter." He is willing to leave the question unresolved and comes
close to saying, mischievously, that it does not matter.[5]

Emerson saw this topic as so close to being insolvable that more than
once he made it the subject of a jest. Thus when a Millerite confronted
him with the news that the world was about to end, he replied, "Let
it go; we can get on just as well without it." On another occasion,
when a sawyer delivered firewood while he was entertaining guests, he
excused himself, saying, "We have to attend to these matters just as
if they were real."[6] Yet, coming again to a consideration of this topic
when he addresses himself to the vital category of Spirit, while conceding that we cannot confront directly the final cause of Nature, he
insists that we can, in perceiving that Nature stands "as the apparition of God," receive from Nature the lesson of worship. Here again
Emerson seems to be proposing that matter is not a substance but a
phenomenon. Orthodox critics in his own day, however, agitated by
the heresy of romanticism, charged that Emerson, at this moment, proclaimed himself a pantheist. A close scrutiny of Emerson's presentation of his views shows that, on the contrary, eschewing the position
of the pantheist, who sees God in the world, he identified the Idealism
to which he inclined as a belief that "sees the world in God."

In the concluding portion of *Nature* Emerson returns to his first
theme, the assertion of self, this time calling for independence not
merely from established norms but from the dictates of the Understanding. He urges increased reliance on intuition, which elsewhere he
identified as the moral sense, mounting in this way to perfection of
unity. In the verse epigraph he wrote for the second edition of *Nature*
(1849), Emerson, touching on the miracle of evolution even before
men had come to wrestle with the term, had said:

And, striving to be man, the worm
Mounts through all the spires of form.

In anticipation of that declaration, Emerson had found in the spiral a device on which to structure *Nature*. Through its successive stages he carried his readers higher and higher in concentric progress to the portals of the universal All.

This last exhortation seems to have justified *Nature* in the eyes of Orestes Brownson, who wrote George Bancroft on 24 September 1836 that Emerson, in *Nature*, "has a presentiment of social progress which is really cheering." Most readers, perhaps because of what Francis Bowen, who taught philosophy at Harvard, then called Emerson's "cloud-capt phraseology," and Holmes, much later, spoke of as "the language of one who is just coming to himself after having been etherized," felt as free as Brownson did to interpret *Nature* according to their own moods. Thus Alcott thought it "a beautiful work . . . the production of a spiritualist, subordinating the visible and outward to the inward and invisible," and Carlyle declared it to be "the true Apocalypse." This was an overwhelming response to a book which Emerson had modestly introduced him to as "an entering wedge, I hope for something more worthy and significant." Holmes ventured to say also: "*Nature* is a reflective prose poem. It is divided into eight chapters, which might almost as well have been called cantos." He further described it as "vague, mystic, incomprehensible, to most of those who call themselves commonsense people."[7]

Yet, starkly given, Emerson's message would not have been palatable to such readers. His style compelled even the alienated Francis Bowen to concede at the outset of his critique that the book offered "beautiful writing" and "shows of surpassing beauty" to his dazed readers. One notable passage may suffice to account for Bowen's reluctant seduction:

I see the spectacle of morning from the hill-top over against my house, from day-break to sunrise, with emotions which an angel might share. The long slender bars of cloud float like fishes in the sea of crimson light. From the earth, as a shore, I look out into that silent sea. I seem to partake its rapid transformations; the active enchantment reaches my dust, and I dilate and conspire with the morning wind. How does Nature deify us with a few and cheap elements! Give me health and a day, and I will make the pomp of emperors ridiculous. The dawn is my Assyria; the sunset and moonrise my Paphos, and unimaginable realms of faerie; broad noon shall be my England of the senses and the understanding; the night shall be my Germany of mystic philosophy and dreams.[8]

Thus did Emerson conspire to overwhelm his critics and make ridiculous their pompous strictures. If his style was then only a shield, it functioned so effectively that *Nature* is secure in its reputation as a literary masterpiece even when men have ceased to be agitated over the break with orthodoxy that it announced.

Give me insight into today, and you may have the
antique and future worlds.

28. ''The American Scholar''

OSTERITY remembers 31 August 1837 as a day of unblemished triumph in Emerson's life. On that day he delivered ''The American Scholar'' oration to the Harvard chapter of Phi Beta Kappa — ''the most influential address ever made before an American college audience.''[1] A litany of the praises spoken in tribute to this address, brought together without reference to time, would create the impression that its success had been instantaneous and overwhelming. In fact, it was not. Acclamation came only after the address was reassessed in times remote from the inhospitable age that first received it. That it had to wait so long to receive its due carries out a grim kind of logic. The invitation to Emerson to give the address had itself been an afterthought. The first choice of the selection committee had been Jonathan Mayhew Wainwright, a clergyman of noncontroversial reputation. On 22 June, Wainwright asked to be relieved of the commitment. Only then did Cornelius Felton, as spokesman for the committee, ask Emerson to take on the burden. Even though it meant setting aside travel plans, Emerson accepted.

Emerson cannot have been too pleased with the opportunity offered. The prescribed topic was hackneyed. Year after year, back to the time of his boyhood, Harvard's Phi Beta Kappa oration focused on the same subject — the American scholar. Other speakers, on other occasions, moreover, had made it their theme. William Ellery Channing in 1830, for example, in his *Remarks on American Literature,* had urged that his countrymen assert their independence from the tyranny of European letters. No one can have believed anything worth saying on the subject remained to be said. Wainwright cannot have supposed he was relinquishing a gem of an opportunity.

Today, commentary on the oration invariably notes that Oliver Wendell Holmes hailed it as "our intellectual Declaration of Independence."[2] This calls up a vision of Holmes running into the Harvard Yard as the lecture ended, trumpeting the news that an event of world-shaking significance had just taken place. But Holmes, who never claimed to have been in Emerson's audience on that occasion, first used his ringing phrase in his biography of Emerson, published in 1884, two years after Emerson's death. And, presently, he revised his opinion downward, so that in *Over the Teacups* it had become merely "our literary Declaration of Independence."[3]

Holmes's biography also assured us that young men who did hear the address left the hall "as if a prophet had been proclaiming to them 'Thus saith the Lord.'"[4] If that was so, then the fact was artfully hidden till Holmes reported it, almost fifty years later. Holmes also reminded us that James Russell Lowell, who *was* present when the address was given, had said that it "was an event without any former parallel in our literary annals, a scene to be always treasured in the memory for its picturesqueness and its inspiration." But Lowell had said this in *My Study Windows* in 1871, early enough, it is true, for Emerson to have read his words with some chance of grasping their significance, but long after it had ceased to matter. In that same passage, Lowell also had said: "What crowded and breathless aisles, what windows clustering with eager heads, what enthusiasm of approval, what grim silence of foregone dissent!"[5] The phrase "foregone dissent" calls us up short because it reflects the mood of a substantial part of Emerson's audience, especially those theologians whose ire had been piqued the previous year by the publication of *Nature*. Later they adjudged "The American Scholar" a secular rendering of the "transcendental nonsense" subsequently given full disclosure in the "Divinity School Address."

Emerson delivered his address to a morning audience. That night, at the society's dinner, Edward Everett spoke, hurrying over Emerson's address in ambiguous phrases to focus attention instead on the superior intellectual attainments of Emerson's two dead brothers, Edward and Charles. "We have listened with delight," Everett said, "to a train of original remark and ingenious speculation, clothed in language the most exquisite, and uttered with a natural grace beyond the reach of art." Such lubricious phrases cannot have failed to gratify Emerson's most implacable foes. Only at the close of his statement did Everett, while in no way acknowledging the merit of Emerson's observations, halfway make amends with a toast: "The orator of the day; — the beauty of living excellence recalls to us the memory, but alleviates the loss of that which we deplore.''[6] The tribute really was to Emersons dead and gone.

The audience Emerson had addressed had been well infiltrated with men like the Reverend John Pierce, born on the eve of the Revolution and, for many years, self-appointed chronicler of Harvard anniversaries. Pierce made his own judicious summing up of that morning's oration:

> Rev. Ralph Waldo Emerson gave an oration, of 1¼ hour, on
> ''The American Scholar.'' It was to me in the misty, dreamy,
> unintelligible style of Swedenborg, Coleridge, and Carlyle. He
> professed to have method; but I could not trace it, except in his
> own annunciation. It was well spoken, and all seemed to attend,
> but how many were in my own predicament of making little of it
> I have no means of ascertaining. Toward the close, and indeed
> in many parts of his discourse, he spoke severely of our depen-
> dence on British literature. Notwithstanding, I much question
> whether he himself would have written such an apparently inco-
> herent and unintelligible address, had he not been familiar
> with the writings of the authors named above.[7]

Pierce's acerbic assessment of ''The American Scholar,'' which reflected the views of much of Emerson's audience, is forgotten while Holmes's estimate is repeated whenever the speech is mentioned. No matter that Holmes was right and Pierce wrong; what concerns us is that posterity remembers as a triumph an occasion that was not a triumph.

Asked to state the burden of ''The American Scholar,'' most readers would seek its essence in the phrase, ''We have listened too long to the courtly muses of Europe.'' Emerson had urged his countrymen to end their dependency on European literature and direct their efforts to producing a literature distinctively American. Some might reflect that this brought fresh emphasis to a theme he had touched upon earlier, on 14 January 1836, in ''Modern Aspects of Letters'': ''A degree of humiliation must be felt by the American scholar when he reviews the constellation of great geniuses from Chaucer down who in England have enlarged the limits of wisdom, and then returns to this country where Humanity has been unbound and has enjoyed the culture of Science in the freedom of the Wild and reckons how little has been here added to the stock of truth for mankind.''[8] They even might recall that this theme had long preoccupied Emerson in his journal. Thus, on 10 June 1834 he wrote: ''We all lean on England, scarce a verse, a page, a newspaper, but is writ in imitation of English forms.''[9] In ''Power'' he would say, ''As long as our people quote English standards they dwarf their own proportions.'' And: ''As long as our people quote English standards, they will miss the sovereignty of power.''[10] Within himself such thoughts engendered a reform. On 15 November 1834 he wrote, ''Henceforth I design not to utter any speech, poem or book that is not entirely & peculiarly my work.''[11]

This theme, though it stood paramount even in Pierce's impressions, was no more novel to Emerson's listeners than was the title of the address. All Harvard people knew Edward Tyrrel Channing had stressed the theme in his Harvard rhetoric classes for a dozen years. Find your subject matter, and a style commensurate with it, in your own country, he had told his students, because English ideals no longer serve American needs. Emerson knew this topic was frazzled and probably introduced it only because the title of the address mandated such a declaration and he did not want to disappoint the expectations of his listeners. But he confined his mention of it to a brief passage coming at the conclusion of the address. Moreover, in seventy-five minutes he used the word ''American'' only four times. For him the word ''scholar'' was a synonym for Man Thinking, and Man Thinking was his true subject. And he meant not merely men in his own country, in his own time, but men everywhere and in future times, as well. Reaching out beyond national boundaries to make his appeal to mankind, then and always, he urged each generation to do its own thinking and not be held hostage by the past. ''If the single man plant himself indomitably on his instincts and there abide,'' he said, ''the huge world will come round to him.'' If any one phrase is central to the address, it is that one, and that had nothing to do with American image-building. Emerson had no wish to pioneer American literary novelties but to foster an individualism that men everywhere could have recourse to, each man ''inspired by the Divine Soul.'' At most, a nation of men so directed would be a beacon to mankind, not a coven guarding secrets inaccessible to others. This was in keeping with Emerson's goal of fostering the development of the complete universal man. Emerson's theme is summed up in a phrase that he introduced later into ''Schools in American Literature'' (1850): ''The great man, even whilst he relates a private fact personal to him, is really leading us away from him to an universal experience.''[12] If Emerson can be reproached for visualizing his scholar as contemplative rather than as an active reformer, that limitation can be ascribed, without prejudice, to his determination to address himself not to man's particular needs but to his universal ends. Localized, his scholar would merely be committed to some particular social action and, accordingly, locked in place at some lower stage of growth. Emerson's message comes back always to his unwavering conviction that the reformation of society must begin with the reformation of the individual.

On 14 August 1837 Margaret Fuller had written Emerson from Providence to suggest that since her vacation time coincided with his Phi Beta Kappa address, she should meet him afterward and go back to Concord with him. This would not be her first visit because the visit Harriet Martineau had urged on the Emersons had come to pass in July 1836, and Emerson had seen enough of Margaret then to realize that hers was a mind of the first magnitude. Her proposal now he saw as opportune. Hedge's Club was meeting at his house on 1 September. To introduce this representative woman into that company would be something to see. "What can you not mould them into in an hour!" he exclaimed when he wrote to her on the seventeenth to endorse the particulars of her proposed incursion.[13]

On 1 September, with nearly a score of visitors under his roof — including Elizabeth Peabody, Sarah Ripley, Elizabeth Hoar, John Sullivan Dwight, James Freeman Clarke, George Ripley, Convers Francis, and Hedge — Emerson had the audience he had lacked the day before, friends who placed the worth of the individual above the weight of unexamined tradition.[14] Clarke, writing later that same day to his fiancée, said: "Yesterday we had a noble discourse by Mr. Emerson on the American Scholar. . . . Henry Hedge said they had not had so sweet a song sung to them for many a year."[15] No doubt the substance of Emerson's address was a topic much to the fore among those who gathered at Concord. And no doubt Margaret shone. But the one fact of that meeting that seems best remembered is that Lidian, assuming that the appetites of her guests must be at least as keen as their intellects, set for them a midday meal that consisted of beef, boiled mutton with caper sauce, ham, tongue, corn, beans, macaroni, tomatoes, lettuce, cucumbers, applesauce, puddings, custards, fruit, and nuts. If good nourishment could contribute to the rise of the American scholar or to the completion of the universal man, then Lidian had done her part well.

On 24 October Emerson could write in his journal: "I find in town, the Φ.B.K Oration, of which 500 copies were printed, all sold, in just one month."[16] That the address had stirred greater interest than *Nature* had did not mean, as Emerson knew, that public opinion had swung over to his support. Edward Everett Hale has left us a realistic account of how things really stood:

It was my good fortune to hear, in 1837, the address which Dr. Holmes calls the Declaration of Independence of American Literature — the Phi Beta Kappa oration of July at Cambridge. So I can remember the surprise — shall I say the indignation — which the simple, solid, disconnected phrases of that address awakened among those who heard. I remember the covert criticism of the gay dinner-party which followed. I remember how after-wards men and women freely said he was crazy. Alas, I have on paper my own school-boy doubts whether he appreciated the occasion![17]

Doubts indeed! Hale had written in his diary, afterward, that Emer-son was "half-crazy" and his speech "not very good and very tran-scendental."

When a copy of "The American Scholar" reached Carlyle, he re-sponded on 8 December 1837 with a burst of enthusiasm that made the comments of others, whether good or bad, a matter of indifference to Emerson:

> My soul had sunk down sorrowful, and said there is no articu-late speaking then anymore, and thou art solitary among stranger-creatures? — and lo, out of the West comes a clear utterance, clearly recognisable as a m[an's] voice, and I *have* a kinsman and a brother: God be thanked for it! I coul[d have] *wept* to read that speech; the clear high melody of it went tingling thro' my heart; I said to my wife 'There, woman!' She read; and returned and charges me to return for answer, 'that there had been nothing met with like it since Schiller went silent.' My brave Emerson! And all this has been lying silent, quite tranquil in him, these seven years. . . . May God grant you strength, for you have a *fearful* work to do![18]

In the years just ahead, when Emerson wanted to express his high-est approval, he used Carlyle's phrasing, acclaiming "my brave" Henry Thoreau and "my brave" Jones Very.

29. The Cherokee Expulsion
All the Other Holy Hurrahs

*O*N 19 April 1838, the sixty-third anniversary of the Concord fight, Emerson, like his grandfather on that fateful day, was given the chance to fight for an ideal. In his journal he made an anguished entry: "Then is this disaster of Cherokees brought to me by a sad friend to blacken my days & nights. I can do nothing. Why shriek? Why strike ineffectual blows?"[1]

The matter of the Cherokee was one that Emerson had been familiar with for some time. As would happen with abolition, which, as a popular cause touching on the grievances of an oppressed minority, it in several ways paralleled, Emerson faced up to it slowly and reluctantly. He had neither the stamina nor the inclination to commit himself to campaigns on social issues, stubbornly insisting that the first step to remedying social ills was for men to reform themselves. He groaned, he writhed, yet in the final test he did not flinch.

Several years before, during Andrew Jackson's presidency, the Cherokee reputedly had signed a treaty with the U.S. government by which they had agreed to relinquish their lands and submit to being resettled beyond the Mississippi River. The majority of the Cherokee insisted they had entered into no such agreement. The "sham" treaty was dated 1835, but even before that their removal had been a hot issue. Although the ancient homeland of the Cherokee, in that region later designated as northern Georgia, northeastern Alabama, and southeastern Tennessee, had been theirs beyond the memory of man, throughout many years their right to it had been contested by white settlers. After prolonged strife the Cherokee had sought to placate their foes by adopting their standards of civilization. They invented their own written language and within three years were making general use of it. They drew up and adopted their own constitution and, under it, through an elective democratic process, ruled themselves ably. They converted to Christianity, chose well-educated leaders, and schooled their children. Yet the state of Georgia, by means of a state lottery, raffled off their lands, denied them the right to assemble, and stripped them of all legal rights.

On 24 January 1831 Emerson wrote to Edward that Charles was "all alive upon this nefarious Indian Subject. U.S. versus Cherokee." He himself seemed to have no position at all on the issue but did respect Charles's judgment and was impressed when, a week later, Charles successfully promoted an indignation meeting in Cambridge "to assert the claims & protect the rights of the poor Indians, whom Georgia assails."[2] But this was just a week before Ellen Tucker Emerson died and Emerson must be excused for taking no greater interest in the Cherokee at that time.

On 5 March 1832 Emerson, writing to Charles, mentioned that he had himself gone to a Cherokee indignation meeting on the night of 29 February, at the Federal Street Church, and had been impressed by Cherokee who had spoken there on their own behalf.[3] Since Samuel Hoar also spoke, Emerson may have attended in deference to him. On a later occasion he went to Boston specifically to look at the Sac and Fox Indian delegation at the State House. These Indians, however, he pronounced "so savage in their headdress & nakedness that it seemed as if the bears & catamounts had sent a deputation."[4] Emerson wanted a touch of the genteel in his noble savage.

Although in 1832 the Supreme Court, under Chief Justice John Marshall, handed down a sweeping decision declaring unconstitutional all state laws discriminating against the Cherokee, the issue was a key one in the presidential election that year. The roster of those supporting the Cherokee was impressive — Henry Clay, Daniel Webster, Sam Houston, Davy Crockett, and Edward Everett being but the most notable among them. In the intervening years, however, those favoring expulsion were not silent. By the time Martin Van Buren became President in 1837, Georgia and Alabama were posing a threat of war should expulsion be interfered with. This was an ultimatum that, if yielded to, would create the likelihood of new defiance, especially if the slavery issue heated up further.

President Van Buren, with a country in the grip of a financial panic, did not need an insurrection to contend with as well. He yielded, and on 10 April 1838 ordered Major General Winfield Scott into Cherokee country with instructions to use force of arms, if necessary, to expel them.

Whoever it was who put before Emerson on Patriot's Day 1838, in such disturbing terms, the plight of the Cherokee — it could have been any one of several people, though report favors Cynthia Thoreau, Henry's mother — he or she must have sounded the right note of urgency because, when Concord held its own protest meeting on the issue three days later, it was Emerson who stood before the audience to present the Cherokee's side of the question.[5] Samuel Hoar and other leading Concordians said their piece, too. With uncharacteristic forwardness Emerson stayed on hand to guide this congress of the concerned toward formulation of a resolution to be sent to their representatives in Washington. Apparently, he had thought to let his involvement end with that, but Mrs. Nathan Brooks and Cynthia Thoreau would not let him go until they had extracted from him a promise to write, and dispatch immediately, to President Van Buren on behalf of them all a letter condemning the Cherokee ouster.

The next day, visibly distressed, Emerson wrote in his journal:

> This tragic Cherokee business which we stirred at a meeting in the church yesterday will look to me degrading & injurious do what I can. It is like dead cats around one's neck. It is like School Committees & Sunday School classes & Teachers' meetings & the Warren street chapel & all the other holy hurrahs. I stir in it for the sad reason that no other mortal will move & if I do not, why it is left undone.
>
> The amount of it, be sure, is merely a Scream but sometimes a scream is better than a thesis.[6]

That same day Emerson wrote the letter his friends had sought. He did not enjoy doing it. He told his journal on 26 April:

> Yesterday went the letter to V[an]. B[uren]. a letter hated of me. A deliverance that does not deliver the soul. . . . This stirring in the philanthropic mud, gives me no peace. . . .
>
> I fully sympathise, be sure, with the sentiment I write, but I accept it rather from my friends than dictate it. It is not my impulse to say it & therefore my genius deserts me, no muse befriends, no music of thought or word accompanies. Bah![7]

But revulsion did not stay the force of Emerson's blows. Of the Van Buren letter, Robert Gay says: "It is a remarkable document and should be read by anyone who has thought that Emerson was "pigeon livered and lacked gall to make oppression bitter.'"[8] Conceived of as an open letter to Van Buren, it was sent to Congressman John Reed, a friend of Samuel Hoar's, and printed, through Reed's intercession, in the

Washington *Daily National Intelligencer* on 14 May. Concord's *Yeoman's Gazette* published a variant version of it on 19 May so that Emerson's fellow townsmen could see what fury they had unleashed. Small wonder that a few months later they inducted Emerson into the town's oldest and most exclusive society, the Concord Social Circle.

Emerson's letter, despite its purpose, is, at the outset, touched with that ethnic bias of which he was never wholly free, a fact that, paradoxically, makes it yet more admirable that he gave the victory to his conscience and wrote the letter.[9] He first argued that the Cherokee merited indulgence because of "the painful labors" they had undertaken "to redeem their own race from the doom of eternal inferiority." After recapitulating the events leading up to the expulsion of the Cherokee, scheduled for a month hence, Emerson courageously closed with the issue itself. The leaders of the nation, with Van Buren's ready complicity, "are contracting to put this active nation [the Cherokee] into carts and boats, and to drag them over mountains and rivers to a wilderness at a vast distance beyond the Mississippi." That fact is appalling. "Such a dereliction of all faith and virtue, such a denial of justice, and such deafness to screams for mercy were never heard of in times of peace and in the dealing of a nation with its own allies and wards, since the earth was made." Emerson deplored overstatement. Here, one gathers, he was striving to accommodate the indignation of those around him. But that was not the end of his use of exaggeration. In what was surely the most wrathful statement he ever wrote, he said now, addressing the President directly, "You, sir, will bring down that renowned chair in which you sit into infamy if your seal is set to this instrument of perfidy; and the name of this nation, hitherto the sweet omen of religion and liberty, will stink to the world."

This crescendo of indignation climaxed not much after the midpoint of the letter. Through its remainder Emerson sought a dispassionate tone which effectively leaves that one statement rearing up, like a stark and menacing pinnacle, out of the midst of a serene and manicured plain. Along the way he made another blundering racist statement by raising "the immortal question whether justice shall be done by the race of civilized to the race of savage man." With Emerson's help the Cherokee were being pushed back into the realm of primitivism, all unaware to him.

Only in his closing statement did Emerson find words in which to frame his thoughts in an utterance characteristically his own:

A man with your experience in affairs must have seen cause to appreciate the futility of opposition to the moral sentiment. However feeble the sufferer and however great the oppressor, it is the nature of things that the blow should recoil upon the aggressor. For God is in the sentiment, and it cannot be withstood.

Man's infinitude, compensation, and the universal soul were massed collectively to do battle. Even a chief executive must give way before such odds. "The potentate and the people perish before it, and as its executor, they are omnipotent."

Van Buren may never have seen Emerson's letter. That this letter and protests from many other sources, including 15,668 of the 18,000 people who made up the Cherokee nation, were unavailing did not surprise Emerson. When Cabot suggested that he include it, in 1878, in his *Miscellanies,* Emerson objected, saying it was only a "shriek" of indignation.[10]

In the same notebook that in 1835 had served as a repository for materials intended for his "Historical Discourse" on Concord, Emerson wrote a rough draft of the letter he was to send to Van Buren. It is scarcely more indignant than the final version but is clumsily written and, on that account, seems harsher.[11] In the later version Emerson made the disgrace that would befall the nation something the President himself would be accountable for. That thought was reserved for the penultimate sentence of the letter, three pages thence — a final salvo. Obviously, Emerson had decided, it was better to get the worst over with at once and to suggest, instead, at the close of the letter, that the President's experience might well preserve him from the error in prospect.

Ironically, Emerson placed this letter among earlier notes in which he recorded the systematic takeover of Indian lands by his Concord forebears in the seventeenth century, the war with the Narragansett, and the eventual total extirpation of the Pequot. "Indians are bad neighbors," he says there.[12] But he credits fear of them as a benefaction to the early settlers. To preserve themselves from that danger they were compelled to stand together.

For Emerson, the Cherokee matter was beyond sentiment and simply a humiliation for America. Attempting to redress the situation with mere words was, to him, a further humiliation. He spoke of the "burlesque character" such a letter, by its very nature, must have. Once again the people of Concord had stood him on the head of a sugar barrel and made him declaim a piece for the benefit of his fellow townsmen. Yet he did what he had to do, and did it well.

With a vermillion pencil mark the day.

30. The Address at Divinity Hall

*I*N 1838 Louis Daguerre had perfected his process just in time to capture an historic event, the first such ever photographed — the coronation of Queen Victoria on 28 June 1838 at Westminster Abbey. The event all but captured the world. It did not ensnare Emerson, however, for he was engrossed with a matter that interested him more. He was working on an address to be given to the seniors at the Harvard Divinity School on 15 July, the month before Commencement. Although he seemed to strike it off at white heat, the completed address would show none of the marks of hasty work. In fact, contrary to his usual practice, Emerson fell back on his rhetorical training and made a regular division of his topic under traditional headings. What he had to say, he knew, would not set well with some of his auditors. An impeccable form would advise them that the speaker was not intoxicated by his ideas and reeling out of control.

Emerson had, in fact, chosen his topic before the occasion to address the Divinity School had arisen. The discourse may have come together swiftly, but the ideas had been pondered for some weeks. They came to him at first on 18 March, a Sunday and, for him, a long and tedious day of churchgoing. And they were thoughts quite contrary to those that the preaching he had heard was meant to inspire. That night he wrote: ''At Church all day but almost tempted to say I would go no more. . . . The snowstorm was real, the preacher merely spectral. Vast contrast to look at him & then out of the window.'' The preacher had been Barzillai Frost. Predictably, Emerson scorned the obvious pun and went on: ''I ought to sit & think & then write a discourse to the

American clergy showing them the ugliness & unprofitableness of theology & churches at this day & the glory and sweetness of the Moral
Nature out of whose pale they are almost wholly shut." Not only did
Emerson recall this idea when later he had an address to write, he
went back to the journal entry and assimilated much of it into the
address.[1]

Three days after being Frost-smitten he was asked by students at
the Divinity School to come talk with them. On 1 April he reported
the visit in terms that show he had not abandoned his earlier thoughts:

> I went rather heavy-hearted for I always find that my views
> chill or shock people at the first opening. But the conversation
> went well & I came away cheered. I told them that the preacher
> should be a poet smit with love of the harmonies of moral nature:
> and yet look at the Unitarian Association & see if its aspect is
> poetic. They all smiled No.[2]

This meeting evidently was meant to be preliminary to Emerson's
formal appearance at the Divinity School in July, for it postdated a
letter that Emerson received, asking him, on behalf of the Senior Class,
to deliver on the evening of 15 July, "the customary discourse, on
occasion of their entering upon the active Christian ministry."[3] The
phrase "the customary discourse," was surely formulaic, just as the
invitation to deliver the Phi Beta Kappa address the previous year
referred to the American Scholar as "the customary topic." Since
Emerson had not given customary treatment to that topic on that occasion, and, as was well known, was unlikely to give any topic customary treatment, the likelihood is that, when he met with the students
soon after their invitation and sounded them out on their feelings about
the Unitarian leadership, he knew then that they wanted him to deliver an address that would shake up the establishment. His audience,
he realized, would come to more than the seven students who comprised the class and their guests. The little chapel on the second floor
of Divinity Hall could seat about a hundred people. Emerson correctly
surmised that every seat would be taken and that the faculty of the
school would fill the front pews. If he wanted to get a message to those
who governed this Unitarian citadel of conservatism, he could hardly
contrive a better opportunity. Moreover, since he was a figure of controversy, curiosity alone should fill the pews.

Emerson's central thesis in *Nature,* and again in his "American
Scholar" address had been that man can be free only if he disengages
himself from the past. That he might now extend the perimeters of
this advice to include as well the traditions of institutionalized religion does not seem to have occurred to the school authorities or, if it

did, they discounted it, supposing that Emerson would be reluctant to put forward such a proposal to such an audience. His student hosts can hardly have been so idyllic in their expectations. Most likely they were counting on fireworks. But then they could afford them. Unlike the established ministry they did not have a constituency to placate. The ministry, of course, was within its rights. To dispute from this pulpit the divinity of Christ as it was traditionally understood had to be the height of impropriety. Emerson was not blind to the risk but, as a calculated indiscretion, was willing to venture it to make certain his views were known.

The ideas Emerson had to advance were, as he well knew, not so novel as some people would think. They had simply not yet caught sufficient notice. The missing key, a dramatic presentation given in striking language, was what Emerson proposed to supply.

On 8 July Emerson wrote in his journal:

> We shun to say that which shocks the religious ear of the people
> & to take away titles even of false honor from Jesus. But this
> fear is an impotency to commend the moral sentiment. For if I
> can so imbibe that wisdom as to utter it well, instantly love & awe
> take place. The reverence for Jesus is only reverence for this.
> . . . When I have as clear a sense as now that I am speaking
> simple truth without any bias . . . all railing, all unwillingness to
> hear, all danger of injury to the conscience, dwindles & disappears.
> I refer to the discourse now growing under my eye to the Divinity
> School.[4]

As early as 1819, preaching before a Baltimore audience on the occasion of the ordination of a future president of Harvard, Jared Sparks, William Ellery Channing had said: ''We see God around us because He dwells within us.'' And again, ''God's infinity has its image in the soul.'' In 1829 Channing stated: ''There is the moral principle, that which should especially be called a man's self, for it is clothed with a kingly authority over his whole nature. . . . Its very essence is impartiality. It has no respect of persons.'' When Emerson, in the ''Divinity School Address,'' contends that the moral sentiment is ''divine and deifying,'' and asserts further that ''The soul knows no persons,'' he is not striking out into unknown territory but essentially is paraphrasing Channing's ideas.[5]

Well before Emerson spoke at Harvard, Orestes Brownson had said in print, ''Christianity was not a new revelation with Jesus.''[6] Neither Channing nor Brownson had been treated afterward as pariahs for saying what they had said. Nor was Samuel D. Robbins made to face the wrath of the community when, three months before Emerson gave his "Divinity School Address," in his article "Thoughts on Unity, Progress, and Government," published in Brownson's *Boston Quarterly Review*, he set forth what proved to be the central theme of Emerson's address, and, evidently, its immediate source. Robbins declared:

> The inspiration of nature is the music in all our hearts. . . .
> Individual minds are the best interpreters of the Divinity. The
> original thinkers, the single-eyed, the holy-hearted, are the purest
> conductors of infinite truth, the Christs of God. The word is
> incarnate in every God-child. . . . Creeds change, and dynasties
> crumble in the dust, but man shall always be priest and king . . .
> so long as he shall obey the oracle of his own spirit, and fulfill the
> unwritten commandment of his Godlike spirit.[7]

The truth is, in the midst of a war going on between two fiercely contending factions, Emerson made of himself a shining mark. At Harvard for some time there had been a power struggle between those who espoused the Edinburgh moral-sense philosophy, championed early by Levi Frisbie and Levi Hedge, under whom Emerson had studied; and those who upheld the Scottish realists and Locke and William Paley. Andrews Norton was the standard-bearer of this second faction. What Emerson was saying was being said also by Frederic Henry Hedge, Levi's son, and by Furness, Ripley, Parker, Brownson, and others. These were the men spoken of now as transcendentalists. Arthur Schlesinger explains why only Emerson commanded attention: "He had the gift of crystallizing the impulses of the day and disclosing them with a profundity and richness of suggestion that made even those who had already voiced them wonder at facets they had overlooked and beauties they had not suspected."[8]

Emerson was not capable of the close reasoning his fellow transcendentalists engaged in, but the insights that sprang from his prose, unheralded yet unforgettable, seemed to illustrate the cause he advocated. Here was man brilliantly proclaiming his spontaneous intuitions caught in unassailable aphorisms — truth distilled in incomparable rhetoric. Emerson transferred the speculations of transcendentalism out of the coin of conjecture into the hard currency of verified wisdom, making it one with the lore of the ages, even as epigrams distill moral truths. Obviously the rationalists had to take him out of action or face the prospect of being put to flight.

Even before Holmes got around to calling "The American Scholar" "our intellectual Declaration of Independence," Moncure Conway accorded, perhaps excessively, equivalent status to Emerson's talk at Divinity Hall, identifying it as "that address which stands in the moral history of America where the Declaration of Independence stands in its political history.''[9] The speech was given, as planned, on Sunday evening, 15 July 1838. The Henry Wares, father and son, both holding professorships in the Divinity School, were there, Dean John Gorham Palfrey was there, and so was Andrews Norton. A fair representation of the Transcendental Club was there, too — Hedge, Parker, Ripley, Elizabeth Peabody, and, possibly, William Ellery Channing. That contingent alone was enough to set Norton's teeth on edge. If he had known that when Emerson spoke next at the Divinity School, in a distant day, his son and daughters would be there as part of Emerson's coterie, he probably would have had a seizure where he sat.

In strictly theological terms, the basic message of the Divinity address was that man by responding intuitively, through Nature, to the moral sentiment expresses his divinity. Christ taught that ''God incarnates himself in man.'' Christian leaders have failed their fellowman because they have neglected to explore ''the Moral Nature . . . as the fountain of the established teaching in society.'' They have fossilized Christianity by putting too much emphasis on formal ritual. True faith is attained only when a man experiences a personal awareness of the Supreme Spirit dwelling within him. These arguments led Emerson to two controversial conclusions. Endowing all men with divinity and the capacity to attain to a knowledge of moral truth without the aid of a mediator relegated Christ to a human condition. Insisting on the self-sufficiency of the soul repudiated the authority of the church and, consequently, ecclesiasticism as well.[10]

Chapman says that Emerson ''was not unconscious of what function he was performing'' when he delivered this address and, consequently, could not have been surprised to hear it reported that he was seeking to overthrow the authority and influence of Christianity.[11] Indeed, a letter Emerson wrote to Carlyle on 6 August finds him unperturbed by the commotion stirred: ''I have written and read a kind of sermon to the Senior Class of our Cambridge Theological School a fortnight ago; and an address to the Literary Societies of Dartmouth College. . . . And both these are now in press. The first I hear is very offensive. I will now try to hold my tongue until next winter.''[12]

James Russell Lowell, who at the time of the address was at Concord, where the college authorities had ''rusticated'' him for coming drunk to chapel, blended his classmates' unfavorable reports on the address into his Class Poem. The poem, written in August on his return to Cambridge, read in part:

> *Woe for Religion too, when men, who claim*
> *To place a "Reverend" before their name,*
> *Ascend the Lord's own holy place to preach*

In strains that Kneeland had been proud to reach. . . .
When men just girding for the holy strife . . .
Invite a man their Christian zeal to crown
By preaching earnestly the gospel — down . . .
And tamely hear the anointed Son of God
Made like themselves an animated clod![13]

Because of having been rusticated, Lowell was not at liberty to read his poem at Harvard. Therefore he had it printed and sent a copy at once to Emerson, together with a letter more remarkable for its ingenuity than its seeming ingenuousness. The letter was requisite, for Lowell had, in fact, been the object of Emerson's cordial notice during the period of his Concord exile. Lowell began by owning astonishment that his friends could suppose he "could wilfully malign a man whose salt I had eaten, and whose little child I had danced on my knee." He told Emerson also that he had "spoken so highly of you in private," his friends found it difficult now to reconcile his public utterance with what he had said before. His way out of this dilemma was to insist that he had only spoken as his conscience directed. Here he was reaching Emerson at a vulnerable point because this argument was Emerson's own justification for having said what he said at Divinity Hall. He concluded his defense by asking not that Emerson pardon his offense but rather that he acquit him of the charges brought against him.[14]

Lowell had put his case well. On receipt of the letter, Emerson wrote Lowell at once, indulging his youthful verve: "I cannot find a word . . . in relation to me which the license of the occasion does not more than excuse, & I find some words there wh. make me much your debtor." Emerson was familiar with the reckless tone that showed itself in the rhetoric of the Commencement season, but probably found more satisfaction in Lowell's resourcefulness in defending himself than in his excesses in attacking him. "I love," he exclaimed, "the spirit of your letter." With the exoneration came an invitation: "If you should pass through Concord, I beg you will come & see me. I am vain eno' to think that nobody knows so many pleasant walks in it as I."[15]

During the time he had lived in Concord, Lowell had accompanied Emerson on several walks. From time to time Emerson lent him books. In fact, when he was writing his Class Poem he still had with him in Cambridge an edition of Tennyson lent him by Emerson. And in that interlude he had spoken well of Emerson, describing him as "a very pleasant man in private conversation." But he had also concluded that Emerson's reputation was inflated: "After all I'd heard of him, as an Eagle soaring in pride of place, I was surprised to see a poor little hawk stooping at flies or at least sparrows & groundlings."[16] Though uneasy all along about Emerson's theological views, he had no quarrel with his practical opinions.

Had Emerson seen a letter Lowell had written on 23 July to Nathan Hale, Jr., his classmate, he might not have found time to answer Lowell at all. There Lowell said:

> Speaking of a plentiful lack of wit — did you hear R.W.E.'s sermon . . . ? I hear that it was an abomination. . . . Only imagine if — every time he oped his lanthorn jaws, with "sage saws of books" (for almost all he says he steals), some shrill voiced Powell from the other side of the room were to . . . discharge a similar reply — by Jove! it would be rare sport! They say . . . that man sees himself in everything around him, if E. could see *him*self & it didn't drive him crazy (if indeed in that respect he isn't past mending) why — amen.[17]

While Lowell might not seem entitled to the extenuation he cajoled from Emerson, justification can be found for the difference in tone that distinguishes his letter to Emerson from his letter to Hale. Lowell was the son of an orthodox clergyman. Neither at nineteen nor later did he have leanings toward transcendentalism. Since Hale shared his conservative theological orientation, undoubtedly the facetious vein he fell into when he wrote to him reflected, in part, his desire to please Hale.

In fairness to Lowell, between the time he wrote the first letter and the time he wrote the second, a few things happened to sober his views. During his stay in Concord, he corresponded often with his friend and classmate George B. Loring. On 9 August Lowell wrote to him: "I must go down and see Emerson, and if he doesn't make me feel *more* like a fool it won't be for want of sympathy *in that respect*. He is a good-natured man, in spite of his doctrines. He traveled all the way up from his house to bring me a book which had been sent to me *via* him." With Loring the flippancy he exhibited in his letter to Hale was not appropriate. Loring urged Lowell to exercise restraint in passing judgment on Emerson and to rein in his prejudices.[18]

On 27 August the *Boston Daily Advertiser* carried an unsigned article, "The New School in Literature and Religion," readily identifiable as from the hand of Andrews Norton. For two years now, since the publication of *Nature*, Norton had been wary of Emerson. Back then he had characterized transcendentalism as "absolutely and not remotely, of infidel tendency and import."[19] In his newspaper article Norton deplored Emerson's address as a particularly reprehensible example of the evil forces at work to draw men away from Christianity. That Emerson rejected "all belief in Christianity as a revelation" was obvious to Norton. Only slightly less certain, in his estimation, was the likelihood that Emerson also denied the existence of God. Never did his soubriquet, "the Unitarian pope," seem more merited than when Norton all but formally excommunicated anyone who, in the guise of a Christian teacher, repeated Emerson's ideas. The students who had invited him, though they may have acted in good faith, were "accessories . . . to the commission of a great offence."[20]

Even among those who agreed with Norton some were dismayed at the vehemence of his attack. Theophilus Parsons, destined for a professorship in the Harvard Law School and, even then, a lawyer of note, replied to Norton in a letter published in the *Advertiser* on 30 August. He questioned Norton's means, not his ends. To confront error with "anger, derision, intolerance, and blind and fierce denunciation" would not rout error. What Norton had perhaps missed was Emerson's recommendation, reminiscent of Puritanism itself on its first appearance, that those who saw the need of change should not "project and establish a Cultus with new rites and forms," but rather undertake to breathe "the breath of new life . . . through the forms already existing."[21]

Until Norton spoke out, reaction to the address had been, for the most part, temperate. That state of affairs now dramatically altered. When Lowell wrote to Hale, people were tipping this way and that on the address, with no great expression of feelings being apparent. Now pressure had built up and there was an explosion of sorts. Lowell's poem, a product of the quiescent period, came into print after hostilities had broken out. Lowell had, as Emerson himself put it, offered "strictures on the Address," but did not mean to take up cudgels against its author.[22] Only when Lowell saw Emerson under assault did Emerson's dignity as a person fully dawn on him. Looking back at his upstart attack in his Class Poem, Lowell, long years later, by then having succeeded to terms of cordial if not intimate friendship with Emerson, wrote:

> *Behold the baby arrows of that wit*
> *Wherewith I dared assail the woundless Truth!*
> *Love hath refilled the quiver, and with it*
> *The man shall win atonement for the youth.*[23]

To Lowell's further credit, although during his stay in Concord he boarded with Barzillai Frost, was tutored by him, and came to regard him as trivial-minded, he maintained a circumspect silence on the portrait of Frost given by Emerson in his address.

Too prudent to reply publicly to Norton, Emerson was nevertheless shaken by the ferocity of an attack that Perry Miller characterizes as "so unprecedented an act that it could have been inspired by nothing less than pure rage."[24] On 19 October 1838, prompted perhaps by the table talk of some Divinity School students who came to dinner the day before, Emerson finally set down his views of the matter. They were not mild:

> The great army of cowards who bellow & bully from their bed chamber windows, have no confidence in truth or God. Truth will not maintain itself, they fancy, unless they bolster it up & whip & stone the assailants; and the religion of God, the being of God, they seem to think dependent on what we say of it. The feminine vehemence with which the A[ndrews]. N[orton]. of the *Daily Advertiser* beseeches the dear people to whip that naughty heretic is the natural feeling in the mind whose religion is external. It cannot subsist, it suffers shipwreck if its faith is not confirmed by all surrounding persons. . . . The aim of a true teacher now would be to bring men back to a trust in God & destroy before their eyes these idolatrous propositions: to teach the doctrine of the perpetual revelation.[25]

The same drama had been enacted in Boston two hundred years earlier. Then the advocate of perpetual revelation was Anne Hutchinson. Norton's role, at that time, fell to the lot of a clergyman from Concord, Peter Bulkeley, Emerson's forebear. Thus did the past mock the present.

The reaction of some of Emerson's listeners to his address had been all he could have wished for. On returning home Theodore Parker had written to his friend George Ellis: "It was the noblest of all his performances. The noblest and most inspiring I ever listened to." In his journal he reflected further: "So beautiful, so just, so true, and terribly sublime was his picture of the faults of the church in its present condition. My soul is roused."[26] Elizabeth Peabody also was elated: "There never before had been a discourse there that so justified the foundation principle of the Divinity School" — as enunciated by Channing when the school was dedicated.[27]

Previous to Norton's blunt attack, much of the criticism directed against Emerson's address had passed around by word of mouth. Miller designates it "a whispering campaign."[28] This term, however, implies a tactical assault and that it was tactical is doubtful. Conservative Bostonians did not know quite how to go about attacking one of their own, and found it awkward to engage in such an undertaking. Clearly Emerson did not seek it. The idea of being embroiled in public controversy was repugnant to him. After attending the Phi Beta Kappa gathering at Harvard on 31 August, he remarked in his journal, speaking of himself in the third person: "The vulgar think he would found a sect & be installed & made much of. He knows better, & much prefers his melons & his woods." A week later he reflected further: "All that befals me in the way of criticism & extreme blame & praise, drawing me out of equilibrium, — putting me for a time in false position to people & disallowing the spontaneous sentiments, wastes my time, bereaves me of thoughts, & shuts me up within poor personal considerations."[29]

By November, with the application of judicious amounts of self-deprecation, he had virtually isolated himself from the tempests blowing without. On the eighth he wrote: "Let me never fall into the vulgar mistake of dreaming that I am persecuted whenever I am contradicted. . . . Besides, I own, I am not often inclined to take part with those who say I am bad or foolish, for I fear I am both."[30]

While no organized campaign was mounted against Emerson as a result of the Divinity address, various individuals did indeed speak their mind about it. Cornelius Felton, who had invited Emerson to give "The American Scholar" address, found his remarks now "full of extravagance and overweening self-confidence, ancient errors disguised in misty rhetoric, and theories which would overturn society and resolve the world into chaos."[31] Dean Palfrey, later allied to Emerson in friendship, was rumored to have said that what was not folly in the address was downright atheism.[32] In the *Biblical Repertory and Princeton Review*, a voice of Presbyterian conservatism, Professor Alexander wrote of the address: "We want words with which to express our sense of the nonsense and impiety which pervade it." As the man responsible for it, Emerson was unmistakably "an infidel and an atheist."[33] In Cincinnati, James Freeman Clarke and Christopher Cranch, both of whom ultimately would throw in their lot with Emerson, having then heard only contradictory accounts of the reception the address had received, dealt with it somewhat ambivalently in the November issue of *The Western Messenger*. On a first reading Clarke "did not discover anything in it objectionable at all." He thought that some obscure passage in the address must have been misunderstood by Emerson's accusers. He urged that Emerson be given a fair hearing, free from name-calling. Yet, at the same time, the editors of the *Messenger* seemed to sidle away from Emerson, concluding that the New School, which they, rather in spite of themselves, had come to be identified with, looked for leadership not to Emerson but to Channing.[34]

That autumn Emerson got his fairest hearing, in print, from Orestes Brownson. Brownson began by replying to Norton's *Daily Advertiser* attack with a counterthrust in the *Boston Morning Post*, a warning, really, to those who might take Norton's attack as a signal to launch an all-out attack to proceed at their own peril. "It is as the advocate of the rights of the mind,'' Brownson said, ''as the defender of personal independence in the spiritual world, not as the Idealist, the Pantheist, or the Atheist, that he is run after.''[35]

In Brownson's opinion newspapers did not offer a proper forum for theological controversies. Consequently, readers who wanted Brownson's extended views on this matter found them in the October issue of his *Boston Quarterly Review*.[36] Brownson began by deploring ''the abuse which had been heaped upon Mr. Emerson.'' Christian charity, he pointed out, required others to allow him to express his opinion. If we took exception to it, the right course to follow was to express our dissent calmly and respectfully. He next acknowledged his admiration for Emerson's courage: ''We love bold speculation; we are pleased to find a man who dares tell us what and precisely what he thinks, however unpopular his views may be.'' Not content with that tribute, Brownson then extolled Emerson's integrity: ''Mr. Emerson is the last man in the world we should suspect of conscious hostility to religion and morality. No one can know him or read his productions without feeling a profound respect for the singular purity and uprightness of his character and motives.'' While Brownson did urge ''a certain reserve in all speculations, something like timidity about rushing off in an unknown universe,'' he skillfully circumvented the whole mountain range of Emerson's dissenting beliefs by identifying as ''the real object'' and ''real end'' of Emerson's address a goal no reasonable man could object to:

His real object is not the inculcation of any new theory on man, nature or God; but to induce men to think for themselves on all subjects, and to speak from their own full hearts and earnest convictions. . . . To provoke men to be men, self-moving, self-subsisting men, not mere puppets . . . is a grand and praiseworthy work, and we should reverence and aid, not abuse and hinder him who gives himself up soul and body to its accomplishments.

That the ''Divinity School Address'' and many of Emerson's other discourses and essays continue to engross readers in the twentieth century is due largely to this spirit of free inquiry that Brownson so eloquently identified. We are enthralled even as those in his audiences were, not by closely reasoned arguments (such always were few), but by his questing spirit, the glad and surging force of his rhetoric, pouring from an ardent soul filled with the joy and wonder of existence.

At the conclusion of a magnificent defense of Emerson, Brownson in a single sentence encompasses the essence of Norton's strictures and, even as he allows for their validity, proclaims their inconsequence:

In calling, as he [Emerson] does, upon the literary men of our community . . . to assert and maintain their independence throughout the whole domain of thought, against every species of tyranny that would encroach upon it, he is doing his duty; he is doing a work the effects of which will be felt for good far and wide, long after men shall have forgotten the puerility of his conceits, the affectations of his style, and the unphilosophical character of his speculations.

Emerson may have been startled to see his daring theological constructions thus swept casually into the dustbin, but, since he himself chose to put great emphasis on the paramount importance of allowing men to say what they believe, he was in no position to protest. That men someday would go to the "Divinity School Address" not to ponder his theological arguments but to contemplate a notable instance of a man courageously speaking his mind to a hostile audience, without fear of consequences, might have surprised him, but it would not have dismayed him. He had not really produced arguments to uphold his "heresies." As for those heresies, Cabot said: "Emerson did not think very highly of his address; he had not said what he most wished to say. . . . He was trying to place the reverence for Jesus upon true ground, out of reach of the reaction that was sure to set in when the claim to an exclusive revelation should lose its force."[37]

31. Storm in Our Washbowl
Presumption of Heresy

*W*HEN, in mid-October 1838, Emerson described to Carlyle the furor his "Divinity School Address" occasioned as "the storm in our washbowl," Carlyle, without ever having seen a copy of the address, loyally wrote back: "You are even to go on, giving still harder shocks if need be; and should I come into censure by means of you [as, in fact, he already had], there or here, think that I am proud of my company." In February 1839 Carlyle received, only a few days apart, first a copy of Norton's newspaper attack and then a copy of the address itself. On 8 February he wrote to Emerson: "I find in this . . . that noblest self-assertion, and believing originality which is like sacred fire, the *beginning* of whatsoever is to flame and work; and for young men especially one sees not what could be more vivifying."[1]

Here Carlyle added a perceptive note that others had missed. Emerson's address was not directed primarily to those who were responding to it, the Divinity School faculty, the Boston Association of Ministers, the editors of theological journals. It was pitched to the minds of those who had invited him, the graduating students, and its high excitement was designed to stir them, to induce them to think for themselves, to speak out not from their memories but from their perceptions. That an address upholding the superiority of the intuitions had led, however, to a competition among logicians was a fact that caused Emerson some surprise. But even if that had not been its intended result, it had brought out into the open the paramount issues of the day, and men were speaking at last from their earnest convictions. He found satisfaction in that.

The members of Emerson's family reacted predictably to the "Divinity School Address." Aunt Mary saw it as conceived "under the influence of some malign demon," and would have it consigned to oblivion.[2] William took it in stride. Lidian did, too, regretting that her husband should be traduced, yet rejoicing because, so far as she could tell, Emerson had not "felt a moment's uneasiness on his own account" as a result of the charges raised against him.[3] Uncle Samuel showed the most practical interest. To Aunt Mary he wrote: "It is not necessary to assent to everything he says — but all, even such as I, can understand enough to be moved to adoration and worship of the true, the beautiful and good."[4] Early in August he wrote to Emerson from Waltham, owning truthfully that "we have heard about the wicked thing, alias Ms, from friends & enemies — & some awful things are said." While he had not been intimidated by anything he had heard, he was in possession of the manuscript and had examined it closely. Told by Emerson that he was making arrangements to have it printed, Samuel spoke up in his plain, honest way:

> Now I do not wish you to print this, in some respects, the greatest effort you have yet put forth — It will do no good — it will not enlighten the blind, nor calm the angry, nor sooth the mortified — and if you print only for the few who ask it, you *must* make alterations, cut out exaggerations &c &c, which will cause it not to be the same that was heard. Now it is yours — print it, & it is the worlds. Well be it so — the world needs to be enlightened — but I don't want to see you classed with Kneeland, Paine &c, bespattered & belied —[5]

Cabot claims that Emerson "was surprised to find his intention so far mistaken as to leave many . . . to suppose that he was trying to belittle the character of Jesus." He says rather that Emerson thought the time was near when men no longer would believe that Christ was God and that he wished to establish beforehand other grounds for the reverence of Jesus so that men would not turn away from him. In July 1838, in fact, Emerson told his journal: "Since the parrot world will be swift to renounce the name of Christ in amends to its pride for having raised it so high, it behooves the lover of God to love that lover of God." Elizabeth Peabody later reported that Emerson cut from his text, when editing it for delivery, a passage which conveyed this thought. She asked him to reintroduce it into the printed text. "No," he told her, "these gentlemen have committed themselves against what I did read."[6]

The address came from the press on 21 August. Originally it was not to be published but merely printed for the use of the students.

Because of the interest it had stirred, however, Emerson elected to publish it. He even regretted that it was not on heavier paper, for it was likely to be passed about a good deal. It sold for twelve and a half cents a copy. He would not grow rich from it.

Once the deed was done, Uncle Samuel stood firmly behind him and found himself caught in an awkward dilemma. In October Emerson planned to visit the Ripleys on the Sabbath, indicating that he did not wish to preach. At other times since his approbation, he had preached when he visited Ripley's church. As Ripley saw it, if Emerson came now and did not preach, "it would give the very wrong impression, that I was unwilling to have you hold forth from my pulpit — which never can be so." He therefore invited Emerson to come prepared to preach or to stay away. Since by then other newspapers had entered the fray, the *Boston Courier* labeling him "misguided" and the *Christian Register* editorializing on his views, Samuel had shown great moral courage in standing by him. By mid-October matters had deteriorated still further. Rumor circulated that Abner Kneeland, the "convicted blasphemer," had read Emerson's address to his congregation on a recent Sunday, contending that he could say nothing himself that would be as instructive. Samuel's anxiety for Emerson grew: "The whole band of clergymen have raised their voice against him," he said, "with a very few exceptions and the common people, even women, look solemn and sad, and roll up their eyes. . . . 'Oh, he is a dangerous man; the church is in danger; Unitarianism is disgraced.'. . ."[7]

While Emerson would not allow himself to be brought into open debate about his address, he did consent to exchange views on the subject, privately, with Henry Ware, Jr. No less so than Emerson, Ware took the high road in controversy. The four letters that passed between them over three months' time, beginning on 16 July and ending on 8 October, rival, for respect and tact, a diplomatic correspondence. The two men seemed to be dancing a subdued minuet. Ware initiated the correspondence. While he commended Emerson's "lofty ideas and beautiful images of the spiritual life," he owned sorrow over the direction in which Emerson's mind was moving and expressed anxiety lest his "unqualified statements" imperil Christianity. "You will," he concluded, "excuse my saying this, which I probably should never have troubled you with if, as I said, a proper frankness did not seem at this moment to require it."[8] With the imminent collapse of Christianity in prospect, one might suppose that Ware did not need to justify himself.

Emerson's reply was written twelve days later. In the interval he had delivered an oration at Dartmouth, "Literary Ethics." One could readily believe that he had passed the time instead seeking phrases that would match Ware's in propriety and sensibility. He had found Ware's letter "just what I might expect from your truth & charity combined with your known opinions." He now raised a point that Ware could not controvert since he had first chosen to raise it. While it had caused him pain, Emerson said, to say things in the presence of "dear friends and benefactors" that were contrary to their beliefs, since these were his convictions he had felt honor-bound to express them: "I thought I would not pay the nobleness of my friends so mean a compliment as to suppress my opposition to their supposed views out of fear of offence." He closed by thanking Ware for "this renewed expression of your tried toleration and love." This round was Emerson's.[9]

On 23 September, Ware delivered at the Divinity School a sermon, "The Personality of the Deity." As soon as it came from the press, he sent a copy to Emerson with a covering letter explaining that, while he had sought in his sermon to controvert views which Emerson had advanced, he did not see himself as having truly entered the lists to engage Emerson in combat. In the first place he was not familiar with the ideas on which Emerson's views were grounded. Coming down to specifics, he mentioned the issue central to his remedial sermon: "I do not know by what arguments the doctrine that 'the soul knows no persons' is justified in your mind." Ware probably spoke at the bidding of his colleagues. "I esteem it particularly unhappy," he confessed, "to be thus brought into a sort of public opposition to you, for I have a thousand feelings which draw me toward you."[10]

Here it seemed that Boston's tradition of good breeding, momentarily lost sight of by Norton, was reasserting itself. Now that Emerson had accounted for his apparent lack of circumspection by saying that he had spoken as he did, not because he held his friends in contempt but in deference, rather, to their nobility, there seemed no reason why Ware and Emerson could not thrash out the matter as angels might.

That Ware believed, however, that some step had to be taken to counteract the influence of Emerson's address cannot be doubted. Even as, on the night of 13 September, he was working on his own sermonic response, he had been interrupted in his study by a young Tutor in Greek at Harvard, a graduate of the Divinity School, Jones Very. Under the influence of the "Divinity School Address" Very saw himself as the teacher Emerson had called for, and had come to announce the revelations his own intuitions had brought to him through the Holy Spirit, at the same time denouncing Ware because Ware harkened to his own will and not "to the will of the Father." Two days later, Very, obviously deranged, had to be sent home to Salem.[11]

In November, unaware of the courteous exchange that had taken place between Emerson and Ware, the editors of the *Christian Examiner* put both Divinity discourses under scrutiny. "Emerson's notions," they decided, "so far as they are intelligible," were "neither good divinity nor good sense.'' They recommended that henceforth the faculty should be privileged to veto ''the nomination of the students, against the probability of hearing sentiments . . . altogether repugnant to their feelings, and opposed to the whole tenor of their own teachings.'' As for Ware's sermon, they dutifully acclaimed it

> a strong and lucid statement of a doctrine which lies at the very foundation of religion, and will tend to disabuse the minds of many respecting the true character and tendency of a set of newly broached fancies, which, deceived by the high sounding pretensions of their proclaimers, they may have thought were about to quicken and reform the world.[12]

Ware must have cringed when he read this since it was the sort of personal attack he had hoped to avoid. Moreover, by then he had in his possession Emerson's noble reply to his letter with its enclosure.

Emerson had written the letter that closed the correspondence on 8 October. Having read Ware's sermon, he could say: ''I did not feel any disposition to depart from my habitual contentment that you should say your thoughts, whilst I say mine.'' But now enough for the amenities. Here was his opportunity to make his case with ''the good and wise men in Cambridge and in Boston'' who thought of making him ''into an object of criticism.'' With remarkable agility he established his disinclination to debate while, simultaneously, he affirmed his faith in the superiority of intuition to understanding. He seemed to plead, in fact, a functional incapacity to be other than he was and to claim the privileges that went with such a condition. In what is certainly the most remarkable and disarming letter he ever wrote, he told Ware:

> I have always been from my very incapacity of methodical writing a chartered libertine free to worship & free to rail ; . . . never esteemed near enough to the institutions & mind of society to deserve the notice of the masters of literature & religion. I have appreciated fully the advantage of my position for I well knew there was no scholar less willing or less able to be a polemic. I could not give account of myself if challenged I could not possibly give you one of the ''arguments'' on which as you cruelly hint any position of mine stands.[13]

In this context the word *cruelly* is startling. Ware's almost groveling mildness (several contemporary accounts characterize him as ''saintly'') invites us to believe that Emerson used the term in humorous reproach. That in turn tells us the tone of the entire paragraph ; Emerson is writing in a vein of mocking self-deprecation, yet, in so doing, throwing himself on the mercy of his persecutors. His cordiality is all but boundless. Who could scowl at such a man? Surely not Ware.

Emerson continued: "When I see myself suddenly raised into the importance of a heretic, I am very uneasy when I advert to the supposed duties of such a personage who is expected to make good his thesis against all comers." To remind Ware that he was not locked in a battle unto death with a demon from the pit, Emerson gave him a further verbal nudge. "I certainly shall do no such thing," he said, declining his presumed duties as heretic. But he would continue to be himself: "I shall go on just as before seeing whatever I can, & telling what I see."[14]

Emerson could not let Ware go without a gentle tweaking. He assumed that, in the future as in the past, he would find in the works of Ware and his peers confirmation of his own perceptions and realize that "my nonsense is only their own thought in motley."[15] Thus he left Ware with a paradox. Either he was more orthodox than they realized or they were more heretical than they realized. Had he chosen to do so, he might have cited the matter of the personality of the Deity as an instance where his heresy was more orthodox than their orthodoxy. In denying God's personality he sought to affirm the infinitude of a nature that went beyond the powers of man's comprehension. Channing seems to have grasped Emerson's true intentions. Of Ware's sermon Channing remarked that Ware was "fighting a shadow; for Mr. Emerson expressly says, and makes a great point of it, that God is *alive*, not *dead;* and would have the gospel narrative left to make its own impression of an indwelling life, like the growing grass." Channing was not comfortable with Emerson's deemphasis of the New Testament miracles and apparent outright rejection of the personality of God but accepted the "Divinity School Address" otherwise as "an entirely justifiable and needed criticism on the perfunctory character of service creeping over the Unitarian churches." He did not have far to seek to find those who took issue with him. His assistant at the Federal Street Church, Ezra Stiles Gannett, was one of those who thought the Divinity School faculty should vote itself a veto so that the likes of Emerson's address could not happen again (as though miracles were daily happenings!). "The shepherds of Harvard," Gannett explained, "could hardly be expected to allow the wolf to carry off the lambs in their very presence, even at the invitation of the innocents themselves."[16]

But if Ware was willing to believe that, with his sermon, the scales had again been brought into balance, Andrews Norton was not. Long before he had a "Divinity School Address" to lambast, Norton had made himself the foe of the cause that had culminated in the address. In a letter of 12 February 1838, to Dr. George Rapall Noyes, concerning a lecture on Episcopal ordination that Noyes then had in preparation, Norton had written: "No clergy will be supported among us to teach transcendentalism, infidelity, and pantheism."[17] Soon after the first anniversary of the "Divinity School Address," on 19 July 1839, Norton mounted the same pulpit to speak to the graduates — his topic being "A Discourse on the Latest Form of Infidelity," a formal refutation of the ideas put forward by Emerson the previous year. He said:

> It has been vaguely alleged, that the internal evidences of our religion are sufficient, and that miraculous proof is not wanted. . . . Nothing is left that can be called Christianity, if its miraculous power be denied. . . . The denial that God revealed himself by Christ . . . the rejection of *historical* Christianity, is, of course, accompanied by the rejection of all that mass of evidence, which, in the view of a Christian, establishes the truth of his religion.

Norton next considered Emerson's claim that every man is "a newborn bard of the Holy Ghost." "A wise man," he said, "will remember what he is . . . A creature of a day, just endued [*sic*] with the capacity of thought." He went on: "There can be no intuition, no direct perception, of the truth of Christianity. . . . The evidence of these facts is not intuitive . . . the generality of men have never been able by their unassisted reason to obtain assurance concerning them. . . . There is . . . no mode of establishing religious belief, but by the exercise of reason."[18]

To do Norton justice, he was speaking from provocation and his remarks were not addressed to Emerson alone. The time and place merely made it seem so. Late in 1837 he had published *The Evidences of the Genuineness of the Four Gospels,* a labor of many years. In his *Boston Quarterly Review* in January 1839 Orestes Brownson published a review of the book in which he lamented "certain demonstrations of uncharitableness on his [Norton's] part toward some of our friends," and insisted that Norton had failed to make his case. Norton, by his adherence to Locke, denied "to man all inherent power of attaining to truth." His commitment was thus to a philosophy that blocked "all free action of the mind, all independent thought, all progress, and all living faith."[19] This was like saying that Norton's chef d'oeuvre was worthless. The scope of Norton's Divinity School address, therefore, had to be broad enough to encompass Brownson's strictures on his *Gospels* book, Brownson's defense of Emerson, and the address with which Emerson had set into motion twelve months of controversy.

Having resolved not to engage in polemics, Emerson made no attempt to counter Norton's arguments. Since his supporters felt that they should be answered, George Ripley, a transcendental Unitarian minister with impressive scholarly credentials, stepped into the arena, replying with three open *Letters* published over the next two years.

The first of these, *The Latest Form of Infidelity Examined,* offered his most effective argument, that is, that Harvard was out of touch with the perceptions that now engaged men's minds. Harvard paddled in quiet eddies while the mainstream flowed elsewhere. Cleverly, Ripley displayed his knowledge of the philosophic theologians of Germany whom Norton, with less knowledge of them than Ripley had, had sought to dismiss. He concluded with a solid endorsement of Emerson by insisting that "the principle that the soul has no faculty to perceive spiritual truth, is contradicted by the universal consciousness of man." Norton, of course, rose to this bait and, when it seemed his "steel-cold intelligence" was driving Ripley into a corner, Theodore Parker, but lately ordained a Unitarian minister, writing under the name of Levi Blodgett, entered the lists, winning for himself new respect as a consistent and logical thinker. Parker's unmistakable partiality to transcendentalism (he was soon to deny the authority of the Bible and be branded an "infidel"), was not merely a rebuke to Norton but an embarrassment for him because, as recently as 1836, Parker had been his student. Conservative theologians, who long had held suspect the Harvard Divinity School, made the most of this fact. Thus Professor Noel Porter, who taught moral philosophy at Yale, ruminated aloud: "Where learned Mr. Parker his philosophical system? Where did he discover that man himself might be so inspired, that his God could give him no added inspiration? . . . Mr. Norton will start up with his customary promptness, and reply: 'Not from me — not from me!' "[20] Norton was learning that logic was a double-edged sword.

Of the "Divinity School Address" Dr. Nathaniel Frothingham, brother-in-law of Edward Everett and one of Boston's most respected preachers, had observed soon after Emerson spoke: "Some said it thundered, others that an angel spake."[21] But the pro-angelic faction was not making policy at Harvard. As Emerson's son Edward noted in 1903: "Nearly thirty years passed by before it was felt at the University that Mr. Emerson was a safe or desirable person to be called upon to take any active part in its function."[22] Only in 1867 did the barriers topple. Then Emerson became an Overseer at Harvard, was asked once more to give the Phi Beta Kappa address, and was made an honorary Doctor of Laws. Three years later he was asked to lecture at Harvard, on philosophy. The president of Harvard who caused that to happen and later built an Emerson Hall in the Harvard Yard, to house the philosophy department, was Charles W. Eliot, Andrews Norton's nephew. By that time, not in small part because of the direction in which Emerson had set things moving many years before, a radically new climate prevailed. Octavius B. Frothingham, Nathaniel's son, recalled the "Divinity School Address" now as "Emerson's exquisite chant." Henry James, as might be expected, assessed Emerson's apostasy in terms intimately his own. He found:

a sort of drollery in the spectacle of a body of people among whom the author of "The American Scholar" and the Address of 1838 at the Harvard Divinity College passed for profane, and who failed to see that he only gave his plea for the spiritual life the advantage of a brilliant expression. . . . They might have perceived that he *was* . . . not in the least a secularizer, but in his own subtle insinuating way a sanctifier.[23]

Possibly Nathaniel Frothingham's assessment of the "Divinity School Address" lingered in Emerson's memory. Possibly some response stirred within him when he contemplated Washington Allston's painting of Uriel, one of the seven archangels and their principal messenger — he who was given the responsibility of conveying the light of God to the chosen people, he whose name means "light of God." Possibly he remembered that Milton, in Book III of *Paradise Lost,* identified Uriel as the "interpreter" of God's will and described him as "The sharpest-sighted spirit of all in heav'n," his vantage point being the all-viewing sun itself. Possibly he was struck by Aunt Mary's comment that a piece he had done for *The Dial* was marked "by the spear of Uriel." Possibly he took every one of these factors into account. We cannot say. What we do know is that in 1845, when the controversy initiated by the "Divinity School Address" had subsided and resentment toward Emerson within Harvard's community of scholars had hardened into an unalterable attitude, Emerson wrote an allegorical poem, "Uriel," in which he reflected on the fate that had befallen him, reaffirmed his adherence to his controversial beliefs, and predicted his ultimate vindication.

In "A Masque of Reason" Robert Frost acclaimed "Uriel" as "the greatest Western poem yet." In September 1945, however, in a conversation with Reginald L. Cook, Frost had characterized the poem in less awesome terms as a "bugaboo poem that is meant to scare people." In this same conversation he fondly characterized Emerson himself as "a great disturber of the peace." Frost realized, of course, that "Uriel" was a statement central to Emerson's beliefs.[24] The shrewdest of Emerson's contemporaries, Frederic Henry Hedge, pinpointed as the probable origin of "Uriel" "the discussions of the Boston Association of Ministers."

The central paradoxes of the poem, the utterance of which lead to Uriel's expulsion from the community of angels, are given in the lines:

> *"Line in nature is not found:*
> *Unit and universe are round;*
> *In vain produced, all rays return;*
> *Evil will bless, and ice will burn."*[25]

These lines constitute a poetic restatement of the antithesis of Understanding and Reason, that is, Logic and Intuition, which is central to
Emerson's argument in the Divinity address. Once again he is attacking the notion that truth as perceived is static and not susceptible to
reappraisal. To Emerson, roundness, or the circle, was always important because it carried with it the idea of steadily broadening limits.
Truth was like God himself, of whom Saint Augustine said, as Emerson reported, "His center is everywhere, His circumference is nowhere."

In his essay "Love" Emerson came at the same idea in this way:
"In the procession of the soul from within outward, it enlarges its
circles ever, like the pebble thrown into the pond, or the light proceeding from an orb." In "Circles" Emerson, in undertaking to describe
the role of the genius, states for us, in fact, his justification of Uriel
which, in turn, can be seen to be his justification of the stance he took
in his "Divinity School Address":

> The new statement is always hated by the old, and, to those
> dwelling in the old, comes like an abyss of scepticism. . . .
> Beware when the great God lets loose a thinker on this planet.
> Then all things are at risk. . . . There is not a piece of science but
> its flank may be turned tomorrow; there is not any literary
> reputation, not the so-called eternal names of fame, that may not
> be revised and condemned. The very hopes of man, the thoughts of
> his heart, the religion of nations, the manners and morals of
> mankind are all at the mercy of a new generalization. Generaliza-
> tion is always a new influx of the divinity into the mind. Hence
> the thrill that attends it.[26]

In "Uriel" Emerson says:

> *A sad self-knowledge, withering, fell*
> *On the beauty of Uriel;*
> *In heaven once eminent, the god*
> *Withdrew that hour, into his cloud* . . .[27]

This "sad self-knowledge," however, connotes not failure but superior
knowledge. In confronting again, in a superb poem, the matter that
occasioned the "Divinity School Address," while at the same time
showing that his true plea all along had been for freedom of inquiry
and tolerance of new ideas, Emerson affirmed that he was, after all,
capable of confounding his foes and emerging, in this protracted al-
tercation, with the laurels of victory secure.

32. "Literary Ethics"
A Silver Shower of Eloquence

*A*month after he had agreed to speak on 15 July to the Divinity School, and the same week he sent off, with great aversion, his letter to President Van Buren concerning the expulsion of the Cherokee, Emerson, "with great delight," accepted an invitation to give an oration to two campus literary societies on 24 July at Dartmouth College.[1] At the time he saw Dartmouth as compensation for the disagreeable business of "stirring in the philanthropic mud," a reference to the Cherokee affair. It took a while for him to realize that the Dartmouth commitment was more truly coupled with his Divinity School commitment and that he had the burden of preparing simultaneously two major addresses. By 30 April he was already turning over in his mind ways to make the two addresses complementary. He would tell the Divinity students to seek moral perfection not in historical Christianity but in the precepts made known to them by their own intuitions. He would tell the Dartmouth students to supplant tradition with intuition as their sovereign guide. He wrote:

> Could not the natural history of the Reason or Universal Sentiment be written? One trait would be that all that is alive and genial in thought must come out of that. Here is friend B[arzillai]. F[rost]. grinds & grinds in the mill of a truism & nothing comes out but what was put in. But the moment he or I desert the tradition & speak a spontaneous thought, instantly poetry, wit, hope, virtue, learning, anecdote all flock to our aid. This topic were no bad one for the Dartmouth College boys whom I am to address in July.[2]

Although Emerson, subsequent to delivering his Dartmouth oration, entitled it "Literary Ethics," his true topic was, as he surmised it might be, a secular rendering of the central thesis of his address to the Divinity School. Despite the convenience of working on a previously considered theme, however, the address progressed only in slow stages, and without any real satisfaction. Indeed, the night before it was scheduled to be delivered, with its author by then physically present in Hanover, he was still referring to it, in a letter to Lidian and Ruth, as "the undone address," and owning forthrightly, "I can't say I admire it much & since I have come hither & seen some of the young men, I think it unfit."[3]

Contrary to what might be expected, the Dartmouth oration stirred no controversy. That was no fluke of fortune. While the "Divinity School Address" was a frontal attack made on Harvard theology by one of its own and its polemical emphasis unmistakable, at Dartmouth Emerson was among strangers and neither assigned any personal significance to his remarks nor was suspected of having done so. Moreover, since the Dartmouth oration was not given its final form until after the "Divinity School Address" had been delivered and notice had of its reception, Emerson saw no need to touch off a second charge of explosives. With the first address he had obviously realized his objective. His correct and chosen move now was to position himself on a pinnacle that stood above the scene of turmoil.

Holmes noted, too, that the solid traditionalism of Dartmouth left it relatively impervious to any iconoclastic views Emerson might have uttered there: "If there were any drops of false or questionable doctrine in the silver shower of eloquence under which they had been sitting, the plumage of orthodoxy glistened with unctuous repellents, and a shake or two on coming out of church left the sturdy old dogmatists as dry as ever." The plain truth is, had Emerson wanted at Dartmouth to build upon the controversy he had begun in Cambridge, he would have been hard put to get results. Said Holmes: "The extreme difference between the fundamental conceptions of Mr. Emerson and the endemic orthodoxy of that place and time was too great for any hostile feeling to be awakened by the sweet-voiced and peaceful-mannered speaker."[4]

The day after he delivered his oration, Emerson, writing from Dartmouth — where clearly there had been no movement afoot to hustle him on his way — told Lidian: "Tell Elizabeth [Hoar] our speech is better than she thinks, and I have no doubt some of it found ears in the crowd."[5] In his address Emerson affirmed the lofty role of the scholar. He called upon the students to live up to their highest inspirations. He praised originality and creativity. He encouraged the scholar to discipline himself and "to solve the problem of that life which is set before *him*." And, in a sterling paragraph that is said to have set the young Gladstone afire when he came upon it in an Oxford bookshop, he declared:

You will hear every day the maxims of a low prudence. You will hear that the first duty is to get land and money, place and name. "What is this Truth you seek? what is this Beauty?" men will ask, with derision. If nevertheless God have called any of you to explore truth and beauty, be bold, be firm, be true. When you shall say, "As others do, so will I. I renounce, I am sorry for it, my early visions; I must eat the good of the land and let learning and romantic expectations go, until a more convenient season;"— then dies the man in you; then once more perish the buds of art, and poetry, and science, as they have died already in a thousand thousand men. The hour of that choice is the crisis of your history; and see that you hold yourself fast by the intellect.[6]

This, in fact, is one portion of Emerson's message that has proved timeless.

Emerson had spoken, also, about "the enveloping Now," and the "infinitude and impersonality of the intellectual power," of "spontaneous sentiment," of "the too officious activity of the understanding." He said that religion "is yet to be settled on its fast foundations," and that "by virtue of the Deity, thought renews itself inexhaustibly every day, and the thing whereon it shines, though it were dust and sand, is a new subject, with countless relations." And he told them that a man "is great only by being passive to the superincumbent spirit." Here were heresies enough to have kept busy a dozen synods in seventeenth-century New England, but, in 1838 at Dartmouth, stronghold of orthodoxy though it was, they seem to have gone unremarked. Holmes supplies the probable answer: "Such was his simplicity of speech and manner, such his transparent sincerity, that it was next to impossible to quarrel with the gentle image-breaker."[7] With the exception, of course, of the Harvard Divinity faculty.

At the same time he had copies printed of the "Divinity School Address," Emerson also published the Dartmouth oration. Presently, relying on the kind offices of an itinerant Italian portrait painter, he sent ten copies to Carlyle. On 7 November 1838 Carlyle reported receipt of the gift and disclosed that the artist and he "read it over dinner in a chop-house at Bucklersbury, amid the clatter of some 50 stand of knives and forks." Later, under more suitable conditions, at Chelsea, Carlyle reread it. Reasonably enough, he did not find it on a par with "The American Scholar" (though Jane thought it superior to that work). Yet he designated it "a right brave Speech: announcing, in its own way, with emphasis of full conviction, to all whom it may concern, that great forgotten truth, *Man is still Man*. May it awaken a pulsation under the ribs of Death!''[8] That final asseveration would have made a worthy toast at the Bucklersbury chop-house.

33. Convers Francis
A Quickening Refreshment

$\mathcal{D}$URING a twenty-four-year period beginning on 22 September 1838 and ending in August 1862, just eight months before his death, Convers Francis recounted in his journal six visits to Emerson at Bush. Since, over a four-year period beginning in the summer of 1836, Francis attended fully half of the thirty meetings of Hedge's Club, he may have been to Bush on other occasions as well, but, if so, of these he left no record.

The most memorable of the visits Francis made to Bush was the first, an overnight visit soon after Emerson spoke at the Divinity School. To fraternize with Emerson at that time was tantamount to espousing his cause and called for considerable pluck. That Francis would show such courage is not surprising in a man who, though not a speaker on public issues, had the boldness, even sooner than Emerson did, to deplore from his pulpit the assassination of the abolitionist Elijah Lovejoy.

"Returned to Mr. Emerson's," Francis began his entry, "and spent the night. There was abundance of good talk, which I hardly know how to report."[1] Francis may literally have meant that. After attending Emerson's lecture "Ethics" on 16 February 1837, he had said:

His style is too fragmentary and sententious. It wants the requisite words or phrases of connection and transition from one thought to another. . . . This defect, and his habit of expressing a common truth in some uncommon (is it not sometimes slightly fantastic?) way of his own, are the reasons perhaps that it is so difficult to retain and carry away what he says. I find that his beautiful things are *slippery,* and will not stay in the mind.

In his journal entry for 22 September 1838, Francis said:

> What a pure noble, loving far-reaching spirit is Mr. E.! When
> we were alone, he talked of his Discourse at the Divinity School,
> and of the obloquy it had brought upon him: he is perfectly quiet
> amidst the storm, to my objections and remarks he gave the most
> candid replies. . . . The more I see of this beautiful spirit the
> more I revere and love him; such a calm, steady, simple soul,
> always looking for truth and living in wisdom, and in love for
> man, and goodness, I have never met.

Thus Francis accounted for the respect and admiration that sensible
men always would have for Emerson, even when they took exception
to his views. Emerson said nothing for advantage or effect. He spoke
always the truth as he saw it, cost what it may. Francis continued:

> Mr. E. is not a philosopher, so called, not a logic-man . . . he is
> a *seer* who reports in sweet and significant words what he sees; he
> looks into the infinite of truth, and records what there passes
> before his vision . . . but do not brand him with the names of
> *visionary,* or *fanatic,* or pretender: he is no such thing, — he is a
> true, godful man, though in his love of the ideal he disregards too
> much the actual.[2]

The word *fanatic* was not a random choice. Only twelve days before,
Francis had been to tea at the home of "a family belonging to the
straitest sect of Boston conservatism." He related: "I found they had
been taught . . . to abhor and abominate R. W. Emerson as a sort of
mad dog: and when I . . . told them he was full of piety and truthfulness . . . they laughed at me with amazement — for no such sounds
had penetrated their *clique* before."

Convers Francis was not a precocious young man bent on shocking
the gifted few with improbable assertions. He was a man of moderate
views, wary of theological extremes. That same year, on 28 March he
had heard Emerson's lecture "Holiness," and seemed reconciled to
what Emerson said chiefly because he was reluctant to take him literally. He began by deploring those who dismissed Emerson outright:
"This is the lecture, which . . . alarmed some people not a little, as
certain parts of it were supposed . . . to border close upon atheism.
. . . So far from this lecture containing anything like atheism, it seemed
to me a noble strain of fervent, lofty, philosophical piety. It was, like
its topic, *holy.*" Francis then, with his own interpretation of Emerson's intentions, undertook to extricate him from the situation others
saw him in: "The only idea of impersonality in the Deity, which he

impugned, was, I think, the vulgar idea, which considers God as occupying space : — the personality which consists in a *will* and *consciousness* . . . he seemed to me to express or take for granted, though, it is true, some of his incidental expressions might look differently.'' Francis was willing to ascribe such perplexities to Emerson's novel use of language. ''I thought,'' he conceded, ''that in one passage of the lecture he seemed to take away the distinct, individual existence of man, as a conscious being, after death, and resolve him into the All, the Divine Soul : but my impression is probably erroneous.'' In truth, Francis was too carried away to want to hold Emerson to strict account for anything he had said. ''I wish exceedingly to see Mr. E. in private,'' he concluded, ''and hear him expound these matters more with all the sweet charm of his delightful conversation. After return from Cambridge, read and wrote, but not much ; my head and heart were too full of Mr. E's lecture for that.''

Francis came out of a conservative tradition. His father, like Thomas Emerson, had been a baker. He was eight years older than Emerson and had been brought along in his formation for the ministry by the same men who later watched over Emerson's vocation — John Thornton Kirkland, Ezra Ripley, and Samuel Ripley. Family ties strengthened that relationship. Samuel and he were brothers-in-law, his wife, Abby, being Sarah Bradford Ripley's sister. He was ordained in 1819, to be pastor of the Unitarian church in Watertown, Massachusetts. His parish abutted that of Samuel Ripley in Waltham, and, during the twenty-three years of his Watertown pastorate, and thereafter, there was frequent contact between the two families.

By temperament Francis was a scholar. He built up one of the finest private libraries in greater Boston, and his liberality in loaning his books was legendary. He familiarized himself with the German philosophers and encouraged Emerson's German studies. Emerson, no doubt through the Ripleys, was early aware of Francis; writing to his brother William on 14 February 1819, he spoke of Francis's settlement at Watertown.[3] In 1833, Sarah Ripley wrote to Aunt Mary on 4 September : '' We have had a delightful visit of two days from Waldo. . . . He has some stout advocates. A lady was mourning the other day to Mr. Francis about Mr. Emerson's insanity. 'Madam, I wish I were half as sane,' he answered, and with warm indignation.''[4]

In the spring of 1837, Francis and Emerson exchanged pulpits for a weekend, Emerson preaching at Watertown and Francis going to East Lexington. The way was opened for this gesture when, on 19 September 1836, Francis joined Hedge, Emerson, and the others in starting the Transcendental Club. The task of moderating the meetings regularly fell to Francis as senior member. In the club's first year Francis published a tract, *Christianity as a Purely Internal Principle*, in which he contended that true Christianity shows itself not through forms or rituals but by the personal virtue of individuals. He perceived in Emerson a living exemplar of Christianity practiced as it ought to be. Emerson may have been indebted to Francis for his formulation of the concept of the Over-Soul, for it was Francis who, in a review of Alexander Crombie's *Natural Theology* in the *Christian Examiner* of May 1832, endorsed the belief that "the human soul is a particle of the Divine Mind."

When Emerson arranged for American publication in 1838 of Carlyle's *Critical and Miscellaneous Essays,* Francis cooperated. Emerson wrote Carlyle on 6 August: "To one other gentleman I have brought you in debt, — Rev. Convers Francis . . . who supplied from his library all the numbers of the *Foreign Review* from which we printed the work. We could not have done without his books, and he is a noble-hearted man, who rejoices in you."[5]

There was a time when people looked to Francis for active expression of radical opinions. He was the brother of Lydia Maria Child, a vociferous abolitionist who never hesitated to mount the barricades for a cause she adjudged worthy. People supposed Francis would prove to be of the same stamp. Yet, by temperament, he shunned controversy. He was kindly and erudite, but prudent. Octavius B. Frothingham attributed to him a Confucian summation of his position — "He who defies public opinion, like the man who spit in the wind, spits in his own face."[6] Emerson's defiance could be accounted for in these terms, but at no time did Francis regard his behavior as ludicrous.

Francis made his alleged break with the New Thought when in 1842 Theodore Parker fell under censure for theological views that seemed to many indistinguishable from atheism. As an indigent young man, Parker had sought out Francis and asked him to direct his studies. Francis put his magnificent library at his disposal and skillfully channeled his omnivorous tastes. When satisfied that Parker was ready, he procured him a scholarship to the Divinity School. At Parker's ordination in 1837, Francis delivered the sermon.

When, also in 1842, Henry Ware, Jr., resigned the Parkman Professorship of Pulpit Eloquence and Pastoral Care at the Divinity School, it was given to Francis. Some accounts suggest that Francis failed to speak out in Parker's defense because he did not want to jeopardize the appointment. But Parker himself helped persuade him to accept it, arguing, quite soundly, that Francis would help to liberalize the school.[7] Parker even concluded that they should not see each other because "I do not wish to stand in your way; I will not knowingly bring on you the censure of your brethren."[8] For all that, when Francis accepted the mandate of the Boston Association of Ministers and canceled an agreement to exchange pulpits with Parker, Parker was embittered. "Francis fell back on acct. of his Professorship," he stated in his diary.[9] Later, he recast this thought in terms which suggest that he had dropped not merely his Christian affiliation but the common feelings of humanity: "Poor old gentleman," he said of the man who made his education possible, "he is dead, but thinks benevolently, as a corpse."[10]

In his desire to show tolerance toward the old empiricists with whom he disagreed, as well as toward the proponents of intuitive philosophy, among whom he counted himself, Francis seemed to some of those enrolled at the Divinity School as "too all-sided." Perry Miller concluded that Francis, "intellectually capable of understanding the new ideas, and apparently of embracing them . . . fell away when the social hazards became too great."[11] Moncure Conway, who came to the Divinity School as a student in the following decade, portrayed him in slightly kinder terms: "Dr. Francis was a florid old gentleman, good-natured, tolerant, mystical, and, but for the extent to which his functions had wrapped him in bandages, might have been progressive. . . . We all liked Dr. Francis personally."[12]

Pondering the difficult balance Francis sought to maintain, Henry Steele Commager says: "A thorough and precise scholar, discriminating and urbane. . . . A conservative in everything concerning society and politics . . . he was a liberal in all that concerned theology and religion. . . . The orthodox regarded him as dangerous and the heterodox felt that he lacked courage."[13] Octavius B. Frothingham saw Francis's role as positive: "To him successive classes of divinity students owed the stimulus and direction that carried them into the transcendental ranks. . . . Had he been as electric and penetrating as he was truthful and obedient, high-minded and sincere, hearty and simple, he would have been a force as well as an influence."[14] Frothingham emphatically dissociated Francis from those who defected from the transcendentalist movement, who "had either too little courage of conviction, or too little conviction, to depart from accustomed ways or break with existing associations." Lydia Child measured her brother's intellect in different terms: "You have," she told him, "the highest peaks of your mind at least a little gilded with transcendentalism."[15]

Francis's relations with Parker after 1842 offer further proof that his defection was exaggerated. During 1843–1844, while Parker was in Europe, Francis and George Ripley, between them, filled Parker's pulpit. This was no small gesture because Parker's nonconformity now was so notorious even Emerson discouraged a close association with him and protested when Parker claimed him as an editor of his *Massachusetts Quarterly Review* in 1847. In 1859, as death drew near, Parker wrote to Francis to acknowledge his debt to him.[16]

A scrutiny of Francis's remarks on Emerson over a quarter of a century illustrates the steadfastness of which Francis was capable. When on 8 February 1837 he made an entry in his journal concerning Emerson's essay "Michael Angelo," he had already spent time with Emerson at meetings of the Boston Association of Ministers and of Hedge's Club. Declaring the article to be "exquisite," he continued, "Was ever a mind cast in a finer mould, than E's? He seems to have already anticipated the purity of the spiritual state." On 16 February he said, "There is a charm about this man's mind and his composition, which I know not how to explain, except by saying that it is the charm of hearty truthfulness and the simplicity of a pure, far seeing soul." Emerson's "Human Culture" series, which opened in Boston on 6 December 1837, found Francis ecstatic: "To hear Mr. E. and to see the varying expressions on his heavenly countenance, while truth radiates from him, rather than is uttered by him, seems like breathing a better atmosphere than that of the world." When the series ended on 7 February, Francis concluded that Emerson throughout had "spoken of high things . . . as one filled with the pure inspiration of truth."

Although Francis's ability to judge the integrity of Emerson's mind cannot be gainsaid, there can be no doubt that the manner of Emerson's presentation intrigued him fully as much as did the matter and, to a degree, procured his indulgence. He was struck by the surprising turns of phrase Emerson was capable of, as when he characterized original sin and the origin of evil as "the mumps, measles and whooping-cough of the soul." At a meeting of the Transcendental Club at George Ripley's, on 29 May 1837, Emerson's distinction was brought home to Francis when those present were asked to define religion. One characterized it as a "sentiment," another "a faith in reason." Emerson, however, left these lexicographers far behind. He said religion is "the emotion of shuddering delight and awe from the perception of the infinite."

On the occasion of the first visit that Francis made to Concord, Emerson was entertaining a second guest, John Lewis Russell, a cleric-naturalist, and later a Fellow of the American Academy. Emerson said in his journal that he had had "A good woodland day or two with John Lewis Russell who came here, & showed me mushrooms, lichens, & mosses." He described Russell enigmatically as "A man in whose mind things stand in the order of cause & effect."[17] The previous day, he offered a hint of how he had reacted to Russell's indoctrination: "I say as I go up the hill & thro' the wood & see the soliciting plants I care not for you mosses & lichens, & for you, fugitive birds, or secular rocks! Grow, fly, or sleep there in your order, which I know is beautiful, though I perceive it not; I am content not to perceive it." A little further on in that same day's entry, he observed: "If people would live extempore nobody would be uninteresting but they live from their memory instead of from their impulses."[18] Francis, quite as well as Russell, could have supplied the impulse that prompted Emerson to record this remark. Along with the vast lore he commanded, he also, like Russell, was committed to order. That fact occasioned those curious observations which Francis scattered throughout his journal concerning Emerson's scorn for organization and logic.

In his journal Francis, recording the events of the second and final day of his visit, gives us an intimate glimpse of Emerson, gently exasperated, in the company of these two men of logic: "Mr. Russell was continually giving us information and excellent remarks. I laughed heartily at a quotation made by Mr. E. in his arch, quiet way; Mr. R. had told us of a naturalist, who spent much time and pains in investigating the habits and nature of the *louse* on the *cod-fish;* 'O star eyed science' said Mr. E. 'hast thou wandered there?'"

At the opening of Emerson's winter lecture series on 6 December 1837, Francis was patiently indulgent: "The fault is that of too quick and easy generalization — the natural fault of a mind that dwells habitually on ideas and principles. But every sentence in it was a gem of thought. His description of the *ideal,* the universal aspiration toward the *better,* was admirable, and, what some of his statements are not, it was clear." On 22 February 1838, in Cambridge to hear Emerson's "The Head" (that is, the culture of the intellect), Francis had a pleasant surprise: "The lecture, on the whole, I think superior to any I have heard from Mr. E., more methodical, and coherent."

On 7 November 1840, visiting Concord with his sister-in-law Sarah Ripley, Francis stayed overnight at Bush. The two men sat up late talking, and Emerson read to him excerpts from Carlyle's letters. Francis was struck more by the way Carlyle expressed himself than by his ideas. Francis had a way of screening out ideas that were disagreeable to him. Predictably, therefore, his and Emerson's minds did not interact well. With puzzlement, Francis wrote: "In conversation somehow I cannot get very nigh to Mr. Emerson: but after all, is not every person, by nature of the case, *insular, alone,* as to the intellect? do people ever come together, except through the affections? I suspect not."

When Emerson's *Essays* (First Series) was published in March 1841, he sent Francis a copy. Francis read it at once and decided that Emerson was Emerson and must be accepted on his own terms. Gone were the objections to his apparent incohesiveness:

Emerson's illustrations are arguments; they are not patched, or laid on the composition, but grow up from within it, as parts of the essential structure. There is in his mode of writing a constant use of figurative or allusive words, so that his sentences oftener

suggest than tell his meaning; and this, I think, is the main cause
of the alleged obscurity of his writings.

So much for the manner. As to the matter:

> There will doubtless be a great outcry from some quarters about
> the sentiments expressed in these Essays, and with some of them
> certainly I can by no means agree. . . . It is of little consequence
> whether you agree with Mr. E. or not: he is the most *suggestive*
> writer we have and stirs the reader's mind more than any other, —
> and that is a great merit, worth all the smooth proprieties, and
> approved commonplaces in the world.

Here Francis, rallying his forces, moved to that high ground where
Emerson's most discerning admirers subsequently joined him. Emerson compels men to think, and in that fact he finds all the justification
he needs.

A reading of the *Essays* (Second Series), in December 1844, found
Francis acknowledging and accepting Emerson's uniqueness in a
statement that is a model of succinctness: "How nobly and beautifully
he speaks out from a world, which seems to be all his own! such an
exquisite master of English expression is nowhere else to be found. I
have tried in vain to analyze his mind: does it not defy analysis?"

Early in 1848, while Emerson was in England, Francis read in
Blackwood's Edinburgh Magazine an article favorable to Emerson. The
antiquarian in him was pleased to note that the anonymous critic compared Emerson's effective use of an occasional "curiosity of reflection" to Sir Thomas Browne's use of the same device. On 5 August
1848, soon after Emerson's return, Francis paid him a two-hour visit.
Understanding well now that Francis had an assimilative, retentive
mind, not a mind that was truly speculative, Emerson passed a gossipy
interval with him. Carlyle had long stood high in Francis's regard and
Emerson took care not to disillusion him. "He said," Francis related,
"that the authorship and literature of Carlyle were only accidental
appendages to his strong, burly, earnest, intense soul, which was made
for action rather than for writing."

Again in the company of Sarah Ripley, Francis called on Emerson
on 28 July 1855 and, sure enough, "R.W.E. talked a good deal of
Thomas Carlyle. . . . He read a letter . . . most characteristic and
amusing, in which C. complains, in his own quaint way, of his disappointment about Frederick the Great, of whom he is making a book,
and who turns out, he says, to be no hero to him." Thus did Emerson
find it necessary to deal with earnest scholars and men of science for
whom knowledge of concrete facts was the one end worth pursuing.

The years were winding down for Francis. Yet, while his vision narrowed, he directed it sharply. On 7 April 1858 he heard Emerson lecture on self-possession at Boston's Freeman Place Chapel. Caught up with his own research and professional duties at the Divinity School, he had not heard Emerson lecture for nearly eighteen years, with the sole exception of the slavery issue lecture given at Tremont Temple on 27 January 1855. The comments Francis made now on Emerson were a sincere attempt on his part to describe Emerson as he believed him to be at this stage of his career. For that reason alone his opinion is important to us. That the views he expressed here are the views of someone taking a second look at Emerson, after a gap of many years, gives them further significance, especially since they are the remarks of an unprejudiced observer of superior intelligence. Francis here recognizes truths about Emerson that Emerson, by this time, had come to see as valid, though another dozen years would go by before others would acknowledge their substance. Francis remarked that Emerson had, some time since, come to the limits of his precocity :

> Many years ago that strain of the poet-philosopher fell upon my ear often, and it always brought a charm with it. Now, after a long interval, heard again, it seemed just the same thing. The subject was ''Self-possession,'' and I think there was no idea which I had not found in his lectures from 15 to 20 years ago, and the very words were about the same. . . . I had hoped to find by this time something else ; but, I doubt, Mr. E. never gets or has got beyond the old thought, however good that may be. The fault of his manner of discussing a subject seems to be that he never makes any progress in the subject itself : he empties before you a box or bag of jewels as he goes on, which you may take and make the most you can of. . . . He might as well begin anywhere else and end anywhere else, as where he does begin and end. The mind of the hearer has not the satisfaction of moving steadily on till the consummation is effected.

Only in the last part of his assessment did Francis fall back on his own demands for organization and method as an explanation for Emerson's failure to evidence continued growth and development. That he would try to account for it in these terms was, of course, predictable and, in the light of his own understanding, justifiable. Adjunctive to this mind-set is the happy assessment Francis made of Emerson's ''Man with the Hoe'' remarks made on 29 September 1858, at the Middlesex County Fair at Concord : ''It is quite noticeable what a *practical* man he is, — just what people generally think he is *not*.'' It seemed to him that this was an Emerson he could get to know better : '' I wish

I had the privilege of seeing him more than I am ever likely to do in a world where every man has his own peculiar work, which drives him to the wall.''[19] There is a touch of wistfulness here, suggesting that Francis senses that the role he had chosen had been a limiting one.

Emerson and Francis were to meet twice more when Francis came to Concord to visit Sarah Ripley, who, with her husband, had moved from Waltham to the Old Manse in 1845. The first of these meetings came in August 1859, when Francis made an evening call on Emerson. They talked on topics Emerson knew Francis would find agreeable, Carlyle and Tennyson. Francis used the word "charmingly" to describe Emerson's manner while conversing with him on this visit, as he did again in August 1862, when Emerson received him in the company of Sarah Ripley. On that occasion the William Emersons were present, as were Ellery Channing and Elizabeth Peabody. Francis found them "most pleasant and high company," but, once more, Emerson made letters their topic, this time Matthew Arnold's upbraiding of F. W. Newman for translating the *Iliad* in ballad meter, which the pedantic literalness of his diction made yet more deplorable. Emerson seems never to have tried to think in Francis's presence but to have accounted him a shop-talk visitor. Books were their particular bond.

In November 1862 the *Eclectic Review,* marking the British appearance of *The Conduct of Life* (1860), published an extensive and complimentary appraisal of Emerson's writings. Francis read it and recorded the fact in his journal on 3 January 1863. Still mindful that Emerson had evolved no formal system of thought, he referred to the piece as a "would be philosophical article," yet, even so, it pleased his vanity that the British would accord such notice to "one whom *we* have known from his boyhood all the way from his growth up to fame." These were his last words on Emerson. He died three months later.

Like Mary Moody Emerson, Francis had shaken his head in dismay at some of Emerson's ideas, but even as she was proud of her unconventional nephew so was Francis. And the pride of both rested, ultimately, on their admiration for his personal virtue and their knowledge of his dedication to his ideals. He could not be faulted for speaking the truth as he understood it.

Four years after Francis's death, Emerson again was in the good graces of his alma mater. Francis, despite the frowns of Andrews Norton and Francis Bowen, had always kept a door open to Emerson. Through him, Divinity students at Harvard had found reassurance that Emerson's influence need not be thought of as pernicious. Francis did not live to see Emerson exalted anew at Harvard, but much credit goes to him that at last it came about.

34. Jones Very
A Treasure of a Companion

$\mathcal{O}$ N 29 October 1838 Emerson wrote in his journal, "J. Very charmed us all by telling us he hated us all."[1] The man he was speaking of was a houseguest who had already been with the Emersons for the better part of a week and only the week before that had ended a month's stay at the McLean Hospital for the Insane. Emerson knew this and realized that a visit from Very would be an adventure. Since he had great expectations for Very, he was willing to risk it.

The October visit was Very's third to Emerson's house. That same year, on 4 April, he had lectured on epic poetry at the Concord Lyceum. Emerson had done the inviting and had made up for the meager ten-dollar fee the Lyceum paid its lecturers by entertaining the visitor at dinner.

Very knew something of Emerson because he had bought a copy of *Nature* when it came out, in 1836, just after he graduated from Harvard, second in his class. Since then he had been filling his appointment as Tutor in Greek to Harvard freshmen. Emerson knew a little about Very, too. He was from Salem, and Elizabeth Peabody, always pleased to boost a fellow townsman, thought she saw great promise in him. The day following his first visit, Emerson wrote to her to commend her "sagacity." Very was "remarkable." He himself was rendered "anew in such company." A few days later, accompanied by Cornelius Felton and a selection of Harvard friends, Very returned unannounced. To show off this new marvel, Emerson invited Thoreau, Rockwood Hoar, and Barzillai Frost to join the visitors. He relished the encounter. That his friends did is less certain, for Emerson once said of Very: "When he is in the room with other persons, speech stops, as if there were a corpse in the apartment."[2] Very's unusual appearance cannot have helped matters. He was tall and angular. A towering hairline drew the eye first to a massive sweep of forehead. Skin of an alabaster smoothness covered high cheekbones accentuating eyes that were brooding and intense. These were set well apart by a broad, straight nose that, in maturity, drew attention away from protruding ears that must have been the schoolboy's bane. A purposeful set to his mouth proclaimed obdurateness, yet lent resoluteness to his chin. Thus the explanation for Dr. George B. Loring's quip on hearing that Very was a believer in the resurrection of the body: "I would not be, if I had his body."[3]

Very was enrolled in the Divinity School, but his ideas on "sin" and "love," to mention but two of his topics on this occasion, were hardly conforming. Edwin Gittleman, Very's biographer, suggests that his divergencies may have spurred Emerson to introduce much novelty into the address he gave at Divinity Hall a dozen weeks later.

The circumstances in which Jones Very was raised sponsored individualism. He was the oldest of six children born out of wedlock to first cousins, both Verys. His mother, described as "a tiger of a woman," was a strident, self-proclaimed atheist. To be a prolific unwed mother in Salem in the nineteenth century was no role for the faint of heart. Possibly life would have been different for Very had his father lived to see him grow to maturity. He was a shipmaster who took an interest in Jones, bringing him along on a voyage to Russia when he was ten, and casting him in the role of cabin boy the next year when he sailed a ship to New Orleans. But he died on his return, and that ended Very's experience of a calling his family had held to for generations.

Peculiar days intervened between Very's second and third visits to Concord. If Very's ideas may have emboldened Emerson to be daring when he spoke to the Divinity School, the "Divinity School Address" itself certainly hastened Very into a state that his friends hoped was mystical and his foes were certain was lunacy. The change in him was apparent in September 1838, when he began his third year as Tutor in Greek and discoursed on religion, in Emersonian terms, with his students. He soon asserted that he was the Son of God and that the Second Coming of Christ was at hand. At this point Harvard sent him home to Salem to recover his health. Once in Salem, however, Very concluded that he himself was the Second Coming and undertook to baptize Elizabeth Peabody and a selection of local ministers. On that account, Charles W. Upham, one of the ministers, had Very taken by force to McLean. A remote cousin of Emerson's, Upham had been in Emerson's class at Harvard. In 1836 he had arranged for Emerson to deliver the series of lectures in Salem, but now repudiated him as an atheist.

Very needed attention, certainly, but was released from McLean after a month when the staff there concluded that he was a danger to no one. But he was a danger to Emerson. Upham and other Salem ministers fixed on Emerson as the person responsible for Very's derangement. A born instigator, Upham was capable of much mischief. Some years later, in fact, he maligned Hawthorne and cost him his surveyorship.[4] When word of Upham's present machinations carried to Emerson, Elizabeth Peabody urged Emerson to speak in his own defense. He stood his ground instead. As his son Edward was later to observe, "Whether native or acquired by training, Mr. Emerson always had courage at the right time."[5]

As Very was being removed to McLean, he had told his captors his greatest regret was that he could not give Emerson his revelation. That was all Emerson's detractors needed to hear to be convinced that his teachings had engendered Very's madness.[6] They were unaware, as Emerson was, that Very was obsessed with the idea that he must save his mother from her atheism. When the fervor of his mysticism rekindled her faith, he did, in fact, achieve his goal, which could well have been the real matter obsessing him.

What Emerson did know about at this time was a dissertation on Shakespeare that Very had completed and forwarded to him shortly before his crisis came. This work struck him as profound, so much so that he wrote to his friend William Furness about it: "There is a young man at Cambridge, a tutor, Jones Very, who had written a noble paper on Shakespeare. . . . I am distressed to hear that he is feared to be insane. His critique certainly is not."[7]

Through this time letters were passing among anxious Bostonians, speculating on the damage Emerson had done and expressing concern lest Very had spread the contagion to his students. One of the few to uphold Emerson was Charles Stearns Wheeler, Thoreau's friend and later Emerson's as well. Wheeler had succeeded to Very's tutorship at Harvard. "Very does not believe even as Emerson does," he pointed out. "Very bases all his insane notion of Christ's second coming in him upon the authority of the Bible. Emerson's faith allows no authority . . . to any man or book."[8] In support of Wheeler's argument, it can be remarked that on 1 September, well in advance of Very's crisis, Emerson had written to Aunt Mary: "There is a young man at Cambridge named Jones Very who I think would interest you. . . . He has been here twice yet be not uneasy on that account for he does not agree to my dogmatism."[9]

Emerson could not forget that when he resigned his pulpit, men said he was deranged, nor that they repeated the slander when he gave his address at Divinity Hall. To let his name be linked with Very's was to court further criticism. That was a risk he was willing to run. He was a man who stood his ground.

On his post-McLean visit to Emerson, Very brought with him an essay on *Hamlet*, completed during the time of his confinement. While ordinarily this would have been their principal topic of conversation, just now Emerson was more interested in assessing the state of Very's mind in keeping with other criteria. Although he caught in Very's thought and speech "a certain violence," he found him less agitated than he had expected him to be. Writing to Elizabeth Peabody, he averred: "I wish the whole world were as mad as he."[10] He had found that if one dealt with Very "with perfect sincerity," he had truths and insights of permanent value to communicate.

Emerson was selective in what he chose to record in his journal of his conversations with Very. One account, in fact, was withheld until November 1841, at which time Emerson wrote: "When J[ones] V[ery] was in Concord, he said to me, 'I always felt when I heard you speak or read your writings that you saw the truth better than others, yet I felt that your Spirit was not quite right. It was as if a vein of colder air blew across me.' "[11] Emerson explained that his thoughts were constitutional and that he could not relinquish them without violating his conscience. "After some frank & full explanation," Very yielded the point.

Emerson returned frankness for frankness, admitting to Very that he had a cold nature. Possibly he thought the intense Very could thaw it. Instead, Very drew back, proclaiming the last day of his stay, Sunday, 28 October, "a day of hate." "He discerns," Emerson wrote that night, "the bad element in every person whom he meets which repels him."[12] For his part, Very charged Emerson with grasping truth when he should merely receive it passively. And in Lidian he found a want of true consistency, catching her up at some point in conversation with the rebuke, "Your thought speaks there, & not your life."[13] All this culminated in his affirming a hatred that enveloped them all. To his annoyance this declaration did not put them to rout. "Sincerity is the highest compliment you can pay," Emerson told him, happily fitting an aphorism to the occasion. Lidian, to whom Very seemed especially drawn on this visit, seemed equally content with his low opinion of them. His vulnerability appealed to her. Her husband had no vulnerable points. Through the years, recalling Very, Lidian would say, "How he sat there with a piece of gingerbread in each hand, so innocent and unconscious! and how beautifully he was talking."[14] A man with gingerbread in each hand must expect no one to take him seriously.

That night, there was a customary gathering of Sunday school teachers at Emerson's house, and Very rounded out the day in a fashion much in keeping with what had gone before. He "fronted the presiding preacher," Emerson reported with undisguised glee. The minister had made a windy, dogmatic statement. Very "blew away all his words in an instant, — unhorsed him . . . tumbled him along the ground in utter dismay."[15]

The next morning Very wanted to present himself at Harvard, in the futile hope that he could be reinstated as tutor. Emerson drove him as far as Waltham, concerned perhaps, as for a small child, to turn him loose in the world. Yet that night he reflected: "In dismissing him I seem to have discharged an arrow into the heart of society. Wherever that young enthusiast goes he will astonish & disconcert men by dividing for them the cloud that covers the profound gulf that is in man."[16]

Ten days after Very left, Emerson wrote Margaret Fuller: "Very has been here himself lately & staid a few days confounding us all with the question — whether he was insane? At first sight & speech, you would certainly pronounce him so. Talk with him a few hours and you will think all insane but he. . . . He is a treasure of a companion."[17]

Three days later Emerson began a journal entry on "Great Men" with the avowal: "I like the rare extravagant spirits who disclose to me new facts in nature. . . . Men of God have from time to time walked among men & made their commission felt in the heart & soul of the commonest hearer." A somewhat jumbled list follows in which Very's name appears, though whether as a great man or as a discerning critic of a great man — Shakespeare — is not clear.[18] Less open to ambiguity is a journal entry for 25 November, in which Emerson identifies Very as an *ab intra* speaker and then singles out Christ and Swedenborg as others who taught *ab intra,* concluding, finally: "How great the influence of such! how it rebukes, how it invites & raises me."[19]

Emerson not only had listened to Very, he found in his views confirmation of his own trust in the moral sentiment. On Very's departure, Emerson had written in his journal: "We are wiser, I see well, than we know. If we will not interfere with our thought but will act entire or see how the thing stands in God, we know the particular thing & every thing & every man."[20] Emerson could not have been disturbed, therefore, when Very wrote him, on 30 November: "I was pleased to hear that my stay with you was improving, and that you love that which is spoken by the word. . . . Every scribe instructed in the kingdom . . . shall hear the word of the Father. . . . You seem desirous to hear." He ventured further: "When you shall have bound the strong man within you (that is, your will) then you . . . can plunder the goods of the evil one."[21]

Emerson's response to this letter was conditioned by a new factor. Hitherto he had seen none of Very's poetry. He either knew nothing of it or supposed it was inconsequential. His astonishment was great, therefore, when Very sent him in early November copies of two of his most recent sonnets, published in a Salem newspaper. Very, he saw now, had an important dimension he had not hitherto taken into account. If Very could justify himself in these terms, the scoffers might yet have to withdraw in confusion. Emerson suggested that Very should publish a volume of his prose and verse and offered to assist in this enterprise, aware, surely, that no author, no matter how will-less, could be indifferent to such an invitation.

In May 1838, following his two earlier meetings with Very, Emerson had invited him to a meeting of the Transcendental Club at Caleb Stetson's house in Medford. There Very had met Hedge, Ripley, Alcott, Parker, Dwight, and Bartol. The conversation centered around the topic of mysticism. Entries in Very's journal show that he was then much concerned with the necessity of keeping the body in subjection "so that we may live purely as spiritual beings."[22] Alcott, at least, would have found this fascinating. In fact, the following January, after sharing a bedchamber with Very on an overnight visit to the home of a mutual friend in Lynn, Alcott wondered if Very was not carrying his renunciation of the flesh to the point where he was physically dying.[23]

The members of the club next saw Very immediately after his tumultuous autumn. The date was 5 December. Very, at Emerson's invitation, had come to Boston to hear Emerson's talk "Doctrine of the Soul" at the Masonic Temple. The club planned an informal meeting at Bartol's house following the lecture, and Very agreed to attend, no doubt to the gratification of members eager to ascertain for themselves his state of mind. Word had carried to Very that William Ellery Channing, with the same object in view, was looking for a chance to talk with him on "religious matters." To oblige Channing, Very came to town early and called at his home, where he found Channing in the company of James Freeman Clarke, then visiting Boston, and Wendell Phillips. The clergymen, at least, were impressed with Very's desire to let the Holy Spirit speak through him while he wholly relinquished his own will. Channing gave him a generous hearing. In fact, he let him talk for three hours. Phillips was impressed most by Channing's patience through this interval. But Channing was impressed with Very's exalted state. He wrote to Elizabeth Peabody: "To hear him talk was like looking into the purely spiritual world — into truth itself." It was as though Very had "attained self annihilation and become an oracle of God." James Freeman Clarke was of much the same mind. He saw no evidence of derangement: "We . . . saw only the workings of a mind absorbed in the loftiest contemplations, and which utterly disregarded all which did not come into that high sphere of thought." Very's contention "that all sin consists in self-will, all holiness in an unconditional surrender of our own will to the will of God" Clarke recognized as an argument often advanced by those striving for spiritual perfection.[24]

Very's session at Channing's, supplemented by the stimulation Emerson's lecture offered, left him primed for discussion at Bartol's. Alcott carried away impressions that seemed to confirm the independent judgments of Channing and Clarke: "He is a mystic of the most ideal class. . . . How few there are of sufficient insight into the soul to apprehend the facts of which he speaks. . . . He will be deemed insane by nearly every man."[25] Perhaps so. Yet, in the course of that one day Very's sanity and exalted spiritual state had been vouched for by Alcott, Channing, and Clarke. Emerson had not only provided the occasion for Very to reemerge after the scandal of his alleged madness, he had the good fortune to have a board of superior examiners conclude that Very was in a state much removed from madness.

That night, following the lecture and club meeting, Emerson brought Very back to Abel Adams's house, where Adams gave them adjoining bedchambers. Very used the occasion to reconsider what he took to be his leniency toward Emerson's views. Emerson recalled: "Early the next day in the grey dawn he came into my room and talked whilst I dressed. He said 'When I was at Concord I tried to say you were also right; but the Spirit said you were not right.' " Very may have owed Emerson a debt of gratitude for giving him a chance to vindicate himself, but he was more certain than ever, as Clarke expressed it, that "he *knows* the truth which he delivers."[26]

Led by the Spirit, Very waited six months before seeking Emerson's help in publishing a book. Although the Spirit prescribed an aloofness that caused Very to communicate with Emerson through Washington Very, his brother, and Elizabeth Peabody, a hint of hard common sense crept into the negotiations when Very, through Washington, urged that word of the forthcoming book be speedily communicated to Harvard so that some of his erstwhile students, soon to be graduated, could be appealed to as potential buyers. Rather grandly, Very was ready to transfer the whole burden of editorship to Emerson, and for "some months" he did not expect to visit Concord, since the Spirit did not prompt him to go. Emerson, however, did not realize that, as a poet, Very had merely recorded the utterances of the Spirit and thus what he had written was not alterable. That Emerson supposed it was was enough to draw Very out of seclusion. On 14 June 1839 he showed up at Concord for an editorial conference that extended through the next three days. Very found himself besieged. Emerson was adamant. Among the more than two hundred poems he had found only sixty-six that merited publication. When Very insisted that these, at least, must appear as they had been conveyed to him by the Spirit, Emerson overruled him: "We cannot permit the Holy Ghost to be careless and . . .

to talk bad grammar,'' he said. He insisted that if his editorial advice
was heeded, they were going to have ''a little gem of a volume.''[27]

What happened is indicated by Emerson in his review of the published book in *The Dial* two years later. There Emerson said of Very:
''He is not at liberty even to correct these unpremeditated poems for
the press; but if another will publish them, he offers no objection. In
this way they have come into the world.'' Something led Very to stand
aside while Emerson formulated the book according to his own literary judgment. Since the book that resulted is made up of Very's more
tranquil statements, it seemed designed to reassure its readers that
Very was a devout and simple man, able to express natural and spiritual truths with considerable poetic ardor. There would be those who
thought that Emerson — who, when he edited the work of others, consistently selected the tone — muted Very's message to show that Very's
exposure to his ideas had worked him no injury. In his review of *Essays and Poems,* indeed, he seems to confirm this view:

> The author . . . casts himself into the state of the high and
> transcendental obedience to the inward Spirit. He has apparently
> made up his mind to follow all its leadings, though he should be
> taxed with absurdity or even with insanity. In this enthusiasm he
> writes most of these verses, which rather flow through him than
> from him.[28]

From this point of view, Emerson, by judicious selection, had undertaken to restructure Very's image. Yet we must remember that Very
had backed off from some of the extreme views he had formerly held
and, in fact, would not have found relevant to his present state of
mind some of the ideas he had expressed when his mania was cresting.
Furthermore, the atmosphere had cleared and few blamed Emerson
anymore for Very's crisis. Emerson, then, in editing Very as he did,
was acting not in his own interests but in Very's. If he could produce
a book that showed Very as a gifted writer whose bent was not toward
madness but toward mysticism, then there was hope that Very would
be embraced anew by a community at present wary of him. Emerson
knew such storms could be weathered. And, of course, he was right.
Very's high state of excitement was past. He would not thereafter
reiterate the extreme claims he had made concerning himself. The book
Emerson compiled truly resembled the man Very now was and would
be. We can observe, further, that since posterity has had the chance to
examine the whole of Very's literary output, Emerson's editorial
judgment has been upheld. He suppressed no masterpieces. Even his
assertion in his *Dial* review that Very's poems show ''no pretension to
literary merit . . . have little range of topics, no extent of observa-

tion'' is not wide of the mark. His conclusion that Very's sonnets were laudable as ''the breathings of a certain entranced devotion'' remains their best defense.

On 16 June 1839 Emerson wrote enigmatically of his guest: ''Here is Simeon of Stylite, or John of Patmos in the shape of Jones Very, religion for religion's sake, religion divorced, detached from man, from the world, from science & art; grim, unmarried, insulated, accusing; yet true in itself, & speaking *things* in every word.''[29] On the seventeenth Very set out for home, and Emerson wrote to Elizabeth Peabody to let her know that, counseled by the Holy Spirit, Very was ending his visit. Emerson's feelings about the visit were positive: ''He has been serene, intelligent and true in all the conversation I have had with him, which is not much.'' Since it was Very in that posture whom Emerson wished to portray in the book, he was content. Very's behavior while at Concord convinced Emerson that he had a mandate to produce a book that would benefit him. And he meant to act without delay. He told Elizabeth Peabody: ''I shall go to town this week & settle what I can of the printing of his books.''[30]

On 22 June, Elizabeth herself arrived for a visit with the Emersons and wrote at once to her sister Sophia a report on Emerson's labors: ''He is in a delightful state of mind; not yet rested from last winter's undue labors, but keenly industrious. . . . He says Very forbids all correcting of his verses; but nevertheless he selects and combines with sovereign will.'' She learned also that Emerson shared Hawthorne's opinion that Very was ''always vain.''[31] So much for the supposition that Very, innocent, humble, and unsuspecting, was exploited by Emerson to benefit himself.

Little, Brown, at Emerson's behest, published Very's *Essays and Poems* that same September. It created no sensation. In his *Dial* review Emerson dismissed Very's early poems as unimportant. Perhaps he was thinking of these when, on 28 September, he wrote cryptically in his journal, amid other entries, ''I hate Early Poems.''[32]

One reason Very had been reluctant to visit Emerson in June was his conviction that he was passing a year in a state of grace which called for his withdrawal from society until September 1839. With publication of *Essays and Poems* the year of grace ended and he was free to return to the world. He visited Emerson again in Concord to ask for a letter authorizing his publisher to give him advance copies of his book. He made no acknowledgment of the role Emerson took in making the book possible.

In May 1840, Very came again to the Emersons', this time to attend a meeting of the club. Hedge, Alcott, Thoreau, Fuller, and others came too. Alcott, formerly engrossed in Very, noted this time that Very said nothing ''worth repeating.'' Very himself seems to have sensed that he no longer fitted in and bothered no further with the club after that. Emerson might have anticipated this. On 9 April Very had visited him and they walked together to Walden Pond. Once again Emerson pronounced him a "treasure of a companion." But something had changed. Very no longer felt God-directed. The result was he had become a dull fellow. He went back to Salem where he lived quietly for another thirty-two years, his kindly, careworn face a melancholy reminder to those who saw it of the afflatus that had, for a brief moment, exalted him before it departed forever.

The Very interlude ultimately was embalmed in a passage in Emerson's essay on friendship:

We parry and fend the approach of our fellow-man by compliments, by gossip, by amusements, by affairs. . . . I knew a man who under a certain religious frenzy cast off this drapery, and . . . spoke to the conscience of every person he encountered, and that with great insight and beauty. At first . . . all men agreed he was mad. But persisting . . . he attained to the advantage of bringing every man of his acquaintance into true relations with him. . . . Every man was constrained by so much sincerity to the like plain-dealing, and what love of nature, what poetry, what symbol of truth he had, he did certainly show him. . . . To stand in true relations with men in a false age is worth a fit of insanity, is it not?[33]

Like a comet, Very had come out of the unknown to streak across Emerson's line of vision for a brief moment and then vanish back into darkness. But his stay lasted long enough for him to cast a brilliant light on Emerson's goals, enabling him to see them thereafter as he had not seen them before, without human taint, wholly ideal.

35. The East Villagers
A Great Heat and a Great Light

*F*ROM May 1835 until February 1838, nearly as long a period as he had served as pastor of Boston's Second Church, Emerson was minister to the Unitarian parish in Lexington's East Village, eight miles from his house in Concord. Every Sunday he preached two sermons to the parish, the first in the morning, the second in the afternoon. His commitment was for twenty-four Sundays annually. Of the many parishes where he preached, no other parish, save the Second Church itself, made so great a call on his services.

Lexington's East Village was primarily a farming community. The parish there had been lately organized because the Villagers did not want to travel to the other end of town where the Lexington meeting house stood. For their services they made do with the upstairs hall of the Village Lyceum, a small building with a Greek portico.[1] To preach there Emerson drove down from Concord each Sunday morning in a chaise. The road was rutted and dusty and interrupted with occasional creeks that had to be forded. Sometimes Lidian accompanied him, or Elizabeth Peabody. At least once Margaret Fuller was his companion. On that occasion, during the noon meal, to the edification and mystification of his parishioners, Margaret discussed poetry with him.

On 2 November 1837 Emerson wrote to Carlyle: "I find myself so much more and freer on the platform of the lecture-room than in the pulpit, that I shall not much more use the last; and do now only in a little country chapel at the request of simple men to whom I sustain no other relation than that of preacher."[2] The East Villagers were "simple men," as Emerson said, yet he knew how to reach them. Typical was the remark he made one Sunday to his congregation. He was reading them a sermon he had written some years before. He paused, then said softly, ''The sentence which I have just read I do not now believe.'' Asked about their fondness for their unconventional preacher, one of the Villagers explained : ''We are very simple people, and can understand no one but Mr. Emerson.[3]

Sometimes Henry Hedge or Convers Francis or John Sullivan Dwight filled Emerson's pulpit for him. When the Villagers asked him to become their permanent pastor, he offered them Dwight in his stead, explaining that he did not wish to continue in the ministry.[4] But Dwight did not want to remain a minister either, so that, finally, Charles Follen succeeded Emerson. With evident relief Emerson wrote to William on 14 March 1838, ''I have relinquished my ecclesiastical charge at E. Lexington & shall not preach more except from the Lyceum.'' Stating his resolution more broadly, he said, ''My pulpit is the Lyceum platform.'' Thus he spoke at the start of a career that would see him acclaimed ''the most venerable lyceum speaker of them all.''[5]

The choice of Charles Follen was apt. Emerson and he had been the finalists in 1829 when the Second Church was seeking a new minister.[6] When Ellen was dying, Follen had filled Emerson's pulpit for him. They were allied in friendship and also in notoriety. Follen was German-born, but his wife, Eliza Cabot, was a member of one of Boston's first families. When they married, the Cabots gave money to Harvard to create a professorship in German (the first such at an American university), with the understanding that Follen would hold it. By the time the fund was depleted, Follen, an outspoken abolitionist, had become controversial. Harvard did not renew him. But the Cabots continued to stand by him, and when he took the East Village parish they put up much of the money needed to build a meeting house. Follen built one that suited his own taste — an octagonal-shaped edifice that recalled the church he had worshiped at in his homeland.

The fifteenth of January 1840 was set as the date for the dedication of the new building. On 7 November 1839, Follen wrote to Emerson to ask him to participate in the service. He could either pray or preach. Emerson chose to preach.

Just three days after Follen wrote to Emerson, Emerson wrote his poem ''The Problem.'' This poem did almost as much as the address at Divinity Hall to spread Emerson's fame. It marked the turning point in his life as a writer, even as the address marked the turning point in his life as a churchman. Henceforth he would follow a course that would allow him sufficient freedom of thought and action.

In early January Follen had to take his wife to New York to undergo major surgery, but he was determined to preside at the dedication of the new building and sent word that he would return to Boston, by boat, on the morning of the fifteenth. Although a sleigh was kept in waiting for him in Boston at the dock throughout the morning, his vessel, Commodore Vanderbilt's popular steamer the *Lexington,* failed to arrive when due, and the dedication ceremonies went ahead without him. John Pierpont, pastor of the Hollis Street Church at West Medford, another stormy petrel, gave the formal dedicatory sermon, leaving Emerson free to reflect on the event in his own distinctive way.

In "The Problem" a notable passage reads:

> *The hand that rounded Peter's dome*
> *And groined the aisles of Christian Rome*
> *Wrought in a sad sincerity;*
> *Himself from God he could not free;*
> *He builded better than he knew;—*
> *The conscious stone to beauty grew.*[7]

In his "Address to the People of East Lexington on the Dedication of their Church," Emerson explored the same theme in prose:

> Know then that your church is not builded when the last stone, the last rafter and clapboard is laid, not when we have assembled, not when we have adhered to the customary rite, but then first is it a church when the consciousness of his union with the Supreme Soul dawns on the lowly heart of the worshipper — when the church becomes nothing and the priest nothing for all places are sacred and all persons; when he sees that virtue goes out from him and hallows the ground whereon he stands — then instantly the humble church is made alive; its deadwood and stone are warmed and lighted by thought and love. It is alive and maketh alive — it ennobles and binds in one the inmates. It is a point of civilization, of culture, of poetry, of knowledge by which a whole community is educated. It propagates influences to remote countries and to all history. . . . Out of this narrow circuit may a great light and a great heat go that shall enkindle all men. Your hands which have wrought with such energy and visible success may they find that they knew not what they did, that the effect has vastly transcended the cause and the builders gladly disclaim the praise when they see another and a higher spirit which is more themselves than their hands or their purposes taking up their deed and making it divine.[8]

Robert Spiller and Wallace Williams, mindful of Emerson's almost mystical regard for circles, call to notice early evidence of that interest in other passages in this address:

In alluding to "the graceful circumference of these walls" which in turn may be "circumscribed by a higher truth," Emerson anticipates the central images of "Circles." But he alludes also to the design of the building which, unconventionally octagonal, approximates a circle: the physical church is but a "narrow circuit" out of which a great light and a great heat may go.[9]

From the dedication ceremony in East Lexington, Emerson proceeded to Boston, where he was to lecture that night at the Masonic Temple on "Reforms." There he learned why Dr. Follen had failed to appear that day at his new church. During the night, while traversing Long Island Sound, the *Lexington* had caught fire and burned to the water's edge. Before it sank, panic had taken hold among those on board. Of the more than one hundred and fifty passengers and crewmen making the passage, only four survived. Dr. Follen was among those who perished.[10]

When news of the disaster spread through Boston, William Ellery Channing announced a memorial service in tribute to him. Many Bostonians, however, saw Follen's hard death as a judgment on him. Pressure, therefore, was brought to bear on Channing and he dropped plans for the service. Even then, some stern moralists were not satisfied. One of them, Convers Francis was told, thought it a pity that Ralph Waldo Emerson had not gone down with the *Lexington*.[11]

36. Christopher Pearse Cranch
Aurora Shootings and Summer Lightning

*O*N the morning of 9 August 1840, Theodore Parker and George Ripley set out from West Roxbury on what they estimated would be a two-day walking trip to Groton, a town thirty miles northwest of Boston. The Groton Convention, a gathering of religious extremists — the Millerites, who were getting ready for an Armageddon a scant three years away, and the Come-outers from Cape Cod, a shouting sect, with mystical leanings so original that they shouted even at Millerites — was in progress and Parker wanted to form his own conclusions about it. Since 1837, when he was ordained so that he might serve as pastor at the Spring Street Church, Parker had been living in West Roxbury. Ripley was there for the summer, boarding with his wife, Sophia, Richard Henry Dana's sister, on a milk farm.[1] Though he still was pastor of Boston's Purchase Street Church, he was close to resigning from the ministry and already dreaming about buying the milk farm and implanting a utopian colony upon it — as, in fact, he would do the following spring. This scheme made him curious about the strange assembly at Groton. Some of the ideas of the extremists might have a practical application to the plans he was evolving.

On their way the two walkers collected a third companion, Christopher Pearse Cranch, who had been preaching that winter in South Boston. Cranch had visited Parker, whom he called "the very athlete of scholars," at his parsonage in West Roxbury and found his views in harmony with his own. He also had sought out Ripley at the Purchase Street Church and, on Sunday nights, made it his habit to stop by the Ripleys' at nine for baked potatoes, ale, and good conversation.

Cranch was a Virginian by birth but only because his father, a Bostonian, had been appointed to a federal judgeship in Washington, D.C., forty years before, by his uncle, John Adams, then occupying the White House.[2] Pearse, as he was known, was less interested in the gathering at Groton than he was in the planned stop in Concord, to see Emerson and, the travelers hoped, to persuade him to accompany them on the remaining stage of their journey.

On 19 June, Pearse had written John Sullivan Dwight, who had been his classmate at the Harvard Divinity School, that he intended soon "to visit Emerson, and he shall impart some knowledge of the different 'wandering voices' which fill the air and woods."[3] He had had such a visit in mind for some time. In early March he had written to Emerson, offering him two poems, "Stanzas" and "To the Aurora Borealis," for the first issue of *The Dial*, a new journal with a transcendental orientation being edited by Margaret Fuller, with generous assistance from Emerson. He probably had been invited to contribute when he had called on Emerson in Concord in the last weeks of 1839. At that time he had written a poem that characterized Emerson's transcendental insights as "rocket-winged" meteors and "Aurora shootings mixed with summer lightning." This latter image he developed now in his aurora poem, with transcendental intuitions becoming the "Wild Aurora . . . Reaching upwards from the earth / To the *Soul* that gave it birth."[4] Emerson, of course, did not know that this was a companion poem to one about himself, and wrote back, on 4 March, to assure Cranch that it was brilliant. He went on: "I recognize with joy your sympathy with me in the same tastes and thoughts. . . . If my thoughts have interested you, it only shows how much they were already yours. Will you not, when our fields have grown a little more invitingly green, make a leisure day and come up hither alone, and let us compare notes a little farther."[5]

The first issue of *The Dial* was published on 1 July 1840 and both of Cranch's poems were in it. High time, then, that he should act on Emerson's invitation and present himself again at Concord. Besides, he had already confessed a discipleship that called for more personal contact. In the letter he sent with the poems he wrote, "I have owed to you more quickening influences and more elevating views in shaping my faith, than I can ever possibly express to you."[6]

The Cranches were drawn to the arts. Pearse's older brother John (Pearse was the tenth of thirteen children) was a portrait painter. Emerson's first acquaintance with the family had come in 1833, when, while in Italy, he met John, then studying art in Rome. In addition to being related to the Adamses (the judge's mother was Abigail Adams's sister), the Cranches were related to William Furness, a fact in itself that would have assured them a place in Emerson's esteem.[7] One of

Pearse's aunts was married to Noah Webster. His sister Abby married their cousin, William Greenleaf Eliot, Unitarian minister and founder of Washington University, in St. Louis, and would count among her grandchildren T. S. Eliot. Pearse tried the ministry, poetry, criticism, and painting, in the latter enterprise identifying with the Hudson River School, which was not wholly arbitrary since he married his cousin, Elizabeth De Windt of Fishkill-on-the-Hudson. Pearse's facile skills kept him from concentrating his efforts long enough to achieve success at any one thing. Emerson himself would eventually sum up the problem in a letter he wrote to Pearse on 2 May 1874: "I have always understood that you are the victim of your own various gifts; that all the muses, jealous each of the other, haunt your brain."[8] The "always" was not quite so. Emerson initially entertained great expectations for Cranch.

Cranch graduated from the Divinity School in 1835. Approbated to preach, over the next year he occupied many pulpits, including Hedge's in Bangor, Maine. In December 1836, shortly after arriving in St. Louis, where he had gone to preach, he read and was enraptured by Emerson's *Nature*.[9] A measure of his adulation can be taken from a letter he sent to Emerson, along with two poems for *The Dial*, on 12 September 1841. Emerson made separate copies of the lengthy poems for Margaret Fuller so that she would not see the extravagant things that Cranch had said about him in the letter. Cranch spoke of his "enthusiastic admiration and love" of Emerson's work, and then said further: "The rare beauty of your style is but the first charm of your books to me. They are wells of deep truth, which I feel as if I could never exhaust." To Margaret, Emerson wrote about the "most ungraceful daubing of our poor merits in the letter prefixed."[10] To Cranch he sent dutiful thanks for his "kind and extravagant estimate" of his "poor pages."[11]

As acting editor of *The Western Messenger* in Louisville, Cranch had written on "The American Scholar" in November 1837, commending Emerson as "the man of genius, the bold deep thinker, and the concise original writer." With a fervor that suggested his Virginian upbringing rather than his New England heritage, he proclaimed Emerson an "elevated and fervent spirit" whose message was to "be pondered by every professor and student in the country."[12]

Early in February 1840, once again in Boston, Cranch told a correspondent that he had been attending Emerson's "Present Age" lectures, a private series of ten lectures given at Boston's Masonic Hall, which Emerson had begun two months earlier, on 4 December. "Emerson," he said, "is to me the master mind of New England, at least so far as depth and wonderful beauty in thought, rare and eloquent delivery go. His name will stand the test of time."[13] In December Cranch had written "The Prophet Unveiled," an extravagant poem which, when it was published in his *Poems* in 1844, can only have caused readers to wonder why Cranch had draped his prophet in the single veil of anonymity when his identity was so starkly apparent. If Emerson had felt daubed by Cranch's personal letter in 1841, he must have felt drenched in 1844 by this latest tribute:

> *Kindly he did receive us where he dwelt . . .*
> *Unveiled he stood; and beautiful he moved*
> *Amid home-sympathies . . .*

After pausing to affirm Emerson's alliance with Nature, Cranch riveted on Emerson a lover's attention:

> *In the mild lustre of the long-lashed eye,*
> *And round the delicate lips, how artlessly*
> *Broke forth the intuitions of his mind.*
> *I listened and I looked, but could not find*
> *Courage or words to tell my sympathy*
> *With all this deep-toned wisdom borne to me.*[14]

Cranch revealed that Emerson's *"visible* presence" cast a spell over him. He found his mind so instantly perceptive that his own utterances became but a broken reiteration of Emerson's. The superior course, he saw, was to receive Emerson's words in grateful silence. Yet he did not feel as Emerson himself had when he visited Coleridge and Wordsworth, that he was audience to a declamatory exercise. Emerson was not shackling him but loosening his bonds.

For nearly fifty years young men, awed by what Emerson had written, came, usually unbidden, to Emerson's door and were received with patience and encouragement. Again and again, with surprising consistency, in memoirs, essays, and letters they sought to recreate a sense of what they had experienced. Each had carried away a feeling of lyric exaltation, of mystical pride and grandeur. Yet Cranch, alone among them, undertook to share with others an intimate record of those special feelings and impressions.

When Ripley, Parker, and Cranch reached Concord, they called first on Ezra Ripley, then nearing his ninetieth year. Fortified by Ezra's admonition that they should not become "egomites," they then retraced their steps to Emerson's house, where they were given tea. Since George Ripley was business manager of *The Dial,* he commanded Emerson's ear. He seems also to have dropped a few preliminary hints about his plans for his milk-farm utopia because, when he visited Concord again, in October, to discuss the plan in detail, it was at Emerson's invitation.

Cranch must have regretted not having "come up hither alone." He would have liked to have talked to Emerson about matters of common interest. That summer he had been preaching in Quincy. The previous week, on 2 August, his father's Harvard classmate and kinsman John Quincy Adams remarked in his diary that he had heard Cranch preach and that he "gave out quite a stream of transcendentalism most unexpectedly." In the same entry Adams deplored the doings of "A young man, named Ralph Waldo Emerson (a son of my once-loved friend William Emerson, and a classmate of my lamented George), who, after failing in the everyday occupation of Unitarian preacher and schoolmaster, starts a new doctrine of transcendentalism, declares all the old revelations superannuated and worn out, and announces the approach of new revelations and prophecies."[15] Cranch never read the former President's diary, but, on a visit to Maine in April, he had heard Emerson dismissed as "crazy," and in July had had to write to his father, Justice Cranch, to scotch rumors that infatuation with the German philosophers had left his religious faith in tatters. To John Sullivan Dwight, after remarking on the strictures of the orthodox, Cranch disclosed that he was "nursing my wrath for some fit occasion to blaze out on them in righteous zeal for the good cause!"[16]

At the time of his Concord visit, Cranch was experiencing the onset of a mental depression brought on, perhaps, by theological perplexities (in his letter to Dwight he said mockingly, "renounce R.W.E. and all his evil works") that he would not be free of for another three years. He needed a quiet day with Emerson, but did not get it.

The day had its joyful moments, however. Emerson read poetry to them, some of it his own. He also read favorite verses by Ben Jonson, whose songs he thought second to none in the English language.[17] And they had walked to Walden Pond and to Sleepy Hollow, huckleberrying as they went. Cranch seems, for a while at least, to have rallied his spirits, for Emerson, thirty-four years later, would recall: "I well remember your speech to the frogs, which called out all the eloquence of the inhabitants of the swamp, in what we call Sleepy Hollow in Concord, many years ago."[18] This must have been a Concord first. Even Thoreau, a confirmed frog-listener, did not attempt to engage them in dialogue.

On the morning of 10 August, the Groton pilgrims, having passed the night as Emerson's houseguests, set forth for the convention of enthusiasts. Alcott, who, drawn by Emerson, had moved his family to Concord four months before, accompanied them. Emerson stayed put. He had no need to seek out eccentrics. More than his share sought him out. Of the Millerites, though, he made a mild exception, taking an interest in their New Advent hymns and advising Margaret Fuller that, in his deteriorating state, he was ready to subscribe to their journal, *The Midnight Yell.*[19]

Even before 22 October 1843, Miller's doomsday, arrived, two of the visitors to Groton, Ripley and Alcott, would launch enterprises that would link them to other eccentrics of the times — Brook Farm and Fruitlands. While Ripley was adapting his community to Fourier's scheme of management, Emerson told his journal that he deplored "Millerism & Fourierism & other of our superstitions."[20] Yet, re-signedly, he told Margaret, "It is a part of our lesson to give a formal consent to what is farcical, and to pick up our living & our virtue amidst what is so ridiculous, hardly deigning a smile, and certainly not vexed."[21]

Exhilarated by the happenings at Groton, the four theological mav-ericks decided to stage in Boston itself a Groton-type convention, a blanket invitation to which would be issued to all interested parties to "examine the validity of the views which generally prevail in this country as to the appointment of the first day of the week as the Chris-tian Sabbath, and to inquire into the origin, nature, and authority of the institutions of the Ministry and the Church as now existing."

That call for the new convention was made, through the agency of the Friends of Universal Reform, in William Lloyd Garrison's *Liber-ator* on 16 October 1840. Alcott, appointed to issue the call, was but one of twenty-four signatories, among whom were such earnest re-formers as Abby Kelley, Henry C. Wright, and William Henry Chan-ning. Edmund Quincy, a man of impeccable credentials, was desig-nated chairman, and the courageous Maria Weston Chapman, secretary. The site selected for the convention was that "temple of free discus-sion," the Chardon Street Chapel.

What came about was a nine-day convention — a veritable novena of dissent — separated into three three-day sessions held between No-vember 1840 and October 1841. The Sabbath was discussed at the first session, the ministry at the second, the church at the third.

The Friends of Universal Reform seems to have been a heading that William Lloyd Garrison used for many of his calls. While he did not initiate this convention (having just returned from Britain in late Au-gust), he played a conspicuous role in the first session, moved the con-vening of the second, and, in his counsels at the third led his foes to identify him as a leader of "an infidel convention" and an antinomian of Emerson's ilk.[22]

The convention never published a report of its proceedings, nor, Emerson relates, did it pretend "to arrive at any *Result,* by the expression of its sense in formal resolutions, — the professed object of those persons who felt the greatest interest in its meetings being sim-ply the elucidation of truth through free discussion."[23] Fortunately, however, Emerson attended every session and, in the ninth issue of *The Dial,* in July 1842 — the first issue published under his editorship — gave an overview of it. "As an historian of the times," he explained, "one would certainly want to be there." He went, also, it seems, in high good humor, expecting something of the sideshow that Groton had offered. To Lidian he wrote, two days before the first session opened (Lidian had escaped to Plymouth): "Waldo wishes you would come home and that it would not be Sunday — he certainly would vote against the good Day in the Chardon Street convention."[24]

Hitherto, Chardon Street had occupied an intimate place in Emerson's thoughts. There he had boarded with Abel Adams when he became minister of the Second Church. There Ellen and he had lived for a time. On 15 August 1831 Emerson had written Edward: "I am trying to learn to find my own latitude but there is no horizon in C[hardon] St. If I was richer I wd. have an observatory. I am trying to learn the ethical truths that always allure me from my cradle till now & yet how slowly disclosed."[25] Curious was the turn of events that, almost a decade thence, led Emerson back to Chardon Street to a battle among Uriels for possession of the theological heavens.

Perhaps at no other time than in this hectic decade of reform could so remarkable an assemblage have been brought together in nineteenth-century Boston. Although Emerson made no attempt to reproduce any part of the speeches or declarations made at the convention, he did create a sense of the mix of people there and of the mood prevailing. While such a convention could only have been instigated by those who represented the New Thought, men of such sober reputation as William Ellery Channing and James Russell Lowell attended the sessions and did not feel compromised. Emerson said:

> The faces were a study. The most daring innovators, and the champions-until-death, of the old cause, sat side by side. The still living merit of the oldest New England families, glowing yet, after several generations, encountered the founders of families, fresh merit, emerging, and expanding the brows to a new breadth, and lighting a clownish face with sacred fire.[26]

The local clergy, of course, seeking to rebut heretical opinions, took from the sessions some of the spontaneity that had made the Groton Convention such a success, but they were put to rout by what Edmund Quincy described as "the most singular collection of strange specimens of humanity that was ever assembled."[27] In a passage that has been described as "a locus of Emerson's humor," Emerson glossed for posterity Quincy's observation, attesting to its reasonableness:

> If the assembly were disorderly, it was picturesque. Madmen, madwomen, men with beards, Dunkers, Muggletonians, Come-

outers, Groaners, Agrarians, Seventh-day-Baptists, Quakers, Abolitionists, Calvinists, Unitarians, and Philosophers, — all came successively to the top, and seized their moment, if not their *hour,* wherein to chide, or pray, or preach, or protest.

Word of the convention had traveled far: "The singularity and latitude of the summons drew together . . . men of every shade of opinion, from the straitest orthodoxy to the widest heresy, and many persons whose church was a church of one member only."[28]

Father Edward Taylor had his moment, and Edward Palmer, the "No-Money" advocate who, while his houseguest, Emerson found to be both ridiculous and noble. Parker spoke also, as did Ripley, Very, and Abigail Folsom, who Emerson amiably identified as "that flea of Conventions." Thoreau was there, but merely to listen and observe. Emerson, on the last day of the first session, decided to speak, but the convention prorogued before he could make his wishes known. At the subsequent sessions the desire never revived. Conway surmised that Emerson's silence changed nothing: "Although Emerson did not ascend the tribune nor open his lips, in a sense he made a majority of the speeches."[29]

Conway saw the convention as a "pentecost of the new gospel," and that "new born bard of the Holy Ghost," Emerson himself, as the medium through which much of the inspiration flowed. Emerson's summation showed that he realized this:

> There was a great deal of wearisome speaking in each of those three days' sessions, but relieved by signal passages of pure eloquence, by much vigor of thought, and especially by the exhibition of character, and by the victories of character. These men and women were in search of something better and more satisfying than a vote or a definition, and they found what they sought, or the pledge of it, in the attitude taken by the individuals of their number . . . in the lofty reliance on principles, and the prophetic dignity and transfiguration which accompanies, even amidst opposition and ridicule, a man whose mind is made up to obey the great inward Commander.[30]

That declaration led him to consider Alcott's part in the convention.

Alcott spoke at every meeting. A phoenix sprung from the ashes, he surprised everyone and enjoyed what was surely his finest hour as "the foremost man at the Convention."[31] When Alcott's *Conversations with Children on the Gospels* had appeared, the *Boston Daily Advertiser* had excoriated him. Now, in that same publication, the editor's son, Edward Everett Hale, a recent Harvard graduate, lauded him in handsome terms: ''We have never heard any exposition of the transcendental doctrines so intelligibly made or placed in so favorable an aspect.''[32]

At the final session of the convention, in October 1841, a committee was appointed to call for a Bible Convention to review the credibility and authority of both the Old and New Testaments. Emerson and Alcott agreed to serve on this committee. The resultant convention, conceived of as a three-day event, opened on Tuesday, 29 March 1842, at the Masonic Temple, and closed the same day. The subject, Emerson concluded, was unpopular. He salvaged what he could by persuading an unlettered mechanic from South Marshfield, Nathaniel H. Whiting, to draw up a text of the speech he gave that day. To Emerson it had seemed an admirable illustration of what the untutored mind was capable of when guided by the inner counsels of the soul. Whiting had closed his speech with these ringing words:

> The Soul is its own authority, is bound by its own laws, does not live in the past, but is now. . . . When this great truth shall fill the human heart, and be shadowed forth in human life, then the morning of the Universal Resurrection will dawn, then man shall arise from his groveling position, among the coffins, the bones, and ashes of the buried Past, and live, and grow, and expand, in the bright sunlight of that Eternity in which he dwells.[33]

Alcott had been Emerson's oracle at the Chardon Street Convention. At the Bible Convention that lot fell to the Marshfield mechanic. Daniel Webster's standing as Marshfield's most illustrious orator was not imperiled.[34]

The four nondelegates who went to Groton from Concord on 10 August 1840 in pursuit of ''an adventure,'' as Cranch termed it, partook more than they meant to of the spirit of those around them. Such individualism was contagious. In the months that immediately followed each would sufficiently alter direction to make the orthodox apprehensive. Cranch, having not yet been ordained, by summer had adopted a new calling — landscape painting. Only his courtship of his cousin Elizabeth De Windt, John Adams's great-granddaughter, made him hesitate to make the final break. Some of the impetus came from Emerson. Cranch proclaimed the *Essays* (First Series), published 20 March 1841, as ''a living fountain to me.'' In September he laid his problem before Emerson: ''Whether I turn artist or not, I become more and more inclined to sink the minister in the man, and abandon my present calling *in toto* as a profession.''[35] Emerson replied on 1 October: ''That at all hazards you must quit the pulpit as a profes-

sion, I learn without surprise, yet with great interest and with the best
hope. The Idea that . . . unites us all, will have its way and must be
obeyed."[36]

Poems written by Cranch for *The Dial*, appearing in each issue, secured him status as *The Dial*'s poet laureate. Emerson expressed the
hope that the submissions would continue but made no comment on
Cranch's aspirations to paint. Possibly he had seen the caricatures of
himself that Cranch had done in his *Western Messenger* days and
thought it inappropriate to dwell on Cranch's sketching abilities.

Early the next year, Cranch's contributions to *The Dial* ceased. In
the brief time Emerson had known him, Cranch had run through two
enthusiasms and flung himself into a third. He seemed unable to stay
with anything for long. While Emerson was later to advance his solacing theory of muses in conflict, at this stage he seems to have been
disappointed that Cranch was proving a shallow find. In 1843, in response to a query from Cranch, who wished to publish his collected
poems in book form, Emerson told him he must be prepared to meet
the expenses of publication out of his own pocket. Cranch brought the
book out the year following — dedicated to Emerson. A copy was sent
to Emerson, which he acknowledged, commending Cranch for his tune-
fulness, sweetness, elegance, and metrical regularity. Pointedly, however, he told Cranch that he would like to sit down with him and "talk
over . . . very frankly this whole mystery and craft of poesy."[37] He
must have communicated to Cranch some sense of the real state of
affairs as he saw it, because Cranch rarely wrote poetry thereafter.
Yet, ironically, he was to attain to a vicarious immortality as a poet
when Emerson echoed the final stanza of "Stanzas" ("Enosis") in
lines 232–239 of his own, magnificent "Threnody."

Cranch's marriage and his long stays in Europe, totaling some thirteen years, put a true seal of remoteness on his later correspondence
with Emerson. On 20 March 1855 he wrote to Emerson expressing regret that "minds . . . most nearly related to spirit" must exist apart.[38]
Emerson must have grimaced to find Cranch calling in payment on
that long-ago compliment. The difference in their respective minds
had been clear to Emerson for some time.

Like a retired thespian harkening back to the inspirations that had
drawn him into the theater, Cranch, in later years, would recall with
sober awe the impact Emerson had had on him when first he was groping toward fulfillment. Thus, in the days after the Civil War, he told
the Theodore Parker Society that Emerson's *Nature* had been for him
"like the sunrise." Still greater had been the impact of the "Divinity
School Address." It "struck a loftier, deeper, more inspiring harmony
. . . like a chapter from the Prophets."[39]

In 1874 Cranch put in verse form some of the ideas encountered in

Emerson's essay "Compensation," and gave the results the same title. That same year he dispatched to Emerson a landscape he had done expressly for him. Cranch's covering letter spoke of "the lifelong debt of thanks I owe you for all that your works have been to me." Having made the circuit of the arts, he was drifting back to his old moorings. Graciously Emerson opened to him the hospitality of Bush. He invited the Cranches to come dine with him in Concord, and fetched them himself from the depot in his carryall. That was 14 October 1874. Occasionally they met after that, at the Radical Club, though neither had had a new radical idea in some time. Both were present at the Whittier dinner at which Mark Twain performed to his own dissatisfaction though perhaps to no one else's. On that occasion, a journalist, looking over the assemblage, concluded that Emerson was the most venerable-looking but that Cranch looked the most poetic![40]

On 12 November 1879 Cranch once more attended a lecture by Emerson, this time at the home of Professor C. C. Everett. Emerson's topic, "Memory," was an unfortunate choice, since his daughter had to stand by to see that he did not read the same page twice, and he had to read her lips to know what to say next. For Cranch to see Emerson in this state was only to pound fond memories into rubble. That was their last encounter.

In the scheme of Cranch's life Emerson shrank to a pleasant distraction. Ten years younger than Emerson, Cranch survived him by ten years. Yet for his allotment of years he had little to show. Still a month from publication at the time of his death was his article "Emerson's Limitations as a Poet," in which he repeated the usual arguments meant to show that Emerson was not a major poet. In the same era the same arguments were being put forward to explain why Walt Whitman and Emily Dickinson were not poets of eminence. To Emerson, as prose stylist, he consigned those attributes he withheld from Emerson as poet:

> Each sentence wears a precious jewel in its head. Every fact has a leading into other facts, and all radiate out into principles; so that nothing is unimportant, but each in turn becomes the center of a nurturing thought. Thus Imagination, or the symbolizing faculty, is always present in his pages, and makes him . . . a poet and "prophet of the soul." This dual vision . . . sets him outside of, if not above, most of the accredited thinkers of this century.[41]

To Cranch, Emerson was, further, the "great teacher of the century." On learning of Emerson's death, Cranch wrote "Ralph Waldo Emerson," an elegy with which, he believed, he "exceeded his own limitations as a poet." Forty years earlier, Cranch had written "The

Prophet Unveiled.'' That he thought his later poem superior is melancholy evidence of his diminished horizons. Yet he was right when he said of Emerson: ''The age to come will feel thy impress given / In all that lifts the race a step above / Itself.''[42]

In 1884 Cranch produced a carefully measured argument to account for Emerson's renown. While much that he sought to build otherwise has crumbled, this still holds:

> The ''Divinity School Address'' was of course the greatest rock
> thrown into the sociological current, dividing the conservatives
> from the so-called transcendental movement. And we all know how
> long the two streams ran and tumbled and frothed divergently.
> And some of us are old enough to note how different their later
> blending and confluence is. . . . I feel that I have lived from the
> beginning to the end of a wonderful revolution in thought.[43]

37. Brook Farm
The Kingdom of the New Spirit

*A*T their August 1840 meeting, Emerson had told George Ripley of his dream of founding a free university in Concord. In October, Emerson's turn to listen came. At the beginning of the month he told Margaret Fuller to fix a day to come to see him, in Ripley's company.[1] Ripley's wife, Sophia Dana, came too, and Bronson Alcott. Ripley was there to sell Emerson on his social plans. Here was something more ambitious than an experimental university — a whole community where transcendentalists could live together to their mutual benefit. Ripley had not come to explore with the others the feasibility of his ideas. From them he wanted only head-nodding agreement.

Emerson knew what to expect, yet he did not set his mind against it. He even imagined himself disposed to be receptive if the right appeal was made. "I wished to be convinced," he said next day in his journal, "to be thawed, to be made nobly mad by the kindlings before my eye of a new dawn of human piety."[2] If that is so, it was a notable departure from any feelings he had entertained before. His facetious tone suggests he was jesting; it tells us, certainly, that Ripley's presentation had not won him over. He prided himself on being a cake of ice and he still remained one. Of course, a noble scheme would have been difficult to reject out of hand. But Ripley made the mistake of addressing Emerson not as a pursuer of the ideal but as a man of means from whom he wanted a pledge for a ten percent investment toward an initial outlay of $30,000.

Emerson's reception can hardly have kindled any hopes in Ripley. Emerson said: "Not once could I be inflamed, — but sat aloof &

thoughtless, my voice faltered & fell.''[3] The rudiments of Ripley's plan had become known to him a few weeks before. On 26 September he had told of his wariness in his journal: ''Perhaps it is folly, this scheming to bring the good & like minded together into families, into a colony. Better that they should disperse and so leaven the whole lump of society.''[4] By temperament Emerson was ill suited to community households. During most of the twenty-five years after his father's death, he had known boardinghouse living. And his own home, after he married Lidian, often was run like a guest house. But from all this experience he learned merely how to isolate himself in the midst of many. Neither by measure of health or inclination did he have the stamina to deal with the share of manual labor that would fall to his lot as a member of a communal society. For the work that he could do he needed solitude and independence. ''Solitude,'' he believed, ''is more . . . benevolent than the concert of crowds.'' These were his principal reasons, touching on his own needs, for not committing himself. There were additional reasons, concerning others, to be considered as well. Lidian was a homemaker. Even now their limited means compelled her to improvise to encompass their needs. To ask her to take up a barebones life-style would be unreasonable. His mother had also to be considered. Through long years of deprivation he had nursed the hope that someday he could establish her in comfortable surroundings, ridding her of her burden of cares. He had done that and now was not about to undo it.

Emerson sometimes felt harassed by his duties as a responsible man of property and capable householder. In ''Literary Ethics'' he asked, ''Why should you renounce your right to traverse the star-lit deserts of truth, for the premature comforts of an acre, house, and barn?'' The prospect of being able to center his attention on the life of the mind and spirit enticed Emerson. He had supposed Ripley's plans conspired toward such ends. He was dismayed to be told otherwise. This ''room in the Astor House'' that Ripley offered him meant merely substituting one material situation for another. ''I do not wish,'' he insisted, ''to remove from my present prison to a prison a little larger. I wish to break all prisons. I have not yet conquered my own house. It irks & repents me. Shall I raise the siege of this hencoop & march baffled away to a pretended siege of Babylon?'' To join Ripley's society would be, at best, an evasive action, an attempt to hide his ''impotency in the thick of a crowd.'' He saw no merit in allying himself with a ''select, but not by me selected, fraternity.''[5]

The Concord conferral came early in Ripley's planning stage. He had not yet taken steps to purchase the West Roxbury milk farm he wanted as the site for his community. Yet Emerson, from the moment Ripley's plans were revealed, had begun a tally of reasons that stood in the way of his joining. In effect, he had elected not to become a member of Brook Farm before it had achieved its Brook Farm identity.

Ten weeks went by before Emerson communicated his decision to Ripley. He did not keep Ripley on tenterhooks merely to create an impression that he was giving the proposal every consideration. Nor was he toying with Ripley. Through those weeks he repeatedly prodded those arguments against joining Ripley that he had instantly mustered when Ripley laid the proposal before him. On 23 October he argued, ''If I am true . . . the very want of action, my very impotency, shall become a greater excellency than all skill & toil.'' Thus he justified his reluctance to fall in step with Ripley. On the twenty-sixth he breached his own battlements: ''When I go into my garden with the spade & dig . . . I discover that I have been defrauding myself all this time in letting others do for me what I should have done with my own hands.'' He envied cook and sawyer their self-sufficiency: ''They can contrive without my aid to make a whole day & whole year; but I depend on them.'' That was a compelling argument only if Ripley's community would sponsor self-sufficiency in its members. Emerson doubted that it would.[6]

When another two years had elapsed, he would see things in these terms: ''Brook Farm will show a few noble victims, who act & suffer with temper & proportion, but the larger part will be slight adventurers & will shirk work.''[7] Actually, Emerson was not weighing the experiment in terms of his own involvement. Rather, subtracting himself as either a participant or a backer (and he knew Ripley was as anxious to recruit his prestige as his presence), he weighed the experiment's chances for success and concluded it was doomed. To commit himself to a fatally flawed enterprise would be foolhardy.

Emerson had help in reaching this conclusion. He talked it over with his neighbor Edmund Hosmer, the most practical, reasonable farmer he had ever met. Intuition was a mighty force but, at times, no substitute for that hard common sense that is grounded in long experience. Hosmer did some plain speaking. ''No large property can ever be made by honest farming,'' he said. By their very integrity gentleman farmers would fail. Their one hope was to entrust to a shrewd foreman the selling of their produce, taking care not to make ''any scrupulous inquiry'' into his methods. Since, in Hosmer's opinion, this approach would not be acceptable to ''Mr. Ripley and his coadjutors,'' Brook Farm had no chance of prospering. Hosmer also felt that if all received the same amount of pay for their labor, those who had an interest-paying investment in the community would not work as hard as those who did not. Skilled laborers, without capital, were better workers. Their skill was their capital and they were entitled to interest on that. As Hosmer saw it, if he ran his farm as Ripley planned to run his, he would soon be destitute. Emerson conveyed the gist of Hosmer's arguments to Ripley, who ignored it probably because he believed Hosmer's counsel had cost him Emerson's support. Indeed, Hosmer's hard-driving practicality must be credited with having given substance to Emerson's disinclination to give Ripley his active endorsement. As for Hosmer, he later attended parties at Brook Farm and enjoyed them, unperturbed by the naiveté of the party-givers.[8]

Not wanting to stifle Ripley's enthusiasm, Emerson, in the early stages of planning, had been unwilling to discourage him. In fact, notwithstanding Hosmer's counseling, he may have believed at that time that, for Ripley and others, the plans were feasible. And Ripley, hearing nothing to the contrary, concluded that he had recruited Emerson. When confirming word did not come, however, Ripley wrote him on 9 November, advising him of the progress made since their Concord encounter. Suspecting that Emerson was wavering, he took care to remark that he appreciated Emerson's preference for self-sufficiency since he shared like convictions. But these he was ready to disregard, and wondered if Emerson was of the same mind.

How Lidian looked on Brook Farm we may gather from a letter Emerson wrote to her on 15 November, when Lidian was spending a few days in Boston visiting her brother: "The 'Community' question is in full agitation betwixt Mr Ripley Mr Alcott & me & if you wish to have a voice in it & not to find your house sold over your head or perhaps a troop of new tenants brought suddenly into it you must come & counsel your dangerous husband."[9] This may have been an invitation to Lidian to sow the seeds of discouragement, yet the tone is sufficiently bantering as to suggest that Lidian had no true cause for anxiety. More significant is the allusion to possible tenants. As a way of getting a taste of Brook Farm living without a Brook Farm commitment, Emerson would soon invite the Alcotts to share his home.

The frenzy that saw Brook Farm and Hopedale founded in Massachusetts in 1841, Northampton in 1842, and Fruitlands, New Harmony, Oneida, and a dozen other utopias, most of which produced dystopian results, not long after, was soon recognized by Emerson for what it was. In 1844, in "New England Reformers," he would specify that a union among men, to be effective, "must be inward, and not one of covenants."[10]

Ripley would have to wait another five weeks for his answer. But, after three weeks, Emerson was close to formulating it. He discussed it in a letter to Margaret Fuller, sent on 1 December. Although Margaret had no capital to invest and no household to uproot, she too had misgivings about the "Community." To her Emerson said: "For the 'Community' I have given it some earnest attention & much talk; and have not quite decided not to go. But I hate that the least weight should hang on my decision, — of me, who am so unpromising a candidate for any society. At the name of a society all my repulsions play, all my quills rise & sharpen.''[11]

The next day, 2 December, Emerson wrote William: ''We are absorbed here at home in discussion of George Ripley's Community,'' and mentioned, with seeming offhandedness, that Ripley wanted him to enroll in his company and put some money into it. Although he went on to say that there ought to be some way to ''get the same advantages without pulling down my house,'' he conceded, as well, that he was ''very discontented with many of my present ways & bent on mending them.''[12] He also briefly outlined the scheme, making it sound thoroughly harebrained. Obviously, he wanted a stern warning from William to have nothing to do with it. William obliged and, for good measure, urged him, if he was determined to make a change, to settle on Staten Island, where he himself now lived. William's letter may have reassured Emerson, but it played no part in his decision-making. Before it came he had already notified Ripley that he would not join him in the great adventure.

In a curious document, allegedly written by Emerson on 12 December, and supplied to James Elliot Cabot by William Henry Channing in a copy made by Margaret Fuller, Emerson examined the reasons that had caused him to keep the door open on Ripley's invitation. In doing so he managed to sound like Saint Francis embracing Lady Poverty:

> Instead of being the hero of ideas and exploring by a great act of trust those diviner modes which the spirit will not fail to show to those who dare to ask, I allow the old circumstances of mother, wife, children, and brother to overpower my wish to right myself with absolute Nature. . . . I should like to put all my practices back on their first thoughts. . . . But how will Mr. R's project help me in all this? It is a pretty circuitous route, is it not, to the few, simple conditions which I require? . . . I only wish to make my house as simple as my vocation.[13]

Here, then, is the very crux of that dilemma which, through the autumn of 1840, gave Emerson so much cause for concern.

Evidence of Emerson's psychic struggle during this period is found in his record of a dream entered in his journal that October: ''I dreamed that I floated at will in the great Ether, and I saw this world floating also not far off, but diminished to the size of an apple. Then an angel took it in his hand & brought it to me and said 'This must thou eat.' And I ate the world.''[14]

Criticism has exhausted much ink explicating this passage. It is a record of Emerson's guilt for having used disaffection for the Lord's Supper as a pretext for resigning his pastorate at the Second Church. It is one with his morbid, metaphoric allusions to man's need to devour food to sustain life. It is a variant version of his alleged homosexual parable of the Siphar trees, a theme localized later in an 1853 journal entry in which he acclaims the stubborn resistance to assimilation shown by the Saxon race.[15] A world devoured, a race that balks at being devoured — the same principle is involved but, whereas before it was yielded to passively, it is now contested.

Discussing this dream, Joel Porte remarks:

> Though it might seem that Emerson was here simply symbolizing for himself his necessary recapitulation of Adam's primal sin — eating the fruit of worldly knowledge, but this time with divine sanction — other possibilities suggest themselves. His dream might also represent a figuration of the "Idealism" section of *Nature,* where man, "the immortal pupil," finds himself so dilated and deified that the whole world does indeed circulate through him, totally engulfed "in the apocalypse of the mind." In this view, Emerson's dream might be seen as a kind of rehearsal of that tremendous sense of spiritual power which had inspired his first book (and which, to judge by his later journal entry, would largely evaporate in the mid-1850's: " 'Twere ridiculous for us to think of embracing the whole circle when we know we can live only while 50, 60, or 70 whirls are spun round the sun by this nimble apple we are perched upon. Can the gnat swallow the elephant?'').[16]

Since Emerson brooded, intermittently, on the severity of his father toward his children, it could be urged that his interest in the myth of Saturn prepared the way for his world-apple dream. In March 1835 he wrote in his journal: "Saturn, they say, devoured his children, thereby presignifying the man who thought & instantly turned round to see how his thoughts were made. The hen that eats the egg." In a preface Emerson wrote to *Plutarch's Morals,* published in 1871, Saturn's act is again recalled when he quotes a passage from Plutarch (as quoted by Bacon!): "I had rather a great deal that men should say, There was no such man at all as Plutarch, than that they should say that there was one Plutarch that would eat up his children as soon as they were born, as the poets speak of Saturn." What shudders Carlyle must have provoked in Emerson when, on 7 May 1852, he remarked of Margaret Fuller: "Such a predetermination to *eat* this big Universe as her oyster or her egg, and to be absolute empress of all height and glory in it that her heart could conceive, I have not before seen in any human soul.''[17]

In pondering the significance of Emerson's dream, an obvious interpretation has gone unnoticed. During his early school years he had come under the instruction of Lawson Lyon, a taskmaster remembered in later years as ''a severe teacher, high-tempered, and flogged the boys unmercifully.'' When some aspect of the earth was Lyon's topic, an apple, as a visual aid, became his terrestrial globe. When he had achieved his object, he then devoured the apple with grim relish.[18] This exercise was often repeated, the opportunity to intimidate his charges by devouring the world before their eyes in fierce gulps being, it seemed, the true occasion of the lesson. This hard, mean-spirited man, enacting this sadistic ritual, must have seemed to his timid charges an ogre out of folklore, an invincible giant who exacted a fearful toll from those who encountered him on his own ground. Even as Emerson was traumatized by Lyon's dramatic demonstration, the world as he knew it was swallowed up when his father died, his books sold at auction, and comforts exchanged for hardships. In the fate of the first parents, seduced by an apple, and driven forth from hospitable Eden into an inhospitable world, there was an evident parallel to be seen.

Emerson dreamed that he ate the apple that was the world just at the time he was under pressure from George Ripley to relinquish the world he had reconstituted, the first stable environment he had known since the world his father provided was consumed. Ripley addressed his appeal to Emerson on 16 October. On 25 October he recorded his dream. To Emerson, Brook Farm was a suspect Eden. He was not prepared to trade a world he was sure of for an uncertain one. This time the decision rested with him, and he cast himself as Lyon — he would not be the devoured but the devourer. The world was his and he would internalize it.

All too soon Emerson was to find that the world he thought was his was not. His son, Waldo, died, and something of himself went with him — ''the largest part of me,'' he says, in ''Threnody.'' His world, a veritable universe, was being diminished:

> *For this losing is true dying;*
> *This is lordly man's down-lying,*
> *This his slow but sure reclining,*
> *Star by star his world resigning.*[19]

Much later, when Emerson told his fellowman, ''Hitch your wagon to a star,'' he was urging that men commit themselves not to a perishable world, a star that can be consumed, but to an ideal which can only be strengthened by man's desire to possess it.

Prior to recording his world-apple dream, Emerson had written in his journal: "The method of advance in nature is perpetual transformation. Be ready to emerge from the chrysalis of today, its thoughts & institutions, as thou hast come out of the chrysalis of yesterday."[20] Thus, even then, he was thinking not of the horror of a world perishing but rather of the positive act of discarding one identity to assume another.

In the penultimate stanza of "The World-Soul" the universal mind, as man responds to it and surrenders himself to its dictates, is seen to supplant the physical world with the ultimate reality, an enduring superior world:

> *When the old world is sterile*
> *And the ages are effete,*
> *He will from wrecks and sediment*
> *The fairer world complete.*[21]

Thus is the dilemma of a world devoured resolved. The World-Soul assimilates man, and he is One with Divinity. Operating on that plane, Emerson could hardly have realized himself spiritually in an environment in which man's physical needs were, by reason of circumstance, the engrossing concern.

Emerson's letter of regret was sent to Ripley on 15 December. With a single deft stroke, he apologized for making Ripley wait for an answer and made the apology do double duty as a compliment, thus undertaking to mitigate the impact of a decision contrary to Ripley's expectations. The design of Ripley's new enterprise, he said, had appeared to him "So noble & humane, proceeding . . . from a manly & expanding heart & mind," that it had become for him "a matter of conscience" to examine it sympathetically. "Very slowly & I may almost say penitentially" he had decided not to join. As he had done in his opening paragraph, he again diminished the impact of what he had said by expressing satisfaction in knowing that so many others had flocked to Ripley's standards that his defection would count for nothing.[22]

That at least two variant drafts of this letter exist is not surprising. As with the Van Buren letter, Emerson took pains with it. Indeed, his Ciceronian skill in handling his arguments is so ably managed no one could doubt his classical training. Here is clear proof that Emerson, when circumstances required, could produce closely reasoned arguments expertly joined.

In the third paragraph of his letter, Emerson, making an all but parenthetical reference to difficulties which the community, as a feasible enterprise, posed for him, shifted responsibility for the decision he had made to his own failings. He had grown attached to Concord and if his work fell short of what he hoped to accomplish, that failure devolved on his "own sloth & conformity," not on his "townsmen or . . . social position." Then came a master stroke: "It seems to me a circuitous and operose way of relieving myself of any irksome circumstance to put on your community the task of my emancipation which I ought to take on myself."

A number of neatly set up arguments now followed. He wished to make manual labor a part of his daily regimen but this he could do without displacing his family and himself. He lacked the stamina needed to effect rapidly the changes in himself that were desirable. Living as he did now, he could better conceal his failure to reform himself. Ripley and his associates would be disappointed in him if he lived among them. Thus: "If the community is not good for me neither am I good for it." He concluded with a final, bolstering assurance: "Of all philanthropic projects of which I have heard yours is the most pleasing to me." Literature's gain was diplomacy's loss. Ripley would never get a more gracious refusal.[23]

To crowd Brook Farm out of his thoughts, Emerson projected for himself three alternative plans. In the spring he would bring the Alcotts under his roof and they would carry out, in modest fashion, their own experiment in communal living. Lidian agreed to this proposal but, since Abba Alcott, being of sound mind, did not, nothing came of it. He would try the experiment of manual labor. His want of robustness defeated this plan. The Emersons and their servants would share their meals together. Lacking Emerson's way with words, the servants turned him down with a flat no, a refreshing alternative, in its way, to the flood of ink Emerson had consumed turning down Ripley. Through the years Emerson carried in firewood for the fireplace in his study, and, at bedtime, raked out the embers. That amounted to a symbolic act. Those embers were all that remained to Emerson of his projected reforms. Yet, for Emerson, the decision he made had to be the right one. The following spring Brook Farm came to pass. Fate allotted it a single septenniad before it too was reduced to ashes.

Ripley was not easily reconciled to building a dream in which Emerson had no part, at least no financial part, for not the least laudable demonstration Emerson made of his rhetorical skills in the severance letter was his success in encompassing the subject with a philanthropic thoroughness that seemed entire yet, at no point, spoke of even a token contribution to attest to his faith in the worth of the enterprise. In December 1841, Ripley again asked Emerson to join the community and to invest in its stock at $500 a share, five percent interest guaranteed.[24] By then, Emerson had been instructed by the example of his servants. He answered with a flat no.

38. Bronson Alcott
The Plato Skimpole

*T*o remain Bronson Alcott's friend called for heroic patience. In no way did Emerson better show that he possessed such patience than by making Alcott's cause his own for almost fifty years.

Alcott's great failing was his ego. Emerson understood this full well, not at once perhaps, but soon enough. Much of the time he accepted Alcott for what he was. Occasionally he registered a mild protest, as though speaking of the failings of a child who had not yet arrived at the age of reason.

In the spring of 1842, when Alcott was preparing to go to England (his passage paid by Emerson), Emerson paused to consider the man he had known for seven years: "Unhappily, his conversation never loses sight of his own personality. He never quotes; he never refers; his only illustration is his own biography. His topic yesterday is Alcott on the 17 October; today, Alcott on the 18 October; tomorrow, on the 19th. So will it be always."[1] In Paris, in May 1848, Emerson momentarily found more engrossing than the revolution going on around him his memories of Alcott's colossal egotism: "Alcott said to me," he wrote, " 'You write on the genius of Plato, of Pythagoras, of Jesus, of Swedenborg, why do you not write of me?' "[2] Wisely, Emerson did not grow anxious awaiting a change in Alcott.

Between September 1828 and July 1835, when he first met Emerson, Alcott had heard Emerson preach and lecture several times and was enough impressed to be glad to make his acquaintance when Emerson appeared one night at his quarters on Somerset Place, having come there to meet a visitor from Philadelphia. An autodidact himself, Alcott was delighted to discover that while Emerson was "scholarlike," the man was "not lost in the scholar."[3] In October 1835, when Emerson was barely a month in his new home, Alcott came for a weekend visit. The elegant manners that he had picked up from the plantation gentry while touring the Southland as a peddler — a deportment Carlyle later cruelly dubbed "Cockney gracefulness" — seemed to Emerson the essence of refinement. Here was a find: a man, as Emerson took pains to describe him in March 1842, "very noble in his carriage to all men, of a serene & lofty aspect & deportment in the street & in the house, of simple but graceful & majestic manners."[4] In an era when men were seeking the true nobleman of Nature, Emerson suspected he had found him. In his journal on 21 October, after Alcott's departure, Emerson characterized him reverently — "A wise man, simple, superior to display, & drops the best things as quietly as the least."[5] Alcott had hidden his ego well on this visit. He had been oracular, of course, but Emerson (or "Mr. Emison," as Alcott called him then and always) had not minded that, supposing that he saw exhibited in Alcott a living embodiment of someone whose utterance flowed directly from the World-Soul.

After a visit from Alcott in June 1836, Emerson had more ecstatic conclusions to report, tinged, however, with faint qualifications, as though reservations were appearing that he felt it his duty to stifle: "Mr. Alcott has been here with his Olympian dreams. He is a world-builder. Ever more he toils to solve the problem, Whence is the World? . . . He cannot recall one word or part of his own conversation or of any one's, let the expression be never so happy."[6]

At the end of the month, when he wrote to William, Emerson had no reservations about Alcott. "He is a great genius," he said. "So thoroughly original that he seems to subvert all you know & leave only his own theories."[7] A month later Emerson petitioned Hedge to let Alcott into the Transcendental Club, even though he had had no theological training. "You must admit Mr. Alcott over the professional limits, for he is a God-made priest. That man grows upon me every time I see him."[8] For his part, Alcott found Emerson's perfect sincerity and simplicity constituted the highest expression of the religious spirit. When that same summer, in July, Margaret Fuller came into Emerson's circle, he introduced her to Alcott and she agreed to take Elizabeth Peabody's place at the Temple School, the experimental school that Alcott had started in Boston. Margaret, however, hesitated to attach to Alcott the same value Emerson did. She was wary and was not sure why. She reflected: "I wish I could define my distrust of Mr. Alcott's mind. . . . There is something in his view of every subject, something in his philosophy which revolts my common sense or my prejudices."[9] She argued this point with Emerson. He would not concede it. On 19 May 1837 Emerson wrote to her: "Mr. Alcott . . . is the great man & Miss Fuller has not seen him." That same day, writing in his journal, he had more to say. Alcott was "The most extraordinary man, and the highest genius of the time. . . . The steadiness & scope of his eye at once rebukes all before it, and we little men creep about ashamed."[10]

When a public outcry was raised against Alcott after publication of his *Conversations with Children on the Gospels,* in the spring of 1837, Emerson came at once to his defense, and even Margaret Fuller thought the attack preposterous and discouraged Hedge from joining in when rumor carried to her that he would. Much of the clamor came from the *Boston Daily Advertiser* and from Andrews Norton. Norton's verdict on Alcott's book was that "one-third was absurd, one-third blasphemous, and one-third obscene."[11] When Emerson addressed a letter of protest to the *Daily Advertiser,* Nathan Hale refused to print it. Emerson then sent the letter to the *Courier,* where, though hedged with disclaimers, it was published.

After mounting criticism forced the closing of the school in 1839, Emerson sought in vain to find Alcott a teaching post. Presently came Emerson's offer to shelter the Alcotts in his own home. Though Abba Alcott and Emerson were blood relatives, through her mother, Dorothy Sewall (Emerson's great-great-grandmother, Hannah Sewall, was the niece of Judge Samuel Sewall, Dorothy's grandfather), she knew her husband's response to such an arrangement would be exploitative. Emerson was already paying their rent (fifty-two dollars a year) at Hosmer's Dove Cottage, a half mile from his own house, and she elected not to deepen the obligation.[12]

During Alcott's first summer in Concord, his "Orphic Sayings" were published in July, in *The Dial*'s first issue. These at once became an object of widespread ridicule, described, with some justice, by one observer as being "like a train of fifteen cars with one passenger." Passively, Alcott gathered all the parodies to make a scrapbook. But Emerson, who already — after futile efforts to edit Alcott's *Psyche* — had doubts about Alcott's writing ability, was beginning to wonder if Alcott could ever earn his bread by his pen. It took only six months of Alcott as near neighbor for Emerson to conclude, "A. is a tedious archangel."[13]

Emerson liked Alcott's educational theories, however, and later incorporated some of them into his essay on education. Typically, when he found that Alcott had a following in England, he set about raising what he called the "Alcott-Voyage-fund" to send him there to visit Alcott House, a school named in his honor. When others failed to see the merit of the venture, Emerson took on additional lecture commitments and paid Alcott's passage himself. That was in the spring of 1842.

Once in England Alcott, despite a cautionary letter Emerson sent to them, had no trouble enlisting some of his British admirers as sponsors for another of his chimerical schemes. Though Emerson sent Carlyle a letter that made out the best possible case for the indigent dreamer, he proved harder to convince. On 31 March 1837, when the prospect of Alcott's going to England had not yet arisen, Emerson had written to Carlyle: "A man named Bronson Alcott is great, & one of the jewels we have to show you." On 31 March 1842, when the journey was all but certain, Emerson wrote to Carlyle in a far different vein:

> There is shortly coming to you a man by the name of Bronson Alcott. . . . I do not wish to bespeak any courtesies or good or bad opinion concerning him. You may love him, or hate him, or apathetically pass by him, as your genius shall dictate: Only I entreat this, that you do not let him go quite out of your reach until you are sure you have seen him and know for certain the nature of the man.

The previous week, Emerson had asked himself how he should prepare Carlyle for Alcott's advent and eulogized him with scant restraint: "Where he is greeted by loving & intelligent persons, his discourse soars to a wonderful height. . . . He so swiftly & naturally plants himself on the moral sentiment in any conversation that no man will ever get any advantage of him." As events were to develop, it was well that Emerson, when writing to Carlyle, fell back on his usual practice of understating things.[14]

On 19 July Carlyle reported the results of his first encounters with this latest American visitor: "He is a genial, innocent, simple-hearted man, of much natural intelligence and goodness, with an air of rusticity, veracity, and dignity withal, which in many ways appeals to me." For most of two years that had been Emerson's own opinion of Alcott. But Carlyle went on, showing that he had already advanced to the next stage of acquaintance with Alcott: "He comes before one like a kind of venerable Don Quixote, whom nobody can even laugh at without loving!" There had, nonetheless, already been a falling out between them, Alcott having preached vegetarianism to Carlyle with messianic zeal. Matters came to a crisis when, on the occasion of Alcott's being his overnight guest, Carlyle procured strawberries for his breakfast as a treat, and Alcott mingled them with mashed potatoes.[15]

Writing to Carlyle in October, Emerson voiced the fear that Alcott "through his more than a prophet's egotism, and the absence of all useful reconciling talents," was doomed to accomplish nothing in life. In his first draft of this letter Emerson had said he did not know whether Carlyle's failure to see Alcott's nobility was Alcott's failure or Carlyle's own. Alerted, perhaps, by his knowledge of the caprices of which Alcott was capable, he omitted this passage from the letter sent. That was fortunate because the break between Carlyle and Alcott had already come. In fact, though Emerson was not privy to this knowledge, on 2 August Alcott had written to Abba, saying, ''I have seen . . . Carlyle again, *but we quarreled outright,* and I shall not see him again.''[16]

In November, after Alcott had gone home, Carlyle wrote to Emerson, commending his allusion to Alcott's ''more than prophetic egoism'' and observing, ''I consider him entirely unlikely to accomplish anything considerable, except some kind of crabbed, semi-perverse, though still manful existence of his own ; which indeed is no despicable thing.'' The following March, Carlyle warned Emerson against extending his patronage to Charles Lane and Henry Wright, the would-be utopians who, bent on founding a transcendental paradise, had gone back to America with Alcott. ''Bottomless imbeciles,'' he warned ominously, ''ought not to be seen in company with Ralph Waldo Emerson, who has already *men* listening to him on this side of the water.''[17]

By now Emerson did not need Carlyle to tell him that. On 26 October he had written in his journal : '' A. is a singular person . . . whom all good persons would readily combine, one would say, to maintain as a priest by voluntary contribution to live in his own cottage. . . . But for a founder of a family or institution, I would as soon exert myself to collect money for a madman.''[18] He could call instances of Alcott's impracticality readily to mind. Once he gave him twenty-five dollars for household essentials. Alcott spent it on elegant stationery. On another occasion Mrs. Alcott put by twelve dollars for a much-needed winter shawl. Her husband, commissioned to make this purchase, came home with an edition of Plato instead.

In the ensuing year Emerson watched the Fruitlands venture sprout, wither, and die without ever having flourished at all. While his humanity would not permit him to shun the company of the utopians, as Carlyle had urged, the results of the undertaking were much as he expected them to be. In the waning days of the ludicrous happening he wrote its epitaph : '' Alcott came, the magnificent dreamer, brooding as ever on the renewal or reedification of the social fabric after ideal law, heedless that he had been uniformly rejected by every class to whom he has addressed himself, and just as sanguine & vast as ever.''[19]

With the collapse of Fruitlands Alcott fell into that interval of despair whimsically documented later by Louisa May in her *Transcendental Wild Oats.* In October 1844, Alcott was again in Concord with plans for yet another transcendental community. On 4 October a wary Emerson wrote to William : '' The dreaming Alcott is here with Indian dreams that I helped him to some house & farm in the Spirit Land !''[20] This proposal was merely the opening phase of yet another appeal to

Emerson for assistance. Even as William pleaded with him not to contribute even cheap acres to Alcott's newest fantasy, Alcott was reporting his success to his brother Junius: "Emerson has offered to buy me a few acres and build me a plain house."[21] He would yet have his utopia. He wanted Junius to throw in with him on this plan. But Junius, even without this stimulus, had reached the end of his tether. He became deranged and ended his life by throwing himself into the churning wheels of the factory where his brother Ambrose worked. Lane, on hearing the news, suggested that Bronson's troubles also might be ascribed to madness. Reflecting on his words later, Alcott conceded mildly that it might be so.

In April 1845 the Alcotts moved into Hillside, a house a short distance from Emerson's, its purchase made possible by a bequest Abba received from her father and a gift of five hundred dollars from Emerson, who donated, as well, a few acres across the road from the house.

When, after three years, Alcott withdrew again to Boston, Emerson took occasion to ask himself what it was that he got from Alcott. He concluded: "Alcott is a certain fluid in which men of a certain spirit can easily expand themselves & swim at large. . . . He gives them nothing but themselves. . . . Me he has served now these twelve years in that way; he was the reasonable creature to speak to, that I wanted." When others had asked him to enumerate Alcott's achievements, he had been confounded. "Alcott," he saw now, "is a man of unquestionable genius, yet no doctrine or sentence or word or action of his which is excellent can be detached & quoted." Now, at least, Emerson had an hypothesis to account for this enigma. He afterward added a further insight: "It were too much to say that the Platonic world I might have learned to treat as cloud-land, had I not known Alcott, who is a native of that country, yet I will say that he makes it as solid as Massachusetts to me."[22]

Emerson was pleased to see that others also sought to justify their espousal of this dreamer: "My friends begin to value each other," he wrote, "now that A[lcott] is to go; & Ellery [Channing] declares, 'that he never saw that man without being cheered.' & Henry says, 'He is the best natured man he ever met. The rats & mice make their nests in him.'" Thoreau's feelings toward Alcott were not always so amiable. After his death, Emerson noted: "He loved sufficiency, hated a sum that would not prove; loved Walt [Whitman] and hated Alcott."[23]

This time Alcott left Concord not to pursue another fantasy but because he could not make ends meet. In Boston a post awaited his wife that would bring them income. She would be "a visitor to the poor," a job to which, assuredly, she would bring great understanding.

With Alcott's departure, the spell he cast on Emerson somewhat dissipated.[24] In the spring of 1855, when he came to Emerson seeking money to go to England to trace his ancestors, Emerson put his foot down firmly but creatively: "I set my face against it, & told him I would not only not help it, but I would try to persuade his friends at P[rovidence] to withhold their money from this, & give it a new direction, namely to make it the basis of a permanent, if small, fund for his support at home."[25] The idea for such a fund actually originated in a conversation between Emerson and Longfellow. What they had in mind was "a small annuity that may at least secure him a philosophic loaf every day." Since Alcott would never be other than he was, he might as well have the freedom to follow his natural bent.

Emerson had come again to the view that Alcott was unusual enough to deserve to be subsidized on a modest scale. Even as he sent out appeals to likely donors, he wrote: "Alcott. . . . I was struck with the late superiority he showed. The interlocutors were all better than he; he seemed childish & helpless. . . . But by & by, when he got upon a thought, like an Indian seizing by the mane & mounting a wild horse of the desart, he overrode them all."[26] Nor did the vindication stop there. It ran on in tandem with the fund-collecting. Alcott, Emerson was convinced, was a medium through which the moral sentiment revealed itself. "The comfort of Alcott's mind," he wrote in April 1856,

is, the connexion in which he sees whatever he sees. He is never dazzled by a spot of colour, or a gleam of light, to value that thing by itself ; but forever and ever is prepossessed by the undivided One behind it all. . . . For every opinion or sentence of Alcott, a reason may be sought and found, not in his will, or fancy, but in the necessity of nature itself. . . . I shall go far, see many, before I find such an extraordinary insight as Alcott's.

So much merit did he see in Alcott's curious gifts, his failings, by comparison, came to little : "He has his faults, no doubt, but . . . some that are most severely imputed to him are only the omissions of a preoccupied mind."[27]

The "Alcott Fund" did not prove to be one of the great causes of that era, being overwhelmed rather by the preference many showed for the Kansas Aid Fund. By July 1859, Emerson could report a total of $501 donated. Of this sum he had given $100. The dollar donation came from Thoreau.[28]

"Father decides to go back to Concord," Louisa May noted in her journal in August 1857; "he is never happy far from Emerson, the one true friend who loves and understands him."[29] Orchard House, close by Hillside, was bought in early autumn. The price was $950. Of that sum Emerson stood security on a note for $450. In October the Alcotts took temporary quarters near the town hall where they stayed till the following July, when Orchard House, which Louisa's *Little Women* would make famous, was ready for them. Alcott was fifty-eight, an age at which the dreams of most men begin to wane. But Alcott had another thirty years to live and such successes as he would enjoy in life lay largely ahead of him. At fifty-nine he was appointed superintendent of schools for Concord. The post was chiefly honorary and carried with it an annual stipend of only $100 a year, yet he stepped into the role with the earnestness of a great thespian, going from school to school to talk to the students and to counsel the teachers, and preparing annually a report that could have been a text for educators. And beyond this glory lay the glory of his own Concord School of Philosophy. Emerson had once expressed the hope that he would survive Alcott so that he could see to it that justice was done to his life. That was not to be. Yet in bringing Alcott to Concord, Emerson made it possible for Alcott to live out some of his dreams and that was a greater thing to have done.

To most men Alcott, proclaiming truths that neither they nor the enunciator himself could afterward recall, was an unconscious parody of Emerson's complete universal man. To Emerson, Alcott was an authentic transmitter of the dictates of the moral sense, and in that function, affirmed his great worth. In fact, Alcott's true service to Emerson was his confirmation, by his long dependency on him, of those virtues of friendship which Emerson supposed were his most conspicuous deficiencies — trust, loyalty, understanding, forgiveness, the accepting without complaint of another's burdens. Taken in aggregate, these illustrate the capacity to love. Emerson thought that he lacked this capacity, yet had he not possessed it to a fullness few men ever attain to, Alcott would surely have perished.

39. Margaret Fuller
An Accomplished Lady

*A*FTER Margaret Fuller paid a call on Thomas Carlyle, in Chelsea, on 7 October 1846, Carlyle, who perversely had made up his mind to dislike her (possibly because of his disappointment with Alcott), described her, begrudgingly, in a letter to his brother John as "a *strange* lilting lean old maid, not nearly such a bore as I expected." For Emerson, however, in a letter written on 18 December following, Carlyle found more enthusiastic terms. Margaret was now "A high-soaring, clear, enthusiast soul; in whose speech there is much of all that one wants to find in speech. A sharp subtle intellect too; and less of that shoreless Asiatic dreaminess than I have sometimes met with in her writings. We liked one another very well, I think." After Margaret's tragic death, Carlyle would recall her as "rather a good woman," and own, "I remember I was somewhat hard upon her and certain crotchets of hers."[1]

Carlyle need not have been so remorseful. The first impression Margaret made on people usually was unfavorable and Emerson's first impression of her had been decidedly so. In 1851 he set down his own original reaction to her when in July 1836 — invited, for propriety's sake, as Lidian's guest — she had come to Concord for an extended visit: "Her appearance had nothing prepossessing. Her extreme plainness — a trick of incessantly opening and shutting her eyelids — the nasal tone of her voice — all repelled; and I said to myself, we shall never get far."[2] On 12 August, the day following her departure (her visit had lengthened into three weeks), Emerson described her in his journal as "a very accomplished & very intelligent person."[3] Margaret had improved on acquaintance. There was a reason for that. She worked at it. She had moved in on Emerson, not merely physically, but mentally, spiritually, and emotionally, determined to make a conquest of him. No one, with the exception of Ellen Tucker, succeeded in so engrossing his mind for a time.

To William he wrote, while the visit was still on: "An accomplished lady is staying with Lidian. Miss Margaret Fuller . . . is quite an extraordinary person for her apprehensiveness her acquisitions & her powers of conversation. It is a great refreshment to see a very intelligent person."[4] Later, assessing her impact, Emerson said: "She studied my tastes, piqued and amused me, challenged frankness by frankness, and did not conceal the good opinion of me she brought with her, nor her wish to please. She was curious to know my opinions and experiences. Of course, it was impossible long to hold out against such urgent assault."[5] Emerson knew he was being wooed. But he let himself be won.

Margaret's manner was not the sole thing that at first made him wary of her. Her reputation put him on his guard as well. He observed:

> Margaret made a disagreeable first impression on most persons, including those who became afterwards her best friends. . . . This was partly the effect of her manners, which expressed an overweening sense of power, and slight esteem of others, and partly the prejudice of her fame. She had a dangerous reputation for satire.
> . . . This rumor was much spread abroad, that she was sneering, scoffing, critical, disdainful of humble people, and of all but the intellectual. I had heard it whenever she was named. It was a superficial judgment. Her satire was only the pastime and necessity of her talent, the play of superabundant animal spirits.[6]

Margaret Fuller's mind was as remarkable as Emerson believed it to be and almost as remarkable as Margaret believed it to be. "I have not," she told her friend Samuel Gray Ward one day, "seen any intellect that would compare with my own." Her problem, as she saw it, was how to nurture her genius. To her cousin James Freeman Clarke she had written in 1833: "How often have I thought if I could see Goethe, and tell him my state of mind, he would support and guide me! He would be able to understand." The year before she confronted Emerson, she wrote in her journal: "I sigh for an intellectual guide. . . . I had hoped some friend would do — what none has ever yet done — comprehend me wholly, mentally and morally, and enable me better to comprehend myself." She wondered if Harriet Martineau might become that guide. At one remove, in fact, Harriet did, because it was at Harriet's urging that the Emersons finally had invited Margaret to come on a visit. "Who would be a goody that could be a genius?" Margaret inquired of Emerson when she came to know him.[7]

Margaret's father, a lawyer and sometimes a congressman, had educated her as he would a son, and she had met the challenge, becoming a master of several tongues. While her fair contemporaries dallied with Ann Radcliffe or Fanny Burney, she read through classical literature and the accumulated philosophical works of the West. The loss of her father in October 1835 corresponded to Emerson's loss of his brother Charles the following May. Both needed surrogates. Emerson was auditioning Alcott for the part when Margaret appeared. Though she presently took Alcott up on his invitation to assist him at the school he had opened in Boston, her estimate of him was much lower than Emerson's. That led Emerson to proceed with more caution in taking up Alcott's cause. Margaret's prudence led him to realize that there was less to Alcott than he had at first supposed. Alcott's manner had beguiled him. That was not unusual. Emerson dearly prized fine manners, and even titled British visitors observed that Alcott comported himself in a fashion that would have been commendable in a peer of the realm.

Like Alcott, Margaret Fuller talked better than she wrote, but, unlike him, the substance of what she said did not lift away like a vapor after she had spoken. Of Margaret as a conversationalist Hedge related:

Her conversation . . . I have seldom heard equalled. . . .
Though remarkably fluent and select, it was neither fluency, nor choice diction, nor wit, nor sentiment, that gave it its peculiar power, but accuracy of statement, keen discrimination, and a certain weight of judgment. . . . Her speech, though finished and true as the most deliberate rhetoric of the pen, had always an air of spontaneity which made it seem the grace of the moment.[8]

In December 1836 Margaret succeeded Elizabeth Peabody as Alcott's coadjutor at the Temple School and taught there until the next April, when, bankrupted by his critics, Alcott had no funds to pay her to continue. During that winter Margaret attended Emerson's lectures in Boston, and in April and early May was again a houseguest of the Emersons. While she was there, Emerson benefited from half a dozen German lessons she gave him — rather like a dose of sulfur and molasses forced on a schoolboy. This Emerson reported as but one "among the many things that made her visit valuable and memorable."[9] For her part, Margaret wrote to a friend, Jane F. Tuckerman, of the effect Emerson had on her: "The excitement of conversation prevents my sleeping.''[10] Otherwise, Margaret's report of benefits, at this time, concerns what she got from his discourses. She wrote Clarke: "His influence has been more beneficial to me than that of any American. . . . From him I first learned what is meant by an inward life. . . . Several of his sermons stand apart in memory, like landmarks in my spiritual history.''[11]

Margaret hoped most on this second visit to pierce Emerson's reserve. Although she failed, she did not abandon her aim. Home again, in Groton, she wrote him a bold letter. This, without prejudice, Emerson endorsed, "What shocking familiarity." He then sponsored her membership in the Transcendental Club.

Margaret went away from Concord proclaiming its merits from the housetops — "Concord, dear Concord, haven of repose, where headach — — vertigo — — other sins that flesh is heir to, cannot long pursue.''[12] Lidian would have found this hard to credit.

In June 1837 Margaret went to Providence to teach and there she stayed, save for occasional visits to Boston, for the next year and a half. This interval encompassed the period in which both "The American Scholar" address (which she heard) and the "Divinity School Address" (which she did not hear) were written, delivered, ridiculed, and defended. Letters passed between them, but for Margaret that was not enough. "I want to see you and still more to hear you," she wrote.[13]

The correspondence underwent a subtle metamorphosis. Carl Strauch describes the letters from 16 September 1836, when the correspondence began, to 12 December 1837, as "merely pleasant.''[14] From 4 May to 12 October 1838, he finds Emerson holding Margaret at arm's length. Such phrases from her letters as "Yours is an image in my oratory . . . and I must pray," may have startled him and counseled wariness, or he may have regarded the liberties Margaret was taking with him as presumptuous. Ordinarily he did not invite familiarity from anyone. Lidian could not address him as Waldo; Margaret not only could but did.

The third phase in the Emerson-Fuller correspondence began on 21 October 1838 and ran to 30 March 1840. In this interval Emerson, while acclaiming Margaret as "my vivacious friend," supplemented his mounting cordiality with an outpouring of tributes and imaginative flourishes.[15] This phase started as Margaret's Providence stay was drawing to a close and a new Boston interlude was under way. Settling in Jamaica Plain, on Boston's outskirts, she wrote, translated, and in November 1839 began a series of "Conversations," which fared well enough to be given in two series annually, one starting in November, the other in March, during the ensuing five years. Just prior to the start of this labor, on 20 October 1839, Margaret, with Alcott, paid Emerson an overnight visit on which Emerson reported ambivalently:

"They brought nothing but good spirits & good tidings with them of new literary plans here. . . . What is good to make me happy is not however good to make me write. Life too near paralyzes art."[16]

From late March to early August 1840, Emerson's correspondence with Margaret mostly concerned *The Dial,* which Margaret, in November 1839, on a promise of active assistance from Emerson, had agreed to edit. That same summer Emerson also poured his energies into "Friendship," an essay the grist for which he had now not only from his friendship with Margaret, but from Margaret's friends, who had constituted themselves his instant coterie. These friends, whom Margaret displayed, said Elizabeth Hoar, as "a necklace of diamonds about her neck," included Samuel Ward, Caroline Sturgis, and Anna Barker.[17] All three, like Margaret, were charged up with those emotional anticipations which, in that era, constituted a kind of prenuptial mating dance. Margaret thought she was in love with Ward, seven years younger than she was (*she* was seven years younger than Emerson), and Ward seemed to encourage her but became betrothed instead to Anna Barker, whose beauty took even Emerson's breath away. Caroline appeared to encourage Ellery Channing, but, when the signals flickered, he turned away to become betrothed, instead, to Ellen Fuller, Margaret's sister. Then suddenly Emerson, trolling with the lure of Platonic love, found that Caroline and Margaret both had fixed on him as a romantic object. Worse still, he found himself to a degree responsive. And so "Friendship" became the drafting board on which he sought to mark his course.

On 22 June, Emerson wrote to Ward: "I am just now finishing a Chapter on Friendship . . . on which I would gladly provoke a commentary."[18] His objective was to recruit Ward as someone who could interpret his high motives to the others lest they misconstrue them. In the finished essay there are ideas and phrases culled from letters he wrote to the Fuller circle. He also incorporated into the essay passages written in the second person as though personally addressed to them. "High thanks I owe you," he said, at one point, "excellent lovers, who carry out the world for me to new and noble depths, and enlarge the meaning of all my thoughts." But he said as well:

It would indeed give me a certain household joy to quit this lofty seeking, this spiritual astronomy or search of stars, and come down to warm sympathies with you; but then I know well I shall mourn always the vanishing of my mighty gods. It is true, next week I shall have languid moods, when I can well afford to occupy myself with foreign objects; then I shall regret the lost literature of your mind, and wish you were by my side again. But if you come, perhaps you will fill my mind only with new visions; not with yourself but with your lustres, and I shall not be able any more than now to converse with you.[19]

Here Emerson was specifying the plane on which their love must exist.

The project of the "Friendship" essay forced a crisis in his relations with both Margaret and Caroline. In his biography of Margaret, Emerson tells us:

> In the summer of 1840, Margaret underwent some change in the tone and direction of her thoughts, to which she attributed a high importance. . . . She made many attempts to describe her frame of mind to me, but did not inspire me with confidence that she had now come to any experiences that were profound or permanent. . . . There was a certain restlessness and fever, which I did not like should deceive a soul which was capable of greatness.[20]

A journal entry of 16 August put this commentary in sharper perspective. Emerson and Margaret had both just been with Anna Barker, whose marriage to Sam Ward was announced for October. To lose a man she loved to a friend she loved had set up a turmoil in Margaret that she subdued only with difficulty: "She taxed me . . . with inhospitality of Soul. She & C[aroline] would gladly be my friends, yet our intercourse is not friendship but literary gossip. I count & weigh but do not love. . . . However often we have met, we still meet as strangers." He continued:

> I thought of my experience with several persons which resembled this: and confessed that I would not converse with the divinest person more than one week. M[argaret] insisted that it was no friendship which was thus so soon exhausted, & that I ought to know how to be silent and companionable at the same moment. She would surprise me, — she would have me say & do what surprised myself. I confess to all this charge with humility unfeigned. . . . Yet would nothing be so grateful to me as to melt once for all these icy barriers, & unite with these lovers. . . . This survey of my experience taught me anew that no friend I have surprises, none exalts me.[21]

Dutifully, that same day — 16 August — Emerson tried to apply to his friendship with Caroline the insights Margaret had given him, writing her not to establish the stronger emotional ties she craved, but to propose instead a brother-sister relationship:

> You & I should only be friends on imperial terms. We are both too proud to be fond & too true to feign. But I dare not engage my

peace so far as to make you necessary to me as I can easily see any establishment of habitual intercourse would do, when the first news I may hear is that you have found in some heaven foreign to me your mate & my beautiful castle is exploded to shivers.[22]

Two weeks later he would use this same image — "a flash of lightning shivers my castle in the air" — when telling Margaret how Anna Barker's engagement had affected him. One does not take images out of stock to describe a deep emotional setback. Caroline and Anna both were much younger than Emerson. He enjoyed the company of both but was in love with neither. He wrote to them as he did so as not to wound their sensibilities. For him it was a game of Platonic love.

Emerson's letter to Caroline continued:

But that which set me on this writing was the talk with Margaret F[uller] last Friday who taxed me on both your parts with a certain inhospitality of soul. . . . I confess to the fact of cold & imperfect intercourse, but not to the impeachment of my will and not to the deficiency of my affection. If I count & weigh, I love also. . . . You give me more joy than I could trust my tongue to tell you. . . .

But I do not get nearer to you. Whose fault is that? Come & live near me whenever it suits your pleasure & if you confide in me so far I will engage to be as true a brother to you as ever blood made.[23]

Although on 13 September Emerson advised Margaret, "I write my letters lately to Caroline, with whom I have agreed that we are brother & sister by divine invisible parentage,"[24] as early as 20 August, in a follow-up letter to Caroline, he sought to move their relationship to the plane of the ideal, in effect taking her out of emotional contention:

When we fear the withdrawal of love from ourselves by the new relations which our companions must form, it is mere infidelity. . . . So, dear child, I give you up to all your Gods. . . . You shall not give me so great a joy as by the finding for yourself a love which shall make mine show cold and feeble — which certainly is not cold or feeble.[25]

No patron mistaken for a swain ever extricated himself from his dilemma with greater tact. Without hurt Emerson had pointed Caroline in the direction that would lead to her marriage to William Tappan and such comforts as the Tanglewood estate, which their heirs would bestow as a gift on the Boston Symphony Orchestra in the next century.

Margaret was not so easily managed. ''I shall never go quite back to my old arctic habits,'' he told her on 29 August. Then he turned to the matter that most pained her then: ''Ward I shall not lose. My job for him is very great. . . . But ah! my friend, *you* must be generous beyond even the strain of heroism to bear your part in this scene & resign without a sigh two Friends.'' To offer to Margaret, in place of what she had lost, a brother-sister relationship would, of course, have been ludicrous. Emerson spoke instead of the highest love, Celestial love — ''we can retreat always upon the Invisible Heart upon the Celestial Love,'' he assured her. If Margaret and he were to go on together, this was the path they must travel.[26]

By late September, however, the pact Emerson thought they had made began to come apart. On 25 September he sought to mend it:

Now in your last letter, you . . . do say . . . that I am yours & yours shall be. . . . I on the contrary do constantly aver that you & I are not inhabitants of one thought of the Divine Mind, but of two thoughts. . . . Those who swell in the same truth are friends; those who are exercised on different thoughts are not, & must puzzle each other, for the time.

But Margaret replied with a ''we are to be much to one another'' letter.[27]

Some of Margaret's letters from this interval have not survived. A journal entry Emerson made on 26 September supplies a probable reason:

You would have me love you. What shall I love? Your body? The supposition disgusts you. What you have thought & said? Well, whilst you were thinking & saying them, but not now. I see no possibility of loving any thing but what now is, & is becoming; your courage, your enterprize, your budding affection, your opening thought, your prayer, I can love — but what else?[28]

He can only have written this with Margaret in mind. Lidian, of course, had no role in this competition.

With the pressure building Emerson shifted tactics, writing now to Margaret in an exalted, lyrical mood. He began to sound not like Emerson the fellow traveler who would pursue, with her, the steep trail that led to Celestial love, but like Emerson the essayist, discoursing to a discriminating lyceum audience. Signaling retreat, he said: ''He must be divorced & childless & houseless & friendless a churl & a fool if he would accompany with the Cherubim & have the Alone to his friend.'' On 7 October he was more cautious still: ''I am capable I know, of pure satisfaction from my friends, and yet it is oftenest

only a momentary glow & nobility they awaken, and when I reach my
own hearth, I am no more than when I left it." Nine days later, when
Margaret came to call with George Ripley for George's discourse on
his milk-farm utopia, no chance was offered for the Platonic friends
to review the progress of their friendship. "I should gladly have talked
with you another day," Emerson wrote Margaret afterward, "that we
might have brought things to speech somewhat more reverently than
in a cold room at abrupt & stolen moments. Yet what would another
day have done to reconcile our wide sights?" Emerson's suggestion —
"Let us float along through the great heavens a while longer" — hardly
suited Margaret's designs at this stage. Margaret wanted no part of
cloudland now. She wanted matters between them set on a firm basis.[29]

On or about 24 October Emerson received from Margaret a letter,
no longer extant, that drew from him a dramatic reply with which he
brought to a sudden close the dialogue about love she had been pursuing with him with mounting excitement. Some hint of the move Margaret made to raise the emotional temperature is given in Emerson's
memoir of their decade of friendship:

> When I found that she lived at a much faster rate than mine,
> and which was violent compared to mine, I foreboded rash and
> painful crises, and had a feeling as if a voice cried, *Stand from
> under!* — as if, a little further on, this destiny was threatened
> with jars and reverses, which no friendship could avert or console.
> This feeling partly wore off, on better acquaintance, but
> remained latent; . . . she remained inscrutable to me; her strength
> was not my strength, — her powers were a surprise.[30]

The watershed letter of 24 October read in part:

> I have your frank & noble & affecting letter, and yet I think I
> could wish it unwritten. I ought never to have suffered you to
> lead me into any conversation or writing on our relation. . . . I
> was content & happy to meet on a human footing a woman of
> sense & sentiment with whom one could exchange reasonable words
> & go away assured that wherever she went there was light & force
> & honor. . . . But tell me that I am cold or unkind, and in my
> most flowing state I become a cake of ice. I can feel the crystals
> shoot & the drops solidify. . . . It is not for me to bring the
> relation to speech. . . . Ask me what I think of you & me, — & I
> am put to confusion. . . . You cannot communicate yourself to me.
> I hear the words sometimes but remain a stranger to your state of
> mind. . . . I see not how we can bear each other anything else than
> good will though we had sworn to the contrary. . . . Speak to me

of every thing but myself & I will endeavor to make an intelligible reply. . . . I see very dimly in writing on this topic. . . . Do not expect it of me again for a very long time.[31]

Whatever Margaret's expectations were, that ended them.

The correspondence between Emerson and Margaret moved now to matters that had engaged them before the essay on friendship had tried their friendship to the breaking point. Fortunately, *The Dial* beckoned, leaving little time to dwell on the past. By 30 October Emerson was already oriented toward the duties *The Dial* entailed. "I write myself into letters, the last few months," he told Carlyle, "to three or four dear & beautiful persons my country-men & women here. I lit my candle at both ends, but now will be colder & scholastic."[32]

The following March and April Emerson was enough at ease to attend four of Margaret's "Conversations" on Greek mythology, which he playfully described as Margaret's "Parlortorio." Caroline Healey Dall said that Emerson, at the second "Conversation," "pursued his own train of thought. He seemed to forget that we had come together to pursue Margaret's." Possibly Emerson acted out of mischief because, on 14 March, he began a letter to Margaret with the observation: "The young people wished to know what possessed me to tease you with so much prose, & becloud the fine conversation."[33]

The relaxed mood that had come into their relation did not mean there would be no relapses. In October 1841, when Margaret came to Concord to work with Emerson on *The Dial*, she moved into her usual room, the "red room" across the hall from his study. One night when, in quest of a book, she entered the study in his absence, she wrote him a letter instead, telling him:

> I like to be in your library when you are out of it. It seems a sacred place. I came here to find a book, that I might feel more life and be worthy to sleep, but there is so much here I do not need a book. When I come to yourself, I cannot receive you, and you cannot give yourself ; it does not profit. But when I cannot find you the beauty and permanence of your life come to me.

She then yielded to an impulse to allude to what had happened between them : "I want to say while I am feeling it . . . — how long it must be before I am able to meet you. — I see you — and fancied it nearer than it was, you were right in knowing the contrary. How much, much more I would fain say and cannot." Yet she had come to accept him on his own terms : "I am too powerfully drawn while with you, and cannot advance a step, but when away I have learned something. Not yet to be patient and faithful and holy, however, but only have

taken off the shoes, to tread the holy ground.'' Margaret's pilgrimage
to Celestial love was under way. This document Emerson endorsed as
a ''from room to room'' letter.[34]

On 13 October, possibly after finding the ''room to room'' letter,
Emerson wrote in his journal:

> I would that I could . . . give the lights & shades, the hopes &
> outlooks that come to me in these strange, cold-warm, attractive-
> repelling conversations with Margaret, whom I always admire,
> most revere when I nearest see, and sometimes love, yet whom I
> freeze, & who freezes me to silence, when we seem to promise
> to come nearest.[35]

There are days when the great are near us.

40. My Good Henry Thoreau

INCE Emerson, like most thinkers, had "several more lives to live" than he had time to live them, he not only drew on the resources of others but, without conscious persuasion or awareness, sent others forth to live on his behalf those unrealized lives he could not himself pursue. His understanding of creative assimilation allowed him to regard such delegated lives as a personal resource, quite as was the work his hired hands did for him tending his orchard or splitting his kindling. Emerson looked upon Thoreau — who, in fact, first served him as a man-of-all-work — as such a resource. Unlike others who received from Emerson similar silent commissions, however, Thoreau was not content to augment Emerson's personality on more than a short-term basis. His struggle to individuate himself would be for both men the most dramatic experience of their lives.

Emerson had not yet met Thoreau when he outlined for him the life he was to live. On 28 March 1835 he wrote in his journal: "If life were long enough among my thousand & one works should be a book of Nature. . . . It should contain the Natural history of the woods around my shifting camp for every month in the year. . . . No bird, no bug, no bud, should be forgotten on his day & hour."[1] This was something Emerson never was able to do for himself, but Thoreau, as his surrogate, could and did.

We can only conjecture the circumstances bringing together the two men: the patrician Emerson, newly arrived in Concord; the plebeian Thoreau, born there. Dr. Ripley may have asked Emerson, in 1835, to make the appeal to First Church that led to Thoreau's receiving the

Penn annuity, the same Winthrop land scholarship that had benefited
the Emerson brothers when they were Harvard undergraduates. Chances
are that Thoreau did no disciplined thinking about Nature until he
read Emerson's *Nature*, since those Harvard exercises which he wrote
prior to its publication pay the subject no heed.

Emerson's letter asking for scholarship aid for Thoreau was one
that any man of reputation might write for a deserving young man in
his community. There was no intimacy between them until, upon his
graduation from Harvard in 1837, Thoreau came home to Concord.
The common belief is that Lucy Brown, Lidian Emerson's luckless
sister (who had been boarding with the Thoreaus), recommended him
to Emerson on the basis of something he had written. By that autumn
the friendship between the youth of twenty and the man of thirty-
four was growing. The first of Emerson's many mentions of Thoreau
appeared in February 1838. The entry for 17 February is notable:
"My good Henry Thoreau made this else solitary afternoon sunny with
his simplicity & clear perception. . . . Everything that boy says makes
merry with society, though nothing can be graver than his meaning."[2]
On 25 April they walked together to Fairhaven Cliff and Emerson
experienced Nature with a fullness he had not known before. Thoreau's company had to be a factor. Emerson was beginning to see how
Thoreau might serve him.

In the summer of 1838, dubbing Thoreau "a brave fine youth,"
Emerson said of him, "I delight much in my young friend, who seems
to have as free and erect a mind as any I have ever met." A year later
he had fixed on Thoreau as a poet, that coveted status which he reserved for those moving toward unity with the World-Soul. A Lam-
mastide entry reports his jubilation: "Last night came to me a beautiful poem from Henry Thoreau, 'Sympathy.' The purest strain & the
loftiest, I think, that has yet pealed from this unpoetic American forest." As plans for *The Dial* evolved, Emerson saw a place in them for
Thoreau. To William he wrote on 26 September 1839: "My Henry
Thoreau will be a great poet for such a company, & one of these days
for all companies."[3]

Later Thoreau would say that he was "born in the most estimable
place in all the world, and in the very nick of time," that is, just in
time to enjoy the inestimable advantage of Emerson's friendship and
counsel.[4] Myriad sources attest that Thoreau, in the initial stages of
this friendship, fell completely under Emerson's spell. When Lowell,
rusticating at Concord in expiation for his Harvard misdemeanors,
visited Emerson on 11 July 1838, he wrote his friend George Bailey
Loring a day later: "I saw Thoreau last night & it is exquisitely amusing to see how he imitates Emerson's tone & manner. With my eyes
shut I shouldn't kn[ow] them apart."[5] That same year, Emerson's

cousin David Greene Haskins, who had known Thoreau at Harvard, garnered a similar impression, as he later related:

> I happened to meet Thoreau in Mr. Emerson's study at Concord. I think it was the first time we had come together after leaving college. I was quite startled by the transformation that had taken place in him. . . . In his manners, in the tones and inflections of his voice, in his modes of expression, even in the hesitations and pauses of his speech, he had become the counterpart of Mr. Emerson. Mr. Thoreau's college voice bore no resemblance to Mr. Emerson's, and was so familiar to my ear that I could readily have identified him by it in the dark. . . . I remember to have taken the opportunity . . . of listening to their conversation with closed eyes, and to have been unable to determine with certainty which was speaking. . . . I do not know to what subtle influence to ascribe it, but, after conversing with Mr. Emerson for even a brief time, I always found myself able and inclined to adopt his voice and manner of speaking.[6]

During this visit, Emerson told Haskins that Thoreau was "*the* man of Concord," and, what is more pertinent to our understanding of their relations, said, "We could not do without him."

On 15 January 1848, Ednah Littlehale (Cheney) told of attending one of Alcott's "Conversations" the night before: "Thorault [*sic*] . . . is all overlaid by an imitation of Emerson, talks like him, puts out his arms like him, brushes his hair in the same way, and is even getting up a caricature nose like Emerson's. Yet he has something in himself — else he would be altogether disgusting and ridiculous; as it is, 'tis funny."[7]

Many would note how remarkably Thoreau's handwriting came to resemble Emerson's.[8] And Henry Seidel Canby concluded that the style and structure of his prose, as well, took shape under Emerson's influence: "The habit of composing by sentences or brief paragraphs inconsecutive as the flashes of perception which they recorded, he probably borrowed from him. . . . The plan of selecting and arranging these paragraphs in a loose pattern about a theme, he certainly learned from Emerson."[9]

Edward Emerson suggested that his father's impact on Thoreau was as natural as Perugino's on Raphael. Ellery Channing saw himself similarly influenced. He once wrote to Emerson: "Mrs. Whitman told me . . . that I am exactly like yourself — like by the very gait, air, voice, turning of the eyebrow, etc."[10] Conway acknowledged the similarities linking Thoreau to Emerson, but insisted that they were not fundamental:

I perceived that he [Thoreau] was not in the least like his
parents, but closely resembled Emerson. His features, expressions,
tones of voice, were more like those of Emerson than any likenesses I have known between brothers. . . . But because this
influence was in the least part personal, the resemblance of Thoreau to Emerson was as superficial as a leaflike creature to a leaf.
Thoreau was quite as original as Emerson.[11]

Four years into their friendship, Emerson rebuked Thoreau for not
venturing beyond the perimeters of the world according to Emerson :
"I told H[enry] T[horeau] that his freedom is in the form, but he
does not disclose new matter. I am very familiar with all his thoughts, —
they are my own quite originally drest. But . . . he has not yet told
what that is which he was created to say." Thus Emerson wrote in the
fall of 1841.[12] Thoreau had been living with the Emersons since the
previous April, but Emerson still had not had from Thoreau the originality he wanted. Such energy as flowed between them passed from
him to Thoreau.

Canby supposes that "like all teachers . . . he [Emerson] loved best
in his pupil the extensions of his own personality." Porte carries this
argument further :

Especially in the early days of their friendship, Emerson seems
frequently to have looked upon Thoreau almost as a physical
extension of his own being, or as a potential source of new physical vitality. . . . His close identification with the potentialities and
aspirations of the younger man enabled him to feel thoroughly
represented by Thoreau, in the sense of being reproduced in a new
shape which would be both an enlargement and a transformation
of his own nature.[13]

Perhaps that is the answer. Emerson wanted not merely to be extended in Thoreau but to be expanded by him. In his journal Emerson
wrote, in 1852, that expansions and concentrations made up the whole
history of the intellect, the expansions being "the claims or inspirations from heaven to try a larger sweep, a higher pitch then we have
yet tried, and to leave all our past, for this enlarged scope." Thoreau
"insisted much on expansions." Emerson believed that some men could
snap "the staunch iron hoops that bind us" and set "all the particles
dancing each round each." Thoreau, he thought, could do this for him.
In the summer of 1848, however, sailing home from Europe, Emerson
qualified his readiness : "Thoreau is like the woodgod who solicits the
wandering poet & draws him into antres vast & desarts idle, & bereaves
him of his memory, & leaves him naked, plaiting vines. . . . Very se-

ductive are the first steps from the town to the woods, but the End is want & madness.'' Here Emerson attests more to his own limitations than to Thoreau's excesses.[14]

In the winter of 1840–41, the Emersons had had an Irish youth, Alexander McCaffrey, living with them as odd-jobs man. But Alexander was homesick and sullen, and when Thoreau agreed to move in with them in the spring, Emerson gladly released him.[15] On 26 April Thoreau noted crisply in his journal, ''At R.W.E.'s.''[16] Neither man was ready yet to intimate what was hoped for from this new arrangement. Only on 1 June did Emerson open up to William on the subject: ''I work with him as I should not without him, and expect now to be suddenly well & strong though I have been a skeleton all the spring until I am ashamed.''[17] If Emerson needed a tonic then, apparently Thoreau was that tonic. His stamina grew and he lived another forty-one years, his last full day on earth, 26 April 1882, marking the exact anniversary of the start of Thoreau's residency in his household.

If Emerson at this time thought of Thoreau as primarily a poet, Thoreau saw no reason to dispute him. Even though the months immediately ahead brought a heavy burden of woes — the death of his brother John, whom he cherished, and the death of Emerson's son, Waldo, whom he especially prized — he held to his purpose. If others did not value the results, Emerson did. Of the thirty-one appearances Thoreau made in *The Dial*, seventeen were as a poet. As late as the first week of September 1842, Emerson still was congratulating himself on his find: ''It is much to know that poetry has been written this very day, under this very roof, by your side. . . . Behold all day from every pore these auroras have been streaming.''[18] But listening to the trill of this songbird did not make up the whole of their life together. In this same season, Emerson admitted to Hawthorne, the new tenant at the Old Manse, that having Thoreau in his house was an inconvenience. Hawthorne manfully commented: ''It may be well that such a sturdy and uncompromising person is fitter to meet occasionally in the open air, than to have as a permanent guest at table and fireside.''[19]

In 1842 Thoreau recorded in his journal some of the positive virtues of his patron-mentor:

Emerson again is a critic, poet, philosopher, with talent not so conspicuous, not so adequate to his task [as Carlyle's]; but his field is still higher, his task more arduous. Lives a far more intense life; his affections and intellect equally developed. Has advanced farther and a new heaven opens to him. . . . His personal influence upon persons greater than any man's. In his world every man would be a poet. Love would reign. Beauty would take place. Man and Nature would harmonize.[20]

In September 1842 Emerson had felt privileged to have a poet under his roof. By November much of his enthusiasm had ebbed away. "Last night," he wrote on the eleventh, "H[enry] T[horeau] read me verses which pleased if not by beauty of particular lines, yet by the honest truth. . . . Their fault is, that the gold does not yet flow pure, but is drossy & crude." Evidently the gold never did flow. On his deathbed Thoreau told Channing that he had burned much of his poetry on a hint from Emerson that it was inferior. The mood this act engendered was not reversible. The following February, when Emerson asked him about his poetry, he answered summarily, "I have not remembered to write any for some time; it has quite slipped my mind."[21]

Thoreau was soon to set out for New York to seek his fortune while living with the William Emersons on Staten Island and earning his keep tutoring seven-year-old Willie. He did not bring to this commitment, however, his usual enthusiasm. His brother's death, the unresponsiveness of editors to poetry he submitted, Emerson's winnowing of his portfolio, any one of these factors, or all of them, may have initiated his deflation. Yet another factor made its contribution. Of Thoreau, Emerson earlier had reflected: "Though we pine for great men, we do not use them when they come. Here is a Damascus blade of a man, such as you may search through nature in vain to parallel, laid up on a shelf in our village to rust and ruin."[22] The stimulus of Emerson's presence had kept Thoreau burnished and fit for battle. But without Emerson to second him he was reluctant to engage the enemy.

Emerson must have been conscious of Thoreau's adulation of him when he made him a member of his household. And he must have known that in binding Thoreau close he was courting an element of hazard. Yet he was eager to turn to good purpose this energy directed toward himself. Initially, that seems to have happened. Thoreau was his "benefactor," making him strong and well. But Thoreau likewise had needs. Without conscious calculation on the part of either man, Emerson had become his role model. The intimacy that shared living quarters made possible found him anxious to deepen their association and to instate himself more perfectly in Emerson's good graces.

That summer of 1842 Emerson had sent his "Plato Skimpole," Bronson Alcott, off to England. In Alcott's absence, holding the ground for Plato, he was plunging ahead with his essay on friendship. The air must have been filled with it. Certainly Emerson's letters were. His Platonic correspondences with Caroline and Margaret were under way, and the friends Margaret had shared with him were caught in the same churning swirl of spiritual flirtations, though at times raised to the brink, seemingly in danger of spilling over into the sensual. To Thoreau, at this time, Emerson must have spoken about what was most on his mind, Platonic love and Celestial love, love directed toward the Soul of Souls. Conceivably, realizing that Thoreau was enamored of him on the level of the ideal, Emerson strove to redirect his adulation to that higher love. Concomitant to that, Thoreau's extrapolations on the subject of friendship were certain to be enlightening since, in prior times, he had often made it his theme, as the rediscovered journal of 1840–1841 attests. He by no means came uninformed to this New England game of courtly love, played out in painful Calvinistic terms.

Long before Margaret did, Thoreau understood the situation between Emerson and Lidian. One could not live under the same roof with them without realizing that Lidian felt shut out of much of her husband's life and longed to share more fully in it. Edward Emerson concluded that Thoreau treated Lidian like "a sort of lady-abbess," or "a priestess," showing her "chivalric devotion." Edward made these distinctions long before Canby suggested that Thoreau was infatuated with her. He probably was merely being heedful of her reputation. After all, when Emerson went to Europe in 1847–1848, it was Lidian who invited Thoreau to live at Bush as "man-of-the-house" (Edward's unguarded term). Edward says also that in 1841 Thoreau, "by Mr. Emerson's invitation, came to live in his family like a younger brother."[23] Here he is picking up a term — "brother" — that Thoreau's correspondence with Lidian made suitable and Emerson's correspondence with Caroline made inevitable.

Thoreau's first stay with the Emersons lasted two years. During that time Emerson was often absent and when at home either shut in his study, writing, or entertaining houseguests and visitors. Thoreau must have been disappointed that they could be together only occasionally. To woo Lidian Platonically was, for him, an agreeable alternative. Even as it gave her a new sense of her own worth, it would afford him the opportunity to interact with the mind of the person nearest to Emerson and thus contribute to his understanding of Emerson. At the same time, he would be engaging in an exercise in friendship of the very kind that Emerson permitted himself.

Lidian probably did not grasp fully the nuances of such relationships. Emerson can hardly have discussed with her, with any thoroughness, the brother-sister relationship he had arranged with Caroline or Margaret's desire to raise the temperature of their relationship. That Thoreau would have heard of these matters from Emerson is improbable. But in the summer of 1842, when Thoreau's feelings for Lidian seem first to have been recognized, Channing, who had access to Emerson's correspondence with Caroline and may quite easily, through his wife (Margaret's sister), have known of the letters and exchanges that passed between Emerson and Margaret, was also a houseguest of the Emersons. Since discretion was never one of his marked attributes, he probably divulged to Thoreau — with whom he speedily became friendly — all that he knew.

However much Thoreau realized that occupying Lidian with his suit would uplift her spirits, this end cannot have been viewed by him as a calculated objective. He would have seen as sniveling and mean-spirited a courtship embarked on as a diversionary tactic. As Platonic swain he would have been wholly in earnest.

In late January 1843, when Emerson went to New York to lecture, letters from Thoreau pursued him. Thoreau's stay was in its closing phase and he took inventory:

> I have been your pensioner for nearly two years, and still left free as under the sky. It has been as free a gift as the sun or the summer, though I have sometimes molested you with my mean acceptance of it, — I who have failed to render even those slight services of the *hand* which would have been for a sign at least; and, by the fault of my nature, have failed of many better and higher services. But I will not trouble you with this, but for once thank you as well as Heaven.[24]

No hint of a struggle against overpowering infatuation lurks in this passage, and Thoreau was too upright to lament small services neglected if the specter of a major abuse of hospitality hung over him. On 12 February, again writing to Emerson, he said, "How mean are our relations to one another! Let us pause till they are nobler."[25] With this statement he stepped up his exploration of the meaning of friendship, which, thereafter, almost to the close of his stay, was his chief topic. There was no infatuation to contend with.

Thoreau went to Staten Island to live with the William Emersons and to tutor Willie in May 1843. Only then did his courtship — with that touch of anguish which separation gives, adding to its visibility — materialize.

Emerson had sent Thoreau to Staten Island with great hopes, telling William on 6 May 1843: "And now goes our brave youth into the new house, the new connection, the new City. I am sure no truer & no purer person lives in wide New York; and he is a bold & a profound thinker though he may easily chance to pester you with some accidental crotchets and perhaps a village exaggeration of the value of facts."[26] Emerson could not profile Thoreau so accurately and yet be wrong in pronouncing him pure of heart.

Lidian was the first person Thoreau wrote to, other than his own family, after his arrival in New York. His letter, sent on 22 May, is a curious blend of courtly compliments, therapeutic tributes, and home-sickness. For the latter, a flare-up of tuberculosis, activated by a cold caught en route to New York, may have been to blame. Thoreau wrote:

> I think of you as some elder sister of mine. . . . You must know
> that you represent to me woman, for I have not traveled very far
> or wide. . . . I thank you for your influence for two years. I was
> fortunate to be subjected to it, and am now to remember it. . . .
> You always seemed to look down at me as from some elevation, —
> some of your high humilities, — and I was the better for having to
> look up.

Thus Thoreau paid homage to her whom he identifies as his representative woman, a title that takes her out of contention as someone to
whom he is drawn by the hunger of the flesh. He could not have described more explicitly an affection conceived in the loftiest terms.
    Thoreau next moved to tactful consideration of Lidian's dark moods:

> You must not think that fate is so dark there. . . . Your
> moonlight . . . though it is a reflection of the sun, allows of bats
> and owls and other twilight birds to flit therein. But I am very
> glad that you can elevate your life with a doubt, for I am sure
> that it is nothing but an insatiable faith after all that deepens and
> darkens its current.

Thus, with a metaphysical conceit that is simultaneously a paradox,
Thoreau sought to uplift Lidian's spirits. Although Emerson had no
patience with Thoreau's paradoxes, the wisdom of this one would not
have escaped him.[27]
    Lidian's reply to this letter of 22 May is not extant, but Thoreau's
reply to it, on 20 June, makes clear its contents. Thoreau's compliments had swept Lidian out to sea. She relished them. Yet she took
pains now to set their relationship in the context of courtly love. Submissive wife that she was, she must have let Emerson see Thoreau's
letter and let him dictate the terms of her response, because the letter
Thoreau describes is such a letter as Emerson himself wrote to Caroline when her Platonic feelings toward him overflowed. Since Emerson
had no wish either to deprive Lidian of the new faith in herself engendered by Thoreau's chivalric wooing or to humiliate Thoreau by dis-
puting his intentions, his task was not easy. Thoreau's reply attests
that, nonetheless, Emerson skirted these hazards successfully:

> Your voice seems not a voice, but comes as much from the blue
> heavens as from the paper. I feel as if it were a great daring to go
> on and read the rest, and then to live accordingly. . . . I am
> almost afraid to look at your letter. I see that it will make my life
> very steep, but it may lead to fairer prospects than this. . . . My
> dear friend it was very noble in you to write me so trustful an
> answer. . . . The thought of you will constantly elevate my life.

For another few paragraphs, Thoreau went on, eager to acknowledge his gratitude for the exalted terms in which Lidian had responded to him. Lidian could have framed her reply without consulting Emerson, yet the response her letter drew from Thoreau corresponds so exactly to the response Emerson's letter to Caroline invited the probability is high that he counseled Lidian in formulating her arguments. He understood that Thoreau was platonizing and must emerge from that sensitive experiment without trauma. That Thoreau should have sent a letter addressed to both the Emersons on 8 July, in which he said, "But know, my friends, that I a good deal hate you in all my most private thoughts — as the substratum of the little love I bear you," does not mean that he had taken umbrage at Lidian's dismissal of his suit. He is merely paraphrasing Jones Very's "day of hate" remark, which had been a source of amusement to them all. It tells us, rather, that the tension was going out of their correspondence and a more assured mood supplanting it.[28]

Thoreau gave Staten Island a six-month trial. Nothing went as planned. His first month there his illness sequestered him. William and his wife had neither warmth nor humor and took no interest in his fortunes. No fortunes, in fact, appeared. The prospects he looked for in New York never opened up. Even little Willie did not take to him. In November he sought Concord to spend Thanksgiving with his family. An upsurge of joy made him realize how wretched he had been away from home. He returned to New York, packed, and departed. Indigenous to Concord, he could not flourish in alien soil.

When Thoreau settled into his old life again, his friends were uneasy about his prospects. In May 1844, Emerson wrote in his journal: "If I cannot show his performance much more manifest than that of the other grand promisers, at least I can see that, with his practical faculty, he has declined all the kingdoms of this world. Satan has no bribe for him."[29] Channing took a more aggressive approach. He wrote Thoreau the following March: "I see nothing for you in this earth but that field [near Walden Pond] which I once christened 'Briars'; go out upon that, build yourself a hut, & there begin the grand process of devouring yourself alive. I see no alternative, no other hope for you."[30] (Had Channing counseled himself as wisely he would not now be no more than a wearisome footnote in the history of Concord idealism.) Thoreau took his advice at once and began his climb to renown. In 1844 Emerson bought land on the margin of Walden. Thoreau now proposed to clear it and reforest it with pines, if, in exchange, he might build a hut there and live in it. Emerson gave his approval and before March was out Thoreau was wielding an ax against the scrub. On Independence Day, the hut was ready and Thoreau moved in for another two-year stay as Emerson's guest, on a tract of land he made so distinctly his own that Emerson assigned it to him in his will.[31]

At the other end of the Walden stay, on 6 August 1847, Emerson, his hopes for Thoreau revived, would tell Furness: "I write because Henry D. Thoreau has a book in print. Henry D. Thoreau is a great man in Concord, a man of original genius & character . . . master of all woodcraft, & an intimate associate of the birds, beasts & fishes, of this region."[32] *A Week on the Concord and Merrimack Rivers* was finished and Emerson again felt the pride of fatherhood. A grand promiser had, at last, realized his promise, or so it seemed: publication of Thoreau's book had to wait another two years when early prospects fell through.

Earlier that year, a piece Thoreau had written on Carlyle appeared in *Graham's Magazine*. Copies were dispatched to Carlyle, who read it "with due entertainment and recognition," acknowledging that "A vigorous Mr. Thoreau, — who had formed himself a good deal upon one Emerson, but does not want abundant fire and stamina of his own; — recognizes us, and various other things, in a most admiring great-hearted manner; . . . I like Mr. Thoreau very well; and hope yet to hear good and better news of him." When he himself was not Thoreau's subject, however, Carlyle found it impossible to sustain an interest in his work. On 13 August 1849 he commented to Emerson, "I got Thoreau's Book, and meant well to read it, but have not yet succeeded, tho' it went with me thro' all Ireland: tell him so, please. Too Jean-Paulish, I found it hitherto." Carlyle did not take notice of Thoreau again.[33]

Thoreau's immediate reason for leaving Walden was to be "man-of-the-house" at Bush while Emerson lectured in England. Confidently, he wrote to the distant Emerson: "Lidian and I make very good housekeepers. She is a very dear sister to me."[34] He was reviving the old Platonic sport. There was little chance now for that. Stricken with hepatitis, Lidian was a bed patient for three months. If Thoreau's peculiar disquisition on "A Sister" was written in this interval with Lidian in mind (as Canby alleged), he could not have chosen a more forlorn object for veneration. Lidian's grandson Alexander Forbes told a friend many years later that "Grandmamma thought Thoreau was rather silly." If "A Sister" was placed in her hands when jaundice had brought her spirits to their lowest ebb, she had ample reason for thinking so. There is no hard evidence that "A Sister" was written to Lidian or even that it was written at this time. Allusions to sun and moon and morning star, which might seem to link the old letters and the new essay, need not detain us. Moon allusions appear repeatedly in the Caroline–Waldo–Margaret correspondence — a metaphysical property that had become the common resource of this pocket of Platonists.[35]

In September 1849 Thoreau's confidant, Channing, told Thomas Wentworth Higginson (his brother-in-law) of his own altered view of

Emerson: ''Emerson is a terrible man to deal with, — one has to be armed at all points. He threshes you out very soon; is admirably skillful, able to go anywhere or do anything. Those nearest him feel him hard and cold. . . . Women do not like him; he cannot establish a personal relation with anyone, yet he can get on agreeably with everyone.''[36] This estimate of Emerson was grossly unfair, but such remarks, repeated often enough to Thoreau by Channing, may have succeeded in poisoning their well of friendship. An entry Thoreau made in his journal on 24 November 1850 shows the process at the opening phase:

> I have certain friends whom I visit occasionally, but I commonly part from them early with a certain bitter-sweet sentiment. That which we love is so mixed and entangled with that we hate in one another that we are more grieved and disappointed, aye, and estranged from one another, by meeting than by absence. Some men may be my acquaintances merely, but one whom I have been accustomed to regard, to idealize, to have dreams about as a friend, and mix up intimately with myself, can never degenerate into an acquaintance.[37]

Thoreau's growing harshness eroded Emerson's almost infinite patience. In 1851, in an undated journal entry, he wrote: ''He is a boy & will be an old boy.'' In June that year Emerson expressed a milder concern about Thoreau's failure to realize himself: ''Thoreau wants a little ambition in his mixture. Fault of this, instead of being the head of American Engineers, he is captain of a huckleberry party.'' Emerson knew little about what Thoreau was doing. He himself, carrying family responsibilities, labored incessantly. By contrast, Thoreau must have seemed a drone.[38]

In December 1851 Thoreau was still clinging to his friendship with Emerson:

> Last night I treated my dearest friend ill. . . . Instantly I blamed myself, and sought an opportunity to make atonement; but the friend avoided me. . . . I doubt now, in the cool morning, if I have a right to suppose such intimate and serious relations as afford a basis for the apology I had conceived. . . . Yet I am resolved to know that one centrally, through thick and thin; and though we should be cold to one another, — though we should never speak to one another, — I well know that inward and essential love may exist under a superficial coldness. . . . Methinks our estrangement is only like the divergence of the branches which unite in the stem.[39]

Yet he complained also of Emerson's "palaver," and declared, "It is the misfortune of being a gentleman and famous. . . . One of the best of men and wisest. . . . Repeating himself, shampooing himself!"[40]

Late in January 1852 a nettled Thoreau wrote of Emerson: "My friend invites me to read my papers to him. Gladly would I read if he would hear. . . . To associate with one for years with joy who never met you thought for thought! An overflowing sympathy while yet there is no intellectual communion." Soon after, he said further: "I should value E[merson]'s praise more, which is always so discriminating, if there were not some alloy of patronage and hence of flattery about it." Either Thoreau had learned from Lidian to see slights where none was intended, or Emerson, seeing those around him as a resource that fed his art, made such responses inevitable.[41]

Channing, as a sniper, was much more undeviating and authentically spiteful. "He [Emerson] has no love of Beauty or knowledge of it; he gave that all up after he wrote *Nature*. He is now all humanitarian; he is besides every shrewd Yankee merchant, — that's what he is."[42]

Thoreau's animosity seemed to keep pace with Channing's almost as if empathy with Emerson waned as empathy with Channing grew. On the eve of Emerson's fiftieth birthday, Thoreau complained: "Talked, or tried to talk, with R.W.E. Lost my time — nay, almost my identity." A hint that Thoreau and Channing nurtured each other's fancied grievances against Emerson came in Thoreau's journal entry: "I asked W.E.C. yesterday if he had acquired fame. He answered that, giving his name at some place, the bystanders said: 'Yes, sir, we have heard of you. . . . Your name is mentioned in Mr. [Emerson]'s book.' That's all the fame I had, — to be made known by another man." Thus might the spitefulness of both men be accounted for — Emerson's reputation continued to increase while fame passed them by.[43]

John Albee's visit to Emerson in May 1852 yielded a candid account of Emerson's and Thoreau's behavior toward each other in this stressful period: "Emerson continually deferred to him and seemed to anticipate his view, preparing himself obviously for a quiet laugh at Thoreau's negative and biting criticisms. . . . He was clearly fond of Thoreau; but whether in a human way, or as an amusement, I could not then make out."[44] Considering Thoreau's testiness, even limited good will from Emerson is notable. Emerson had to justify to himself his loyalty to Thoreau and did so by one of those exceptional feats of will with which he could repudiate anger. "Thoreau gives me," he concluded, "in flesh & blood & pertinacious Saxon belief, my own ethics. He is far more real, and daily practically obeying them, than I."[45]

In June 1853 Emerson found a new way to account for Thoreau's contrariness: "H[enry] is military. H[enry] seemed stubborn and im-

placable; always manly & wise, but rarely sweet. One would say that,
as Webster could never speak without an antagonist, so H[enry] does
not feel himself except in opposition."[46] If Thoreau was not crossing
swords with Emerson, he was crossing pens with him. This entry came
within days of Thoreau's complaint that Emerson was abducting his
identity.

When *Walden* was published in 1854, Emerson commended it: "All
American kind are delighted with *Walden*."[47] Thoreau himself entered a season of "great expectations," supposing that his public,
henceforth, would allow him no peace. But the world let him be, and
his disappointment must have been great.

Even as Thoreau waited for *Walden* to appear, he was in a state of
high irritability vented mainly on Emerson. On 16 April Thoreau wrote:

> When I meet one of my neighbors these days, who is ridicu-
> lously stately, — being offended — I say in my mind, "Farewell! I
> will wait till you get your manners off. Why make politeness of so
> much consequence when you are ready to assassinate with a
> word? I do not like any better to be assassinated with a rapier
> than to be knocked down with a bludgeon. You are so grand that I
> cannot get within ten feet of you."[48]

Much of that had to be rhetoric. It was written at a time when Thoreau was canvassing the town with a petition urging that Emerson
commit himself to a series of lectures at the Lyceum. The next year
Emerson recruited Thoreau to proofread *English Traits* when a lecture tour kept him from doing it himself. And when he saw that Thoreau's health was poor, he invited him into his home, to convalesce.

There were snappish moments, however, when winter came again.
At the end of February, with an exasperation he had not shown before
and would not show again, Emerson wrote:

> If I knew only Thoreau, I should think cooperation of good men
> impossible. Must we always talk for victory, and never once for
> truth, for comfort, and joy? Centrality he has, and penetration,
> strong understanding, and the higher gifts, — the insight of
> the real, or from the real, and the moral rectitude that belongs to
> it; but all this and all his resources of wit and invention are lost
> to me, in every experiment, year after year, that I make, to
> hold intercourse with his mind. Always some weary captious
> paradox to fight you with, and the time and temper wasted.[49]

With Thoreau's petulance and verbal combativeness went a kind of
boyish compulsiveness rooted in the feelings of inadequacy that want

of recognition brought. Had Thoreau been Concord's sole writer in residence he might have considered himself a success. With Emerson there, he stood in his shadow. He had hoped *Walden* would bring him equivalent status. It had not done so. To confirm that he was his own man he had now always to assert himself. "It is curious," Emerson wrote in April 1856, "that Thoreau goes to a house to say with little preface what he has just read or observed, delivers it in lump, is quite inattentive to any comment or thought which any of the company offer on the matter, nay, is merely interrupted by it, & when he has finished his report, departs with precipitation." Emerson was not sneering at this hit-and-run didacticism, but expressing dismay.[50]

In his own mind Thoreau took up deeper brooding on the crisis things had come to. Through all this interval Channing's marriage to Ellen Fuller had been in a state of upheaval and Thoreau, as Ellery's near neighbor and chief confidant, had had to bear with his moods. The quarrels, estrangement, reconciliation, and, at last, in 1856 Ellen's sickness and death were shadows on Thoreau's life throughout this period. His concurrent differences with Emerson were a phantom reenactment of what was happening to Channing. Just as Thoreau had had the symptoms of tetanus when his brother John had died of tetanus, he manifested the symptoms of estrangement when Channing and Ellen were estranged. When this happened, he internalized the problem with real hurt to himself. Clearly Thoreau's proclivity for identifying with others, though less overt now, still persisted.

Despite his domestic troubles, Channing seems to have found time to nurture fancied grievances against Emerson, making, no doubt, full disclosure of them to Thoreau. Writing on 23 December 1856, apparently to Elizabeth Hoar, Channing marveled: "How strange it seemed to hear W[aldo], lecturing on friendship. If he knew all the hearts he has frozen, he might better read something on the fall of human hopes."[51] In an undated letter, sent also to Elizabeth, sometime later, Emerson's failure to reciprocate friendship again was Channing's bitter theme:

> To Emerson I have sacrificed one half of my life . . . to be near his remorseless hand which like the keen scissors of the fates, cuts with remediless stroke, at once my life & joy. A fearful price I have had to pay for loving him. . . . I know too well that we who love him have no share in his heart. . . . Under the unsparing hand of this terrible master, I have become like a statue, a machine, in which no part of myself is left. . . . To love the gods is too great for the price which it costs.[52]

On 28 March 1856, in the privacy of his journal, Thoreau foretold a grand renunciation:

> Farewell, my friends! My path inclines to this side the moun-
> tains, — yours to that. For a long time you have appeared farther
> and farther off to me. I see that you will at length disappear
> altogether. For a season my path feels lonely without you. . . .
> The memory of me is steadily passing away from you. My path
> grows narrower and steeper and the night is approaching. . . . I
> accept that everlasting and salutary law, which was promulgated
> as much that spring when I first knew you, as this, when I seem to
> leave you.[53]

The very grandness of this statement, complete with its mystifying
allusions to an "everlasting and salutary law," suggests an exercise
done, not in anguish, but with deliberation, as though the writer was
expounding a thesis rather than stating a fact. The word "seem" in
the concluding phrase, which gives a spectral substance to the whole
utterance, negates it as effectively as if its author, after writing it,
had blotted out his lines with India ink.

In February 1857, in four journal entries made over a sixteen-day
period, Thoreau brought his spectral estrangement from Emerson to a
final crisis and purging. He spared himself nothing and effected an
efficient catharsis. On the eighth the great renunciation was formally
promulgated:

> And now another friendship is ended. I do not know what has
> made my friend doubt me; but I know that in love there is no
> mistake, and that any estrangement is well founded. . . . I am
> sensible not only of a moral but a grand physical pain, such
> as gods may feel, about my head and breast. . . .
> Certainly there is no event comparable for grandeur with the
> eternal separation, if we may conceive it so, from a being that we
> have known. . . . With one with whom we have walked on high
> ground, ever after. We have tried so many years to put each other
> to this immortal use, — and have failed.
> I am perfectly sad at parting from you. I could better have the
> earth taken from under my feet than the thought of you from
> my mind.

On the sixteenth Thoreau assured himself: "Some persons are enveloped and confined by a certain crust of manners, which, though it
may sometimes be a fair and transparent enamel, yet only repels and
saddens the beholder; since by its rigidity it seems to repress all further expansion." On the nineteenth a phase of self-reproach arrived:
"A man cannot be said to succeed in this life who does not satisfy one
friend." On the twenty-third he stated his justification: "I say in my

thought to my neighbor who was once my friend, 'It is no use to speak the truth to you. You will not hear it. What then shall I say to you?' "

Having come to the bottom of his protests, Thoreau now began to scale the walls of the pit he had dug:

> At the instant that I seem to be saying farewell forever to one who has been my friend, I find myself unexpectedly near to him; and it is our very nearness and dearness to each other that gives depth and significance to that "forever." Thus I am a helpless prisoner, — and these chains I have no skill to break. While I think I have broken one link, I have been forging another.[54]

Indulging in word play that would not have occurred to a mind authentically distraught, Thoreau thereupon announced that the "ship" of Friendship has broken apart in the storm — "I hope to make a sort of raft of Friendship, on which, with a few of our treasures we may float to some land." Conceits do not embellish great crises of the soul, even when that great exemplar of self-reliance, Robinson Crusoe, supplies their wherewithal. What Thoreau really was concluding was his long exercise of Platonic friendship with Emerson. Henceforth they were to be friends on normal, human terms. Platonizing was for the young and they were no longer young.

While all this high drama was being recorded in their respective journals, Emerson and Thoreau had continued to pursue their relations with no visible breach. In 1853, when Ruth Emerson died, Thoreau fetched Bulkeley home and, through the period of the funeral, acted as his tender guardian. As usual, Emerson and Thoreau walked together, talked together, shared meals together, and were mutually involved in town activities. Even in the February 1857 crisis, while Thoreau wrestled with renunciation, Emerson amiably referred to him in a letter as one of his "two gossips" (Alcott being the other). The record of their walks together between May 1856 and May 1858 includes visits to Walden Pond and Walden Woods, Sawmill Brook, Goose Pond, Flint's Pond, Conantum, Fairhaven Cliff, Wyman's Orchard, the "Red Chokeberry Lane," Concord River, Estabrook Farm, Everett's pasture, Cyrus Smith's, Peter Hutchinson's, and the auction of the scientific curiosities of Perez Blood. If foes fraternize thus, what ground would they have covered had they been friends?

Emerson was one of those who came often to Thoreau's bedside through the late winter and spring of 1862, as he lay dying of the scourge that so often had taken from Emerson those whom he loved. On 2 April he told Thoreau, with delight, that the ice still was holding on Walden and he had crossed it on that very day. Thoreau, disputatious even at the point of death, recalled that it held one year until the eighteenth. Emerson made note of the fact and dutifully went back to the pond on the eighteenth to find the ice indeed was still holding, though the day was warm. Here was news Henry would like to hear. He so liked to be vindicated. But Henry himself was not holding. He could not walk unassisted or see to read. His study bed was moved to the parlor and from there he greeted the friends who came daily to see him. He died at nine in the morning of 6 May.

To the surprise of many, though he had signed off long since, Thoreau was buried from the First Parish Church. Emerson wanted it so. In Italy Unitarians were called Naturalists. If Thoreau was not the one, he was the other, and could not object to being buried as one. On the ninth the coffin stood in the vestibule of the church. Andromeda, fashioned into a wreath — symbol of eternal life — crowned the fragile sleeper. Thoreau knew all the flowers but loved andromeda best. The choir sang a hymn that Channing had written for this occasion. Then Emerson, in a "broken, tender voice," gave the eulogy, preparation of which had occupied most of his waking moments since Thoreau's struggle had ceased. A selection of Thoreau's thoughts had appeared the previous day in the *Boston Daily Advertiser*, but prepared no one for the frank and heartfelt words spoken now.

Louisa May Alcott, mindful of the gift-book virtues, approved the manner of Emerson's discourse, but not the matter. "Good in itself," she said, but "not appropriate to the time or place." Sophia Thoreau, Henry's sister and lone survivor, was not put off. She had not lived with him all her life without knowing what he would have liked. To Thoreau's friend Daniel Ricketson, who had been too grief-stricken to come to the funeral, she wrote: "Mr. Emerson read such an address as no other man could have done. It is a source of great satisfaction that one so gifted knew and loved my brother, and is prepared to speak such brave words about him at this time."[55]

James and Annie Fields were among the mourners. Annie wrote afterward: "Emerson made the simple ceremony one never to be forgotten by those who were present." For her, the depth of Emerson's sincerity routed every other consideration. "Happy," she wrote,

> were they who heard him speak at the funeral of Henry Thoreau.
> At whatever periods he first framed his intuitions upon the future
> in prose, on that day a light was flashed upon him which he
> reflected again upon the soul of his listeners, and to them it
> seemed that a new-born glory had descended. Whatever words are
> preserved upon the printed page, that spirit of what was given
> that day cannot be reproduced.[56]

What a pity that Louisa missed all this.

Emerson spoke other words that day which were remembered also.

The coffin was carried to the New Burying Ground, at the fringe of Sleepy Hollow. There Thoreau was buried with his mother's people — the Dunbars — not on a summit, not on a slope, but at the level. School children by the hundreds crowded around to blanket the coffin with wildflowers, which many could name because Thoreau had made the names known to them. As the shadows of the coming dusk lengthened, Emerson turned away, his resonant whisper muted by sadness. "He had a beautiful soul," he said. And, as he always did when grief touched him, he spoke the words a second time — "He had a beautiful soul."

Emerson had more thinking to do about Thoreau now that he was in his grave and the common tributes paid. *The Atlantic Monthly* awaited the manuscript of the eulogy since many wanted to know more about Thoreau and to know what Emerson said that had so deeply stirred the mourners. The finished piece was a selective account that emphasized Thoreau's stoicism and "haughty independence." This emphasis was in the spoken eulogy but now was more pronounced. Thoreau's negative side was well documented, while his positive side was skimped. From this document, for many years, men garnered what they believed to be the quintessential Thoreau. From its tone, for many years, Thoreau's posthumous reputation was determined. As he did with other essays, Emerson structured his essay on Thoreau around notations on the subject found throughout his journals, some going as far back as 1843. Unfortunately, some of these perceptions came at times when Thoreau's querulousness or seeming want of purpose had exasperated Emerson. The illustrations that Emerson, after his usual practice, now clustered around these perceptions seemed to complete a likeness of a man who was humorless, disputatious, wanting in social graces and the poetic temperament — and "rarely tender." Perhaps deliberately, while he acknowledged that "occasional traits" — not further specified — were consistent with Thoreau's Gallic heritage, Emerson found that Thoreau's salient traits otherwise derived from "a very strong Saxon genius." Nothing was said of his Scottish antecedents though he had been much in the company of his Dunbar kin. Those of his traits which most exasperated Emerson — his stubbornness, hard-headedness, obdurateness, and contumacy — would, in a company of Scots, seem to confirm a heritage consistent with their own. Since in English letters such traits in Scotsmen often were the butt of stringent humor, Emerson may have wished to disengage Thoreau from an accepted stereotype. After all, no classification would suffice to account for Thoreau. Furthermore, Emerson had seen enough Scotsmen, including Thomas Carlyle, to know that Thoreau could not be explained by that single label.

Emerson's most unexpected conclusion came in his disclosure that Thoreau was deficient in those qualities which made friendship possible. He wrote: "His first instinct on hearing a proposition was to controvert it. . . . This habit, of course, is a little chilling to the social affections. . . . Hence, no equal companion stood in affectionate relations with one so pure and guileless.'' Emerson's final few words appeared to mitigate this account of Thoreau's flawed relations with others but, once made, the point was not to be undone. Nor did Emerson truly want it to be. It too well described what he believed his own relations with Thoreau finally to have been. In attestation of this he restated it, later in the essay: ''I think the severity of his ideal interfered to deprive him of a healthy sufficiency of human society.''[57]

Quite as remarkable to Emerson as Thoreau's alienating severity was his ''Noble Purity,'' to which he several times adverts. He ''was sincerity itself, and might fortify the convictions of prophets in the ethical laws by his holy living.'' Emerson seemed anxious to make this fact known, almost as though there were some who might dispute it. With seeming fastidiousness, though he draws on Elizabeth Hoar's remembrances of Thoreau and on those of Ellen and Edward, one could not tell from his essay that Lidian also knew him. Neither is her name mentioned nor any reminiscences of Thoreau recounted that could be attributable to her. To have touched, however delicately, on the Platonic Thoreau would, of course, have rent the fabric of the essay, which seemed meant to exclude the possibility that Thoreau was capable of striking a wooing stance, even with the most exalted motives in view, or, for that matter, experiencing affection of any kind. Emerson's Thoreau ''had no temptations to fight against, — no appetites, no passions. . . . He did not like the taste of wine, and never had a vice in his life.''[58]

In his closing statement, Emerson said: ''The country knows not yet, or in the least part, how great a son it has lost.'' Nor, it seems, did Emerson, who supposed then that Thoreau had left ''in the midst his broken task,'' with the work he was meant to do undone.[59]

To the eulogy given at the church Emerson appended excerpts from Thoreau's journal that he culled from a selection Channing earlier had copied and now lent him as a source of stimulation. The collection brought him the first hint of a Thoreau of larger dimensions than he knew of. Soon Sophia Thoreau lent him the journals themselves and these contributed insights that went into his *Atlantic* revision of the eulogy.

In June Emerson introduced into his journal a paragraph he would plunder for the *Atlantic* piece:

Henry Thoreau remains erect, calm, self-subsistent, before me, and I read him not only truly in his Journal, but he is not long out of mind when I walk, and, as today, row upon the pond. He chose wisely no doubt for himself to be the bachelor of thought

& nature that he was, — how near to the old monks in their
ascetic religion! He had no talent for wealth, & knew how to be
poor without the least hint of squalor or inelegance. Perhaps he
fell, all of us do, into his way of living, without forecasting it
much, but approved and confirmed it with later wisdom.[60]

Into his own journal Emerson now introduced lustres from Thoreau's journal, which, in their epigrammatic form and vigor, recalled
Emerson's old habit of drawing up lists of the best that was said and
thought by other men. In this task he may have been stimulated also
by Thoreau's legacy to him — seventeen of the books of Oriental thought
given him by the British aristocrat Thomas Cholmondeley.

Perusal of the journals also induced a mild speculation: "If we should
ever print Henry's journals, you may look for a plentiful crop of naturalists. Young men of sensibility must fall an easy prey to the charming of Pan's pipe."[61]

The next year, as he was preparing for Fields the volume called
Excursions, made up of selections from Thoreau's works, Emerson wrote
on 24 June:

In reading Henry Thoreau's Journal, I am very sensible of the
vigor of his constitution. That oaken strength which I noted
whenever he walked or worked or surveyed wood lots, the same
unhesitating hand with which a field-laborer accosts a piece of
work which I should shun as a waste of strength, Henry shows in
his literary task. He has muscle, & ventures on & performs feats
which I am forced to decline. In reading him, I find the same
thought, the same spirit that is in me, but he takes a step beyond,
& illustrates by excellent images that which I should have conveyed in a sleepy generality.[62]

Once *Excursions* appeared, Emerson began work on an edition of
Thoreau's letters and poetry. Toward this labor he showed the same
solicitude he had shown earlier for Carlyle's publications in America.
Thoreau seemed to have been constantly in his thoughts. John Burroughs would remark later that in Emerson's journal for 1864 (as
edited by Edward Emerson and his nephew, Waldo Forbes), Thoreau
figures in ninety-seven paragraphs, far oftener than any of the other
one hundred and sixteen men mentioned in the journal that year.[63]

Emerson changed his mind about the extent to which Thoreau had
left his task unfinished but continued to believe that Thoreau should
come before the world as a stoic. As was true of his profile of Margaret
Fuller, he wanted his notion of what his subject was like to prevail.
He had failed, however, to reckon with Sophia Thoreau, who could be

as strong-willed as her brother. She wanted Henry's tender side disclosed and insisted that passages in his domestic letters that showed him at such times should not be suppressed. "It did not seem quite honest to Henry," she afterward explained, "to leave out such passages."[64] Possibly Emerson meant merely to individuate Thoreau by portraying him as an obdurate loner. That was, in fact, how many people saw him. Indeed, when Thoreau nursed his father through his last illness, his own mother said, "But for this I should never have seen the tender side of Henry." To portray Thoreau as "a most perfect piece of stoicism" was not, in Emerson's eyes, to denigrate him. He did not see the stoical virtues as truly reprehensible.

Emerson also, and with full justification, had shown no signs of relenting from his judgment of Thoreau's poetry. He limited his selection to ten poems, explaining to Fields: "I send all the poems of Thoreau which I think ought to go with the letters. These are the best verses, and no other whole piece quite contents me." Spurning Emerson's advice, Sophia introduced her own favorites into the selection, but not without Emerson's telling her, "You have spoiled my Greek statue."[65]

Once *Letters to Various Persons* achieved publication in 1865, Sanborn rebuked Emerson for having printed too few poems, but Emerson assured him that he had picked the best and that it would be no service to Thoreau's reputation to print any of the others. In 1887 the British-born physician Samuel Arthur Jones, after reading the book, jotted his comments in a notebook. Emerson's selective portrait of Thoreau irked Jones. "It's a pity," he deplored, "that Thoreau's truthfulness did not infect his editors."[66]

Emerson was not satisfied when Channing published his *Thoreau, the Poet-Naturalist* in 1873, nor was Sophia, who acted through Emerson to recover her brother's journals from Channing, who had borrowed them and, in her opinion, made too free a use of them. Upon her death in 1876, they went to Harrison Gray Otis Blake, to whom she had bequeathed them. Emerson found Blake trustworthy. In fact, when Sophia, soon after Thoreau's death, lent his letters to Blake, Emerson was not alarmed. He saw Blake as "a man who would even return a borrowed umbrella."[67] Yet he questioned Blake's judgment. When Blake published selections from Thoreau's journals in the *Atlantic*, Emerson was not pleased. In his opinion neither the best selection had been made nor the best arrangement followed. Thoreau at last had Emerson's ringing endorsement, but, as he saw it, if the world was to admire Thoreau, it should be in the Emerson redaction.

Nature itself seems . . . to invite us to explore the meaning of the conspicuous facts of the day.

41. The Waterville Oration

W̶HEN, on 22 March 1841, Emerson received a letter from Waterville College in Maine,[1] asking him to give an oration to the Erosophian Adelphi, a literary society, on 11 August, he wrote to George Bradford asking for information on Waterville, wondering, no doubt, if a little Baptist college would be receptive to an Emersonian address. George assured him that he could accept without qualms. Emerson next wrote to Margaret Fuller, asking, "Do you know that in August I am to go to Waterville a Baptist college & deliver a literary oration to some young men? For which of my sins?"[2]

As early as 20 April Emerson had tentatively chosen a topic for his Waterville oration. "Would it not be well," he speculated in his journal, "to write for the young men at Waterville a history of our present literary & philosophical crisis, a portrait of the parties & read the augury of the coming hours?"[3] After that, however, until the second week of July, he did not actively consider the matter again.

On 8 July, affirming that "I shall quickly learn whether the spacious ever murmuring sea beach will write an oration for me," Emerson showed up at Worrick's Hotel, at Nantasket Beach on Boston's South Shore. Worrick's was an elegant public house opened in 1826 by William Worrick, who officially named it "The Sportsman." Emerson did not acknowledge it under that designation. Later Nantasket would become a thriving resort community, thickly settled in summer, but in 1841 Worrick's was Nantasket's sole hotel and its patrons had the beautiful five-mile-long beach much to themselves. During the presidencies of Adams, Jackson, and Tyler, Worrick's was the preferred holiday haven of Daniel Webster and other notables. By the 1890's it was but one in a row of hotels and inns sprawled along the Nantasket beach. These have all disappeared. Yet Worrick's, though it passed through many transformations, becoming a private residence in 1867 and later a gaming house, remains. Today, once more it is a house of good repute.[4]

Emerson had sought out Nantasket for two reasons. He needed a place to rest and a place to work. With him he brought a satchel full of books and writing supplies. But before he could work he needed to relax. Boston was sweltering in a heat wave. That night, writing to Lidian, he said he had "jumped into the water at once."[5] Although this was the obvious thing to do at Nantasket in the midst of a summer heat wave, for Emerson it was remarkable. Most of his life, until then, he had loathed salt water, never being able to banish from his mind the immersions his father had forced on him in early childhood. Even when he visited Lidian's relatives in Plymouth, in a house that stood but a few hundred feet from the salt sea, he never thought to bathe there. But he had set his mind on a combination holiday and working session and, in the heat, bathing in the sea was the obvious thing to do. Moreover, he had come to Nantasket in quest of inspiration and was hopeful that, in the soothing environment the seashore offered, it would be forthcoming.

On the third day of his holiday Emerson was able to report to Lidian, who was at home in Concord between holidays of her own, that on his twice-daily walks to the beach his eye was taken with "a profusion of roses growing out of the rifts of the rocks." To his transcendental mind, the symbolism was inescapable: "They seem to say, 'So shall it be unto thee also.'!"After another two days, writing to Caroline Sturgis, he supplied further evidence that he was finding at the seashore the composure and inspiration he sought. "I like the sea. What an ancient pleasant sound is this of the rubbing of the sea against the land."[6]

For Emerson the experiment seemed to be working out as he had hoped it would. It had been a bold one, for in a letter to Margaret Fuller he conceded that he had gone to Nantasket with a definite antipathy to overcome:

> I am here making a sort of peace offering to the god of waters against whom, ever since my childhood — imprisoned in streets & hindered from the fields & woods — I have kept a sort of grudge. Until lately, every landscape that had in it the smallest piece of the sea, seemed to me a little vulgarized. . . . Now . . . this beach & grand sea line receive me with a sort of paternal love.

Emerson's use here of the word "paternal" is striking. It can be remarked that there was a small piece of the sea — a saltwater pond —
on the grounds of his father's parsonage. At Nantasket Emerson had
found consolation beyond his expectations, yet essential to his purpose.
He could scarcely have hoped to pass his time there profitably if his
old grudge against the sea persisted. Possibly, since his mission was to
prepare an address that put him in the paternal role of counseling the
young, he realized it was time he saw his ancient experience of the sea
through his father's eyes and not as a mewling child. His reconciliation seems entire. "I gaze & listen by day, I gaze & listen by night,"
he told Margaret, "and the sea & I shall be good friends all the rest
of my life." To Lidian, a week into his holiday, he wrote of the sea:
"Nothing can be so bland & delicious as it is. I had fancied something
austere & savage, a touch of iron in it, which it hardly makes good."[7]
Nine years later, asked by Josiah Quincy for some reminiscences of
his father, Emerson replied that he remembered only

> a somewhat social gentleman, but severe to us children, who twice
> or thrice put me in mortal terror by forcing me into the salt water
> off some wharf or bathing house, and I still recall the fright with
> which, after some of this salt experience, I heard his voice one day
> (as Adam that of the Lord God in the garden), summoning us to
> a new bath, and I vainly endeavoring to hide myself.

Since Emerson could recall few things about his father, if he was to
tell Quincy anything at all, this experience would have to be one of
his remembrances. That he is able to refer to it openly and even drolly,
to compare himself not to Isaac being readied for sacrifice — a blameless victim — but to the transgressing Adam, suggests that Emerson
now realized his father had acted as his adult wisdom decreed. He
himself had been at fault. Because he overcame his terror of the sea
and with it his resentment of his father, it does not follow that the
memory of that traumatic experience was forever expunged. He had
found a way of dealing with it; he had, in fact, come to a healthy
acceptance of it.[8]
A marked feature of Emerson's Nantasket letters to Lidian is that
in them, he refers to his mother more than he did during any other
period of absence from home. Ruth, at seventy-two, had found the
summer heat oppressive. By 20 July Emerson's anxiety concerning
her health was evident. To Lidian he wrote: "I do not like what you
say of Mother's fasting & languor in the heats — It is time her son
should come home —"[9] Ruth was, in fact, more on her own than usual.
Lidian was five months pregnant and unwell. Elizabeth, who ordinarily lavished on her a daughter's care, had gone to Vermont to visit

friends. Concerned that Ruth might feel forsaken, Emerson told Lidian that his letters to her were meant for his mother also.[10] If any of his letters reached Concord after Lidian had gone to Plymouth, it was understood that Ruth could open them.

A further factor may account for Emerson's concern for his mother at this time. Experiencing, at long last, amiable feelings toward his father, he was frustrated in not being able to convey them. He could make his mother the beneficiary of those feelings, however, and did so. In the Waterville oration he would say, significantly:

A man should know himself for a necessary actor. A link was wanting between two craving parts of nature, and he was hurled into being as the bridge over that yawning need. . . . His two parents held each of them one of the wants, and the union of foreign constitutions in him enables him to do gladly and gracefully what the assembled human race could not have sufficed to do.[11]

Conscious of his debt to both parents for bringing into existence the unique being that was himself and mindful of his failure in the past to do justice to his father, he strove now to make amends through his mother.

Another passage in the address contributes a further insight into Emerson's state of mind at that time:

An individual man is a fruit which it cost all the foregoing ages to form and ripen. . . . The history of the genesis or the old mythology repeats itself in the experience of every child. He, too, is a demon or god thrown into a particular chaos, where he strives ever to lead things from disorder into order.[12]

Balancing now his memory of being forced off a wharf into saltwater by his father, he substitutes the positive experience of "being hurled into being" as a bridge and being "thrown into a particular chaos" to accomplish positive ends possible to him alone.

Long before confronting the sea at Nantasket, Emerson had unconsciously taken his deceased father as his role model. His father had had a beautiful speaking voice and was a notable sermon-giver. Emerson had cultivated these same aptitudes. His father had taught school on his way to the ministry. He had done that, too. His father had been pastor of Boston's First Church; he became pastor of Boston's Second Church. His father had been chaplain of the state Senate and a member of the Boston School Committee; these offices fell to him as well. And figuratively he had given reality to another of his father's ambitions — his dream of founding a nondenominational church. As Concord had been his father's place of origin, now he sought to find there his own identity. The stage was set for the final act of reconciliation. Where better to bring it to pass than by the salt sea, itself a symbol of catharsis and purification?

In a remarkable letter he wrote to Caroline Sturgis from Nantasket on 13 July, Emerson said: "You know I was baptised in Walden Pond — here is a better font & if you were here, I would say, O angel friendly to my life what hindereth that I be sprinkled again?"[13] Thus he announced himself ready to be born anew there where Nature, through the sea, manifested that it existed to a universal end. In "The Method of Nature," his Waterville oration, Emerson would announce the fact of that baptism. Acclaiming "The doctrine of this Supreme Presence," of the universal mind suffusing the universe, he said, "I praise with wonder this great reality which seems to drown all things in the deluge of its light." Emerson's fear of drowning, implicit in his fear of the sea, here yields to an image of drowning as a gain, as the infusion of his mind into the universal mind. "What man seeing this," he asks, "can lose it from his thoughts, or entertain a meaner subject? The entrance of this into his mind seems to be the birth of man."[14]

Emerson brought home from Nantasket a seaweed collection and an outline of an oration. He also brought home the serenity of a wholeness previously lacking. Emerson's father had grown up fatherless and never was easy as he pondered what kind of man his own father had been. His psychic estrangement was never resolved. Such was his customary manner that he appeared to repudiate his father's theological and social stance. Like William, Waldo also had grown up fatherless. Never having personally experienced, in his remembrance, a father's love, and able only to recall his severity, Emerson especially relished the opportunity given him to be a loving father to little Waldo. A relationship had been given him that two generations of Emersons had been denied. At Nantasket, even as he came into a tranquil relationship of acceptance with his own father, Emerson's thoughts toward Waldo continued to intensify. In his letters, he inquired dutifully for both children but Waldo especially was in his thoughts. On 11 July he wrote Lidian: "I need no animal magnetism to see Waldo & Ellen, on the way to school, or on the way to the barn. Yet I wish to hear of them whatever you can tell me." On the eighteenth he mentioned only Waldo: "I wish I had him here to see the ships go by." On the twentieth, as his visit was nearing its close, he advised Lidian, "In the pocket of the coat I will put a pebble from the beach for Waldo."[15]

The following September, when Dr. Ripley died — described then by Emerson as "the patriarch of the tribe" — Emerson took Waldo to see the body on the day of his passing. The titular grandfather gone, his ties with the preceding generations severed, Emerson felt even more keenly his ties with the new generation, embodied in Waldo, being pulled taut. Events were focusing his mind more and more on this relationship, and from it he garnered new confidence to follow the dictates of the spirit within him. In the context of these events Waldo's sudden death in January, the green sprig shorn just four months after the oak, at ninety, had fallen, came to Emerson as a staggering blow. Having healed at last the wound of being left fatherless — of having been betrayed by his father's desertion, as perhaps he saw it — now, at the very time he had recaptured a father-son relationship, with himself in the ascendant role, he had been left sonless. The anguish that came to him then would never truly retire.

On his arrival at Nantasket on 8 July, Emerson at once chartered a boat to take him deep-sea fishing at dawn. Heavy bookings and heavy weather kept him ashore the first two days, but on the third day he caught a cod, a flounder, a pollock, a perch, and two haddock. Ashore again, he wrote to both Lidian and Margaret, reporting with Munchausen extravagance his fisherman's luck. He also socialized some, especially with Lowell and Maria White, whom Lowell was courting. Although Maria, a few years later, married Lowell, it was upon Emerson, at the end of her stay, that she bestowed her collection of pressed seaweed.

On 11 July Emerson spoke finally of a tentative beginning to his bookish labors. Two days later he cited some progress even though his fishing expedition had intervened. The next day, again writing to Lidian, he said, "I have got into a pretty good way of reading & writing at last." But then, although at the end of only the first week of his two-week vacation, he intimated that his hopes of achieving at Nantasket what he came there to do were fast ebbing: "I have accomplished some reading that has been lying in wait for me a year or two & so I have not lost the whole time, & I see at least how such materials as I have will work into an oration although I have not had any of those visitations of the high Muse."[16]

Despite his misgivings, the "sea change" Emerson was seeking was taking hold. On 13 July he told Caroline Sturgis that "this satiating expanse," the sea, was "the only thing on earth that compares with the sky in contenting the eye, wh. it more contents beheld from the shore than on the ocean," a description he recast, experimentally, in subsequent letters to Margaret and Elizabeth.[17] From these exercises there evolved a striking passage in the Waterville oration:

> The ocean is everywhere the same, but it has no character until seen with the shore or the ship. Who would value any number of

miles of Atlantic brine bounded by lines of latitude and longitude? Confine it by granite rocks, let it wash a shore where wise men dwell, and it is filled with expression; and the point of greatest interest is where the land and water meet.[18]

When Emerson sought inspiration, he often turned to letter-writing to set his mind pulsating. In ''Friendship'' he explained:

> Our intellectual and active powers increase with our affection. The scholar sits down to write, and all his years of meditation do not furnish him with one good thought or happy expression; but it is necessary to write a letter to a friend, and, forthwith, troops of gentle thoughts invest themselves, on every hand, with chosen words.[19]

At Nantasket he wrote letters daily, several of considerable length. During his second week there, Lidian kept him in a state of uncertainty by revamping her plans to visit Plymouth, finally expanding them to include him. ''But for this journey of yours, I mt. have spent my remaining days of the fortnight a little differently,''[20] he told her with that bland resignation which, in his emotional vocabulary, stood proxy for reproachfulness. Here it implied that he would have been writing his oration. Yet, to Sam Ward, he had a different story to tell:

> Is it the picture of the unbounded sea, or is it the lassitude of this Syrian summer, that more and more draws the cords of will out of my thought and leaves me nothing but perpetual observation, perpetual acquiescence and perpetual thankfulness? . . . I have seen enough of the obedient sea wave forever lashing the obedient shore. I find no emblems here that speak any other language than the sweep and abandonment of my woods and blueberry pastures at home.

Elsewhere he disclosed that he knew such moods often masked real activity: ''We do not know to-day whether we are busy or idle. In times when we thought ourselves indolent, we have afterwards discovered that much was accomplished and much was begun in us.''[21] In Nantasket he had, in fact, succeeded in inviting the Muse, but time had still to pass before he realized he had done so.

Once through the Plymouth ordeal — consoling there Lidian's brother and his wife on the recent loss of their infant son — and home again in Concord, he wrote Margaret Fuller of his rhapsodic hopes for completing the much-desired oration: ''I . . . flew home again yesterday, to write my oration. . . . Under this soft moon kissing the trees over the bones of my ancestors, in fields where I still seem to hear David's Psalter on the cadences of the evening wind, I will make new prayers to the local or universal muse.''[22] Emerson now was coming into the requisite mood to write an address suffused with a soaring lyricism that gives it a distinction all its own.

In 1841 Waterville College, founded only in 1813, was a mere speck on the academic horizon. Some fame was beginning to attach to it as the alma mater of the murdered Elijah Lovejoy, but the distinction it would gain as the place where Emerson delivered his ''The Method of Nature'' oration was something that neither town nor gown was then qualified to appreciate. Doubtless Emerson foresaw this, but practical as well as ethical reasons nonetheless enjoined fastidious preparation. While working on his first series of *Essays*, published the previous January, he had written no new lectures, nor had he written any during the six months that had elapsed since the *Essays* appeared. At Nantasket word had come from Carlyle that an English edition of the *Essays* was about to appear and that he himself had written a preface for it. As a result Emerson's reputation was much enhanced. ''The Method of Nature,'' marking as it did Emerson's reemergence on the lecture platform, was, accordingly, an event that raised questions. Had growth come with success? Would he command a wider public? What strategy would he use to disarm his critics? To most of these speculations Emerson would have been indifferent. Yet he must have felt a heightened responsibility to measure up to the expectations that the *Essays* raised. But the responsibility he especially felt was to his audience. He meant it when he told Carlyle that he was going to Waterville for the sake of the ''boys'' who had invited him.[23] No matter that much that he had to say was beyond them. He could count on certain phrases sending a thrill through a youthful audience, to initiate a process of change. That was enough to start with. Full enlightenment could come later. His constituency was youth. To that constituency he had directed both ''The American Scholar'' and the ''Divinity School Address.'' He wanted to catch young men at the threshold of life and point them in the right direction.

Repeatedly, Emerson referred to ''The Method of Nature'' as an oration, and it was as a classical oration that he wrote it. It has a formal exordium and peroration and all the requisite in-between segments. His listeners had received a classical education and Emerson paid them the compliment of casting his remarks in a form they could identify and relate to. He laid out a program of life that best could be followed by those who as yet had not committed themselves to conventional goals. And a letter to Lidian shows that he knew it would not be concrete enough for some.[24] Still, whatever stir the *Essays* had made on their appearance, Waterville cannot have known much about

Reverend William Emerson, from
an engraving in the *Polyanthos*,
May 1812, with notation by his son
Ralph Waldo Emerson.

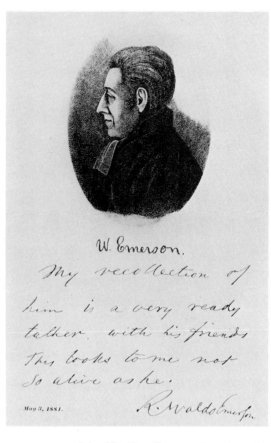

W. Emerson.
My recollection of
him is a very ready
talker, with his friends
This looks to me not
So alive as he.

May 3, 1881.

R. Waldo Emerson

Ruth Haskins Emerson, Emerson's mother,
at eighty. *Courtesy, Concord Free Public
Library.*

John Haskins, Emerson's maternal
grandfather.

Ezra Ripley at eighty, 1832. *Courtesy, First Parish Church, Concord.*

John Clarke, William Emerson's predecessor at Boston's First Church. This portrait looked dow on the Emersons at mealtime in Emerson's boyhood.

The First Church of Boston, 1810.

The Old Manse, built by William Emerson, 1770.

Edvardus-Gardiner Davis
Jacobus-Ferdinandus Deering
Archibald Dunbar
Andreas-Leonard Emerson
Carolus Flagg
Josua-Barker Flint
Gulielmus-Henricus Furness
Ezra-Stiles Gannett
Gulielmus Gragg
David-Priestley Hall
Edvardus-Brooks Hall
Gulielmus-Byrd Harrison
Alfredus-Woodward Haven
Johannes-Cole Hayden
Tilly-Brown Hayward
Isaacus-Lothrop Hedge
Gulielmus-Kneeland Hedge
Payson Kendal
Benjamin Kent
Ingalls Kittredge
Calvinus Lincoln
Gulielmus Oakes
Georgius Barber Osborn
Carolus Paine
Josephus Palmer
Augustus Peirce
Daniel-Hall Peirce
Gulielmus-Taylor Potter
Gulielmus-Georgius Read
Johannes Rogers
Nathanael Russell
Georgius-Washington Sargent
Stephanus Schuyler
Gulielmus-Rufus Smith
Gulielmus-Lawrence Stearns
Enos Stewart
Johannes-Grosvenor Tarbell
Horatius Townsend
Gideon Tucker
Adolphus-Eugenius Watson
Henricus-Goodwin Wheaton
Daniel-Kimball Whitaker
Johannes-Adams Williams
Franciscus-Henricus Williams
Jacob Wyeth
Alexander Young

1821.

Georgius-Washington Adams
Samuel Alden
Johannes Angier
Robertus-Woodward Barnwell
Allard-Henricus Belin
Horton Bethune

Gulielmus-Henricus Blake
Oliver-Hunter Blood
Cyrus Briggs
Henricus Bulfinch
Carolus Bunker
Warren Burton
Johannes-Milton Cheney
Gulielmus-Parker Coffin
Richardus Corbett
Loring-Pelham Curtis
Gulielmus-Bradley Dorr
Radulphus-Waldo Emerson
Radulphus Farnsworth
Enoch Frye
Johannes-Lowell Gardner
Amos-Gordon Goodwin
David-Wood Gorham
Robertus-Marion Gourdin
Johannes-Gaillard-Keith Gourdin
Samuel Hatch
Josephus-Bancroft Hill
Johannes-Boynton Hill
Gulielmus Hilliard
Georgius-Johonnot Hubbard
Georgius-Brooks James
Carolus Jarvis
Theodorus-Russell Jenks
Thomas-Jones Johnston
Theodorus Keating
Edvardus Kent
Fredericus-Gore King
Henricus Lane
Fredericus-Percival Leverett
Edvardus-Greely Loring
Franciscus-Cabot Lowell
Samuel-Hall Lyon
Josephus Manigault
Georgius-Barrell Moody
Mellish-Irving Motte
Henricus-Manly Neyle
Gulielmus-Foster Otis
Georgius-Alexander Otis
Johannes Pope
Gulielmus Pope
Georgius-Williams Pratt
Josias Quincy
Benjamin-Tyler Reed
Johannes-Furness Tilton
Benjamin Tucker
Andreas Turnbull
Carolus-Wentworth Upham
Gulielmus Withington
Nathanael Wood

Concord Center, 1837.

View from the Old Manse of the Battle at the North Bridge, April 19, 1775.
William Emerson's field in foreground. A. Doolittle, 1775.

Facing page: Catalogue, Harvard College, 1821.

Staircase, Winslow House,
Plymouth, where Lidian, in
1834, had a vision of Emerson
as her bridegroom. *Courtesy,
Concord Free Public Library.*

Lidian Emerson in her later
years. *Courtesy, Concord Free
Public Library.*

Facing page:
Ellen Louisa Tucker, miniature
painted by Sarah Goodridge, 1829.
*Courtesy, Concord Antiquarian
Museum.*

Emerson at his writing table. A photograph taken in October 1879.

Detail from Margaret Fuller
Ossoli Memorial, Mount
Auburn Cemetery, Cambridge,
Massachusetts.
Photograph, Joe Ofria.

Elizabeth Hoar with, perhaps,
her nephew, Charles Emerson
Hoar, c. 1850. *Courtesy,
Concord Free Public Library.*

Bush, Emerson's Concord home. His study is the room to the right of the front
door, ground level.

Emerson, c. 1842.

Emerson as lecturer, painted by
David Scott, Edinburgh, 1848.
Original in Concord Free Public
Library.

Emerson, sketched by "the Jane
Austen of Sweden," Fredrika Bremer,
1851. *Courtesy, Concord Free Public
Library.*

Emerson, 1857.

Emerson, 1859.

The Adirondac Club, painted by
William J. Stillman, August 1858.
Emerson stands alone in the center.
Original in Concord Free
Public Library.

Handbill distributed on Emerson's return to
Concord, 1873. *Courtesy, Concord Free Public
Library.*

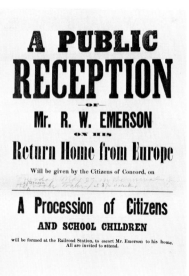

Thomas Carlyle and Emerson's grandson,
Ralph Emerson Forbes, 1872.

Facing page:
Emerson, with son
Edward and grandson
Charles Lowell Emerson,
1876. *Courtesy, Concord
Free Public Library.*

Graves of Ralph Waldo Emerson and his wife, Lidian, Authors' Ridge, Sleepy Hollow Cemetery, Concord. *Photograph, Joe Ofria.*

Old Corner Bookstore, Boston, 1887.

it. Emerson could not have felt under any special constraint to meet specific expectations there. In fact, if Waterville had known much about him, he probably would not have been invited at all. He was free, then, to write what he wanted with a view of giving a meaningful message to those who sent for him.

To E. P. Whipple, a widely admired lecturer and literary critic, Emerson once described, with evident amusement, the circumstances that marked his visit to Waterville. His stagecoach, still the chief mode of travel in New England, pulled into town late at night after most people had gone to bed. No one was sure whose guest Emerson was to be. Emerson told Whipple:

> The stage-driver . . . stopped at one door, rapped loudly; a window was opened; something in a night-gown asked what he wanted; the stage-driver replied that he had inside a man who *said* he was to deliver the lit-ra-rye oration to-morrow, and thought he was to stop there; but the night-gown disappeared, with the chilling remark that he was not to stay at *his* house. Then we went to another and still another dwelling, rapped, saw similar night-gowns and heard similar voices at similar raised windows; and it was only after repeated disturbances of the peace of the place that the right house was hit, where I found a hospitable reception.

The following evening, when Emerson delivered his oration, the audience was about as receptive as the disturbed sleepers had been the previous night. "The address," Emerson told Whipple, "was really written in the heat and happiness of what I thought a real inspiration; but all the warmth was extinguished in that lake of iced water," a strange destiny to overtake an oration which had its beginnings by the briny Atlantic, in the dog days of July. Nonetheless, the humor of what happened was not lost on Emerson. Whipple recalled: "He seemed intensely to enjoy the fun of his material discomforts and his spiritual discomfiture."[25]

Three days later, when the local newspaper, *The Watervillonian*, assessed Emerson's oration, his impressions of his audience were confirmed. Said its reporter: "Of this performance we hardly know in what terms to speak. . . . An honest farmer probably expressed the opinion of the generality of those who heard it — 'It is quite likely that the oration contained a great deal of *science;* but even if it did not, no one could know the fact.' "[26]

The subsequent history of "The Method of Nature" somewhat compensated Emerson for the apathetic reception it got at Waterville. Emerson sent several copies to Carlyle in November. Carlyle owned that he had reservations: "I do again desiderate some *concretion* of these beautiful *abstracta*. It seems to me they will never be *right* otherwise; that otherwise they are but as prophecies yet, not fulfillments." But he considered its merits: "The new *Adelphi* piece seems to me, as a piece of Composition, the best *written* of them all. People cry over it; 'Whitherward? What, What?'" From Lowell, likewise, the oration received warm praise. But only when Whipple said that he thought "The Method of Nature" the best of all his college addresses did Emerson acknowledge that he himself held it in high regard.[27]

Emerson began his oration by saying that nothing served the interests of America better than "the fit consecration of days of reason and thought." Since his hosts had provided such an occasion, they could assume he included them in the company of scholars who embodied "the spiritual interest of the world."[28] Yet temptations lay athwart the scholar's path — "the material interest is so predominant as it is in America." He did not join Blake in deploring "the dark Satanic mills." "I do not wish," he said, "to look with sour aspect at the industrious manufacturing village, or the mart of commerce." But he saw that machines could be used to degrade laborers; "Let there be worse cotton and better men." Here his auditors were urged to make their presence felt: "the scholar must be a bringer of hope, and must reinforce man against himself." Men might scorn the scholar but heaven justified him. "It seems to me," he said, "the wit of man, his strength, his grace, his tendency, his art, is the grace and the presence of God." Yet men let themselves be sidetracked, turning away from the universal to the particular.

If man's intellect recoils from universality, Nature does not. "That which once existed in intellect as pure law, has now taken body as Nature. It existed already in the mind in solution; now, it has been precipitated, and the bright sediment is the world." Accordingly, an inquiry into the method of Nature may instruct man in ways of meeting his highest obligations. But, in fact, it does not lend itself to analysis; "That rushing stream will not stop to be observed." We can surmise this much: "Nature can only be conceived as existing to a universal and not to a particular end. . . . There is in it no private will, no rebel leaf or limb, but the whole is oppressed by one superincumbent tendency, obeys that redundancy or excess of life which in conscious beings we call *ecstasy*," since "the universal does not attract us until housed in an individual." Because such is the method of Nature, "So must we admire in man the form of the formless, the concentration of the vast."

Emerson now revealed that "When nature has work to be done, she creates a genius to do it." He is here "to do an office which nature could not forego." Moreover, "What are the thoughts we utter but the reason of our incarnation?'' So awed was Emerson by this miracle that he resorted to biblical language to describe it further: "Here art thou with whom so long the universe travailed in labor; darest thou think meanly of thyself whom the stalwart Fate brought forth to unite his ragged sides, to shoot the gulf, — to reconcile the irreconcilable?'' That his listeners registered no positive response to this invitation to recognize their exalted role in the scheme of creation seems hard to credit.

Man's status defined, Emerson went on to consider how man manifests in his behavior the method of Nature: "His health and erectness consist in the fidelity with which he transmits influences from the vast and universal to the point on which his genius can act.'' The spirit is "our unseen pilot. . . . If the man will exactly obey it, it will adopt him, so that he shall not any longer separate it from himself in his thought, he shall seem to be it, he shall be it.'' Yet in man there is "a mischievous tendency'' to turn away from his universe of ends and stand by the particular ends gained. If he rests "in his acts'' the voice of the divine wisdom gradually fades until at last he can no longer hear it. When he listens "with insatiable ears, richer and greater wisdom is taught him.'' Moreover, "His health and greatness consist in his being the channel through which heaven flows to earth, in short, in the fulness in which an ecstatical state takes place in him.'' It is the nature of "this ecstatical state . . . to direct a regard to the whole and not to the parts.'' Men must be guided by an awareness of this fact: "There is no office or function of man but is rightly discharged by this divine method, and nothing that is not noxious to him if detached from its universal relations.''

He warned against assigning to our actions either utilitarian or pleasurable ends: "Man must be on his guard against this cup of enchantments, and must look at nature with a supernatural eye. By piety alone, by conversing with the cause of nature, is he safe and commands it.'' He opined that "ecstasy is the law and cause of nature,'' that "Things divine are not attainable by mortals who understand sensual things.''

Emerson's last major piece before "The Methods of Nature'' had been "Man the Reformer.'' Inevitably, now, he saw fit to assess reform efforts in terms of his present argument, and, by implication, to account for his own reluctance to lend his authority and active support to practical projects of reform. Reforms drew us away from that universe of ends which constituted our proper concern: "He who aims at progress, should aim at an infinite, not at a special benefit. The reforms whose fame now fills the land, . . . fair and generous as each appears, are poor bitter things when prosecuted for themselves as an end.'' The fact is, "there is no end to which your practical faculty can

aim, so sacred or so large, that if pursued for itself, will not at last
become carrion and an offense to the nostril. The imaginative faculty
of the soul must be fed with objects immense and eternal. Your end
should be one inapprehensible to the senses." Emerson then made the
startling promise that the man who is "whole and sufficient" through
his attachment to universal ends will "exert magnetism" which will
be everywhere felt, even by those at a distance, and, indeed, be inescapable.

Lest his listeners fear that they would leave the world's work undone if they turned away from particular ends, Emerson paused now
to define history in terms of his teachings: "What is all history but
the work of ideas, a record of the incomputable energy which his infinite aspirations infuse into man? Has anything grand and lasting been
done? — Who did it? Plainly not any man, but all men: it was the
prevalence and inundation of an idea." To illustrate his thesis he considered two events of paramount importance in American history, the
coming of the Pilgrims and the War of Independence. Boldly he asserted that the Pilgrims came not to establish civil liberty, a church,
or a prosperous plantation but to foster "the growth, the budding and
expansion of the human race." The war, he said, "was not begun in
Concord . . . but was the overflowing of the sense of natural right in
every clear and active spirit of the period." This argument led him to
consider the example offered by the founding fathers of New England. They did not work for selfish ends, and we can be instructed by
their example. "A man was born not for prosperity, but to suffer for
the benefit of others, like the noble rock-maple which all around our
villages bleeds for the service of man."

The work of true reform can be done by adopting the methods of
Nature. If universal ends are pursued, under the guidance of "this
immanent force," men will be brought to "health and reason." How,
specifically, may men secure "the attainment of gifts so sublime?"
They must act on what they know. "The only way into nature is to
enact our best insight. Instantly we are higher poets and can speak a
deeper law. Do what you know, and perception is converted into character." Here, indeed, was advice meant to send young men forth into
life motivated to elevate the condition of humankind.

Emerson was certain that the soul is eternal and that its qualities
"circulate through the Universe" and "hold the key to universal nature." To know that that divine force sustains us gives us "courage
and hope." By responding to its guidance we go out "through universal love to universal power."

Young men on Commencement Day hardly could look for a more
positive message. They were told to choose lofty ideals and not to relinquish them. For a pattern they were to look to the method of Nature. The unseen pilot, "the mighty and transcendent soul" that was

the divinity within them, would enable each man "to deliver the thought of his heart from the universe to the universe," to do the work of Nature he was created to do.

Writing to Lidian on 2 August 1841, Emerson said, "I am quite sure my Waterville Speech . . . will betray my spectral life."[29] Rusk, accepting Emerson's gingerly offered observation at face value, said that "The Method of Nature" was "one of Emerson's most spectral" speeches.[30] But spectral evidence is more easily asserted than validated. Since Emerson knew what he wanted to say at Waterville and said it with an eloquence he never elsewhere surpassed, this charge rests really on his thrice reiterated reluctance to define in the oration things which he regarded as undefinable — first genius, then the method of Nature, and, finally, the natural history of the soul. Yet to have defined these things would have been limiting and that would have contradicted the thesis on which the oration is built, that men, guided by the universal mind, can act without recourse to other authority.

Holmes, addressing himself to questions this oration raises, chose to sidestep controversy, observing merely: "There are many expressions in this Address which must have sounded strangely and vaguely to his Christian audience." He illustrated his point by quoting the most mystifying passage of all: "Are there not moments in the history of heaven when the human race was not counted by individuals, but was only the Influenced, was God in distribution, God rushing into multiform benefit?" Proceeding to ground where every reader could follow him, he added, with delicious understatement: "It might be feared that the practical philanthropists would feel that they lost by his counsels."[31] Firkins saw the oration as a depository of ideas not confronted elsewhere by Emerson either in his journals or essays. He contended that Emerson's insistence that man must model himself on Nature, "seeking only the expression, by elastic and changing methods, of the divine force which he embodies," was disheartening and perplexing information to give to his Waterville audience.[32]

Edward Emerson, commenting on the Waterville oration, said aptly: "Had the oration been called a sermon and given on Sunday, its heresy would have been challenged, but, as often happened, Mr. Emerson found that on a week-day people would listen even with pleasure to words against which on Sunday they would have been on their guard."[33] He made this observation in glossing Emerson's assumption that God's divinity is found within us. To multiply the charge of heresy against him it can be further observed that, in urging his listeners to "worship the mighty and transcendent Soul," he was reiterating the invitation extended in the "Divinity School Address" for men to break free of institutionalized worship. "The Method of Nature" thus is a true companion piece to the Divinity Hall address, pursuing its premises to compatible conclusions.

42. Waldo
As the Mist Rises

*I*T was that week in winter when Walden Pond usually freezes over, the last week of December and, in fact, the last day of the year, 1879. Louisa May Alcott was alone in the house on Main Street that she had bought for her family two years before. Thoreau had died there, and her mother had also, just twelve days after they moved in. Her sister Anna, a widow, had gone to Boston. Bronson, her father, now eighty, disregarding the numbing slap of Arctic cold, had gone to the post office on the Milldam. May, who lately had given birth to a daughter in Paris, was ill and he was hoping for news.

Emerson was also abroad that cold morning. From his own house, a mile away, he had walked to Alcott's. Soon to be seventy-seven himself, and sometimes befuddled in his thinking, he was nonetheless a vigorous walker. On this particular morning his stride could not have been particularly vigorous because his mind was clear enough about his mission, and his mission was a mournful one.

On her deathbed on that rainy Sunday when she died, Abba Alcott had looked fondly at May's picture and waved her hand repeatedly, saying, "Good-by, little May, good-by!" Summoned downstairs now by a servant, Louisa found Emerson waiting in the parlor where Thoreau had died, his eyes fixed on that same picture. Usually his color was good. Today, despite the frigid weather, his face was pale. And his eyes glistened with tears the wind had not put there. In his hand he held a cablegram. Ernest Nierecker, May's husband, had sent it to him rather than to the house on Main Street, because he thought Emerson would find some way to break the news gently. Yet how did one soften such a message? May had died two days before.

Here was a role Emerson was not equal to. To have understood the purpose of his mission only made it more difficult. "My child," he began, "I wish I could prepare you . . ." He hesitated, then went on, "But alas, alas!" His voice broke. He could find no words to continue. Instead, he held out the cablegram. Louisa read it. She had been expecting the worst for some days. The bleak words said what she thought they would. "I *am* prepared," she told Emerson and she thanked him for coming himself. "He was much moved and very tender," Louisa wrote later in her journal. "I shall remember gratefully the look, the grasp, the tears he gave me; and I am sure that hard moment was made bearable by the presence of this our best and tenderest friend."[1]

Once before, Louisa had shared with Emerson an intimate moment of grief. In January 1842, soon after his fifth birthday, Emerson's son, Waldo, fell ill with scarlet fever. The rapid progress of the disease, bringing death within seventy-two hours, left Emerson stunned. After Emerson's own death, Elizabeth Hoar's brother George said, "I remember, as if it were yesterday, that winter morning in my early youth when the messenger came to my father's door before sunrise, bearing his written message to one of the household [Elizabeth], 'Everything wakes this morning except my darling Boy.'"[2] In his journal Emerson wrote: "I woke at 3 o'clock, & every cock in every barnyard was shrilling with the most unnecessary noise. The sun went up the morning sky with all his light, but the landscape was dishonored by this loss. . . . Every tramper that ever tramped is abroad, but the little feet are still."[3]

Waldo died at eight-fifteen on the night of 27 January, with Emerson sitting at his bedside, holding his hand. "He gave up his little innocent breath like a bird," he wrote later. Louisa Alcott was just nine years old then. For her, that morning, Emerson had only the starkest message. She recalled:

> My first remembrance is of the morning when I was sent to
> inquire for little Waldo, then lying very ill. His father came to
> me, so worn with watching and changed by sorrow, that I was
> startled, and could only stammer out my message. "Child, he is
> dead!" was his answer. Then the door closed, and I ran home to
> tell the sad tidings. . . . That was my first glimpse of great grief,
> but I never have forgotten the anguish that made a familiar
> face so tragical, and gave those few words more pathos than the
> sweet lamentation of the "Threnody."[4]

That Emerson would make so unadorned a statement of the facts to Louisa is a true measure of his anguish. Notable also, in the brief letters he sent at this time to tell others of his loss, was his frequent repetition of phrases, even as he said "alas, alas," when May died. The phrase, "Farewell & Farewell," appears in letters to William, Dr. Jackson, and Margaret Fuller. "My darling, my darling!" occurs in the letter to Abel Adams, and "My boy, my boy," in his letter to Aunt Mary. The usage seems elegiac. Repetition occurs also in "Threnody," the poem he wrote on Waldo's death: "The lost, the lost, he cannot restore . . ." Normally Emerson shunned repetition. Yet there is a tradition, probably universal among mankind, of the grief-stricken repeating phrases in a chant or refrain; most memorable, of course, in David's "O Absalom, my son, my son Absalom! Would God I had died for thee, O Absalom, my son, my son!" Judge Hoar would write later: "I think I was never more impressed with a human expression of agony than when Mr. Emerson led me into the room where little Waldo lay dead and said only, in reply to whatever I could say of sorrow or sympathy, 'Oh, that boy! that boy!' "[5]

To Carlyle, Emerson had written on 18 March 1840: "The boy has two deep blue wells for eyes, into which I gladly peer when I am tired. Ellen, they say, has no such depth of orb, but I believe I love her better than ever I did the boy." Yet when Ellen came down with scarlet fever the day Waldo died, Emerson did not show the same concern he had had for Waldo. In a letter written next day to Elizabeth Peabody, he told her of Waldo's death and concluded: "With him has departed all that is glad & festal & almost all that is social even, for me, from this world. My second child is also sick, but I cannot in a lifetime incur another such loss."[6]

Emerson's adulation of Waldo was apparent from the outset. On 31 October 1836 he wrote in his journal: "Last night at 11 o'clock, a son was born to me. Blessed child! a lovely wonder to me, and which makes the Universe look friendly to me." In April, when Waldo at five months was wheezy and fretful with a cold, Emerson's anxiety was unmistakable: "Ah! my darling boy, so lately received out of heaven leave me not now! Please God, this sweet symbol of love & wisdom may be spared to rejoice, teach, & accompany me."[7]

"Who is rich or happy but the parent of a son?" Emerson asked Cincinnati friends nearly twenty years after Waldo's death.[8] The little boy became for Emerson a source of continuing delight. On 26 April 1838 he wrote: "Lidian came into the study this afternoon and found the towerlet that Wallie had built half an hour before, of two spools, a card, an awl-case & a flourbox top, each perpendicularly balanced on the other, and could scarce believe that her boy had built the pyramid."[9] Houseguests would find Emerson's study inaccessible during his working hours, but never Waldo. A family friend described Waldo to Cabot as: "A domesticated sunbeam, with his father's voice, but softened, and beautiful dark blue eyes with long lashes. He was his father's constant companion, and would stay for hours together in the study, never interrupting him.''[10]

''I like my boy,'' Emerson wrote in his journal on 9 July 1839, ''with his endless, sweet soliloquies & iterations, and his utter inability to conceive why I should not leave all my nonsense, business, & writing, & come to tie up his toy horse, as if there was or could be any end to nature beyond his horse.''[11] One of Waldo's playmates would in after years recall:

> One day Waldo and I were in the hay-mow, up-stairs, when we heard below a most solemn and awful voice, — though very sweet: 'Little Boy Blue, — where is little Boy Blue?' Waldo's great blue eyes opened wide; in wonder and amaze he looked all about him, though he knew well it was his father down-stairs. He did not once stir nor move from the place.[12]

This episode contrasts significantly with Emerson's account of his efforts to conceal himself from his own father when William sought to force him into the salt sea.

Weighing the impact of Waldo's death on Emerson, Snider suggested:

> In the loss of his boy Waldo the discipline of death struck him a more poignant blow than he had ever before experienced, more than even in the passing of his dearly loved wife and brothers. This child he deemed the heir of his Genius and greater — the very proof and presence of the divine descent into human being. Thus young Waldo may be called his father's transcendental son and gave to the latter a living evidence of the truth of his doctrine before his eyes. Moreover in this crushing stroke Emerson again was made to feel the transitoriness of personality which deep experience wrote itself into his conviction, whence it passed to his outer writing.[13]

Jonathan Bishop, weighing the tragedy in other terms, concludes that Emerson's first creative period coincided largely with the brief span of Waldo's lifetime (1836–1842) and suggests that Waldo's death ''seems to have been the end of something essential in Emerson.''[14]

In the fall of 1841 a daguerreotyper came to Concord. John Thoreau, Henry's brother, correctly surmising that Emerson would prize a likeness of Waldo, took him for a sitting. His thoughtfulness was something Emerson never forgot. The resulting daguerreotype shows a well-favored boy, with the pensive, appraising eyes of his father, and a set to his mouth that suggests both sensitivity and resoluteness. He

appears to be the remarkable boy Emerson described in his journal on
the day of his funeral:

> This boy, in whose remembrance I have both slept & awaked so
> oft, decorated for me the morning star, & the evening cloud . . .
> touched with his lively curiosity every trivial fact & circumstance
> in the household the hard coal & the soft coal which I put into
> my stove; the wood, of which he brought his little quota for
> grandmothers fire; the hammer, the pincers & file he was so eager
> to use; the microscope, the magnet, the little globe, & every trinket
> & instrument in the study . . . the nests in the henhouse and
> many & many a little visit to the doghouse and to the barn, — For
> every thing he had his own name & way of thinking, his own
> pronunciation & manner. And every word came mended from that
> tongue. A boy of early wisdom, of a grave & even majestic
> deportment, of a perfect gentleness.[15]

John Thoreau could not speak of Waldo's death because he died
suddenly himself, on 11 January. But Henry, who "had been one of
the family for the last year . . . and possessed his [Waldo's] love and
respect" felt the loss keenly. Barely recovered himself from grave illness, he wrote now to Lucy Brown: "As for Waldo, he died as the
mist rises from the brook, which the sun will soon dart his rays through.
Do not the flowers die every autumn? . . . it seemed the most natural
death that could happen. His fine organization demanded it, and nature gently yielded its request."[16]

In time Emerson came to agree with Thoreau. On 4 February he
wrote to Caroline Sturgis:

> The innocent and beautiful should not be sourly and gloomily
> lamented, but with music and fragrant thoughts and sportive
> recollections. Alas! I chiefly grieve that I cannot grieve. Dear boy,
> too precious and unique a creation to be huddled aside into the
> waste and prodigality of things; yet his image, so gentle, so rich in
> hopes, blends easily with every happy moment, every fair remem-
> brance, every cherished friendship, of my life.[17]

"Emerson," Cabot said, "gave much more of his time and thought
to his children, from their infancy, than was usual with busy fathers
in New England forty years ago, or is, perhaps, now." He drew Waldo
readily into things. The day before he was stricken, Emerson had taken
him to the new church. The sudden reversal of events was overwhelming: "On Sunday," he wrote, "I carried him to see the new
church & organ. & on Sunday we shall lay his sweet body in the ground."
For the moment his philosophy failed him: "Sorrow makes us all chil-

dren again, — destroys all differences of intellect. The wisest knows nothing."[18]

Three days after Waldo's funeral Emerson had written to Margaret:

We are finding again our hands & feet after our dull & dreadful dream which does *not* leave us where it found us. Lidian, Elizabeth, & I recite chronicles words & tones of our fair boy & magnify our lost treasure to extort if we can the secretest wormwood of the grief, & see how bad is the worst. Meantime the sun rises & the winds blow Nature seems to have forgotten that she has crushed her sweetest creation and perhaps would admonish us that as this Child's attention could never be fastened on any death, but proceeded still to enliven the new toy, so we children must have no retrospect, but illuminate the new hour if possible with an undiminished stream of rays.[19]

On 20 March Emerson seemed to be groping toward, if not acquiescence, then, at least, a realization that other interests must take over his thoughts:

The chrysalis which he brought in with care & tenderness & gave to his Mother to keep is still alive, and he most beautiful of the children of men is not here. I comprehend nothing of this fact but its bitterness. Explanation I have none, consolation none that rises out of the fact itself; only diversion; only oblivion of this & pursuit of new objects.[20]

A month and a day passed before Emerson could write to Carlyle. Evidence of a concern with his grief that made him insensitive to the feelings of others is apparent in the harsh opening phrase with which he excluded the childless Carlyle from comprehending the sorrow of a bereaved parent: "You can never sympathize with me; you can never know how much of me such a young child can take away."[21]

We know what Emerson thought he had lost in the death of Waldo. That his loss and the world's loss were the same is less sure. It is doubtful that Waldo would have outshone his father. It is not even likely that he was in any recognizable sense "the heir of his Genius." Waldo took life literally. When Emerson brought him to the circus, the boy watched the clown playing his pranks with the ringmaster with, one suspects, the same lowering look caught by the daguerreotyper, then tugged at his father's sleeve, saying, "Papa, the funny man makes me want to go home." "I and Waldo," Emerson noted, "were of one mind."[22]

His family zealously preserved anecdotes about Waldo. Taken in aggregate, they show him as all too human. Ellen "got pushed" because she stepped inside his sand castle. He lunged for her when she toppled his house of blocks. He had a ranting fit when some of his cutouts were by mischance destroyed. He decided that he did not want to accompany Mrs. Mumford, the housekeeper, to church because her face and arms were red and she ate at an unpainted table. When the threat of punishment loomed, he reconsidered. Told once that a spider found accidentally crushed by a closing door was probably "happy," with normal boyish exuberance he procured a beetle to dispatch in the same fashion. For parts of his toy house he came up with mystifying nomenclature — "the interspeglium," "the coridaga." These were, he explained, "names the children could not understand."

The night Waldo fell ill, he asked his mother to write to cousin Willie telling him not to send him any more presents, "unless he wanted to very much," since he had so many things already. Recalling the lessons in renunciation Ruth Emerson gave her own children, one finds it likely that Waldo was coached to decline Willie's toys. Only lately Emerson was disturbed to hear him wishing for "something to play with that no one ever had before." In fact, he took occasion to comment on it in a lecture he gave in the past month: "*Ennui* . . . shortens life, and bereaves the day of its light. Old age begins in the nursery, and before the young American is put into jacket and trowsers, he says, 'I want something which I never saw before' . . . What has checked in this age the animal spirits which gave to our forefathers their bounding pulse?"[23]

But Waldo had a sense of his own importance. Thoreau made him a wooden whistle. He was blowing it when there was a rattle of distant thunder. "My music makes the thunder dance," he disclosed with an assurance Dr. Ripley might have envied. Waldo also supposed that the bell he was making would wake up the world once it was rung. Waldo had imagination, but it was sobriety and certitude that made it memorable. He could hardly have avoided it. He was adored by everyone, and he knew it. His parents doted on him. His grandmother, who taught him reading and spelling, "loved him dearly." Thoreau turned out all sorts of toys for him. Margaret and Caroline, when they came, showered him with caresses. When Aunt Lizzy (Elizabeth Hoar) came, he dropped everything — "playmates, playthings, and all" — to run to her.

Waldo was not spoiled. There was too strong a tradition of discipline in the Emerson family for that to have happened. But he knew he was cherished and had a strong sense of privilege. It may be recalled that when he was born, Elizabeth petitioned to have him named Charles.[24] The name would have suited him. Charles Emerson approached life with sobriety, earnestness, and intensity. In young manhood Emerson had deplored what he saw in himself as a bent toward "silliness." There was nothing of that in Charles, nor in Waldo either.

To lose Waldo at five was a heartbreaking ordeal for Emerson. But given Waldo's temperament, he would not have been for Emerson later the companion he had hoped for.[25] His sober virtues were of the kind that produce efficient citizens like his uncles, not free spirits like his father. Had he survived to maturity, Emerson might have found him a stranger to much that he held dear.

The same day Waldo fell ill, Emerson had written to William that he was soon to undertake a new course of lectures, in Providence, "so far will the love of *paying debts* draw me."[26] This obligation he conscientiously met, masking his feelings to deliver five lectures between 10 and 17 February. From Providence, however, after delivering the first of these lectures, he wrote to Lidian that his audience had been small and that "If it do not grow larger, I shall have to go to New York, I think, to make another adventure to retrieve my losses." He noted, also, that he was due to make "report of my success" to Alcott the Saturday following. The fact is, he was putting himself through this ordeal to raise money for his "Alcott-Voyage-fund." His heart was not in lecturing just now, but what he could not do for himself he could do for his friend. He therefore next undertook, without inducement from any quarter, to try his fortune as a lecturer in New York City, asking William to book him in some hall there for six lectures on "The Times," to be given over a two-week period. The undertaking succeeded. The series netted him close to two hundred dollars. He gave Alcott three hundred and seventy-five dollars. Fifty of it he cadged from friends; the rest of it came from his own pocket. On 8 May the dreamy philosopher sailed to England.[27]

In what Emerson may not have recognized as a vindication of his theory of compensation, the New York venture set in motion circumstances that gradually gave new purpose to his life. He saw that the success he had enjoyed when he went by invitation to lecture in New York in 1840 was something he could build upon. Furthermore, on this visit he was discovered by Henry James, who immediately extended to him the umbrella of his friendship and hospitality. With this powerful advocate acclaiming his merits he was assured, henceforth, both recognition and respect in New York. Nor was James the only new friend he found on this visit. He met for the first time Horace Greeley and Albert Brisbane. Greeley would emerge as an important ally. If Brisbane was unable to recruit him into the ranks of the Fourier Socialists, Emerson could at least understand better George Ripley's later infatuation with that movement.

The Providence lecture series likewise brought Emerson a new, supportive friend, Charles King Newcomb, subsequently a Brook Farmer

and already a protégé of Margaret Fuller's. Variously described as a
sentimental mystic and unattached Catholic, Newcomb seemed to
Emerson an important new find. In February, when he was in Providence, and afterward, in March, he was made acquainted with Newcomb's romantic tale "The Two Dolons." During the spring Newcomb
recast this tale to make little Waldo a pattern for his hero. To this
end, Lidian, at Emerson's urging, sent Newcomb letters in May in
which she set down some of her own thoughts about Waldo. The manuscript, sent from Brook Farm, reached Emerson early in June. Lidian was delighted with it. "My wife," Emerson wrote Newcomb, "was
made happy by finding so friendly and eager an ear for her anecdotes
of her sweet Boy." Emerson thought it must go at once into *The Dial*
and urged Newcomb to come stay with them at Bush while he worked
on the conclusion of the tale. To Margaret, Emerson insisted that some
sentences in "The Two Dolons" were so admirable that they were
"worth the printing of *The Dial* that they may go forth." Grief, of
course, marred his judgment. Newcomb's tale is all but unreadable.[28]

However mediocre his writing talents, Newcomb served a useful
function in bringing Emerson to a sense of acceptance of his loss. On
16 June 1842 Emerson wrote in his journal:

> Newcomb took us all captive. . . . Charles is a Religious Intel-
> lect. Let it be his praise that when I carted his MS story to the
> woods, & read it in the armchair of the upturned root of a pinetree
> I felt for the first time since Waldo's death some efficient faith
> again in the repairs of the Universe, some independency of natural
> relations whilst spiritual affinities can be so perfect and compen-
> sating.

Of Newcomb Emerson said, in high tribute: "In the total solitude of
the critic, the Patmos of thought from which he writes in total uncon-
sciousness of any eyes that shall ever read this writing, he reminds me
of Aunt Mary." Select company, indeed, for young Newcomb.[29]

"The Two Dolons" was published, in part, in *The Dial* for July
1842. There was no second part. Newcomb never got back to it. The
passage thought to apply best to Waldo begins:

> He was a beautiful boy, with long, auburn-brown hair, a fair
> and delicate complexion, light blue eyes, and eyelids which at the
> side-view lay gently-heavily folded over his eyes, as if the eyes
> were homes, like heaven air, for two little heavenly fairies, like a
> spring-fountain in the fresh meadows for little fishes, and the lids
> were curtains which opened them to the world and covered them
> from mortal sight, like a cave opening into a forest.[30]

Even allowing for the predisposing environment he was in when he read it, that Emerson would find such a passage solacing is instructive.

Carlyle, striving manfully to acknowledge Emerson's loss, had retreated into almost conventional words of Christian consolation:

> There is nothing to be said, — nothing but what the wild son of Ishmael, and every thinking heart, from of old have learned to say: God is great! He is terrible and stern; but we know also He is good. 'Though He slay me, yet will I trust in Him.' Your bright little Boy, chief of your possessions here below, is rapt away from you; but of very truth HE is with God, even as we that yet live are, — and surely in the way that was BEST for him, and for you, and for all of us. Poor Lidian Emerson. . . . May good Influences watch over her, bring her some assuagement. As the Hebrew David said, 'We shall go to him, he will not return to us.'[31]

At this tragic time, Carlyle had reverted, almost instinctively, to the comfortable formulas of a theology he had elsewhere rejected. If Emerson chose to linger over Newcomb's mawkish transcendental effusions sooner than Carlyle's old-line Covenanter sentiments, at least he was showing consistency.

Two years after Waldo's death, Emerson still had not found the efficient faith he longed for. To Margaret, on 30 January 1844, he wrote:

> When, last Saturday night, Lidian said, "It is two years today," I only heard the bell-stroke again. I have had no experience, no progress, to put me into better intelligence with my calamity than when it was new. . . . But the inarticulateness of the Supreme Power how can we insatiate hearers, perceivers, and thinkers ever reconcile ourselves unto? It deals all too lightly with us low-leveled and weaponed men. Does the Power labor as men do with the impossibility of perfect application, that always the hurt is of one kind and the compensation of another? My divine temple, which all angels seemed to love to build, and which was shattered in a night, I can never rebuild. . . . Yet the nature of all things, against all appearances and specialities whatever, assures us of eternal benefit. But these affirmations are tacit and secular; if spoken they have a hollow and canting sound. And thus all our being, dear friend, is evermore adjourned.[32]

For one final time Emerson gave way to that distraught state which he signified unwittingly with reiterative phrases — "Patience, and patience, and patience!" He closed with a promise to copy out for Mar-

garet his "rude dirges to my darling," these being the long poem
"Threnody," in the opinion of Holmes, "a lament not unworthy of
comparison with 'Lycidas' for dignity."[33]

Alfred Noyes has called "Threnody," the poem in which Emerson
allowed his readers a unique glimpse of his intimate feelings, "perhaps the most beautiful and profound poem in American literature, a
poem whose music is wrought to the heights of prophetic inspiration."
Here, in Noyes's estimate, Emerson had come to true renown: "if he
had written nothing else, it would eventually confirm his right to a
place among master-singers. It is cosmic in its range, human in its
grief, and divine in its hope."[34] In "Threnody" Emerson assures Waldo
a place of permanency in the annals of mankind that a lifetime of
virtue and service might not have secured him. And in doing this
Emerson universalized his own sorrow so ably that "Threnody" may
be accounted, of all his achievements, the one that most surely perpet-
uates a sense of its author's worth.

To Aunt Mary, Emerson wrote, only hours after Waldo's death:
"My darling & the world's wonderful child, for never in my own or
another family have I seen any thing comparable, has fled out of my
arms like a dream. He adorned the world for me like a morning star,
and every particular of my daily life. I slept in his neighborhood &
woke to remember him."[35]

The first one hundred and seventy-five lines of "Threnody" were
written in 1842 — a record of Emerson's love for this "wonderful
child," and of his grief and his inability to understand why such a
tragedy had to befall him.[36] Here we are allowed to approach Emerson
in the act of creation in a way not vouchsafed us at any other time.
He had gone before to journal entries and to letters for phrases and
ideas that he then reshaped for passages in essays and poems, but it
seemed that these materials had always been meant for that use. His
journal, he had said, was his Savings Bank. The 1842 segment of
"Threnody" glitters with phrases, themes, and perceptions culled from
his immediate reactions to his loss as he struggled to articulate them,
first as the sun rose on a new day and, again, two days later, when he
returned home from the Hillside Burying Ground. There the small
coffin had been placed with Ezra Ripley's in the vault to which those
who loved him would lift their eyes in sorrow and affection as they
came and went from the Milldam. These thoughts, these phrases, were
not laid by as salvageable insights meant to be utilized to good advantage at some later date. Possibly, without recognizing his intent, he
benefited from a habit so long-standing it had become a natural reflex.
He may have felt compelled to record those moments of intimate perception as a way of keeping inviolate the memory of his grief. More
likely, we have here an illustration of Emerson's spontaneous feelings,

long encouraged to assert themselves unencumbered by affectation or labored logic. Nowhere did he better disclose his responsiveness, under stress, to the promptings of Nature. Again and again he was to achieve pure pitch, sounding a note so indisputably right that he attains a Shakespearean perfection in fusing thought and expression. Images of wind and fire, bud and bird, brook, star, snow house, kennel, tramper, crowing rooster, dawn, and a world dishonored are scattered like fiery gems through those first letters and first journal entries, destined to be brought together in an authentic expression of grief that becomes not poetry ingeniously contrived but the statement of a mind responding with limpid validity to the dictates of a sincerely experienced emotion.

One hundred and fourteen lines make up the concluding meditation of "Threnody." In this second movement the poet reports a measure of reconciliation to his loss and reveals both a sweetness and tenderness of nature that transcend the petulance of grief. "The mysteries of Nature's heart" have triumphed over "the blasphemy of grief." The poet believes no muse adequate to the task of articulating those mysteries. Nonetheless, they have borne away the encompassing shadows. Emerson seems almost to open the Madonna's embrace to Waldo when he expresses the hope "That thou might'st cherish for thine own / the riches of sweet Mary's Son, / Boy-Rabbi, Israel's paragon." For that moment Emerson consigns Waldo to a Christian heaven. And in the last meditation he attains to a Miltonic serenity and reconciled acceptance. "My servant Death," he acknowledges, "with solving rite, / Pours finite into infinite."

Emerson believed that man, in his quest for the ideal, comes to the highest state of spiritual awareness when he sees and knows nothing save God as the essence interpenetrating all matter. In "Experience" he discloses that an approach to this state had helped to reconcile him to Waldo's death. "Grief too will make us idealists," he said, even if such knowledge comes to us "with the costly price of sons and lovers." Here he says, too: "In the death of my son, now more than two years ago, I seem to have lost a beautiful estate, — no more. I cannot get it nearer to me. . . . it does not touch me; something which I fancied was part of me, which could not be torn away without tearing me nor enlarged without enriching me, falls off from me and leaves no scar."[37]

The wound appeared closed, but the beautiful estate Emerson had lost was Paradise and he could no more stifle remembrance of it than mankind can expunge its collective Edenic longings.

Fifteen years after Waldo's death, Sleepy Hollow Cemetery was consecrated, and Emerson, having bought a lot on what was to become known as Authors' Ridge, made arrangements to have his mother's coffin and Waldo's coffin removed from Dr. Ripley's tomb and reburied on the ridge. The season was summer, the time early July, with a bright sun moving up the sky in mid-morning. At Sleepy Hollow the ground had been prepared and slabs of granite placed in readiness to cover the two coffins. Then, boldly, Emerson asked the undertaker to open Waldo's coffin so that, this one last time, he could look upon his "hyacinthine boy." Had Waldo lived he would now have been twenty. The pathetic dust Emerson looked at in this one final effort to rout death can have conveyed to him no real sense either of the impermanence of death or the finality of life. When the coffin was closed again, he picked from a neighboring white oak tree a handful of leaves and, after the burden was lowered into the grave, strewed them on the lid.

In February 1870 William Furness, who had lately buried a son of glowing promise, had come to Boston but Emerson failed to see him. Emerson wrote to Sam Bradford on 4 February: "William Furness when he was here never showed me his face though I pursued him in Cambridge & Boston for two days in vain. He had his grandchild with him . . . & the poor little boy must suddenly be carried home to die. I almost fear to see him after such griefs as he has had."[38] A sense of his own anguish of long ago enabled Emerson to understand all too well Furness's heartbreak now.

Emerson, believing the world was in a state of constant flux, affirmed in *Nature:* "Nature is not fixed but fluid. Spirit alters, moulds, makes it. The immobility or bruteness of nature is the absence of spirit; to pure spirit it is fluid, it is volatile, it is obedient."[39] The idea of permanent flux was introduced by Heraclitus, adopted by Plato, and transmitted to the Neoplatonists, whence came Emerson's first exposure to it.

Emerson introduced flux into his theory of nature much as the earlier philosophers introduced it into theirs. For him, this flux was meaningful. In consonance with Plotinus's doctrine of emanation, flux in the material world became an emanation from the Divine One. He elaborated: "Every natural fact is an emanation, and that from which it emanates is an emanation also, from every emanation is a new emanation. If anything could stand still, it would be crushed and dissipated by the torrent it resisted, and if it were a mind, would be crazed." Consequently Emerson urged that man move with the flow of life: "We see the foaming brook with compunction: if our own life flowed with the right energy, we should shame the brook."[40]

Yet Emerson also modified the traditional theory of flux. He saw flux as a river flowing in an upward spiral. Vivian Hopkins says that for Emerson "spirit is energy projected from intellect, constantly flowing through matter and rendering it more alive; and implicit in this Plotinian idea of 'the flowing' is the concept of upward ascention."[41] Despite this upward sweep, however, in the notion of flux there is implicit a pessimistic view of the physical world that may or may not be within man's experience at a given time. Flux, thus defined, is believed by some critics to have eroded Emerson's confidence in compensation, and swept him into the currents of skepticism as he entered middle life. Waldo's death, it is suggested, provided the wedge of doubt that gave such speculations substance in his mind. Yet, if this were so, then "Threnody" never was.

43. Henry James
An Independent Right Minded Man

*T*HE correspondence between Emerson and Henry James, which began in 1842, continued for thirty years. Nothing, therefore, could have been more natural than Elliot Cabot's application to James, when he began work on Emerson's biography, for permission to read those of James's letters found among Emerson's papers. And nothing could have been more unexpected than James's reply. "Emerson," he said, "always kept one at such arm's length, tasting him and sipping him and trying him, to make sure he was worthy of his somewhat prim and bloodless friendship, that it was fatiguing to write him letters." James had always been disappointed in the "maidenly" letters he got from Emerson and doubted that he had ever sent him a serious letter in return. James had high expectations at the start of their friendship. In these he had been mistaken. "It is painful," he concluded, "to recollect now the silly hope that I had, along the early days of our acquaintance, that if I went on listening something would be sure to drop from him that would show me an infallible way out of this perplexed world. For nothing ever came but epigrams; sometimes clever, sometimes not."[1]

Cabot declined to accept this letter as written. James survived Emerson only by a few months and Cabot surmised that he was out of sorts when he made such declarations. But Cabot misjudged James. From the first days of their friendship James genuinely loved Emerson, but as a man, not a thinker. Emerson's scorn for analytical reasoning was alone an impassable gulf between them. James wanted Emerson to account for his views. Emerson would own he was "awed and distanced'' by James's argumentative ways. The fact is, James had come to Emerson as a theologian seeking discourse with another theologian only to find that Emerson had little experience of theology as James understood it. To Emerson the stringency of James's views harkened back to an earlier age. Eventually he told James: ''I find or fancy . . . that you have not shed your last coat of Presbyterianism, but that a certain catechetical and legendary Jove glares at me sometimes in your pages, which astonishes me in so sincere and successful a realist.''[2] Not until a paper on Emerson that James had written in 1881 was published, however, did it become clear that James's letter to Cabot was not the crotchety reply of a man whom failing health had alienated, but, rather, James's considered estimate of his friendship with Emerson. James's endorsement of Emerson was, almost from its inception, on the terms he stated after Emerson's death.

The friendship had begun on 3 March 1842. That evening, in New York City, Emerson had lectured on ''The Times.'' James was in the audience, and so enraptured with what he heard that he sought his writing desk immediately on his return home, and wrote Emerson a note that would have turned the head of a reigning diva:

> I listened to your address this evening, and as my bosom glowed
> with many a true word that fell from your lips I felt erelong
> fully assured that before me I beheld a man who in very truth was
> seeking the realities of things. I said to myself, I will try when I
> go home how far this man follows reality — how far he loves truth
> and goodness. For I will write to him that I, too, in my small
> degree am coveting to understand the truth which surrounds me
> and embraces me. . . . I will further tell him that to talk famil-
> iarly with one who earnestly follows truth . . . has never been my
> lot for one half-hour even; and that he, therefore, if he be now the
> generous lover of truth and of her friends which he seems to be,
> may give me this untasted pleasure, and let me once feel the
> cordial grasp of a fellow pilgrim and remember for long days the
> cheering Godspeed and the ringing laugh with which he bounded
> on from my sight at parting.[3]

James fell victim to the usual misconceptions that attend infatuations. The Emerson he was addressing did not, in some particulars, resemble Emerson as he actually was. James supposed Emerson to be, like himself, a disputatious theologian who would defend, with relentless logic, his intuitions. For men so motivated a bounding step and ringing laugh might be wholly suitable. Nothing could have become Emerson less.

Even in this state of delirious supposition, however, James's common sense took hold long enough for him to establish that he was attracted to Emerson not because of his ideas, but rather because Emerson hewed to the truth as he understood it. "I will tell him," James said, ". . . that I chiefly value that erect attitude of mind about him which in God's universe undauntedly seeks the worthiest tidings of God, and calmly defies every mumbling phantom which would herein challenge its freedom."[4] Not even in his state of high elation, then, did the youthful James (he was then just short of thirty-one) momentarily surmise that he could look to Emerson for complete enlightenment. At the most he hoped to join forces with a fellow seeker of the truth.

Although James included in his letter an invitation to Emerson to visit him at his convenience at Washington Place, Emerson was committed to give five more lectures over the next eleven days and James, taking that into account, evidently sought him out, for on 5 March Emerson told Lidian he had received a long visit from James, "a very manlike thorough seeing person."[5] Since James came to each of his lectures, their acquaintance thereafter grew rapidly. To Margaret, on 10 March, Emerson could report that James was "a very intelligent person . . . an independent right minded man," and, moreover, brother-in-law to Anna Barker Ward's brother, a fact that drew him to the fringes, at least, of their intimate circle.[6] When Emerson did visit the Jameses at Washington Place, so tradition went in the James family, he climbed the stairs to the nursery to give his blessing to the newborn William.

James, however, hoped to have something from Emerson that was not Emerson's to give. Before the year was out we find him writing to "the Invisible Emerson, the Emerson that thinks and feels and lives . . . and not to the Emerson that talks and bewitches one out of his serious thought when one talks to him, by the beautiful serenity of his behavior." He went on to complain:

Whenever I am with you I get no help from you. . . . I am led . . . to get hold of some central *facts* which may make all other facts properly circumferential, and *orderly* so — and you continually dishearten me by your apparent indifference to such law and central facts: by the dishonor you seem to cast upon our intelligence, as if it stood much in our way.[7]

James later would describe Emerson's mind as "feminine" because Emerson relied so exclusively on intuitive knowledge. He saw in Emerson a childlike innocence. William Stafford says: "Emerson, James is convinced, never had the impulse to break any of the ten commandments. He could not, *ergo*, have had a conviction of personal sin. James had such a sense, and, upon meeting Emerson, was at once overjoyed at meeting so much innocence and goodness, hoping therefrom to discover how one 'got that way.' "[8]

By late 1843, James would good-naturedly rebuke Emerson for his failure either to explain or defend his views. "Oh you man without a handle!" said James. "Shall one never be able to help himself out of you, according to his needs, and be dependent only upon your fitful tippings-up?" Emerson apparently thoroughly enjoyed this tweaking and, when James set out for Europe with his family on 19 October 1843, Emerson prepared his way with an enthusiastic letter of introduction to Carlyle. It served its purpose well, for Carlyle wrote Emerson on 17 November: "James is a very good fellow, better and better as we see him more. Something shy and skittish in the man; but a brave heart intrinsically, with sound earnest sense, with plenty of insight and even humor. He confirms an observation of mine . . . that a stammering man is never a worthless one."[9]

Prior to this, Emerson effected a meeting of James with Thoreau in June 1843, during Thoreau's Staten Island stay. The two men at first liked one another. "He is a man," Thoreau wrote Emerson on 8 June, "and takes his own way, or stands still in his own place. I know of no one so patient and determined to have the good of you. It is almost friendship, such plain and human dealing." On that first visit they had three hours of "solid talk" and James offered Thoreau the freedom of his house. The attachment did not last, James presently concluding that Thoreau "was literally the most childlike, unconscious and unblushing egotist it has ever been my fortune to encounter in the ranks of manhood." Eight years older than James, Emerson had let the age gap make no difference in their relationship. Six years older than Thoreau, James made of that gap an unbridgeable chasm.[10]

When the Jameses reestablished themselves in New York in 1847, Emerson's visits resumed. Young Henry, in the next century, would recall that their sole guest room always was respectfully referred to as "Mr. Emerson's room," and, for his readers, materialized an episode from this period of his life:

I "visualize" at any rate the winter of our back parlor at dusk and the great Emerson — I knew he was great, greater than any of our friends — sitting in it between my parents, before the lamps had been lighted, as a visitor consentingly housed only could have done, and affecting me the more as an apparition seriously and, I held, elegantly slim, benevolently aquiline, and commanding a tone alien, beautifully alien, to any we had round-about, that he bent this benignity upon me by an invitation to draw nearer to him, off the hearth rug, and know myself as never yet, as I was not indeed to know myself for years, in touch with the wonder of Boston.[11]

Emerson seems to have benefited from these visits as well. After stopping over with James in New York, he wrote in his journal on 6 April 1850: "Henry James was true comfort, — wise, gentle, polished, with heroic manners, and a serenity like the sun." In November of 1851, he wrote: "He is the best man and companion in the world." In the meantime, James had found a new foundation on which to rest their friendship. Writing to Emerson in the summer of 1849, he had said: "I never read you as an author at all. Your books are not literature but life, and criticism always strikes me, therefore, as infinitely laughable when applied to you." Thus James conferred on Emerson as a thinker a kind of diplomatic immunity.[12]

In this same period James's zeal for social reform was growing and he found himself impatient with Emerson because Emerson had no confidence in the process of "hurrying up the cakes." Yet, as always, he admired Emerson's personal graces, saluting him as "the best and most memorable" of men and insisting "your life is a very real divine performance."[13]

In December 1858 James came to Bush, as Emerson's guest, to sit in on one of Alcott's "Conversations." Not divining that an Alcott "Conversation" was, in fact, a monologue, James began to interrogate Alcott, supposing that he, at least, could be made to defend his intuitions with logic. Alcott fell silent and the dialogue now became a Jamesian monologue, but only until he berated self-conscious ethics (to which he assigned the label "Morality") as pernicious. Thereupon Mary Moody Emerson, at eighty-four at last again under Emerson's roof, supposing that James had assailed the moral law, sprang from her chair and ran at him like a terrier to shake him by the shoulders even as she vigorously denounced his views. It may be that his shoulders shook merely with laughter, for even Thoreau, who was present, commended his good temper. James grinned as he assured Aunt Mary that he esteemed the moral law not a whit less than she did. Possibly as a carry-over from this incident, Emerson responded mischievously, at a later date, when George Bradford told him that James's daughter, Alice, had "a highly moral nature" — "How in the world does her father get on with her?"[14]

James was in Paris when, in 1856, he first read *English Traits*. He disliked it but only because he thought Emerson's "own stand-point is too high to do justice to the English," whom he looked upon as "an intensely vulgar race." He had not forgotten that his own antecedents were Irish. James's assessment of *English Traits* did not diminish by an iota his affection for Emerson. In the late summer of 1859, smitten with grief at the consequent separation, he brought his two youngest sons, Wilky and Bob, to Concord to be educated at the school that Franklin Sanborn had started there a few years earlier under Emerson's sponsorship. We may put it down to Jamesian excess, however, that he claimed to have found on his arrival at Bush, "the Concord Pan himself in the midst of his household, breezy with hospitality and blowing exhilarating trumpets of welcome." Such antics were beyond Emerson's social range.[15]

In 1868, when James, then living in Cambridge, was about to set out for a visit to Bush, he wrote to his son William, then in Germany :

> Emerson's unreality to me grows evermore. You have got to deal with him as with a child, making all manner of allowances for his ignorance of everything above the senses, and putting such a restraint upon your intellect as tires you to death. . . . He has no sympathy with nature, but is a sort of a police-spy upon it, chasing it into hiding-places, and noting its subtlest features, for the purpose of reporting them to the public ; that's all. He is an uncommonly sharp detective, but a detective he is and nothing more. He never for a moment drops his office, loses sight of himself, and becomes drowned in the beautiful illusion, but is sure always to appear as a fisherman with his fish upon his hook. The proof of all this is that he breeds no love of nature in his intellectual offspring, but only the love of imitating him and saying similar cute things about nature and man. I love the man very much, he is such a born natural ; but his books to me are wholly destitute of spiritual flavor, being at most carbonic acid gas and water. . . .[16]

The new note here is that James has come to conclude that Emerson's rapport with Nature, notwithstanding his determination to live in the senses, was superficial. James perhaps was spurred to these reflections because he was then compiling some reflections on Emerson, which in due course he asked leave to read to the Emersons — without Emerson himself being present! He shared these observations, about 1872, with a few other intimate audiences, but they stayed otherwise unpublished among his papers until William James released them to *The Atlantic Monthly* in 1904. Here, as was to be expected, his amiable feelings toward Emerson as a person, not as a man of ideas, predominate.

> I shall have ill succeeded in my task if I fail to convince you that Mr. Emerson's authority to the imagination consists, not in his ideas, not in his intellect, not in his culture, not in his science, but all simply in himself, in the form of his natural personality. There are scores of men of more advanced ideas than Mr. Emerson, of subtler apprehension, of broader knowledge, of deeper

culture; but I know of none who is half so interesting in himself,
none whose nature exhibits half so clear and sheer a reconciliation
of infinite and finite.[17]

Yet in 1869, on 5 March, Annie Fields reported in her diary: "Henry
James came . . . and had gone so far as to abuse Emerson pretty well
when the latter came in. 'How do you do, Emer-son,' he said, with his
peculiar intonation and voice, as if he had expected him on the heels
of what had gone before." In this same period we find James writing
to Annie to decline an invitation to hear Emerson lecture, and asking
with that facetiousness which always seemed to imply less than it said:

> Who *did* contrive the comical title for his lecture — 'Philosophy
> of the People'? I suspect it was a joke of J[ames]. T. F[ields]. It
> would be no less absurd for Emerson himself to think of philoso-
> phizing than it would be for the rose to think of botanizing.
> Emerson is the Divinely pompous rose of the philosophic garden,
> gorgeous with colour and fragrance.[18]

To the rose, since it would not yield the nectar he sought, James brought,
together with his taste for nectar, his sting as well.

In his piece on Emerson, prepared soon after Emerson's death and
published in 1885, allowing always for those high spirits which his own
waning health could not stifle, James took in the whole of their friendship in a panoramic sweep that encompassed thirty years.[19] After 1872
nothing passed between them. Emerson's declining health could account for that, but, above and beyond, their need to communicate with
each other had ceased. Here we have, fully extruded, the points succinctly advanced in James's letter to Cabot and variously touched upon
all the way back to the first letter sent in March 1842. James romps
through the relationship and somehow, as always, manages to suggest
that while sounding Emerson has been like thumping a hollow tub
which gave back only the echoes of his own efforts, his affection for
the man was in no way lessened.

"Good heavens!" he said, touching on the early stages of their
friendship,

> how soothed and comforted I was by the innocent lovely look of
> my new acquaintance, by his tender courtesy, his generous lauda-
> tory appreciation of my crude literary ventures! and how I used
> to lock myself up with him in his bed-room, swearing that before
> the door was opened I would arrive at the secret of his immense
> superiority to the common herd of literary men! I might just
> as well have locked myself up with a handful of diamonds, so far

as any capacity of self-cognizance existed in him. I found in
fact, before I had been with him a week, that the immense superiority I ascribed to him was altogether personal or practical — by
no means intellectual. . . .

James next made it appear that he had been taken in by Emerson :

At first I was greatly disappointed in him, because his intellect
never kept the promise which his lovely face and manners held out
to me. He was to my senses a literal divine presence in the house
with me ; and we cannot recognize literal divine presences in
our houses without feeling sure that they will be able to say
something of critical importance to one's intellect. It turned out
that any average old dame in a horse-car would have satisfied my
intellectual rapacity just as well as Emerson. . . . Though his
immense personal fascination always kept up, he at once lost all
intellectual prestige to my regard. I even thought that I had never
seen a man more profoundly devoid of spiritual understanding.

This charge he clarified at once : "This prejudice grew, of course, out
of my having inherited an altogether narrow ecclesiastical notion of
what spiritual understanding was." He persisted : "I could make neither head nor tail of him according to men's ordinary standards — the
only thing that I was sure of being that he, like Christ, was somehow
divinely begotten." With that magnanimous phrase, James obliterated
all the strictures he had leveled against Emerson to that point. But he
at once resumed his attack. Emerson was "fundamentally treacherous
to civilization. . . . He had no conscience . . . and lived by perception.
. . . In his talk or private capacity he was one of the least remunera-
tive men . . . absolutely destitute of reflective power."

Now James again altered direction. Emerson was "a show-figure of
almighty power in our nature . . . he was destitute of all the apparatus of humbuggery . . . he unconsciously brought you face to face
with the infinite in humanity." In thus describing the basis on which
he came to terms with Emerson, James pointed the way for posterity
to follow. The inspiration Emerson offered would ultimately be found
not in his ideas but in the "transparent absence of selfhood" manifested in his unblemished innocence.

44. Hawthorne and Hosmer
A Walk to Walden

*T*HE day was Sunday, 14 August 1842. Margaret Fuller was about to arrive for a visit with the Emersons that would stretch into forty days. Thoreau was already living under their roof and had been for most of the past sixteen months. Newly settled at the Old Manse were the Hawthornes, Nathaniel and Sophia, who had moved in directly after they were married, on 9 July. Over the weekend the Hawthornes were entertaining George Hillard and his wife, Susan. The night before, the clerical ghost that haunted the Manse had walked again. Sophia and Susan were thrown into a fright by it. Hillard was, too. But it came and went without Hawthorne noticing. He was on the sofa meditating at the time and refused to believe what the others told him. But ghosts that scribbled sermons at Nathaniel's study desk or ground coffee in the kitchen seemed to pose no great hazards and a night's sleep was sufficient to exorcise them or at least all major apprehensions concerning them.

For breakfast they had, with flapjacks, whortleberries from the neighboring hill and perch and bream from the neighboring river, both berries and fish procured through the industry of Hawthorne, who felt enough like Emerson's ''new born Adam'' (though he would have disavowed the comparison) to believe himself truly imparadised. About nine o'clock, before the heat of the day was up, with Hillard at his side, Hawthorne set out for Emerson's house, where he meant to inquire for directions to Walden Pond, which, thus far, he knew only by reputation. Since his arrival, Emerson had been looking in on him almost daily. Although Hawthorne always let Emerson do most of the talking, a situation Emerson did not relish, he had occasionally, as neighborliness required, visited the Emersons, but cutting cross-country, around Jones' Hill to do so, thus bypassing the town and the people in it. Neighborliness did not come easy to Hawthorne.

Hillard had been one of Charles Emerson's Harvard classmates and, afterward, Charles Sumner's law partner. He was now trying to recover for Hawthorne the $1,400 he had invested in Brook Farm. His office was a mecca for literary people, most of whom came by to see him, sooner or later, not for legal counsel but for friendship's sake. Much of Hillard's time went to writing memoirs and biographies of various notables who caught his interest, though his one sure contribution to literature would be the fund he collected several years later to free Hawthorne of financial worries while he was writing *The Scarlet Letter*. Hillard was frail and stooped and looked like Lincoln long before Lincoln was prominent enough for anyone to think of making the comparison. Emerson eventually would scorn Hillard because he upheld the Fugitive Slave Law, but that was a decade away and cast no shadow on this bright Sabbath morn.

When the strollers reached Emerson's house, he drew them inside. He insisted on escorting them to Walden himself but thought it best for appearance's sake to postpone their walk until the villagers bound for church had passed on their way. Hawthorne was incredulous. A man who scoffed at foolish consistencies should not accommodate so readily to the sensibilities of others. Emerson had from him no intimation of what he was thinking but later, in a journal entry, Hawthorne had a quiet laugh at this "scruple of his external conscience." That Emerson merely wished to avoid visiting discomfiture on others did not occur to him.

Arlin Turner has suggested that Hawthorne may have made this entry in his journal to tease Sophia, who thought of Emerson as the most perfect man in the world.[1] If so, Hawthorne saw some advantage in keeping the joke going, for on 22 August, writing in the journal about a surprise encounter with Emerson in Sleepy Hollow the previous afternoon, he noted that Emerson, "in spite of his clerical consecration, had found no better way to spend the Sabbath than to ramble among the woods."[2]

Once the coast was clear, the three men set out for Walden. Emerson took them there by way of Edmund Hosmer's farm, half a mile east of Bush and an equal distance from the pond, on Sandy Pond Road.[3] Not by chance did he lead his companions aside to visit Hosmer. Hosmer had also been part of the tour when he brought Jones Very to Walden on 9 April 1840.

To Emerson, Hosmer was a rare find. Although he was less than five years Emerson's senior, Edward Emerson identified him as "the oracle'' his father ''constantly consulted.''[4] Brook Farm was but one of many topics they had considered together. In ''Agriculture of Massachusetts,'' which he had just published in the July 1842 issue of *The Dial*, Emerson, taking on the ways of Hesiod, had described Hosmer sympathetically and offered readers his commonsense views about farming — in this instance basically an expansion of notations made concerning a visit to Hosmer's on the afternoon of 22 April 1842.

> This man always impresses me with respect, he is so manly, so
> sweet-tempered, so faithful, so disdainful of all appearances,
> excellent and reverable in his old weather-worn cap and blue frock
> bedaubed with the soil of the field, so honest withal, that he
> always needs to be watched lest he should cheat himself. . . . Toil
> has not broken his spirit.[5]

Hosmer, in Emerson's eyes, was a fine specimen of unspoiled nature deserving to be exhibited quite as much as the fine pond they were going to. ''He is a man of a strongly intellectual taste,'' boasted Emerson, ''of much reading, and of an erect good sense and independent spirit which can neither brook usurpation nor falsehood in any shape.'' While one of Hosmer's three sons drove the oxen, Hosmer had held the plow, and Emerson had walked up and down the field with him, talking as the farmer sank his furrow. Even as this happened, Hosmer's keen mind cleaved a clear path through the problems of the day. ''I believe,'' Emerson allowed, ''that my friend is a little stiff and inconvertible in his own opinions, and that there is another side to be heard; but so much wisdom seemed to lie under all his statement, that it deserved a record.'' And Edward Emerson said: ''Mr. Hosmer was a farmer of the old New England type, versed in agriculture and domestic economics . . . and the ally called in by Emerson in dealing with the interesting but to him puzzling management of his increasing acres.''[6]

When George and Burrill Curtis forsook Brook Farm in 1844 and, lured by the attraction of Emerson, came to Concord to live, it was Hosmer, at Emerson's behest, who took them into his own home and, in exchange for a few hours' labor each day, enabled them to bask under Emerson's influence, which included sitting in on the philosophical conversations held at Emerson's house on Monday nights.

While living with Hosmer, in May 1845 George and Burrill earned a niche in literary annals when they accompanied Hosmer and his sons to Walden Pond, where they helped Thoreau frame up and raise the roof of his historic hut. During the previous autumn and winter, until, in January 1845, he successfully negotiated the purchase of a house (later Hawthorne's Wayside) for them, Hosmer had opened his home to the Alcott family, again on an appeal from Emerson, after the collapse of the Fruitlands fantasy.

The "spicy farming sage," who conducted his own affairs with such unerring common sense, must at times have felt he was presiding over a combination haven and counseling service for would-be and has-been utopians. He had shielded Emerson, but the most he could do for Emerson's friends, the Curtis brothers and the Alcotts, was to help set them on their feet again after they tripped and sprawled. Hosmer must have found Thoreau's self-sufficiency a welcome alternative. In *Walden* Thoreau said: "On a Sunday afternoon, if I chanced to be at home, I heard the cronching of the snow made by the step of a long-headed farmer, who from far through the woods sought my house, to have a social 'crack'; one of the few of his vocation who are 'men on their farms.' " The visitor was Hosmer, glad, obviously, that one utopia had been founded at his doorstep so that he could offer its sole occupant on-the-spot counseling while the experiment was in progress rather than having to pick up the pieces after the damage was done. In his journal Thoreau wrote: "Human life may be transitory and full of trouble, but the perennial mind whose survey extends from that spring to this, from Columella to Hosmer, is superior to change."[7] Beyond question Thoreau shared Emerson's high opinion of Hosmer, notwithstanding an awareness of the limitations of Hosmer's mind. Once when a group of friends, Hosmer included, gathered at Bush for philosophical discussion, Emerson wrote in his journal the next day, 11 February 1838, "At the 'teacher's meeting' last night my good Edmund after disclaiming any wish to difference Jesus from a human mind suddenly seemed to alter his tone & said Jesus made the world & was the Eternal God. Henry Thoreau merely remarked that 'Mr Hosmer had kicked the pail over.' "[8] The night before Thoreau died, Hosmer, at Thoreau's request, kept a vigil at his bedside.

After his August 1842 encounter with Hosmer, Hawthorne put down some definite reservations in his journal. Although he described Hosmer as "short and stalwart and sturdy," he surmised that Emerson's praise had touched Hosmer's ego:

> I was not impressed with any remarkable originality in his views, but they were sensible and characteristic. . . . The simplicity of his character has probably suffered by his detecting the impression he makes on those around him . . . he inevitably assumes the oracular manner. . . . Mr. Emerson has risked the doing him much mischief by putting him in print, — a trial which few persons can sustain without losing their unconsciousness.[9]

Hawthorne may have been a little put off when Emerson first introduced him to Hosmer, recognizing him as the same man who had come to the Manse to advise him on a drainage problem.

In this interval Emerson recorded in his journal a number of Hos-
merisms, which, since he judged them worthy of preservation, may be
taken as typical of the Delphic utterances Hawthorne was audience to.
On 11 August Emerson wrote: "Queenie says that according to Edmund [Hosmer] it was a piece of weak indulgence in the good God to
make plums & peaches." Three months later, on 11 November, he wrote:
"Edmund Hosmer . . . finds that the Irish . . . are underselling him
in labor. . . . He does not see how he & his children are to prosper
here, & the only way for them is to run, the Caucasian before the
Irishman."[10]

Making almost daily visits to the Old Manse, Emerson had been
striving to rout Hawthorne's natural reticence and draw him into the
community. Hawthorne saw this as an attempt on Emerson's part to
take command of him. He felt the attraction. "It was impossible," he
said, "to dwell in his vicinity, without inhaling, more or less, the
mountain-atmosphere of his lofty thought, which, in the brains of some
people, wrought a singular giddiness."[11] His antidote was to retreat
into mockery. Contrasting Hosmer and Emerson, he said:

It would be amusing to draw a parallel between him and his
admirer, Mr. Emerson — the mystic, stretching his hand out
of cloud-land in vain search for something real; and the man of
sturdy sense, all whose ideas seem to be dug out of his mind, hard
and substantial, as he digs potatoes, beets, carrots, and turnips, out
of the earth.[12]

Turner reminds us that "From the day of his arrival" in Concord,
Hawthorne "noticed the extent to which the community revolved about
Emerson." As Melville would say of himself a dozen years hence, he
did not want to "oscillate in Emerson's rainbow."[13]

As a gardener, Emerson was so incompetent that a delegation of
farmers once waited on him to discover the methods he pursued to
grow "such poor specimens of such fine varieties [of apples]."[14] On
that account alone Emerson was disposed to hold in esteem so able a
farmer as Edmund Hosmer. Yet, however meritorious Hosmer's farm
lore was in Emerson's eyes, that fact was incidental to what he saw as
Hosmer's true worth. While the soul, Emerson contended, has the capacity to communicate directly with stores of universal truth, it is
through Nature that that capacity exercises itself. Hosmer, he was convinced, communed with Nature and his wisdom came from the store
of universal truth Nature made accessible to him. Thus in Hosmer's
gnomic insights Emerson found his belief in the moral sentiment vindicated.

From Hosmer's farm, Emerson and his two companions went on,

through woodland paths to Walden Pond, halting often to pick and devour enormous blackberries growing in profusion up slope and down dale. When they came in sight of the pond, Hawthorne was surprised. Its size did not impress him nor should it have since he had grown to manhood in a seacoast town and had lived in Maine and explored New Hampshire and seen much larger bodies of inland water. But the clearness of the water pleased him. Twice daily, and sometimes oftener, he swam in the Concord River, which flowed past the Manse. The river was sullen in its flow. Its banks waylaid the unwary with sucking ooze and festering vegetation. Walden's shore was pebble-strewn, and the sand beneath the waters white. Emerson had accomplished his undertaking. He had led Hawthorne and Hillard to the pond they sought. He could now fade into the forest, if not like a friendly Wampanoag, then at least like a discreet well-wisher.

Emerson gone, Hawthorne and Hillard wasted no time in stripping and plunging into the pond. Hawthorne pronounced himself scoured clean of the "mud and river slime," that "had accumulated on my soul."[15] They returned to the Manse for dinner, then napped. At teatime there was a downpour that discouraged further walking, but they brought in heaps of clematis to fill all the vases in the house, letting fall upon the sill a raindrop asperges from the freshened blossoms. They sat up late telling ghost stories.

45. Margaret Fuller
A Member of the Household

*O*N 10 August 1842 Margaret Fuller, who was making slow progress on "Romaic and Rhine Ballads," a long article promised for *The Dial,* asked Emerson if she could come for a month's visit, not as a guest but as a member of the household. Thoreau was then living with the Emersons. And Ellery Channing, married to Ellen Fuller the previous October, was their houseguest while looking for a place in Concord to settle for the winter. Moreover, Lidian, solicitous for the welfare of Edith, her infant daughter, and mourning still for Waldo, was having dental surgery and feeling wretched. But Emerson told Margaret by all means to come, and she came for forty days — a penitential interlude that was, at times, exactly that for all concerned. "Well, now please to come," Emerson had replied, "for this I have always desired that you will make my house in some way useful to your occasions & not a mere hotel for a sleighing or summering party." Margaret's ground rules raised the amusing prospect of monastic quiet descending over Bush. Said Emerson: "I admire the conditions of the treaty, that you shall put on sulkiness as a morning gown, & I shall put on sulkiness as a surtout, and speech shall be contraband & the exception not the rule."[1]

Margaret arrived on the evening of the seventeenth, a figure stepping out of the fog which, that night, inundated the meadows and low reaches of the Lexington Road. The Emersons had the red room prepared for her — across the hall from Waldo's study. The next afternoon Emerson and she walked to Walden Pond and stayed until sunset. "I feel more at home with him constantly," she remarked in her journal, "but we do not act powerfully on one another."[2] The next night they walked to the river under the light of the moon. Both reported the incident in their journals, Emerson mildly noting: "Last night a walk to the river with Margaret and saw the moon broken in the water, interrogating, interrogating."[3] Despite his endorsement of silence, Margaret disclosed that he had had much to say: "Looking at the moon in the river he said . . . how each twinkling light breaking there summons to demand the whole secret, and how 'promising, promising nature never fulfills what she thus gives us a right to expect.'" She disclosed that "[We had] an excellent talk: We agreed that my god was love, his truth." The lines of demarcation established when Emerson turned the flow of their Platonic correspondence still were being observed.

On the twenty-fourth Margaret wrote: "Waldo and I have good meetings, though we stop at all our old places. But my expectations are moderate now: it is his beautiful presence that I prize, far more than our intercourse." The next day she wrote to an unidentified friend concerning Emerson:

> After the first excitement of intimacy with him, — when I was made so happy by his high tendency, absolute purity, the freedom and infinite graces of an intellect cultivated much beyond any I had known, — came with me the questioning season. I was greatly disappointed in my relation to him. . . . He had faith in the Universal, but not in the Individual Man. . . . But now I am better acquainted with him. . . . As I look at him more by his own law, I understand him better. . . . He . . . makes me think.[4]

What Emerson was not to achieve with Hawthorne, he was achieving with Margaret.

Yet on 27 August, after her brother Richard arrived for a visit, Margaret admitted that she relished his company "after these fine people with whom I live at swords points." The day was cold. Rain fell in torrents. Margaret passed the afternoon with Emerson, in his study. To keep off the chill he had donned a blue cloak and looked, to the worshipful Margaret, "as if he had come to his immortality, as a statue."[5] Charged up by Emerson's presence, Margaret, before the day was done, put the finishing touches on her piece on ballads — which ran to eighty pages.

An extended season of rain now broke upon them, sweeping away the vestiges of summer — "black rain," Margaret called it, that kept everyone indoors and set the stage for successive days of drama in a household that held a pent-up mixture of strange mortals.

Sunday, the twenty-eighth, Margaret spent much of the day alone in the red room, feeling sad and listless. In the evening Ellery sought her there. The weather had smote his vulnerable spirits. He was sullen and testy. The Emersons were new to him and Margaret was, too. In the best of times he was prone to black humors. The effort he had been making to be agreeable came to an end. He lashed out at Margaret. She was artificial, he said, "too ideal." Margaret found the attack stimulating. Anything was a welcome change from the weather. Ellery probably retreated in a mood gloomier still than it had been. Margaret, soaring, made a new entry in her journal. She took inventory of her current views of human nature. The result was a workable blend of Emersonian idealism and Christian orthodoxy that neither Emerson nor Andrews Norton would have found satisfactory but that did well for her:

> The spirit ascends through every form of nature into man, and no doubt here should make the complete instinctive man before unfolding his higher nature. But it was no accident that the serpent entered Eden, that the regular order of things was destroyed, that a painful throe accompanies every precious truth. When the soul has mastered it all . . . then there shall be no more breaks, no sluggishness, no premature fruit, but every thought be unfolded in its due order. Till then let us stand where our feet are placed and learn bit by bit, secure that it must be the destiny of each man to fill the whole circle.

A break in the weather brought a general elevation of moods. On the opening day of September Margaret went for a woodland walk with Emerson. There they lingered till sunset. Emerson used the occasion for another discourse on Celestial love, the only kind of love he would risk talking about now with Margaret. She disclosed: "W[aldo]. took his usual ground. Love is only phenomenal, a contrivance of nature. . . . The soul knows nothing of marriage, in the sense of a permanent union between two personal existences. . . . There is but one love, that for the Soul of all Souls . . . *the Soul*."

Yet at last a personal note slipped in. He said every married woman demanded of her husband "a devotion day by day that will be injurious to him, if he yields." And he added, "Those who hold their heads highest would do no better if they were tired," a clear reference to Lidian, always vain about her fine carriage and notorious for her aloofness. This final sally, made "with a satirical side glance," told Margaret that he was referring to Lidian. Prudently she let matters rest there. Yet it was a moment of intimate disclosure between them. Thereafter Emerson could speak mockingly of Lidian to Margaret, always in oblique terms, knowing full well that she understood the difficulties his marriage posed for him.

Margaret had good cause to tread softly where Lidian was concerned. Feverish, swollen of face, medicated, Lidian had been keeping to her room since Margaret's arrival. During the first days of her stay, Margaret, as merely another "member of the household," let Lidian be. She was caught up with her ballads essay and supposed Lidian would appear when she chose to. But at last she went to Lidian's room to visit her, with results she had not foreseen:

> When I *did* go in, she burst into tears, at sight of me, but laid the blame on her nerves, having taken opium &c I felt embarrassed, & did not know whether I ought to stay or go. Presently she said something which made me suppose she thought W[aldo]. passed the evenings in talking with me, & a painful feeling flashed across me, such as I have not had, all has seemed so perfectly understood between us. I said that I was with Ellery or H[enry]. T[horeau]. both of the eve gs & that W[aldo] was writing in the study.

Margaret had to make her own adjustments to what had happened. "L[idian]. knows perfectly well," Margaret assured herself, "that he has no regard for me or any one that would make him wish to be with me, a minute longer than I could fill up the time with thoughts." Lidian had suggested that Emerson enjoyed Margaret's company more than he did her own. Margaret faced that charge squarely: "As to my being more his companion that cannot be helped, his life is in the intellect not the affections. He has affection for me, but it is because I quicken his intellect." She was not going to let this confrontation spoil her visit. "I dismissed it all," she wrote with ringing finality, "as a mere sick moment of L[idian]'s."

But, on the other side of the rainy spell, more trouble awaited Margaret. The succession of lowering days had worn on Lidian's nerves. At dinner on 1 September she asked Margaret to accompany her on an afternoon walk, her first outing since her illness. Margaret had already promised to go for the walk with Emerson and told her so, meaning to add that she would adapt her plans so that she could go walking first with her. Before Margaret got that far, Lidian burst into tears. An awkward scene followed:

> The family were all present, they looked at their plates. Waldo looked on the ground, but soft & serene as ever. I said "My dear Lidian, certainly I will go with you." "No," she said, "I do not want you to make any sacrifice, but I do feel perfectly desolate, and forlorn, and I thought if I once got out, the fresh air would do me good, and that with you, I should have courage, but go with Mr E[merson]. I will not go."

With patience Margaret won her over. Through the crisis Emerson's
behavior continued to offer a textbook illustration of his philosophy:
"Waldo said not a word: he retained his sweetness of look, but never
offered to do the least thing. I can never admire him enough at such
times; he is so true to himself." On 21 June 1838, Emerson had written in his journal: "I hate scenes. I think I have not the common
degree of sympathy with dark, turbid, mournful, passionate natures."[6] He was as good as his word.

Margaret not only went walking with Lidian before she strolled into
the sunset with Emerson, but also, on the day following, as she related: "I stole the morning from my writing to take Lidian and then
Mamma [i.e., Ruth Emerson] to ride." Lidian seized on both occasions
to describe, at length, Emerson's shortcomings as a husband. Margaret
put them down to Lidian's failure to account for Emerson's needs:

> I think she will always have these pains, because she has always
> a lurking hope that Waldo's character will alter, and that he will
> be capable of an intimate union; now I feel convinced that it
> will never be more perfect between them two. I do not believe it
> will be less: for he is sorely troubled by imperfections in the
> tie, because he don't believe in any thing better. — And where he
> loved her first, he loves her always.

Margaret, then, had no plans to exploit the division between Emerson
and Lidian. She tried to give Lidian sound advice — "take him for
what he is, as he wishes to be taken." That was Lidian's best course.
But she could not see it. In this period of her grieving, Emerson might
well have spent more time with her than he did, but he knew she had
a mountainous hypochondria that no amount of attention ever would
dispel.

Momentarily distracted by Lidian's problems, Margaret discovered
that Ellery also was in need of placating. For two or three days he
was "in a real pet" with her, sulking and unwilling to meet her glance.
She searched her memory, trying to discover what "trifling thing"
had set him off. She concluded that he had made overmuch of her
playful banter with Emerson, especially when he overheard her telling
Emerson of her disappointment when she missed a chance to go walking with him. But Ellery was no purist. A letter came from Caroline
Sturgis, inviting him to visit her at Naushon, an island off Woods
Hole.[7] Since Caroline had been in love with Ellery herself and was
bitter about his marriage to Ellen, the invitation promised trouble.
But he said he had "a duty" to go. Margaret agreed, her logic being
that a wife, be it Lidian or Ellen or anyone else, should defer to her
husband's needs — not exactly the thesis one would look for from the

woman who within the year would publish "The Great Lawsuit: Man vs. Men. Woman vs. Women," remembered as "the most radical feminist document yet produced in America."[8] But Ellen was not there to speak for herself. She was, however, on her way east from Ohio to join Ellery, and expected shortly. She would hardly be pleased to learn, on her arrival, that Ellery was keeping an island tryst with his cast-off sweetheart. Ellery saw no problem. He would get back before Ellen reached Concord. With that blithe assurance he took his leave.

Margaret had found it hard to be objective about Caroline's invitation. She herself had once been infatuated with Caroline and still had strong feelings toward her. The next day her feelings were given a further trial. Passing through Boston, Ellery had sent Sam Ward back to spend the day in Concord. Margaret's feelings for Ward were akin to Ellery's for Caroline. In previous meetings with him since he married Anna Barker, there had been coolness between them. Though vaguely she thought the business endeavors that came with his marriage (Anna had refused to marry him until he made a responsible business commitment) had tarnished him, relations between them again were cordial. At best Ward's visit was but the idyll of a day. And after he was gone the rains came again and new darkness lay upon the household, befitting the melodramatic entanglements it was almost daily witness to.

In the blackest of rains they waited for Ellery's return. He had stayed past his self-appointed deadline and Ellen's arrival was fast approaching. Margaret passed along her jitters to Lidian and Mamma, who came and sat in the red room with her where even small talk failed. Earlier, in the dark afternoon, Emerson had come in to share with her his latest journal entries on marriage, sentiments relevant to their earlier conversations, such as "Marriage should be a covenant to secure to either party the sweetness and the handsomeness of being a calm continuing inevitable benefactor to the other." That was all very well, but would Ellen think so when she arrived and found that her husband was with Caroline? Margaret did not think so. Neither did Emerson. He assured them that Ellen and Ellery would arrive together, but Margaret could see that he was as anxious as she was.

In the midst of a deluge, the stage stopped before the door. Margaret almost fainted with mortification when she heard Ellen, at the threshold, asking Emerson, "Is Mr. Channing here?" Lidian and Mamma were close to tears. Emerson, upset now for Margaret's sake, ushered Ellen in. Margaret momentarily satisfied Ellen with a vague account of Ellery's whereabouts. As soon as occasion offered, Emerson got Margaret aside and volunteered to set out at once for Boston, the dark and the rain notwithstanding, to get what news he could of Ellery. His sympathy went to her heart, but she dissuaded him with a firm no. In the middle of the night Ellen got up and rummaged in her luggage for Ellery's picture, which she put on the mantel where she could see it. In the mood she was in, Margaret wondered why since it was "an ugly thing." To aggravate matters, Ellen prattled on about Ellery: "He values Cary's [mind] very much: he reads her letters a great deal. Do you know whether he has seen her?" With forbearance Margaret refrained from saying, "He's with her right now." The next day Ellery appeared. Nonplussed, Margaret reported, "Waldo looked radiant & H[enry]. T[horeau]. as if his tribe had won a victory."

On Monday, 19 September, Margaret told her journal: "I gave the aft^n & eve g to Lidian." She might have been speaking of a humanitarian obligation dutifully discharged. Conversation with Lidian did not carry her to any new frontiers. "Nothing makes me so anti-Christian & so anti-marriage as these talks with L[idian]," she owned. "She lays such undue stress on the office of Jesus & the demands of the heart." Lidian, after complaining that Emerson failed to meet her wants, had opined that "Christ would if he were there." She knew that Margaret was an ardent theist and perhaps thought she could be reached on this basis if not on any other.

This ordeal was compensated for in full two days later when Emerson visited the red room at nightfall to read to Margaret a poem he had been working on. Margaret was now in the last days of her visit and there was poignancy in her thoughts about the niceness of the routine Emerson and she had worked out during her stay:

This is to me the loveliest way to live that we have. I wish it would be so always that I could live in the red room, & Waldo be stimulated by the fine days to write poems & come the rainy days to read them to me. My time to go to him is late in the evening. Then I go knock at the library door, & we have our long word walk through the growths of things with glimmers of light from the causes of things. Afterward, W[aldo]. goes out & walks beneath the stars to compose himself for his pillow, & I open the window, & sit in the great red chair to watch them.

Lidian was more understanding than either Emerson or Margaret realized. During her visit, Margaret, as a kind of spiritual concubine, had been having the best of Emerson. At the most Lidian had shown only a sporadic uneasiness about it. But even the paradise of the red room was not perfect. In a curious postscript, left tantalizingly unexplained, Margaret ended her description of her nighttime idyll with this sharp complaint:

The only thing I hate is our dining together. It is never pleasant and some days I dislike it so that I go out just before dinner &

stay till night in the woods, just to break the routine. I do not
think a person of more complete character would feel or make the
dinner bell such a vulgarity as W[aldo]. does, but with him
these feelings are inevitable.

Obviously there was more to deal with at Emerson's not-so-festive board
than Aunt Mary's harangues or Lidian's tears.

Late that night Emerson appeared in the red room again. He had
more lines to read but found that Margaret had been weeping. Lidian
had stopped by to visit her and that was the source of her tears. Emerson innocently supposed that their subject had been the dead Waldo,
whom Margaret had cherished as though he were a son of her own.
Margaret told Emerson that there was another cause for her tears.
Readers of her journal were left to surmise for themselves the substance of Lidian's tear-provoking remarks, but Margaret was not certain that she had done the right thing in telling Emerson as much as
she did because he "walked in deep shadow for one or two days after."

Lidian's shadow was, in fact, in these days ominously Gothic. She
still dressed in heavy mourning for Waldo and wore a mood to match.
Earlier that day — a chill and somber day offering a foretaste of winter — Margaret had dined with the Hawthornes and gone boating with
them. Hawthorne, fully capable of a shrewd surmise about what life
with Lidian must have been like, said he had been surprised to encounter her abroad at the noon hour. "It seemed scarce credible," he
observed, "you could meet such a person by the light of the sun."
Margaret conceded: "She does look very ghostly now as she glides
about in her black dress, and long black veil." Hawthorne had, in fact,
caught sight of Lidian visiting a world she seldom entered. She shunned
bright sunlight as she would a pestilential rain.

Margaret caught for posterity a glimpse of Lidian in a more representative excursion abroad:

> The other eve g I was out with her about nine o'clock; it was a
> night of moon struggling with clouds. She asked me to go to the
> churchyard, & glided before me through the long wet grass,
> and knelt & leaned her forehead on the tomb. The moon then burst
> forth, and cast its light on her as she prayed. It seemed like the
> ghosts of a mother's joys, and I have never felt that she possessed
> the reality. I felt that her child is far more to her in imagination
> than he ever was in reality. I prayed, too; it was a good moment &
> will not be fruitless.

Gothicism, in 1842, lived beyond the pages of gift books and annuals.
On Saturday the Emersons had a swarm of guests to tea — Sophia
Hawthorne and her mother; Sarah Clarke, James Freeman Clarke's

sister and Margaret's cousin; Margaret's brother, Richard, and sister,
Ellen, with Ellery; and the poet Ellen Sturgis Hooper, Caroline's sister, of whom Margaret would say after her death six years later, "I
have seen in Europe no woman more gifted by nature than she." Ellen
Hooper's daughter Clover (the ill-fated Mrs. Henry Adams) remembered her mother as "our lady of Emersonian thought and sentiment." In a poem she wrote about Emerson, Ellen, awed by his emotional stability, saluted him as "Dry-lighted soul."[9]

Of this farewell tea, Margaret wrote afterward: "It was not very
pleasant, rather a mob, though all fine people." But Emerson and she
escorted Mrs. Peabody and Sophia back to the Manse, then "took a
long moonlight walk," which made up for her earlier discomfiture. "I
can't think about what passed all the time," she noted later, "I have
only an indefinite recollection of the moonlight & the river. We were
more truly together than usual."

Margaret passed the next morning reading Emerson's journals and
was in his study talking to him from the end of the dinner hour until
dusk fell. Spending six weeks mostly in a room a few feet from his
study door had not been without hazard for them both, but especially
Margaret. What she was feeling now was not Celestial love for the
Soul of Souls. "I ought to go away now," she wrote, "these last days
I have been fairly intoxicated with his mind. I am not in full possession of my own. I feel faint in the presence of too strong a fragrance.
I think, too, he will be glad to get rid of me."

Lidian and Ruth accompanied Margaret to Boston on the morning
of the twenty-sixth, a Monday. On the way Margaret had a heart-to-
heart talk with Lidian. She came away convinced that allowances had
to be made for Lidian. Her state of mind showed that she needed help.
Nearly thirty years later Lidian underwent extensive diagnostic eval-
uation, and the examining physician concluded that her chronic ill
health was psychosomatically induced. Margaret reached that conclusion in 1842. Although her presence at Bush had contributed to Lidian's recent anxieties, she held herself blameless. "I shall never trouble
myself any more," she wrote, "it is not just to her." Her magnanimity did not end there: "But I will do more in attending to her, for I
see I could be of real use. She says she feels I am always just to her,
but I might be more."

As her visit ended Margaret's thoughts continued to center on
Emerson. "Farewell, dearest friend," she said, addressing him in the
pages of her journal,

there has been dissonance between us, & may be again, for we do
not fully meet, and to me you are too much & too little by
turns, yet thanks be to the Parent of Souls, that gave us to be born

into the same age and the same country and to meet with so much of nobleness and sweetness as we do, & I think constantly with more and more.

Notwithstanding such barriers as Emerson could devise, Margaret did not despair of sponsoring in him a conflagration of true affection. On 16 October 1842, she wrote to him: "Now don't screw up your lip to an ungracious pettiness, but hear the words of frank affection as they deserve *'mente cordis'* Let no cold breath paralyze my hope that there will yet be a noble and profound understanding between us."[10] With Emerson, Margaret played a double game, speaking to him with an intimacy and boldness no one else dared adopt with him, and, at the same time, professing to adopt his ideal of transcendent love so that he could not reproach her with being stalled on the plane of the personal.

This effort of Margaret's pleased Emerson. In March 1843, under the heading "Margaret," he wrote in his journal:

It is a great joy to find that we have underrated our friend. . . . I have never known any example of such steady progress from stage to stage of thought & of character. An inspirer of courage, the secret friend of all nobleness. . . . Her growth is visible. . . . She rose before me at times into heroical & godlike regions, and I could remember no superior women, but thought of Ceres, Minerva, Proserpine. . . .[11]

Once Margaret grasped the rules of the game as Emerson wanted it played, she met his conditions beyond all expectation. No wonder Lidian paced her room in frustration, and tore her hair, and wrung her hands, and wept. No one could match the pace Margaret was setting.

The year following Margaret's visit Lidian became pregnant again. One of the journal entries Emerson made while Margaret's visit was under way — perhaps for Margaret's benefit, since he made her privy to the contents of his journal — read: "I have so little vital force that I could not stand the dissipation of a flowing & friendly life; I should die of consumption in three months. But now I husband all my strength in this bachelor life I lead."[12] From that Margaret was free to conclude that Emerson and Lidian lived as brother and sister. The birth of a son, Edward, on 10 July 1844, was compelling evidence to the contrary. Thereafter, Emerson was much caught up in the life of his family, with Margaret gradually receding from view. She came no more on long visits.

The Fuller journal is a kind of minor miracle. Margaret had a unique opportunity to report on the Emerson household, at close range, at a time when Emerson was coming to the fullness of his powers. Moreover, she was there, not as a guest but as someone temporarily inducted into the family. And she brought to her task an intelligence of the first magnitude. Finally, she kept the journal as a discipline, and not to fill idle hours. Only as her labors neared their end did she protest, saying, "Oh I am tired of this journal: it is a silly piece of work. I will never keep another such. . . . This meagre outline of fact has no value in any way." No value except to take us deeper into Emerson's household and deeper into his psyche than anyone else ever was able to penetrate. And from this near collision of souls Emerson drew energy to confront a broader destiny, both as an artist and as a man.

Although contact between them diminished during Margaret's years abroad, the Emersons were yet prepared to offer her, together with her husband and child, shelter under their roof when she decided to return to America in 1850. That could have been a memorable chapter in Emerson's life. Margaret was forty, the Marchese Giovanni Angelo Ossoli, son of a Vatican official, twenty-nine. Though amiable, he was without intellectual pretensions. "She talks, and he listens," said Elizabeth Barrett Browning, who knew both well. When Ossoli took up sculpturing, he was observed to have wrought a human foot with the great toe on the wrong side. Their friend Joseph Mozier characterized him as "half an idiot."

The news that all three Ossolis had perished in the sea when their ship was wrecked off Fire Island, on 19 July 1850, staggered Emerson. Memories and impressions crowded his mind first, and then the pages of his journal. "To the last," he wrote,

> her country proves inhospitable to her; brave, eloquent, subtle, accomplished, devoted, constant soul! . . . The timorous said, What shall we do? how shall she be received, now that she brings a husband & child home? But she had only to open her mouth, & a triumphant success awaited her. . . . I have lost in her my audience. I hurry now to my work admonished that I have few days left.[13]

Emerson soon agreed to collaborate with William Henry Channing and Sam Ward in preparing the memoirs of Margaret and editing selections from her letters. With James Freeman Clarke substituting for Ward when Ward decided to withdraw, the work went speedily forward. As he reconsidered Margaret's life in terms of this undertaking, Emerson came to a new estimate of her. He wrote: "All that can be said, is, that she represents an interesting hour & group in American cultivation; then, that she was herself a fine, generous, inspiring, vinous, eloquent talker, who did not outlive her influence; and a kind of justice requires of us a monument, because crowds of vulgar people taunt her with want of position.''[14]

In 1853, a year after the memorial appeared, Emerson came righteously to Margaret's defense:

> Margaret Fuller having attained the highest & broadest culture that any American woman has possessed, came home with an Italian gentleman whom she had married, & their infant son, & perished by shipwreck on the rocks of Fire Island, off New York; and her friends said, ''Well, on the whole, it was not so lamentable, & perhaps it was the best thing that could happen to her. For, had she lived, what could she have done? How could she have supported herself, her husband, & child?'' And, most persons, hearing this, acquiesced in this view, that, after the education has gone far, such is the expensiveness of America, that, the best use to put a fine woman to, is, to drown her to save her board.[15]

Even then there were suspicions, of which Emerson was aware, that Margaret had had, at most, a common-law marriage with the father of her child. Not until fifteen years later did Hawthorne draw, in his Roman journal, his severe portrait of Margaret, and even this was not published until Emerson was two years in his grave. Yet it says bluntly what Emerson had heard whispered:

> She had a strong and coarse nature, which she had done her utmost to refine, with infinite pains; but of course it could be only superficially changed. . . . Providence was, after all, kind in putting her and her clownish husband and their child on board that fated ship. . . . There was something within her that she could not possibly . . . re-create or refine . . . and, by and by, this rude old potency bestirred itself. . . . I do not know but I like her the better for it; because she proved herself a very woman after all, and fell as the weakest of her sisters might.[16]

The real reason Emerson, Channing, and Clarke prepared their *Memoirs* was to discourage just such assessments.

One hundred and fifty pages, nearly half the content of volume one of the two-volume *Memoirs of Margaret Fuller Ossoli,* were written by Emerson. In addition he took a leading role in selecting passages from Margaret's journals, letters, and writings, published and unpublished, for inclusion in the second volume. Margaret's heirs, designating him ''her spiritual representative,'' gave him complete freedom to gather and edit as he saw fit whatever materials were needed for his purposes. They had not reckoned with Emerson's lofty aims. He had just published *Representative Men* (1850) and found irresistible the desire to portray Margaret as the complete representative woman. "All the art, the thought, and the nobleness in New England," he declared, "seemed, at that moment, related to her, and she to it."[17] If she was not the complete universal woman, she was, within her particular world, the radiant central figure.

To vindicate his thesis, Emerson, aided by his collaborators, took astonishing liberties with the trunkfuls of letters and papers sent to him from many quarters. Many documents conveying an image of Margaret that could not be reconciled with the likeness (of Margaret) her editors wished to convey were either destroyed outright, cropped, or obliterated. Fistfuls of pages were torn from her notebooks. Sentences and paragraphs were shifted from one document to another.[18]

Of Margaret, Alcott wrote in his journal: "We have had no woman approaching so near our conception of the ideal woman as herself."[19] It was this "ideal woman" whom Emerson and his collaborators memorialized. No doubt they proceeded as they did, partly out of sentiment and partly out of the desire not to visit further affliction on her family to whom they generously consigned all the royalties from the book. Even at that, Margaret's mother wept because Emerson had said that Margaret was not beautiful.

Not all those who read the *Memoirs* were pleased with the idealization. Thomas Wentworth Higginson, writing almost as though he had perused the 1842 journal (which the vandalizing hands of the memoirists had not encountered), observed: "I do not think that Mr. Emerson with his cool and tranquil temperament did justice to the ardent nature that flung itself against him."[20]

John Jay Chapman offered a bolder estimate of Emerson's portrait of Margaret, going back to the relationship itself:

> If it were not pathetic, there would be something cruel in
> Emerson's incapacity to deal with Margaret Fuller. This brilliant
> woman was asking for bread and he was giving her a stone. . . .
> No one understood her need. One offered her Kant, one Comte,
> one Fourier, one Swedenborg, one the Moral Law. You cannot feed
> the heart on these things.[21]

Chapman obviously had not read the 1842 journal. The thing Margaret most wanted of Emerson he could not give her — himself.

46. Nathaniel Hawthorne
A Pedestrian Excursion

*A*FTER Hawthorne's death in May 1864, Emerson wrote in his
journal:

> I have felt . . . that I could well wait his time . . . and might one
> day conquer a friendship. It would have been a happiness, doubt-
> less to both of us, to have come into habits of unreserved inter-
> course. It was easy to talk with him, — there were no barriers, —
> only, he said so little, that I talked too much, and stopped only
> because, as he gave no indications, I feared to exceed. . . . Now it
> appears that I waited too long.[1]

Emerson then recalled: "I have forgotten in what year, but it was
whilst he lived in the Manse, soon after his marriage, that I said to
him, 'I shall never see you in this hazardous way; we must take a long
walk together. Will you go to Harvard and visit the Shakers?' "[2]
Hawthorne agreed and they had set forth on their two-day excursion,
Emerson remembered, "on a June day." As to the month, Emerson's
memory failed him also, but understandably so. Although autumn came
early and a killing frost had taken Hawthorne's beans and squash
plants in mid-September, he related that "there has since been some
of the most delicious Indian-summer weather that I ever experienced — mild, sweet, perfect days, in which the warm sunshine seemed
to embrace the earth, and all earth's children, with love and tenderness."[3] Little wonder that Emerson, thinking back to this "blue and
gold mistake," believed they had been wooed by the "sophistries of

June," when, in fact, they had made their visit on 27–28 September 1842.

Although Hawthorne and Emerson were neighbors for several years, then and later, the walk to Harvard was the only walk of substance they ever took together. Emerson's recollections of their conversational exchanges explains why. They liked each other, respected each other, but did not share a common outlook. The record each man kept of what Hawthorne called their "pedestrian excursion" illustrates their disparity of interests. Two weeks elapsed before Hawthorne entered the event in his journal. He gave it a paragraph and admitted he had forgotten the details:

> Mr. Emerson had a theological discussion with two of the Shaker brethren; but the particulars of it have faded from my memory; and all the other adventures of the tour have now so lost their freshness that I cannot adequately recall them. Wherefore let them rest untold. I recollect nothing so well as the aspect of some fringed gentians, which we saw growing by the roadside, and which were so beautiful that I longed to turn back and pluck them.[4]

Hawthorne did recall that his overnight excursion with Emerson occasioned his first separation from Sophia since their marriage, eleven weeks before. Only lately, he had written in his journal, "My wife is, in the strictest sense, my sole companion, and I need no other."[5] Sophia was equally clinging, but Hawthorne gave her little choice. Earlier that month Sarah Ripley invited her to a party in Waltham and to stay overnight. "If she wishes to go," Hawthorne said, "she shall go, and spend the night, away from her poor desolate husband."[6] Sophia elected to stay home.

For Hawthorne the Shaker interlude was a wrench. Next to that fact, the thing he remembered best about the journey was his safe arrival back at the Manse. A pleasant realization had then dawned on him. This was "the first time that I ever came home in my life; for I never had a home before."[7]

Since Emerson had initiated this adventure and meant to use it to get to know Hawthorne better, predictably, on his return, he introduced a detailed report on it into his journal. His spirits seemed high. To Sam Ward he wrote on 30 September: "Hawthorne and I visited the Shakers at Harvard, made ourselves very much at home with them, conferred with them on their faith and practice, took all reasonable liberties with the brethren, found them less stupid, more honest than we looked for, found even some humor, and had our fill of walking and sunshine."[8]

Their steps took them first to West Concord past the site of Concord's most impressive industry, the Damondale factory, which made "domett" cloth, a superior combed flannel. Legend had it that when Damon showed his improved flannel to his former employer, the man exclaimed, "Domett [i.e., damnit], it will sell," whereupon Damon adopted that name for his fabric. If Emerson repeated that story to Hawthorne, Hawthorne did not find it memorable.

Emerson was not at his fittest. He had a bronchial infection and a croupy cough. But the warm spell suited him. He even surpassed his later remembrance and spoke of it as July weather. Unlike Hawthorne, who, working at his custom-house job, had come to loathe the heat of the sun and would remember the walk to Harvard (some thirty-nine miles round trip) as "an arduous journey," Emerson rejoiced in the abundant sunshine and felt the urge to walk in it until he dropped in his tracks from exhaustion.[9] The rich fullness of autumn awakened a sensate response. His eyes feasted on thorn bushes laden with red berries, on boughs bending under their load of apples, and on rampant grapevines drenching the air with their heavy, drowsy odor. The day was a Tuesday, yet no one was on the road or in the fields that lay along the road. Dwellings were equally scarce. They saw only the private ways that led to houses of prosperous landowners who could afford to live out of sight of their neighbors.

That they talked we know, for Emerson said: "We were in excellent spirits, had much conversation, for we were both old collectors who had never had opportunity before to show each other our cabinets, so that we could have filled with matter much longer days."[10] Unlike Emerson's usual walking companions, Hawthorne was Emerson's near contemporary. Conceivably, they had a mutual interest in many topics that would not have interested Emerson's younger friends. And there was Brook Farm. Emerson had held aloof from the experiment. Hawthorne had plunged in and found out at last what Emerson had surmised from the outset. There was a topic to fill a morning. Nor would Margaret Fuller have gone unmentioned. During her stay with the Emersons her path had crossed Hawthorne's several times. She had proposed to the Hawthornes that they take in her sister, Ellen, and her husband, Ellery Channing, also newlyweds, as boarders at the Manse. Hawthorne's response had been an emphatic "No!" Hawthorne, at other times, both before and after his walking tour with Emerson, had delivered himself of strong pronouncements on Margaret. At a later time, Hawthorne said of Emerson in his journal: "He seemed fullest of Margaret Fuller," the pun on her name implying, no doubt, his own reservations concerning the subject.[11] Yet an afternoon spent at Sleepy Hollow in Margaret's company, on 21 August 1842, had left him temporarily under her spell; he wrote to her a few days later,

"There is nobody to whom I would more willingly speak my mind, because I can be certain of being thoroughly understood."[12]

The impression is given that, in their banter with one another, Hawthorne and Emerson assumed an Irvingesque mode. No incident had arisen to give drama to their stroll. They agreed "that it needed a little dash of humor or extravagance in the traveler to give occasion to incident in his journey."[13] They had provoked nothing, not even leaving themselves open to some adventure by asking for a cup of milk at some local farmhouse. Emerson cited this lost opportunity possibly because, a few weeks before, he had asked for milk and irked his benefactors when he offered to pay for it.

The theme of a rural journey; an allusion, culled from Wordsworth, to the "huts where poor men lie"; speculations, not at all usual with Emerson, about blushing country maidens languishing for love; and the pleasing fancy that Hawthorne and he could "even get entangled ourselves in some thread of gold or grey," that is, get caught up in the plaintive concerns of youth or age, all suggest that Emerson extended himself in Hawthorne's company, meeting him on what he judged to be his own ground, in the environs of pastoral romance and sentiment. He could even have articulated his "entangled" image as he groped to find the key to acceptance that Hawthorne warily withheld, because several months later, Sophia, writing to her sister Mary, in alluding to the conquest Anna Barker Ward made of Emerson when both were dinner guests at the Manse, remarked: "He was truly 'tangled in the meshes of her golden hair,' for he reported in several places how beautiful it was."[14]

Emerson and Hawthorne broke their journey with a tavern stop. Emerson lamented that the camaraderie once characteristic of taverns was a thing of the past. The Temperance Society had wrought the change. Jokes and politics, which kept the barrooms in a warm and pleasant uproar, had ceased. Taverns were cold places now and inhospitable. "H. tried to smoke a cigar," Emerson said, "but I observed he was soon out on the piazza."[15] Whether he was asked to smoke outside or the bleakness of the environment ejected him, Emerson did not specify.

Emerson did not align himself with the temperance movement but did make temperance his topic on one or two occasions. That he was not a teetotaler himself does not mean that he played the hypocrite. Temperance did not mean total abstinence but use of alcohol in moderation. The movement, in New England, did not come about without ample provocation. In 1763 Boston merchants estimated that in Massachusetts the annual per capita consumption of rum was four gallons.[16] As time passed the situation worsened. The month before Emerson died, Louisa May Alcott told her journal: "Helped start a

temperance society; much needed in C[oncord], a great deal of drinking, not among the Irish, but young American gentlemen, as well as
farmers and mill hands.''[17] No family was immune. Both John Adams
and John Quincy Adams had sons who died drunkards. Emerson remembered fondly the Malaga he drank in his student days at Harvard.
In adulthood his drinking was limited to a glass of wine at dinner
when guests were present. When Bret Harte visited him, he face-
tiously proposed that they make ''a wet night'' of it over a glass of
sherry and was amused when Harte was taken aback at the suggestion.[18] Bush, after all, was not Roaring Camp.

In his journal in March 1832, Emerson disclosed that he had spent,
over the past year, twenty dollars on wines and liquors. He wished the
money had gone instead for a good print from which he could derive
continuing pleasure. That was merely a reflection on values. At fifty-
six he wrote: ''I abstain from wine only on account of the expense.''
In ''The Poet'' he said, ''The spirit of the world, the great calm presence of the Creator, comes not forth to the sorceries of opium or of
wine. The sublime vision comes to the pure and simple soul in a clean
and chaste body. That is not an inspiration, which we owe to narcotics,
but some counterfeit excitement and fury.''[19] Emerson had not lived
among those who frowned on strong spirits. His grandfather John
Haskins had been a prospering distiller. He deplored the abuse of alcohol; he had no wish to exclude its use altogether.

In Stow the travelers had a midday meal, then went the last stage
of their journey, arriving at the Harvard Inn not on foot, however,
but in a wagon, being transported by a venerable Harvardian who not
only recognized Emerson but remembered when his father had been
Harvard's pastor, in the previous century. Thus it was that Emerson,
grandson of a privateersman, and Hawthorne, whose great-grandsire
had followed the same calling and whose gait, in Channing's opinion,
was like that of a pirate, were brought into town with such ceremony
as in past times attended a pair of buccaneers being borne in a cart to
the gallows on Boston Common. Nor did this well-wisher part from
them until he had made their presence known to general and doctor
and other notable citizens and commended them to the landlord's care.
That was enough to send them early to their slumbers.

For Emerson, who at other times had benefited from the good will
that memories of his long-dead father engendered, the experience sat
well. For Hawthorne, who schemed to come and go unseen among his
fellowmen, this exposure must have approximated a session in the
pillory.

The next morning, at six-thirty, the cool air of the beginning day
snapping them awake, the two celebrities slipped away from the Harvard Inn, not even pausing for a meal. They still had three and a half

miles to go to the spot where the Shakers, some two hundred strong, had implanted themselves. Later, when Charles Lane and Alcott were questing a site for their projected utopia, Emerson recalled the fortuitous choice the Shakers had made of a locale, sending Lane to have a look for himself, with the results that followed. The Shakers, in fact, had settled in Harvard in 1781, and the results they got from improved farming methods were so striking that farmers throughout the district had long been adopting their innovations.

Hawthorne remembered that Emerson upon their arrival had drawn out two of the Shaker brethren, Seth Blanchard and John Cloutman, but after a few days could recall no particulars. For his part, Emerson, put down by his respiratory problems and conscious that Hawthorne had left to him this matter of eliciting from the Shakers a statement of their basic beliefs — "Hawthorn[e] inclined to play Jove more than Mercurius" — did not pursue his inquiries too energetically. He found it more to his taste to have a frank and homely discussion with them, especially when he found that the two men were articulate. He recorded none of their comments but ended significantly: "The conversation on both parts was frank enough; with the downright I will be downright, thought I, and Seth showed some humor."[20]

The Harvard Shaker community, compared with Brook Farm would, of course, have different lessons to communicate to Hawthorne than to Emerson. It was but one of several Shaker villages in America. These shared among them insights in practical management as well as in spiritual formation. Accordingly, the system of communal living which they had evolved had far greater sophistication than anything Ripley and his followers had been able to achieve. Moreover, having existed for sixty-one years, the Harvard settlement had had ample time to confront and confound those common hazards that thwarted communal settlers.

When the visitors had eaten, Cloutman brought them on an extended tour of inspection — vineyard, herb room, pressing room, orchard, barn, and much more. Emerson, whose fondness for fresh fruit had led him to lay out an orchard behind his own house, took especial satisfaction in inspecting the groaning Shaker orchards, the peach, apple, and pear trees abundantly laden in this season of harvest, and the pungent vineyard, arbors creaking under cascading panicles of white and Isabella grapes. That these would disappear into Shaker wine cellars, however, was unlikely. Alcohol was tolerated for medical purposes only. The records of their apothecary show that hemp was the medication most often prescribed to soothe the sometimes tingling nerves of the celibate community. Without grasping the true significance of this therapy, many of the Shakers were dependent on marijuana.

Hawthorne could recall having quaffed, at the Shakers' settlement at Canterbury, New Hampshire, a tumblerful of hard cider that had left his head swimming. On the strength of it he had jovially spoken of joining the sect. But in "The Canterbury Pilgrims" and "The Shaker Bridal" he made clear his actual repugnance for the Shaker way of life, which he thought offered men comforts that did not differ in essentials from those allotted to beasts of burden. Hawthorne had additional reasons for his coolness toward the Shakers. In an account of a visit he made to the Shaker community at Hancock, New York, on 8 August 1851, in the company of Melville and the brothers Duyckinck, he dealt in specifics. Examining their bedchambers, he discovered that in each room "were two particularly narrow beds, hardly wide enough for one sleeper, but in each of which . . . two persons slept." Having had to share a bed in boyhood with a homosexual uncle, Hawthorne would have found this arrangement odious. In addition, "There was no bathing or washing conveniences in the chambers; but in the entry there was a sink and washboard; where all their attempts at purification were to be performed. This fact shows that all their miserable pretense of cleanliness and neatness is the thinnest superficiality." A further thought is more characteristic of Hawthorne: "Their utter and systematic lack of privacy is hateful to think of." He concluded: "The sooner the sect is extinct, the better, I think."[21]

To see the Shaker community through the eyes of a charter member of Brook Farm gave Emerson ample reason for this September outing, but a further, intimate concern also must have influenced his choice of a destination. His double first cousin, Rebecca Hamlin, daughter of Robert Haskins, his mother's brother, and Rebecca Emerson, his father's sister, had on the death of her husband a few years before gone to live in the Harvard Shaker community. With her she had taken her young daughter, Mary. In 1840 Rebecca had paid the Emersons a visit. Since Emerson relates that Cloutman told him that Shakers entertained "without price all the friends of any member who visit them," we may conjecture that Emerson and Hawthorne were received as guests of Rebecca and Mary and passed some time with them. Some years later, after Rebecca's death, when Lidian learned that Mary wanted to leave the community because she had fallen in love with a young Shaker, she convinced the reluctant Shakers that they should let the young couple depart in peace. That Emerson should have Shaker kin must have amused Hawthorne, but it would have been as uncharacteristic of him to scoff at the fact as it would have been for Emerson to conceal it.[22]

Fortified with good Shaker nourishment — though vegetarians, the Shakers normally lived to a great age, touched by few illnesses — the hikers set out for Concord at a comfortable gait that brought them to their doors before four in the afternoon. During their pedestrian excursion understanding had grown between the two men. Hawthorne especially had benefited. Until he had spent that afternoon in the forest with Margaret Fuller, he had been wary of her; the time together had caused him to revise his opinion of her. He had been wary as well of Emerson, fearful even that Emerson meant to collect him for his coterie. Thus on the Shaker visit, to hold Emerson at a distance he exercised a studied aloofness, having recourse, without contrariness, to amiable observations that left him his own man. Since Emerson had no wish to dominate Hawthorne, he was willing to leave Hawthorne's views unchallenged. To end up repeatedly having the last word gave Hawthorne all the assurance he needed to know that Emerson would not, either by his natural magnetism or by powers consciously applied, annex him.

In December, Sophia, whose good will toward Emerson was never in dispute, wrote to a friend, Mary Foote, telling her of the tranquillity of their lives and how it was not truly disrupted by the advent of occasional visitors such as the ethereal Elizabeth Hoar "and Mr. Emerson, whose face pictured the promised land (which we were then enjoying), and intruded no more than a sunset, or a rich warble from a bird."[23]

In April 1843, upon learning of her sister Mary's unexpected engagement to Horace Mann and their imminent departure for Europe, Sophia went to Boston to help with preparations. Hawthorne found himself on his own and resolved to talk to no one in her absence. But Emerson came by for a visit and he relented. The trial of solitude and silence, indeed, had left him eager for conversation. Brook Farm had reconstituted itself into a Fourierist Phalanx, and Hawthorne did not approve. This was the year the Millerites said the world would end. Both Emerson and Hawthorne suspected that the days of Brook Farm, at least, were numbered. They talked of that. They talked of Margaret Fuller and, Hawthorne would afterward recall, possibly with some exaggeration, Emerson affirmed her to be "the greatest woman of ancient or modern times."[24]

At that time Emerson and Sam Ward were preparing for publication a volume of Ellery Channing's poetry. Hawthorne had been put off by Ellery's petulance and thought he had not felt the hand of discipline enough as a child. He did not give high marks to Ellery's lyric effusions and may have said so now. What he did want to see published, however, was a history of Brook Farm, tracking its successive phases. Emerson, while in full agreement, did not envisage any such book as *The Blithedale Romance*.

After Emerson left, Hawthorne went into the yard to chop wood. A billet struck him, giving him, for the next several days, a conspicuous black eye. That fact did not keep him from writing in his journal and recording positive feelings about Emerson. This talk with Emerson he saw as the best he ever had had with him. Emerson was "electric."[25] He conceded furthermore that he "stimulates us to fulfill our destiny. . . . He helps us most by helping us to help ourselves."[26]

One evening a week the Emersons received a selection of friends. By preference at such times, Emerson liked to sit in a corner of his study, leaning forward, narrow shoulders hunched, head cocked parrotwise, alert eyes fixed in turn upon those members of the company who brought news and opinions. Sometimes his own opinion was called for, or, with a pithy phrase, he contributed a perception, but he did not like to take the floor, preferring rather that others should. On an autumn night in 1842, Hawthorne had steeled himself to come and be among Emerson's guests. So somber were his ways, however, that Emerson, by contrast, seemed convivial. Hawthorne sat awhile in the shadows, back from the fire, then finally rose and walked to the window and stood, his back to the others, gazing out at the bleak and slumbering landscape. At the first hint that the gathering was breaking up, he slipped toward the door, bade the Emersons good night, and was gone. Emerson smiled as he watched young George Curtis staring after Hawthorne in some surprise. "Hawthorne," he explained, "rides well his horse of the night."[27]

Emerson and Hawthorne were at first shoved toward one another by mutual admirers. Each submitted to the ordeal and waited for something to happen, but nothing did. On 23 June 1839 Elizabeth Peabody, that great promoter of causes, including this one, wrote to her sister Sophia, Hawthorne's future bride: "I was hardly seated here, after tea yesterday, before Mr. Emerson asked me what I had to say of Hawthorne, and told me that Mr. Bancroft said that Hawthorne was the most efficient and best of the Custom House officers. . . . Mr. Emerson seemed all congenial about him, but has not yet read his writings."[28] Previously Elizabeth had sought to remedy that situation by pushing Hawthorne's *Footprints on the Seashore* on him. He told his journal — 16 June 1838 — "I complained that there was no inside to it. Alcott & he together would make a man." Hawthorne's fiction is mentioned in a journal entry for 18 September 1839, but only to note a failing: "It is no easy matter to write a dialogue. Cooper . . . Dickens, and Hawthorne cannot."[29]

If Emerson resisted Hawthorne, Hawthorne succeeded equally well in holding himself aloof from Emerson's spell. In October 1842 Sophia wrote to her mother, with pride: "Miss [Elizabeth] Hoar says that persons about Mr. Emerson so generally echo him, that it is refreshing to him to find this perfect individual, all himself and nobody else." Hawthorne knew he required nothing of Emerson. He conceded that once he might have gone to him as to a master but since his marriage he was no longer looking for answers: "Being happy, I felt as if there were no question to be put, and therefore admired Emerson as a poet of deep beauty and austere tenderness, but sought nothing from him as a philosopher."[30]

Emerson seems to have assigned an ambivalent value to Hawthorne's failure to need him. The very September in which he walked to Harvard with him, he wrote in his journal: "N. Hawthorne's reputation as a writer is a very pleasant fact, because his writing is not good for anything, and this is a tribute to the man."[31] When *The Scarlet Letter* was published, Emerson admitted to E. P. Whipple that it was "a work of power," but he repudiated it. "It is ghastly," he said, reinforcing the judgment "with a repulsive shrug of his shoulders."[32] "No one ought to write as Hawthorne did," he told Charles Woodbury. He scorned "the sad in literature."[33]

Inevitably *The Blithedale Romance*, with its portrayal of Margaret Fuller in the tragic Zenobia, stirred Emerson's ire. It was "untrue," he said. He expanded this argument until it encompassed his larger argument: "Hawthorne lived afar from us. He was always haunted by his ancestry. . . . His gait and moods were of the sea. He had kinship to pirates and sailors."[34]

Blithedale made of Emerson a belated champion of Brook Farm. He told Annie Fields: "Ever since Hawthorne's ghastly and untrue account of that community . . . I have desired to give what I think the true account of it."[35] One wonders if Emerson would have included in that account a record of the visit he made to Brook Farm to investigate the rumor that free love was being practiced among some of the younger members of the community.

Whether Hawthorne set his stories locally or elsewhere made no difference to Emerson. He still did not like them.

Our Old Home, Hawthorne's English sketches, published in 1863, was contrasted, by some readers, with Emerson's *English Traits*. Emerson apparently never read farther than the dedication. It, and a letter written by Hawthorne, were addressed to Franklin Pierce. Emerson cut both letter and dedication from the copy of the book presented to him. Pierce, he believed, with many, had sided with the South on the slavery issue. James T. Fields had warned Hawthorne that the dedication would ruin the book's chances but, with his usual tenacity, Hawthorne said he would sooner sacrifice the profits of the book than capitulate to keep the "goodwill of such a herd of dolts and mean-spirited scoundrels."[36] As Hawthorne received from a flying billet on William Emerson's battlefield a greater wound than William ever received there, so now he confronted enemy fire with the fortitude William lacked. Emerson ought to have respected him for this, but he did not. The smoke of battle had temporarily obscured his vision.

In his journal Emerson wrote: "Ellery thinks that he is the lucky man who can write in bulk, forty pages on a hiccough, ten pages on a man sitting down in a chair; like Hawthorne, &c, that will go." "I never read his books with pleasure," he said on another occasion, then added enigmatically, "they are too young." In a different mood, he told Channing that they were "too pathetic."[37]

On learning of Hawthorne's death Emerson wrote: "As he always appeared to me superior to his own performances, I counted this yet untold force an insurance of a long life. Though sternly disappointed in the manner and working, I do not hold the guaranty less real."[38]

In 1874, when Lowell appeared at a Saturday Club dinner, after a long absence in Britain as U.S. minister to the Court of St. James's, Emerson told him: "We have had two great losses in our Club since you were last here — Agassiz and Sumner." Lowell, who thought Hawthorne was "our greatest imaginative genius," responded, "Yes, but a greater than either was that of a man I could never make you believe in as I did — Hawthorne."[39]

Emerson always found Hawthorne an enigma to fathom. On that September excursion he finally had reached him but probably never knew it.

47. A Look at Emerson
The Face I Shave

*W*HEN Emerson was seventy-six, Daniel Chester French undertook to produce a bust of him. Although almost fifty years younger than Emerson, French had already come to renown as sculptor of the statue of the Minuteman that stood at Concord's North Bridge, a commission Emerson had helped to win for him. A Concordian by long adoption, French over the years had had many chances to observe Emerson at close range. Emerson's features, he said, had "an almost child-like mobility that admitted of an infinite variety of expression and made possible that wonderful 'lighting-up' of the face so often spoken of by those who knew him." But Emerson was old now, and what French called his "glorifying expression" came only rarely and fleetingly. "Why didn't you tell me? I could have put it on," Emerson told him when French said the bust displeased him. "Put it on! Oh, Father, you couldn't," Ellen said. "Oh," Emerson said, smiling, "an old cock can."[1]

To accommodate French, one of the ground-floor rooms at Bush was turned into a temporary studio. Beginning in March 1879, French, coming daily, took a month to complete the modeling. If Emerson knew his face was giving French problems, he never said so. "This is as easy as sleeping," he said once as he watched the sculptor at work.

Emerson was not always pleased with his own photographs. Thus when Herman Grimm asked him for a photograph, Emerson wrote back: "You asked for my photograph head, and I tried yesterday in Boston to procure you something; but they were all too repulsive."[2] But Emerson liked sculpture and perhaps had a better feeling for it. He was close to the mark when he said of the bust of him done in 1854 by John Crookshanks King, "It looks as harmless as a parsnip." For French he had only compliments. When he came forward to inspect the bust after one of the sittings, he was characteristically self-deprecatory : "The trouble is, the more it resembles me, the worse it looks."[3] Later, gazing at the finished bust, he said, "That is the face I shave." Elliot Cabot agreed. He was often in Emerson's company when the bust was being done. He did not expect French to recapture Emerson's prime. The French bust was, he said, "the best likeness of him . . . by any artist (except the sun), though unhappily so late in his life."[4]

"My portraits," Emerson remarked once to Conway, "generally oscillate between the donkey and the Lothario."[5] Few remarks could have encompassed more ground. Yet it reveals nothing about his actual appearance.

In a moment of ill temper, Julian Hawthorne described Emerson as ugly, misshapen, awkward, and shambling. Compared with what others said of his appearance, this was unusually severe, perhaps even for Julian, because he went on then to say that Emerson gave the impression of beauty — like sunlight coming into a room — and to ascribe to him "the grace of movement of a natural king."[6]

A careful sifting of the myriad descriptions of Emerson that accumulated over the years, especially in his middle decades when he lectured widely, yields a plausible likeness of the man as he was.

Emerson's audiences often did not find in the man who stepped before them the man they had expected to see. Their first impression was that a changeling had been sent in his place. He was tall, "six feet in his shoes," Edward said, but, as he grew older, he did not straighten himself to that height. His bone structure was small and his head — he wore a size six and seven-eighths hat — noticeably so, perhaps because it was long and narrow and his facial features contrastingly large. When he lectured in San Francisco in 1871, the *Daily Evening Bulletin* said his was "a head constructed on the utility rather than the ornamental principle."[7] His shoulders were narrow and sloping. This aspect of his appearance often was remarked; more so because he carried one shoulder higher than the other and carried his head slightly forward and a little to one side, a trait he shared with Nathaniel Hawthorne, who, however, had a massive head. Acknowledging this trait of Emerson's, French said he made a special effort to "perpetuate the peculiar sideward thrust of the head or the neck that was characteristic of him conveying an impression of mental searching." Head-leaning evidently was in the Yankee genes. It was claimed as a Cotton trait, too, apparent in the descendants of John Cotton, of whom Lidian was one. Fanny Appleton Longfellow — as the sister of Thomas Gold Appleton, Boston's ranking wit, too quick of wit herself to be unaware of the cruelty of what she was saying — once alluded to Emerson's "falling voice and shoulders."[8]

If there is a hint of caricature in contemporary allusions to Emerson's appearance, it must be conceded that Ichabod Crane aspects were not lacking. Emerson had large, protruding ears, which, even though he hid them under his thick mop of brown hair, could not, on account of his scrawniness, be effectively concealed. John Trowbridge said that, observed from behind, "they stood out from his head like wings borrowed from the feet of Mercury." From the front, said Trowbridge, these ears, viewed in conjunction with his nose, were "sidewheels to that prow."[9]

Emerson's nose was taken into account by all viewers. In 1832, when, as a school committeeman, he was making the rounds of Boston's schools, a twelve-year-old who encountered him said her first thought was, "What a nose!" It challenged the vocabularies of those who beheld it. To one it was "a very prominent Wellington nose"; to another, "the high predacious nose of the Emersons." In 1847 Carlyle, in an uncharitable mood, sketched his face in these terms: "A delicate, but thin pinched triangular face, no jaws nor lips, lean hook-nose; face of a *cock*." Holmes, unable to resist a flash of wit, dropped his normal reverence toward Emerson to say it was "a nose somewhat accipitrine, casting a broad shadow." Emerson himself understood the problem. In 1878, when someone showed him an engraving done of him by Wyatt Eaton, he said, "I will show you what this man looks like." Thereupon he got up from the dinner table, disappeared into his study, then came back with a volume of Herrick open to a page which showed that poet in profile, endowed, beyond question, with an enormous Roman nose. Pointing to it, Emerson acknowledged it as his own true likeness.[10]

Emerson's high forehead once was described as "sinewy." His photographs suggest it was not a vulnerable point. His chin was described by John Burroughs as "massive" and "benevolent," and by Holmes as "shapely and firm." Such a chin could be counted as asset, given the prominence of his nose. His neck, however, because of his sloping shoulders seemed longer than most. Lidian once said that what most impressed her the first time she saw him was the length of his neck. She accounted it a virtue. But, then, Lidian was Lidian.[11]

Emerson never wore a beard. When he came into his prime, beards were so much out of fashion that Joseph Palmer, the reformer, was persecuted for wearing one. But conformity would not have induced Emerson to go beardless if he had wanted a beard. When Ellen told him she was glad he never wore one, he replied, "I had none to wear." Until he was in his sixties his hair stayed brown and thick. Grayness did not predominate until after the illness that cost him his hair.

There was little agreement about Emerson's complexion. Some sources speak of his cheeks as being "fresh-colored, an Emerson trait." When Herman Grimm met him in Europe in 1873, he was struck by his "bright coloring," which he thought more characteristic of a man of fifty than of seventy.[12] Yet Clough wrote in 1848 that Emerson's coloring was "lank and sallow." Holmes thought his was a "complexion bred in the alcove not in the open air." During cold weather Emerson always kept a fire built up in his fireplace. Despite his frequent Nature walks, his overheated study would have robbed his complexion of ruddiness.

Seen in repose, Emerson's mouth was impressive. His lips, the lower one a little prominent, were delicate and severe. Holmes noted in them a "look of refinement . . . rarely found in the male New Englander." The mouth itself was wide but becoming and fascinating in its way, "carrying," said Holmes, "a question and an assertion in its finely finished curves."[13]

Rose Hawthorne found Emerson's use of his eyebrows remarkable: "The arch of his dark eyebrows sometimes seemed almost angry, being quickly lifted, and then bent in a scowl of earnestness; but as age advanced this sternness of brow grew to be, unchangeable, a calm sweep of infinite kindness."[14]

His eyes were Emerson's most arresting feature. "Eyes of the strongest and brightest blue," so Holmes described them. Edith Emerson told Holmes, "My sister and I have looked for many years to see whether anyone else had such absolutely blue eyes, and have never found them except in sea captains." Others were struck by the use he made of them. When he looked at you, he looked into you; on that much there is general agreement. It was, Burroughs said, an "unflinching" look. In Britain in 1857 the *Scottish Review* reported that "His eye has a frosty glitter, like that of a cold-bit basilisk." Emma Lazarus, who never met Emerson until she was his houseguest in 1876, even then paid homage to his "eagle eyes." Cabot contributed to that analogy:

> When anything said specially interested him, he would lean towards the speaker with a look never to be forgotten, his head stretched forward, his shoulders raised like the wings of an eagle, and his eye watching the flight of the thought which had attracted his attention, as if it were his prey, to be seized in mid-air and carried up to his eyry.[15]

Charles Woodbury described Emerson's eyes as "piercing." When he was excited "his look was illuminated, and betrayed by turns the sagacity of the man of affairs and the 'vision' of the clairvoyant." It occurred to Woodbury that Emerson had "the same inquisitive peer" common to "business men of the first order." Yet he caught other moods, too. In moments of tranquillity his eyes were "as limpid as a clear pool." They were, as well, "tender, shrewd eyes that, until the very end, kept so much sunshine in them."[16]

As a young man, Emerson decided it was unseemly to laugh aloud. In those years he accused himself of having "a silly streak" and may have thought that controlling his laughter was one way to subdue it. On her first visit to the Emersons, Margaret Fuller set it as a conscious goal to make Emerson laugh. She succeeded, but to his dismay. "She made me laugh more than I liked," he protested later. Accounts of Emerson's stifled laughter are both varied and intriguing. Fields said that when Emerson laughed inwardly, "his eyes left their wonted sockets and went to laugh far back in his brain." Holmes said, "His eyebrows and nostrils and all his features" reflected his struggle to suppress an audible demonstration of his mirth when the humor of something struck him." James Thayer described his struggle against a mounting urge to laugh as a "ground swell."[17]

For the laughter that he suppressed Emerson compensated with a smile that shed benedictions on all recipients. "The whole street," said John W. Chadwick, "seemed to be lighted up and cheered and brightened with the ineffable sweetness of his face." In England in 1848 Henry Crabb Robinson owned that he had gone to an Emerson lecture determined to dislike him but was conquered by his "radiant visage." Holmes linked Emerson's smile to his alert and questing mind: "his whole look irradiated by an ever active inquiring intelligence." Recalling Emerson as he appeared when he met him in Florence in the spring of 1873, Herman Grimm offered this picture: "A tall spare figure, with that innocent smile on his lips which belongs to children and to men of the highest rank."[18] Hawthorne spoke of him as one transfigured: "a pure intellectual gleam diffused about his presence like the garment of a shining one." Rose Hawthorne made this attempt to communicate the exact experience of his smile:

My earliest remembered glimpse of him was when he appeared — tall, side-slanting, peering with almost undue questioning into my face, but with a smile so constant as to seem like an added feature. . . . I wondered if I should survive. I not only did so but felt better than before. It then became one of my happiest experiences to pass Emerson upon the street. Yet I caviled at his self-consciousness, his perpetual smile. I complained that he ought to wait for something to smile at. . . . After a time, I realized that he always had something to smile FOR, if not to smile AT; and that a cheerful countenance is heroic. By and by I learned that he always could find something to smile at, also; for he tells us, "The best of all jokes is the sympathetic contemplation of things by the understanding, from the philosopher's point of view."[19]

Holmes perhaps saw this when he said:

Without a certain sensibility to the humorous, no one should venture upon Emerson. If he had seen the lecturer's smile as he delivered one of his playful statements of a runaway truth, fact unhorsed by imagination, sometimes by wit, or humor, he would have found a meaning in his words which the featureless printed page could never show him.[20]

Some observers in the cities through the West where Emerson lectured ascribed to him "old fashioned courtesy," "a quaint look, bearing, and manner," and even "little oddities" of behavior. Hawthorne said Emerson's manner was "without pretension . . . encountering each man alive as if expecting to receive more than he could impart."[21]

Edward Emerson, appraising the busts of his father made by Sidney H. Morse and French, concluded that, in both works, "the face has a very different expression according to the side looked at, one representing Emerson the thinker and speaker, the other Emerson among his friends." Bliss Perry, considering this matter further, came to this view: "His [Emerson's] features were slightly asymmetrical. Seen from one side, it was the face of a Yankee of the old school, shrewd, serious, practical. . . . Seen from the other side, it was the face of a dreamer, a seer."[22]

One explanation for the impact Emerson's appearance made on most people is found in remarks French addressed to Cabot soon after Emerson's death: "I think it is very seldom that a face combines such vigor and strength in the general form and plan with such exceeding delicacy and sensitiveness in the details." Emerson had large, strong features. Samuel Worcester Rowse was particularly successful in catching these in his original sketch of Emerson. Burroughs thought these strong features, placed, as they were, on a small head and face, resulted in an appearance that was "more feature than face, with a corresponding alertness and emphasis of character." This is in harmony with French's conclusion: "No face was ever *more* modeled than was Mr. Emerson's; there was nothing slurred, nothing accidental; but it was like the perfection of detail in great sculpture; it did not interfere with the grand scheme."[23]

Yes, he has his dark days, he has weakness, he has
waitings, he has bad company, he is pelted by storms
of cares, untuning cares, untuning company. . . .
He shall not submit to degradation, but shall bear
these crosses with what grace he can.

48. Thomas Carlyle
The Road of the Druids

*E*ARLY in June 1856 Emerson wrote to William, saying that the
Stonehenge chapter of *English Traits* would go next to the printer
and, with that, the book would be almost done.[1] That this chapter was
being written nearly eight years after the journey it recounted is not
significant. It came at the end of the book because it dealt with the
last days of Emerson's most recent visit to Britain. But the chapter
had called for special pains. Emerson had gone to Stonehenge in Carlyle's company and, for all he knew, he was describing their final encounter. There is, in fact, a valedictory note to it which suggests that
both men had been touched with a melancholy expectation that they
would not see each other again. Contemplation of a ruin from an extinguished era also gave them a sense of transiency and an awareness
of the fleeting consequence of many things that formerly had seemed
to them of paramount importance.

Emerson's formal lecturing in England, which had begun the previous November, closed with a talk at Exeter Hall, London, on 30 June
1848. He was booked to sail for America on the *Europa* two weeks
thence and meant to use the intervening time for sight-seeing. To Lidian he wrote, on the twenty-ninth, that prospects were good that Carlyle would accompany him to Stonehenge — which led the list of places
he wanted to see — the following week. Although Carlyle summered
annually in neighboring Hampshire, he had never been to Stonehenge
either.

Emerson also told Lidian that when he gave his penultimate lecture
at Exeter Hall on the twenty-eighth, the committee in charge had seated

Carlyle directly behind him. This Emerson described as "a thing odious to me."[2] On such occasions Carlyle emitted snorts, grunts, guffaws, and rumbling asides. In fact, Carlyle's future biographer, James Anthony Froude, whose first glimpse of Carlyle was vouchsafed him at Emerson's last London lecture, recalling the occasion later, remembered best that aspect of his behavior — "I heard his loud, kindly, contemptuous laugh when the lecturer ended."[3] Emerson did not realize it then, but such behavior foretold the greater ordeal of spending four days as Carlyle's traveling companion. This would be the sole journey Emerson and Carlyle would make together. For Emerson it would not precisely replicate Boswell's travels with Johnson to the Outer Hebrides, but certain parallels undoubtedly prevailed.

The interval between Emerson's first and second visits to England had seen a gulf gradually widening between himself and Carlyle, yet they corresponded regularly with little cause to anticipate the strain that showed itself once Emerson returned to England. In fact, at considerable bother to himself, Emerson had looked to the publication of Carlyle's works in America and, as a direct consequence, had provided, at times, that margin of income which kept the Carlyles above the poverty level. As often as he recalled this, Carlyle was grateful, but sometimes it slipped his mind. For that matter, Emerson's solicitude for Carlyle's interests did not make him a blind admirer. On 7 December 1835 one of his journal entries read: "Carlyle's talent I think lies more in his beautiful criticism in seizing the idea of the man or the time than in original speculation. . . . He seems merely to work with a foreign thought not to live in it himself."[4]

In 1838 he reread Carlyle's *French Revolution* and said: "He squanders his genius. . . . Why should he trifle & joke?" He spoke here not as a scion of the Puritans but as a critic. He had discerned in Carlyle "some inequality between his power of painting, which is matchless, and his power of explaining, which satisfies not." On 12 July 1842 he expanded his objections: "I always feel his limitation, & praise him as one who plays his part well according to his light. . . . Carlyle is worldly, and speaks not out of the celestial region of Milton & Angelo."[5]

Between 1833 and 1847 Emerson heard nothing from the Carlyles to suggest that their enthusiasm for him was waning. Adding a postscript to her husband's letter to Emerson on 7 November 1838, Jane said: "I read all that you write with an interest which I feel in no other writing but my husband's."[6] In August 1843, when she asked Carlyle to give William Macready a letter of introduction to Emerson, she inquired: "Who is there else worth knowing in America?" On that occasion Carlyle described Emerson to Macready as a man "of truly notable faculty and worth, one of the clearest, shrewdest, most

simple-hearted and friendly of men, — in quiet but invincible opposition, as I conjecture, to the whole current of American things. There
is no man in that country so well worth seeing, that I have heard of."[7]
For good measure Carlyle added that most of his American friends,
other than Emerson, "belong, alas, alas, to the species Bore." The truth
is, Emerson had sent many Yankees to call on the Carlyles and the
Carlyles had grown weary of them. On 28 November 1843 Jane wrote
to her uncle, John Welsh: "Yankees form a considerable item in the
ennuis of our mortal life. I counted lately fourteen of them in one
fortnight, of whom Dr. Russel [Le Baron Russell, through whose efforts *Sartor Resartus* achieved publication] was the only one that you
did not feel tempted to take the poker to."[8]

At the end of July 1847 Emerson, at forty-four, announced to Carlyle with mock-heroic solemnity, "In my old age I am coming to see
you." He was coming, in fact, at Carlyle's urging. He had been cold
to invitations to speak in England until Carlyle promised to secure
him London engagements. Emerson went on to ask for permission to
call on the Carlyles — "I shall not stay but an hour," he promised.
This was high comedy. He had been a houseguest of the Carlyles when
he was unknown to them. And he would be now. That was certain.[9]

Despite his tactfulness, Emerson must have wondered if he had
somehow succeeded in provoking Carlyle's displeasure because, when
he sailed on 5 October, no reply to his letter had yet come. A comedy
of errors had taken over. His letter, gone astray, did not reach Carlyle
until 27 September, too late for a reply to reach him in Concord. Carlyle's letter of 15 October was entrusted to Alexander Ireland, with
instructions to give it into Emerson's hands "on the instant when he
lands" in England.[10] Ireland, editor now of the *Manchester Examiner*,
entrusted the letter to his assistant, Francis Espinasse. Espinasse, mis-
informed about the arrival time of Emerson's ship, mailed the letter
to him. The ship arrived on 22 October and Emerson was in Liverpool
two days before the letter found him. Nonetheless, there could be no
mistaking the genuineness of Carlyle's welcome. That much came
through intact. He spoke of the delay that had kept Emerson's letter
out of his hands until 27 September as "one of the most unpleasant
mistakes that ever befell me." He said further: "In verity your Home
while in England is here. . . . My Wife has your room all ready; —
and here surely, if anywhere on the wide Earth, there ought to be a
brother's welcome and kind home waiting you! . . . by night or by
day you are a welcome apparition here, — foul befall us otherwise!
. . . Come soon; come at once."[11] After placating Ireland with a two-
hour visit, Emerson hastened on to London.

While Carlyle was absent from Chelsea, Jane had written him: "I
have been in a pretty mess with Emerson's bed, having some appre-

hensions he would arrive before it was up again. The quantity of sewing that lies in a lined chintz is something awfully grand."[12]

Emerson's visit, even before it began, seemed marked for misfortune. The confusion brought Carlyle to a state of near-distraction. He had told Ireland that his invitation simply had to reach Emerson on time — "I shall be permanently grieved otherwise; shall have failed in a clear duty (were it nothing more), which will never probably in my life offer itself again."[13]

At ten o'clock at night on 25 October Emerson rapped on the door at 5, Cheyne Row. Jane herself opened it to receive him. In the hall behind her, a lamp in his hand, was Carlyle. Ever the gruff peasant when he sought nonchalance, he exclaimed, "Well, here we are, shovelled together again!" Carlyle's letter had promised, "You shall not be bothered with talk till you repose; and you shall have plenty of it, hot and hot, when the appetite does arise in you." But this reunion had no such reasonable beginning. Emerson disclosed:

> We had a wide talk that night, until nearly 1 o'clock, & at breakfast next morning, again. At noon or later we walked forth to Hyde Park, & the palaces, about two miles from here to the National Gallery, & to the Strand, Carlyle melting all Westminster & London into his talk & laughter, as he goes. . . . An immense talker, and, altogether as extraordinary in that, as in his writing; I think, even more so. . . . My few hours' discourse with him, long ago, in Scotland, gave me not enough knowledge of him; & I have now, at last been taken by surprise by him.[14]

He observed further: "Carlyle has a hairy strength which made his literary vocation a mere chance, and what seems very contemptible to him. I could think only of an enormous trip hammer with an 'Aeolian attachment.' "[15] That was dangerously close to calling Carlyle a windbag.

Undertaking to describe Carlyle to Lidian, Emerson sought an analogy in the Irishman who kept their garden: "Suppose that our burly gardener, Hugh Whelan, had leisure enough on the top of his day labor, to read Plato, Shakspeare, & Calvin & . . . should talk scornfully of all this nonsense of books he had been bothered with, — & you shall have the tone & talk & laughter of Carlyle." He concluded that his blustery host was "not mainly a scholar, . . . but a very practical Scotchman, such as you would find in any sadler's or iron-dealer's shop, & then only accidentally & by a surprising addition the admirable scholar & writer he is."[16]

This visit — Emerson's only overnight stay with the Carlyles during the nine months of his time abroad — extended over four days. He

had intended to remain into the next week but cut his visit short, perhaps, with his superior capacity for reading nonverbal gestures, surmising, as in fact was so, that Carlyle was distressed at the prospect
of a visit of that duration. Though Carlyle assured him later that "your
room" was being kept in readiness, he did not occupy it again. And it
was more than the chintz lining that kept him away. Before the four
days of his visit were up, Emerson was confiding to his journal that
better or wiser men than the friends he had left behind in Concord
were not to be found. Carlyle, he knew, would not suit them. Emerson's warranty for this view was Carlyle himself. Writing to his sister
Jean, after Emerson left England the following summer, Carlyle said:

> He zealously assured me of many deep (silent) friends in
> America; but I answered that for that very reason, I ought to
> continue silent to them, and never behold them in the body:
> if they once found what 'a fiery ettercap' I was, and how many of
> their delightful philanthropies I trampled under my feet, it
> would be a great vexation to both parties of us![17]

Here are forecast Carlyle's own sharp differences with Emerson over
the slavery issue, which brought the near-rupture of their friendship.
  While still at Chelsea, Emerson wrote Lidian of Carlyle: "He talks
like a very unhappy man, profoundly solitary, displeased & hindered
by all men & things about him, & plainly biding his time, & meditating
how to undermine & explode the whole world of nonsense which torments him."[18]
  After Emerson set off for his lecture tour in the North, Carlyle
wrote:

> Emerson is now in England, in the North, lecturing to Mechan-
> ics' Institutes, &c.; in fact, though he knows it not, to a kind of
> intellectual *canaille*. . . . Very *exotic;* of smaller dimensions, too,
> and differed much from me, as a gymnosophist sitting idle on a
> flowery bank may do from a wearied worker and wrestler passing
> that way with many of his bones broken. Good of him I could
> get none, except from his friendly looks and elevated exotic polite
> ways; and he would not let me sit silent for a minute. . . . But
> we will try a little farther. Lonelier man is not in this world that I
> know of.[19]

Between autumn and spring a few brief letters went between the
two men, with Carlyle wishing Emerson well on his lecture tour and
reminding him that his room awaited him when his labors were done.
"Thanks that you keep the door so wide open for me still," Emerson
replied, with "exotic" politeness.[20] One night, on his return, he did

invite himself to dinner, but for lodgings he let his London publisher, John Chapman, accommodate him in his house on the Strand.

One March morning Jane Carlyle had business that took her to the Strand. Chancing to pass Chapman's, she mistook it for a Strand bookshop of the same name and entered. On making herself known, she was sent up three flights of stairs to the top-floor apartment where, waiting to receive her, she found Emerson, who supposed she was paying him a courtesy call. Breathless from her climb, flabbergasted at the mischance that brought her there, she was in all but a state of stupor as a gratified Emerson, hailing her as "a noble child," ushered her in and then insisted on taking her on what Henry James later would call a "complete domiciliary tour." Since Carlyle lately had told him that Jane was housebound by illness, Emerson must have been flattered to think that she had emerged from her seclusion to assure herself that he was comfortably situated. Jane had no choice but to stay on for the half hour customarily allotted a social call. She seethed to think that Emerson supposed she had sought him out in his aerie.[21]

In late April, at Lincoln's Inn Fields, in the company of Dickens and others, Emerson and Carlyle had dinner together. Emerson found him depleted and jumpy. In fairness to Carlyle, a stubborn cold succeeded by a throat infection had harassed him through the late winter and spring.

Behind the scenes, erosion was taking its toll. Espinasse told the Carlyles that Emerson had cautioned him not to let his fascination with *Sartor Resartus* and *The French Revolution* corrupt his style. He spoke of Emerson's great popularity in the North and praised the high ethical ideal Emerson advocated. Carlyle retorted that Emerson's ethics consisted largely of prohibitions. Espinasse, who had a sharp, observing eye, had noticed also that the only time Emerson lost his self-possession was when Carlyle's name was mentioned. To Espinasse, Emerson confided his concern for Carlyle, saying that while Carlyle had a heart as large as the world, morbidity was gaining on him.

Espinasse's small talk led to predictable results. Jane's indignation "knew no bounds and, for some time, she scarcely could speak of Emerson with patience." Espinasse put this down to "a certain wifelike jealousy," concluding that she had come to see Emerson "as a sort of rival to her husband."[22] When, in Manchester, a young Greek merchant, Stavros Dilberoglue, told her of his admiration for her husband, she reported that fact to Carlyle. This fellow was one of his admirers, she said, "but still more, I am afraid, of Emerson's." The resentment was not all on Jane's part. Only a few days after Emerson's visit Carlyle wrote to Lady Harriet Ashburton, describing Emerson as "A pure-minded elevated man: *elevated,* but without breath, as a willow is, as a reed is; no fruit to be gathered from him."[23]

Joseph Slater says that the affection the Carlyles had had for Emerson now "cooled into something between disenchantment and mocking repudiation."[24] Those who suggest, as Andrew Symington does, that Jane's estimate of people often was taken over by her husband find support in Jane's letter written to Lady Harriet at that time. She also used the reed analogy, and went further, telling Lady Harriet that two days' exposure to the conversation of "this Yankee seraph" had taken its toll "and now I have escaped to my bedroom, to *bathe my head* in *cold water*."[25] Then came perhaps the true source of Jane's provocation. Emerson refused to be riled. In his innocence he supposed Carlyle and his wife lived "on beautiful terms."[26] Even had he been capable of ire he would have adjudged it inappropriate to bring disharmony into their tranquil bower. Jane, with quite other intentions, gave witness to his heroic restraint: "Polite and gentle, this Emerson certainly is; he avoids with a laudable tact, all occasions of dispute, and when dragged into it by the hair of his head (morally speaking) he *gives* under the most provoking contradictions, with the softness of a feather-bed."[27]

To his Irish friend Gavan Duffy, Carlyle revealed an almost imp-like rage at being thwarted by Emerson's angelic calm. In a dramatic passage Duffy records Carlyle's scornful evocation of Emerson: "[Emerson] bore, however, with great good humor the utter negation and contradiction of his theories. He had a sharp perking little face, and he kept bobbing it up and down with 'Yissir, yissir' (*mimicking*) in answer to objections or expositions."[28] During the preceding months, when Emerson was in England, Carlyle occasionally had flared up at him directly. When Emerson disputed Carlyle's visualization of Cromwell, Carlyle "rose like a great Norse giant from his chair — and, drawing a line with his finger across the table, said, with terrible fierceness: 'Then, sir, there is a line of separation between you and me as wide as that, and as deep as the pit.' "[29]

Of all this state of affairs Emerson could not have been entirely unaware when he drew Carlyle into his plans to visit Stonehenge. Maybe that destination was agreeable to them both because they saw it as neutral ground — a place that predated all their concerns and would survive them as well. Eight years later, fleshing out his account of the Stonehenge sortie, Emerson chose to remember that Carlyle, in the presence of the great Stone Age monument, "was subdued and gentle." He was also melancholy, apparently, because immediately following this estimate, Emerson adds that Carlyle, at Stonehenge, was moved to say, "I plant cypresses wherever I go, and if I am in search of pain, I cannot go wrong."[30]

Emerson had not waited until Carlyle was ready to accompany him to Stonehenge to begin his whirlwind tour of sites of renown. On 4 July he visited Stoke Poges, Eton College, and Windsor Castle — where he inspected, in turn, the private apartments of Queen Victoria, St. George's Chapel, and the Royal Mews — and climaxed the day with a visit to Virginia Water, George IV's miniature lake. The whole of 6 July was given over to Cambridge.[31] Finally, on Friday, 7 July, Carlyle and he set forth in fine weather, not only "on the road of the Druids," but on a touring circuit that would include, by design, Stonehenge, Salisbury and Winchester cathedrals, Wilton House, and, finally, in weather turned foul but, quite possibly, better in keeping with Carlyle's moods, a day at Bishop's Waltham as guests of historian Arthur Helps.[32] They went by train to Salisbury and by carriage to Amesbury, where they took lodgings at the George Inn, which both Dickens and Hazlitt had recommended to them. There they had a dinner that Carlyle, writing to Jane that night, identified as "whale-blubber mutton and old peas."[33] Thus dubiously fortified, they set out on foot to cover the two-mile walk to Stonehenge.

Earlier, as their train was passing through Hampshire, the passion of American tourists for seeking out works of art while in Europe had been their topic. Emerson commended it. Carlyle deplored it. With a broad swipe of his scorn he indicated that a vacuous civilization needed only stark accommodations to shelter it. Science did not escape Carlyle's contempt either. That the number of stars in the sky and the number of hairs in his eyebrows alike meant nothing to Confucius had his robust approval. That Americans "run away to France" to experience the gratifications Gallic culture afforded he heartily condemned. Americans "manfully staying in London" could learn much more.[34]

Emerson refused to be baited. He conceded amiably that he "was easily dazzled." Everywhere he turned he found confirmation of Carlyle's high opinion of English culture. But then, employing perhaps what Carlyle later denigrated as his "sly low-voiced sarcasm," he craftily allowed that, once home again, he would resume believing that the future of the Anglo-Saxon race rested with America "and that England, an old and exhausted island, must one day be contented, like other parents, to be strong only in her children."[35] Later, at Bishop's Waltham, when heavy rain kept them indoors, Emerson pursued his taunting of Carlyle by readily producing for inspection "an American idea" when asked if there was such a thing: "I opened the dogma of no-government and non-resistance, and anticipated the objections and the fun. . . . I can easily see the bankruptcy of the vulgar musket-worship . . . and 'tis certain as God liveth, the gun that does not need another gun, the law of love and justice alone, can effect a clean revolution." In *English Traits* he suggests that his arguments "made some impression on C." He could afford to be generous.[36] He had gotten under Carlyle's skin but had not allowed Carlyle to get under his.

Mead believes that Emerson's record of what passed between Carlyle and him "is incomplete." That seems certain. Francis Espinasse said that Carlyle, on his return from Stonehenge, denounced Emerson's limitless *laissez-faire*, saying that, carried to its inevitable conclusion, it would prevent a man from doing so much as "rooting out a thistle."[37] Espinasse admired Emerson and that fact annoyed both the Carlyles. Indeed, on 18 January 1848 Jane had written Carlyle, then at the Grange: "There was one [letter] last night from Espinasse — too much of Emerson, whom he 'likes much better than he did.' In reply to my charge that Emerson had no ideas (except mad ones) that he had not got out of you, Espinasse answers prettily, 'but pray, Mrs. Carlyle, who has?'"[38] That the Carlyles had begun to resent Emerson's success as well as his nature is a fact to keep in mind as the circumstances of the four-day tour are noted.

The walk to Stonehenge across Salisbury Plain and contemplation of the serene ruins, "with their strange aspect and groupings," stirred a Wordsworthian response in Emerson. From a distance they appeared "Brown dwarves on a vast Wiltshire down. Gray stones on a gray evening, here were they, nettles & butter cups at their feet within the enclosure, larks singing over them & the wind old as they ringing among the conscious stones." He hailed it as "a quiet temple of Destiny," and compared its trilithons — "the simplest & surest structures" — to Achilles' tomb on the plain of Troy.[39] Carlyle approved of the trilithons, too. They offered him shelter so that he could get his cigar lit. "Far and wide a few shepherds with their flocks sprinkled the plain." At Tottenham Emerson had lately visited Turner's home and seen collections, there and elsewhere, of Turner's paintings. He saw now those landscapes anew: "At Stonehenge, it was impossible to forget Turner's pictures. In the English landscape the combed fields have the softest look, & seem touched with a pencil & not with a plough."[40] It bothered him, when examining the great ruin, that "The geologist had pecked at every stone."[41] As for Carlyle, what he saw thrust him into a Gothic mood. He reflected on "the larks which were hatched last year, and the wind which was hatched many thousand years ago."[42] In the twilight, in the raw, wet weather, they walked back to the inn and Carlyle went grumbling to bed when he found there was no milk for his tea.

Next morning, accompanied by a local authority on Stonehenge whom Emerson had recruited, they returned to the site in a dog-cart, with Carlyle in a state of high dudgeon because no more suitable vehicle was available. When Emerson had heard all his guide had to tell of the alleged astronomical stones and alleged sacrificial stone, the two companions continued on to Wilton Hall, where Sir Philip Sidney had written his *Arcadia*. As they drove along, Carlyle heaped imprecations on the heads of those who reserved Salisbury Plain for sheep-grazing, when thousands of Englishmen needed jobs and food. No matter that the land was not arable and that to turn the soil would rob it even of its present usefulness. Carlyle preferred to see things his way.

At Wilton Hall, predictably, Carlyle upbraided the modern statuary observed in a quadrangle cloister. At Salisbury Cathedral, a Presbyterian wariness of pipe organs still active within him, Carlyle opposed inspecting the choir and they did not do so.

After their rainy Sunday at Bishop's Waltham, the travelers, with the helpful Arthur Helps (later Sir Arthur), went on to Winchester, where they toured the cathedral. Beforehand, however, at Winchester's outskirts, they visited the Church of Saint Cross and, in pursuance of ancient custom, asked for and received free bread and beer. The Scotsman's grumpiness again was evident. Emerson relates: "This hospitality of seven hundred years' standing did not hinder C. from pronouncing a malediction on the priest who receives £2000 a year, that were meant for the poor, and spends a pittance on this small beer and crumbs."[43] No matter that Saint Cross distributed bread and beer to more than seven thousand visitors annually. Carlyle preferred his reckoning, or perhaps he thought the priest should duplicate the miracle of the loaves and fishes.

William of Wykeham is buried at Winchester, and Carlyle patted the hands of the marble effigy recumbent upon the tomb. There, too, Jane Austen is buried. Neither man remarked the fact, nor should we suppose they would have. She was remote from the interests of both.

The megaliths of Stonehenge had awakened in both men a sense of the fleeting character of human existence. Approaching Stonehenge, they first had passed Old Sarum — "a bare, treeless hill," Emerson remarked, "once containing the town which sent two members to Parliament, — now, not a hut."[44] Here, in prehistoric times, had stood the great fortress of Old Sarum, before the arrival of the Romans an important trade center in Britain and, later, the home of the kings of Wessex, a citadel for Alfred and Edgar. In the eleventh century it was a bishopric and the site of a cathedral. In the thirteenth century, New Sarum (the Salisbury to be) was built and Old Sarum began its decline toward extinction. In this context the two men reflected that the megaliths "had long outstood all later churches, and all history." Emerson perceived himself coming there "to visit the oldest religious monument in Britain, in company with her latest thinker."[45] Carlyle found that "The spot, the gray blocks and their rude order, which refuses to be disposed of, suggested to him the flight of ages, and the succession of religions."[46] Neither would give expression to the reality Emerson's visit to England had made apparent, the struggle under way to determine which of them would prevail — Carlyle with his wrathful judgments or Emerson with his creed of optimism. Neither man could know that, dead a hundred years, Emerson would tower against the skyline while Carlyle had dwindled to a speck.

After Carlyle bade Emerson good-bye, he noted in a journal entry: "Gave Emerson a 'Wood's Athenae;' parted with him in peace. A spiritual *son* of mine? Yes, in a good degree, but gone into philanthropy and other moonshine."[47] There was reason enough for Carlyle's contentiousness — the disciple was not always submissive to the master. When another week had passed, Carlyle wrote to Jean:

> Emerson . . . is a man who praises everything, and in a languid kind of way is *content* with everything. . . . I found him very amiable, gentle-minded, sincere of heart; but withal rather *moonshiny*, *un*practical in his speculations, and it must be confessed a little wearisome from time to time! The things and persons he took interest in, were things generally quite of the *past tense* with me; and the best I could do generally was to listen to such psalmodyings as those of his *without* audibly wishing them at the Devil! He got among a poor washy set of people chiefly, 'friends of humanity' &c — to keep wide *away* from whom is my most necessary struggle here, — so in fact I have not had very much relation to him at all; and as he sedulously keeps the peace with all mortals, and really loves me very well, I managed without difficulty to keep the peace to him; and our parting was altogether friendly.[48]

Clearly, unlike Jane, Carlyle saw that Emerson's unalterable amiability was the real guarantor of their friendship.

That Emerson was imperturbable in the face of Carlyle's rancorous outbursts does not mean that he was untouched by them. He came to realize, however, that Jane was the true sower of discord. Espinasse concluded: "Emerson's admiration for her abated visibly, till at last he was heard to say that the society of 'the lady' was worth cultivating mainly because she was the person who could tell you most about the husband."[49] Perhaps some word of Jane's enmity carried to him. She had, after all, disclosed it to many confidants. She told Emerson's friend Joseph Neuberg that, amiable though Emerson was, she found it impossible to get up the least interest in him or affection for him.[50] Of Jane her friend Caroline Fox said: "She thought no good would come of Mr. Emerson's writings, and grants that he is arrogant and shortcoming." Jane further insisted that Emerson's later writings were "affected, stilted, mystical."[51] When G. S. Venables called one night on the Carlyles, they received him with an elation that mystified him. As he was departing Jane explained their conduct. "When the bell rang, both Carlyle and I said, 'It's Emerson,' and [when] you were shown in instead we couldn't help expressing our feeling of relief."[52]

Expanding on her feelings about Emerson to Lady Harriet, Jane said:

> I hardly know what to think of him, or whether I like him or not. The man has *two* faces to begin with which are continually changing into one another like *dissolving views,* the one young, refined, almost beautiful, radiant with what shall I say — 'virtue its own reward'! the other decidedly old, hatchet-like, crotchety, inconclusive, like an incarnation of one of his own poems.[53]

In addition to being able to discern two faces, Jane was expert, also, in wielding a two-edged sword, smiting man and poet in one action.

When Emerson first saw the Carlyles on his return to England, he thought they had altered little in fourteen years. But he soon saw that the superficial impressions he had gathered during his fleeting visit to Craigenputtock had not prepared him for the Carlyles as he came to know them now. Carlyle had developed into a bitter cynic and pessimist. Nor was Emerson the person he had been fourteen years before, either. The Carlyles then had looked on him as a defenseless innocent to be sheltered beneath their wings. At times Jane caught now glimpses of that first visualized Emerson. But, that the idealistic Emerson should coexist with the Emerson who was to be heard in London by an audience of a thousand and paid tribute to with thunderous applause was a paradox she could not accept. Emerson seemed to have come to renown without any compromises. To Jane, that had to be an illusion, fostered by hypocrisy. Only a Janus identity could explain him.

Carlyle is alleged to have made an attempt to dissolve Emerson's optimism by taking him on a tour of the fetid stews and gin shops of sprawling London and to the Houses of Parliament, where, Carlyle fervently believed, the worst iniquities of the kingdom daily unfolded. At the end of this ordeal, he thundered at him, "Well, do ye believe in a devil noo?"[54] Certainly, having survived the devil that was Carlyle, Emerson could have survived this devil also.

Asked by Starr King, a fellow Bostonian, "What is Carlyle doing these days?" the newly returned Emerson told him, "Oh, he sits in his four-story house and *sneers.*"[55] Emerson did not exaggerate. In 1851, attending a London dinner honoring Browning, James T. Fields found himself seated next to Carlyle. " 'Isna there a place called Concord that is near ye? — What like is it?' " Carlyle asked him curtly. " 'A pretty little New England town,' " Fields began, " 'of no political consequence but lively and pleasant as a residence.' " Carlyle snorted like a balked bull. " 'Pretty! — lively! — ye ken I had fancied it to be a dull, dreary place wi' a drowsy river making believe to creep through it, slow and muddy and stagnant, like the folk that inhabit it.' "[56]

In 1856, at Cambridge, on 25 February, Richard Henry Dana heard Emerson speak on Stonehenge and Carlyle, from the manuscript he would introduce into *English Traits*. Dana's reaction is interesting: "According to his account, which is, doubtless, as favorable as possible, Carlyle must be a conceited, dogmatical, pugnacious, ill-bred man, sceptical in great matters, opinionated and positive in little ones."[57] Either Emerson substantially modified this material before sending it to his publisher, or read it in a tone rich in nuance. Or possibly Dana was acute enough to sense what the true state of affairs had been. At any rate, four days spent with Carlyle at the start of his visit and four days spent with him at its close had tested Emerson's survival abilities, had Dana but known it, fully as much as two years before the mast would have done.

Lord Macaulay conjectured later that Emerson's second visit to England gave Carlyle and Emerson the chance to find each other out, with the result that they ceased to care for one another. He was closer to the mark than either man would allow. To Carlyle's credit, he subsequently realized that his own viciousness was no match for Emerson's virtue, and blamed himself — rightly so — for the coolness that had engulfed their friendship. On 6 December 1848, five months after they parted, he wrote Emerson: "Of one impression we fail not here: admiration of your pacific virtues, of gentle and noble tolerance, often sorely tried in this place! Forgive me my ferocities." And even more abjectly, he said in a letter sent on 19 April 1849: "O, forgive me, forgive me all trespasses, — and love me what you can!"[58]

More than a year later, on 19 July 1850, when Emerson had let a year and a half go by without writing to him, Carlyle took up the theme on an expanded basis:

> Tho I see well enough what a great deep cleft divides us, in our
> ways of practically looking at this world, — I see also (as probably
> you do yourself) where the rock-strata, miles deep, unite again;
> and the two poor souls are at one. Poor devils! — Nay if there
> were no point of agreement at all, and I were more intolerant of
> 'ways of thinking' than I even am, — yet has not the man Emer-
> son, from old years, been a Human Friend to me? Can I ever
> forget, or think otherwise than lovingly of the man Emerson?[59]

Despite the desperation and pathos of this letter, Emerson did not hasten to answer it.

Conceivably Emerson was irked by "The Present Time," the first of Carlyle's *Latter-Day Pamphlets*, published in 1850. Alluding to the United States here, he had said: "What great human soul, what great thought, what great noble thing that one could worship, or loyally admire, has yet been produced there? . . . They have begotten, with a rapidity beyond recorded example, Eighteen Millions of the greatest *bores* ever seen in this world before, — that hitherto is their feat in History.''[60] Many Americans, including Sam Ward, took this as a hint not to call on Carlyle. Ward, with consummate tact, succeeded in letting Carlyle know that he was returning to America with a letter of introduction from Emerson, which he had thought it prudent not to present. The point was not lost on Carlyle, who advised Emerson of his humiliation in a letter sent on 14 November 1850, and assured him, ''Any friend of yours . . . carries with him an imperative key to all bolts and locks of mine, real or imaginary.''[61]

A reply to Carlyle, a pamphlet written by Elizur Wright, who identified himself as ''One of the 'Eighteen Millions of Bores,' '' was sent to Carlyle at Cheyne Row. Carlyle refused to read it, but Jane did and concluded that the handwriting in which it was addressed was Emerson's own. Whether it was or not, Emerson congratulated Ward on snubbing Carlyle, telling him in a letter written on 3 December 1850, after the receipt of Carlyle's letter, ''I am, I think, quite compensated for your leaving Carlyle unvisited, by the fine vengeance of it.''[62] In effect, acting on Jane's inclination, Carlyle had ''taken a poker'' to the Americans. Emerson felt it had been wielded against him as well. His humaneness in not ending his correspondence with Carlyle stands as compelling testimony to the authenticity of his compassion.

On 30 August 1851 Carlyle forwarded to Jane a letter from Emerson in which Emerson discoursed on the theory and practice of optimism. Carlyle sneered at it for ''singing plainly a mild 'blessed (not accursed) are they that are at ease in Zion.' Of which I do not believe a syllable.'' Of the letter, he said further: ''A word or two about poor Mt Fuller's death is all there is of any value in it.''[63] Forgetting his plea for forgiveness, Carlyle still could sharpen his talons on Emerson.

A softer mood, though slow in coming, finally came. In 1856 Emerson sent Carlyle a copy of *English Traits* upon its publication. Carlyle at once acclaimed it as the best book written on England by an American. He took no offense at Emerson's portrayal of him on their four-day holiday nor should he have since Emerson had depicted him without spite. Carlyle's letter of acknowledgment ended: ''O my friend, save always for me some corner of your memory; I am very lonely in these months and years.''[64]

Despite these moves toward reconciliation, during the Civil War years the ''great deep cleft'' widened when Carlyle's sympathies came in on the side of the Confederacy. Only Jane's illness in 1866, soon to be followed by her death on 19 April, brought a conciliatory letter from Emerson, asking Carlyle to ''use your old magnanimity to me, & punish my stony ingratitudes by new letters from time to time.''[65] The following autumn Carlyle caught him unawares by sending him, via a young friend, George Smalley, an affectionately inscribed photograph. Emerson was nonplussed. Ignoring other gifts and letters the visitor brought, he took up the photograph. "It was Carlyle himself who sent me this?" he asked. "Yes," Smalley told him, "you see the inscription and the date." Emerson persisted, "But you did not ask him for it? It was his own thought?" The visitor assured him that the idea was wholly Carlyle's own. Emerson caressed the picture as though it were a fragile jewel. "Thank you," he said, visibly moved, "you could have brought me nothing I should so much value."[66]

But their correspondence, which saw its best days when Carlyle was using Emerson to promote his books and protect his interests in America, never rallied. Accordingly, it came as a surprise to Emerson when, in November 1869, after nearly three years of silence between them, he received from Carlyle a letter informing him he had talked with Charles Eliot Norton, then in England, and told him he wanted to make a gift to "some institution in New England" of the books he had used while researching *Cromwell* and *Frederick the Great*. Norton nominated Harvard as a fitting recipient. Since Carlyle specified that he was making the gift as a way "of testifying my gratitude to New England (New England, acting mainly through one of her sons called Waldo Emerson)," he chose not to confirm Norton's choice until Emerson made his preference known. Emerson chose Harvard also, telling Norton, "I see no bar to the design, which is lovely and redeeming in Carlyle, and will make us all affectionate again." He immediately told President Eliot of the plan, and Eliot confirmed acceptance of the gift at a meeting of the Corporation summoned especially for that purpose. At Carlyle's request the gift was not announced, not because of modesty but rather because he did not want his judgment to become a matter of controversy in the press.[67]

Even as the details of the gift to Harvard were being negotiated, Emerson's *Society and Solitude* was published. There was no mistaking the warmth of the inscription he wrote in the copy he sent to Carlyle: "To the General in Chief from his Lieutenant."[68]

49. Persons of Mark and Genius
British Admirers

*I*N nineteenth-century Great Britain the social situation produced a high yield of nonconformists. These "oddly shaped mortals" (to use Hawthorne's term for Emerson's following) rallied in droves to Emerson's standard during his visit of 1847–1848, a fact Carlyle had been quick to deplore. Three separate contemporary accounts describe an assortment of such votaries whom Emerson brought together for a dinner party on Sunday night, 30 January 1848. Beyond a scant reference in a letter to Lidian written on 10 February, Emerson never described this dinner, possibly because the first of these guests arrived a day early and the last of them left a day late, and he may well have gone for two days without sleep.[1]

January 1848 found Emerson settled in comfortable rooms that he was renting from a Mrs. Massey, at 2, Fenny Street, Higher Broughton, a half hour's walk from the center of Manchester. Higher Broughton was not quite the rural retreat Emerson had found in Boston's Canterbury, but each house had its garden, and beyond his windows stretched a tranquil vastness of Lancashire countryside interrupted only by the long ramparts of far-extending hills and the sinuous meanderings of the River Irwell. Emerson may well have chosen the site in a moment of homesickness, and that same mood may have prompted him to schedule his dinner party, an event so reminiscent of gatherings at Bush.

That no record survives of the delectables served at the Fenny Street festivities would not be curious if we were not so meticulously informed about all other aspects of the evening. We know that the dreamy

young poet Henry Sutton favored a diet of roots and water, and that
Emerson, in deference to Sutton's tastes, had had a vegetarian meal
prepared for him — even though Sutton had told him, "I like Alcott
much better than I do you." We know that Thomas Hornblower Gill —
a poet also and a hymn writer — an angular, Jack-in-the-box of a fellow, the very incarnation of awkwardness, swept his dinner plate into
his lap while dramatically gesticulating to his host, and, subsequently,
while essaying a toast, let his wineglass spring from his clutch and
spread gouts of goriness over his neighbor's shirt. But no clue survives
as to what platter or plate contained. Mere gustatory gratification must
have been remote from the thoughts of men who feasted usually on
spiritual delights.

The night was rainy. On such a night, in the dead of winter in the
bleak North country, only heroes would venture far from their hearth-
stones. But many of these people had entertained Emerson. Each, in
his own fashion, reverenced him or supposed that he should. As Mrs.
Massey prepared the meal, she must have wondered if anyone would
show up to eat it. When one by one the guests appeared, she may have
wished they had stayed away. Not until Mrs. Hudson received the
clientele of Sherlock Holmes would an English housekeeper again open
her door to so motley a succession of visitors.

Even Emerson was surprised when George Searle Phillips arrived.
Phillips was impoverished and lived at such a distance Emerson had
invited him only to acknowledge his fierce idealism. But he met his
own needs, walking from Huddersfield, twenty-five miles away, much
of his progress taking him through stormswept Yorkshire moors. Phillips's fortunes, frustrations, and solitary ways had made him a cynic.
His account of the funny Fenny Street convocation, which, skirting
sacrilege, he caricatured as a parody Last Supper, guaranteed that the
event would not be forgotten. A lot of spleen would go into his account, so much, in fact, that he published it behind the nom de plume
of January Searle.

Emerson had prepared himself for a quiet, receptive evening, listening, taking note, eager for what was striking and new, but in no sense
dominating. That was his way with guests, especially such guests as
these. They may have thought they had come to sit at the feet of the
master, but their real intention, as Emerson knew, was to bring themselves to his further notice.

Phillips's arrival singled him out at once. On that account alone,
Emerson, beaming, brought him about, introducing him to his companions of the evening. "There are some men here," he explained sotto
voce, "to whom I should like more particularly to introduce you, as
persons of mark and genius." From the devastating portraiture Phillips subsequently provided, it is reassuring that Emerson seems to have

held his guests in varying degrees of esteem. Yet, in truth, we have no assurance that some of Emerson's "persons of mark" are not among those whom Phillips marked for extinction.

Alexander Ireland got off lightly. Ireland was, in effect, Emerson's business manager in England and had attended to all the tedious details of arranging this British tour. Phillips began by saying that Ireland was "dark" and "bilious," but then the rhetoric swung in Ireland's favor — "kind intelligent black eyes, a friendly, genial face, and a most true and affectionate nature." The *Manchester Examiner* owed much of its success to his competence. Not only did Ireland love books and the fine arts, he "had one of the finest and rarest private libraries in the city." Since Ireland obviously did not transport his library about with him, Phillips must have formed his opinion outside the context of the Fenny Street gathering. He also knew something else about Ireland — "He loved Emerson, and was beloved by Emerson." Since Phillips himself reverenced Emerson, Ireland's high standing with Emerson impressed him and he flung no vitriol in his direction. He spared, likewise, Ireland's friend John Cameron, whom Emerson described as "the most erect & superior mind I have found here."[2] For reasons unknown he also passed over in silence an affluent German merchant, Joseph Neuberg. Not only did Neuberg not fit into Carlyle's description of Emerson's coterie as a "poor washy set of people," when Emerson afterward introduced him to Carlyle, he became Carlyle's researcher, amanuensis, and intimate over many years.

Six of Emerson's guests were Scotsmen. This further exposure to the Scottish mind was advantageous to Emerson since he was about to set out for Edinburgh for engagements that would keep him in Scotland during much of February. Chief among the Scots, next to Ireland himself, was W. B. Hodgson, a doctor of laws and, at that time, principal of a high school at Chorlton on Medlock. Of Hodgson, who he granted was "a great classical scholar,"[3] Phillips said, reducing him almost to simian status: "Clad in complete black, and bushy with a quantity of whiskers and dark hair, he was always skipping and grinning about Emerson."[4] Hodgson, who had found Emerson his lodgings on Fenny Street and lived nearby, had relieved him of the practical arrangements for the dinner. On the night of 30 January he called himself to Phillips's notice only because he gravitated to the company of his countrymen. These included Thomas Ballantyne, editor of the *Examiner*, born in Paisley, Scotland. Once a Lancaster weaver, Ballantyne was "a hard, iron man." Another was William MacCall, like his host an erstwhile Unitarian minister. Phillips had no fondness for him, finding him "brilliant as a Vauxhall exhibition — full of metaphysics and poetry, which last he was constantly repeating, or rather singing in a half musical, half savage Scotch drawl — a man of talent, genius, and many capabilities; but acrid, fierce, egotistical, and intolerant of interruption."[5]

Of the Scottish faction, that guest who especially came under Phillips's astringent gaze was George Dawson, who, lecturing in a somewhat ranting fashion on Carlyle, Wordsworth, Goethe, and others, was then enjoying a vogue. "There was one man there," Phillips said of Dawson, with ominous reticence, "about whom we shall say no more than that he reminded us of Judas at the Last Supper."[6] Although Ireland, on reading this estimate, insisted it was "most unjust," Emerson seems not to have taken notice of Dawson at all. Perhaps the need to balance off his portrait of Henry Sutton induced Phillips to characterize Dawson as he did. After describing Sutton as "a thin, timorous young man . . . with strange, mystic eyes," who "lived on roots and water," Phillips conceded that Sutton was, after all, "A beautiful gentle-natured young man — a poet also, as well as a preacher and an apostle. He sat at the right hand of Emerson . . . the St. John of the company."[7]

If we were to accept Carlyle's description of the third chronicler of the evening, Espinasse, as "an Edinburgh semi-Frenchman," then that would add half a Scotsman to the company. But Phillips would have him an *isolato,* pivotally placed in the midst of the gathering, "digesting all that passed, and sneering in his Mephistopheles moods at much that was worthy of reverence." Phillips does his best to portray him as, at very least, a Gothic villain in the customary Mediterranean mold — a "dark, Shakespear-browed young man, with the general *physique* of a Spaniard. He wore eye glasses, and seemed to belong to nobody but himself. Now and then he uttered some cold remark, which fell upon the company like ice; he enjoyed the confusion and silence which he had caused. Or he would utter some witty sayings, which made everybody laugh, and him smile sardonically."[8]

Phillips reserved his cruelest barbs for Thomas Hornblower Gill, the guest who came a day early to assure himself intimate conversation with Emerson. In a letter written to Lidian on Christmas Day, Emerson told her, "At Birmingham, I saw a young man of genius, Thomas Hornblower Gill, who outweighed all Birmingham for me."[9] Perhaps, having preempted privileged status in Emerson's quarters, Gill made himself superior to the rest of the company. Whatever the cause, Phillips enlisted all the powers of his pen to caricature him as an English Ichabod Crane: "a tall, thin, ungainly man, about thirty years of age, speaking in squeaks at the top of his voice, making all kinds of grimaces and strange gesticulations, with a small Puritan head, which was more than half forehead." Emerson was just about to introduce Phillips, newly arrived from his brutal tramp across the moors, to the other guests when this apparition strode before him. Gill, perusing

Plato, had come upon a passage he wanted to share at once with Emerson. His intrusion determined Phillips's mood for the evening.

Standing aside, Phillips lets Gill account for himself:

> Without more ado he put the volume within half-an-inch of his eyes, and read the passage. After which he commenced a long dissertation upon it — twisting his body into all conceivable and inconceivable forms, rolling up the whites of his eyes, and moving his head from shoulder to shoulder with extraordinary activity. . . . Emerson sat silent and listening, with that calm pale face of his, the eye thoughtful but not excited, and the mouth occasionally lighted up with a faint moonlight smile. He was evidently pleased, and so were all who listened to that wonderful six feet of brain and nerves.

Nor was much exception taken to what Gill said: "An occasional objection made the speaker stop — roll up his small, twinkling, swinish eyes; turn his head, which seemed to be hung on a swivel, — and then, with rapid recognition, and rapid speech, start off again in eager, genuine earnestness, and overwhelming energy of lung, throat, and tongue."

Gill had no sooner ended his discourse and collapsed into a chair than Emerson led Phillips forward to introduce him. Gill at once jack-knifed upward, his head collapsing forward on his extended hands, then spiraled erect and turned so that, with his fundament, he bowed in Phillips's direction, his head saluting the window opposite. Then he telescoped again into his chair. "That man," an undismayed Emerson now informed Phillips, "is a fine scholar, has a fine mind, and much real culture. He is well read in literature, in philosophy, in history; and has written rhymes, which, like my friend Ellery Channing's, are very nearly poetry." Emerson seemed to be making the best of an awkward moment.[10]

One aspect of the evening Phillips found irreproachable — the conduct of his host. Ireland relates that Emerson had been the epitome of attentiveness to the guests he had assembled, "and made them feel, as was his wont, that *he* was the favored one of the party, and that *he* especially was imbibing much wisdom and benefit from their discourse."[11] He moved among them not as a teacher but as a receptive listener. Yet when dinner was over, his guests, over his protests, had prevailed and he read to them — though the ink was scarcely dry — his lecture on Plato. No matter that Gill could talk profoundly on the subject. Emerson's first overtures to Plato had begun before Gill was born and his paper was the product of long years of rumination. Even Espinasse, who had felt that the evening had jangled along discordantly, was satisfied that Emerson on Plato had made everything right again.

After Emerson spoke, Phillips went out of doors, strutting about, umbrella elevated against the rain, a cigar set between his teeth. He was, Ireland observed, "an inveterate smoker."[12] He returned hours later. Only two guests had lingered, the lovable Sutton and the ludicrous Gill. They sat up through the night. It became, as Phillips suspected it would, a time of enchantment, for Emerson had gathered about him three disciples, each of whom had contributed to the enjoyment of his first weeks in England, and whom he cherished for their promise. Among friends now, in conditions reminiscent of Concord, he remembered Concord, and spoke of Thoreau's promise. Only after all four had eaten breakfast with Hodgson did these last three dinner guests depart.

On his long journey back across the moors, Phillips must have felt his prospects enriched with the opportunity to write about the night when the goblins walked with Ralph Waldo Emerson and, under his spell, had their restless souls restored to peace.

Phillips's own restless soul fared less well. He lived out his last days in New York, in a madhouse. Yet we must not suppose his was a topsy-turvy view of a Mad Hatter party at Fenny Street. Although Ireland was dismayed when he read Phillips's account of the evening, he swallowed hard and commended his "life-like sketches of his fellow-guests."[13]

Catherine Stevens Crowe's dinner party at her Edinburgh home, which came to pass just two weeks after the dinner at Fenny Street, was another matter.

Thomas De Quincey had walked ten muddy miles from his house at Lasswade to be at Mrs. Crowe's table that rainy Sunday evening. Catherine Crowe, herself a scholar and author of local renown, was one of those who helped to extricate De Quincey from his many troubles, but now she was deceiving him slightly. He thought he was coming to dinner with just Mrs. Crowe and Dr. Samuel Brown, another of his benefactors. "He sometimes soars and indulges himself" in such circumstances, his friends said, "but rarely in company."[14] Mrs. Crowe was staging her dinner party at the behest of Dr. Brown, a would-be Paracelsus, whose houseguest at the moment was Ralph Waldo Emerson. De Quincey had been invited because Emerson wanted to talk with him, but he had not been told that. Had he known a stranger awaited his coming, the shy and skittish De Quincey would never have come.

One more celebrity completed the roster of guests — David Scott, the dour Scottish painter of whom Margaret Fuller had said, "What he does is bad, but full of a great desire."[15] Scott was the son of a thwarted engraver and the grandson of a thwarted sculptor and, at his studio at Easter Dalry, on Edinburgh's outskirts, worked amid an array of paintings, some of them massive, which together made up the chronicle of his own frustrations. When he was a child, his four brothers died within the space of a few weeks. Although later other children arrived, his parents never were reconciled to their loss and David never escaped from under the weight of their gloom. Like a rift in the clouds that usually engulfed him, Emerson's essays momentarily brought him hope and confidence. He noted in his diary: "In Emerson I find many things that meet conclusions formed, and feelings expressed by myself. He is a less sectarian and more unfettered doctrinist than I have yet met." Scott's wary Scottish mind, however, insisted on a ground plan Emerson could not provide — "As yet, however, I have not arrived at the basis (if he has indeed defined such) of the superstructure of his mind." Scott illustrated what Emerson himself had commented on: "There is no elasticity about Scotch sense it is calculating and precise."[16]

Scott was scheming now to get Emerson to commit himself to sit for a portrait. Scott actually held portrait-painting in small esteem, his own tastes running to epic themes like *Achilles Addressing the Manes of Patroclus* and *Vasco da Gama Encountering the Spirit of the Cape,* but he had in his inward eye an image of Emerson that he wanted to capture in oils. In a letter home, groping for a parallel that would help Lidian visualize Scott, Emerson described him as "a sort of Bronson Alcott with easel & brushes a sincere great man, grave, silent, contemplative, & plain."[17]

As for De Quincey, he was compromised from the start. He arrived soaked to the skin, but Mrs. Crowe had no change of clothes to offer him. Emerson took him in carefully, remarking "his extremely plain and poor dress." With wholesome Yankee practicality, however, he concluded that the rain really could not worsen such attire and that the refinement of De Quincey's manners was such that what he wore was of no consequence. The man himself Emerson saw as "a small old man of seventy . . . a very gentle old man, speaking with the utmost deliberation and softness."[18] De Quincey was, in fact, sixty-two, still writing well, and with yet another eleven years to live.

Emerson and De Quincey seem to have exchanged only a few commonplaces before gravitating to others in the company. As Emerson assessed De Quincey with his retentive eye, De Quincey was sizing him up with approval. Emerson's trait of not pushing himself on people served him here to excellent advantage. When an awkward moment arose for Emerson, it was De Quincey who effected his rescue. Philip James Bailey's *Festus* came into the conversation. Emerson denied him the title of "true poet," and asked if anyone could recall a single good line Bailey had written. Leaping to the defense of his countryman, Scott declaimed the line, ''Friendship hath passed me like a ship at sea.'' De Quincey at once disqualified Scott's choice, saying ''that tautology of 'ship' & 'friendship' would ruin any verse.''[19] To be thus summarily refuted cannot have built Scott's confidence in the presence of the master dispenser of confidence, but it forged a sure link between Emerson and De Quincey, which, after all, had been the goal of the evening.

Emerson's record of other remarks De Quincey made that evening seems to be of things De Quincey fed into the general flow of conversation — bits about his literary preferences, his publishers, and his penchant for losing valuable books and manuscripts (including five manuscript volumes of Wordsworth's unpublished poems!), rather than responses elicited in direct exchanges with Emerson, but the evening ended with De Quincey's inviting Emerson to join his three daughters and himself for dinner, six days thence.[20]

From Scott came an invitation to come to breakfast next morning. He wanted to get a start on the sittings without delay, for, in the course of the evening, he had forcibly drawn from Emerson the commitment he wanted. At Easter Dalry Emerson found a second guest, Dunlop of Brochloch, a Scottish laird who had journeyed among the Indian tribes of the American interior and saw enough merit in the Indian way of life that Emerson thought the news worth relaying to Thoreau.

After breakfast Emerson had his first sitting. To Lidian he reported:

> He is a grave colossal painter, surrounded with huge pictures in his hall of a studio, in a Michel Angelo style of size & of anatomical science. This man is a noble stoic sitting apart here among his rainbow allegories, very much respected of all superior persons, but far from popular as a painter, though his superiorities are all admitted.[21]

Scott's finished portrait of Emerson is of a somberness bordering on gloom. Of it Sanborn said: ''The coloring is too dark for the milder tints of Emerson's complexion, and there is a dark shadow under the eyes that contradicts the genial smile they so often flashed forth.''[22] To lift the shadows Scott thrust a rainbow into the sky above Emerson's head. Scott had an affinity for rainbows.

Emerson sat again for Scott, enabling him to finish a portrait that the public accepted as successful.[23] A little more than half length, it shows Emerson, clad in an outer coat, in his lecturing attitude, with his right hand clenched in a fist, a gesture peculiar to him when he spoke. His left hand is extended in a healing gesture. Those who knew Emerson were glad Scott chose to portray him in this expressive attitude. Emerson animate seemed to them more natural than Emerson in repose.

When Scott was finishing the portrait, he made an entry in his diary: "Portrait of Emerson nearly done during his stay here. My first impression of him was not what I expected it would have been. His appearance is severe, and dry, and hard. But, although he is guarded, and somewhat cold at times, intercourse shews him to be elevated, simple, kind and truthful."[24] Here, in capsule form, is a description of Emerson such as it took Margaret Fuller weeks to formulate.

Over the next six days Emerson gave five more lectures, three in Edinburgh and two in Glasgow, scurrying back and forth between the two cities and accepting as many invitations as possible to acquaint himself with the culture of both places. On Saturday, in the company of Dr. Brown, he dined at De Quincey's, where he was favorably impressed by De Quincey's three well-bred daughters and his son Francis, a medical student. With further conniving they got De Quincey to go back with them to Mrs. Crowe's and then to attend Emerson's final Edinburgh lecture, "Eloquence." Emerson was intrigued at De Quincey's anxiety lest this Edinburgh incursion thrust him again into the company of his arch-enemy, Mrs. McBold, she of the comic-strip name. But nothing untoward occurred and De Quincey enjoyed himself sufficiently to dine with Emerson again, the next day, at Mrs. Crowe's. At tea-time they were joined by the tragedian Helen Faucit, celebrated for her Antigone and for her beauty, which Emerson acknowledged and commended. When Emerson took the train to Dundee on Monday, De Quincey came along with Dr. Brown to the railroad station to see him off. He had quite given over his week to this agreeable "foreigner," as he designated him. When Emerson had gone, De Quincey wrote to Coleridge's son Derwent, recommending Emerson and describing him as someone who "knew your illustrious father personally, and honored him," and as a distinguished author of fascinating books. The De Quincey who thought so well of Emerson was not the vague old man Emerson took him to be but a vigorous writer then in his most prolific decade. His masterpiece, *The English Mail-Coach*, would be published the following year. It speaks well of Emerson that he could engage De Quincey's notice so completely at this time.

On Sunday Emerson had sat for Scott a final time but departed without seeing the completed portrait. In July, a few days before sailing for home, Emerson wrote Scott from London. "I carry with me," he wrote, "a bright image of your house and studio, and all your immortal companions therein, and I wish to keep the ways open between us, natural and supernatural. If the Good Power had allowed me the opportunity of seeing you at more leisure, and of comparing notes of past years a little!"[25]

Emerson did not see his encounter with David Scott as a chance to be the subject of a distinguished portrait but as an opportunity to help the troubled younger man and give him the assurance he needed to realize fully his ambitions. That chance never came. Nine months later, on 5 March 1849, Scott died. He was forty-three. Yet Emerson had served him and he had served Emerson better than either man knew. If Scott is remembered at all, it is for his portrait of Emerson as orator, our one likeness of Emerson in his most characteristic public attitude.

In 1869 Scott's brother William sent the portrait to the United States. Asking price was $1,000, or $700 if Emerson or any of his friends wished to buy it. Emerson declined, saying it was beyond his means. Lowell urged Harvard to buy it for its portrait gallery but could find no one at Harvard who liked it well enough.[26] Some thought it hard in drawing and color. Some suggested that the rainbow be painted out. In 1873 it was bought for $800 by Rockwood and Elizabeth Hoar and Reuben Rice and given to the Concord Free Public Library, where it hangs still in the main reading room. Lidian declared it a good likeness. Alcott and Sanborn liked it, too. Edward Emerson thought the picture "wooden" but redeemed by the rainbow. "He recognized," Edward explained, "that my father stood for Hope, and he put the rainbow in the background — the symbol of hope."[27]

50. Into the Lake District
Martineau and Wordsworth

*W*ITHIN days of his arrival in England in 1847, Emerson was lecturing to Manchester and Liverpool audiences. Among those who urged him to come for a visit when a break in his schedule allowed was Harriet Martineau.[1] A decade had passed since she acclaimed Emerson in *Retrospect of Western Travel*. They had not corresponded but, through mutual friends, continued to be aware of each other.

The Knoll, Harriet's house at Ambleside, the gift of friends, was built to her specifications while she was traveling in Egypt. She had been living there only six months when Emerson came to visit, on 27 February 1848. She had wanted to live at Ambleside to be near Wordsworth and that fact worked to her advantage. The prospect of seeing Wordsworth again was an inducement to Emerson's coming.

If visitors were disappointed not to find Wordsworth living in a wild, romantic setting, they were agreeably surprised at the congenial environment the strenuous Harriet had created for herself. The front windows, facing southwest, offered a view of the tortuous Rothay and its grassy banks. In the distance craggy Loughrigg Fell and Brow Head rose up against the skyline. Harriet had taken command of her home and environment with a sureness of purpose that surprised those who did not realize she was fulfilling a long-postponed ambition. When Emerson wrote Carlyle from Ambleside that Harriet ''is most happily placed here, & a model of housekeeping,'' he was making but a bare statement of the facts.[2] Rain or shine, before day dawned, Harriet was out on a rural ramble that might cover several miles. By seven-thirty she was at her desk where she worked till two. As with Emerson, guests notwithstanding, her mornings were her own, for writing.

One early morning Harriet carried to Emerson the season's "first green spray of wild currant."[3] And she saw that he rode horseback with her about the countryside, to look upon meandering Windermere and the valley of the Rothay, at Todd Crag and lofty Wansfell.

The visit to Wordsworth came on the afternoon of Emerson's first full day at Ambleside. Entrenched though he was in Tory ways, Wordsworth was not annoyed to have Harriet set up her outpost in the Lake District. The novelty of the doings of "the good Harriet," as he dubbed her, were a diversion. At seventy-seven diversions, even for a poet laureate, were growing fewer. The able lady and her American guest went to Rydal Mount on foot. As he had fourteen years before, Emerson approached unannounced. The stroll through countryside splotched with the gleaming blades of bluebells and copper clusters of cuckoopint, along the post road to Rydal Chapel, then up the steep flank of Wordsworth's Mount, turned out to be the best part of the day.

Dora Wordsworth, who had cared for her father over many years, had lately died. Wordsworth's grief was so intense that other members of the household feared for his sanity. Alone in his room he gave way to long crying spells, interspersed with sobs. Emerson knew nothing of all this. Harriet and he found the poet sleeping on a sofa ; rousing him, they were confronted by a man less than affable. "He seemed a little short & surly as an old man suddenly waked before he had ended his nap," Emerson said. The mood was set. The cogs of encounter were out of synchronization and, during the ninety minutes the visit lasted, would not mesh smoothly. "Bitter old Englishman that he is," Emerson exclaimed. And he ran through a checklist of Wordsworth's dislikes. He was "bitter on Scotchmen," and on the French, too. "No Scotchman can write English," he said and then named several, including Carlyle, "a pest of the English tongue." And neither could Gibbon write. He granted Tennyson "a right poetic genius," but charged him with "affectation."[4]

Emerson retreated to the high ground of the immortals. Did Wordsworth think that "If Plato's *Republic* were published as a new book today in England," it would find any readers? Wordsworth thought that it would not but, after a pause — "with that conceit that never deserts a true born Englishman" — averred, "And yet, we have embodied it all."[5]

Emerson's journal account sounds, at that point, a condescending note. "His opinions of French, English, Irish & Scotch, &c. seemed rashly formulized from little anecdotes of what had befallen himself & Mrs. Wordsworth in a diligence or a stagecoach, when their precious selves went a traveling." After taking note of Wordsworth's "weatherbeaten face, face corrugated, — especially the large nose," he paid the British elite the dubious compliment of excluding Wordsworth from their company. The entry ends with a few anecdotes touching on Wordsworth's "stingy" ways, although Emerson generously recorded Harriet's defense of Wordsworth's thrift: "H[arriet]. M[artineau]. represented the Wordsworths as having served the whole neighborhood, not at all by their cultivation, but by setting a good example of thrift, & a good careful decent household."[6]

When he had called on Wordsworth in 1833, Emerson was an unknown. Now he measured up ably to Harriet's description of him ten years before. Yet to Wordsworth he was no different. Although Emerson cannot have heard of Wordsworth's dismissal of his essays until Harriet told him, he knew that he was not being received as a literary artist or brother poet. Wordsworth, in fact, never mentioned Emerson's poems during their time together.

Outside the pages of his journal, Emerson reported the encounter as a positive experience. In *English Traits,* Wordsworth, abruptly awakened, was merely "at first silent and indisposed." Asterisks are substituted for Carlyle's name in the "pest of the English tongue" passage. The allusion to "their precious selves" disappears altogether. "Complacency" succeeds "conceit" in the "true born Englishman" allusion.[7]

In his account in *English Traits,* Emerson not only altered the tone of his journal entries, he took occasion to define Wordsworth's place in English letters:

> I do not attach much importance to the disparagement of Wordsworth among London scholars. . . . He lived long enough to witness the revolution he had wrought, and to 'see what he foresaw.' There are torpid places in his mind, there is something hard and sterile in his poetry, want of grace and variety, want of due catholicity and cosmopolitan scope: he had conformities to English politics and traditions; he had egotistic puerilities in the choice and treatment of his subjects; but let us say of him that, alone in his time, he treated the human mind well, and with an absolute trust. His adherence to his poetic creed rested on real inspirations. The Ode on Immortality is the high-water mark which the intellect has reached in this age. New means were employed, and new realms added to the empire of the muse, by his courage.[8]

Wordsworth would have been surprised to know that, a century hence, his name would be coupled with Emerson's as one of the two writers of the greatest importance in the nineteenth century.

51. Scott, Dickens, and Others
How Insipid Is Fiction

*E*MERSON devoted a lecture to a novelist only once and that was before an audience that had come together to mark the centennial of Scott's birth. To the surprise of no one who knew of Emerson's disdain for fiction, he seemed more eager to praise Scott's poetry than his prose. But, at length, he confronted Scott as storyteller:

> The tone of strength in Waverley at once announced the master, and was more than justified by the superior genius of the following romances, up to the *Bride of Lammermoor.* . . . Other painters in verse or prose have thrown into literature a few type-figures; as Cervantes, De Foe, Richardson, Goldsmith, Sterne and Fielding; but Scott portrayed with equal strength and success every figure in his crowded company.[1]

During the Divinity School interval when Emerson went south for his health, he had the temerity to write to Aunt Mary: "If I read the *Bride of Lammermoor,* a thousand imperfect suggestions arise in my mind, to which cd. I give heed, I shd. be a novelist." He knew how Aunt Mary would recoil at that. He could not forget her avowal: "How insipid is fiction to a mind touched with immortal views!"[2]

As early as 1820, when *The Abbot* appeared, Emerson had written in his journal that it "must be to its author 'a source of unmixed delight & unchastened pride.'" To Boynton Hill he wrote in the summer of 1823, "Qentin [*sic*] Durward is a very respectable novel. . . ." Still, years later, after rereading it, he confessed in his journal:

I felt indignant to have been duped & dragged after a foolish boy & girl, to see them at last married & portioned, & I instantly turned out of doors like a beggar that has followed a gay procession into the castle. Had one noble thought opening the abysses of the intellect, one sentiment from the heart of God been spoken by them, I had been made a participator of their triumph, I had been an invited and an eternal guest, but this reward granted them is property . . . which is rude and insulting to all but the owner.[3]

This repudiation had been shaping up for some time. In 1829 he wrote, ''Walter Scott is the grandpa of the grown up children.''[4] In the lecture ''Modern Aspects of Letters,'' given on 14 January 1836, after conceding that Scott brought enjoyment to many readers, he described him as ''a very careless and incorrect writer.'' He continued: ''In the high and strict sense of Imagination he can scarcely be said to exercise that faculty. . . . He has been content to amuse us. He has not aimed to teach. Let it not be said that this is not to be expected from the novelist. Truth will come from every writer, let the form be what it may, who writes in earnest.''[5]

Convers Francis disputed Emerson's estimate of Scott in January 1838, afterward relating: ''I had some debate with him for saying that Walter Scott sometime was not *real*, but acted the fine gentleman. The *spiritual* men, I find, are not disposed to do justice to Scott, because he lived so in the phenomenal, the outward; they will not allow him to be a *true man*, because he was not what they require.''[6]

In Italy in 1833, when Emerson read Alessandro Manzoni's *I promessi sposi*, he offered a broad clue to his standards for judging fiction: ''I hear from day to day such hideous anecdotes of the depravity of manners, that it is an unexpected delight to meet this elevated & eloquent moralist.'' In 1841, he informed his journal: ''A novel may teach one thing as well as my choosings at the corner of the street which way to go, — whether to my errand or whether to the woods, — this, namely, that action inspires respect; action makes character, power, man, God.''[7]

Emerson saw *Uncle Tom's Cabin* as a book he must read because only the illiterate were ignorant of it. Yet not until January 1853, while he himself was cooped up in a cabin in Illinois, was he able to report to Lidian that he had finally read it. The choice of occasion was a happy one. That week, at Springfield, Abraham Lincoln was in his audience.[8]

The genius of Jane Austen escaped Emerson altogether. In August 1861 he wrote:

I am at a loss to understand why people hold Miss Austen's novels at so high a rate, which seem to me vulgar in tone, sterile in artistic invention, imprisoned in the wretched conventions of English society, without genius, wit, or knowledge of the world. Never was life so pinched & narrow. The one problem in the mind of the writer in both the stories I have read, *Persuasion,* and *Pride and Prejudices,* is marriageableness. . . . Has he or [she] the money to marry with, & conditions conforming?[9]

The squabble over Ellen's estate would have made this a painful subject for Emerson.

Charlotte Brontë had Emerson's approval because she offered guidelines for conduct. *Shirley,* he concluded, "must cultivate its readers."[10]

Since Emerson was in Dickens's company on several occasions, both in England and America, and relished him, it would seem that Dickens might eventually have been exempted from the condemnation Emerson made of most novelists. He was not. A glance, in 1838, convinced him he did not want to read "the poor Pickwick stuff."[11] The next year he wrote:

I have read *Oliver Twist* in obedience to the opinions of so many intelligent people as have praised it. The author has an acute eye for costume; he sees the expression of dress, of form, of gait, of personal deformities; of furniture, or the outside & inside of houses; but his eye rests always on surfaces; he has no insight into Character. For want of key to the moral powers the Author is fain to strain all his stage tricks of grimace, of bodily terror, of murder, & the most approved performances of Remorse. It all avails nothing. There is nothing memorable in the book except the *flash,* which is got at a police office, & the dancing of the madman which strikes a momentary terror. Like Cooper & Hawthorne he has no dramatic talent. The moment he attempts dialogue the improbability of life hardens to wood & stone. And the book begins & ends without a poetic ray & so perishes in the reading.[12]

Never elsewhere did Emerson essay so intimate a critique of a novel. Never elsewhere are the limitations of his Puritan yardstick so glaring.

Dickens arrived in Boston for the start of his first American tour on 22 January 1842. Emerson was invited to a testimonial dinner in his honor, and to a private reception for him that Elizabeth Peabody had arranged. But on 27 January little Waldo died, and so Dickens came and went unnoticed by Emerson.

The first copies of *American Notes,* that dubious progeny of Dickens's tour, reached New York on the *Great Western* on 6 November 1842. A day later an American edition went on sale. The book's abusive tone made it a sensation. By 10 November a Boston firm reported a sale of seven thousand copies in a single day. On 25 November Emerson damned it in his journal: "Yesterday I read Dickens's *American Notes.* It answers its end very well, which plainly was to make a readable book, nothing more. Truth is not his object for a single instant."[13] Later, he spoke a better word for it when he decided it had redeeming social value. Dickens had "held bad manners up, so that the churls could see the deformity."[14]

When Emerson spoke at the Athenaeum's Annual Soirée in Manchester, England, on 18 November 1847, he was told that Dickens was in his audience. That expectation accounts for his allusion to *Dombey and Son,* a few sentences into his address: "There is no land where the sun shines, that Dombey does not; no land where paper exists to print on, that it is not found. No man who can read, that does not read it, &, if he cannot, he finds some charitable son or daughter of Adam who can, & hears it." Yet Emerson's integrity would not allow him to appear before his audience as a fiction lover. He appended a further observation: "But these things are not for me; these compliments, though true, would better come from one who felt & understood these merits more." He might have spared himself this discomfiture. Dickens, it turned out, was not in his audience after all.[15]

The next April the long-delayed encounter between Emerson and Dickens came to pass. John Forster, editor of the *Examiner* and in due course biographer of Dickens and Landor, arranged a dinner party at his home at Lincoln's Inn Fields on 25 April, to bring together Emerson, Carlyle, and Dickens. To Lidian, Emerson wrote on 4 May, recording the pleasing impressions Dickens had made: "I met Dickens at Mr. Forster's and liked him very well, did not much observe the dandy of which every one speaks, in him. He was cordial & sensible." A frank discussion occurring at this dinner was not reported to Lidian but was described in the journal that night:

> There were only gentlemen present, & the conversation turned on the shameful lewdness of the London streets at night. Carlyle said, & the others agreed, that chastity for men was as good as given up in Europe. . . . I said, that, when I came to Liverpool, I inquired whether the prostitution was always as gross in that city, as it then appeared? . . . C[arlyle]. & D[ickens]. replied, that chastity in the male sex was as good as gone in our times; &, in England, was so rare, that they could name all the exceptions. . . . I assured them that it was not so with us; that, for the most part, young men of good standing & good education with us, go virgins

to their nuptial bed, as truly as their brides. Dickens replied, 'that incontinence is so much the rule in England, that if his own son were particularly chaste, he should be alarmed on his account, as if he could not be in good health.'[16]

At home in October, when Emerson drew up a list of the fifty most notable people he had seen while abroad, Dickens's name went on the list (by error, twice, in fact). In 1853 he procured *Bleak House* for Ellen, and read it. Otherwise, mentions of Dickens in his journal and correspondence are scant.

Before Dickens opened his second American tour in Boston in December 1867, Emerson dined with him at the Fieldses' house on Charles Street. Once again, with the exception of Annie, who, looking ''like a pensive Burne-Jones portrait,'' presided at one end of the table, Dickens on her right, it was an all-male gathering — Louis Agassiz, Holmes, Longfellow, Norton, Judge Hoar, George Washington Greene, and, of course, Emerson and Fields. Annie would recall that Dickens ''bubbled over with fun,'' yet was bored by Holmes, who got his ear and would not let him go. ''I was sorry for this,'' she said, ''because Holmes is so simple and lovely, but Dickens is sensitive, very.'' Dickens recovered, however, and presently ''gave the most irresistible imitation of Carlyle.''[17]

On Saturday, 22 February 1868, Emerson finally had an opportunity to hear Dickens read. The reading was ''Dr. Marigold.'' This time Annie took care to describe Emerson's reactions:

> Mr. Emerson came down to go, and passed the night here; of
> course we sat talking until late, he being much surprised at
> the artistic perfection of the performance. It was queer enough to
> sit by his side, for when his stoicism did at length break down,
> he laughed as if he must crumble to pieces at such unusual bodily
> agitation, and with a face on as if it hurt him dreadfully — to look
> at him was too much for me, already full of laughter myself. . . .
> When we came back home Mr. Emerson asked me a great many
> questions about C.D. and pondered much. Finally he said, ''I am
> afraid he has too much talent for his genius; it is a fearful
> locomotive to which he is bound and can never be free from it nor
> set at rest. You see him quite wrong, evidently; and would
> persuade me that he is a genial creature, full of sweetness and
> amenities and superior to his talents, but I fear he is harnessed to
> them. He is too consummate an artist to have a thread of nature
> left. He daunts me! I have not the key.''[18]

The Fieldses had been seeing much of Dickens during his prolonged Boston stay. They had served a long apprenticeship catering to the many literary figures who came within their purview, and Dickens was now the full beneficiary of the attentions, honors, appreciation, and deference they were capable of. They were with him every available moment. They saw that he met everyone worth meeting. They were in his audience at every reading, not merely in Boston but often elsewhere. Once he managed to get off to Longfellow's to dinner. Otherwise the only hospitality he accepted, while in Boston, was that extended by the Fieldses. Dickens and Fields customarily took a seven-mile walk together every day and Fields would return home bursting with what Dickens had said. ''Whatever unpleasant is said of Charles Dickens I take almost as if said against myself,'' Annie said. ''It is so hard to help this when you love a friend.''[19] Thus she thought. But Emerson was not to be shaken from his own contrary assessment.

An unusual compliment that Emerson paid Dickens when he lectured on natural aristocracy at the Universalist Church in Cincinnati, on 20 May 1850, stirred the ire of at least one member of his audience. Discussing genius among men of letters, he said: ''The eminent examples are Shakespeare, Cervantes, Bunyan, Burns, Scott, and now we must add Dickens.'' L. G. Curtiss, editor of the *Cincinnati Daily Commercial*, wrote the next day that he had ''remained long enough to hear him utter one unmistakable absurdity and left.'' He wanted to know ''how much Dickens paid Ralph Waldo Emerson for classing him with Shakespeare.''[20]

The days are ever divine.

52. George Eliot and Her Circle

*T*HE day he returned to London from his holiday with Carlyle, Emerson wrote to Charles Bray, a silk and ribbon manufacturer of Rose Hill, Coventry, to accept his standing offer for a visit. Emerson and Bray, author of *The Philosophy of Necessity* (which Emerson had read with enthusiasm), had known each other only through an exchange of letters. But in London, Emerson had dined with Mrs. Bray's sister, Sarah Hennell, whose brother, Charles C. Hennell, then deceased, was the author of *An Inquiry Concerning the Origin of Christianity*, which undertook, after the manner of Renan, to rend the gospels. Also present had been the poet Wathen Call and his wife, Charles Hennell's widow. Call, once, at Coleridge's bidding, an Anglican priest, and now, at his own bidding, a rationalist, was a figure of some notoriety to the foes of freethinking. Mrs. Call, the daughter of R. H. Brabant, financial founder of the *Westminster Review*, had mastery of Hebrew, Greek, German, and French. To Hennell and her belonged credit for discovering Marian Evans (the future George Eliot), then living obscurely in Coventry, at Birdgrove. Subsequently she collaborated with Marian in translating David Friedrich Strauss's *Leben Jesu*, Marian's first step toward prominence. Conversation with the Brays and their circle obviously would not stop with silks and ribbons.

Even though Mrs. Bray, who had herself done a little book on conduct, manners, and duties for children, was "full of the preparations for our great juvenile fete on Thursday," she was enthralled to realize they were to have "the great spirit amongst us."[1] Immediately on receipt of Emerson's letter, she "ran upstairs to put the best room in order," for the guest whose advent was announced for that very night. Little did Emerson realize how English bedchambers fluttered at his approach.

Sarah Hennell, who fitted strangely into this freethinking family since she produced many religious mystical works, had reported to her sister what it was like to meet Emerson. After Emerson had come and gone, Mrs. Bray, in turn, reported her impressions to Sarah: "I feel as you do now how much greater his thoughts, which we had before, have become from the corroboration they have received from his presence. I have quite a grateful feeling that he has been under this roof, though only for a few hours."[2]

Others in Coventry who caught a glimpse of Emerson during this visit were similarly impressed. The daughter of a conservative minister told Moncure Conway that they found it reassuring that "this heretic [was] not a man of the world, like Voltaire and Gibbon, but one whose righteousness exceeded that of the orthodox."

Charles Bray himself met Emerson's train. Already longing for home, Emerson took readily to the Brays' pleasant domestic environment. "He looked round the drawing-room," Mrs. Bray recalled, "and said, 'Coventry is a very nice place.'" With unerring tact he put things at once on a familiar footing. "The next morning was so easy and pleasant," said his gratified hostess, "that I wondered where all my awe had gone to." They sat in the garden beneath a luxuriant acacia tree, and Emerson spoke of the rocking horse he was fetching home for his daughters, and the crossbow bought for Edward.[3]

Upholding his reputation as a thinker, Emerson spoke of deeper matters, too. Indian mythology became his subject, a topic that formed part of his interest in Hindu thought. Charles Lane, who had arrived in Concord in 1843 with a sizable personal library of Oriental books, had quickened that interest and, after the failure of Fruitlands, had given it opportunity for growth when he sold most of those books to Emerson.

Incursions into the Oriental scriptures did not mold Emerson's thought, as some have believed. During his formative years he knew the writings of the Orientals only at second hand and his philosophy took shape without reference to them. In fact, in 1822 he characterized Hindu religious thought as stemming from "indolence and ignorance."[4] His earliest writings, including his first volume of essays, contain few references to the Orient, none of any importance. After having developed his own most significant ideas, Emerson, beginning in 1837, undertook a reading program that included texts from Hinduism, Islam, Buddhism, Zoroastrianism, and Confucianism.[5] From that time onward references in his journal to Oriental thought are numerous. By 1845 he considered himself steeped in the subject. Yet, from what he read he assimilated only what harmonized with his own system.[6] As he himself said in his journal in 1857, "We read the orientals but remain occidental."[7]

Conversation with the Brays was interrupted by the arrival of Marian Evans, who had been invited to meet the man whose essays had been solacing companions to her lonely hours. Marian was, at twenty-nine, a strong-faced woman whose perceptive, attentive eyes quickly identified her to Emerson as a woman of intellect. With Marian there to round out the company, the Brays were anticipating "a nice quiet day" with Emerson, but that was not to be. Unexpectedly their number was increased with the arrival of Edward Fordham Flower, the frequent mayor of Stratford-on-Avon, and his wife, Celina Greaves Flower, sister of Alcott's lamented booster James Pierrepont Greaves. Flower, like the other members of this circle, knew Emerson only through his books, but on 7 July he had written to Emerson inviting him to come see Stratford, Kenilworth, and Warwick Castle. Emerson, upon his return to London on the tenth, had countered with the suggestion that Flower look in on him while he was in Coventry.

So the Flowers came, just after breakfast on the twelfth, determined to carry Emerson off to Stratford. The Brays, perceiving that Emerson was charmed at the prospect of such an abduction, at once adapted their plans and all set out for Stratford. A train took them there. On the return journey they rode back in an open carriage, Emerson paired off with Marian. The camaraderie the carriage ride induced saw Emerson at his best. "He talked as if we had been old friends," Mrs. Bray remembered. He was much taken with Marian, whose strong, clear mind and breadth of knowledge would remind Carlyle of Margaret Fuller. Several times Emerson told Bray of the admiration he felt for her. "That young lady has a calm, serious soul," he said. Marian was no less explicit in expressing her positive estimate of the visitor. "I have seen Emerson," she said, writing to Sarah Hennell, "the first *man* I have ever seen." On the carriage ride, Emerson asked her, "What *one* book do you value most?" Marian answered, "Rousseau's *Confessions*." Emerson's head snapped back, his eyes assessing her with fresh enlightenment. "So do I," he said. "There is a point of sympathy between us."[8]

The travelers got back to Coventry in time for tea. Sitting by the low windows opening from the drawing room on a resplendent garden, Emerson told these new friends, "If the law of love and justice have once entered our hearts, why need we seek any other?" For a family whose Sunday night service might consist of a piano rendition of Handel's *Messiah*, this was exactly right.[9] In his brief encounters through England Emerson had perfected an oracular manner that intrigued those eager for some cherished memory of him. The above utterance was culled from Mrs. Bray's notebook. Earlier, dining with Sarah Hennell, Emerson had shunned an invitation to disputation with ''The children of the gods never argue.''[10] Over such a line few would presume to trespass.

On 24 April 1873, as guest of George Howard, later Earl of Carlisle, Emerson lunched again with Marian Evans, then at the pinnacle of her fame as a novelist. To the man mystified by the homage paid to the works of Austen, Dickens, Thackeray, and Hawthorne, that, of course, was of no consequence. On the contrary, it seemed to him a matter of regret that Marian had failed to live up to the promise given in the Birdgrove years.[11]

53. Arthur Hugh Clough
A Strange Balance to Adjust

*J*N July 1848 Emerson's departure from England was delayed when he learned that the ship he intended to sail on was bound for New York. He transferred his booking to the *Europa*, which was sailing for Boston a week later. Even though he was besieged on all sides with invitations he wanted to accept, he still took time to let a young Welsh friend, Arthur Hugh Clough, know of his change of plans. Clough had known Emerson only for a dozen weeks, but neither that fact nor an age gap of sixteen years seemed to make any difference to either of them. Clough was looking for a leader and believed he had found one in Emerson. Not surprisingly, therefore, he decided to go to Liverpool to see Emerson off. Emerson was delighted. Clough's friendship gave him assurance that the seed scattered in Britain had not fallen on barren ground.

When the hour for sailing neared, Clough went on board with Emerson and paced the deck with him. He confessed a sense of loss. Emerson was going away and leaving people like himself without a leader. "Carlyle," Clough complained, "led us into the wilderness and left us there." He liked that phrase and would repeat it to others. Yet from others it can never have drawn the response it drew from Emerson. "That is what all young men in England have said to me," he said to the young man whom he saw as "a new and better Carlyle." With that he laid a hand on Clough's head and declared, "I ordain you Bishop of all England, to go up and down among all the young men, and lead them into the promised land."[1] Here, of course, was no Pentecostal moment in Clough's life. Emerson would never, had he meant to give Clough a true commission, have sought to consecrate him a bishop or to confuse his task with that which the Lord had given Moses. His tone had to be consoling and amiable. Clough needed bolstering. Emerson no more than Clough made a record at this time of the anointing. We know of it because Emerson later told Edward Everett Hale about it. The gesture was meant to be neither sacrilegious nor smug. He was simply telling Clough that he understood his feeling and was solicitous, also, for the future.[2]

Ten days after he arrived in England in the fall of 1847, Emerson had launched two concurrent lecture series that saw him hurrying between Liverpool and Manchester during the first three weeks of November. Although he had accommodations in both cities, he soon found himself responding to a flood of invitations. One of these had taken him to the home of Samuel Bulley, a Liverpool admirer, where, during the evening, he heard his host read excerpts from ''A Consideration of Objections against the Retrenchment Association,'' an ethical pamphlet that urged immediate succor for famine-stricken Ireland. The pamphlet was the work of Arthur Hugh Clough, a Fellow and Tutor at Oriel College, Oxford. Clough's sister Anne, another of Bulley's guests that night, had gone to hear Emerson speak earlier at the Liverpool Mechanics Institution, and Clough, who was smitten with Emerson's *Essays,* had lately written her: ''I wish I was with you to go and hear Emerson — I don't know what chance I have of seeing him.''[3] Anne's response was to tell him to invite Emerson to Oxford and see what came of it. Clough did as he was told, dispatching an invitation to Emerson on 26 November. ''Your name,'' he wrote, ''is not a thing unknown to us — I do not say it would be a passport in a society fenced about by Church Articles — But amongst the juniors there are many that have read & studied your works, & not a few that have largely learnt from them, & would gladly welcome their author.''[4] Clough's frankness probed Emerson at a vulnerable point. He wrote back to say that when, in the coming year, a gap opened up in his schedule, he would visit Oxford. True to his word, on 30 March, just before noon, Emerson arrived at Oriel College for a two-day stay.[5] His visit was to be a fleeting one, but he would use the time to good advantage, learning much and laying the foundation for a lasting friendship with Clough.

On the first day Emerson dined at University College with Dean Stanley, a future dean of Westminster, and his Fellows. The next morning he was the breakfast guest of the Regius Professor of Divinity, William Jacobson, and treated to the company of more deans and Fellows. At Clough's rooms that afternoon he had tea, and in the evening dined at Exeter College. The morning of his departure, Clough, Charles Daubney, a botany professor at Oriel, and others were his companions at breakfast. Time had been found, of course, to take him on walks about Magdalen and Christ Church and on a tour of the college buildings. The Bodleian and the Randolph Gallery especially held his attention. At Clough's rooms, James Anthony Froude and Francis Palgrave, still in the pre-dawn of their renown, had been tea-time guests. According to notations Clough made afterward in his diary, the topics of conversation were well suited to Emerson's tastes, being chiefly Carlyle, the Gita, Swedenborg, and Plato. Evidently they spoke of Wordsworth as well. After Clough's death, Emerson told his widow: "He interested me more than any other companion, when I first knew him, in 1848, by his rare freedom & manliness. . . . I remember we met cordially on his high appreciation of Wordsworth."[6]

Froude was sufficiently taken with Emerson to write him, after he returned to London: "Your . . . visit here, short as it was, was not without its service to us; you left luminous traces of your presence in the words you scattered. . . . In a few years I hope even here in Oxford you will see whole acres yellow with the corn of your sowing."[7]

To his friend Thomas Arnold, Clough wrote on 16 July 1848 of Emerson's impact on himself and the Oxonians:

> He is very Yankee to look at, — lank and sallow, and not quite without the twang; but his looks and voice are pleasing, nevertheless, and give you the impression of perfect intellectual cultivation, as completely as would any great scientific man in England — Faraday or Owen, for instance; more in *their* way, perhaps, than in that of Wordsworth or Carlyle. One thing struck everybody, — that he is much less Emersonian than his Essays.[8]

Emerson's own impressions were no less amiable. In a letter to Lidian of 2 April he noted: "They all showed me the kindest attentions . . . but much more, they showed me themselves, who are many of them very earnest, faithful, affectionate; some of them highly gifted men; some of them, too, prepared & decided to make great sacrifices for conscience sake."[9]

Emerson and Clough were together on three occasions in London during the month of April; in May they were almost constantly together in Paris, where they had gone — first Clough, then Emerson — to catch a glimpse of the Revolution. For most of a month there they dined together daily, and, under Clough's guidance, Emerson overcame that Puritan wariness of Gallic ways that had made him shrink from Paris fifteen years before. Grateful to this resourceful cicerone, who talked to him with such ease about the current political upheaval on the one hand, and the perennial "loose and easy conventions" of Paris, with special insights into "the grisette estate," on the other,

Emerson identified him to Lidian as "my chief dependence," and more graphically in his journal as "the best *pièce de resistance,* and tough adherence, that one could desire."[10]

Clough was a high-spirited youth, brawny and outgoing. At Rugby, Thomas Arnold had esteemed him as he would a son. Some said he had stood as model for Arthur in *Tom Brown's Schooldays.* He was the most prominent boy at Rugby in his time and when he left, nearly every boy shook hands with him. He was five feet ten, massive in build. Yet, as the son of a cotton merchant of modest means, he had had to drive himself to come to recognition. He said later: "As a boy I had less of boyish enjoyments of any kind whatever, either at home or at school, than nine-tenths of boys; certainly, even as a man I think I have earned myself some title to live for some little interval."[11]

Emerson could relate to the history of Clough's boyhood because it paralleled his own, yet that Emerson supposed that in manhood he was entitled to exact from life the equivalent of the recreations never claimed in youth is inconceivable. Indeed, after skirting this possibility with Clough — was a visit to a bordello broached? — Emerson wrote in his Parisian journal: "When I balance the attractions of good and evil, when I consider what facilities, what talents a little vice would furnish, then rise before me . . . the dear and comely forms of honor and genius and piety in my distant home, and they touch me with chaste palms moist and cold, and say to me, You are ours."[12] Actually, Emerson found satisfaction in noting that vice brought with it its own retribution. Posters advertising cures for venereal diseases met his eye everywhere in Paris. French promiscuity made no inroads on this most proper of proper Bostonians.

In December 1848 Emerson came upon a book in a Boston bookstore, *The Bothie of Toper-na-Fuosich,* a pastoral in hexameters, the work of Clough. In their time together Clough had given no hint that he had written such a poem, nor had he, in his conduct, revealed to Emerson that exuberant side of his character apparent here. Emerson was astonished. As he later told to Clough:

This poem is a high gift from angels that are very rare in our mortal state. It delights & surprises me from beginning to end. I can hardly forgive you for keeping your secret from me so well. . . . How could I know or guess that you had all this wealth of expression, this wealth of imagery, this joyful heart of youth, this temperate continuity, that belongs only to high masters.

At Emerson's urging Longfellow read *The Bothie,* as well he might since Clough admitted that he got the idea to rhapsodize in hexameters after reading *Evangeline.*[13] Lowell read it, too. Both liked it.

Emerson had still further reason for elation. One of his young men seemed to have established himself as a writer of consequence. Clough's furtiveness alone marred the perfection of the day. Even that proved an illusion. "How could I tell you of my Pastoral-to-be," he wrote Emerson, "when it had not been thought of ? — It was only begun in September : & when I left you on the deck of your Steamer I had no thought of that or any other new poem." Emerson must have found amusing Clough's confession that he had hesitated to send him *The Bothie* because at Oxford the verdict was that it was "indecent & profane, immoral & (!) Communistic."[14] Clough could not foresee that Emerson's tastes were catholic enough to embrace even *Leaves of Grass,* which, as it turned out, Clough's own tastes were not. *The Bothie* actually menaced not morals but class distinctions. Its protagonist defies his social class to marry a rural maid and go with her to New Zealand to homestead. If Clough was not "a high master" of poetry as Emerson adjudged him to be, at least he showed possibilities as a Brook Farmer.

On 17 June 1852 Clough wrote a letter to Emerson that made Emerson's heart leap with joy. Said Clough : "I entertain thoughts of emigrating to your side of the Water." He thought he might find his footing in America teaching English and the classics but approached the subject with boyish diffidence — "I dare say you have little need of strange teachers."[15]

Emerson knew that Clough's retreat from religious orthodoxy would militate against his procuring an appointment at Harvard, but he knew, also, that there was money to be made tutoring boys preparing for college and those undergoing the ordeal of rustication. For that reason he urged Clough to come : "Do you take the first ship or steamer for Boston, come out & spend two or three months here in my house. I will defend you from all outsiders, initiate you step by step into all the atrocities of republicanism." Although Emerson's enthusiasm would outrun his ability to deliver, Clough found in his words the assurance he was looking for and decided to come. "You cannot come wrong," Emerson told him elatedly, ". . . your chamber is all ready."[16]

Clough sailed for Boston from Liverpool, not in the summer, when Emerson invited him, but on 30 October, when Emerson's busiest season of lecturing was fast approaching. On the crossing he had for fellow passengers Thackeray and Lowell, both of whom took a proprietary interest in him. When he reached Concord, however, in mid-November, he found himself without the sponsorship he had expected. On 24 November Emerson would travel to the Midwest, visiting sixteen cities and delivering thirty-one lectures in the space of ten weeks. Manifestly, during Emerson's absence Clough would have little to gain by making Concord the seat of his activities. If he was going to prepare boys for college, he would do better to locate in Cambridge. The plan to accommodate him at Bush was not pursued.

On that initial visit Emerson took Clough about to give him a feeling for the Concord world and to introduce his Concord friends. The first day Clough seemed uneasy. "A Mystic called Allcott [*sic*] accompanies me," he said cryptically, in his journal, as though he were a medium speaking of his spirit control.[17] Sunday a note of enthusiasm appeared in his journal: "Loads of talk with Emerson all morning. Breakfast at eight displays two girls and a boy, the family. Dinner at 2:30." When Emerson walked him through the woods to show him what he regarded as Concord's "chief ornament," Clough reported the sight with what is surely the coolest dismissal Walden ever received: "Walk with Emerson to a wood with a prettyish pool."[18] Indeed, Concord itself seemed bleak to him, as well it might to a stranger coming upon it in mid-November:

> Concord is very bare (so is the country in general); it is a small
> sort of a village, almost entirely of wooden houses, painted white,
> with Venetian blinds, green outside, with two white wooden
> churches — one with a stone facade of Doric columns, however.
> . . . There are some American elms, of a weeping kind, and
> sycamores, i.e. planes; but the wood is mostly pine — white pine
> and yellow pine — somewhat scrubby, occupying the tops of
> the low banks, and marshy hay-land between, very brown now. A
> little brook runs through to the Concord river.[19]

The note Clough struck here was a fair clue to the difficult kind of houseguest he was and a reliable indication that he would not find in America his permanent home. In a sense history was repeating itself. Between the ages of six and nine Clough had lived in Charleston, South Carolina, where his father had hoped to settle his family. Clough's mother, however, isolated herself as completely as she could from American influences. During that interlude, Arthur became his mother's constant companion and confidant. She reminded him repeatedly that he was a Briton. He passed much of his time in her room reading about the glories of Britain's past. It was her influence that had kept him apart from boyish games and amusements. And it was her influence now that made him bristle on first contact with Emerson's world.

Possibly Clough's decision to come to America was part of his effort to identify more with his father. Yet, once he was there, the conditioning received from his mother overwhelmed his good intentions. He thought as he had been taught to think as a child. Little wonder that one line he is remembered for is "the horrible pleasure of pleasing inferior people." The marvel is that Emerson, seen in the environment

of what Clough thought of as his dowdy world, was not diminished in
Clough's eyes. Clough was taken up by some of Boston's foremost people, fraternizing easily with Charles Eliot Norton, Longfellow, Lowell,
Cornelius Felton, Channing, Horatio Greenough, George Ticknor,
Sumner, Parker, Thoreau, Francis Child, Palfrey, and Hawthorne, yet
he insisted, "Emerson is the only profound man in the country," concluding further, "I more and more recognize his superiority to everybody I have seen."[20] The likelihood is that Emerson had become for
Clough a surrogate father figure. Unfortunately, in terms of the welfare of his aspirations, with Emerson's departure for the West, Clough,
once again deprived of a father's presence, fell back on his mother's
thinking.

Clough's mother had been intensely devout. His flight from orthodoxy, and, by implication, the break with the past made by the hero
of *The Bothie*, may have been part of his attempt to escape her influence. Thirty-three years old when he arrived in America, Clough had
a head of hair that was already snow-white. To Moncure Conway, who
saw Clough pass the Divinity School almost daily on his way to visit
the Nortons at Shady Hill, it seemed like a halo. He concluded that it
was "set there by a long spiritual struggle, and marking a costly victory."[21]

On Sunday afternoon, during Clough's first visit to the Emersons,
guests came at tea-time. Clough recorded the fact without elaboration:
"At 6:30, tea and Mr. Thoreau, and presently Mrs. Ellery Channing,
Miss Channing, and others."[22] When Clough's friend Thomas Cholmondeley visited Concord two years later, he was so taken with Thoreau he deserted Emerson. Quite otherwise, the author of *The Bothie*
was immune to Thoreau's homespun appeal. Emerson continued to have
the full focus of his attention.

With the start of his lecture tour in the offing, on Saturday, 20
November 1852, at three o'clock, Emerson in Clough's honor tended a
dinner for twelve at the Tremont House. Writing to his fiancée, Blanche
Smith (a double cousin of Florence Nightingale's), Clough reported
that the dinner was "very swell," with "all the notables" on hand.
These included Hawthorne, Longfellow, Lowell, Greenough, Parker,
Sumner, Ward, and Channing. At the conclusion of the dinner (the
"superb menu" included canvas-back ducks and Madeira), Clough, in
the company of Emerson and Hawthorne, returned to Concord for a
three-day visit.[23]

On Tuesday Clough was moving from his Boston hotel to Cambridge, where he had taken lodgings on Garden Street, near the Harvard Yard. Having begun the day in Concord, he paused, when he got
back to Boston, to make a journal entry: "I am rather tired this morning — Emerson's breakfast is before ½ past seven; & I had to get up

to pack before break^{ft} & it has been snowing. . . . I am not sorry to be spared the month's stay there which I had been invited to; it w^d probably have been a bother to her."[24] Clough then had quickly divined what the home situation was with Lidian. Probably his own mother's neuroses had supplied him all the clues he needed. In fairness to Lidian, though, Clough's peremptory manner and condescension would have grated even on cast-iron sensibilities. Perhaps, too, his peacock apparel, including some gorgeous dressing gowns, which, Norton confessed, ravished his eye from the instant he saw them, disconcerted her too. Life, for Lidian, had cloaked itself in a somber hue.[25]

The next morning Emerson set off on the first stage of his lecture tour. It was the day before Thanksgiving, Emerson's favorite holiday. This year he would not be having duck turnovers, which he stipulated should be prepared because it was a family tradition that went back to his boyhood. But his commitments came first, before Thanksgiving, before custom, before Arthur Hugh Clough.

Clough did not go to Bush again until 19 February, when he came on a weekend visit from which he salvaged some positive feelings:

> Just back at Cambridge after my visit to Emerson. I was rather *sleepless* there, but it is very good to go to him. He appears to take things very coolly, and not to meddle with religious matters of any kind. Since visiting him, I feel a good deal more reconciled to mere 'subsistence.' If one can only have a little reasonable satisfactory intercourse now and then, subsistence may be to some purpose. But to live in a vain show of society would not do long. The Boston people have been too well off and don't know the realities. Emerson is really substantive.[26]

Clough had, in fact, been placed in an awkward situation. His means were slender and remained so while he taught and prepared articles for *Putnam's* and the *North American Review* and worked at revising Dryden's translation of Plutarch's *Lives*. Those whom Clough was acquainted with and with whom, by education and preference, he was disposed to associate had ample resources to draw on. Only their natural, Puritan parsimony narrowed the gap between them.

A typical evening found Clough summoned to Craigie House by Longfellow to dine with Norton, Lowell, and Felton. With the Nortons he developed a family intimacy. At Shady Hill he participated in an evening of private theatricals, contributing "a nice little epilogue" for one of the productions. At Elmwood, over dinner, Lowell's father supplied engrossing table talk, telling of his audience with George III; of his presence at Napoleon's coronation as emperor — scarcely your usual chitchat.[27] One night in early January, Clough joined Felton,

Dana, and Longfellow for an eight o'clock dinner at Elmwood. At ten o'clock Fields and Thackeray joined them. It was one o'clock before the party broke up.[28]

Well might Emerson's rustic life-style have seemed a refreshing alternative to someone who felt a need to substitute the *Bothie* ethic for the glitter of the social whirl.[29] Yet Clough's friends did not help matters. To Lowell he seemed one of life's butterflies, one of those whom, because of the pleasure they bring, society should be willing to subsidize.

Grateful, comforted by the readiness with which the Cambridge elite embraced him socially, torn between his ideals and a yearning for the plenitude this society knew, Clough still at times let his innate arrogance surface. Thus, as dinner guest of Jared Sparks, president of Harvard, after telling Mrs. Sparks to no avail the correct pronunciation of his name, he made one last emphatic try, turning back from the door at the end of the evening and approaching her to say loudly and firmly, "*Cluff*, madame, *Cluff!*"[30]

Clough stayed with the Emersons the weekend of 10 April and, on the twenty-fifth, meeting Emerson in Boston by chance, took a stroll with him and joined him at Ward's for dinner. On 14 June he dined again at Longfellow's, this time in the company of Emerson, Lowell, Norton, and Longfellow's brother Sam, all of them there to pay homage to Hawthorne, who was about to sail for England to take up his post as American consul at Liverpool. Norton afterward reported that Clough showed up "dressed in such a superb and radiant manner" that Hawthorne was "dazzled" by his appearance and driven into new depths of moroseness. Accustomed by now to Clough's snideness, Norton noted with satisfaction: "Clough and I were as usual, and we had such a good time that even he was able to praise it."[31] To own that he enjoyed himself in such company can hardly be counted a show of magnanimity on Clough's part.

Hawthorne's ship, the *Niagara,* was to sail on 6 July. No one suspected then, least of all Clough, that he would be crossing on the same run.[32]

Another weekend at Bush lay ahead, in the prime of June. On Tuesday, 21 June, back again in Cambridge, where he was staying at Shady Hill while the Nortons were at Newport, Clough made his notations about the visit: "I came back from Emerson's yesterday, after a pleasant Sunday — only Mrs Emerson never gives one any meat on Sunday — so that dinner is a sort of mess of cocoa — bread & butter & strawberries & cream — however one does."[33] It was, of course, the peak of the strawberry season in Concord. In their innocence the Emersons supposed they entertained handsomely with strawberries. Indeed, when the Hawthornes at length returned from Europe, the Emersons had a strawberry party to welcome them back. But Clough, who boasted that he had acquired in America a taste for soda water (presumably with whiskey), must have found strawberries a tame repast.

When he set out for Cambridge on Monday, Clough cannot have known that he would never see Concord or the Emersons again. Indeed, on this visit, he had "established his valise" at Bush, leaving there articles of clothing he expected to use on subsequent visits. But a letter from Lady Ashburton overthrew all his calculations. At Carlyle's urging she had secured Clough a clerkship in the British Council Office, in the Education Department. It paid three hundred pounds a year. That was better than any prospect America offered. Once back in London, Clough wrote to Emerson: "I came off . . . on the very shortest notice — telegraphed, packed, & decided all between 9 a.m. & 5 p.m."[34] In Clough's defense, it can be observed that he was gone for days before anyone, Emerson included, missed him.

Townsend Scudder says, "For years Emerson could not recover from the grief of this astonishing desertion." That is true. But Scudder insists that Emerson "locked in a cupboard some articles of clothing which Arthur had failed to gather before his hasty departure" to "serve as hostages for his return."[35] That is not true. Emerson retained the things on Clough's advice, for on 22 July Clough wrote him from London: "I hope you will keep the items of clothing which I left with you as an auspice of a future coming —"[36]

Emerson was not overwhelmed by Clough's flight, but he did lament it. And he wondered as well at Carlyle's role in providing the occasion for it. Yet he did not suspect the extent of Carlyle's complicity. "I beseech you not to commend his unheroic retreat," Emerson wrote Carlyle on 10 August.[37] In his return letter on 9 September Carlyle assured him,

> I did not, and will not, try to influence him in his choice of countries; but I think he is now likely to continue here, and here too he may do us some good. Of America, at least of New England, I can perceive he has brought away an altogether kindly, almost filial impression — especially of a certain man who lives in that section of the Earth.[38]

Carlyle further sought to placate Emerson by intimating that he might himself visit Emerson at Concord when *Frederick the Great* was finished. Perhaps Emerson's dismay at Clough's move left him chagrined:

> I was glad to see Clough here, with whom I had established some kind of robust working-friendship, and who had some great permanent values for me. Had he not taken me by surprise and

fled in a night, I should have done what I could to block his way. I
am too sure he will not return. . . . The sphere of opportunity
opens slowly, but to a man of his abilities and culture — rare
enough here — with the sureness of chemistry. . . . He had made
himself already cordially welcome to many good people, and would
have made his own place.[39]

Emerson's declaration that he would have done what he could to block
Clough's departure, had he known that it was in prospect, can be accepted at face value. Clough must have sensed as much. His precipi-
tateness suggests that he dared not risk a confrontation with Emerson.

Clough's flight still was Emerson's topic in March 1854. He wrote
him then: "If you had all the testimonies which I could furnish of the
grief of your friends here . . . I think you would . . . come again over
the sea." That next summer when Clough married Blanche Smith, his
Boston friends, at Felton's prompting, sent the Cloughs a box of wedding gifts. The Emersons contributed a silver candlestick. Two years
later Emerson sent Clough a copy of *English Traits*. With disarming
self-deprecation, meant no doubt to assure Emerson of his continuing
filial regard, Clough responded: "I think you praise us too highly — I
was anxious for more rebuke — and profitable reprimand."[40]

When, in 1857, his Boston friends started *The Atlantic Monthly*,
Clough promised to contribute. Emerson thereupon declared that it
had been worth founding if only for that result.[41] Clough's *Amours
de Voyage*, a narrative poem, was serialized in the magazine over several issues, beginning in February 1858. For it he got "a handsome
sum," the only money his poetry ever brought him. Emerson's hopes
for Clough were dashed with the final canto. Clough's vacillating hero
lost heart and went down to defeat, an outcome all too relevant to
Clough's own history.

Letters from Clough continued to reach America — to Lowell, to
Professor Child, and a stream of them to Norton freighted with that
news of politics and literature that delighted London ears and Boston
ears as well.[42] But Clough's correspondence with Emerson languished
because Emerson himself did not uphold it. His disappointment in
Clough was something he would not hide. It was probably this annoyance that disposed him to discount rumors that Clough's health had
broken. But tuberculosis ravaged his lungs. He went to Italy and at
Florence died, at forty-two, on 13 November 1861, nine years to the
day after Emerson received him at Concord.

"He may do us some good," Carlyle had said to Emerson when he
had successfully manipulated Clough's return. He had fetched Clough
"out of the wilderness," he thought, not some perilous scriptural vastness but one of Emerson's contriving. Since Clough had earlier told

Emerson that Carlyle had led him into the wilderness, it seems to have been his fate to be shunted between wildernesses. Clough's only comment to Emerson concerning Carlyle, when he got back to London, was to say he had found him "more than usually bilious." Nonetheless, he was thick with Carlyle after that, a frequent visitor at Cheyne Row and in Osborne's view, "one of the most patient and unself-assertive of disciples."[43]

Carlyle was pleased with this son whom he had snatched from Emerson's clutches. When Clough died, he wrote sorrowfully to Froude: "A mind more vivid, more ingenious, more veracious, mildly radiant, I have seldom met with, and in a character so honest, modest, kindly. I expected great things of him."[44] It did not occur to him that the subservience he exacted from Clough did not mandate greatness.

In "Thyrsis" Clough's lifelong friend Matthew Arnold memorialized him. His own poetry could not do that. Even Emerson has been criticized for seeing in *The Bothie* more than was there.

After Clough's death, Emerson wrote to his widow, praising him but taking care not to claim too much for him. Tactfully, he spoke of Clough's unrealized potential, of "a power that was only augmenting by its reserves & delays." In 1865, when Mrs. Clough asked him for reminiscences of Clough for a memoir she was preparing, Emerson did not provide them. He wrote to her a year later, after receiving a copy of the published book, explaining that he had sent nothing because he could recall nothing of sufficient weight to warrant its inclusion, and he touched again on Clough's fatal procrastination, "that extraordinary recoil" that might have profited "a grand career," but proved "a barrier to a short march."[45] In Emerson's lexicon, Clough's deficiency could be defined as a lack of courage, a failing he did not readily forgive.

54. Fredrika Bremer
David's Heart with David's Songs

$\mathcal{S}$HE was nearly fifty, a semi-illustrious spinster, plain enough to be considered homely. Fredrika Bremer was a Swedish author who wrote what were called "fireside novels." But her books were popular and were translated into several languages. One American admirer, Walt Whitman, could think of no other novels better calculated "to melt and refine the human character."[1] Fredrika was educated, well-read, had a discriminating knowledge of the arts, and could express herself in half a dozen languages. As a Christian close to orthodoxy, she knew a gulf loomed between Emerson and herself, yet she longed to meet him. "I have as yet never gone a step to see a literary lion," she wrote to her sister Agatha soon after arriving in America in the fall of 1849, at the start of a two-year, fact-finding tour, "but Emerson this pioneer in the moral woods of the New World, who sets his ax to the roots of the old trees to hew them down, and to open the path for new planting — I would go a considerable way to see this man."[2]

Fredrika had heard that Emerson was "a man of singular beauty," but that fact did not explain her interest in him since, as she put it, "the time is long since past when I wished very much to please men."[3] She suspected, however, that Emerson was, himself, the complete universal man he was seeking, "true and beautiful . . . very handsome and tall of stature," and it was for that reason that she plotted to see him. Doors everywhere opened to Fredrika, in her own right a literary personage. The question then was not whether she would see Emerson, but how.

In New York, Fredrika fell in with the Springs, Marcus and his wife, Rebecca. The Springs were Quakers and, so Fredrika heard, as "Socialists and Abolitionists," allied to the liberal movement in America. Spring, moreover, was an acknowledged philanthropist and one of the principal backers of the North American Phalanx at Perth Amboy, New Jersey, an American experiment in Fourierism. In 1846 Margaret Fuller had gone to Europe with the Springs, paying her way, in part, by tutoring twelve-year-old Eddy Spring. A well-wisher told Fredrika that through the Springs she could meet William Henry Channing and, through Channing, gain access to Emerson. The hint was enough. By 7 November 1849 Fredrika could report to Agatha that Channing had suggested a meeting with Emerson.[4]

Fredrika was off to Boston to celebrate Thanksgiving there on 26 November, and then to follow up invitations to visit "the Lowells, the Emersons, and many others."[5] The Lowells were putting her up at Elmwood for an extended stay, but, for the moment, the best she had been able to arrange for in Concord was an overnight visit with Elizabeth Hoar. Fredrika owed more to Elizabeth than she realized. Lidian, through Elizabeth, had come to admire the fireside novels and it was at Lidian's behest that Fredrika was invited to call at Bush. Fredrika innocently supposed that what had been arranged was the coming together of two literary minds, Emerson's and her own.

With the Springs, Eddy included (he got in everywhere, even accompanying Margaret Fuller when she went to see Wordsworth), Fredrika went by train to Concord. The day was 3 December. They arrived in the midst of a violent snowstorm that gave Emerson an opportunity for gallantry which no romantic novelist could have failed to relish. Heedless of the falling snow, he strode bareheaded down the path between his snow-decked evergreens to greet the visitors at the gate. Fredrika saw at once that he was "not so handsome as I had imagined him; his exterior less fascinating." His features, she also saw, were "strongly marked," his "complexion pale." But he presented "a quiet, nobly grave figure," an appearance "more significant" really than mere good looks could guarantee.[6]

This initial visit could not have been long since Fredrika's recorded impressions were few. Chiefly, she conveyed to Agatha the impression that while Emerson spared no effort to receive them cordially — "me in particular, as a lady and a foreigner, kindly and agreeably" — he stirred no flutters in her bosom:

> He is a very peculiar character, but too cold and hypercritical
> to please me entirely; a strong, clear eye, always looking out
> for an ideal, which he never finds realized on earth; discovering
> wants, short-comings, imperfections; and too strong and healthy
> himself to understand other people's weaknesses and sufferings.

. . . He interested me without warming me. That critical, crystalline, and cold nature may be very estimable, and, in its way, beneficial for those who possess it, and also for others who allow themselves to be measured and criticized by it; but — for me — David's heart with David's songs![7]

Since Emerson supposed Fredrika was Lidian's visitor, he may not have realized that she had him under such close surveillance. Certainly, he had no idea that she had done so much daydreaming about him before this encounter. For her part, she attested to the reliability of her powers of observation by describing him in terms much the same as those used earlier by Margaret Fuller and Caroline Sturgis.

Lidian must have conveyed to Fredrika some measure of her enthusiasm for the novels that had earned her acclaim as "the Jane Austen of Sweden," because Fredrika actually took her eyes off Emerson long enough to notice her: "Mrs. Emerson has beautiful eyes, full of feeling, but she appears delicate, and is in character very different to her husband." For her attentiveness Fredrika was rewarded with an invitation to return in January as the Emersons' houseguest.[8]

On this visit Fredrika was in Concord till the next afternoon but did not see Emerson again. At the Hoars' she found old Samuel's devotions unappealing: "We went to sleep at the house of a stern old Puritan, where we had long prayers, kneeling with our faces to the wall." We may sympathize with Fredrika's discomfiture but that she should publish the fact in *Homes of the New World* was, in the eyes of those who had received her, unconscionable. "As if," Emerson sputtered when he read it, "— as if Mr. Hoar was expected to pray for her entertainment!"[9] To Emerson Fredrika had assigned a "regal" scorn. She would have been dismayed to know that she had written something that later made her the object of that scorn.

If Fredrika's vision of the physical Emerson was obliterated by the reality, her vision of him as the complete universal man was not so easily routed. She found the man first met in a snowstorm was like a figure encapsulated in a miniature glass ball whose aspect, with a tip of the hand, might suddenly be altered. In a swirl of flakes he eluded her. In a postscript to the letter written to Agatha after the snowstorm visit, Fredrika wrote:

I am not sure that I have judged rightly of Emerson. I confess that I was a little staggered by the deprecating manner in which he expressed himself about things and persons whom I admired. . . . He may be unjust or unreasonable, but it certainly is not from selfish motives; there is a higher nature in this man; and I must see more of him, and understand him better.[10]

Intent on catching further glimpses of her quarry, Fredrika attended at least three of the series of ''Conversations'' that Alcott, now living in Boston again, launched on 9 December, on West Street in a room adjacent to Elizabeth Peabody's bookstore.

Since Alcott accepted questions from those assembled — some of whom sought to confound him — there was not much cohesiveness to the ''Conversations.'' But Emerson usually intervened to give a tone to events, or so Fredrika judged: ''The presence of Emerson never fails to produce a more profound and more earnest state of feeling, and by degrees the conversation arranged itself into something like observation and reply; in particular, through Emerson's good sense in calling upon certain persons to express their sentiments on certain questions.''[11] Fredrika determined that Emerson polarized those present into two factions, the social reformers who believed the perfection of man rested with social institutions, and the individualists who believed each individual must perfect himself before society could be perfect. Fredrika did not realize that every Boston gathering was made up of these two factions.

At the end of that particular evening Theodore Parker offered a recapitulation, bearing down in sardonic terms on Alcott's impractical philanthropic views. The laurels of victory seemed to be his when Emerson intervened. Earlier, when Fredrika herself, in private conversation with Emerson, had found fault with Alcott's thinking, Emerson, in resonant tones deepened for emphasis, had rebuked her: ''Amid all the noise and stir of the present day for outward and material aims, cannot you bear to hear one or two individual voices speaking for thoughts and principles which are neither salable nor yet transitory?''[12] Parker got the same treatment now. Emerson told him, ''That is quite right and would be still more so if we came here to examine a speech from the chair, and not a free, unreserved conversation.'' He thought rather that now that spirit was meant to govern which had prevailed on similar evenings he had been present at in Britain — ''that everybody was welcome to say what he thought right, but that it was forbidden to anyone to make remarks on that which was said.'' As those present realized, no rule better suited Emerson's temperament. Their smiles told Parker that Emerson had carried the day.[13]

Because Emerson, with his mounting authority, could with a few quiet words carry with him a Boston audience, it does not mean that the opposition had capsized. Earlier that same evening one of those present had asked Emerson to explain what he meant by the phrase ''the moral right of victory on earth,'' which the questioner took to be an ''absurd'' phrase at variance with Christian doctrine. Fredrika's account of how Emerson called into play his particular reserve to silence this adversary gives us a rare opportunity to observe at close hand his superior conduct under pressure:

The whole assembly directed their eyes to Emerson. I could
perceive that he breathed somewhat quicker, but when, after a few
moments' reflection, he replied, his manner was as calm, and his
voice, if possible, more gentle and melodious than common, form-
ing a strong contrast to that of the questioner. "Assuredly,"
replied he, "I consider that every one who combats and suffers for
any truth and right will, in the end, obtain the victory; if not in
his first appearance, then certainly in his second."[14]

On 17 January 1850 Emerson personally accompanied Fredrika on
the train from Boston to Concord for the start of her much-antici-
pated four-day visit. This was her first real chance to spend some time
with Emerson. The inexhaustible Springs had kept her on the constant
go with "an incessant shower both of visits and engagements, which
sometimes amused me, and sometimes drove me half to desperation,
and left me scarcely time to breathe." She was heading for Concord
in a sick and feverish condition and through the whole of the train
ride seemed in an utter stupor. She did not realize that Emerson had
served an extended apprenticeship bearing with Lidian's unnumbered
but not untold maladies, but was grateful that "he perfectly understood what was amiss with me, and let me be silent."[15] And this was
the man she had supposed was oblivious to the afflictions of others.

To Fredrika's agreeable surprise, on her arrival she rallied and was
well for the duration of her stay at Concord. She wondered if she owed
her recovery to "the presence of that strong and strength-giving spirit
in whose home I found myself,"[16] but, since Lidian seems not to have
benefited from her proximity to that alleged source of replenishment,
more probably Lidian herself was Fredrika's benefactor. They swapped
accounts of their afflictions and, for both, this was a tonic. Indeed,
from Fredrika, Lidian learned that bananas were "good for the nerves"
and thereafter ate them regularly — with a spoon![17]

Regenerated, Fredrika devoted herself to the study of Emerson's
"strong, noble, eagle-like nature."[18] He soon realized that she knew
his essays and had come to Concord not so that Lidian could know her
but so that she could know him. Moreover, her mental acuity pleased
him. She sought to stimulate him by challenging him. She questioned
his reluctance to take an active role in social reform. And she told him
he should realize that "natures as pure and beautiful as his own"
being the exception, his moral code as subscribed to by others "would
produce conceited and selfish beings."[19] At times her belligerency
"called forth his icy-alp nature, repulsive and chilling."[20] But she
found that when she was not being antagonistic he was consistently
amiable. His demeanor and beautiful voice were as soothing to her as
if she was contemplating a lover. She was gratified that he seemed to

respect her mind. Though flattered by her adulation, Emerson did not lose his objectivity. When Fredrika sought to praise his poems as a true expression of America, he protested: "Oh, you must not be too good-natured. No, we have not yet any poetry which can be said to represent the mind of our world. The poet of America is not yet come. When he comes he will sing quite differently."[21]

Fredrika, who had never met Margaret Fuller, was eager to learn as much about her as she could, in part because she knew of no other American woman so traduced by her foes, so upheld by her friends. With what Fredrika spoke of as "his usual almost alarming candor," Emerson told her of Margaret: "She has many great qualities; many great faults also."[22] Rumors then were widespread that Margaret was not Ossoli's wife. Fredrika was touched that the Emersons and Elizabeth were confident that Margaret had not compromised herself.

Fredrika left Concord to join the Springs in Boston on 21 January. En route, her escort, Lidian's brother, Dr. Charles Jackson, showed her the medal given him by the king of Sweden for the discovery of ether anesthesia — a link between her homeland and the Emersons. As she sped away from Concord, Fredrika had fond thoughts of Emerson — "Lovable he is . . . as one sees him in his home, and amid his domestic relations."[23] That same night she saw him again at West Street, where she went with Marcus Spring to catch the last of Alcott's current "Conversations." At the end of the evening, Emerson talked with her for another hour, not leaving before he promised that he would visit her in New York, where he was going the next day to launch a series of lectures to the Mercantile Library Association.

On 29 January Emerson gave the second of his Mercantile Library Association lectures. That afternoon, true to his word, he visited Fredrika, who was once again under the roof of the Springs. On this occasion she purposely made her own beliefs their topic, hoping to convince him of the existence of a personal God and of personal immortality. She said all she meant to say but was not satisfied: "I cannot usually express myself either easily or successfully until I become warm . . . and Emerson's cool . . . circumspect manner, prevented me from getting into my own natural region. I like to be with him, but when with him I am never fully myself. I do not believe that I now expressed myself intelligibly to him." Untouched by her arguments yet unwilling to demolish them, Emerson repudiated both hypocrisy and presumption on grounds more familiar to the logician than the intuitionist: "I do not wish that people should pretend to know or to believe more than they really do know and believe. The resurrection, the continuance of our being is granted; we carry the pledge of this in our own breast; I maintain merely that we cannot say in what form or in what manner our existence will be continued."[24]

In his lecture that night, "The Spirit of the Times," Emerson extended the force of his remarks by castigating political leaders for acting contrary to their own beliefs and character. Fredrika was in his audience, but few others heard him. A howling northeaster was sweeping across New York and rain spilled down in torrents. Emerson adjusted his delivery to his intimate audience. "One cannot," he said, "fire off one's great guns for so few people."[25]

Beginning in mid-March and ending on 2 April 1850, Emerson gave seven lectures (arranged for by Henry James) in New York, at the Hope Chapel. During that same interval, he gave three lectures, by private arrangement, in Brooklyn at the Female Academy Hall. For this second series, his general manager and press agent was Marcus Spring. Not since 1843 had Emerson invaded New York to such purpose. He did so now, reluctantly, yielding to the combined appeals of James and Spring. Without realizing it he was therewith launched on an expanded program of lecturing that was to encompass much of the decade of the fifties.

Fredrika was present for the Hope Chapel lecture, "Eloquence," given on the fifteenth. This was the most popular lecture Emerson ever gave and was always well received. Fredrika related: "The assembly, in the best possible humor with their lecturer, gave the most lively demonstrations of approval and pleasure."[26] On the twenty-third Fredrika heard Emerson lecture in Brooklyn, despite the winter's worst snowstorm. Storms seem to have provided counterpoint to their encounters.

In the summer of 1851, when she was making ready to return to Sweden, Fredrika came again to Boston. Concluding that she "*must* see Emerson yet once more," that her "soul seemed to require it," she took the train to Concord, where Elizabeth Hoar received her. Together they went to visit the Emersons, neither of whom was at home. Stalking Emerson's study, Fredrika steeped herself in its atmosphere, observing at last a moment of silence, storing up impressions she wanted to keep through the rest of her lifetime. His "spirit seemed to pervade its calm, pure atmosphere." As usual Emerson had left the room "in perfect order."[27] That night Emerson visited her at Elizabeth's and insisted she delay her departure next day so that he could show her Walden Pond and bring her to meet his mother, recently bedridden after shattering her hip socket.

Emerson came for her in the morning in a cabriolet and drove her himself through the woodlands to Walden. They talked as they went. Fredrika wanted to know if New England culture had reached its zenith in the present day. Emerson was sure an influx of new ideas from Europe and Asia augured further growth. She was glad to observe that the Fugitive Slave Law had moved him closer to an active role in reform. Though mindful of Margaret Fuller's tragic death since she had last seen him, she avoided the subject as alien to the mood of the day. When Emerson dismounted and secured the horse's reins to a tree so that he might fetch her a tumbler of clear spring water, she emblemized the gesture in transcendental terms:

> It is precisely this crystal, pure, fresh cold water in his individual character, in his writings, which has refreshed, and will again and yet again refresh me. . . . In long years to come, and when I am far from here, in my own native land, and when I am old and gray, yes, always, always, will moments recur when I shall yearn toward Waldo Emerson, and long to receive from his hand that draught of fresh water.[28]

Fredrika had constructed for herself a Platonic love affair, yet took care not to implicate Emerson by ascribing to him any overt inducements. To acquit herself of any she took pains to establish that her faith had been her buckler, a difference that guaranteed a stand-off between them — ''For wine, warmth-infusing, life-renovating wine, I would go to another. Emerson baptizes in water; another there is who baptizes with the Spirit and with fire.''[29] Yet she could not withhold intimation of an attraction between them that both were too noble to acknowledge: ''I left Emerson with an unmingled sentiment of gratitude for what he has been to me. . . . Never shall I see his equal again.''[30] However much she deplored his theology, Fredrika found nothing to object to in the man:

> Pantheistic as Emerson is in his philosophy, in the moral view in which he regards the world and life he is in a high degree pure, noble, and severe, demanding as much from himself as he demands from others. His words are severe, his judgments often keen and merciless. . . . One may quarrel with Emerson's thoughts, with his judgment, but not with himself. That which struck me most, as distinguishing him from most other human beings, is *nobility*. He is a born gentleman.[31]

We would be missing a valuable dimension had we never seen Emerson through the comprehending eyes of Fredrika Bremer. She was able to report her impressions of him without egoism and with much of the objectivity of a discriminating journalist. Her endeavor puts him in sharper focus for all who would know him.

55. Emerson the Speaker
A Spirit's Tongue

*T*o know Emerson the essayist and poet, we must know Emerson the speaker. His lecture scripts were tried out first at the Lyceum, on a Concord audience. One hundred times in all, he addressed this company of friends and neighbors and, report insisted, was never better than when he spoke to them. But with them he learned what would not go as well as what would go. Ruefully, he owned, "The barber learns his trade on the orphan's chin."[1]

For lecture materials Emerson went first to his "Savings Bank," as he called his journal. Yet even the lecture, polished after it had been heard at Concord and given later to paying audiences, was still a transitional piece, well honed by frequent repetition and finally worked into an essay. Chapman thought this process crucial to the form the essay took:

> It was the platform which determined Emerson's style. He was not a writer, but a speaker. On the platform his manner of speech was a living part of his words. The pauses and hesitation, the abstraction, the searching, the balancing, the turning forward and back of the leaves of his lecture, and then the discovery, the illumination, the gleam of lightning which you saw before your eyes descend into a man of genius — all this was Emerson. He invented this style of speaking.[2]

Alcott came at the same matter from a different direction:

None hears but to admire the stately wisdom and ornate beauty of Emerson's diction. Then in speaking he pleases, practicing a sort of hesitancy between the readings of his paragraphs, as of the springs of locks or choice of keys at the showing of cabinet specimens; seems sensitive at the delay sometimes, and the negligency, as it were, of another — as anxious as we are to get sight of each as it comes forth from the separate drawers, yet hesitating till the gem is out and glittering, so glad to see and admire, and the setting as the jewel itself.[3]

"Though Emerson was an ethical teacher," said Bliss Perry, "he was by no means invariably in the pulpit, either as prose-man or poet." Perry was challenging multitudes. George Woodberry, for example, insisted that Emerson "never ceased to be in garb and manner, the preacher." Richard Adams found *Nature* flawed because its unity is interfered with by "the persistence of the sermon structure." Yet Emerson disclaimed a clerical identity at every turn, typically telling a promoter in Madison, Wisconsin, "I see you write me Rev^d, to which I have no title. Do not advertise me so."[4]

Rather than being a preacher who came before his audiences in the guise of a lecturer, Emerson had begun his career as a lecturer who came before his congregations in the guise of a preacher. During the period of his pastorate at the Second Church, only twenty-five percent of his sermons were concerned with the meaning of religion. Nearly half had for their theme the improvement of character. His ideal, even then, was "ethics without cant." His friend Hedge, himself a minister, said: "Emerson's early sermons were characterized by great simplicity and an unconventional, untheological style, which brought him into closer *rapport* with his hearers than was commonly achieved by the pulpit in those days."[5]

A week after Emerson's death, on 4 May 1882, Boston's Unitarian weekly, *The Christian Register*, reembraced him, saying, "He never ceased to rebuke wrong, to expose shams, to uphold the good, to exhort the highest virtue. He could not get the preacher out of his blood." Holmes was soon to remark perceptively: "Many of the metrical preludes to his lectures are a versified and condensed abstract of the leading doctrine of the discourse. They are a curious instance of survival; the lecturer, once a preacher, still wants his text." Joel Porte confirmed Holmes's assessment of Emerson's manner but noted that typically when Emerson used a thematic biblical text he subverted its traditional meaning.[6]

Some who saw Emerson's work enveloped in the atmosphere of the pulpit would not, on that account, allow him status as an authentic man of letters. Henry Beers concluded: "Emerson was essentially a

prophet and theosophist, and not a man of letters, or creative artist.''
Canby disputed Beers only to insist that preaching, too, can be art:
''In the synthesis of all his faculties and most of all his will [Emerson
was] a preacher — and preaching, good preaching, is literature.''[7]

John Burroughs, once devoted to Emerson, put distance between
them by reordaining him and exiling him to the company of his clerical brethren. He wrote in 1877: ''Emerson is essentially a priest. . . .
His point of view is . . . that of the refiner and selector, the priest's
point of view.'' Twenty-five years later, in *Literary Values,* Burroughs
returned to this thesis: ''He was like a flower escaped from the garden, and finding a lodgment in an adjoining field, but which never
ceased to be a garden flower.''[8]

To complete the indictment, Barrett Wendell argued that Emerson's
legacy from the pulpit thwarted his development as a poet.[9]

Emerson's idiom occasionally betrayed some confusion of identity.
Writing to Carlyle on 31 March 1842, he spoke of his New York lectures (the tour on which Henry James mistook him for a theologian):
''Many persons came and talked with me, and I felt when I came away
that New York is open to me henceforward whenever my Boston parish is not large enough.'' Yet, when in 1847 he wrote in his journal:
''Much as I hate the church, I have wished the pulpit that I might
have the stimulus of a stated task,'' he seemed to have been voicing
his frustrations rather than ruminating on how to reconcile his present
role as lecturer with his past role as preacher.[10]

Emerson's habitual attire was ministerial. In Concord, usually he
wore a gray suit and soft felt hat. For city wear and formal appearances, he wore black clothes. Even after upright collars became the
fashion he preferred to wear his turned over, in the old way, either
because he was indifferent to the change or because he chose not to
appear fashion-conscious.

On the lecture circuit Emerson's attire sometimes was criticized. The
Cincinnati Gazette alluded to ''his plain suit of ill-fitting black.'' After
visiting Emerson at Bush in August 1840, in the company of George
Ripley, Theodore Parker observed in his journal: ''We saw R.W.E.
who looked as divine as usual, in his somewhat slovenly attire.'' The
Cincinnati Times reported, ''He looks and dresses soberly, and has a
quaint look, bearing and manner that reminds us more, though not
much, of pictures we have seen of Anatomy-of-Melancholy Burton, than
any thing else we can recall.''[11]

In old age Emerson garnered an insight concerning apparel that
delighted him: ''I have heard with admiring submission the experience of the lady who declared that the sense of being well-dressed
gives a feeling of inward tranquillity which religion is powerless to
bestow.''[12] But it came too late to benefit him as a lecturer.

Emerson's manner made up for his sartorial shortcomings. The rhetoric of Everett and Webster once had held him in awe. But the instruction he had had from Edward Channing, the example offered by William Ellery Channing, and the affection for frank and simple utterance Montaigne had awakened in him drew him away from all artificial graces, gestures, tricks. Those reporting on his lectures consistently described his manner as modest, simple, mild, serene, natural, earnest, sincere. Henry James once characterized a lecture by Emerson as an instance of "the esoteric made audible." In another phrase James caught what must have been the most striking aspect of Emerson's platform manner. "Instead of treating the few as the many," he said, "after the usual fashion of gentlemen on platforms, he treated the many as the few."[13]

Emerson spoke with complete absorption of the matter at hand and seemed to invite his listeners into his thought processes. Annie Fields, reporting on his public readings, catches for us something of the mood of intimacy of which he was capable: "He would sometimes bend his brows and shut his eyes, endeavoring to recall a favorite passage, as if he were at his own library table."[14] Others believed he advanced his introspective manner a step further. Thus George Gilfillan saw him reducing the many to one — "a public monologist, talking rather to himself than his audience; and what a quiet, calm, commanding conversation it is!" He reflected:

It is not the seraph or burning one you see; it is the naked cherubic reason thinking aloud before you. He reads his lectures without excitement, without energy, scarcely even with emphasis, as if to try what can be affected by the pure, unaided momentum of thought. It is a soul totally unsheathed that you have to do with; and you ask, Is this a spirit's tongue sounding on its way? so solitary and severe seems its harmony. There is no betrayal of emotion except now and then when a slight tremble in his voice proclaims that he has arrived at some spot of thought to him peculiarly sacred or dear. There is no emphasis often but what is given by the eye, and this is felt only by those who see him on the sideview. . . . His eloquence is thus of that high kind which produces great effects with small means, and without any effort of turbulence; still and strong as gravitation, it fixes, subdues, and turns us round.[15]

Margaret Fuller captured the same experiences at a deeper level of insight:

Among his audience some there were — simple souls — whose life had been, perhaps, without clear light, yet still a search after truth for its own sake, who were able to recognize beneath this veil

of words the still small voice of conscience, the vestal fires of lone
religious hours, and the mild teachings of the summer woods.
The charm of his elocution was great. His general manner was
that of the reader, occasionally rising into direct address or
invocation in passages where tenderness or majesty demanded
more energy. At such times both eye and voice called on a remote
future to give a worthy reply — a future which shall manifest
more largely the universal soul as it was then manifest to his
soul.[16]

In comparison, Henry James's remarks on Emerson in the lecture
hall show a flippancy that borders on irreverence. Yet by artfully sub-
verting it, he writes a tribute to Emerson no less admirable than Margaret's:

> His demeanor upon the platform . . . was modesty itself ; not
> the mere absence of display, but the presence of a positive per-
> sonal grace. His deferential entrance upon the scene, his look of
> inquiry at the desk and the chair, his resolute rummaging among
> his embarrassed papers, the air of a sudden recollection with
> which he would plunge into his pockets for what he must have
> known had never been put there, for his uncertainty and irresolu-
> tion as he arose to speak, his deep relieved inspiration as he got
> well from under the burning glass of his auditor's eyes, and
> addressed himself at length to their docile ears instead : no maiden
> ever appealed more potently to your enamoured and admiring
> sympathy. And then when he looked over the heads of his audi-
> ence into the dim mysterious distance, and his weird monotone
> began to vibrate in your bosom's depths, and his words flowed on,
> now with a river's volume, grand, majestic, free, and anon
> diminished themselves to the fitful cadence of a brook, impeded in
> its course, and returning its melodious coquetry upon itself, and
> you saw the clear eye eloquent with nature's purity, and beheld
> the musing countenance turned within, as it were, and harkening
> to the rumor of a far-off but on-coming world : how intensely
> personal, how exquisitely characteristic, it all was.[17]

This effect Emerson communicated not only through his lectures but
through the essays that resulted from the lectures. On 25 October 1860
Herman Grimm, whom he had never met, wrote him: "You write so
that every one reading your words must think that you had thought
of him alone."[18]

Although Emerson disliked extemporaneous speaking, often he conveyed the impression that he was saying what had that moment come

to mind. Lowell said: "He somehow managed to combine the charm of unpremeditated discourse with the visible existence of carefully written manuscript lying before him on the desk." In 1863, when Emerson lectured in Indianapolis, a local newsman confessed admiration for Emerson's device of "seeming to forget the last word or two, always significant . . . and stumbling upon them unexpectedly with an effect that the most elaborate declamation could not produce." This process, in fact, duplicated Emerson's authentic groping for the word he wanted. John Albee said: "He often hesitated for a word, but it was the right one he waited for." Holmes, mentioning a visit to the Saturday Club, recreated the experience for his readers as only he could: "I sat by Emerson, who always charms me with his delicious voice, his fine sense and wit and the delicate way he steps about among the words of his vocabulary — if you have ever seen a cat picking her footsteps in wet weather, you have seen the picture of Emerson's exquisite intelligence, feeling for his phrase or epithet."[19]

Emerson's tentativeness once produced an unexpected response. He visited the Reform School ship and, against his natural preference, gave an impromptu address to the boys on board. A few days later, when their reading instructor was trying to show them the necessity of learning to express themselves with ease and grace, he put on a demonstration of how an awkward speaker might discourse, then asked, "Now, boys, what should you think if you heard a man speak so?" "Should think it was Mr. Emerson," the boys chorused in response.[20]

Emerson's voice itself seems to have been an instrument of such subtle range and force that even listeners who could not follow his thought often came away from his lectures fully gratified. After hearing Emerson lecture, Samuel Bowles wrote to Austin Dickinson, Emily Dickinson's brother, "It is pictures, landscapes, poetry, music, babies, and beautiful women rolled up in an hour of talk. It takes the place of making love in our young days."[21] Whipple approached it from another direction:

> Emerson's voice had a strange power, which affected me more
> than any other voice I ever heard on the stage or on the platform.
> It was pure thought translated into purely intellectual tone, the
> perfect music of spiritual utterance. It was impossible to read his
> verses adequately without bearing in mind his peculiar accent and
> emphasis; and some of the grandest and most uplifting passages in
> his prose lose much of their effect unless the reader can recall the
> tones of his voice. . . . There was nothing sensual, nothing even
> sensuous, nothing weakly melodious, in his utterance; but his voice
> had the stern keen, penetrating sweetness which made it a fit
> organ for his self-centered, commanding mind. Yet though pecu-

liar to himself, it had at the same time an impersonal character, as though a spirit were speaking through him.[22]

Alcott found in Emerson's voice the sounds of Nature — "an organ of marvellous compass . . . dying away like the roar of waves on the ocean shores, or else the whisper of zephyrs in the summer's evening." To Margaret Fuller it was like seasoned "instruments of wood and brass." To Maud Howe Elliott it was "by turns like a silver trumpet and the soughing of the breeze." Yet it was, as well, a voice of authority. N. P. Willis said: "It is a voice with shoulders in it which he has not — with lungs in it far larger than his — with a walk in it which the public never see — with a fist in it which his own hand never gave him the model for." Lowell agreed: "There is a kind of undertow in that rich baritone of his that sweeps our minds from their foothold into deeper waters with a drift we cannot and would not resist."[23]

As for Emerson's gestures while lecturing, they were few. The *Cleveland Daily Plain Dealer* commented: "We had quite as lief see a perpendicular coffin behind a lecture-desk as Emerson." Woodbury said: "He always stood on the rostrum, having cast away all the tricks that orators hold dear, gestureless, save now and then a slight movement of the hand, repelling as from the cold pole of a magnet." This gesture was most commonly reported. John Townsend Trowbridge saw it in these terms: "He had but one gesture, a downward thrust of his clenched right hand, held contorted and tense at his side, and used with unconscious earnestness in driving imaginary stakes."[24]

Ireland also observed, however, "occasionally a slight vibration of the body, as though rocking beneath the hand of some unseen power."[25] This rocking motion originated in Emerson's unconscious habit of periodically lifting himself up on his toes, as a form of emphasis. When in 1866 he spoke to the Encore Club in Quincy, this gesture dramatically called attention to itself. There Emerson spoke from an improvised platform that consisted chiefly of loose planks. Each time he elevated himself on his toes the boards bumped and rattled beneath him, muttering their acknowledgment of the rhetorical adagio and bringing it to the notice of the packed assembly.

Emerson deplored his inadequacies as a lecturer, describing himself as "the worst known public speaker, and growing continually worse." If he was referring exclusively to his want of continuity in his discourse, then many would have agreed with him. Typical was an incident that occurred when he lectured in England on Plato, in 1848. "Can you tell me," one listener whispered to another, "what connection there is between that last sentence and the one that went before, and what connection it all has with Plato?" His neighbor told him, "None, my friend — save in God!" Usually Emerson's listeners were not put off by that difficulty. The *Cincinnati Enquirer* dealt with it once by saying of a lecture that Emerson delivered there: "[We] have toyed in the dark with a string of pearls."[26]

Emerson has been credited with having, along with Lincoln, precipitated the downfall of the tradition of high-flown oratory. The new tradition of natural utterance on the stage, which, given impetus by Edwin Booth, took hold in Emerson's lifetime, owed a major debt to Emerson's example. Emerson did not hold his listeners by any of the familiar devices of rhetoric, nor by physical or verbal gesture, nor by his personal appearance. Even his unique vocal endowments were, of themselves, insufficient to explain the phenomenon of Ralph Waldo Emerson — outstanding lecturer of his age. Yet the evidence that he stood first is overwhelming. In 1868 William Robinson wrote: "Emerson is of all men the one most worth hearing, even better than [Wendell] Phillips with his matchless oratory." Trowbridge said: "Emerson was no orator. . . . he had no gift of extemporary utterance, no outburst of improvisation. But in the expression of ethical thought, or in downright moral vehemence, I believed and still believe him unequaled." Lowell concurred: "I have heard some great speakers and some accomplished orators, but never any that so moved and persuaded men as he."[27]

Thee may sovran Destiny
Lead to victory day by day!

56. Emerson as Lecturer
The Conquest of the West

*T*HURSDAY afternoon, 16 May 1850, found Emerson on board the
steamer *America,* sailing down Lake Erie from Buffalo to Sandusky,
Ohio. He had committed himself to give a series of eight lectures in
Cincinnati and was well on his way to his destination. From Sandusky
a train would take him across Ohio to Cincinnati. Meanwhile, he was
under no pressure. He did not have to speak in Cincinnati till Monday
evening, four days hence. And that suited him since it was the chance
to see something of the West, where he had never traveled before, that
disposed him to accept the Cincinnati invitation.

The invitation that resulted in this journey had come from Ains-
worth Rand Spofford, a young bookstore clerk, and one of the found-
ers of Cincinnati's Literary Club. Spofford, guided by what Emerson
later termed "despotic benevolence," had collected the signatures of a
hundred people who wanted Emerson to deliver a lecture series in
Cincinnati, now, with a population of over 115,000, the biggest city in
the Ohio Valley.[1] To show their sincerity, his would-be sponsors pledged
$150 for Emerson's traveling expenses.[2] In addition to that sum, he
would be given whatever profits the lectures realized. It was well, however, that money was not the prime inducement in luring a reluctant
Emerson from Concord in Maytime. Despite encouraging words from
the press, the lectures were "thinly attended." His total profits from
a three-week visit came to $560.

Spofford's invitation had, in fact, posed a problem for Emerson.
Over the winter just ending he had given three dozen lectures, the last
six of these in Philadelphia, during April. "I incline to refuse," he

494

told William, "as my garden wants me, & my library more."[3] But he did not let these obstacles long detain him. In addition to the chance to see the West, he was further enticed by the prospect of opening up a new territory to lecture in, and the opportunity to show good will to the many New Englanders now implanted in Cincinnati, including two of his own cousins — a Haskins and a Ladd — Bellamy Storer, kin to the Hoars, as well as Edward Cranch, Pearse's brother, all presumably signers of the appeal Spofford had sent to him. Emerson's subsequent western tours were more readily undertaken because on this journey he learned that he would find old friends wherever he went. Thus he would write Lidian in February 1854, from Toledo: "I have found a population of Yankees, out here, and an easy welcome for my Massachusetts narrowness everywhere."[4]

Emerson was not much of a gardener. A Great Lakes cruise suited him better. But suddenly there was a rumble in the bowels of the ship. A boiler had exploded and the *America* was on fire. This was no small matter. The annals of the day abounded in ship tragedies. In fact, by a remarkable twist of fate, on this very day, almost at the same hour, Margaret Fuller, with the Marchese Ossoli and their infant son, was boarding the merchant ship *Elizabeth* at Livorno, Italy, to set out on the journey that would carry all three to shipwreck and death. When the *America*'s crisis came, the ship was ten miles from Cleveland. There could have been panic but there was none. The late edition of the *Cleveland Daily Plain Dealer*, published that same day, described what happened: "The captain very discreetly told the firemen to keep their places, not to alarm the passengers." The ship made for Cleveland, where the passengers were disembarked. Only then was the alarm given. Additional firefighters came aboard, and a three-hour battle ensued. For a time the fire seemed out of hand and preparations were begun for scuttling the ship. Although at last she was saved, the *America* "was considerably charred and no doubt would have burned up had she been at sea."[5]

The same newspaper that carried first particulars of the fire disclosed that Ralph Waldo Emerson, making an unscheduled stopover in Cleveland as one of the passengers forced to disembark from the *America,* had agreed to give a free lecture that night at Empire Hall, for the Cleveland Library Association.[6] His topic was "England," and a good audience, recruited on a few hours' notice, was on hand to hear him. Thus it happened that Cleveland snatched from Cincinnati the distinction of being that city in Ohio which heard the first of sixty lectures Emerson gave in that state over the next seventeen years.

That Emerson could walk away from a burning ship and, minutes later, agree to deliver, that same night, an unscheduled lecture in an unfamiliar city suggests that he had greater stamina than customarily he credited himself with. The following March, indeed, with good cheer, he described to Lidian some of the discomfitures he currently suffered while on tour: "Two nights spent in railcars and the third on the floor of a canal-boat, where the cushion allowed me for a bed was crossed at the knees by another tier of sleepers as long-legged as I, so that in the air was a wreath of legs."[7] On the lecture trail, so long as he did not lose his manuscripts Emerson could come through any ordeal without too much dismay.

Despite his adaptability, Emerson, by inclination, was not a traveler. "I shall be glad to be home again," he wrote Lidian from New York in March 1842. "I was not born for gipseying."[8] On 15 February 1865, on his return from lecturing in Chicago and Milwaukee, Emerson was to make a celebrated entry in his journal:

> 'Twas tedious the obstructions & squalor of travel. The advantage of their offers at Chicago made it needful to go. It was in short this dragging a decorous old gentleman out of home, & out of position, to this juvenile career tantamount to this; "I'll bet you fifty dollars a day for three weeks, that you will not leave your library & wade & freeze & ride & run, & suffer all manner of indignities, & stand up for an hour each night reading in a hall:" and I answer, "I'll bet I will," I do it & win the $900.[9]

On 11 January 1853 Emerson wrote to Lidian:

> Here I am in the deep mud of the prairie, misled, I fear, into this bog . . . by a young New Hampshire Editor, who overestimated the strength of both of us. . . . In the prairie, it rains, & thaws incessantly, & if we step off the short street, we go up to the shoulders, perhaps, in mud. My chamber is a cabin. . . . But in the prairie we are new men just come and must not stand for trifles.[10]

And men marveled that later Emerson could stand the rigors of a meticulously organized camping trip in the Adirondacks, with Lowell, Louis Agassiz, Rockwood Hoar, and others, each man accompanied by his personal guide to render valet service.

To Carlyle Emerson wrote on 11 March 1854: "I went out Northwest to great countries which I had not visited before; rode one day, fault of broken railroads, in a sleigh, sixty-five miles through the snow, by Lake Michigan . . . to reach Milwaukee. . . . I was much made of, as the only man of the pen within five hundred miles."[11] There was some compensation for the punishment endured. Vanity could warm even Emerson.

At Davenport, Iowa, in December 1855, noting his trips to and fro between the Illinois and Iowa shores, Emerson wrote, "I have crossed the Mississippi on foot three times." That same month he noted also: "Yesterday morning in bitter cold weather I had the pleasure of crossing the Mississippi in a skiff. . . . Much of the rowing was on the surface of fixed ice . . . but the long run to the Tepfer House, the volunteered rubbing of our hands by the landlord and clerks, and good fire restored us." On 3 January following, he arrived at Dixon, Illinois, "at 4 in the morning, to take the last & worst bed in the tavern."[12]

By 8 January, Emerson had advanced to Belvidere, Illinois, and again wrote Lidian. He spoke first of the weather, all other concerns now being secondary to that: "Mercury below zero 22°. . . . The cruel kindness of a gentleman at Galena carried me out in a bitter cold sleigh jaunt on the river to see the [Marsden] lead mines. I not suspecting the 5 miles, thinking it 3, it turned out seven; & last night I could hardly speak."[13] Emerson pushed on. January 9 found him in Beloit, Wisconsin: "Fierce cold weather, mercury varying from 20° to 30° below for the last week." He reflected on what all this meant to him as a lecturer:

This climate and people are a new test of the wares of a man of letters. All his thin, watery matter freezes; 'tis only the smallest portion of alcohol that remains good. At the lyceum, the stout Illinoian, after a short trial, walks out of the hall. . . . Well, I think . . . the people are always right (in a sense), & that the man of letters is to say, these are the new conditions to which I must conform.[14]

Emerson did not look upon these noblemen of nature as brimming repositories of infused knowledge, however. "I find," he said, "well-disposed kindly people among these sinewy farmers of the north; but in all that is called cultivation they are only ten years old; so that there is plenty of non-adaptation & yawning gulfs never bridged in this ambitious lyceum system they are trying to import."[15]

On his first visit to Cincinnati, Emerson visited Niagara Falls en route. The falls met his expectations and on later western visits he again put up at Niagara. On 4 January 1863, at the start of an extensive lecture tour, he took a room at Niagara's American House. After inspecting the falls he retired early. To his daughter Edith, on 8 January, he wrote an account of what followed:

At 3 o'clock, was waked by the cry of Fire! within the house. I put on my clothes or some of them, & gathered up my properties

as many & as fast as I could in the dark, & got down stairs
through a cloud of smoke & cinders, and found women clothed in
blankets & barefooted in the hall & in the street, & great distress
everywhere. The house was burned out thoroughly, before all our
eyes, & nothing left but the four walls. All the furniture, &
quantities of clothing, & much money of the guests & of the
proprietor, were lost. I had left my baggage at the Suspension
Bridge, & had with me only my black bag, but contrived to lose
my ticket from Buffalo to Chicago, and some brushes, &c. no
insurance.[16]

At the first light Emerson walked the two miles to the Suspension
Bridge, to retrieve his luggage and continue his journey.

The destruction of the American House gave Emerson pause. With
a clairvoyance he would have been happy to have had invalidated by
future events, he told Edith: "You must not burn up the castle [i.e.,
Bush], &, if it kindles, save the little black trunk under your mother's
bureau, & all the MSS in the study."[17]

As Emerson neared the end of the span of western tours, he showed
he had adapted capably to the conditions the circuit offered. In 1860
he limped westward before he had recovered from a severe sprain. Yet
a month into the tour, after delivering seventeen lectures, he wrote
Ellen from Milwaukee, saying, with undiminished pluck, that he had
"awed my Wisconsin senate . . . with a richer orotund than they had
heard." Its cause was a cold caught in Chicago three days before. In
Washington, Iowa, on 13 February 1867, he noted: "In riding in an
open sleigh, from Oshkosh to Ripon, in a fiercely cold snowstorm driving in my face, I blessed the speed and power of the horses." He blessed
also the pressure he was under. Writing from Milwaukee, on 31 January 1865, he told Ellen: "My Milwaukee days are the correctors of
my MSS."[18]

Storm and cold, fire and mud — these were merely the more dramatic hazards Emerson encountered on tour. Errors in scheduling,
hostile journalists, inquisitors, poor housing, and noisy and unheated
lecture halls were others. Once, in Cincinnati, Emerson was about to
lecture on power when the power failed, the gas lights flickering out
to leave Smith and Nixon's Hall in darkness long enough for a large
part of the audience to give up and go home.

In the winter of 1856 the Ohio River froze from shore to shore. In
Cincinnati, on the night of 4 February, as Emerson was giving his
lecture "Works and Days," the ice broke, wrecking six steamers and
causing extensive destruction and havoc. Much of his audience forsook
the lecture hall to watch the spectacle. The *Gazette* told of one observer who lamented the stupidity of people who chose to take in the

ice show when they might have watched instead, "one good looking Yankee, with a long nose, spouting pantheism, nonsense, mist and mud."[19]

Emerson's heart went out to Jenny Lind (even though, as he meticulously noted in his journal, her gross receipts for ninety-three concerts in America were $176,675.09) when he heard she had had to sing in a hall located over a railroad depot. He had experienced the equivalent. On 18 January 1866 at Rock Island, Illinois, he lectured in Babcock's Hall, located over a livery stable. The *Daily Argus* next day reported: "The only drawback [was] the real painful sensation produced by the slamming of doors; the tramp of heavy feet on stairs and aisles; the rattling of stoves; and the thunder produced by the driving of teams on the noisy planks under the hall." To this orchestration Emerson had lectured on social aims in America, and managed to convince John Saxe, editor of the *Daily Argus*, that he had listened to "the most scholarly production we have heard in Rock Island," and had passed "So purely happy an hour [as] is rarely found."[20]

After so many years, Emerson could not be put off by mere thundering hooves. Nor would he have been disconcerted by the strategy of his promoters, who, to swell his audience, shut down the local skating rink, posting notices which read: "Emerson lectures tonight. Go to Babcock's Hall. There will be no skating." After all, had he not lectured elsewhere where a dance was combined with his lecture and the advertisement read, "Tickets to Emerson and ball, one dollar"?[21] In fairness to his western public, Emerson sometimes had had to lecture under deplorable conditions in his native Massachusetts. On 3 March 1847 he had noted tartly:

> At Lincoln, last night, read a lecture in the schoolhouse. The architect had a brighter thought than ordinary there. He had felicitously placed the door at the right of the desk, so that when the orator is just making a point and just ready to drive the last nail, the door opens at his side & Mr Hagar and Deacon Sanborn & Captain Peck come in, & amiably divide with him the attention of the company. Luckily the sleighbells, as they drove up to the door, were a premonitory symptom, & I was able to rein in my genius a little, whilst these late arrivers were bundling out & stamping their feet before they usurped the attention of the house.[22]

On the night of 17 May 1850, the day after the *America* caught fire, at seven o'clock Emerson left Cleveland, sailing down the lake on the steamer *Saratoga* to Sandusky, where he disembarked at midnight. At five in the morning he was on his way again, traveling southward on the Mad River and Lake Erie Railroad, transferring at Springfield to the little Miami Railroad, which took him on the final stage of his journey to Cincinnati. That day alone he traveled two hundred and eighteen miles.

Before the next weekend arrived Emerson had given three of his scheduled lectures. The third of these lectures, "The Spirit of the Times," he delivered on Friday, 24 May. That afternoon he had been visited in his rooms at the Burnet House — just newly opened and a showplace for elegance — by "a committee to invite Mr. Emerson to meet the Literary Club on some evening convenient to himself for the purpose of a free confab on literary men and matters." One of his visitors was a struggling young lawyer, Rutherford B. Hayes. In his diary that night Hayes recorded a careful description of Emerson as, with his fellow committee members, Isaac Collins and the persevering Spofford, he had observed him at the Burnet House:

> Mr. Emerson is above the middle height, a tolerable figure, but rather awkward; dresses in the *plainly genteel style* — black surtout and pants, black satin vest and cravat, common shoes. His head is not large, forehead low and narrow, hair cut short — a brown color, eyes grayish blue, a rather large nose with deep lines from the nostrils on either side arching around the mouth, but not so as to give an unpleasant expression. Is agreeable in his manners and first address. Talks, as he speaks, freely, and in a somewhat quaint way.[23]

The last lecture Emerson ever gave in Ohio was given at Columbus, on 30 December 1867, when he spoke at the YMCA on manners. Closing the circle begun seventeen years before, he made a visit to the State House to pay a courtesy call on Hayes, who had lately been elected to the first of his three terms as Ohio's governor. A decade later, in June 1877, ignoring his infirmities, Emerson traveled down to Cambridge from Concord to greet Hayes at the Harvard Commencement where, as President of the United States, he was to receive an honorary degree.

As Hayes's political fortunes expanded, so did his appreciation of Emerson. He bought and read his books promptly upon publication, and reread them many times, heavily annotating them. On 22 August 1889, two months after his wife died, Hayes found comfort in reading Emerson's "Immortality." Emerson, Hayes told his friend Mrs. John Herron, was "the best mind of our time and race." The following May, Hayes wrote again to Mrs. Herron, saying: "When I mount my hobby — Emerson — away I am carried. . . . How he prepares one to meet the disappointments and griefs of this mortal life. His writings,

with me, seem to be religion. They bring peace, consolation; that rest
for the mind and heart which we all long for — content.'' An entry in
his diary made two years before his death, on 11 June 1891, shows his
loyalty to Emerson was undiminished: ''Uncle Birchard read John
Ruskin. He was the favorite author with him. Not with me. Mine is
and for forty years has been Emerson.''[24]

Among others who extended a welcome to Emerson on his visits to
Cincinnati were Alphonso Taft and Nicholas Longworth. Taft, a native of Vermont who settled in Cincinnati in 1840, seven years after
graduating from Yale, was attorney general in Grant's cabinet, succeeding to the post Rockwood Hoar had held earlier in Grant's administration. Taft was Emerson's kinsman, being descended from the Reverend Joseph Emerson of Mendon. Alphonso Taft's son William married
Helen Herron, daughter of Hayes's friend, and became twenty-seventh President of the United States. Longworth's grandson Nicholas,
a congressman from Ohio and Speaker of the House under Coolidge
and Hoover, married Theodore Roosevelt's daughter Alice.

Early in February 1860, Emerson was taken on a tour of Longworth's great Catawba wine cellars. There he gathered an insight he
later used in his poem ''May-Day,'' suggesting that as wine, heeding
the call of spring, burst its casks, men, harkening to the memory of
Eden, sometimes sought to repossess Edenic bliss by instituting utopias.[25]

The day after the committee of the Literary Club waited on him in
1850, Emerson visited their rooms for relaxed conversation. Hayes noted
in his diary that Emerson, over the next two and a half hours, encompassed in his remarks everything from British men of letters ''to raising corn and pigs.'' And he confirmed Emerson's assertion that he did
not enjoy being asked to explain transcendentalism. In March 1842,
after meeting Greeley and Brisbane, Emerson had written Lidian:
''They fasten me in their thought to 'Transcendentalism,' whereof you
know I am wholly guiltless. . . . So that I have to begin by endless
disclaimers & explanations.''[26] At the Literary Club Hayes noted: ''Mr.
Emerson seemed quite puzzled, not to say vexed, when speaking of this
subject. It was forced upon him by questions and suggestions.''[27] A
background to Emerson's vexation is preserved in odd jottings. On 29
September 1836, with evident amusement, he told his journal: ''Transcendentalism means, says our accomplished Mrs. B[arlow] with a wave
of her hand, *A little beyond.*''[28] But to his mother he wrote from Providence on 28 March 1840:

You must know that I am reckoned here a Transcendentalist,
and what that beast is, all persons in Providence have a great
appetite to know: so I am carried duly from house to house, and

all the young persons ask me, when the Lecture is coming on
the Great Subject? In vain I disclaim all knowledge of that sect of
Lidian's, — it is still expected I shall break out with the New
Light in the next discourse. I have read here my essay on the Age,
the one on Home, one on Love, & one on Politics, — These seem
all to be regarded as mere screens & subterfuges while this dread
Transcendentalism is still kept back. They have various definitions
of the word current here. One man, of whom I have been told, in
good earnest defined it as 'Operations on the Teeth'; A young man
named Rodman, answered an inquiry by saying 'It was a nick-
name which those who stayed behind, gave to those who went
ahead.'[29]

As for what those designated as New England transcendentalists had
in common, Emerson conjectured: "Perhaps they only agreed in having fallen upon Coleridge and Wordsworth and Goethe, then on Carlyle, with pleasure and sympathy."[30] He had no idea, he owned, who
was responsible for the designation.

On Saturday, 25 May 1850, Emerson was forty-seven years old. To
mark the occasion a delegation from the Literary Club took him some
forty miles to visit Fort Ancient — earthworks, some four or five miles
long, created by the early Mound Builders. His appetite for new wonders sharpened, Emerson, at the end of his stay in Cincinnati, agreed
to go off with his hosts to visit Mammoth Cave in Kentucky. "They
think it a little matter to run down the river to Louisville 133 miles,"
he told Lidian.[31] He seemed eager to accept life on that same grand
scale. So off they went, a party of seventeen at final reckoning, ladies
as well as gentlemen, and three Englishmen among them.

The cave, when they finally reached it, met Emerson's fullest expectations, and the letter he wrote to Lidian concerning it — the longest
he ever wrote to her — detailed all its wonders. With boyish enthusiasm he insisted that Elizabeth should see the letter and his sister-in-
law, Susan. He had added a chapter to Hakluyt, his favorite narrator
of wondrous travels.

The actual journey proved more of an adventure than Emerson had
foreseen. No system of transportation had been set up between Cincinnati and Mammoth Cave to facilitate the movement of so large a party.
At Louisville they waited two days for horses and carriages that never
came, then took passage on the steamer *Mammoth Cave* which took
them 182 miles down the Ohio to Evansville, then up the Green River
to the Barren River, to cast anchor at last at Bowling Green, a distance of another 150 miles. They sailed on Wednesday afternoon and
got to Mammoth Cave on Saturday night, covering the last thirty miles
in a procession of coaches. Passing up the Green River was not unlike

advancing through uncharted regions of the Congo. The stream was narrow, and, panicked by their presence, wild turkeys flew ahead of them from tree to tree. Sometimes they had to pole their way through thick mats of rotting vegetation, each thrust releasing marsh gas, which posed a new fire hazard since it was readily combustible.

All the hardships were forgotten in the fascination of an eighteen-mile walk through the Church, the Coffin Room, Fat Man's Misery, Purgatories, the Valley of Relief, the Vineyard, the Snowball Room, Cleveland's Cabinet, until at last, at the end of fourteen hours, they emerged into Serena's Arbour. The next morning they went into the cave again to spend four hours visiting the Gothic Chapel, the Star Chamber, and Gorin's Dome. On emerging they found, once again, transportation nonexistent. Undaunted, Emerson set out on foot with one of the obliging literati and they walked twenty-one miles before they found a buggy that would take them the rest of the way to Bowling Green.[32]

On his homeward journey, Emerson registered at Planter's Hotel in St. Louis, which proved to be a charnel house, its patrons succumbing wholesale to cholera. Hastily he resumed his journey, only to find that cholera and death had come aboard the riverboat also and traveled with them on the four-day voyage to Galena.[33] Throughout his tour, it seemed, Emerson had been sailing between Scylla and Charybdis. Even so, nineteen days after he set out from Mammoth Cave, Emerson arrived home in Concord unscathed.

In May 1848 Emerson had written in his journal: "I meet in the street people full of life. I am, of course, at ebbtide; they at flood; they seem to have come from the south or from the west or from Europe. I see them pass with envy at this gift which includes all gifts."[34] At forty-five Emerson saw himself depleted of vitality. He never would have supposed himself capable, in the months ahead, of the arduous journey Spofford's letter initiated.

Even as Emerson turned in at his own door, in the South Atlantic the storm was organizing that would shatter the *Elizabeth* and bring death to many on 19 July at Fire Island. Emerson saw in the news of Margaret Fuller's death an omen that he himself "had few days left." In fact, he had another thirty-two years. Had he stopped to consider the facts he would have realized that he had just proved himself a survivor. In the years ahead he would prove it again, many times over.

57. Horatio Greenough
A Man of Great Elevation

*T*o William Emerson, Waldo wrote from Florence, Italy, in April 1833: "Greenough at Florence has more genius, his friends here say, than all the other artists in Italy put together."[1] He meant Horatio Greenough, a young Bostonian who had been studying art in Italy during most of the eight years since he had graduated from Harvard. Emerson's aunt, Lydia Haskins, was married to Greenough's uncle, William Greenough, pastor of a parish in Newton, a Boston suburb. This link was reason enough for Greenough to extend Emerson full hospitality and to carry him off to breakfast and dinner meetings with Walter Savage Landor at his villa on the slope of Fiesole, on the outskirts of Florence.[2]

Greenough, in his own right, was someone to meet. He had just received confirmation from the American secretary of state of a commission to execute a colossal statue of Washington for the Capitol Rotunda. Moreover, he had notions of art that Emerson declared to be "quite the most magnanimous theory of arts and artists, I have ever chanced to hear from one of themselves."[3] Greenough had contended then that modern artists never would thrive until they heeded the example of the ancient Greeks and worked, not in isolation, but as members of a brotherhood inspiring one another. The compatibility Emerson's receptiveness to this theory implied would later be confirmed when the two men explored other ideas together. All but illiterate when it came to theories of art, Emerson had only to hear ideas in harmony with his own thinking to assimilate them without hesitation.

When Greenough's statue of Washington was placed in the Capitol

Rotunda in 1841, few commended it. Greenough had portrayed Washington as Phidias had envisaged Zeus in the statue he wrought for the temple at Olympia. He was seated, the upper half of his body undraped, his right hand pointing heavenwards. While Greenough preferred the heroic tradition, the building where his statue would be housed was neoclassical. Therefore he had produced a statue in keeping with its setting. Emerson thought so, too.

In January 1843 Greenough carried out some experiments in lighting the statue, and Emerson, visiting Washington at the time, took in the spectacle, sitting for two hours on the stone floor of the Rotunda as the lights were moved about. He witnessed more drama than he anticipated. The wooden case that held the lamps caught fire. Fireballs shot through the Rotunda. The lamps melted, producing such a volume of smoke that the whole apparatus had to be hauled outside.[4]

In August that same year, the *Democratic Review* published Greenough's seminal article "American Architecture," in which he insisted that form should follow function. Absent in Europe over the next several years, Greenough did not try to generate interest in his theory in America until he returned home in the fall of 1851. Soon afterward, on 28 December, he wrote to Emerson from Washington, to ask if he might come to Concord to explore his theories with him in depth. Delighted with any theory that put man in harmony with Nature, Emerson invited Greenough to come the following month.[5] Instead, Greenough turned to and wrote a book, *The Travels, Observations, and Experience of a Yankee Stonecutter*, in which he set forth his views. When at last he showed up in Concord for a visit in mid-August 1852, he had already delivered the manuscript to G. P. Putnam, in New York. From Emerson he was looking now not so much for insights as for approval.

He was not disappointed. On 18 August Emerson wrote in his journal:

> Horatio Greenough came here & spent a day . . . a man of sense, of virtue, & of great elevation. . . . His magnanimity, his idea of a great man, his courage, & cheer, & self-reliance, & depth, & self-derived knowledge, charmed & invigorated me, as none has, who has gone by, these many months. I told him, I would fife in his regiment.

To this handsome endorsement, he added a wary note: "His democracy is very deep, &, for the most part, free from crotchets, — not quite, — & philosophical."[6]

Recalling this visit eleven years later, Emerson said:

> He stayed a day & a night, — a most memorable visit. Until that day I had no knowledge of the power of his genius, or the wealth

of his mind. His ingenuity, his variety of knowledge, his eloquence, his power of illustration, his high moral demands, his ideal
democracy, &, through all, the perpetual presence of the Artist,
were an incessant surprise & delight to me.[7]

Emerson was not the only Bostonian to be impressed by Greenough.
The previous January Longfellow had driven into Boston with him to
hear Emerson's lecture "Worship" and liked Greenough better than
he liked the lecture.[8]

At the start of September 1852 Greenough sent Emerson the printed
sheets of his book. Emerson instantly provided his endorsement: "It
is a very dangerous book, full of all manner of reality & mischievous
application, fatal pertinence, & hip-&-thigh-smiting personality, and
instructing us against our will. . . . It contains more useful truth than
any thing in America I can readily remember." Greenough came again
to Concord, on 25 October, and passed the day with Emerson. Referring to that visit, during which they had ranged over a shining array
of topics — Fourier, sex, diet, the Elgin marbles, Puritan aesthetics,
and foreign influences in America — Emerson wrote him: "You have
done me a world of good by a pair of conversations. May I often see
you!"[9]

If Greenough charmed Emerson, it was by his self-assurance and
the novelty of his ideas, not by flattery. He had strong reservations
about Emerson's writings and took no pains to hide them. In March
1851, when first he looked into Emerson's essays, he told Landor that
Emerson so weighed his language as to give more substance to a thing
than was there.[10] With Emerson himself he made no pretext at qualifying his criticism. In his journal Emerson opened his first entry on
Greenough's   first   visit   with   a   disarming   Greenough   aspersion:
"Greenough called my contemplations, &c. 'the masturbation of the
brain.'"[11]

Some hint of the way his conversations with Greenough went came
in an 1868 entry in Emerson's journal: "Horatio Greenough shone,
but one only listened to him."[12] Emerson was enough engaged by
Greenough's urbanity, however, to have him voted into membership in
the Town and Country Club and to invite him to Clough's dinner at
the Tremont House on 20 November 1852. He was not present, however, on 24 November, Thanksgiving eve, when Greenough lectured at
the New Music Hall, on art as related to life, nor for a second lecture
on the same topic, given at the Music Hall on 29 November, having set
forth on his own extended lecture tour. Thus he missed the pitiful
drama that unfolded over the next few weeks.

Greenough aspired to produce a great equestrian monument and had
proposed to raise funds for it with his lectures. But scarcely anyone

came. Total receipts for both lectures were fourteen dollars. Alcott thought the first lecture "admirable" but "far too metaphysical and fine for the few who came to hear." Dana was not so indulgent. He took in both and thought them "the first work of an unbalanced mind." Whatever the character of the first lecture, those who attended the second acknowledged it was "a curious *mixture of incomprehensibleness.*" One friend, concluding that Greenough's mind was giving way, urged him to rejoin his wife and children in Newport. Greenough, instead, next morning passed his time with Alcott, who, relishing a metaphysical conversation, supposed his visitor's incoherencies were new illustrations of "the subtlety and mysticism of his distinctions." Alcott specialized in understanding the incomprehensible. This time he was too generous.[13]

Exercising all his powers of persuasion, Greenough's brother Henry got him home to Newport. There he became violently deranged and had to be brought back to Boston, to the McLean Asylum in Somerville, bound in a straitjacket. At McLean, talking compulsively and without letup in Italian, he entertained successive delusions, his state of excitement compelling the use of lead restraining straps. On 18 December he died. Those who knew Greenough well saw this as the culminating episode in a condition of intermittent insanity that had plagued him for years. To those only lately acquainted with him his madness and death came as a great shock.

Emerson was in Cincinnati when Greenough died. Writing to Carlyle in April, he said, "Our few fine persons are apt to die. Horatio Greenough, a sculptor, whose tongue was far cunninger in talk than his chisel to carve, and who inspired great hopes, died two months ago, at forty-seven years."[14] This may be taken as less a condemnation of Greenough's neoclassical sculptures than a commendation of those ideas which Emerson found so much in harmony with his own.

In 1863, writing to Henry Greenough, Emerson amplified further:

> I . . . in Cincinnati learned what an end had come to all my joy & exultation. It was the more deplorable, that he appeared to be in the perfection of manly power & beauty. I must think that the country has never met so great an intellectual loss as in that life; and I say it in the recollection of his extraordinary conversation, which seemed to me to cast all his works of art with all their excellences into shade.[15]

With consummate tact he was repeating what he had told Carlyle. Greenough's tongue was more cunning than his chisel.

Although Emerson declined an invitation from Greenough's widow to write his biography, he did keep his memory alive, laying stress in

The Conduct of Life and *Society and Solitude* (''Beauty'' and ''Art''),
on the element of functionalism in beauty. He perhaps, as well, introduced Greenough's theories to Frank Furness, William's son. Frank
was the architect who first employed Louis Sullivan, the functionalist
who became the father of skyscraper architecture. Frank Lloyd Wright
also went to Emerson for Greenough's ideas.[16] In *English Traits*
Emerson gave an account of Greenough's theory of structure, fully
crediting him. In 1868, in the introduction to ''Art and Nature,'' he
associated Greenough with Goethe, Winckelmann, and Ruskin, as one
of those who brought to the attention of their fellowman facts that
''are joyful possessions which no man could forego.'' In 1871, when
Emerson drew up his list of ''My Men,'' he included Greenough's
name.[17]

58. Daniel Webster
The Old Titanic Earth-son

*I*N October 1841 Emerson wrote in his journal:

> I saw Webster in the street — but he was changed since I saw
> him last, — black as a thunder cloud, & care worn: . . . I did not
> wonder that he depressed his eyes when he saw me, and would not
> meet my face. The canker worms have crawled to the topmost
> bough of the wild elm & swing down from that. No wonder the elm
> is a little uneasy.[1]

Webster's biographer Irving H. Bartlett has described Emerson, not
without reason, as "the most famous and eloquent of all the Webster
watchers." To Emerson, in young manhood and into middle age, Daniel Webster had been the embodiment of his ideal of the complete universal man. He had watched his rise with pride. When Webster was
sent to Congress in 1822, Emerson wrote to his Harvard classmate
John Boynton Hill, "The good cause has succeeded and we are sending our Giant down among you false Southrons. We are proudly anticipating the triumph of a Northern Interest to be begun or to be achieved
by Mr. Webster." In 1834 he wrote of Webster, "Seemed, when at last
his clarion accents broke, / As if the conscience of the country spoke."
In August 1839, pleased with Carlyle's good opinion of Webster,
Emerson wrote: "He has his own sins, no doubt; is no saint, is a prod-
igal . . . but the 'man's a man for a' that.' "[2]
In 1841, in spite of Webster's lowering looks, Emerson did not side
with his foes but stood by him, maintaining: "It is a bad fact that our

editors fancy that they have a right to call on Daniel Webster to resign his office, or, much more, resign his opinion & accept theirs. That
is the madness of party.''[3]

For personal reasons, too, Emerson had reason to like Webster. Edward Emerson had been tutor to Webster's sons and had studied law
in his Boston office. On 8 August 1839 Emerson told Carlyle: ''Edward read law with him, & loved him . . . & afterwards in sick &
unfortunate days received the steadiest kindness from him.''[4]

By 1843 uneasiness about Webster took hold of Emerson. On 7 February he inventoried Webster's ''admirable'' physical advantages —
''his noble & majestic frame, his breadth & projection of brows, his
coalblack hair, his great cinderous eyes . . . the rich & well-modulated
thunder of his voice.''[5] But Webster's conduct troubled him:

> His speech at Richmond was made to bear a meaning by his
> Southern backers which he did not intend, and I have never
> forgiven him that he did not say, Not so fast, good friends, I did
> not mean what you say. He has missed the opportunity of making
> himself the darling of the American world in all coming time by
> abstaining from putting himself at the head of the Anti-slavery
> interest, by standing for New England and for man against
> the bullying and barbarism of the South.[6]

Emerson did not yet believe Webster capable of utilizing an ambiguity
to win Southern support; nonetheless, his own unflinching sincerity
made him sensitive to Webster's lapse.

In 1843 Webster and Rufus Choate came to Concord, where the county
courthouse was then located, for court week in August, to defend William Wyman, president of Charlestown's Phoenix Bank, against a charge
of embezzlement. A phoenix himself, Wyman had risen intact from
two previous trials concerning this same charge and was finally acquitted on a legal point. Webster carried this process through, even
while struggling with hay fever that caused him to use a dozen hand-
kerchiefs a day.[7]

While in Concord, Webster stayed at the home of John Cheney, one
of Emerson's Harvard classmates, and visited Thoreau's aunt, Louisa
Dunbar, whom, nearly forty years before, he had courted unsuccess-
fully.[8] On Tuesday evening, 15 August, the Emersons held a tea party
for Webster and his fellow jurists and were impressed to see Webster
give Ruth Emerson his arm and escort her across the room.[9] Lidian
had always held him in special regard because, in 1820, he had danced
a set with her when he came to Plymouth to mark the bicentennial of
the landing of the Pilgrims.

Emerson caught the excitement of Webster's visit. ''He quite fills our little town,'' he wrote, ''& I doubt if I shall get settled down to writing, until he is well gone from the county. He is a natural Emperor of men.'' Webster's visit to Bush left pleasant impressions: ''Webster behaves admirably well in society. These village parties must be dishwater to him, yet he shows himself just goodnatured, just nonchalant enough, & has his own way without offending anyone or losing any ground.'' Emerson was impressed as well by Webster's courtroom manner:

> Mr. Webster loses nothing by comparison with brilliant men in the legal profession: he is as much before them as before the ordinary lawyer. . . . His wonderful organization, the perfection of his elocution, and all that thereto belongs, voice, accent, intonation, attitude, manner, are such as one cannot hope to see again in a century. . . . His rhetoric is perfect, so homely, so fit, so strong.

Emerson sat in on a morning session; that sufficed. ''Perhaps it was a mark of having outlived some of my once finest pleasures,'' he reflected, ''that I found no appetite to return to the Court in the afternoon & hear the conclusion of his argument. The green fields on my way home were too fresh & fair, & forbade me to go again.'' Still, he used the occasion to mount a defense of Webster's character:

> It seems to me the Quixotism of criticism to quarrel with Webster because he has not this or that fine evangelical property. He is no saint, but the wild olive wood, ungrafted yet by grace, but according to his lights a very true & admirable man. . . . Were he too prudent a Yankee it would be a sad deduction from his magnificence. I only wish he would never truckle.[10]

Clearly, Emerson was uneasy about Webster's stand on the slavery issue. On 3 September 1843 he disclosed increased wariness, lumping John C. Calhoun, Henry Clay, and Webster together as ''underlings'' who took ''the law from the dirtiest fellows.''[11] Emerson had reason to be perplexed by Webster's behavior. As a strict sectionist, Webster, in 1822, had advocated secession as an alternative to accepting the federal tariff laws. By 1830, however, he had arrived at an understanding of Union which, while it ran ahead of a technical interpretation of the Constitution, anticipated our concept of nationalism as it evolved. Indeed, Bartlett concludes that the nation emerged whole from the Civil War because Lincoln based his ''every action . . . on a devotion to the same principles Webster first had articulated thirty years before.''[12] For many years, thanks to the eloquence of the abolitionists, the view prevailed that Webster sacrificed his integrity to his ambitions to be President. But to posterity it appears that he subordinated those ambitions to the goal of national unity and, by so doing, placed his country forever in his debt.

In the summer of 1844, Mrs. Thoreau and other Concord women persuaded Emerson to give a talk marking the tenth anniversary of the emancipation of the slaves in the British West Indies. But snags developed. The churches did not want to provide accommodations for the lecture. The day was rainy, so it could not be given out of doors, even though Hawthorne offered the grounds of the Old Manse as a site. Moreover, the sexton at the First Parish Church refused to ring the town bell in the church's steeple to announce the event. Thoreau, with gusto, dispatched the difficulties, one after another. He got the use of the courthouse hall for the lecture. He raced about the village, from door to door, giving notice of time and place. Finally, he charged into the church and rang the bell lustily, gathering for Emerson a proper audience for a lecture of high significance.[13] The antislavery people, from thirteen townships in Middlesex County, expected to hear something more from Emerson than a recapitulation of the downfall of slavery in the British West Indies. Emerson did not disappoint them. He did his duty by the announced topic but then made some telling points, based on that success. "Whilst I have read of England," he said, "I have thought of New England. . . . There is a disastrous want of *men* from New England."[14]

Freedom for America's slaves, Emerson argued, could be purchased en masse by the government. The success of the freed West Indian blacks refuted those who said the black race is mentally inferior to the white. He found the seizure of black seamen from Northern ships putting into Southern ports unconscionable and not to be tolerated. His concern with this specific problem was to be visibly quickened a few months later when Samuel Hoar, at sixty-six, went to South Carolina as the personal emissary of the governor of Massachusetts to negotiate the release of the captive seamen. In the company of the ailing Elizabeth, Hoar would be forced by a vigilante committee, threatening to burn his hotel and drag him through the streets to the ship chosen for his departure, to leave Charleston. After first saying that "he had rather his broken skull should be carried to Massachusetts by somebody else than to carry it home safe himself," Hoar reconsidered and left without a struggle. Though Channing thought Hoar's conduct less than heroic, Emerson found it dignified and honorable.[15] He had reflected on the possibilities of martyrdom too often not to realize that it should not be provoked by a reckless gesture. Emerson later joined others in raising his voice in protest at the treatment Hoar received.

Unwittingly, Emerson may have played a more direct role in this drama than he realized. His "Discourse on Emancipation" was, for him, rancorous and even passionate. In the course of it he had branded the governor of Massachusetts "a trifler" because he had failed to take firm action. Apparently the governor's answer to that charge was to dispatch Hoar to Charleston. It was Hoar's experience, Edward Everett Hale said later, that first made Emerson realize that civil war was inevitable. Even Webster interpolated a mention of the episode into his Seventh of March speech in 1850. He left it out of the speech, however, when he delivered it before the Senate, a fact Emerson saw as new evidence of Webster's willingness to truckle to the slaveholders.[16]

On the last day of April 1846 Emerson, attending Edward Everett's inaugural as president of Harvard, was further irritated by Webster: "Webster I could so willingly have spared in this occasion. . . . Well, this Webster must needs come into the house just at the moment when Everett was rising to make his Inaugural Speech. Of course, the whole genial current of feeling flowing towards him was arrested, and the old Titanic Earth-son was alone seen."[17] Everett sat down while the audience gave Webster an ovation.

The next summer Emerson moved farther away from Webster. He reflected: "Webster is a man by himself of the great mould, but he also underlies the American blight, & wants the power of the initiative, the affirmative talent, and remains like the literary class, only a commentator, his great proportions only exposing his defect."[18]

In September of that year, when "Joe," a fugitive slave, was captured in Boston and sent back to New Orleans, Samuel Gridley Howe sought to recruit Emerson for a mammoth protest meeting at Faneuil Hall and, presumably, for a secret Vigilance Committee he was organizing to thwart the slave-catchers. Although Emerson held aloof, he wrote Howe deploring an act that made Boston "a slave-port," and concluded that if Boston's prosperity depended on placation of the South by its "mercantile body," then it was "high time our bad wealth came to an end." In such circumstances, he said, "I am sure, I shall very cheerfully take my share of suffering in the ruin of such a prosperity, and shall very willingly turn to the mountains to chop wood, and seek to find for myself and my children labors compatible with freedom and honor."[19]

By 1849 Emerson's opinion of Webster was plummeting toward zero: "It is true that Webster has never done any thing up to the promise of his faculties. He is unmistakably able, & might have ruled America, but he was cowardly, & has spent his life on specialties."[20] Emerson spoke as one who had experienced a personal betrayal.

It is impossible to pay no regard to the day's events,
to the public opinion of the times, to the stirring
shouts of the parties, to the calamities and
prosperities of our town and country.

59. Social Reform

*E*MERSON declined the role of social reformer long before he was asked to assume that role. In the spring of 1828 he wrote in his journal: "We are very apt to overrate the importance of our actions. . . . Truth says, Give yourself no manner of anxiety about events, about the consequences of actions. They are really of no importance to us. . . . The whole object of the Universe to us is the formation of Character."[1]

By the mid-1830's his fellow members of Hedge's Club were looking to him for leadership and at times were perplexed by his reluctance to engage in public debate on heated issues. Thus Samuel Osgood in January 1837 suggested that Emerson may not "have mingled enough with common humanity," and may have "confounded his idiosyncrasies with universal truth."[2]

In "The American Scholar" Emerson thought to make his position clear: "The office of the scholar is to cheer, to raise and to guide men by showing them facts amidst appearances. These being his functions, it becomes him to feel all confidence in himself and to defer never to the popular cry." May of 1840 found him expanding on this topic: "The world accuses the Scholar of a tendency to idealism. . . . Let ideas obtain and establish their sway again in society, let life again be fair and poetic and we shall gladly be objective, lovers, citizens and philanthropists." In "Spiritual Laws" in 1841 he specified further, "Real action is in silent moments. . . . The object of the man, the aim of these moments, is to . . . suffer the law to traverse his whole being without obstruction."[3]

In his "Lecture on the Times," given on 2 December 1841 at Boston's Masonic Temple, Emerson distinguished two classes, the actors and the students (that is, scholars) : "The actors constitute that great army of martyrs who, at least in America, by their conscience and philanthropy, occupy the ground which Calvinism occupied in the last age, and compose the visible church of the existing generation." The student saw inward reform as the necessary prompter of outward reform. The efforts of the actor, although he did not realize it, were impelled by the inclination within him to live in harmony with the moral law : "The origin of all reform is in that mysterious fountain of the moral sentiment in man, which, amidst the natural, ever contains the supernatural for men. That is new and creative. That is alive. That alone can make a man other than he is." The actor, then, was responding to the same impulse the student was responding to but at a superficial level.[4]

On 19 March 1842 Horace Greeley's *New-York Tribune* took Emerson to task for his presumed aloofness to reform : "We would ask Mr. Emerson whether the Poverty, Ignorance and Misery of the Human Race and the devastated and neglected condition of the Globe are not objects great enough to arouse the Philosopher of the Transcendental School to action." And so the assault continued, painting a grim picture of a suffering world to which Emerson was, presumably, indifferent.

Writing in *The Harbinger* on 7 August 1847, George Ripley, crediting a spurious claim that Emerson was an editor of the *Massachusetts Quarterly Review,* said, not without pique, "The names of those associated with the senior Editor are a guaranty that the *Review* will not be characterized by the profound indifference to the great humanitary movements of the age which forms such a signal defect in the philosophy, as well as the productions, of that gentleman."[5] This was a stinging rebuke coming from the man who had defended Emerson so forthrightly after the "Divinity School Address."

The year following, when Emerson was in England, he fell into the company of the British reformer James J. G. Wilkinson, who reported to *The Harbinger* on 11 April 1848 : "I tried to hint to friend Emerson, that that individuality which he would maintain so inviolate and so high . . . was practically nil in the present confusion . . . but would come forth with power and great splendor under the new social *regime.*"[6] The reformers were applying pressure collectively, trying to shift Emerson away from his role of apparent inaction.

Such criticisms would not cease when Emerson finally spoke out in behalf of the cause of abolition, or even after his death. Chapman insisted that Emerson had been mistaken in supposing that society would be reformed if only men reformed themselves. Self-sufficiency was not a fact and individual spiritual power was not invincible. Charles W. Eliot likewise saw Emerson's noninterventionist posture as unfortunate: "He was but a halting supporter of the reforms of his day. . . . His visions were far-reaching, his doctrine often radical, and his exhortations fervid; but when it came to action . . . he was surprisingly conservative."[7] Eliot was not vouchsafed a true grasp of Emerson's position.

Chapman characterized as the "Emerson madness" the self-will Emerson unleashed. This designation accounted for man's follies so conveniently it would be invoked anew in the twentieth century by Quentin Anderson, who contended that Emerson, by pushing the claims of the Self too far, promulgated "the primacy of the imperial self." By exalting "individual claims" while repudiating the authority of society, the church, and history, Emerson is blamed for having sponsored a commitment to relativism that has carried the modern world to the edge of chaos.[8]

In "New England Reformers" (1844), Emerson said: "Society gains nothing while a man, not himself renovated, attempts to renovate things around him."[9] Here, succinctly given, is the position he embraced. Only when individuals were good would society be good. Goodness could not be imposed from without.

To Carlyle, Emerson wrote on the last day of 1844, "Though I sometimes accept a popular call, and preach on Temperance or the Abolition of Slavery, I am sure to feel, before I have done with it, what an intrusion it is into another sphere, and so much loss of virtue in my own." When the annexation of Texas occurred, Emerson deplored it as "one of those events which retard or retrograde the civilization of ages," but then dismissed it with the buoyant assertion, "The World Spirit is a good swimmer, and storms & waves cannot easily drown him."[10]

Occasionally Emerson spoke as though he disassociated himself from reforms because he thought those who benefited from them were not worth the effort: "The worst of charity is that the lives you are asked to preserve are not worth preserving. Masses! The calamity is the masses." In time, he came to take a more reasonable view: "What we call our root-and-branch reforms of slavery, war, gambling, intemperance, is only medicating the symptoms. We must begin higher up, namely, in education." Now, at last, he sounded like a reformer, and one who had been talking to Horace Mann.[11]

In "Celestial Love" Emerson distilled the essence of his social philosophy in an elevating couplet: "He that feeds men serveth few; / He serves all who dares be true." Edward Emerson recalled that, whenever a domestic crisis called for his father's participation he retreated behind a favorite quotation — "The strength of the Egyptians is to sit still.''[12] Where larger issues were involved, Emerson could transform that thought into the most earnest of declarations:

> The philanthropies and charities have a certain air of quackery. . . . Unless the action is necessary, unless it is adequate, I do not wish to perform it. . . . 'I can sit in a corner and *perish* . . . but I will not move until I have the highest command. . . . Your virtuous projects, so called, do not cheer me. . . . Cannot we screw our courage to patience and truth, and without complaint, or even with good-humor, await our turn of action in the Infinite Counsels?'[13]

Yet Emerson did not wish to be seen as inexorably opposed to reform. In ''The Young American'' (1844), he wrote:

> If a humane measure is propounded . . . that sentiment, that project, will have the homage of the hero. . . . More than our good-will we may not be able to give. We have our own affairs, our own genius, which chains each to his proper work . . . but to one thing we are bound, not to blaspheme the sentiment and the work of that man, not to throw stumbling-blocks in the way of the abolitionist, the philanthropist.[14]

At the start of ''Man the Reformer'' Emerson said he hoped that each of his listeners ''felt his own call to cast aside all evil customs, timidities and limitations, and to be in his place a free and helpful man, a reformer, a benefactor, not content to slip through the world like a footman or a spy.'' He was not announcing a capitulation, for presently he explained: ''The true reformer initiates his labor in the precincts of private life, and makes it, not a set of measures . . . not an impulse of a day, but commensurate with human existence: a tendency toward perfection of being.''[15] He mended not human circumstance but the human spirit.

Emerson had other, more specific charges to levy against reformers than those already noted. A total commitment to reform, he declared, is deleterious to the reformer. He becomes egotistical, self-righteous, and dogmatic. He thinks that the welfare of the world depends upon him exclusively, yet he lets ''the popular judgments and modes of action'' supplant his self-reliance. Moreover, excessive preoccupation with one issue deforms the issue itself: ''If a man fasten his attention upon a single aspect of truth, & apply himself to that alone for a long time, the truth itself becomes distorted.''[16]

As early as 1837, in his first speech on slavery, Emerson sought to make his opinion known:

The professed philanthropists, it is strange and horrible to say, are an altogether odious set of people. . . . The impatience of discipline, the haste to rule before we have served, to prescribe laws for nations and humanity before we have said our own prayers or yet heard the benediction which love and peace sing in our own bosom, — these all dwarf and degrade.[17]

The same note was sounded in ''The Method of Nature,''[18] and it became his theme as well in ''Lecture on the Times'':

The young men who have been vexing society for these last years with regenerative methods . . . all exaggerated some special means. . . . The reforms have their high origin in an ideal justice, but they do not retain the purity of an idea. They are quickly organized in some low, inadequate form, and present no more poetic image to the mind than the evil tradition which they reprobated. . . . Those who are urging with most ardor what are called the greatest benefits of mankind, are narrow, self-pleasing, conceited men, and affect us as the insane do. They bite us and we run mad also. I think the work of the reformer . . . is a buzz in the ear. . . . We do not want actions but men.[19]

Emerson, in ''Self-Reliance,'' observed also that reformers used their grand commitments to shun their immediate obligations:

If an angry bigot assumes this bountiful cause of Abolition, and comes to me with his last news from Barbadoes, why should I not say to him, 'Go love thy infant; love thy wood-chopper; be good-natured and modest; have that grace; and never varnish your hard, uncharitable ambition with this incredible tenderness for black folk a thousand miles off. Thy love afar is spite at home.'[20]

The supposition that Emerson retreated to an ambuscade from behind which he sniped at reformers while himself repudiating any role in reform is misleading. Holmes assessed Emerson's role correctly when he said: ''Nothing is plainer than that it was Emerson's calling to supply impulses and not methods. He was not an organizer, but a power behind many organizers, inspiring them with lofty motive, giving breadth to their views.'' Emerson recognized this fact and even reduced his method to an epigram: ''When he has hit the white, the rest may shatter the target.''[21] He sought only to discourage fanaticism and to make certain that reformers acted on promptings from their moral sense and not from the promptings of zealots. William Emerson's capricious role in the battle of Concord may have stood for him as a graphic illustration of irresponsible enthusiasm.

Given impetus by the representations of Margaret Fuller, the issue of woman's rights became increasingly Emerson's concern. In November 1841, his posture still traditional, he said: "Woman should not be expected to write or fight or build or compose scores; she does all by inspiring men to do all. . . . She is the requiring genius." In March, two years later, he said: "The Muse is feminine. But action is male." Later that month, reporting thoughts engendered by a conversation with Margaret Fuller, he said: "For me, today, Woman is . . . a docile daughter of God with her face heavenward endeavoring to hear the divine word and to convey it to me." Simultaneously she was exalted and subordinated. Lidian would strive to adjust to this difficult role. Margaret never could.[22]

To Paulina W. Davis, who wrote to him in 1850, asking him to take a role in convoking a convention looking toward the procurement of political functions for women, Emerson replied on 18 September:

> The fact of the political and civil wrongs of woman I deny not. If women feel wronged, then they are wronged. But the mode of obtaining a redress, namely, a public convention called by women is not very agreeable to me, and the things to be agitated for do not seem to me the best. Perhaps I am superstitious & traditional, but whilst I should vote for every franchise for women, — vote that they should hold property, and vote, yes & be eligible to all offices as men — whilst I should vote thus, if women asked, or if men denied these things, I should not wish women to wish political functions, nor, if granted assume them.[23]

He declined to attend the convention but agreed to be a sponsor for it so that he would not, by default, "stand in the way of any right." Five years later, Paulina got him to attend that year's convention and to speak. Here he occupied high ground and his listeners knew he found their cause just. Even as his thoughts for his address were taking shape in his mind, he wrote in his journal: "If the women demand votes, offices, and political equality . . . refuse it not. 'Tis very cheap wit that finds it so funny. Certainly all my points would be sooner carried in the state if women voted." At the convention he told his audience: "Let the laws be purged of every barbarous remainder, every barbarous impediment to women. Let the public donations for education be equally shared by them. . . . If you do refuse them a vote, you will also refuse to tax them." By July 1869 Emerson could describe the move toward women's suffrage as "an important step in civilization." That was inevitable. Two months earlier he had accepted a vice-presidency in the New England Woman Suffrage Association.[24]

Snider identifies 1855 as the year in which Emerson launched his antislavery crusade and began "his grand work of self-redemption from his previous partial paralysis both of intellect and will."[25] The boundaries Snider set were too narrow, not taking into account Emerson's role as opinion-maker. But certainly it was in the mid-1850's that Emerson actively declared himself. Edward Emerson relates:

> To all meetings held in Concord for the cause of Freedom, spiritual or corporal, he felt bound to give the sanction of his presence . . . ; he officially welcomed Kossuth and his Hungarian exiles; he entertained John Brown at his house and gave largely from his, at that time very limited, means, to the fund for the furtherance and arming of the Kansas "Free State" immigration.[26]

His rhetoric accommodated his new militancy. In "Affairs in Kansas," a speech he delivered to the Kansas Aid Society on 10 September 1856, he not only deplored the activities of the border ruffians, he dismissed the theory of Manifest Destiny as "bilge-water."[27]

Subscribing ultimately to a belief in ameliorative evolution, Emerson came to see man as the instrument of betterment. Yet when he compared his own approach to reform with that of the announced reformers, he saw that he was to be counted a rainbow or a firefly. These analogies he did not choose haphazardly. All hues are present in the spectrum that is the rainbow; the firefly carries within itself its own source of light. He did not find, in comparing himself with the official reformers, that he appeared to worse advantage. "My reforms," he said, "include, so will outlast, theirs." Even Chapman accepted this view finally. The "great artist," was, after all, "the most educative influence upon the globe." Garrison had carried out his campaign, and had achieved his goals. And when he died his power died with him. Consider, however: "The small, inner, silver trumpet of Emerson caught and sounded the same note, and it continues to sound the note, shaking down the walls of inner Jerichoes of men of later and even later generations."[28]

We shall one day bring the States shoulder to shoulder
and the citizens man to man to exterminate
slavery. Why in the name of common sense and the
peace of mankind is not this made the subject of
instant negotiation and settlement?

---

60. The Completest Man

*O*N 7 March 1850, with the country brought to the brink of war
over the slavery issue, Daniel Webster, addressing the Senate on the
topic "The Constitution and the Union," announced his espousal of
Henry Clay's Compromise. No speech delivered before the Senate, prior
to or subsequent to that time, ever polarized public opinion as did this
"infamous" Seventh of March address, as it was thereafter known.
While later historians are convinced that Webster, by procuring the
Union another decade of peace with this Compromise, tipped the scales
in favor of an eventual Union victory and thus saved his country, his
liberal constituents saw his action as a tragic betrayal, choosing to
believe Webster acted as he did to further his personal ambitions. That
devotion to the Union had been Webster's persistent theme since 1830
did not matter to them. Nor did it matter that up until now he had
several times resigned or refused high office in keeping with his own
declaration that opportunism in public life was "inconsistent with
personal dignity and derogatory to the character of the institutions of
the country."[1]

When, toward the end of March, a letter lauding his stand was forwarded to Webster, carrying the signatures of more than eight hundred
Bostonians, including Holmes, Prescott, Ticknor, Choate, Thomas
Handasyd Perkins, and President Jared Sparks of Harvard, Emerson
remarked in his journal: "I think there was never an event half so
painful occurred in Boston. . . . Many of the names very properly
belong there, — they are the names of aged & infirm people, who have
outlived everything but their night cap & their tea and toast. But I
observe some names of men under forty!"[2]

On 18 September 1850, with Webster, his newly chosen secretary of state, looking on, President Fillmore signed the Fugitive Slave Bill, one of the end results of the Compromise. From that moment Emerson's opposition to slavery steadily mounted. The Harvard editors of his journals relate:

> After passage of this law . . . something snapped within the usual poise and cool eclecticism of Emerson's journalizing, resulting in a continuous cluster of entries for eighty-six manuscript pages in Journal BO — a concentration unique, in length and tone in all of Emerson's journals. . . . He becomes angry, bitter, ironical, and holds this mood for days. He was deeply touched in areas he held inviolate: the higher law's superior claim over political expediency.[3]

Under the heading "Bad Times," in May 1851 Emerson began to disgorge a litany of denunciations: "The Word *liberty* in the mouth of Mr. Webster sounds like the word *love* in the mouth of a courtezan," he wrote. And, again: "The fame of Mr. Webster ends in this nasty law." And: "He has the curse of all this country which he has afflicted." And: "Webster's absence of moral faculty is degrading to the country." In July, at last he found a phrase that caught the fierceness of his indignation: "This filthy enactment was made in the nineteenth century, by people who could read and write. I will not obey it, by God." To him it was "Mr. Webster's law."[4]

Chapman saw what happened in these terms:

> It was the defection of Daniel Webster that completed the conversion of Emerson and turned him from an adherent into a propagandist of abolition. Not pity for the slave, but indignation at the violation of the Moral Law by Daniel Webster, was at the bottom of Emerson's anger. . . . After the 7th of March, 1850, he recognized in Webster the embodiment of all that he hated. In his attacks on Webster, Emerson trembles to his inmost fibre with antagonism. . . . This exhibition of Emerson as a fighting animal is magnificent, and explains his life. There is no other instance of his ferocity. No other nature but Webster's ever so moved him; but it was time to be moved, and Webster was a man of his size.[5]

Emerson once had seen Webster as a born colossus — the man of the century. Chapman contended that Emerson himself had the attributes he had ascribed to Webster:

> He stands on a plane of intellect where he might, under other circumstances, have met and defeated Webster. . . . Their natures

were electrically repellent, but from which did the greater force radiate? Their education differed so radically that it is impossible to compare them, but if you translate the Phi Beta Kappa address into politics, you have something stronger than Webster . . . and Emerson would have had this advantage, — that he was not afraid.[6]

At the end of that tempestuous year, in November 1851, the embattled secretary of state, with less than a year to live, wrote to John Cheney's wife to say that he had meant to visit Concord in October, but "changes that have taken place" had deterred him:

> Many of those whom I so highly esteemed, in your beautiful and quiet village, have become a good deal estranged, to my great grief, by abolitionism, free-soilism, transcendentalism, and other notions, which I cannot [but] regard as so many vagaries of the imagination. These former warm friends would have no pleasure, of course, in intercourse with one of old-fashioned opinions.[7]

Word of Emerson's vituperations, then, had carried to Webster's ears.

In June 1852 the Whig convention at Baltimore passed over Webster to choose Winfield Scott as its presidential nominee. Failing in health, Webster resigned his office and went home to Marshfield. As October advanced, the world heard that death was coming for the great Whig.

At nearby Plymouth, Emerson, there on a visit with Lidian, walked the beach and the streets of the undulating town. On the morning of 24 October, a Sunday, he stood on the shore and looked across Duxbury Bay toward Webster Island, where Webster had his hunting lodge. There, at no greater distance from his house than Walden was from Emerson's, Webster had come often to seek the companionship of the roaring Atlantic and the serenity of Nature. Haze hung on the water. An offshore breeze swept the spray onto orchards and hills and on the man standing on the sandy sweep of beach gazing toward Marshfield. "I supposed, Webster must have passed," Emerson related, alerted surely by local church bells strenuously tolling the event despite angry objections from abolitionist parishioners. Webster had died at two-thirty that morning. In his delirium he had delivered an oration on religious principles and then asked those around him if he had said anything unworthy of Daniel Webster. He had asked also that a lantern be kept lit, hung from the mast of the boat at anchor on the little pond outside his bedroom window, and the flag kept aloft so that he could look upon Old Glory as long as his vision held.

Webster had died, yet, as Emerson afterward reflected, "The sea, the rocks, the woods, gave no sign that America & the world had lost the completest man.'' Despite his hard feelings, Emerson knew one of the great men of the age had died: ''Nature has not in our days, or, not since Napoleon, cut out such a masterpiece. He brought the strength of a savage into the height of culture. A man within & without, the strong & perfect body of the first ages, with the civility & thought of the last. . . . He was a statesman and not the semblance of one.'' To this unstinting epitaph, Emerson, to placate his conscience, added one stinting line: ''But alas! he was the victim of his ambition; to please the South betrayed the North, and was thrown out by both.''[8] One further reflection from Emerson was cited later, by Conway, as Webster's best epitaph: ''He had honor enough to feel degraded.''[9]

At Marshfield, twenty thousand people converged on Webster's estate for a funeral that had to be held out of doors because of the multitude that wanted to witness it. At Faneuil Hall, the use of which had been denied to Webster a year before, a memorial service was attended by other hundreds as was yet another service at the Hollis Street Church. Bunker Hill was draped with a banner reading, ''Bunker Hill Mourns the Departed Patriot.'' Webster's rehabilitation had already begun. But not with Emerson. Through the ensuing years his household observed the seventh of March as a day of infamy.

On the fourth anniversary of Webster's Compromise speech Emerson, at the invitation of the Anti-Slavery Society, stepped before a large audience at the New York City Tabernacle — a veritable nerve center from which antislavery sentiments radiated to the nation — to talk again on the Fugitive Slave Law. Because his audiences were lyceum audiences and lyceums shunned controversy, that law had not been his topic for three years. Emerson had not found it hard to accommodate himself to their tastes. The very first sentences of his Tabernacle address explained why: ''I do not often speak to public questions; — they are odious and hurtful, and it seems like meddling or leaving your work. I have my own spirits in prison; — spirits in deeper prisons, whom no man visits if I do not.''[10] He had other reasons, too. He confided to Furness that his antislavery speeches were the worst in the country — only less bad than slavery itself. Prior to lecturing on slavery at Tremont Temple, he wrote to William on 17 January 1855, ''I am trying hard in these days to see some light in the dark Slavery question to which I am to speak next week in Boston. But to me as to so many 'tis like Hamlet's task imposed on so unfit an agent as Hamlet.''[11] He perhaps was right. On 14 May 1857 Longfellow told his journal: ''It is rather painful to see Emerson in the arena of politics, hissed and hooted at by young law students.''[12] For Emerson, stepping into the reform movement was a painful test of courage from which he did not flinch.

Bliss Perry thought the Tabernacle address ''one of the most magnificent invectives in the English language, marred only by a lack of charity.''[13] An ostensible philosophical detachment was deceptive. Through its early stages Emerson built a careful image of Webster as a god descended to earth. That such a man should betray the hopes of those who looked to him for leadership was appalling. Emerson said: "Mr. Webster, by his personal influence, brought the Fugitive Slave Law on the country. . . . It cost him his life, and under the shadow of his great name inferior men sheltered themselves, threw their ballots for it, and made the law." Emerson went on to single out Webster's tragic lack: "If his moral sensibility had been proportioned to the force of his understanding, what limits could have been set to his genius and beneficent power? But he wanted that deep source of inspiration." This man, whom he once believed was aligned with Nature, was, in fact, estranged from the universal force.[14]

Before 1850 various outrages associated with slavery had not provoked high indignation in Emerson. But something that had been lacking up to now made the Fugitive Slave Law particularly odious to him. Firkins hit upon the probable explanation when he said Emerson detested the law ''because it obliged the Northern men to catch slaves, because it was an interference from without with Emerson's rights, with any man's rights, to obey his own conscience. It attacked the jurisdiction of the moral sentiment.''[15] Emerson, then, objected to the law on transcendental grounds.

On 30 September 1865, after the Civil War was over, Emerson thought once more about Webster and the Fugitive Slave Law:

Now in the time of the Fugitive Slave-law, when the best young men who had ranged themselves around Mr Webster were already all of them in the interest of freedom, & threw themselves at once into opposition, Mr Webster could no longer see one of them in the street; he glared at them, but knew them not; his resentments were implacable. What did they do? Did they sit down & bewail themselves? No; Sumner & his valiant young contemporaries set themselves to the task of making their views not only clear but prevailing. They proclaimed and defended them and inoculated with them the whole population, & drove Mr Webster out of the world. All his mighty genius . . . availed him nothing . . . and he withered & died as by suicide.[16]

Only such a moral conception of what the law embodied could have driven Emerson to the extremes of invective he went to when once he concluded that Webster's truckling had made the law possible. His personal disinclination to involve himself in public issues was a sound one. On this occasion, by laying a moral transparency over a public issue, he found justification for taking a public stand on it. His motivations were sound. His judgment was not. In repudiating Webster on political grounds, under the supposition that he was acting in a moral cause, Emerson mistook the promptings of his emotions for the promptings of his moral sensibilities. But to preserve the integrity of his convictions he could not have done otherwise.

In the spring of 1851, with a congressional election brewing and the Free-Soilers, who opposed the recently enacted Fugitive Slave Law, giving battle to the Whigs, who embraced it, Emerson campaigned boldly for John Gorham Palfrey, former dean of the Harvard Divinity School, former congressman, and now the Free-Soil candidate for the congressional seat in Emerson's district. On Sunday, 4 May, his opening salvo, a blistering attack on the Fugitive Slave Law in general and on Webster in particular, came at Concord. To the abolitionists the news was electrifying. Charles Sumner, who had succeeded to Webster's seat in the Senate, exclaimed, "I have more satisfaction in this voice on our side than in that of any politician."[17] Emerson next took to the road with his address, repeating it the Sunday following at Lexington; on Wednesday, 14 May, at Cambridge; and, two days later, at Fitchburg; and elsewhere on subsequent days, before the election on 26 May, when Palfrey, though carrying Concord, was defeated by his Whig rival. In the summer, Emerson wrote to Carlyle, indicating some satisfaction with his efforts: "In the spring the abomination of our Fugitive Slave Bill drove me to some writing and speech-making without hope of effect but to clear my own skirts."[18]

Emerson, actively campaigning, would at any time have been memorable. His Cambridge appearance, however, crowned this first effort with distinction. The lecture was given in a Cambridgeport hall, and the audience was infiltrated by twenty or more well-dressed Harvard students who came to shout down the lecturer. They represented themselves as proponents of "union-at-all-costs" and "the rights of the South." E. P. Whipple, who was present, has left a graphic account of what occurred:

> They were the rowdiest, noisiest, most brainless set of young gentlemen that ever pretended to be engaged in studying "the humanities" at the chief university in the country. Their only arguments were hisses and groans, whenever the most illustrious man of American letters uttered an opinion which expressed the general opinion of the civilized world. If he quoted Coke, Holt, Blackstone, Mansfield, they hissed all these sages of the law because their judgments came from the illegal lips of Emerson.[19]

And when they did not hiss, they groaned, or cheered, intermittently, for Webster, Clay, Fillmore, Everett, and for "Old Harvard."[20]

James B. Thayer, another member of the Cambridgeport audience, gave Cabot this account of what happened:

> The hisses, shouts, and cat-calls made it impossible for Mr. Emerson to go on. Through all this there never was a finer specta- cle of dignity and composure than he presented. He stood with perfect quietness until the hubbub was over, and then went on with the next word. It was as if nothing had happened: there was no repetition, no allusion to what had been going on, no sign that he was moved, and I cannot describe with what added weight the next words fell.[21]

Whipple developed the same scene with gusto, conveying the spec- tacle the evening offered with greater immediacy:

> It was curious to watch him, as at each point he made he paused to let the storm of hisses subside. . . . There was a queer, quizzical, squirrel-like or bird-like expression in his eye as he calmly looked round to see what strange human animals were present to make such sounds; and when he proceeded to utter another indisputable truth, and it was responded to by another chorus of hisses, he seemed absolutely to enjoy the new sensation he experienced, and waited for those signs of disapprobation to stop altogether before he resumed his discourse. . . . There was not the slightest tremor in his voice, not even a trace of the passionate resentment which a speaker under such circumstances and impediments usually feels, and which urges him into the cheap retort about serpents, but a quiet waiting for the time when he should be allowed to go on with the next sentence. During the whole evening he never uttered a word which was not written down in the manuscript from which he read.[22]

Some reports allege that Emerson so altered the mood of his harassers that "they settled quietly in their seats, and went peaceably home," but neither Whipple nor Thayer reports any such triumph for Emer- son. His triumph came both in the fortitude with which he resisted the impulse to engage in a verbal duel with those bent on unnerving him, and in his pluck in not allowing his hecklers to drive him from the platform.

At this time Free-Soilers were in a minority. Any abolitionist who spoke in Cambridge could expect to be heckled by students, as was Horace Mann when he spoke there. Emerson had anticipated trouble and by handling it with his customary aplomb, came through it not only unscathed but with his reputation enhanced.

Whipple and others wanted Emerson to publish this speech. He refused, "feeling probably," said Whipple, "that, being written under the impulse of the passion of the day, it was no fit and fair summary of the characters of the statesmen he assailed."[23] If this is what he thought, he was right. Phyllis Cole has described this address as "the most enraged and partisan address of his career."[24]

"There is," Emerson began, "an infamy in the air."[25] Each day, he said, he awoke to "the odious remembrance" of the Fugitive Slave Law, "a law which no man can obey or abet the obeying without loss of self-respect and forfeiture of the name of a gentleman." Those who once honored Webster, he contended, now "disown him" for favoring this law. "He who was their pride in the woods and mountains of New England is now their mortification. . . . All the drops of his blood have eyes that look downward." The Shakespearean authority of that line alone communicated to everyone who heard it the immensity of Emerson's loathing for Webster's ignominy. Webster said that he had voted as he did to preserve the Union. "But one thing appears certain to me," Emerson said, "that the Union is at an end as soon as an immoral law is enacted. He who writes a crime into the statute-books digs under the foundations of the Capitol."

Emerson did not concentrate his wrath exclusively on Webster. Boston's aristocracy, "spoiled by prosperity," had countenanced the new law — "All are involved in one hot haste of terror, . . . not a liberal recollection, not so much as a snatch of an old song for freedom, dares intrude on their passive obedience." Those who hitherto had acknowledged Emerson's capacity for producing a fine phrase, even though they did not understand what he was talking about, understood his words well enough now and were stung to be themselves the target of phrases as fine as any Emerson ever had spoken. In his indignation Emerson seemed willing that the Union itself should crumble sooner than the crime of slavery be tolerated further. Seizing on that point and on his spendthrift proposal that the freedom of the slaves be bought at the cost of a billion dollars, his critics argued that he had furnished proof anew that he was deranged.

"The last year has forced us all into politics," Emerson said, and this speech affirmed that his sense of outrage had at last compelled him to act. To stand shoulder to shoulder with Garrison and Phillips would have been alien to his nature. Their vociferous confrontation of the issues approached too closely his notion of rabble-rousing. But his position was clear. With regret, the *Boston Daily Advertiser* advised its readers that Emerson might now "be fairly looked on as a decided abolitionist."[26]

61. Martyrdom

*W*HEN he stood up against the hoots and jeers of his hostile Cambridgeport audience, Emerson cannot have felt that he was placing his head on the martyr's block. Yet the dignity he showed suggests that he welcomed this moment of crisis and had prepared his mind for it.

Over the years Emerson often had considered the subject of martyrdom and hoped he would have the courage to die for the truth he believed in if the time came when he was put to the test. He had courted a dry martyrdom when he made himself a target for abuse by resigning his pastorate, and, again, when he gave his "Divinity School Address." Since he looked at such episodes of dissent as grave and serious business, he took care that they occurred only under extraordinary circumstances. He often expressed views contrary to those of his listeners but did so in a way calculated to gain their tolerance, rather than to provoke them to resentment and hostility. Now he realized that even his exceptional May-time flirtation with the abolitionist cause was not sufficient. Here was a truth that demanded more of him. In the summer of 1852 he wrote in his journal, "I waked at night, & bemoaned myself, because I had not thrown myself into this deplorable question of Slavery, which seems to want nothing so much as a few assured voices." He went on, however, "in hours of sanity, I recover myself. . . . I have quite other slaves to free than those negroes, to wit, imprisoned spirits, imprisoned thoughts . . . which, important to the republic of Man, have no watchman, or lover, or defender, but I."[1]

In boyhood, Emerson once told his brother Charles that he thought he could endure martyrdom, be burned at the stake. Charles answered,

"Yes, but if any one spoke to you on the way there you would be so abashed you wouldn't have a word to say."[2] It is worth noting that Webster, when alluding to his Seventh of March address shortly before his death, invoked the same test of courage: "If I had seen the stake, if I had heard the faggots already crackling, by the blessing of Almighty God, I would have gone on and discharged the duty which I thought my country called upon me to perform."[3]

In his sophomore year in college, although he knew he was placing his future in jeopardy, Emerson had stood by his classmates when they staged their protest strike. That was good conditioning for an aspiring martyr. In "On Showing Piety at Home," preached in the first year of his ministry (and twenty-six times thereafter!), Emerson discussed worthy behavior that bore kinship to martyrdom even while falling short of it. He said: "You may be greatly virtuous even though through the blessing of God, you do not live in times when you must give your body to be burned or to be sawn asunder for your faith. . . . The strict adherence to truth at all risks . . . done out of a solemn sense of duty, done in the Eye of God, is great and venerable."[4]

In 1834, in his journal, Emerson recorded an interior monologue:

Were it not a heroic venture in me to insist on being a popular speaker & run full tilt against the Fortune who with such beautiful consistency shows evermore her back? . . . My entire success, such as it is, is composed wholly of particular failures, — every public work of mine of the least importance having been, (probably without exception) noted at the time as a failure.[5]

The mood is gay. Emerson is hardly claiming that his failures are part of a strategy he is pursuing consciously. Yet, in fact, his failures, sponsored sometimes by his determination to hold firm to his own controversial opinions, did become the underpinnings of his future renown.

In *Nature* martyrdom is a prompt theme:

When a noble act is done, — perchance in a scene of great natural beauty; when Leonidas and his three hundred martyrs consume one day in dying . . . are not these heroes entitled to add the beauty of the scene to the beauty of the deed? . . . When Sir Harry Vane was dragged up the Tower-hill, sitting on a sled, to suffer death, as the champion of the English laws, one of the multitude cried out to him, "You never sate on so glorious a seat!" Charles II, to intimidate the citizens of London, caused the patriot Lord Russell to be drawn in an open coach, through the principal streets of the city, on his way to the scaffold. "But," his biographer says, "the multitude imagined they saw liberty and virtue sitting by his side."[6]

Thus in this transcendental way does Nature confirm the nobility of martyrdom.

In 1837, on 7 November, the abolitionist editor Elijah Lovejoy was shot and killed at Alton, Illinois, defending his press against a mob of incendiaries. In Boston, William Ellery Channing presided at a protest meeting at Faneuil Hall. Championship of Lovejoy was not countenanced in Boston, and Channing had procured use of the hall only with difficulty. Thus when Emerson introduced the subject in his lecture, ''Heroism,'' given at Boston's Masonic Temple on 24 January 1838, it was an act of true courage on his part. George P. Bradford said later that ''a cold shudder seemed to run through the audience at this calm braving of public opinion.''[7] Said Emerson: ''It is but the other day that the brave Lovejoy gave his breast to the bullets of a mob, for the rights of free speech and opinion, and died when it was better not to live.''[8] Emerson had not come slowly to this opinion. On 24 November 1837 he had written almost the same words in his journal.[9]

Writing to Caroline Sturgis on 18 October 1840, Emerson lamented the easy route those in their coterie, himself included, took, safe from the threat of martyrdom: ''See you not, Caroline, that we all . . . have never known a rough duty. . . . The scarred martyrs . . . go silently, yet every victory in their history . . . augments their irresistible attraction for me. . . . I am daily getting ashamed of my life.''[10] Predictably, after declining to go to Brook Farm Emerson reported a sense of guilt because conscience ''beckons me to the martyr's and redeemer's office.''

In ''Character'' (1844), Emerson affirmed that martyrdom can proclaim nobility of character: ''The ages have exulted in the manners of a youth [Christ] who owed nothing to fortune, . . . who, by the pure quality of his nature, shed an epic splendor around the facts of his death which has transfigured every particular into an universal symbol for the eyes of mankind.'' In ''Compensation'' he said, ''The martyr cannot be dishonored. Every lash inflicted is a tongue of fame.''[11]

In the spring of 1851, reacting to the claim of Webster's ally Rufus Choate that the Pilgrims of 1620 would have held the opponents of the Fugitive Slave Law in contempt, Emerson insisted, ''They would have died at the stake before soiling themselves with this damnation.''[12]

June 1856 found him reflecting: ''There are men who as soon as they are born take a bee-line to the axe of the inquisitor. . . . Wonderful the way in which we are saved by this unfailing supply of the moral element.''[13] Ten days before Emerson recorded this thought, Senator Sumner had been brutally assaulted and beaten unconscious, in the Senate chamber, by Congressman Preston Brooks, a Southerner. He had been attacked because of his courageous, if at times strident, diatribes against slavery. Emerson saw that Sumner, unlike himself, had made a bee-line for the inquisitor's axe. The stage was now set for the advent of a yet more spectacular martyr.

Shortly before John Brown carried out his fateful raid on Harpers Ferry, he came to Concord and was received by Emerson. Emerson did not know of his plans, but Brown had been represented to him as a champion of the abolitionist cause and, as such, Emerson welcomed him and wished him well. After Brown was taken prisoner on 18 October 1859, Emerson quoted a young friend, a lady from Kentucky, in his journal: "Mattie Griffith says, if Brown is hung, the gallows will be sacred as the cross." Evidently he repeated the phrase to Bronson Alcott on the night of 30 October, when both were in Thoreau's audience to hear his impassioned "Plea for Captain John Brown," because Alcott, writing in his journal the next day, said, "This is too noble a man to be sacrificed so; and yet such as he, and only such, are worthy of the glories of the Cross." On 7 November, lecturing on courage to a Boston audience, Emerson interpolated into his prepared text a spontaneous observation, reported the next day in the *New-York Daily Tribune* as: "The Saint, whose fate yet hangs in suspense, but whose martyrdom, if it shall be perfected, will make the gallows as glorious as the cross." When on 11 November *The Liberator* reprinted the statement — Emerson's first public comment on the situation — indignation at Emerson's "blasphemous comparison" became national.[14]

In Cincinnati, early in February 1860, a rich Conservative asked Emerson to repudiate the phrase. When he repeated the words as they had been reported to him, Emerson said, "That's about what I said."[15] He would not buy the man's good opinion by going back on his word. His interrogator had meant well. The day before Emerson's arrival, the editor of the *Cincinnati Enquirer* had deplored his coming:

> His appearance upon the stand will be a public scandal. It is but a few weeks since he declared in a speech that John Brown, the hero of the Harpers Ferry insurrection, "HAS MADE THE GALLOWS GLORIOUS LIKE THE CROSS!" The utterance of this blasphemous and traitorous sentiment . . . this insult of every thing which men hold sacred, ought to debar its author from the recognition of any community which has a proper respect for moral and patriotic feelings. . . . Only think of the atrocious sentiment, that John Brown has made his gallows as the cross upon which the Saviour of mankind had expiated, by his sufferings, the sins of a guilty world.[16]

Here a final variation in phrasing should be noted. "The gallows will be sacred [or "as sacred"] as the cross" now has become "has made the gallows glorious like the cross.''[17] At some point Emerson seems to have substituted ''like'' for Mattie Griffith's ''as.'' Whatever the word, he did not like the attendant controversy. When ''Courage'' was published a decade after Brown's hanging, Emerson omitted the remark entirely, ''distance of time having brought the case into a juster perspective.''[18] By then Emerson knew there was in Brown's history a dark chapter that set him at a far remove from Calvary. The indulgent editor of the *Enquirer*'s rival, the *Cincinnati Gazette*, had long since exonerated him, however. In an immediate response to the *Enquirer* he argued that Emerson meant merely that Brown's high purpose ''would give the gallows a higher meaning than as a mere symbol of retribution for common felony.''[19]

More surprising than the Cincinnati brouhaha and the cold shoulder shown Emerson in many quarters (including Philadelphia, where, because of the Brown remark, one of his lectures was canceled) was Hawthorne's entrance into the fray after it was all but forgotten. He was in Europe when Emerson made his speech, but in July 1862 he wrote to *The Atlantic Monthly:*

> I shall not pretend to be an admirer of old John Brown . . . nor did I expect ever to shrink so unutterably from any apophthegm of a sage, whose happy lips have uttered a hundred golden sentences, as from that saying (perhaps falsely attributed to so honored a source,) that the death of this blood-stained fanatic has ''made the Gallows as venerable as the Cross!'' Nobody was ever more justly hanged.[20]

When Hawthorne was advised that Emerson's word had been ''like,'' not ''as,'' he was mollified. The substitution, he found, made ''a considerable difference, as allowing the reader or auditor (if he pleases) to put John Brown at a somewhat lower elevation than Jesus Christ.'' He did not let matters rest there, but added, ''As a mere matter of taste, surely, it had better never been said.''[21] He did not allow for the high feelings rife at the time the remark was made. He cannot have known that on the day of Brown's hanging, an overflow crowd gathered at Tremont Temple, weeping openly before a huge symbol which dominated the hall — a picture of John Brown superimposed upon a black cross![22]

In May 1860, when Theodore Parker died in Florence, Emerson reflected that Parker, a member of the secret committee that sponsored Brown's raid, also had accepted a martyr's fate. For the sake of his ideals he had again and again put himself on the firing line. An alienation had resulted so massive that Boston's Unitarian community refused to pray for him even when he was dying. Emerson wrote of

Parker: "He was willing to perish in the using. He sacrificed the future to the present, was willing to spend & be spent."[23]

With Parker's death a strange deflation came upon Emerson. He seemed to move away from life itself:

> I reached the other day the end of my fifty seventh year, and
> am easier in my mind than hitherto. I could never give much
> reality to evil & pain. But now when my wife says, perhaps this
> tumor on your shoulder is a cancer, I say, what if it is? It would
> not make the gentleman on his way in a cart to the gallows very
> unhappy, to tell him that the pain in his knee threatened a white
> swelling.[24]

The abolitionist movement gave Emerson a further chance, nonetheless, to show his heroic side when Wendell Phillips asked him to speak at the annual meeting of the Massachusetts Anti-Slavery Society, at Tremont Temple, on 24 January 1861. He prefaced his account of what occurred with a new tribute to martyrdom: "The chamber of flame in which the martyr passes, is more magnificent than the royal apartment from which majesty looks out on his sufferings."[25] Phillips addressed the audience first. According to Julia Ward Howe, who was present, as soon as he stepped forward to speak "a perfect hubbub arose in the gallery." Again and again howls, shrieks, and catcalls drowned him out. But he stood his ground, predicting to his companions on the platform that the troublemakers soon would tire themselves out. He proved right and, to the delight of his sympathizers, gave a spellbinding speech.[26]

Unfortunately, Phillips's triumph left the dissidents in the audience aroused and wrathful. The next speaker was Emerson and on him they loosed their indignation. In his journal Emerson wrote afterward:

> Do thy duty of the day. Just now, the supreme public duty of
> all thinking men is to assert freedom. Go where it is threatened,
> and say, 'I am for it, and do not wish to live in the world a
> moment longer than it exists.' Phillips . . . did me the honor to
> ask me to come to the meeting at Tremont Temple, and, esteeming
> such an invitation a command, though sorely against my inclina-
> tion and habit, I went.

When Emerson began to talk, there were hisses and groans and shouts of "Dry up," "Put him out," "Button your coat," and such. Emerson owned humbly: "The mob roared whenever I attempted to speak, and after several beginnings, I withdrew."[27]

Neither Emerson nor Phillips was able to hold long a high opinion of each other. When Phillips spoke slightingly of Samuel Hoar, Emerson's reply was to ignore Phillips's hand the next time he offered it to him. That undoubtedly explains Phillips's later condescending observation: "The chief merit of Emerson's life was that, having talked about heroism all his life, he recognized the hero when John Brown appeared."[28]

Holmes, who saw the significance of Emerson's long love affair with martyrdom, at least in the abstract, said:

> Judged by his life Emerson comes very near our best ideal of humanity. He was born too late for the trial of the cross or the stake, or even the jail. But the penalty of having an opinion of his own and expressing it was a serious one, and he accepted it as cheerfully as any of Queen Mary's martyrs accepted his fiery baptism. . . . His writings, whether in prose or verse, are worthy of admiration, but his manhood was the underlying quality which gave them their true value. . . . There are living organisms so transparent that we can see their hearts beating and their blood flowing through their glassy tissues. So transparent was the life of Emerson; so clearly did the true nature of the man show through it. What he taught others to be, he was himself.[29]

62. Moncure Conway
Euphrasy and Rue

$\mathcal{O}$N 9 November 1852 Ruth Haskins Emerson had a birthday, her eighty-fourth. No notice of it was taken on that day. Emerson was absent from home, and Lidian thought it appropriate that he should be at Bush to celebrate with his mother a birthday which, given her fragile health, might be her last. The following night, when he returned, the "little feast" was duly held. For Ruth the occasion must have been a pleasant one. Customarily, she took her meals in her room. This evening she was carried downstairs, a necessary procedure now when she ventured into that part of the house.

All the family was present, including Elizabeth Hoar, Ruth's long-cherished "adoptive" daughter-in-law and frequent companion. Their tête-à-têtes cannot have always concerned Charles, dead now sixteen years, though Lidian would not have doubted it. In Lidian's mind Elizabeth enjoyed a kind of Grecian-urn immortality, her betrothed ever envisaged in the ideal, in a state of perfection, a notion that Margaret Fuller had taken to be illustrative of the unsubstantial grasp Lidian had on reality. This evening, at least, nothing was said to mar the good cheer that belonged to the occasion, and Ruth felt the benefit of it. She chose not to be carried back to her room. With her son and her nurse assisting her, she rewarded those who had shown her a full measure of affection by *"walking (or rather climbing) up all the stairs from the front door to her chamber."*[1] Waldo that same night wrote to William to share this good news with him.

Emerson had taken more than usual precautions to make certain that his mother's birthday celebration was a time of perfect contentment for her. Her lifetime had been marred with many sorrows and hardships and another had arisen of which he chose to spare her immediate knowledge. A note had come that evening from his cousin David Greene Haskins, the Episcopal minister who had been Thoreau's classmate at Harvard. David's father, Ralph Haskins — he whom Ruth had raised — had died at eleven o'clock the night before. The burial service and interment were scheduled for the next morning. Emerson waited until then to tell Ruth of her loss.

To David Greene Haskins, on 21 May 1880, although by then he had all but ceased to write letters, Emerson wrote in response to David's request for some comments for a sketch he was preparing of his father: "Your father was the admired brother of my mother. I learned from her that I was named *Ralph* for him. . . . He met her affection by careful interest and advice in her affairs from year to year."[2]

That Ralph Haskins had died on Ruth's birthday supplied an added note of poignancy to the news of his passing. Yet Ralph's death was but the first of a series of sad events touching her family which had to be communicated to Ruth in the ensuing months. Four months later, Ruth's sister Elizabeth died; seven months after that, her brother Thomas.

The month following Thomas's death, only a week after her eighty-fifth birthday, while Emerson was meeting a lecture commitment in Charlestown, Ruth herself died unexpectedly. "After living with her so long," Emerson wrote to William, with justifiable dismay, "I feel as if I might have been present at the moment of her departure."[3] But friends she cherished had been with her — Elizabeth Hoar and Sarah Ripley. She went so quietly, they assured Emerson, they had not at once realized that she was gone.

Ralph Haskins's death brought into view other circumstances which attested further to Emerson's natural propensity to be both understanding and thoughtful. "I shall attend the funeral," he told William matter-of-factly. Then, without rancor or recrimination, he went on to touch upon circumstances that would have stirred bitterness and resentment in many bosoms. Twice during Ralph Haskins's last illness Emerson had gone to visit him. On both occasions he was refused access to the sickroom.[4]

No adequate explanation for the coolness of the Haskinses toward Emerson is readily apparent. When Emerson taught school in Roxbury in 1826, David Greene Haskins had been one of his pupils. When David published his book, *Ralph Waldo Emerson: His Maternal Ancestors*, in 1887, he had only pleasant memories of that encounter to record and kind words to say for Emerson himself. Yet he wrote the book to show that Emerson's maternal heritage was not without distinction and it may be that the Haskins side of the family felt at times that the Emersons had neglected them or even looked down on them. In turning back Emerson from his father's bedchamber David was probably trying to bring himself out from under Emerson's shadow by telling him there was one place where his authority did not go.

However stressful the vibrations that rattled Emerson's domestic world, his main preoccupation continued to be his intellectual life. His writing and lecturing engrossed him and stimulation sought him out at Bush in every season with a steady flow of visitors. The world was beating a path to his door long before he made that phrase famous. One such encounter came early in May 1853.

It was a little after twelve, on Tuesday, the third. The young Virginian had waited until then because he had been told that mornings were Emerson's work time and inviolable. To the servant who answered his knock he handed a letter of introduction from John Gorham Palfrey, with a request that he might be allowed to call later in the afternoon. Edith and little Eddy came next to the door. Their father was out, they said, but would be home for his dinner at one. Their mother said he was to stay. The visitor took no persuading. In high spirits he passed the ensuing hour with the children, walking among Emerson's apple and pear trees and sitting in the rustic summer house that, six years before, Alcott with Thoreau's help had built of twenty hemlocks.[5]

Dinner hour was drawing on when the young man from Virginia, Moncure D. Conway, was sent for. Emerson was at the front door to greet him, eyes alight with that kindling welcome remembered by so many who met him. He perused the letter which Conway produced anew. "Surely," he exclaimed, "you are my Virginian correspondent."[6] He was remembering a letter Conway had written him on 4 November 1851, when, at nineteen, Conway told him, "About a year ago I commenced reading your writings. I have read them all and studied them sentence by sentence. I have shed many burning tears over them; because you gain my assent to Laws which, when I see how they would act on the affairs of life, I have not the courage to practice."[7]

When Conway confirmed his identity, Emerson stepped to the door of his study and called "Queenie," summoning Lidian. Both then insisted that Conway should spend a few days with them. Although the offer came as the fulfillment of a dream, Conway could not act on it. Other commitments had a prior claim, but this day in itself, at least, was touched with perfection. He would count it always as the greatest day in his life.

During the morning, Conway had stalked Hawthorne around Concord without finding the courage to speak to him, but at noon he went through with his resolve to approach Emerson, for he had come out from Cambridge, from the Divinity School, for that express purpose. His visit was no whim but the culmination of a process long under way. Emerson had come unexpectedly into his life after he graduated from Dickinson College at eighteen. One morning at Falmouth, Virginia, where his parents lived, he settled himself on a hilltop overlooking the Rappahannock. There in a copy of *Blackwood's* he found a piece about Emerson, a name new to him, and came to an uneasy halt on reading Emerson's words, ''All that Shakespeare says of the king, yonder slip of a boy that reads in the corner feels to be true of himself.'' Emerson might have been talking directly to him.

Conway's people were Virginia gentry. His forebear, John Washington, had been George Washington's granduncle. But Conway now was pointed in a direction that would lead him right out of that world. Somehow, thanks to Emerson's catholicity, Conway found in his ideas a response to his own Methodism, and, never suspecting that his new views were not compatible with those he had been schooled in, he turned from the study of law to enter the Methodist ministry. Concomitant with this new commitment, he broadened his acquaintance with Emerson. He related: ''Soon after leaving home for the charge assigned me by the Baltimore Methodist Conference, I obtained the first series of Emerson's *Essays,* and presently his other works. They were read, between my nineteenth and twentieth birthdays, on horseback, while traveling the roads and woods of a 'circuit' in Maryland.''[8]

Under Emerson's influence Conway saw he was ''mentally traveling to a new point of view.'' On a visit to Washington he talked to Professor Spencer F. Baird (afterward head of the Smithsonian), about the change that Emerson had brought to his thinking. Baird had read Emerson and told Conway: ''Whatever may be thought of Emerson's particular views of nature, there can be no question about the nature in him and in his writings: that is true and beautiful.''[9]

Conway was now at the stage when he needed to address Emerson directly. On the pretext of wanting to know where he could buy a set of *The Dial,* he wrote the letter of 4 November 1851. Emerson was busy then readying the Fuller memoirs for publication. But, from his own experience, he knew the anguish that went with spiritual doubts and wrote back at once, on 13 November, telling Conway:

I believe what interests both you and me most . . . is the morals of intellect. . . . A true soul will disdain to be moved except by what natively commands it, though it should go sad and solitary in search of its master a thousand years. The few superior persons in each community are so by their steadiness in reality and their neglect of appearances. This is the euphrasy and rue that purge the intellect and ensure insight.[10]

"Yours, in all good hope," Emerson said, in closing his letter. Of this phrase Conway said later, "My heart learned this note and sang it to me in many a night of loneliness and poverty."[11]

Over the next year Conway's inquiring spirit drew him into alliance with the Hicksite Quakers and into a developing friendship with William Furness. Before the end of 1852 he broke with the Methodists and early in 1853, disowned by his family, journeyed to Cambridge to begin his studies at the Divinity School.

Before dinner on Conway's unforgettable third of May, Emerson drew him out on the subject of his spiritual odyssey. Conway spoke of the effect that the *Blackwood's* article had had on him. In response Emerson told him: "When the mind has reached a certain stage it may be sometimes crystallized by a slight touch." "The gods generally provide the young thinker with friends," he said further, on learning of the support Conway had received from Furness and the Hicksites. Presently the three children — Ellen, Edith, and Edward — joined them and Emerson debriefed them of the events of the day. "He insinuated that she was a rogue, and she insinuated the corkscrew in his leg,"[12] Emerson suggested mischievously when Edith disclosed that a neighbor had struck an accuser in the leg with a corkscrew. Conway took it as proof of a nimble mind that Ellen saw the joke at once. Estranged then, and for long years to come, from his parents, Conway enjoyed the merry, domestic chatter that passed between parents and children.

Emerson's after-dinner event for Conway and himself was a walk around Walden Pond. For a brief interval before they set out, Conway found himself left on his own in Emerson's study. Like other visitors before him, he drank in the scene hungrily. Three likenesses of Goethe, a portrait and two statuettes, were in the room. On four long shelves along the inner wall enough manuscripts were piled "to furnish a score of printed volumes," or so Conway concluded. These were Emerson's accumulated journals, a project already of thirty-four years' duration. The furnishings of the room seemed to Conway "rather antique and simple." And, indeed, their sole merit was their usefulness. Emerson had neither the money nor the inclination to surround himself with heirloom pieces.

As the two men skirted Walden, Emerson suggested that the best Unitarian ministers were men recruited from other denominations. A lively faith was to be looked for in men whose convictions experience had formed. "I cannot feel interested in Christianity," Emerson said, in terms that would have confounded a creationist. "It seems deplorable that there should be a tendency to creeds that would take men back to the chimpanzee."[13]

Conway marveled aloud that he could ever have credited innate depravity, eternal damnation for the unbaptized, and more. And when

Emerson, turning from these weighty topics to the beauty of the spring day around them, remarked on the glittering arcs of the oars dipping into the pond in sunlight and on the voices of the fishermen who manned them, transmuted into music by distance and by the carpet of water about them, Conway went on to attest to the repugnance he felt when, at Baltimore, he had attended Roman Catholic services. But here he was putting himself in opposition to the pleasant sensations Emerson had reported to Lidian when, ten years before, he had attended high mass in Baltimore's Catholic cathedral. "The Unitarian church," he had told her, "forgets men are poets."[14] Gently now he emended Conway's conclusions. As a sensate experience these ceremonies had their place, "Yet they possess beauty in the distance," he acknowledged. "When one sees them on the stage, — processions of priests in their vestments chanting their hymns at the opera, — they are in their place, and offend no sentiment."[15] Emerson was a long way from a Catholic acceptance of the senses, but a long way too from Conway's Protestant loathing of them.[16] Conway had outgrown the dogma, but not the doggerel, of his Huguenot and Presbyterian forebears. When, in 1882, Conway was told that at Concord's First Parish Church, where Emerson lay in state before burial, a display of pinks, pansies, and roses positioned above him had been arranged to represent an open book, with FINIS inscribed on the final page, he lauded the symbolism inherent in the tribute. By then he had come to terms with the sensate.

Many of the remarks Conway attributes to Emerson on that "most memorable day of my life" reduce to aphorisms. That Emerson spoke to him mostly in aphorisms is unlikely. Yet, of the things Emerson did say, the aphorisms, naturally, would have been most firmly fixed in his memory. And so we are told that when Conway moved away from his topic of Catholic ceremonies, he spoke of a paper he had to prepare on eschatology. Still not quite done with the sensate, Emerson aphoristically replied, "An actually existent fly is more important than a possibly existent angel." And again, still not ready to be drawn to the dry texts of the theologian, Emerson observed, "The old artist said, *Pingo in eternitatem;* this *eternitatem* for which I paint is not in past or future, but is the height of every living hour."[17] Then he fought clear of Conway's abstract concerns altogether, giving the conversation such a turn that even Conway understood his intentions.

Through the bushes and brambles they had come to a side path. Emerson drew up short, peering intently along the way before them through the thicket. "Ah!" he exclaimed, "There is one of the gods of the wood!" "Where?" asked Conway, who saw nothing. Emerson, ignoring the question, was under way again. "Did you see it?" he called back over his shoulder. "No, I saw nothing," the thwarted Conway answered. "What was it?" Emerson had already retreated into his own counsel. He spoke softly. "No matter." Not accustomed to laconic New England ways and forgetful of Emerson's practice of skipping stages of discourse, Conway asked again what it was that he had failed to see. Perhaps Emerson wanted to make him realize that we often miss seeing what we should see, for he merely replied, "Never mind, if you did not see it." Conway's initial reaction was to be piqued but, in the long run, Emerson achieved his purpose. He had moved the conversation to his own ground. Conway conceded that he "very soon was listening to talk that made my eschatology seem ridiculous." From his endorsement of "the supremacy of the present hour," Emerson had moved Conway to the actual experience of it.[18]

At length their steps led them to the ruins of Thoreau's hut, forsaken six summers past. There, not so much for the words spoken as for the power exuded, standing by those visible reminders of a dream that had gone from the particular to the universal, Emerson, in Conway's eyes, seemed for the moment transfigured, "an incarnation of the wondrous day he had given me."[19] Emerson seemed able at will to produce for an aspiring disciple a moment of ecstatic intimacy that grappled that person to him, forever after, with hoops of adamantine. In quest of such experiences men have sought out gurus. A growing number of men could say that while Concord held Emerson men need not travel to the Himalayas.

Two days later Conway sought in vain to see Emerson at a crowded dinner event in Boston only to learn, to his dismay, on his return to Divinity Hall, that in his absence Emerson had come there to pay him a visit.

63. A Harvard Incursion
Loammi's Room

$\mathcal{A}$FTER a winter tour that saw him traveling as far west as Wisconsin to deliver twenty-nine lectures in seven states and in Canada, in little more than seven weeks, Emerson returned to Concord in early March 1854. Aside from a Maine commitment for the end of the month, whatever lecturing he had to do through the rest of the winter would be done in Massachusetts itself. When one such lecture, announced for the Concord Lyceum in March, was rescheduled, word of the change did not carry to Harvard. Accordingly, Moncure Conway persuaded two of his classmates, Henry Gardiner Denny and Loammi Goodenough Ware, to divide with him the cost of renting a sleigh to take them to Concord, on the date originally announced, so that they could be in Emerson's audience.

Neither Denny nor Ware had any special interest in Emerson. They made the run in subzero weather, chiefly as a lark that they could boast about later. When they got to Concord, however, they found the town hall standing dark and empty. Deflated, they went on to Emerson's house, hoping to learn how they had miscalculated. Emerson and Lidian received them sympathetically and at once undertook to make amends. In chairs drawn up before the fire, provided with warm drinks and refreshment, they soon were basking in the splendor of Emerson's conversation.

After his visit the previous May, Conway had come back to Concord and stayed through the summer, his fortunes watched over by Emerson, who found him a place to stay, often had him to dinner, and took walks with him. More than that, he put his library at Conway's disposal, and when Conway's conscience began to bother him over the quantity of books he was borrowing, many of them scarcely procurable elsewhere, Emerson dismissed his concern with the words, "What are they for?" Best of all, Emerson introduced Conway to Sarah Ripley and Elizabeth Hoar and put him under the tutelage of Thoreau. When he did that, he assured him dryly, "You will find our Thoreau a sad pagan."[1]

Over the summer Conway became acquainted with the Gita and the Persian poets and, of course, the German romantics. On one occasion Lidian confided to him that Goethe was "a sort of bogy to her." This was said in Emerson's hearing. He made no comment then but later he told Conway that "Goethe had written some things — *Elective Affinities*, for instance — which could be readily read only by minds which had undergone individual training." In a frivolous moment the Emersons had named their cat Goethe. One day Conway overheard Emerson expelling the animal from his study with the observation, "Goethe, you must retire. I don't like your manners."[2]

Conway relished the opportunity to be with Emerson. He doted on his every word and carried away a liberal stock of anecdotes. "Whom shall we invite to the picnic?" Conway heard Ellen ask her father one day. "All children from six years to sixty," Emerson decreed.[3] On one occasion Conway was with him in the garden when Emerson stopped to point out a favorite plum. "This is when ripe," he said, "a fruit of paradise." Then he searched the tree until he found a ripe plum and on tiptoe fetched it down for Conway to enjoy.

"What, sonny?" Conway heard Emerson exclaim one day to little Eddy, trying to jolly him out of an indisposition. "Your mother says you are not well today. Now what naughty thing have you been doing, for when anyone is sick something *the devil* is the matter." Sometimes Emerson confided to Conway his opinion of others. Of Samuel Hoar, frail and aging, he said, when they passed on the street, "He is a saint. He no longer dwells with us here down on earth." Of the formidable Rockwood, Samuel's son, Emerson owned that he "rather dreaded him . . . on account of his tendencies to argumentative and remorselessly logical talk." This he said with a smile so that Conway knew it was half jest.[4]

Since his family at that stage had disowned Conway for his "heretical" views, the friendship of the Emersons was vital to him, coming when it did. In after years he spoke of Concord as his "second birthplace," and of the Emersons as his "second family."

Although that winter night Emerson sent home happy to Cambridge the sleigh contingent from Harvard, it bothered him that the three young men had been cheated of their expectations. Thus a letter followed Conway back to Cambridge. In it Emerson said he would come some afternoon to Conway's room to read a lecture if Conway could arrange it. That his room should be the setting for an event of such magnitude Conway saw at once was impossible. Its starkness proclaimed his impoverishment. But Loammi's room was another matter. No other room in Divinity Hall approached it for splendor. That became the agreed-upon site and a date was chosen — 27 April. When Emerson arrived, he found awaiting him an audience equal to the occasion. This was not merely Emerson giving a lecture, after all. This was Emerson returning to Harvard after an exile of sixteen years, once again guest of students of the Divinity School. Emerson intended no challenge when he proposed that the students invite him. But he was sending Harvard a signal. Old antagonisms need not divide them. He had come to a new wisdom and Harvard itself was changing. The topic he had chosen was not one calculated to generate controversy. It was simply ''Poetry.''

In addition to his fellow excursionists, Ware and Denny, Conway rounded up for this moment of gentle indiscretion an audience with impeccable credentials — Henry and Fanny Longfellow, James Russell Lowell, John Sullivan Dwight, Charles Eliot Norton and his sisters Jane and Grace (they were not throwing down a challenge to their father, Emerson's old adversary, Andrews Norton; he was several months in the grave), Mrs. Charles Lowell, Franklin Sanborn, and the concert pianist Otto Dresel. Harvard could scarcely construe this event as an episode of student bravado.

When Emerson came to the end of his lecture, his audience was curiously mute. Conway, in retrospect, sought to suffuse that moment with awe. ''Presently,'' he said, ''Otto Dresel moved to the piano and performed several of Mendelssohn's 'Songs without Words.' Those were the only words possible.''[5] He insisted further that Emerson, alluding in this lecture to the Hunterian doctrine of ''arrested and progressive development,'' anticipated, five years before publication of *Origin of Species*, Darwinian evolution. Such a statement does appear in Emerson's ''Poetry,'' but Edward Emerson, after examining the script of the 1854 Divinity School lecture, concluded that Emerson interpolated mention of Hunter into this lecture at some later time.[6] Conway's memory played him one further trick. He placed Clough in Emerson's audience. Clough by then was back in England.

An alternative explanation for the solemnity of mood that overtook those who heard Emerson's lecture came from Longfellow: ''It was full of brilliant and odd things; but not very satisfactory on a first hearing. I hope to read it one day, and perhaps understand it better.''[7] Norton conjectured, plausibly, that the presence of Lowell and Longfellow in his audience affected the substance of Emerson's remarks, putting him under constraint so that he suppressed passages which

deplored the general state of poetry in America in that day.[8] In point
of fact, his audience heard a lecture that had not yet fully evolved.
Indeed, new materials were culled from several later addresses before
it achieved its final identity as "Poetry and Imagination" in 1872, the
form in which it was printed in 1875 in *Letters and Social Aims.*

Conway's account of the fresh tempest Emerson's appearance at the
Divinity School generated can be relied on even if his account of the
lecture itself cannot. Two of his professors, Convers Francis and George
Noyes, called on him to explore the rumors that Emerson had set up a
shadow curriculum within the Divinity School to nurture those who
embraced his "cult." They went away satisfied that nothing untoward
had occurred.[9]

That Andrews Norton's children had been in Emerson's select audience ought to have been indication enough that winds of change were
blowing in Emerson's favor. In fact, many of the fretful would live to
see Norton's nephew Charles W. Eliot, as president of Harvard, embrace Emerson's principles and recruit him for his faculty. Actually,
perhaps because of the wider recognition being granted him outside of
Boston, Emerson had been steadily gaining ground. It was reported
that Henry Ward Beecher, over lunch, once said to Emerson, "Do you
think a man eating these meats could tell what grasses the animals fed
on?" When Emerson said no, Beecher said, "I'm glad to hear it, for
I've been feeding on you a long time and I'm glad my people don't
know it."[10]

Prior to the Divinity Hall lecture, Conway had heard Emerson speak,
probably on 1 December 1853, on the topic "The Anglo-Americans."
This occasion he remembered as "the most vivid experience of my
life." He seems, however, to have been impressed more by Emerson's
manner than his matter because, in reporting on the event, that is
what he focused on. Conway evoked a memorable likeness of Emerson
on the lecture platform:

> I recall no gesture, only an occasional swaying forward of the
> body by an impulse of earnestness. Though nearly every word had
> been written, the manuscript did not hold his eye, which kept its
> magnetic play upon the audience. At one time, indeed, he searched
> his memory for a quotation from Plato which he wished to
> introduce, his hand going to his chin and his face turning aside
> from us as if he would find the words written on the wall. The
> sentence found was well worth the pause.[11]

Young men in Emerson's audiences nearly always took fire. For all
Conway's tendency to swathe his memories in lyricism, especially as
he grew older and found that his affection for Emerson had survived

his affection for his ideas, he was successful in recreating for us a sense of the excitement Emerson stirred in youthful bosoms.

When Conway emerged from the Divinity School in 1854, he took a pastorate in Washington, D.C. Two years later the Unitarian church in Cincinnati came under his management. There he handled the details for Emerson's local lecture series and began publishing a reincarnated *Dial* as a monthly. In support of this venture, Emerson contributed two poems, "Quatrains," and "The Sacred Dance," and an essay, "Domestic Life," given first as a lecture in 1839 or 1840, but never published hitherto.[12] Emerson's patronage was not enough. On 11 February 1860, the *Cincinnati Daily Gazette* dismissed the journal with this estimate: "Thus far *The Dial* has disgraced the name of the respectable, if erratic, periodical which it is a clumsy attempt to revive."

During Emerson's last years Conway made hit and run visits to Concord, first in 1875, when he was Emerson's houseguest for a few days, and again in 1880. To the first visit we owe his account of Emerson's peculiar failure of memory: "He remembered the realities and uses of things when he could not recall their names. He would describe what he wanted or thought of; when he could not recall 'chair' he could speak of 'that which supports the human frame,' and 'the implement that cultivates the soil' must do for plow." Conway found that Emerson, in the midst of company, now did not converse at all, but on a one-to-one basis could be much his old self. By 1880, though, the problem had substantially deepened. Emerson was enough aware to chide his "naughty memory," but, listening, he assumed a brooding intensity as though trying to find passage through some intricate maze. Conway, unable to let mere facts efface his memory of Emerson triumphant, rounded out his account with an indulgent reflection: "Emerson appeared to me strangely beautiful at this time, and the sweetness of his voice, when he spoke of the love and providence at his side, is quite indescribable."[13]

Although he was in England when Emerson died, Conway was able to render one meaningful service to his memory. Carlyle had told Emerson's daughter Edith that "he had never to his knowledge destroyed a scrap of paper on which her father's hand had rested, and all would be sent to her."[14] A memorandum to that effect appeared in Carlyle's will, and Froude, through Carlyle's niece, Mrs. Alexander Carlyle, had dutifully forwarded such letters as he found among Carlyle's papers. But many letters were lacking. Conway discovered that these had been stolen by an amanuensis whom Carlyle had had in his hire. Although Lowell, then U.S. minister to Great Britain, declined to buy back these priceless letters and neglected to advise others that they were for sale, Conway followed up the matter and, with great tact, was able to make true copies of them without causing the thief to take alarm. Charles Eliot Norton, first editor of the Emerson-Carlyle correspondence, acknowledged a special debt to Conway for this assistance.[15]

Despite or because of his blind admiration, Conway's reminiscences of Emerson, in *Emerson at Home and Abroad* and in his autobiography, often are marred by imprecision and a gushing ardor. Emerson did not dread without reason the prospect of Conway's taking over as his biographer and literary executor.[16]

64. Pigeon Cove and the Adirondac Club
Celebrations of the Wild

*T*HE spring of 1856 brought tempestuous times to the country. The Kansas-Nebraska Act of 1854 had made the territory a battle-ground over slavery and Boston preempted a major role in the struggle. There the Emigrant Aid Company was founded and dispatched to Kansas thousands of New Englanders bent on voting the abolitionist ticket. Amos Lawrence, one of the Boston's merchant princes, was a principal manager of the company. He funded the founding of the University of Kansas at Lawrence, Kansas (named in his honor), and there, on 21 May, blood was spilled when proslavers sacked and burned Free-State headquarters. Swift reprisal came when John Brown, armed with rifles provided by Lawrence, three days later slaughtered five proslavery men, and, soon after, vanquished a proslavery vigilante band.

It was on the day following the strife at Lawrence that Charles Sumner was clubbed unconscious by Preston Brooks. Four days later, for the first time since the Cherokee outrage, Emerson addressed an indignation meeting at Concord. In the days immediately ahead, Concord raised $1,360 for Kansas Relief. Emerson gave generously. In the months ahead, Kansas Relief would continue to be an active concern for Emerson, both as an advocate and fund-raiser.

The year was a presidential election year and battle lines were shaping up around the slavery issue. Although Emerson was much involved in last-minute details leading to the publication on 6 August of *English Traits,* it is a measure of his concern that he allowed his name to stand on the list of alternate delegates to the newly formed Republican Party's first national convention, which was held in June and nominated an abolitionist, John C. Frémont, as the standard bearer.

Considering the pressure he was under, we can understand Emerson's amusement when, at this time, he received a letter from a lady in Virginia insisting that he allocate an hour a week to foster her potential. When he answered this letter, seeking to be helpful without making a commitment, he received, in reply, a stern letter of reprimand. That letter alone may have led him to follow the advice of Cyrus Bartol, and go to Rockport for a week-long holiday, his first seaside vacation since the sojourn at Nantasket fifteen years before. Since Delia Bacon chose that same interval to lay siege to Emerson for support of her claims that Bacon wrote the plays attributed to Shakespeare, we can only take it as evidence of Emerson's heroic fortitude that he did not contemplate a total escape to the South Seas.[1]

Emerson's Rockport vacation lasted seven days. This time, unlike his Nantasket visit, his family accompanied him. Edith liked it so well that, ten years later, she chose the same hotel — the Pigeon Cove House — for her honeymoon.

Rockport, Massachusetts, which occupies the tip of Cape Ann, seceded from Gloucester to become a separate town in 1840. Pigeon Cove, Rockport's northerly portion, stands on a rich deposit of magma, the snouts of which protrude everywhere through the thin topsoil. Although Emerson liked swimming well enough to swim daily in the ocean in the hot July weather, climbing on the rocks was the most usual recreation of visitors to Cape Ann in that period. He pursued that sport with relish, too. Thus it was that the day following their return from Rockport, he entered Lidian's room at Bush in a high state of elation. When he found the children sitting with their mother, who was convalescing from Rockport as from an affliction, Emerson held out his journal and made an excited announcement to them all: "I came in yesterday from walking on the rocks, and wrote down what the sea had said to me; and today when I open my book I find that it all reads in blank verse, with scarcely a change. Listen!" He then read the passage that so struck him:

> Returned from Pigeon Cove, where we have made acquaintance with the sea, for seven days. 'Tis a noble friendly power, and seemed to say to me, 'Why so late and slow to come to me? Am I not here always, thy proper summer home? Is not my voice thy needful music; my breath thy healthful climate in the heats; my touch thy cure? Was ever building like my terraces? Was ever couch as magnificent as mine. Lie down on my warm ledges and learn that a very little hut is all you need. I have made thy architecture superfluous, and it is paltry beside mine. Here are twenty Romes & Ninevahs & Karnacs in ruins together, obelisk & pyramid and Giant's Causeway, here they all are, prostrate or half-piled.'

And behold the sea, the opaline, plentiful and strong, yet beautiful as the rose or the rainbow, full of food, nourisher of men, purger of the world, creating a sweet climate, and in its unchangeable ebb and flow, and in its beauty at a few furlongs, giving a hint of that which changes not, & is perfect.[2]

At Rockport, the reconciliation with the sea that began at Nantasket seems complete and fulfilling, even its curative powers, in which his father trusted, at last being acknowledged. Since his estrangement from the sea was fused in Emerson's mind with his estrangement from his father, somehow it was fitting that he should first announce his own good terms with the sea in the presence of his children.

Seven or eight years later Emerson made almost verbatim use of this passage for better than half of his poem "Seashore," keeping its rhythmic flow as well as its images:

> *I heard or seemed to hear the chiding Sea*
> *Say, Pilgrim, why so late and slow to come?*
> *Am I not always here, thy summer home?*
> *Is not my voice thy music, morn and eve?*
> *My breath thy healthful climate in the heats,*
> *My touch thy antidote, my bay thy bath?*
> *Was ever building like my terraces?*
> *Was ever couch as magnificent as mine?*
> *Lie on the warm rock-ledges, and there learn*
> *A little hut suffices like a town.*
> *I make your sculptured architecture vain,*
> *Vain beside mine. I drive my wedges home,*
> *And carve the coastwise mountain into caves.*
> *Lo! here is Rome and Ninevah and Thebes,*
> *Karnak and Pyramid and Giant's Stairs*
> *Half piled or prostrate; and my newest slab*
> *Older than all thy race.*
>   *Behold the Sea,*
> *The opaline, the plentiful and strong,*
> *Yet beautiful as is the rose in June,*
> *Fresh as the trickling rainbow in July;*
> *Sea full of food, the nourisher of kinds,*
> *Purger of earth, and medicine of men;*
> *Creating a sweet climate by my breath,*
> *Washing out harms and griefs from memory,*
> *And, in my mathematic ebb and flow,*
> *Giving a hint of that which changes not.*[3]

Here Emerson allowed himself to be governed by the spontaneity of the mood that invaded him when he made his original journal entry.

His acquiescence made possible a poem that soars above many of his more disciplined lyrical flights into Nature. When one commentator suggested that the poem was Tennysonian, a young friend reported the remark to Emerson. He weighed it, then dismissed it. "It is not Tennysonian," he concluded, "but Pigeon Covean."

Emerson did not have to seek Nature in solitude to encounter the Muse. A sojourn in the wilderness a few years later, in every way alien to the tranquil interlude at Pigeon Cove, had lyric consequences no less fruitful and thorough.

As though in answer to his own query, "What is so rare as a day in June," in August 1857 James Russell Lowell left behind him the bride he had married that June and went off to the Adirondacks with the artist William Stillman and Dr. Estes Howe (Lowell's brother-in-law, with whom he and his wife then were living), on a successful deer hunt. The gratification this sally into the wilderness gave Lowell led him, the next year, to coax from the Saturday Club, a secondary fraternity, the Adirondac Club, meant to flourish in the summer when the activities of the Saturday Club were in abeyance. That Emerson would be drawn into this new club was inevitable since the Saturday Club had, in Holmes's words, "shaped itself around him as a nucleus of crystallization." He had, in fact, brought the club idea to Boston after having enjoyed the courtesy of clubs in London and Paris in 1848. The next year he joined forces with Sam Ward to found the Town and Country Club. This gave way to the Magazine or Atlantic Club, from which emerged both *The Atlantic Monthly* and the Saturday Club. Members of the Saturday Club met on the last Saturday of the month, from three to nine, for dinner and conversation in the mirror room of the Parker House. Day and time were chosen to accommodate Emerson's long-standing habit of visiting the Athenaeum on Saturday mornings and dining afterward with Boston friends. On that account, indeed, the club sometimes was spoken of as Emerson's Club. For nearly twenty years the opportunity the club offered him to meet with Boston's first men of intellect gave Emerson great satisfaction. It gave him added satisfaction to realize that the activities of this club paralleled those of the Anthology Club his father had helped to found when the century was new.[4]

Ten campers made up the membership of the band of improbable hunters that trooped into the wilds in the first days of August 1858 — Lowell and Stillman; Louis Agassiz and Dr. Jeffries Wyman, whom Agassiz had recruited to teach natural history at Harvard; Howe; Dr. Amos Binney; Horatio Woodman (alas, not a woodsman but a businessman); and the three unlikeliest members of the party, the remorselessly logical Rockwood Hoar, soon to take up his seat on the bench of the Massachusetts Supreme Judicial Court; Ralph Waldo

Emerson; and his erstwhile pupil, John Holmes, crippled and seden-
tary, but wittier, Emerson thought, than his brother Wendell, and,
what was more important, a survivor of Lowell's camping trip of the
previous year.[5]

Emerson meant to bring down a deer and, with this feat in mind,
bought a handsome, double-barreled gun and had himself instructed
in its use. Had it not been for that this "philosopher's camp," as Stillman designated it, might have expanded to a full dozen huntsmen.
When Longfellow learned that Emerson would be armed, he begged
off going. He was sure, he said, that somebody would get shot.[6] Thoreau also declined to go. It was in that interval that the gap between
Emerson and himself was widening. He got greater satisfaction out of
japing at Emerson armed and out for blood than the adventure itself
would have afforded him. "The story on the Mill-Dam," he wrote in
his journal, "is that he has taken a gun which throws shot from one
end and ball from the other."[6]

By common assent, Stillman was appointed "captain of the party."
Since ten veteran guides accompanied the ten huntsmen and assumed
the burdens of portage as well as the tedious business of preparing
campsites and readying meals, including dressing and cooking seven
deer slain by the hunters, Stillman's role cannot have been an onerous
one.

The Adirondac Club's errand into the wilderness of course offered
some hardships to these men of city-bred refinement. On Monday night
they arrived supperless at Lake George. On ensuing days they crossed
that lake and Lake Champlain, sailed on Saranac Lake, Saranac River,
Round Lake, and Upper Saranac Lake, at length sleeping in their clothes
in a log house on the loft floor. Rain meanwhile pelted down in cascading torrents, and midges and mosquitoes rapturously devoured them.
Furthermore, fleas that infested the tracker hounds brought by the
guides got beneath their clothing and peppered them with a fusillade
of bites.[7]

Some of the Adirondac party fished, some hunted; Agassiz and Wyman collected and dissected specimens of the fauna and flora. Despite
his avidity for specimens, Agassiz would not shoot at any living thing,
but Emerson on his behalf did magnanimously bring down a peetweet.
Announcing that he must understand this passion to kill, he also went
out at night with his companions, jack-hunting, "stealing with paddle
to the feeding-grounds of the red deer, to aim at a square mist." When
the signal to shoot came, however, unable to see the deer he was commissioned to shoot, he held his fire until the deer successfully took
flight. Otherwise, all he shot was empty ale bottles, using them for
target practice and, along with Agassiz and the others, breaking doz-
ens of them. Thoreau, who later received an account of these exercises

from Emerson himself, thought Emerson had demeaned himself by groveling in the commonplace. "Think of Emerson," he wrote in his journal, "shooting a peetweet (with shot) for Agassiz, and cracking an ale bottle (after emptying it) with his rifle at six rods. They cut several pounds of lead out of the tree. It is just what Mike Saunders, the merchant's clerk, did when he was there."[9]

After two weeks the woodland sojourners had attained appearances to rival their bold conduct. Judge Hoar found apt words to convey that fact when he bolted from the woods ahead of the others and wrote to his wife: "Our party when assembled in costume were a remarkable looking set, considering who they were, and I think anyone of them would have been convicted of piracy on very slight evidence, especially Mr. Emerson."[10] That was said, no doubt, because of all the members of the party, Emerson, reduced to such a state, would have seemed the most severely compromised. Yet, after all, grandfather Haskins had been a privateersman! Emerson was Emerson. His least departure from circumspect ways could not fail to astonish. Still, unlike Thoreau, who had his Puritanical or Covenanter side, Judge Hoar understood how good it was for Emerson to relax his standards on occasion. A delayed adolescence was better than none at all. On that jocose note the judge told his wife: "Neither Mr. Emerson nor I have shot the other and Mr. Emerson has passed for a very creditable woodsman."[11] Emerson, at least, cannot have found that fact surprising. None of the others had, year in and year out, trusted himself in the dead of winter to the rigors of the western lecture circuit. Emerson had developed into both a resourceful traveler and an inured one. Like a true champion of self-reliance, he made the best of things as he found them. He did not complain. Evidently his long-term commitment to the doctrine of compensation was assurance enough that the balm of contentment came, ultimately, to those whom hardships visited.

While this elite band of forest rovers was still in the wild, word carried to them that the last lengths of the cable intended to link Europe and America were now extended along the floor of the Atlantic Ocean. Europe and its muses, both courtly and uncourtly, whether for good or ill just minutes away, now hummed in the ears of America. The sylvan glade echoed as the odd assortment of hunters raised cries of exultation when they received the news.[12] Local pride probably added to their enthusiasm since a fellow Bay Stater, Cyrus Field (whose guest Emerson would be when he visited London in 1873), had initiated the project. The forest seemed a curious place to be for ten men so remarkably qualified to appreciate the significance of the news when they heard about it. Presumably, they had gone there to isolate themselves from the world and now they rejoiced because the world had found new ways to intrude upon them. Thoreau, had he had to endure their lusty cheers, would have seen their behavior as proof that they did not belong there at all. Emerson, however, had no difficulty reconciling this triumph of American technology with a commitment to Nature undefiled. In "The Adirondacs," a poem sponsored by this wilderness experience, Emerson saw in this feat new evidence that man could work in harmony with the laws of Nature. "The lightning has run masterless too long," he proclaimed. The news that it had been harnessed, like the current "pulsating" through the cable, quickens those who receive it. Their "exulting cries," their "burst of joy" flung back from the escarpment about them, in complimentary salute, replicates the nimble pulsations by means of which "man's messages" are being "Shot through the weltering pit of the salt sea."[13] Here is an analogy worked out in transcendental terms.

This poem alone has merit enough to make Emerson's role as peet-weet-slayer, deerstalker, ale-swigger, and bottle-breaker a small price to pay for benefits derived. Thoreau ought to have seen that.

Before the adjournment of this least orthodox of camp meetings, Stillman posed the campers for a painting at Follansbee Pond. Illustrious though many of them were, there can have been no dissent when Stillman accorded Emerson the central place among them. Perhaps, too, Stillman made a conscious decision to group the others but to have Emerson standing apart from them. There, as would be true wherever he found himself, Emerson was a unique personage. In truth, the Adirondac Club would not be remembered at all had Emerson, to assuage Longfellow's anxieties or to avoid scandalizing Thoreau, stayed home. Stillman's portrait was bought by Judge Hoar and given to the Concord Free Public Library, where it hangs today.

The Test of the poet is the power to take the passing
day, with its news, its cares, its fears, as he shares
them, and hold it up to a divine reason, till he sees it
to have a purpose and beauty, and to be related to
astronomy and history and the eternal
order of the world.

65. The Poet's Ear

*A*FTER attending at Concord a Quintette Club concert in January 1861, Emerson made an entry in his journal that reads like something Mark Twain might have written to exasperate his wife: "Because I have no ear for music . . . it looked to me as if the performers were crazy, and all the audience were making-believe crazy, in order to soothe the lunatics, & keep them amused." When he heard Marietta Alboni, the Italian diva, sing in *Cenerentola* in London in 1848, he had dismissed her efforts as "trills & gurgling . . . not only not interesting, but . . . painful . . . surgical . . . functional."[1]

Emerson's tone deafness was an affliction he periodically adverted to. He once wrote his wife that nobody save herself ever had heard him sing. In a piece he wrote for *The Dial,* one phrase begins, "The music of Beethoven is said by those who understand it . . . ." On hearing Chopin play, he said he wished that heaven had given him ears for the occasion.[2]

Emerson was so sure he lacked the faculty for appreciating music, he sought in himself some compensating faculty. On 14 November 1838, under the heading "Musical Eyes," he wrote:

> I think sometimes that my lack of musical ear, is made good to
> me through my eyes. That which others hear, I *see*. All the
> soothing, plaintive, brisk or romantic moods which corresponding
> melodies waken in them, I find in the carpet of the wood, in the
> margin of the pond, in the shade of the hemlock grove, or in the
> infinite variety & rapid dance of the treetops as I hurry along.[3]

At times Emerson tried to reach beyond music to some universal insight: "Not having an ear for music, I speculate on the song and guess what it is saying to other people; what it should say to me. It is Universal and seems to hint at communication more general than speech, more general than music also." Sometimes he attempted to lose himself in it: "So is Music an asylum. It takes us out of the actual & whispers to us dim secrets that startle our wonder as to who we are & for what, whence & whereto. All the great interrogatories like questioning Angels float in on its waves of sound." Further reflection provided yet another compensation. Edward Emerson said: "He . . . pleased himself that no one of us could sing, for he said he thought that he had observed that the two gifts of singing and oratory did not go together."[4]

Tone deafness did not make Emerson an oddity among his contemporaries. General Grant said that he recognized just two tunes — "One is 'Yankee Doodle,' and the other isn't." Hawthorne, Samuel Gridley Howe, Charles Sumner, and Theodore Parker all insisted they had no ear at all. At Harvard, when the singing-master was auditioning Emerson's classmates, he presented himself too. "Chord!" the master called out. Emerson stood perplexed. "Chord! Chord!" the master snapped. "I don't know what you mean," Emerson said. "Why, sing!" the master told him. "Sing a note." "So I made some kind of a noise," Emerson related, and the master said, "That will do, sir. You need not come again."[5] While the note Emerson produced under such provocation could hardly have been melodious, the master's verdict was enough to convince Emerson that he was without an ear for music. In support of the master's judgment, we may consider the comments of Lidian's cousin Mary Miller Engel. At church services, she observed, Ellen did not sing — "She found the places in the hymnal for the others and I shared her book. She had the appearance of singing without making a sound. It seems that she, as well as her father, brother and sister, had little ear for music and she was afraid of singing a false note."[6]

Every now and again, as in June 1838, Emerson made a statement that suggested he was more receptive to music than he realized:

I delight in our pretty church music & to hear that poor slip of a girl, without education, without thought, yet show this fine instinct in her singing, so that every note of her song sounds to me like an adventure and a victory in the *ton-welt*, & whilst all the choir beside stay fast by their leader & the bass viol, this angel voice goes choosing, choosing on, & with the precision of genius keeps its faithful road & floods the house with melody.[7]

Emerson once conjectured: "I think sometimes, could I only have music on my own terms, could I live in a city and know where I could go whenever I wished the ablution and inundation of musical waves, that were a bath and a medicine."[8] He spoke of music as the characteristic modern art and awakened to the wonder of it almost as he did to the daguerreotype. Opera he saw as something that could inspire him to achieve freer and fuller expression in his own work. At York Minster in 1848 he heard Handel played on the organ and was convinced he had never heard anything so grand.

Hawthorne supposedly did not write poetry because he was afraid he would betray his bad ear. Emerson did write poetry and, in so doing, supposedly gave away his bad ear. Firkins, scrutinizing Emerson's prose, remarked: "Emerson's ear seems not to have partaken of the repulsion commonly felt by sensitive ears for the close proximity of similar sounds." As proof, he cited such phrases as "they coldly hold," "The efflux of a June noon," and "If the race is good, so is the place." He thought Emerson's prose survived this flaw but thought "its extension to his verse is unlucky." He illustrated at length:

> Emerson's rhymes are often pitiable: one begins by indignation at such couplings as *nature, feature; forms, worms; hurry, busy; swamp, lamp; realm, film; grace, praise; own, down; coats, spots; alive, give.* But before he has done with us, he contrives to extenuate or efface all these transgressions by such further iniquities as: *thoughts, doubts; god, cloud; hour, slower; power, restore; arms, psalms; likeness, sickness; science, clairvoyance; doeth, knoweth; pronounce, persuasion; Italian, Castilian; generous, rose; draw, proprietor.*

Emerson was as faulty in cadence as in rhymes: "He can write lines that pierce the ear like gimlets." Firkins pointed to the acuminate *t*'s in such a line as "To a beauty that not fades," to confirm his argument.[9]

Yet Emerson's ear cannot have been wholly lacking. Hyatt Waggoner remarked: "In his early journals and even in childhood, as well as in such early poems as 'Indian Superstitions,' he demonstrated his ability to write perfectly regular conventional verses. . . . It is hard to believe that this power deserted him altogether as he matured."[10] That his lapses came with calculation is suggested by Merlin's recommendation that the poet liberate himself from "the coil of rhythm and number." This, however, was not an invitation to embrace anarchy. Emerson said that his mind sometimes was visited by tunes, in varying meters, encumbered with no burden either of words or ideas. And Edward says that walking in the woods with his children, he would recite

poetry to them "and occasionally would try upon us lines of poems
that he was composing, 'The Boston Hymn,' or 'The Romany Girl,'
'crooning' them to bring out their best melody."[11]

Even Firkins credited Emerson with moments of exquisite music:
"Emerson can invest with witchery a line of which the beats are regular as clock-ticks, — 'But if with gold she binds her hair,' or he can
write lines in which only a delicate ear can extricate the fine kernel of
melody from its husk of encasing roughness. 'The rain comes when the
wind calls.' "[12]

Concerning the role of music in poetry, Emerson theorized: "Poetry
aids itself both with music and with eloquence, neither of which is
essential to it." This statement he immediately qualified: "Say rather
that music is proper to it, but that within the high organic music proper
to it are inferior harmonies & melodies, which it avails itself of at
pleasure."[13] Emerson sometimes spurned these "inferior harmonies
and melodies," but "the high organic music" he respected as he respected the integrity of the soul.

Emerson's acute ear for the music of other bards is conceded. Firkins verifies it with an interesting test. He asks, "Could he delight in
pure music, in pure expression, without a pious afterthought?" And
answers:

> The affirmative evidence seems incontestable. He quoted as an
> example of exquisite verse Beaumont and Fletcher's line on
> melancholy, 'Hence all ye vain delights,' a poem surely innocent
> of sanctity. He cites, in illustration of Shakespeare's poetic
> felicity, the equally undidactic lines: — 'What may this mean, /
> That thou, dead corse, again in complete steel / Revisit'st thus the
> glimpses of the moon?'

Firkins acknowledged the pleasure Emerson took in such phrases as
Collins's "Bubbling runnels joined the sound," and Tennyson's
"stammering thunder."[14] Nor should it be forgotten that, in "Poetry
and Imagination," Emerson wrote, "Every good poem that I know, I
recall by its rhythm also."[15]

George Brandes hailed Emerson as a "keen observer" for calling
attention to the two rhythms in *Henry VIII* — one Shakespearean, the
other distinctly not. Emerson conjectured that Shakespeare had re-
written an earlier play, portions of which he kept:

> The first play was written by a superior, thoughtful man with a
> vicious ear. I can mark his lines, and know well their cadence.
> See Wolsey's soliloquy, and the following scene with Cromwell,
> where instead of the metre of Shakespeare, whose secret is that the

thought constructs the tune, so that reading for the sense will best bring out the rhythm, — here the lines are constructed on a given tune and the verse has even a trace of pulpit eloquence.[16]

This is remarkable criticism for a man with no musical ear.

Poets should be lawgivers, that is, the boldest lyric
inspiration should not chide and insult, but should
announce and lead the civil code and the day's work.

66. The Burns Centennial

*I*N December 1858 Emerson was invited by the president of the
Boston Burns Club, John S. Tyler, to attend a dinner at the Parker
House on 25 January to mark the centenary of the birth of Robert
Burns. Although it meant extricating himself from a speaking engagement, he accepted the invitation. He did this perhaps because all literary Boston was turning out to honor Burns and he did not want to
seem indifferent or hostile by staying away. Certainly the occasion
itself was not sufficient to induce him to rearrange his schedule in a
busy season. He was not a great Burns booster. In fact, he once thought
that Burns's fame was "too great for the facts."[1] Eventually, he did
concede that Burns had the "social strength" and magnetism that accompanies greatness and placed him cheek by jowl with Franklin, Homer, Shakespeare, Scott, Voltaire, Rabelais, Montaigne, and Hafiz. Yet,
even then, he found it difficult to count Burns a personal favorite.[2]

That Emerson had things to say at the Burns dinner that would
captivate his audience seemed improbable. Holmes was but one of many
who was caught unawares: "I felt . . . wonder at Mr. Emerson's . . .
marvellous discourse on Burns, whose qualities I should have thought
to be rather 'out of his line' — though very much in mine." Curiously,
Emerson's astonishment paralleled that of Holmes: "I was greatly
surprised at the applause that greeted my speech at the Burns dinner
in Boston the other day. Not having had a very good opinion of this
Scottish songster, I renewed my acquaintance with him by a fresh
reading, and to a better purpose. But I had only a few moments to
prepare myself for speaking."[3] "A few moments," indeed! For more

than a month Emerson had known that he would be asked to pay verbal tribute to Burns at his centenary dinner. Possibly he even knew well in advance that Whittier, Holmes, and Lowell were writing poems to read to the gathering. Considering that Emerson had had to reacquaint himself with Burns before preparing his remarks, he may have had less time than he liked to get the job done, but we need not think of him as scratching out his remarks on a notepad in a Parker House alcove, minutes before the assembled group sat down to eat. Whether by accident or design, however, the manner of his delivery was such that many of those present believed they were witnessing that rarest of events, Ralph Waldo Emerson delivering a brilliant extempore address.

One person who jumped to that conclusion was Judge Hoar, who remembered the Burns address as surpassing in merit the best efforts ''of the chief orators of our time.'' Emerson's audience, Hoar noted, had been an unpromising ''queer mixture'' of scholars, politicians, businessmen, doctors, lawyers, clerics, and poets, the inner core of which was the members of the Burns Club, earnest, dour Scots ''jealous of the fame of their countryman, and doubtful of the capacity to appreciate him in men of other blood.'' Yet, from his first words, Emerson illustrated his own definition of eloquence, ''a taking sovereign possession of the audience.'' Not only was the address so radiant and engrossing ''the company could hardly tolerate any other speaker,'' though several of note were still to follow, Hoar adjudged it, as a tribute to Burns, ''perhaps the best which the occasion produced on either side of the ocean.''[4]

As a wordsmith Lowell was better equipped to assess Emerson's discourse than was Hoar, yet his recreation of the event, even as it eclipses rhetorically the judge's account, substantiates its content:

Every word seemed to have just dropped down to him from the clouds. He looked far away over the heads of his hearers, with a vague kind of expectation, as into some private heaven of invention, and the winged period came at last obedient to his spell. 'My dainty Ariel!' he seemed murmuring to himself as he cast down his eyes as if in deprecation of the frenzy of approval and caught another sentence from the Sibylline leaves that lay before him, ambushed behind a dish of fruit and seen only by nearest neighbors. Every sentence brought down the house, as I never saw one brought down before, — and it is not so easy to hit Scotsmen with a sentiment that has no hint of native brogue in it. I watched, for it was an interesting study, how the quick sympathy ran flashing from face to face down the long tables, like an electric spark thrilling as it went, and then exploded in a thunder of plaudits. . . . I, too, found myself caught up in the common enthusiasm.[5]

That there was a prepared text is attested to by Edward Emerson.[6] While the Burns address is one of Emerson's briefest speeches, the art that went into it is at once apparent. Emerson's method of delivering closely packed ideas to his audience, each almost standing on its own, was ideally suited to an occasion that found him, as one of many speakers, anxious to enlighten his listeners without detaining them. He set the mood by inviting them to believe that he spoke without preparation, relying on the inspiration of his subject. In itself that was a stroke of genius. The Burns he spoke of was a man of spontaneous insight, sprung from Nature, real and unerring. To put him under labored, bookish analysis would seem to violate the wondrous texture of his art and affirmations.

Emerson disarmed the members of the Burns Club by asserting at the outset (and therefore appealing to their sense of courtesy to dispute him) that he was "the worst Scotsman of all."[7] He had, in fact, served an ample apprenticeship in acquainting himself with the Scottish character through a host of Scottish friends, including Carlyle, Ireland, Sterling, and, we might add, Thoreau, whose mother was a Dunbar and grandmother, a Burns. Midway in his remarks, he recalled his bond with Carlyle, identifying him as the only man of their day who, for "his grand plain sense" formed a link in the chain of the greatest masters — Rabelais, Shakespeare, Cervantes, Butler, and Burns. His early infatuation with Scott also must have made a contribution to the responsiveness he had to things Scottish. He identified Burns first as "the poet of the middle class," as the man around whose standards the middle class had formed ranks and marched forward as champions not of political upheaval but of sweeping changes in education and the social order. As "documents in the history of freedom . . . the songs of Burns" stood alongside "The Confession of Augsburg, the Declaration of Independence, the French Rights of Man, and the Marseillaise." He dramatically asserted, in phrases that certainly must have elicited the response Hoar and Lowell described:

> He has made the Lowland Scotch a Doric dialect of fame. It is
> the only example in history of a language made classic by the
> genius of a single man. . . . He had that secret of genius to draw
> from the bottom of society the strength of its speech, and astonish
> the ears of the polite with these artless words, better than art,
> and filtered of all offense through his beauty.

With this exposition Emerson admitted Burns into a rare and exalted company.

These compliments paid, Emerson moved swiftly to his even more admiring conclusion. "The memory of Burns," he exclaimed, "— I am afraid heaven and earth have taken too good care of it to leave us anything to say." Men need not go to books to learn Burns's songs. They pass from mouth to mouth. "They are the property and solace of mankind."

Here was a rhapsodic tribute, a joyous canonization of Burns. Not once did Emerson's foot fall on the mean byways of criticism as he swept Burns up into the company of the immortals. The poet had come to the end of his first century. To have picked one's way among his verses, gauging and assessing, would have been petty. And Emerson was never petty.

Emerson's tribute was reprinted in Britain and on the Continent. Carlyle clipped it from his journals even before a copy sent by Emerson reached him. He was charmed by it. Fifteen years later students at the University of Glasgow nearly elected Emerson to the Lord Rectorship — a shift of a hundred and one votes out of twelve hundred cast would have made the post his instead of Disraeli's. "I count that vote as quite the fairest laurel that has ever fallen to me," Emerson wrote when the news reached him.[8] On his own merit he deserved it, and it could well be that it was in recognition not of his tribute to Burns but his kinship to him that so many thought he should have it. The passion Emerson showed when he delivered his tribute suggests that he had at last made that discovery for himself.

67. William Dean Howells
Such Ire in Heavenly Minds

*I*N August 1860 William Dean Howells, twenty-three years old and five feet four, boyish and ebullient, arrived in Boston from Ohio with plans to visit as many literary luminaries as would receive him, his way paved, he was sure, by the poems he had published in the *Atlantic*. He began with Lowell, who took at once to this western wayfarer, never foreseeing that Howells would one day repay his kindness by procuring for him a favored post in the diplomatic service, that of minister to Great Britain.

Lowell did not skimp. He had Howells to dinner at the Parker House, taking care to make the occasion memorable by recruiting Holmes and Fields to piece out a literary foursome. And he sent him to Concord to see Hawthorne, just back from his long stay in Europe and again in possession of his own Concord house, The Wayside, only a five-minute walk from Bush. In lightning sallies that sprang through the chinks in his shyness, Hawthorne disclosed an instant affinity for him. A climb up Revolutionary Ridge, the mingled incense of cigars, tea, and shared sympathies back at the house, an invitation to come again, and Howells set off down the road, a glow of acceptance suffusing him, bearing proudly to Emerson Hawthorne's scrawled message of approbation — "I find him worthy."[1]

Although he had caught from Hawthorne's manner hints of the reserve usual in those with a Puritan past, Howells sprang along the road brimming with youthful confidence and élan. Evidently, it had not occurred to him that western manners would not have for Emerson the same charm they had had for Hawthorne, who had little experi-

ence of them. To add to that difference, either because of his gauche-
ness or because his country manners triggered in Emerson the same
response Thoreau triggered when at variance with him, Howells was
destined to glimpse Emerson's acerbic side. A severe cold then besetting Emerson made it easier, unfortunately, for that to happen.

Howells would always believe that he was at fault for the bad turn
his visit took. Between seeing Hawthorne and seeing Emerson, he had
looked in on Thoreau. Thoreau, just then "full up on the topic of John
Brown," had been orphic and remote. This remoteness was physically
demonstrated when Thoreau sat him on one side of the room while he
sat against the opposing wall, confronting him. Until that occasion
Howells had seen Brown as a warm and human figure. Thoreau reconstituted him as the embodiment of a universal idea. The conversation
went to pieces and Howells exited, bedraggled and whipped. In that
condition he had presented himself at Emerson's door.[2]

At fifty-seven Emerson already thought of himself as old. And so
he seemed to Howells when he came to the door to receive him, though
Howells was not certain why he so regarded him, since "His hair . . .
was still entirely dark, and his face had a kind of marble youthfulness." Maybe he based his estimate on what he alluded to as Emerson's "vague serenity," which seemed to derive from a sad, shy look
in his eyes and from a mouth of "incomparable sweetness," both grave
and "subtly . . . arch." It was a face that "expressed the patience
and forebearance of a wise man," in which direction the weathercock
of opinion had turned after long years of pointing the other way. For
many years, Howells said, Emerson had been regarded as "a national
joke, the type of the incomprehensible, the byword of the poor para-
grapher."[3] To abide that status must have hastened the serenity and
deportment of age.

Given a chair in Emerson's study, Howells acknowledged his regard
for his intercessor, Hawthorne, and that led to his first surprise. A
nice neighbor, and a man of exemplary character, Emerson conceded,
"But his last book [*The Marble Faun*] is a mere mush." Howells bore
his anguish in silence. One did not dispute Emerson's judgment at his
own hearthside.

Emerson now made the lack of writers in the West his topic. Perhaps recalling that when he himself first traveled among the English,
Britishers seemed to take perverse satisfaction in the paucity of letters
in America, he was not scornful but solicitous. Yet Howells could find
no reasons to explain why western writers were so few. He was beginning to feel he was making a poor showing with Emerson when re-
prieved by an announcement that the noon meal was ready.

When they were done eating, Emerson took Howells on an inspection tour of his garden, a tactic he sometimes had recourse to when he

wanted to be rid of a visitor. Sometimes he was "sorely tried" by visitors, who descended on Bush in droves. Even when he lingered with a pleasing visitor, he could be remorseful afterward. "What is good to make me happy is not however good to make me write," he concluded. Lidian once counseled him to try, when chance visitors came, "to make humanity lovely to them." On some days he did not seem mindful of that injunction. In October 1848 he told his journal: "I find out in an instant if my companion does not want me; I cannot comprehend how my visitor does not perceive that I do not want him. It is his business to find out that. I, of course, must be civil. It is for him to offer to go. I certainly shall not long resist." When a departing guest once missed the stage, Emerson, setting off in hot pursuit, intercepted it.[4]

After the garden tour, Emerson took Howells into his study again. But Howells was not uncomprehending. "I meant to linger," he said, "only till I could fitly get away." Presently he did depart, hastened on his way by two antic statements from his host, made, it seems, with sarcasm and condescension. Emerson asked him if he knew Channing's poems. Howells said he knew them only through Poe's criticisms. He had no idea that Emerson had sponsored their publication and that Poe's ridicule had ruined Channing's prospects. "Whose criticisms?" Emerson asked, his archness much in evidence. "Poe's," Howells naively persisted. Emerson let the word hang in the air a moment while he steadied his lance. Then, his voice rising and descending, the thrust came, impaling his victim. "Oh! *You mean the jingle-man!*"[5] Emerson had used a variant of this indictment in 1846 when disparaging Byron's poetry — "How many volumes of such jingle must we go through before we can be filled, sustained, taught, renewed?"[6] In 1874, asked his opinion of Swinburne, who likewise qualified for membership in his jingle club, Emerson showed what he was truly capable of when out of sorts. He said Swinburne was "a perfect leper and a mere sodomite." Infuriated, Swinburne denounced him as "a foul-minded and foul-mouthed old driveller."[7] By comparison, Howells had escaped with a light dusting off. He had no way of knowing that. He thought he had been overtaken by an avalanche.

During the closing moments of the visit, Howells felt like a spectral visitor, unable to participate in what was happening. "If I had written the criticisms [Poe's] myself," he wrote forty years later, "I do not think I could have been more abashed." Like a voiceless shadow he watched Emerson fetch from a shelf bound volumes of *The Atlantic Monthly* and stare at the poems Howells had published there "with the effect of being wholly strange to them," conceivably a final rebuke to someone whose taste had been formed by the odious Poe.

Poetry continued to be Emerson's topic as he pursued Howells's retreating footsteps to the door: "One might very well give a pleasant hour to it now and then." This, Howells surmised, was Emerson's way of telling him that his work was inferior. Since he had come into Emerson's presence as someone "meaning to give all time and all eternity to poetry," this summary dismissal devastated him.[8]

Howells, who had taken a room for the night at a local inn, gave himself up to brooding, convinced that, in his confused flight, he had shown Emerson discourtesy. He would go back and apologize. Or he would pen an apology. Or he would ask Hawthorne's counsel. He went as far with this last strategy as to lurk in the vicinity of Wayside, watching a contemplative Hawthorne, seated on a log in the gathering dusk, smoking a cigar. But at last he went away without accosting him. The day following, when he got back to Boston, he sought out Fields and told him what had happened. Fields rocked with laughter. The situation did, after all, have its comic side. Howells came to see that and elected to survive.

Years later, when Mark Twain became convinced that he had insulted Emerson, he sought Howells's advice and Howells told him to send Emerson a note of apology. Twain did so but subsequently learned none had been necessary. Emerson could not recall the occasion Twain was concerned about. Perhaps Howells, in advising Twain, was trying to overtake, vicariously, what he judged to be his own ancient remissness. Perhaps on the occasion of his visit to Emerson he had been gauche, but if anyone was ill-mannered that day it was Emerson himself, maybe to test Howells's mettle, or maybe because he rued a day spoiled.

During that visit Emerson seems to have acquired a set impression of Howells that in subsequent years he saw no cause to alter. Long afterward, as editor of the *Atlantic*, Howells persuaded Emerson to submit a poem for a forthcoming issue. When Emerson was tardy in sending back the galleys, Howells asked if he could hold the poem for the following issue. Emerson's retort was to tell him to "send me back my verses & break up the form." Howells was once again a chastened, red-faced boy. He hastily returned the proofs to the sender, "silently grieving that there could be such ire in heavenly minds."[9] If only Howells could have shown consistently in his dealings with Emerson the tact inherent in that sentence, he would have had no trouble with Emerson at all. Although Emerson claimed to loathe ridicule and sarcasm, he conceded that he did, "like puss have a retractile claw."[10] Howells had a talent for providing occasions that caused him to unsheath it.

68. Civil War Years
A Noble Humanity

I have," Emerson once confided to his journal, "the fatal gift of perception."[1] And so he had, for some things, but the faculty did not extend in all directions. His advocacy of abolition, for example, had built slowly. Incident by incident he was pushed toward espousal of the cause of emancipation. His anti-institutional bias, grounded in his conviction that men are best governed from within, made him certain that sound principles came first. If the Union was not an expression of these, then it forfeited all rights to respect. The expulsion of Samuel Hoar from South Carolina, Webster's acceptance of Clay's Compromise, the attack on Senator Sumner, the trial and execution of John Brown, broadened the gulf that separated Emerson from those who placed the Union above the cause of emancipation. Yet he had no wish to see the matter resolved by a clash of arms. In compensated emancipation he saw a way out of the dilemma. Only in the closing phase of the antebellum struggle did he conclude that those who merited compensation were not the slaveholders but the slaves themselves. Once that idea took hold, he was, of course, whether he realized it or not, committed to a solution embedded in internecine warfare.

At no stage of his emergence as a national figure did Abraham Lincoln seek to hide his commitment to the preservation of the Union. That fact alone had made Emerson wary about his candidacy. When William Seward lost the nomination to Lincoln, Emerson, by his own admission, "heard the result coldly and sadly." Lincoln, in his debates with Douglas, had shown that he deplored slavery as an offense against morality, but he still placed the preservation of the Union above the cause of emancipation. To Emerson it seemed that Lincoln stood where Webster had stood. Brown's execution, which carried Emerson to the very apogee of his antinationalism just as Lincoln was coming into prominence, gave Emerson a further reason for scorning Lincoln's priorities.

On Election Day, 1860, Emerson felt sufficiently the pressure of impending events to put aside his scruples and vote for Lincoln. When Lincoln won, Emerson described his victory as "the pronunciation of the masses of America against slavery." When others proclaimed it a victory for the principle of Union, he scoffed.

On 1 February 1862 Sumner brought Emerson to the White House to meet President Lincoln. The previous day Emerson had urged the cause of emancipation in an address delivered before the Washington Lecture Association at the Smithsonian. Conway believed Lincoln and members of his cabinet were present when Emerson spoke, but the evidence is against it.

After Lincoln took office, Emerson periodically recorded misgivings about him, suspecting him of being a rawboned man of the prairies, wanting in refinement and vacillating in judgment. Yet he tried to show patience with him: "If Mr. Lincoln appear slow and timid in proclaiming emancipation . . . it is to be remembered that he is not free as a poet to state what he thinks ideal or desirable, but must take a considered step, which he can keep. Otherwise his proclamation would be a weak bravado, without value or respect."[2]

Emerson's doubts sprang up anew when Lincoln removed Frémont from his command after that general, on his own initiative, emancipated slaves in the territory he had occupied. But the face-to-face encounter at the White House swept away some of Emerson's preconceptions:

> The President impressed me more favorably than I had hoped.
> A frank, sincere, well-meaning man, with a lawyer's habit of
> mind, good clear statement of his fact, correct enough, not vulgar,
> as described; but with a sort of boyish cheerfulness, or that kind
> of sincerity & jolly good meaning that our class meetings on
> Commencement Day show, in telling our old stories over.

He found this impression strengthened by Lincoln's spontaneity and openness: "When he has made his remark, he looks up at you with great satisfaction, & shows all his white teeth, & laughs."[3]

In Emerson's presence Lincoln reviewed with Sumner the circumstances that led to a sentence to death by hanging for a slavetrader named Gordon. With the instincts of a good lawyer Lincoln announced his intention of satisfying himself further about the facts. "All this,"

Emerson remarked with gratification, "showed a fidelity and conscientiousness very honorable to him."[4] Emerson does not suggest that he discussed emancipation with Lincoln but his friends Senator Sumner and John Murray Forbes had Lincoln's ear and, as staunch advocates of emancipation, certainly could have satisfied any questions about Emerson's views that Lincoln might have had.[5] On Sunday, 2 February, Emerson attended church with Seward, now secretary of state, and afterward, at Seward's invitation, accompanied him to the White House for his daily conferral with Lincoln. Lincoln, it turned out, had skipped church to read papers of state. Since Emerson thought the service he had attended was marred by "hopeless blind antiquity of life & thought," he could not fault the President's choice. The two leaders carried out their discussion of urgent matters of state in Emerson's presence, a sure mark of the respect they had for him.

Although the Emancipation Proclamation was promulgated on 22 September 1862 and would take effect on 1 January 1863, Emerson reported some misgivings about it in his journal in October. In Boston the foes of abolition were directing their wrath against Sumner, rather than Lincoln, because, Emerson said, "they do not think him really antislavery." What is more, rumor had it that Lincoln "thinks Emancipation almost morally wrong, & resorts to it only as a desperate measure." Yet he could not gainsay the favorable impression Lincoln had made on him: "We must accept the results of universal suffrage, & not try to make it appear that we can elect fine gentlemen. We shall have coarse men, with a fair chance of worth & manly ability, but not polite men, not men to please the English or French." Since Emerson equated coarseness with naturalness and forthrightness, no fault-finding was implied. There was no way, he concluded, to get Lincoln to "walk dignifiedly through the traditional part of the President of America." He "will pop out his head at each railroad station & make a little speech. . . . He will write letters to . . . any . . . saucy party committee that writes to him, & cheapen himself." But, in what was essential, Lincoln measured up: "Let the clown appear, & hug ourselves that we are well off, if we have got good nature, honest meaning, & fidelity to public interest, with bad manners, instead of an elegant roue & malignant self seeker."[6] Gradually, Emerson was coming to believe that Lincoln was guided by a higher wisdom than he had supposed. Had he acted sooner than he did he would have acted too soon. He had needed victories to make his Proclamation creditable. McClellan's check given Lee at Antietam had provided such a context. In support of Lincoln's conduct, Emerson now quoted Napoleon: "If I had attempted in 1806 what I performed in 1807, I had been lost."

When the Proclamation was issued, Emerson spoke out. Lincoln was "an instrument" of "the Divine Providence"; he "had the courage to seize the moment." It behooved us to "forget all that we thought shortcomings, every mistake, every delay." He had replaced government in the good graces of mankind. The democratic system of government had vindicated itself, and Lincoln had shown himself in harmony with the universal mind.[7]

The country was given one hundred days to get ready for the event. On New Year's Day, 1863, emancipation, sought for so long by so many, would at last be a reality. In no city in the land had men struggled as they had in Boston to make this day come to pass. Thus, in Boston, plans went forward at once to mark the event with suitable festivities. Given impetus by John Sullivan Dwight, the celebration committee decided to stage a Jubilee Concert on New Year's Day afternoon at Boston's Music Hall.[8] Boston's newest and largest hall, first opened in November 1852, the Music Hall, at the corner of Winter Street and Bumstead Place, seated 2,700 and, as in the present instance, could accommodate overflow audiences of 3,000 and more. What was wanted was a program commensurate with the significance of the occasion. Maestro Carl Zerrahn would conduct. The program would begin with Beethoven's *Egmont* Overture. The selections that followed, which included Oliver Wendell Holmes's "Army Hymn" and Handel's "Hallelujah Chorus," would sustain the mood. With a gusto meant to keep high the spirits of those attending, Rossini's Overture to *William Tell* would end the concert.[9] Yet for Dwight this admirable occasion called for something more — a unique expression of the thoughts that filled the hearts of those who, having made abolition their cause, now saw the dream become an actuality. He appealed to Emerson. Would he write a poem and read it to the audience at the Music Hall?

Dwight was asking a great deal. Emerson did not like to write what was not from himself. He had made emancipation his cause, but that did not mean that he could, on demand, write about it in terms in keeping with his standards. Nonetheless, the challenge appealed to him. What Faneuil Hall had been to the cause of American independence, the Music Hall had been to the cause of emancipation. Theodore Parker had preached there. One Sunday a month Wendell Phillips had gone there to champion the cause of abolition. Two years earlier, in January 1861, Emerson himself had spoken to Parker's congregation there on free speech and slavery.

The days that followed brought frustration and discouragement. On the night of 18 December Emerson "made some rude experiments at verses," but was dissatisfied with the results. The next day he wrote Dwight and told him so.[10] Through the ensuing days matters showed no improvement. Part of the difficulty was that, in that season, he was heavily committed to other lectures. Suddenly, with nothing he could call a poem on hand, he realized he had only four days in which to produce one. And even that narrow timespan was soon reduced with the joyous homecoming, on New Year's Eve, of Edward, a freshman at Harvard, whose delicate health was giving his father anxious moments.

To an invitation asking the Emersons to a party on New Year's night at the home of the George L. Stearnses in Medford, Emerson replied: "I am promised, if I can, to bring some verses to the Musical Festival on Thursday & the verses are not written. . . . Forgive me, & pity me, that I cannot come."[11]

On 30 December Emerson sent Dwight a hurried note: "At this hour you must certainly print the programme without my name, as I have had little or no good fortune." He was unable to sleep, he said. Still, he did not wholly despair. If he slept well that night, perhaps he could "at the eleventh hour, pray to be admitted."[12]

A frenzy of activity must have followed. Emerson got beyond the five stanzas entitled "The Pilgrims," which he had written on the eighteenth, and wrote three successive drafts. The third draft contained twenty-nine stanzas, including the original five. These, together with one other stanza from the first redraft, were dropped when Emerson settled on the poem's final version.

Dwight was elated when Emerson arrived at the Music Hall, poem in hand. The atmosphere there was one of high expectation. At the sight of William Lloyd Garrison making his way into the hall, a spontaneous ovation rose from the assembled throng. Maestro Zerrahn tapped to let the audience know the orchestra was ready to play. At that point, Josiah Quincy, Emerson's classmate of Harvard days, stepped forward and announced that Emerson was present and would deliver a new prologue written for the occasion. The audience was jubilant. Emerson himself was ebullient. His nervous fingers fumbled the manuscript and some of the pages flew from his hand and fluttered out into the crowd. This was normal for him, however.[13] He knew he had nothing to fear from this audience, and he read his poem with a confidence that gave a thrill of emphasis to his words, especially to the celebrated eighteenth stanza:

> *Pay ransom to the owner*
> *And fill the bag to the brim.*
> *Who is the owner? The slave is owner*
> *And ever was. Pay him.*[14]

Conway said, "The vast audience listened with hearts aflame." With the last stanza the crowd, among which mingled former slaves, rose to its feet, shouting and singing.[15] Emerson's words had caught what others felt in their hearts but were unable to express.

Emerson's working title for the poem had been "The Pilgrims."

But, when writing to Dwight, he had referred to it as "a sort of Boston Hymn." And that was the title he gave it when he read it at the Music Hall, reminding those who heard it that the cause of abolition owed as much to Boston as the cause of independence owed to Concord. Later commentators have said that Emerson's audience looked upon the "Boston Hymn" as a companion piece to Julia Ward Howe's "Battle Hymn of the Republic." Whether or not they did so, that night Emerson went, after all, to Medford, to the Stearnses' New Year's party, and read his poem again, with Wendell Phillips, Bronson Alcott and Louisa, and Julia Ward Howe herself constituting (along with the Stearnses) his audience. When he concluded, Phillips unveiled a bust of John Brown and Mrs. Howe read her "Battle Hymn." Thus, quite literally, the two hymns were coupled from the outset.

The ardor of the occasion, of course, explains in part the popularity of the "Boston Hymn," which is not one of Emerson's best poems. It is memorable, however, not only for the occasion on which it was first delivered, but for the form it took. The lines of the poem are assigned to God Himself. By implication, Lincoln is his chosen instrument. With God recruited to their ranks, how could Northerners feel other than confident of victory?

When Emerson's "Boston Hymn" was first printed, it was a stanza short. Copying it, Emerson had inadvertently omitted the seventeenth stanza. Perhaps his eye had leaped ahead to the next stanza, to those words which, we are told, deeply moved the men who made up Thomas Wentworth Higginson's black regiment, and provided the chaplain of that regiment a text for a sermon.[16] What these men felt, many felt. Emerson had served his country by those means he best commanded.

Henceforth Emerson's creed of individualism would expand to accommodate a judicious recourse to institutions to help mankind on its upward surge. Such a change of direction could not have been accomplished without some awareness that he had been mistaken in some of his judgments. Never having lashed himself to the mast of his convictions, he was free to repudiate a position he no longer found tenable, yet he could not have done so without some chagrin. His final routing would come with Lincoln's assassination. Then was given him the chance to show true magnanimity.

Patriot's Day, 19 April, was Concord's great festive day. Yet in 1865, that day was a day of lamentation which found Emerson summoned to deliver a eulogy for the newly martyred President. Others were affected by Lincoln's instant apotheosis but how many of them had been seeking, as Emerson had, the complete universal man — the representative man fit to stand in the company of Michelangelo, Shakespeare, Napoleon, and Goethe? Emerson told his listeners: "Old as history is, and manifold as are its tragedies, I doubt if any death has caused so much pain to mankind as this has caused.'' In that modern hour the hopes and fears of mankind were centered on America and her institutions. Lincoln had been ''a man of the people . . . a quite native, aboriginal man . . . no aping of foreigners, no frivolous accomplishments.'' At first encounter he offered no luminous qualities. Yet he proved, ''a man without vices. . . . He had a vast good-nature which made him tolerant and accessible to all. . . . This good nature became a noble humanity . . . with what increasing tenderness he dealt when a whole race was thrown on his compassion.'' Thus was Lincoln purged of that possible flaw that had earlier troubled Emerson, his seeming vacillation over the issue of emancipation. Ironically, Lincoln's commitment to the Union, once accounted a liability, now could be seen as evidence that he stood for the best instincts of his people — an embodiment of Unity. Evidence of recourse to the moral sense and his receptivity to this Divine source of wisdom is found in the insights he imparted to us: ''He is the author of a multitude of good sayings . . . the wisdom of the hour. . . . What pregnant definitions! what unerring common sense! what foresight!'' (Here Emerson may have been contrasting him, in his mind, with Webster, who had, he said, in all his discourses never struck off a memorable phrase.) Lincoln had ''stood a heroic figure in the center of a heroic epoch.'' In him Emerson had found his long-sought-for poet-hero, a ''heroic deliverer . . . a completed benefactor,'' who, accorded the crown of martyrdom, serves ''his country even more by his death than by his life.''[17]

Emerson had long awaited the theophanic who would expend his life to impart new life to others. At times he thought he might be called upon to sacrifice himself, but, with a fateful hesitancy, he ever drew back from the commitment, not perceiving a fitting occasion. When Lincoln appeared, Emerson, like Sir Parsifal, who beheld the Holy Grail but was unmindful of what he saw until the vision was withdrawn, had been slow to understand his worth. ''In a period of less facility of printing,'' Emerson supposed, ''he would have become mythologized in a very few years.'' Notwithstanding this obstacle, the mythologizing process went forward, and, as it did, Emerson came to see that his expectations for the age had been fulfilled in another and that the part he had had in shaping the events of the time was done. From that moment his own light in the firmament began to dim.

69. Charles Woodbury
A Series of Intoxications

*O*n 7 November 1865 Emerson arrived at Williams College to lecture on social aims, the first of six lectures in his "American Life" series. In mid-October he had lectured at neighboring Amherst College and had at once been approached by students representing the Literary Societies at Williams, asking if he would give them a lecture, too. His unannounced arrival now caught them unawares. They hurriedly secured the use of the Methodist meeting house. Then they blanketed the campus with placards announcing the event, posting them even in the campus chapel. They ran, too, from door to door spreading the word and set clanging the college and chapel bells. When it was time for Emerson to speak, a capacity audience awaited him. He seems never to have suspected that it was recruited on short notice by haphazard methods.

Not only did Emerson's hosts enjoy "Social Aims," they persuaded him to stay a week and to give the other five lectures in the series. Emerson, with four lectures delivered and two still to go, wrote to Ellen on the eleventh, expressing pleasure with his reception.

We know more about Emerson's informal get-togethers with the students at Williams than we know about the social side of his visits to other colleges. One of the students who invited him, Charles J. Woodbury, who was then twenty-one, undertook to play Boswell to the visiting celebrity. Initially, at least, Emerson was aware of what Woodbury was doing and raised no objections. It was not as though Woodbury was pirating material for which Emerson had ambitious plans.

Presently Woodbury learned to write down his observations after he had been with Emerson. "I was delighted," said Woodbury, "to discover that his language came back to me without loss or change. It seemed as if my pen was a reed, through which breathed upon the paper his monologue, with the physical impression of his accent, dress, gait, and manner."[1]

A quarter of a century later, working from these notes and from notes made after several visits to Bush between 1865 and 1870, Woodbury prepared a small, unauthorized volume, *Talks with Ralph Waldo Emerson,* which he published in 1890. Edward Emerson received a letter that intimated that Woodbury "was a clever fellow who learned the trick and wrote what would have been probable," but Edward described it as "a remarkable and charming little book."[2] The description is not undeserved. Woodbury had, in fact, quoted from Emerson's published works and repeated information gathered from other sources, but his feeling for Emerson was sound.

Woodbury was struck first by Emerson's approachability. While his professors put distance between themselves and their students:

> Almost before we were alone he had made me forget in whose
> presence I stood. He was merely an old, quiet, modest gentleman,
> pressing me to a seat near him, and all at once talking about
> college matters, the new gymnasium, the Quarterly; and from
> these about books and reading and writing; and all as if he
> continually expected as much as he gave.[3]

This was a new experience for Woodbury. It puzzled him and he concluded it was "a trait of first meeting, and was prepared for it to disappear." The next day, however, he walked with Emerson to Mount Greylock and the Berkshire hills and found his "heartiness and comradry" undiminished. Nor did Emerson discard this mode of behavior later: "Whether I saw him alone or in the presence of others, there was the ever ready welcome shining in his eyes, the same manifest gentleness and persistent preference of others."[4]

"I hope you like walks alone and in bypaths," Emerson remarked to Woodbury, at one point. "You find your best muse there."[5] On the night of 14 November Emerson supplied a corollary to this observation that might have dismayed Woodbury: "These mountains give an inestimable worth to Williamstown and Massachusetts. But, for the mountains, I don't quite like the proximity of a college and its noisy students. To enjoy the hills as poet, I prefer simple farmers as neighbors."[6] That was the poet speaking, not the friend and counselor of youth. By turns Emerson relished each role.

Emerson took other walks with Woodbury and his friends — to Bryant's Glen and to the Natural Bridge, near North Adams.[7] On this latter excursion Woodbury perceived that Emerson "could not take even a walk superficially." He remarked "how indefatigably" Emerson "examined the quality and strata of the rock to determine its comparative age."[8] He saw further that while Emerson took a great interest in Nature, he loathed such deceptions as wood painted to resemble iron fence rails or stone.

One night two students, Stanbrough and Hutton, brought Emerson to the college's observatory. Through a powerful telescope he saw double stars and nebulae and other wonders in the night sky hardly known to him if known at all. "I have rarely been so much gratified," he wrote. "Of all tools, an observatory is the most sublime."[9]

From Emerson Woodbury got many exemplary insights concerning writing and literature, but this information, he realized, was not communicated by Emerson in the ordinary way. "Emerson," he said, "was not what one would term 'talkative.' . . . Seldom one meets a man more held in duress by his own thought. When he was surprised into utterance it was mostly a monologue of oral reflections which seemed to be addressed to a widely read and thoughtful audience, and which always exacted much of the listener." In this context, Emerson's definition of conversation as "a series of intoxications" seems apt.[10]

Emerson's manner intrigued Woodbury. He opined that Emerson's "social bearing was distinguished by an old-school politeness, with just enough polish to divert the suspicion that his retirement had made him rustic; and his slight, half-foreign etiquette was so uplifted by the presence of the moral sense, that his manners were celestial."[11] Woodbury took this to be evidence of the Holy Spirit working through him. Emerson would have qualified that explanation.

If Woodbury thought Emerson spoke always "in the low tone of one accustomed to being listened to," he also credited him with being "an intent listener." If appreciation was deserved, it was forthcoming, yet "a certain resistance" was evident, too. Woodbury says: "Even when his companionship was most gentle and encouraging, it was searching and pungent like the odor and flavor of certain flowers and herbs."[12]

In personal contact, Woodbury believed, Emerson's voice dominated all else. There was an upward pitch to it, yet the anticipated "emphasis of the final pause" never came. To this unusual delivery Woodbury assigned an ethical meaning: "On all subjects we discourse inadequately, and can never come to a period."[13] Emerson spoke "with the accent of a man who insists on this present statement, but who believes that we cannot here come to the whole truth of the thing, and shall never quite find the end of it."[14]

Woodbury responded to some of Emerson's ways with adolescent enthusiasm and awe. Emerson's meticulousness and punctuality surprised and impressed him, so much so that he mended his own ways.

Emerson's talent for instructing through example is further argued:

> He was a most salutary companion. His very nearness was an
> abstention. To him, there was but one foundation of genuine
> courtesy as of genuine character, and that was the moral sense, so
> that though he never preached against bad physical habits and
> morals, his presence did not permit them.[15]

Emerson's domestic side was not lost on Woodbury, either. He spoke
of "the home-like feeling he diffused." And he commented: "He had
the passion for home which is characteristic of all manly natures, and
told me that he believed in large families."[16]

Woodbury was particularly impressed with Emerson's ability to establish rapport with youth: "I asked him once about his boyhood, but
the brief answer gave small glimpse of boyish spirits and joy. . . .
And so not least among the marvels he awakened, was the pleasant
query how one who never was a boy himself could cherish so subtle a
sympathy with a boy's weakness and work and gladness and troubles."[17] Occasionally, Emerson expressed himself to Woodbury in a
disarming, boyish way that shrank the gulf separating youth from age.
Thus, upon inspecting Woodbury's bookshelves, he commented wryly:
"Some mathematical works here, too. What hours of melancholy mine
cost! It was long before I learned that there is something wrong with
a man's brain who loves them."[18] His further self-deprecation of his
epistolary skills is appealing: "It is a fortune to write good letters. I
do not have it. I do not love letter-writing, and do not write letters
readily."[19]

Of all the things Emerson ever said to Woodbury, Woodbury seized
on nothing more eagerly than Emerson's advice on what an aspiring
writer must do to succeed. "Write! Write! There is no way to learn
except by writing." This manifesto he supplemented with practical
suggestions. These sometimes served as a clue to his own goals as a
writer. He said: "The most interesting writing is that which does not
quite satisfy the reader." Later, he amplified: "Do not put hinges on
your work to make it cohere."[20] His passion for the exact word received endorsement in the advice given: "Expression is the main fight.
Search unweariedly for that which is exact. . . . Avoid adjectives. . . .
The adjective introduces sounds, gives an unexpected turn, and so often
mars with an unintentional false note."[21]

In a chapter entitled "Counsel," Woodbury brought together most
of the advice Emerson gave him as an aspiring writer. This, the most
concentrated chapter in the book, needs only Emerson's words to carry
it. Obviously, when he gathered materials for his notebook on Emerson, Woodbury paid closest heed to those things which would best serve

him as a writer. It is ironic, therefore, that he is remembered not for his use of them but only for his record of them.

Despite his respect for the man and the writer, Woodbury was fully awake to Emerson's limitations as a critic. He said: "I do not think of Mr. Emerson as primarily a critic. His was not generally the posture indicated by the word. He was familiar with the laws that determine excellence of form, but sincerity and the satisfaction of the moral sense constituted his criterion."[22] Conscientiously, and without sympathy, he recorded Emerson's disappointing estimates of Shelley, Blake, Dickens, Goethe, Poe, Hugo, Cervantes, and Hawthorne. Concerning Whitman, he looked in both directions simultaneously: "*Leaves of Grass* . . . is a book you must certainly read. It is wonderful. I had great hopes of Whitman until he became Bohemian."[23]

While Emerson's reluctance to engage in polemics was well known, few realized that tenacity rather than diffidence accounted for his reluctance to dispute his views. Woodbury recognized that fact and addressed it in clear terms:

> Once I heard him defend assailed statements; and that occasion afforded a remarkable instance of the tenacity with which he held his views, and the cogency with which he could advocate them. . . . His quiet rejoinders concealed the dark fires of volcanic regions which catch where they are not seen. It was from his example a brief and gentle discussion . . . and not abandoned until all saw that there was positively no hope of eliminating from such pertinacity any position once assumed. But the charm consisted in the quiet reappearance of the arraigned propositions; they came clad always in new language, with illustrations that gave them a new force, but the same indestructible identity.[24]

Woodbury made the most of his brief hours with Emerson. Had he spent as much time with him as Alcott, Sanborn, Channing, or Thoreau did, we would know more about him than we do now, for none of them had the Boswellian impulse he had, or kept themselves so successfully in the background when they wrote about him.

When Woodbury visited Emerson at Bush, Emerson invited him to examine one of the notebooks that contained a wide selection of reflections and comments on "anything and everything" that interested him. Woodbury relates that as he perused it, "In a moment it flashed upon me that I was in the presence of one of the manuscript sources of the addresses, essays, treatises, yea, the books themselves."[25] Acting on this insight he sought to follow an indicated theme through the ensuing pages but soon found that he was attempting the equivalent of trying to follow an uncharted comet through the heavens. Perhaps then the fact was brought home to him that it took more than resolution, purpose, discipline, and perseverance to be an Emerson. Genius could not be taught.

70. Faltering Powers
A Chaos Full of Shooting-Stars

*T*HIRTY years had passed since Emerson had given his first Phi Beta Kappa address at Harvard. Now he had come again to speak, on 18 July 1867, his topic "Progress of Culture." In welcoming back Emerson with an honorary degree the previous year, after his long exclusion, and, more recently, electing him to its Board of Overseers, Harvard adumbrated the possibility of such progress.

Emerson would give eighty lectures in 1867 and travel to fourteen states to give them. This schedule — the most ambitious he had ever pursued in a single year — proved beyond his strength. Symptoms of aging and decay appeared that, within a few years, halted his effective labors. Indeed, at Harvard, on that day of days, matters went strikingly amiss. While ineptitude was nothing new to Emerson, there was more to his poor showing than mere clumsiness or exhaustion could account for. "It began nowhere and ended everywhere, and yet . . . it left you feeling that something beautiful had passed that way," was Lowell's loyal estimate.[1] Annie Fields was loyal, too, but from her we learn more:

> He seemed to have an especial feeling of unreadiness on that day, and, to increase the trouble, his papers slipped away in confusion from under his hand as he tried to rest them on a poorly arranged desk or table. Mr. Hale put a cushion beneath them finally, after Emerson began to read, which prevented them from falling again, but the whole matter was evidently out of joint in the reader's eyes. He could not be content with it, and closed

without warming to the occasion. . . . After the reading he openly expressed his own discontent, and walked away dissatisfied.[2]

Emerson, speaking at Harvard after so long an absence, was bound to be scrutinized closely and every untoward incident magnified, but his failure had been real enough and the fault was not in his material, which was up to his customary standards. After his death, Ellen told Annie Fields what really happened: "The trouble that day was that for the first time his eyes refused to serve him; he could not see, and therefore could hardly get along."[3]

Following this crisis, Emerson reduced his pace. In 1868 he gave, at most, thirty addresses. Only eight of these were out of state, none farther than New York. In that year Lowell heard his lecture "Nature and Art," given in Boston on 12 October. This was the first of six lectures he delivered over the next five weeks. Ticknor & Fields had made the arrangements and for these lectures he was paid $1,655.75, the largest sum he ever got for a lecture series. Ironically, just as he was able to command large fees, his powers deserted him. Lowell reported on this address and, once more, his tone was firmly tolerant:

We do not go to hear what Emerson says so much as to hear Emerson. Not that we perceive any falling-off in anything that ever was essential to the charm of Mr. Emerson's peculiar style of thought or phrase. The first lecture, to be sure, was more disjointed even than common. It was as if, after vainly trying to get his paragraphs into sequence and order, he had at last tried the desperate expedient of *shuffling* them. It was chaos come again, but it was a chaos full of shooting-stars, a jumble of creative forces.[4]

Emerson's pace quickened in 1869. He gave forty-five lectures, but, apart from a sally into upstate New York in a two-week period in winter, all of these were given in Massachusetts or Rhode Island. His western tours were all but at an end. Even the Eastern Seaboard offered a challenge he no longer cared to face. When in November of that year, the Civil War hero General Ambrose E. Burnside asked him to give a lecture in Washington, D.C., for a G.A.R. welfare benefit, he declined, explaining forthrightly that he could only go where his "failing eyes, and other infirmities could be allowed for, and in some way supplemented."[5]

With characteristic kindness, three years later, when Emerson decided that he could accommodate Washington while fulfilling lecture commitments in Maryland, New Jersey, and New York, he did oblige the G.A.R. by lecturing, on 16 January 1872, in Washington, for their welfare fund.[6] His topic was "Greatness." While in Washington, prior to addressing the G.A.R. gathering, "compelled by an artifice," he spoke at Howard University.[7] Impromptu lectures did not suit Emerson and, while he scored a great success with the black students who made up Howard's enrollment, he himself rated the speech as "very poor; merely talking against time." His memory already was beginning to go and, as he did the following April when lecturing at Boston's Mechanics' Hall, he was apt to read the same page twice to his audience without realizing it. When Ellen suggested precautions to avoid such slip-ups, he showed himself curiously resigned to what was happening: "Things that go wrong about these lectures don't disturb me," he told her, "because I know that everyone knows that I am worn out and passed by, and that it is only my old friends come for friendship's sake to have one last season with me."[8]

That Emerson's final sweep through the Middle Atlantic states in 1872 made heavy demands on him is evident from a letter to Ellen sent ten days into the tour. He would lecture in New Brunswick on Monday night, 15 January, then speed on to Washington, give his address to the G.A.R. on Tuesday night, and afterward set out for home the same night. He had not, he said, "yet ciphered the sum to compute the hour of creeping into Bush."[9] The supposition that Emerson was yearning to escape to the haven of home should be resisted, however, because his haste was dictated by a further commitment. On the night of the seventeenth James T. Fields was lecturing at the Concord Lyceum and the Emersons had invited him and Annie to be their overnight guests. As the time drew near, Emerson wrote Lidian to say he doubted he could be home sooner than the eighteenth. Yet it distressed him to disappoint his guests.[10]

The New Brunswick talk, which Emerson had agreed to give for a YMCA benefit for $100 (in Boston he now got at least $275 per lecture), through no fault of his own had had to be rescheduled. His subject was "Attractive Homes." Much of the lecture was culled from old scripts, their disparate origins plainly evident. In fact, the assessment offered next morning in the *New Brunswick Daily Times* suggests that Emerson, inured to being told people did not understand him, had this time chosen to wander where he listeth without heed to unity or coherency.

The manner of Emerson's delivery provoked greater annoyance than the matter. A *Daily Times* editorial supplied a checklist of his failings:

> He stands still while speaking, only twirling his glasses now and then. His words are either not all written or not well remembered, and, digressing from his notes, as he frequently appears to, he

shows a want of fluency in language, and frequently descends to a tone even fainter than the conversational, and a manner unpleasantly hesitant. The consequence was that some of his best *bon mots* were lost, and the connection of his discourse not always perceived.[11]

The concluding part of the lecture was so fragmentary, said the *Times*, no coherent description of its contents was possible. From those parts of the lecture which the *Times* did try to reconstruct, it seems that he cannibalized "Domestic Life," "Concord Walks," "Country Life," "Books," "Hospitality, Homes," "Education," and tossed in, for good measure, a journal passage written four years before. This unreconciled eclecticism all but proclaimed that he no longer could impose even an illusion of order on his material.

Had the audience that jammed St. James's Church that night maintained at least a semblance of attentiveness, Emerson's dignity might have come through unscathed. Instead, it was glaringly restive. Emerson was on his farewell tour, but neither he nor the audience realized that. When he fell short of their expectations, they did not hide their irritation.

More surprising was the reaction of two friends who, earlier in the month, attended Emerson's Baltimore lectures — Walt Whitman and John Burroughs. Burroughs, "dragging Walt" with him, had gone to Baltimore expressly for that purpose. Whitman complained that Emerson was making do with "about the same attitude as twenty-five or thirty years ago." Burroughs owned himself "utterly tired of these scholarly things."[12] Putting their observations into the picture, it seems that Emerson's lecture tour had fallen into a shambles.

Between mid-April and mid-May that year, Emerson earned $1,457 for six "conversations" on literature given at Boston's Mechanics' Hall. The change of name better described and seemed to sanction what Emerson's lectures were fast becoming — unconnected ramblings offered with no pretext of a point to be made.

Those who arranged for the series seem to have made Emerson's convenience their first consideration. The greater part of his audience was made up of women, mostly admirers and disciples. On Monday afternoons, as the hour of three approached, they took their seats in the hall, amused at the handful of men who came, chiefly men who were hoping to find out what Emerson was all about. No one expected him to tangle with great social or political issues. Rather, they regarded him as a comfortable Boston institution. At three o'clock the tempo of the day's business in Boston would soar to a peak. Those inside the hall would hear it as a muffled roar like a distant surf breaking. A writer in the *Boston Journal*, reporting on the second con-

versation, "Poetry and Imagination," given on 22 April, recreates for
us a civilized scene as remote from New Brunswick as the Sistine Chapel
is from Seven Dials:

> A venerable gentleman, well preserved, serene and elegant in
> manner, takes his seat upon the platform of a cosy and comfort-
> able hall . . . and, gently arranging his papers before him, looks
> calmly around him upon the large audience gathered to hear him.
> . . . A red curtain hangs behind him, setting off in sharp relief
> the keen and noble outline of his features — the head thrown
> forward with the poise of daring assertion — and the face now
> animated with all the warmth and enthusiasm of a genuine poetic
> admiration, now saddened and reserved with the diffidence of
> the habitual student and the man of reverie. Side-lights from each
> wing of the stage throw a sharp light upon the ample manuscript
> on the reading desk, for the philosopher and poet is now rapidly
> nearing seventy years of age. . . . There is no other man in
> America who can, by the mere force of what he says, enthrall and
> dominate an audience. Breathless attention is given, although
> now and then his voice falls away so that those seated farthest off
> have to strain every nerve to catch the words. . . . The emphatic
> New Englander listens, incredulously at first, but finishes by
> saying, "That's so!"[13]

A close reading of the *Journal*'s report suggests that Emerson's Mechanics' Hall presentations did not escape the infirmities that marred
his New Brunswick appearance. But Boston understood. This was
Emerson.

The day that Fields was to lecture at Concord, 17 January 1872, the
temperature plummeted toward zero. Boston was frigid and Concord
more so. "Even the horse that carried us from the station to the house
had on his winter coat," said Annie Fields. The deep snow cover gave
everything an Arctic aspect. Ellen and Lidian, prepared for the arrival of the Fieldses, had fires blazing in the fireplaces and a hot supper in preparation. The enthusiasm of their welcome minimized the
consequences of Emerson's absence. And that problem itself soon vanished, for Annie relates:

> After supper, just as the lecture time was approaching, I
> suddenly heard the front door open. In another moment there was
> the dear sage himself ready with his welcome. He had lectured
> the previous evening in Washington, and left in the earliest
> possible train, coming through without pause to Concord. In spite
> of the snow and cold, he said he should walk to the lecture-room as
> soon as he had taken a cup of tea.[14]

Emerson did exactly that. Fields had not completed his first sentence when the door opened and Emerson, beaming, entered and slipped into his seat.

At Bush, after the lecture, a festive evening unfolded. Friends had sent flowers, the fires were built up, and Alcott expanded in the good cheer and talked with some of his old brilliance. Nor did the weary Emerson withdraw to the periphery of things. Annie Fields would remember:

> The spirit of hospitality led the master of the house to be swayed also, for it was midnight before the talk was ended. It was wonderful to see how strong and cheerful and unwearied he appeared after his long journey. "I would not discourage this young acolyte," he said, turning to the lecturer of the evening and laughing, "by showing any sign of discomfort."[15]

And when the Fieldses entered the breakfast room at eight o'clock next morning, Emerson was on hand to greet them.

Over breakfast there was lively chatter. During several days, while away, Emerson had stayed at Senator Sumner's house, the invitation to come there having been hand-delivered to him in Baltimore by Walt Whitman. Sumner had seen to it that Emerson was rushed about Washington — to the Senate Chamber to meet a battery of senators; to Arlington Cemetery; the Smithsonian; the Library of Congress. And there had been dinners galore. Emerson had dined with senators, congressmen, the British ambassador. Something of this had to be reported to Fields and his Annie.

Back through the fields of snow went the Fieldses to the depot, aglow at Emerson's hospitality, refreshed to have looked "upon the same landscape which was the source of his own inspirations." On this occasion the flames of good fellowship and cheer had leaped higher for Emerson than they would again. Five years later he would fend off an invitation to visit the Fieldses when he went to Boston to lecture to an afternoon audience at the Old South (by then needing Ellen to turn the pages for him and to form difficult words for him, silently, with her lips). To Annie, Emerson wrote, "I . . . am grown so old that though I can read from a paper, I am no longer fit for conversation, and dare not make visits. So we send you our thanks, & you shall not expect us."[16]

All the newspapers, all the tongues of today will of
course at first defame what is noble; but you who
hold not of today, not of the times, but of the
Everlasting, are to stand for it.

71. University Lecturer

*I*N the summer of 1869, Charles William Eliot, at thirty-five the
youngest man ever elected to Harvard's presidency, began what was
to prove the most enduring term of service in that office — forty years.
Eliot's election signaled a new era in Harvard annals. From the moment the Harvard Corporation announced its selection, its judgment
was disputed. Eliot was too young. He was a layman and a chemist.
Moreover, he had a fiercely independent nature that threatened those
accustomed to manipulating Harvard presidents — traditionalists who
saw change as a threat to the social order in which they found their
contentment. Born with a raised, liver-colored birthmark covering the
right side of his face down to the corner of his mouth, Eliot had a
compulsive need to prove himself superior to all challengers. When he
was a child, other boys had chased him off Boston Common because of
his disfigurement. But he had not run from anyone in a long time.

If anyone doubted where Eliot stood, he had only to consider his
inaugural address: "The young man of nineteen or twenty ought to
know what he likes best and is most fit for. . . . An atmosphere of
intellectual freedom is the native air of literature and science."[1]
Henceforth an expanded curriculum would offer Harvard men the
benefits of what was already known as "the elective system." The philosopher John Fiske was overjoyed. To his wife he said: "We are going
to have new times here at Harvard. No more old fogyism, I hope."[2]
Fiske's reaction was not limited to himself. In the front row, as Eliot
spoke, sat a responsive Ralph Waldo Emerson, "listening and smiling
and assenting," as the wife of his future biographer, James Elliot
Cabot, wrote to her husband.[3]

Emerson had ample cause to rejoice. From the era when he himself had been a Harvard undergraduate he had advocated such changes as Eliot now promised. Eliot's election had not come about readily, but Emerson, as an Overseer, supported it through successive balloting. Emerson, who, on his sixty-sixth birthday, waited on Eliot as a member of a joint committee of Corporation members and Overseers to advise him of his election, was the youngest member of the board.[4] Little wonder that Eliot, in time, would complain about the "senility" of the board members, and that rebellious students, staging a torchlight rally in the Yard, would display a banner reading, "Average age of Harvard Overseers, 95 in the shade." Eliot was indebted to Emerson not only for his active endorsement but for his inspiration. It was Emerson's own vision that Eliot was committing himself to implement. Eliot knew this and acknowledged it.

"As a young man," Eliot told an audience when he was older than Emerson had been on his inauguration day, "I found the writings of Emerson unattractive, and not seldom unintelligible. . . . I was brought up in the old-fashioned Unitarian conservatism of Boston, which was rudely shocked by Emerson's excursions beyond its well-fenced precincts."[5] Eliot had been practically a babe in arms when Emerson sent shock waves through the Harvard world, yet, from Eliot's later recollections, it might seem that he had stood at the elbow of his uncle Andrews Norton, as he traduced Emerson for his theological excesses. Long after 1838 the face of the Boston establishment remained set against Emerson. On 11 February 1852 Eliot wrote to Theodore Tebbets, a friend enrolled in the Divinity School, greeting him with mock derision as "My young transcendentalist," and disclosing his reaction to a pair of lectures Emerson had given in late January at Boston's Masonic Temple. The views of his parents' generation still were largely Eliot's own:

If my respect for Mr. Emerson was considerably increased by the first lecture ["Culture"] I heard from him, the second completely disgusted me. It was the most rambling, pointless discourse on no subject whatever that I ever listened to. His subject nominally "Worship"; nothing upon that serious subject did I hear, but his lecture was chiefly composed of what were meant to be jokes, but were specimens of exceedingly bad wit and bad taste, and of quotations from old English authors, which were so quaint as to border on the indecent. . . . On the whole, though the room was crammed with people who were hanging on his words with delight, I came to the conclusion that I should stand less chance of hanging if I put the door between myself and my object of indignation. I therefore evaporated after watching the escape of his gas for three quarters of an hour.[6]

Although Eliot, as an analytical thinker, was bothered by Emerson's nonsequential delivery, he was offended more by his theological deviancy. Fortunately, the vapors of his resentment soon began to dissipate, for in his confessional discourse in 1903, Eliot revealed: "When I got at what proved to be my lifework for education, I discovered in Emerson's poems and essays all the fundamental motives and principles of my own hourly struggle against educational routine and tradition, and against the prevailing notions of discipline for the young."[7] In 1924, addressing those who had come together to celebrate his ninetieth birthday, Eliot declared that the idea of the elective system first occurred to him as he pondered Emerson's ideas on self-reliance.[8]

Both in Cambridge and at Northeast Harbor in Maine, where he had his summer home, Eliot kept complete sets of Emerson's works. Eventually, he knew Emerson's essays almost as well as he knew the Bible. One favorite phrase came often to his lips: "Society can never prosper, but must always be bankrupt, until every man does that which he was created to do."[9] By temperament Eliot was both dogmatic and dictatorial. The ameliorating influence of Emerson's belief in the sacredness of the individual enabled him to modify his authoritarian impulses.

Eliot did not merely talk about his debt to Emerson. He sought to repay him. As a young man Emerson had thought how agreeable it would be to teach rhetoric and elocution at some college. In June 1869 the offer finally came. President Eliot caused Emerson to be confirmed as a university lecturer so that he might teach one of seven courses in a new series of philosophical courses, billed as the University Lectures, which Eliot was instituting at Harvard. The other courses were to be taught by Francis Bowen, Emerson's old adversary; Hedge, for even longer his ally; Cabot, his future executor and biographer; C. S. Peirce, G. P. Fisher, and John Fiske. Of these, Fiske may have interested Emerson most, because Fiske was young and an unstinting admirer of his ideas.

At twenty-seven Fiske had already begun to build the reputation that would earn him fame as the foremost expounder in America of Spencer and Darwin, and as a brilliant reconciler of evolution and religion. Through his mother Fiske could claim collateral descent from the great rationalist, John Locke, but he preferred his spiritual kinship with Emerson, whom he credited with recognizing evolution as the Divine plan of creation even before Darwin established its scientific basis.

When Emerson was introduced to Fiske as a colleague in 1869, it was not the first time the two men had met. In 1860 Fiske, then a sophomore at Harvard, had visited Emerson at Bush. Emerson made no record of the visit, but Fiske did. He regarded it as a turning point in his life, and perhaps it was, since no interpreter of science and philosophy, in his time, resembled Emerson more strongly in the certitude with which he acknowledged a Divine First Cause.

Fiske went to Concord in the company of a classmate, Edward Dorr McCarthy, who already was known to Emerson. They made their visit on one of the peak days in September — the fifteenth — but arrived at seven at night just as the family had risen from the tea-time meal with which it customarily ended the day. Emerson himself was not among them, but soon arrived. Though supperless, he received them cordially and insisted they join him at the dinner table.

While Lidian, Ellen, and Edith sat at one end of the table, sewing, Emerson broke bread with his guests at the other. They found him unexpectedly qualified to share in their enthusiasms. Henry Thomas Buckle, then soaring to his brief moment of fame as an historian; Voltaire; Marie François Bichat, the physiologist — Emerson was ready to assess them all. Buckle he rated "the master mind of the age." Bichat evoked raptures. And Fiske reported raptures of his own. "I didn't expect to find him booked on science," he exclaimed, "but I find him tremendously so." Nor did his admiration end there. "I was astonished," he said, "not only at his learning but also by his wisdom and his goodness. I thought him the greatest man I ever saw."

The visitors wanted to hear about Carlyle. From his study Emerson fetched his daguerreotype of Carlyle. And he regaled them with an account of a visit Theodore Parker made to Carlyle on a Sunday night. Parker had found him quite alone, with, however, a huge bowl of whiskey punch for company. With the aid of a tablespoon, the fierce Scot was making steady inroads on it, his face glowing. "Why, Tom, what are you doing?" Parker wanted to know. Carlyle's answer came promptly. "Why, I take a whole bowl of whiskey punch every Sunday night, Theodore, don't you?" Over their virtuous cups of tea, the visitors chuckled at Carlyle's glorious dissipation.

Emerson's "very deep bass voice" rolled over Fiske like a soothing tide. "I felt as much at my ease as I would with an old acquaintance; there was something so charming, so simple and unaffected and exquisitely-bred about Emerson." Fiske went back to Harvard, Emerson's champion for evermore. "Of all the men I ever saw," he told his mother unashamedly, "none can be compared with him for depth, for scholarship, and for attractiveness."[10] The fatherless Fiske had found a role model.

All told, Emerson would give sixteen lectures out of a scheduled eighteen in the spring term at Harvard in 1870, starting on 26 April and lecturing on Tuesdays, Thursdays, and Fridays for five successive weeks, with the final lecture on Thursday, 2 June. The invitation to teach at Harvard was a personal victory for Emerson and he knew it.

He accepted the appointment with pleasure. To a friend he said, "I never was a metaphysician, but I have observed the operations of my faculties for a long time and noted them, and no metaphysician can afford to do without what I have to say."[11]

For several years Emerson had been bringing notes together under the heading "The Natural History of the Intellect." These were intended to result in a book that he envisaged as his chief work. That topic now became the general title of his announced course. He would do for the intellect what Gilbert White had done for Selborne. His introductory lecture was "Praise of Mind." Then followed "Transcendency of Physics," "Perception and Memory" (two on each), five covering, in turn, "Imagination," "Inspiration," "Genius," "Common Sense," and "Identity," two on "Metres of Mind," and three final lectures covering "Platonists," the "Conduct of Intellect" (canceled because he could not shape the material to his satisfaction), and the "Relation of Intellect to Morals." This last lecture Emerson had given two years earlier in Brooklyn.

Emerson may have had expectations that Harvard did not meet. Along with the series he was participating in, Harvard offered a second series, on modern literature, given by Lowell, Francis Child, and others. Since both series ventured into areas hitherto not embraced by Harvard's curriculum, they drew more of a lyceum audience, comprised of graduates and the merely curious, than a true enrollment. One hundred and fifty-five persons, in all, attended one or more lectures in the dual series. Thirty appeared for Emerson's course. But ultimately only four followed the philosophical series through to its conclusion and were examined on it. The fee for each course was $150, the normal tuition fee for those enrolled in the traditional program. Emerson was paid $8.75 per lecture, even though Eliot was, in that very hour, insisting that Harvard must pay its professors a wage worthy of their hire. For such a fee Emerson could have afforded to stay estranged from Harvard.

On the first day Emerson let his students know that they should not look for system in the observations he had to make:

> He who contents himself with dotting only a fragmentary curve, recording only what facts he has observed, without attempting to arrange them within one outline, follows a system also, a system as grand as any other, though he does not interfere with its vast curves by prematurely forcing them into a circle or ellipse, but only draws that arc which he clearly sees, and waits for new opportunity, well assured that these observed arcs consist with each other.[12]

"System-makers," Emerson explained, were "gnats grasping the universe." He did not necessarily have new truths to lay before them, but "anecdotes of the intellect." He would share with them a "farmer's almanac of mental moods," "a tally of things to thoughts." Thereupon his students closed their notebooks. Since there was no pattern of thought to follow, there was nothing for which they could be held responsible. When, at the end of one lecture, Emerson said, "This subject is to be finished next time," Francis G. Peabody entered the remark verbatim in his notebook and then wrote after it, "To what subject does he here refer?"[13]

From the outset Emerson had misgivings about the success of the series. Quoting Scott's "Dinas Emlinn," he told Lidian, when he came home after the first lecture, "I have joined the dim choir of the bards who have been."[14] Part of his difficulty was his aversion to philosophical terms and the necessity which that fact imposed on him of addressing a metaphysical subject in nonmetaphysical terms. Had Eliot asked him to lecture on modern literature the results might have been different. As it was, his enthusiasm for what he had agreed to do waned quickly. The entire undertaking put him in such a state of irritation and weariness that he effectively nullified material meant to be the substance of his future book. When at last his labors ceased, he wrote to Carlyle:

> The oppressive engagement of writing & reading 18 lectures on Philosophy to a class of graduates in the College, & these in six successive weeks, was a task a little more formidable in prospect & in practice than any foregoing one. Of course, it made me a prisoner, took away all rights of friendship, honor, & justice, & held me to such frantic devotion to my work as must spoil *that* also.[15]

Peabody, who bore with Emerson throughout this ordeal, later put it down as one of the great ironies of his lifetime that when Harvard erected a hall of philosophy, it named it Emerson Hall for the man who, on the occasion of this trial, had proved such an "unacademic, unscholastic influence."

Several factors militated against Emerson's achieving, with this series of lectures, the success he yearned for. Age and an awareness of diminishing powers had led him to slow the pace of his activities. Now he was put under the strain of having to deliver sixteen lectures, much of it new material, in fewer than forty days. Moreover, his audience would be looking for a continuity among these lectures which he could not supply. He must have sensed also that those at Harvard who had opposed him through the years were hoping he would founder. Whatever resolve he had to disappoint their expectations must have been speedily dissipated when he saw the sparse turnout of students. As the enrollment dwindled so must his spirit have dwindled too. Unfortunately, he was deprived of a major source of stimulation when a petition from students enrolled at the Divinity School that they might attend his lectures without paying was denied by the university.

Of the seven courses being offered in philosophy, only two, Emerson's and Fiske's, whose topic was "Positive Philosophy," concerned recent philosophical thought. To the new generation, Emerson's views must have seemed the apostasy of bygone days, ideas that scandalized their fathers but could not scandalize them. But Fiske was the voice of newness. Besides, they could make sense out of what he was saying.

To no one's surprise, Emerson made no attempt to examine the students when the course ended. Actually, the course just sputtered out with the sixteenth lecture, two short of his announced goal.

Unwilling to concede that this first attempt to expand Harvard into a true university had been a failure, Eliot reinstituted the series for the 1870–1871 academic year, and Emerson agreed to revise and repeat his lectures, this time for a fee of $340 for the whole course. To ease the burden they were begun on 14 February and extended over nine weeks. To bolster his confidence, Emerson omitted the lectures given previously on perception, identity, and the Platonists, and gave in their place lectures on wit and humor, demonology, poetry, and will and conduct of the intellect. Some of this material he had used for years and he had full mastery of it.

Although Emerson expected to go through this second series with less work and with some pleasure, he was not satisfied that he met these expectations. He marred swatches of good writing by losing his place or misplacing pages. His renewed discouragement is evident in a letter he wrote to Carlyle, on 10 April: "I hope the ruin of no young man's soul will here or hereafter be charged to me as having wasted his time or confounded his reason."[16] By the time he wrote this letter, Emerson had ended his course — one lecture short of the announced eighteen — so that he might accept an invitation from John Murray Forbes to travel, with a party of friends, to California on Forbes's private train. The journey began on 11 April, the date for which Emerson's final lecture had been scheduled. Edith and her husband, who were members of the party, may have conspired to draw Emerson away from his academic responsibilities at that time because it was apparent that they were wearing him down.

If Emerson's expectations for the lecture series were not met, neither were those of President Eliot. In his report announcing discontinuance of the entire program, Eliot revealed that the lectures had proved to be "discursive, heterogeneous, and disconnected," and that was not what the students wanted.[17] Emerson's foes must have been tempted to think that his haphazard methods had spread a pestilence through the ranks of his fellow lecturers.

To James B. Thayer, now a professor at the Harvard Law School and the spouse of one of Uncle Samuel Ripley's daughters, Emerson confided on the journey west that he would have accepted gladly, at any time, a Harvard professorship. That he had proved unequal to the challenge when it came was a bitter end to his dream.

Groups of men who came together to weigh and decide issues, whether as a school committee in Concord or the Harvard Board of Overseers, were all one in Emerson's mind. They were made up of businessmen or men who functioned as businessmen. And so it was that Emerson, as a member of Harvard's Board of Overseers, was satisfied to admire the presentations others made but rarely spoke himself. Yet occasions came when his conscience would not allow him to be silent. Thus we know that he urged that the Harvard curriculum be broadened so that the study of poetry could be given more prominence. There was no better way, he believed, to stimulate the imagination. This meant to him lifting the mind above the level of mere understanding, of fact for fact's sake, into the realm of reason where dawned awareness of the revelations of the universal mind. Such developments could not be left to chance. He knew young men hungered for such an awakening and thought it unconscionable that a restricted curriculum should stunt their development. He was a natural champion of Eliot's free elective system. He further contended that a college education was not the birthright of every youth whose family had the means to send him to college. Why waste money and energy on those whose minds were set against learning or whose capacity for taking it in was limited?

Harvard Overseers were elected to six-year terms, and began them at the close of Commencement Day in the year they were elected. Customarily, they sought reelection to a second term. At the end of twelve years, however, they were expected, in keeping with the statute, to pass a year out of office before standing again for election. Thus would Emerson's fellow Overseer, the Boston banker Henry Lee, come on the board in 1867, take his statutory year of recess in 1879, then take his place on the board again through 1892. It may well have been the resolute Lee who convinced Emerson to cast his surprising vote, on two separate occasions, in favor of continuing compulsory morning prayers at Harvard, even when the majority of the Overseers, Phillips Brooks among them, voted against it. Lee, who thought students were overpampered, declared, ''I am very glad indeed to find some one act which is disagreeable to them, and I should like to compel every one of them to perform it once every day.''[18] This remark came at a time when, as a result of loosening regulations, there was a general breakdown in discipline among the undergraduates. Drastic measures under Eliot's own direction soon had to be taken to restore order. It was in consideration of these facts that Emerson cast his vote as he did. He wanted men free to discipline themselves. But freedom carries with it an obligation to heed the dictates of the moral sentiment. If that obligation is spurned, then society has no choice but to reimpose restraints. Such considerations could overwhelm even the exhortations of the ''Divinity School Address,'' which can in no way be reconciled with compulsory chapel. Experience often counsels prudence. Who, for example, would identify the august Rockwood Hoar, a justice of the Massachusetts Supreme Judicial Court, with the youth who, in 1834, spent long and desperate midnight hours on his back in the belfry of Harvard Hall, resolutely striving to saw off the tongue of the college bell, the agency used to summon students to morning prayers?[19]

When Emerson's second term as Overseer ended in 1879, he was seventy-six and, as the words he loved forsook him, in danger, like the chapel bell, of falling silent. He did not stand for office again.

72. John Muir
Westward Down All the Mountains

$\mathscr{A}$T the close of his Harvard lecture series in 1870, Emerson had refused an invitation from John Murray Forbes to accompany him on a visit to the White Mountains. He wrote:

> The scheme is charming to me, the company and the mountains. And yet it is not to be thought of by me, — I wish it were. I have just come to the end of my Cambridge work, which has been so unusual a strain on my lawless ways of study, that I have been forced to postpone all duties, demands, proprieties, specially letters, to it, and now they will break my doors down if I do not face them. Please give me credit for rare honesty, nay, magnanimity, that I do not run out by the back door and take the train to you. . . . I have the sorrow of a boy that I cannot go.[1]

Such was Emerson's determination in June 1870 to hold to the path of duty.

The inroads that the ensuing months and the responsibilities of his second series of Harvard lectures made on Emerson's strength and spirits were evident less than ten months later when he dealt with John Murray Forbes's invitation to accompany him on an ambitious pleasure tour — a train trip across the continent to California. Ten others would make it a party of twelve: Mrs. Forbes; three daughters, Alice, Sarah, and Mary (Mrs. George Russell); the Forbeses' son William Hathaway and his wife, Edith Emerson; James Bradley Thayer and his wife, Sophia Ripley, Emerson's first cousin; Garth Wilkinson James, son of Henry James; and Wilkie's friend G. Holdredge.[2]

Emerson was now more open — with himself as well as with Forbes — about the serious strain his "Cambridge work" was putting him under. He saw that the journey would benefit him both physically and mentally, but was concerned about the breach of routine it would involve. Tasks and obligations already long postponed would have to be put out of mind altogether. In "Terminus" he had acknowledged a readiness to accept the diminished role advancing years decreed.[3] Now age was asking him to make good that pledge. He capitulated.

With a casual grandeur that came easily to a powerful railroad magnate, Forbes had waiting for his party, when they reached Chicago on 18 April, the *Huron*, a private Pullman. George Pullman himself saw to its provisioning, boasting to them, as they set out on their journey westward, that they could dine as they would at the Parker House. For Emerson that was the signal to slip into the routine of club life, which he so relished. He could handle well the hardship of travel, as he had proved many times. But in the luxurious circumstances that went with being a member of the Forbes party, he could only bask like a melon in the sun. The *Huron* seemed to the travelers a palace car; for Emerson such comforts on the road, after the torments he hitherto had known, constituted a flood of compensation that swept away in an instant memories of decades of constant hardship.

Chicago, rapidly swelling to renown, seemed a happy choice as a departure point for this flying-carpet adventure. Six months thence, a fire storm would lay waste much of the city, but no foreknowledge weighed on the Boston adventurers just as no hint reached Emerson that the advancing foe of years soon would ravage him. "Pray Heaven you may long *keep your right hand steady*," Carlyle wrote to him on learning that Emerson, on the eve of his journey, was uneasy about some of his writing commitments.[4] He did not know it, but Emerson had good cause for concern.

Emerson, for the most part, dispensed with note-keeping on this journey, in all having less to say about the impressions garnered in six weeks than he had written earlier about his two-day visit to Mammoth Cave. But James B. Thayer took notes enough to publish them, two years after Emerson's death, as *A Western Journey with Mr. Emerson*. Thayer made much of Emerson's extraordinary amiability. A young lady in the party had put the question to him: "How *can* Mr. Emerson be so agreeable, all of the time, and not become tired and annoyed?" And she had not overstated the facts. Several days in a Pullman, even a palace Pullman, cooped up with others ought to have given Emerson a chance to show his bad side. None was revealed because he had none. Said Thayer: "He was always accessible, cheerful, sympathetic, considerate, tolerant; and there was always that same respectful interest in those with whom he talked, even the humblest, which raised them in their own estimation." Thayer sought an explanation for Emerson's behavior in his philosophy:

> One thing particularly impressed me, — the sense that he seemed to have a certain great amplitude of time and leisure. It was the behavior of one who really *believed* in an immortal life, and had adjusted his conduct accordingly; so that, beautiful and grand as the natural objects were among which our journey lay, they were matched by the sweet elevation of character and the spiritual charm of our gracious friend.[5]

The nearest approach Emerson made to a complaint was to express regret that not a single wild buffalo strode into view as they crossed the prairies. Conceivably, too, in his own oblique fashion, Emerson maneuvered Forbes into making a side trip to Salt Lake City, especially if Carlyle's comment, "I fear you won't see Brigham Young" (written in a letter sent *after* Emerson's return), reflects some earlier exchange between them on the subject of the Mormons.[6] At Salt Lake City on 19 April (in an observance markedly different from the Patriot's Day commemoration going on back in Concord), they called on Young, and Emerson came away able to tell Carlyle: "Our interview was peaceable enough, and rather mended my impression of the man."[7] He counted it in Young's favor that, on the previous Sunday, he had given a sermon that "avoided religion, but was full of Franklinian good sense." Forbes, who weighed the encounter between Emerson and Young with the practiced eye of a tycoon, was struck by a contrast he had not anticipated in a meeting between two men of God: "The Prophet . . . was a burly, bull-necked man of hard sense, really leading a great industrial army. . . . The chief interest of the scene was the wide contrast between these leaders of spiritual and material forces."[8]

The travelers were no sooner settled at the Occidental Hotel in San Francisco on 21 April when Horatio Stebbins, the local Unitarian pastor, swooped down on them, full of plans. Next day they must come with him to the Cliff House to observe the sea lions basking on the rocks, and the day following, Sunday, Emerson must speak to his congregation. Emerson accommodated both wishes. In an account of the sea lions that he sent to his grandson Ralph Emerson Forbes, he established that he had seen them properly, both with his naked eye and through a spyglass. Over the next nine days he spoke four times at Stebbins's church, delivering well-seasoned lectures — "Immortality," "Society in America," "Resources," "Greatness" — which he brought with him in the expectation that he would be asked to speak. Philosophical discourses were not everyday fare for San Franciscans,

but Emerson was Emerson and they were determined to make the most
of it. At breakfast, on the morning of the twenty-fourth, the day after
he spoke on immortality, he shared the merriment of his friends when
they read in the *Alta California:* "All left the church feeling that an
elegant tribute had been paid to the creative genius of the Great First
Cause, and that a masterly use of the English language had contributed to that end."[9]

If Emerson realized that he was the first American author to have
spanned the continent as a lecturer, he never said so. But he appreciated the $500 he received for his efforts. Prices were high in San
Francisco, but he could now spend as the whim took him without scandalizing his New England conscience or returning part of his strip of
gingerbread.

That same week, another Concordian, Carrie Augusta Moore, was
the star of a roller-skating exhibition in San Francisco. She sent
Emerson free tickets and promised to repeat her act if he got there
after curtain time. He never arrived at all. If a circus clown's antics
could dismay him, the antics of a roller-skater might well have appalled him.

The stay in San Francisco was interrupted by another side trip, by
wagon and horseback to the Yosemite Valley, begun on 2 May. John
Murray Forbes found himself alternately amazed and nonplussed by
Emerson's conduct. He later told Holmes:

> I wish I could give you more than a mere outline picture of the
> sage at this time. With the thermometer at 100° he would some-
> times drive with the buffalo robes drawn up over his knees,
> apparently indifferent to the weather, gazing on the new and
> grand scenes of mountain and valley through which we journeyed.
> I especially remember once, when riding down the steep side of a
> mountain, his reins hanging loose, the bit entirely out of the
> horse's mouth, without his being aware that this was an unusual
> method of riding Pegasus, so fixed was his gaze into space, and so
> unconscious was he, at the moment, of his surroundings.[10]

By 5 May they were settled in at Leidig's Hotel in the valley, and
by the eighth had carried out several exploratory sallies to see the
expected views. This party of literati, notwithstanding Emerson's
presence among them, was not especially geared to offer, in equal measure, grandeur of response to the grandeur of spectacle Yosemite offered. Their talk was more about books and the great artists of the
past than the wonders of Nature crowding in on them. Emerson, at
least, was not impervious to its impact. While on horseback, he had
looked with satisfaction on the Royal Arches and the Half Dome,

drenched in sunlight, and conceded: "This Valley is the only place that comes up to the brag about it, and exceeds it."[11]

To the better-informed Yosemite dwellers, a new wonder had come to the valley — Emerson himself. As tourist he might sit on the porch of the Casa Nevada Hotel and look at the spectacle of the Nevada Fall and the Giant Stairway, but, once returned to base camp at Leidig's, he was the spectacle. Many hung back in the shadows, whispering and indulging a sense of awe usually reserved for some manifestation of divinity.

Among the shadow lurkers was a young naturalist usually contemptuous of those who came to gawk at his valley. This was John Muir, who at the age of eleven had migrated to Wisconsin's Fox River locale from Scotland; who at twenty-two had begun four years of special studies at the University of Wisconsin; and who at thirty-three was now on the threshold of what he was to regard as one of the two supreme moments of his life, his meeting with Emerson. Although Muir's later travels would take him to the Caucasus, Siberia, Manchuria, India, Egypt, New Zealand, Australia, and the Arctic, nothing was going to impress him as much thereafter except an encounter with a *Calypso borealis* blooming in a Canadian swamp.

Muir had read few of Emerson's essays. Thoreau was unknown to him. But his friend Jeanne Carr, who taught botany at the San Mateo School, had written him to say that Emerson was coming to the valley, where he would be "in your hands, I hope and trust."[12] Emerson had corresponded with Mrs. Carr with a view to getting her husband, Ezra, to edit Thoreau's journals. She told Emerson that Muir was one of his spiritual sons and should be, on that account, received by him. Muir knew this but, in his shyness, had held back until he learned that Emerson's party was leaving the valley in a day or two. Realizing he was letting a unique opportunity slip away, he stifled his bashfulness and brought a note to Leidig's to be given to Emerson. He did not let on that the note-bearer and the note-writer were one and the same, and, bewhiskered and rough-clad, he was taken for a local menial.

Muir's note reads like something he labored over. He concealed his timidity behind near-brashness. He took refuge in cultist jargon, all but summoning Emerson to witness wilderness rituals over which he, as Nature's high priest, would preside. His tone was peremptory and naive. He offered not an invitation but a challenge:

> Do not thus drift away with the mob, while the spirit of these
> rocks and water hail you after long waiting as their kinsman and
> persuade you to closer communion. But now if Fate or one of
> those mongrel & misshapen organizations called parties compel you
> to leave for the present, I shall hope for some other fulness of

time to come for you. . . . I invite you to join me in a month's
worship with Nature in the high temples of the great Sierra
Crown beyond our holy Yosemite. It will cost you nothing save the
time and very little of that for you will be mostly in eternity. . . .
In the name of a hundred cascades that barbarous visitors never
see . . . in the name of all the spirit creatures of these rocks
and of this whole spiritual atmosphere Do not leave us *now*.[13]

A man of world renown, elderly, in declining health, traveling as
the guest of a solicitous friend, with a party made up largely of kith
and kin and esteemed by them, could hardly disappear into the wilderness for a month with a stranger. There was something arbitrary
and irritating about Muir's tone, akin to the possessiveness of a de-
manding lover, which blanketed the whole of his relationship with
Emerson, not only in this brief valley interval but even later, when
they exchanged letters. Thayer resented it and other members of the
party did, too, but Emerson, responsive to the sincerity and purpose
behind the swagger, met Muir's appeal with predictable generosity.
An appeal from ardent youth was a fire bell he could not ignore, and
he acted predictably.

The next morning, instead of sending a messenger to bring Muir to
him, he mounted, with a little assistance, his piebald mustang, and
rode over to Hutching's Mill, where Muir lived. The young man was
tall, lank, and bearded. His rough clothing was one of the things about
him that caused local residents to think of him as peculiar and, though
harmless, something of a ne'er-do-well. Thayer, who accompanied
Emerson that morning, perhaps to make certain that he was not ab-
ducted by some wild man of the mountains, did not find Muir's appearance reassuring. Emerson, however, with his long experience of
Thoreau, felt no apprehensions. Predictably, once contact had been
made, Muir's shyness had given place to a breathless eagerness that
found him all but tripping over his feet in his desire to share with
Emerson the treasures he had garnered at Yosemite. By some curious
quirk of logic he seemed to think he could invest Emerson with his
own boyishness. Perhaps Muir looked beyond externals and in the rapport Emerson readily established with him, as he did with other young
people, caught that youthfulness of spirit which Emerson, even at seventy, still could draw on.

Muir's lodgings were no less peculiar than the man. High on the
outside of the mill, just under the gable, he had fastened a cable-car-
like room, a "hang-nest," he called it. Beneath it the mill stream
grumbled, and beyond it the great sweep of the valley plunged westward. To approach this aerie Emerson was expected to inch his way
up a succession of sloping planks treaded with slats for traction, like

a hen ladder. This Emerson did, with characteristic complacency, as if
gamboling in the treetops was for him a normal recreation. Having
initiated Emerson to this extent into his private world, Muir now seemed
anxious to grapple him to it by a reckless bestowal of gifts — his rock
specimens, his dried plants, and pencil sketches in abundance, of peaks,
and glaciers, and towering trees. But Emerson had no wish to plunder
Muir's cherished treasures. For one thing, he knew he was not capable
of relishing them as Muir did. Later Muir would realize this. When
finally he read Emerson's essays, he saw Emerson was a poor naturalist. After Emerson got back to Concord, packages of specimens from
Muir would follow him through the mails but, for the moment at least,
he was able to come down from the hang-nest without a sample case of
Yosemite's wonders.

Those first two years of what would lengthen into the decade that
Muir spent in the Yosemite Valley had invigorated him both in body
and spirit. In him Emerson beheld a man of great enthusiasm and
vitality. That very zest, however, so intoxicated Muir that he seemed
scarcely able to recognize the limitations of others. Emerson was better
than twice his age, yet Muir could envisage no obstacles to his proposal
that Emerson should rough it in the wilderness with him in the weeks
ahead. He importuned him with what Thayer described as "amusing
zeal."[14] And when Emerson respectfully declined, Muir was sure he
held back solely because "his party, full of indoor philosophy, failed
to see the natural beauty and fullness of promise of my wild plan and
laughed at it in good-natured ignorance, as if it were necessarily amusing
to imagine that Boston people might be led to accept Sierra manifes-
tations of God at the price of rough camping."[15] True enough, Emerson had appeared to consult with his companions on the feasibility of
the adventure, but he could not for a moment have supposed that they
would sanction it.

During the two ensuing days Emerson again visited the mill and
mounted the plank to the hang-nest to chat in seclusion with Muir.
What Muir wanted of Emerson, as Emerson well knew, was the sympathy of perfect understanding. The description of Emerson Muir wrote
more than forty years later shows that he found it: "Emerson was the
most serene, majestic, sequoia-like soul I ever met. His smile was as
sweet and calm as morning light on mountains. . . . A tremendous
sincerity was his."[16] For his part, Emerson saw in Muir a living embodiment of his complete universal man. On his return to Concord a
month later, one of the first entries Emerson made in his journal was
a list of "My Men." On this list were eighteen names, nearly all of
men he had known over many years. Carlyle's name was first on the
list. Muir's name closed it.[17]

When it came time for his party to move on, Emerson asked Muir to ride with him as far as Clark's Station, and then, next morning, to continue on to the Mariposa Grove of Big Trees, south of the valley. The stubborn Scotsman made one further try to outmaneuver Emerson's guardians. He suggested that the two of them should camp out alone for the night under the giant trees. "Yes, yes, we will camp out, camp out," Emerson said.[18]

On the way to Clark's Station, a distance of twenty-five miles, the party chatted about literature concerning which, Thayer thought, Muir knew too little. And Muir chatted about the sequoia and their lesser coniferous cousins, about which, Thayer thought, Muir knew too much. Once Muir aptly quoted a line from Emerson's "Woodnotes" — "Come listen what the pine tree sayeth" — to lure him aside from the party to a high forest ridge where unbroken ranks of sugar pines, tall and grand, marched in seeming endless procession. Emerson saluted them with a compliment that tickled Muir: "Oh, you Gentlemen Pines!"[19]

When, early in the afternoon, they arrived at Galen Clark's tavern and the party began to dismount, Muir revealed that Emerson had elected to camp with him that night beneath the glorious sequoias. The news did not sit well with Emerson's companions. The women were shrill in their protests — "Mr. Emerson might take cold!" Overruled, Emerson capitulated and was escorted, Muir grimly noted, to the "carpet dust and unknowable reeks" of Clark's hostelry.

Muir knew when he had been outflanked. Nonetheless, he did not retreat into the forest to bind up his wounds. He came along, forlornly, to Clark's, reeks notwithstanding. Emerson, deflated by the turn events had taken, "hardly spoke a word all the evening." Yet, however withdrawn he was, since this was Muir's last chance to be with him, Muir was glad of his company.

The next morning the party rode up the trail into the Mariposa Grove, where they dutifully measured the girth of the trees with tape lines or galloped through the openings fire had bored in their vast trunks. At times Emerson, responding as a poet to the wonders about him, dissociated himself from these exercises to saunter about "as if under a spell," with Muir as his silent, respectful companion. Later Emerson would tell him that "solitude is a sublime mistress, but an intolerable wife." In each other's company, they knew something of the sublimity of solitude. Awe kept Emerson mute, and when at last he spoke, it was to confirm that awe. To Muir he whispered, "There were giants in those days."[20]

Galen Clark himself presided over the grove. To commemorate Emerson's visit, he invited him to choose a name for the finest of the trees not yet named. Samoset seemed right to Emerson — the name of an early New England sachem. If the white man had hewn down the primeval forests that Samoset knew, at least Samoset could be commemorated in a tree that had lifted itself proudly to the skies centuries before the white despoilers had laid their axes to American forests.

The party now made last adjustments of saddles and gear, preparing to move out. Muir saw his duty and made one last unsuccessful appeal to the Yankee sachem. "I wanted to steal him," Muir afterward admitted.[21]

Muir stood watching as the riders withdrew, following them with his firm, free step to the edge of the grove. He watched as they mounted the ridge, his clear blue eyes riveted on Emerson, who, almost as though attesting to his reluctance to leave, held back, trailing the others. One by one the riders disappeared over the crest of the ridge till Emerson alone was still in view. There at the crest, he turned his horse and halted. Then he drew off his hat and with it waved to Muir one last sign of farewell. The day was 11 May 1871. They would not meet again. "It was," Muir said, "the afternoon of the day and the afternoon of his life, and his course was now westward down all the mountains into the sunset."[22]

An unfamiliar surge of loneliness swirled now around the man whom another traveler in that same season credited with "marvelous nerve and endurance."[23] "So sure had I been," Muir recalled later, "that Emerson of all men would be the quickest to see the mountains and sing them."[24] Muir was a man accustomed to realizing his goals. Despite his melancholy, he returned to the heart of the grove and there made a bed of sequoia plumes and fern, then gathered wood for a fire. At sundown he lit his fire and saw the day ending well: "Though lonesome for the first time in these forests, I quickly took heart again — the trees had not gone to Boston, nor the birds; and as I sat by the fire, Emerson was still with me in spirit."[25] He did not know that Emerson, descending the western slope of the Sierra, after his last farewell, had assured his companions, "There is a young man from whom we shall hear." But he would learn from a mutual friend that, later still, home again in Concord, Emerson had confided he was sorry he had been prevented from sleeping in the Mariposa Grove.

The next week, in Oakland, Jeanne and Ezra Carr sat in their cottage on a night made blacker than other nights by a dense fog that seemed to swallow up the whole world. Then a commotion at their back door aroused them. They opened it to be greeted by Emerson, standing at their threshold, his cloak pulled tightly about him. He could not come in. His daughter and her husband had already crossed on the ferry to San Francisco. "But I," he said, "could not go through Oakland without coming up here to thank you for that letter to John Muir."[26] He had lost his way in the fog, he revealed, but had persevered so that he could personally thank Jeanne for making possible the meeting with Muir.

A gift of cedar flowers sent by Muir to Emerson, early in the new year, brought a cordial reply from Emerson the following month. He had put off writing Muir and sending copies of his *Essays,* though he had promised to do so. But Muir should not construe his procrastination as indifference. ''I have,'' Emerson wrote, ''everywhere testified to my friends, who should also be yours, my happiness in finding you — the right man in the right place — in your mountain tabernacle.''[27] His adoption of Muir's cultist idiom was in itself a subtle Emersonian compliment. Truly, Muir approached Nature with a reverence due Divinity.

In his letter Emerson let Muir know that he saw him as an exceptional man in a society that produced too many commonplace men. He had been waiting, he said, for Muir's ''guardian angel'' to end his exile and send him with his ''ripe fruits so rare and precious into waiting society.'' He continued: ''I know that society in the lump, admired at a distance, shrinks and dissolves, when approached, into impracticable or uninteresting individuals, but always with a reserve of a few unspoiled good men, who really give it its halo in the distance.'' He invited Muir to be his guest at Bush. ''You must find your way to this village, and my house,'' he modestly insisted. ''And when you are tired of our dwarf surroundings, I will show you better people.''[28]

Muir still could not quite give over his vision of Emerson as his camping companion, gamboling through the wilderness. His January letter asserted: ''What prayers push my pen for your coming, but I must hush them all back for our roads are deep blocked with snow-bloom.''[29] By 18 March 1872, when he wrote again, he was bustling with plans. No promoter of paid tours could have been more enthusiastic:

> Come to our mountain fountains. Come to Yosemite. Last year you left against law. . . . There are no apologies in Nature else you would owe her one. You cannot be content with last year's baptism 'Twas only a sprinkle. Come be immersed. . . . I cannot understand the laws that control you to Concord. You are called of the Sierras.[30]

In his thoughts he infused Emerson with his own zest and strength:

> If you will come about June & stay until October I will have a hut & horse ready for you. . . . You will have a tent & be warm every night in a sheltered grove or on the plushy bank of a glacier meadow. Do you know the manners of mountain clouds? those angels of lakes & streams? — We will travel like them lingering about rockwalls & brows — waving softly along glacial curves

from mountain to mountain, from dome to dome, halting about the skirts of forests, poising on slender peaks in full exposure to the powers of fountain light.[31]

Muir's "glacial-daisy-gentian meadows," however enticing, lay forever beyond the perimeter of Emerson's world.[32]

On 26 March, Muir again wrote Emerson, repeating his invitation. An earthquake occurred while he was writing his letter and, though it can hardly have been a further inducement to Emerson to fall in with his plans, Muir treated him to a detailed account of it. Other letters followed in April and May, the letter writer stimulated by two books of his essays Emerson had sent. After that, Emerson let the correspondence lapse.

Muir had said in a letter he wrote to Emerson on 6 July 1871, "I would willingly walk all the way to your Concord if so I could have you for a companion," that is, as a companion on a journey he was about to make to the High Sierra east of Yosemite.[33] But, actually, in answer to Emerson's invitation to come visit him in Concord, Muir said he had another two or three years' work to do on glaciers and mountain structure at Yosemite before he could even think of coming east. The prospect of having to cope over that interval with Muir's passionate appeals to come tent with him and be his fellow hiker must have given Emerson serious pause. Perhaps, as well, he perceived that Muir was prone to lead more than follow and seemed to be contemplating a relationship in which Emerson sat at his feet, and not the other way around. Muir's marginal notes on Emerson's essays support that assumption. His voice here is irritable and snappish, his judgment, often petty. Emerson wrote, "It never troubles the sun that some of his rays fall wide and vain into ungrateful space." Muir demurs: "How do we know that space is ungrateful?" Emerson said: "Nature 'takes no thought for the morrow.'" Muir counters with, "Are not buds and seeds thought for the morrow."[34] Emerson, Muir concluded, had much to learn about the natural world. Thoreau's quibbles, Emerson had found, were quite enough for one lifetime. He could dispense with Muir's.

One service that Emerson rendered Muir did not go unrecognized. "He said most about Thoreau," Muir had remarked. He had even implied a willingness to transfer to Muir the task he had had Ezra Carr in mind for — the editing of Thoreau's manuscript journals. Now, in 1872, Muir finally read *Walden*. He liked this "open-eyed Thoreau" and praised his "pure soul." Yet, even about Thoreau he had reservations. Thoreau's appreciation of Nature began in abstract metaphysics. He did not have enough direct experience of the wild.

In June 1893 Muir at last came to Concord, where he dined with

Edward Emerson, was shown through Emerson's house, and climbed Authors' Ridge, at Sleepy Hollow, where he laid flowers on the graves of Emerson and Thoreau. It was, he concluded, the most beautiful graveyard he had ever seen. "I could not help thinking," he wrote, "how glad I would be to feel sure that I would also rest here."[35] For someone so certain that Emerson and Thoreau never had seen Nature as he saw it, this was a rare admission. He did own, however, that Authors' Ridge had a further appeal for him that had nothing to do with Emerson and Thoreau. It was identifiable as a glacial drift.

Sailing on the Nile in 1873, Emerson was pleased when the obliging young son of some other touring Americans rowed him ashore.[36] In May 1903 that same youngster, now grown to manhood, quietly slipped away from Washington, D.C., heading for a secret destination — the Mariposa Big Trees, the very spot where Muir and Emerson parted. There, by prearrangement, he met John Muir, and the two men, John Muir and Theodore Roosevelt, President of the United States, disappeared alone into the wilderness for three days, Roosevelt confidently boasting that he "could foot it or rough it" with Muir or anyone else.[37] Later Muir told Roosevelt how he had pleaded in vain with Emerson to make the same trip with him. "You would have made him perfectly comfortable," said Roosevelt, "and he ought to have had the experience."[38]

Back in San Francisco, Emerson, who earlier could not find time to see Carrie Moore cavort on roller skates, found leisure to visit an opium den where, not surprisingly, his transcendental serenity stood out in sharp contrast to the stupor of the addicts. In Thayer's company, he visited, as well, the lowest theater in town — evidently, judging from its popularity with the miners, the equivalent of the strip joint of a later day. Serenity unruffled, he emerged to pronounce it "flat and dreary." He could scarcely have said otherwise after having seen so recently the peaks of Yosemite and John Muir's dried specimens. The coarser aspects of Californian life could not disturb Emerson's equilibrium. Filtered through a transcendental sifter, California showed the glint of gold: "California is teaching in its history & its Poetry the good of evil, & confirming my thought, one day in Five Points in New York . . . that the ruffians & Amazons in that district were only superficially such, but carried underneath this bronze about the same morals as their civil & well dressed neighbors."[39]

In "Chivalry," a final talk given for Horatio Stebbins on 18 May, Emerson let the local pundits catch him up in an anachronism when he spoke of the *Mayflower* Pilgrims reading *Pilgrim's Progress,* a feat even more marvelous than their flight across the Atlantic, since Bunyan was not born until 1628. Sight-seeing was beginning to take its toll.

Reluctant to scandalize his fellow townsmen, Emerson never appeared on the Milldam smoking a cigar. Walking from Bush toward the Milldam, he sometimes did smoke one, however, but always extinguished it and hid it on a fence rail to be retrieved on his return. As a club on wheels, the *Huron* was another matter, and there Emerson availed himself of its full privileges. Thayer relates: ''On this journey Mr. Emerson generally smoked a single cigar after our mid-day dinner, or after tea, and occasionally after both. This was multiplying, several times over, anything that was usual with him at home.''[40] During the weeks in California, of course, the travelers saw nothing of the *Huron*, but it picked them up at Lake Tahoe on 20 May and Emerson had another leisurely week of club living as they made their way east.

Beyond observing that Emerson ''was extraordinarily temperate in his Diet,'' Thayer only once supplied particulars. He could not overlook Emerson's Yankee predilection for apple pie at breakfast and recreated a rare glimpse of Emerson indulging himself :

At breakfast we had, among other things, pie. This article at breakfast was one of Mr. Emerson's weaknesses. A pie stood before him now. He offered to help somebody from it, who declined ; and then one or two others, who also declined ; and then Mr. ——; he too declined. ''But Mr. ——!'' Mr. Emerson remonstrated, with humorous emphasis, thrusting the knife under a piece of the pie, and putting the entire weight of his character into his manner, — ''but Mr. ——, *what is pie for?*''[41]

Emerson arrived back in Concord on 30 May to find his house under quarantine because the upstairs maid was down with smallpox. He could communicate with Lidian only by standing in the yard and calling to her from a distance. Worse still, Edward, in his absence, had been stricken with a milder form of the same disease. His lungs had abcessed and he now looked like a dying consumptive. Until the quarantine was lifted and Emerson could return home, several days later, he stayed at the Old Manse, anxious and brooding. More weeks passed before Edward was out of danger. Worry undid much of the good the journey had done. The signs of strain returned. Cabot notes, ''the descent was steady from this time.''[42]

73. Bush Ablaze
A House Not Built with Hands

*A*T five-thirty in the morning, 24 July 1872 — the hour seeming earlier to many because of the pall of rainclouds that lay over Concord — Emerson awakened to the crackling sound of fire. He saw that his closet was ablaze and that smoke and fire were billowing down from the attic above. Lidian was sleeping downstairs, in the red room, and, as he thrust on some clothes, he cried out news of the danger in a terrifying voice. Befuddled by sleep, Lidian thought at first that he had been stricken in the night with some dreadful malady. When she realized that the house was on fire, her anxiety left her. A husband was important, a house was not.[1]

Even as Lidian dressed, piling on short down skirts, a dress of black alpaca, and a mantilla, without removing her nightdress, Emerson, bootless and half clad, rushed past the door of her room and in hard rain ran down the path to the front gate, calling out in his deep and sonorous voice to alert his neighbors to the tragedy. His calls were heard at a considerable distance. For the next several hours he would be both heated by exertion and soaked by the pouring rain, laying the groundwork for chills and fever. People passing on the road had seen the fire, and soon, a third of a mile away, the First Parish bell rang out to summon volunteers and the fire company.

Even before Lidian emerged from the red room, neighbors were streaming in and out of the house carrying furniture and clothing, books and manuscripts to safety. By touch alone, in the smoke-filled study, courageous young men, holding their breath, felt for volumes they could not see and brought them to safety. As well as he could,

Emerson assisted with and directed the operation. To his grief charred pages from the attic — the remnants of letters stored there and his father's sermons — fluttered through the air and were carried far and wide by the wind. Later, Ellen Tucker's letters were found to be only slightly charred, but while the fire raged Emerson must have feared the worst for them.[2] His own papers and books fared better. Disarranged though they were, they were intact. Louisa Alcott and her sister May stood guard over them with a keen sense of responsibility. Seeking to ease the tension, Emerson jested with them. "I see my library under a new aspect," he said as he surveyed the wet bundles. Quickly he went on, "Could you tell me where my good neighbors have flung my boots?"[3]

None of Emerson's own children had been there to help. Ellen, usually at home, was visiting friends at Beverly Farms. Edward was in England, a student at St. Thomas Hospital. Edith and her family were on the high seas, returning from England. Sam Staples stopped Lidian on the stairs, on her way to Ellen's room to save what she could. There was a camphor trunk under Ellen's bed, she told him, full of shawls. A man ran in and got it out safely. But a little later the roof, in which a hole had been chopped to let the smoke out and the water in, collapsed, along with a chimney, and another neighbor, trying to save what he could, saved himself only by the skin of his teeth. "The whole town came to our help," Emerson told John Murray Forbes on the twenty-sixth, in the first letter he wrote after the fire, "& never were household goods from least to largest so tenderly removed and cared for."[4]

The efforts of many kept the work of destruction from being total, but all Ellen's clothes were lost and cherished letters from Lidian. The upper portion of the house was gutted, yet the rooms on the first floor, though damaged by water and smoke, were largely spared. The house was uninhabitable now, but could be restored. What could be saved, was saved. Years later, when relatives gathered, Ellen would produce, to read, charred letters from long-dead kinsmen.

At one point while the fire raged, Emerson had stood back and exclaimed, "But isn't it a magnificent blaze!" Magnificent or otherwise, the blaze's cause was a mystery. A chimney abutted the closet where Emerson first saw the flames. But it was midsummer and the fireplaces in that part of the house had not been used for many weeks. There was a suspicion that a domestic hired the day before had, while prowling in the attic, touched off the fire by scorching the dry beams with a kerosene lamp.

By eight-thirty the fire was stayed. Only then were Emerson and Lidian willing to leave the scene. The rain had ended and the day was brightening, but their home was a sorry ruin. It was still framed in by the four walls and the trees about the house were intact, spared by the rain, but, with the roof gone, the house lay open to the elements. The Emersons themselves showed the effects of the disaster. Emerson, bone-weary and still but partially dressed, was ready to collapse. His journal entry for that date bespeaks his exhaustion. "House burned," it said. That was all. Lidian had tripped over the facing of her skirt so many times that it had torn loose and dropped down around her feet, exposing the bottom of her nightdress and the hastily donned down skirts.[5] Annie Keyes pinned it up for her and John Keyes took them home in his wagon and gave them a warm breakfast. Sarah Ripley's daughter Elizabeth insisted that they should stay at the Old Manse, the house that had welcomed Emerson before in times of trial.

Word of the disaster traveled speedily from friend to friend. On the afternoon of the fire, Francis Cabot Lowell, who had been Emerson's classmate at Harvard, came over from Waltham to see for himself what Emerson's circumstances were and to offer the Emersons the hospitality of his own home.[6] Judge Hoar, who had gone to Boston early that morning and did not learn about the fire until he got there, went immediately to the insurance office to ascertain what coverage Emerson had. The value of the house had been set at $5,000. It was insured for but half that. Hoar next ascertained the state of Emerson's savings account. Not satisfied with what he learned, he transferred a sizable sum of his own money into it. Then he returned to Concord and sought out the Emersons to offer sympathy and help. Even then, with others, he was scheming to find means for them to rebuild.

On seeing Emerson, Judge Hoar could tell his ordeal had exacted a heavy price. He did not know then, however, that that morning Emerson had "felt something snap in his brain."[7] Most probably, he had suffered a mild stroke. In the days that followed, his memory failed at an accelerated rate and every hair on his body fell out. Many months were to pass before it grew back again.[8] That afternoon Judge Hoar inspected the house, then swept out the barn himself so that salvaged furniture could be stored there. Temporarily, Emerson's books and papers had been stored in a room under the town library. The judge had these removed to a room in the courthouse, choosing one that could be used also for a study.

At the Manse, Lowell and his daughter Nina stayed for tea, and Lidian mentioned that she did not grasp the true pathos of the day's events until she saw "the procession of homeless rats," driven out of the house by the fire, "starting across the field into the wide world." She owned herself cheered, though, by the realization that the rats soon would establish themselves in other households. Nina, appalled, probably wondered if something had snapped in Lidian's head. She knew nothing of Lidian's great fondness for animals. ''I have suffered more from the sufferings of animals,'' Lidian said once, ''than I ever have from my own.''[9]

Further invitations came in the days immediately following. James Elliot Cabot, then summering at Beverly Farms, offered the use of his winter home in Brookline. At Newport, Anne Lynch Botta, one of Emerson's New York admirers, expressed her eagerness to receive them. James and Annie Fields offered them shelter at their home on Charles Street. To Annie, Lidian wrote a week after the fire:

> We are most happily settled in the ''Old Manse,'' where our
> cousin, Miss Ripley, assures us we can be accommodated — to her
> satisfaction as well as our own — until our house is rebuilt. . . .
> I should not use such a word as ''calamity,'' for truly the whole
> event is a blessing rather than a misfortune. We have received
> such warm expressions of kindness from our friends, and have
> witnessed such disinterested action and brave daring in our town's
> people, that we feel — in addition to our happiness in the sympa-
> thy of friends in other places — as if Concord was a large family
> of personal friends and well-wishers.[10]

The Emersons had more to be thankful for than Lidian acknowl-edged. A day or two after his first visit, Lowell appeared again at the Manse and, on his departure, left an envelope with Emerson. In it Emerson found a check for $5,000 from Lowell, his children, and a few other friends. It was intended for their current needs. Lowell had made the gesture, Emerson said afterward, ''like the great gentleman he is, and let us have his visit without a word of this.''[11] To Lowell, Emerson wrote on 2 August: ''Your wonderful note bewilders me. I am accustomed to the kindness and nobility of my friends, but a gift like this I hardly dare to receive. Let me sit and think of it. It seems to imply a sacrifice somewhere which I ought not to permit. Let me think of it twice. . . . Meanwhile let me enjoy my wonder at the good-ness of my friends.''[12] Lowell was a millionaire cotton manufacturer whose industry had, a few years before, helped provide the North the sinews of war. When he died, two years later, Emerson wrote a lengthy profile of him in his journal.[13] Before the Civil War Lowell had been one of those who opposed the abolitionist movement. Emerson could forgive him his conservatism even as Lowell could forgive Emerson his radicalism. When Emerson identified him as ''A man of a quiet inward life, silent and grave, but with opinions and purposes which he quietly held and frankly stated,'' he might have been describing him-self. Of his munificence when Bush burned, Emerson wrote, ''The character of the giver added rare value to the gift, as if an angel brought you gold.'' An offer of a further $5,000 came from Caroline Sturgis Tappan, hard on the heels of Lowell's gift. This Emerson refused, protesting that no more money was needed. He would find, however, that many good friends thought otherwise.

Moving back to the Old Manse gave Emerson a sense of the circle closing. He had worked on *Nature* while he was there, at the outset of his writing career. Now, living there again, he sensed that his writing days were done and expressed regret that the essays and pieces he had intended to write would never be written. The state of his papers, of course, did not ease his state of mind. Daily, both morning and afternoon, he went to the courthouse to try to sort out the mess. He rejoiced when Alcott brought to him two books which he was certain had been lost, his father's *History of the First Church* and Rantoul's *Nineteenth of April Oration.* Yet Emerson reproached himself for not remembering to rescue Fustel de Coulanges's *Cité antique* and Taine's *English Literature,* which, for safekeeping, he had stored in chocolate bags.[14] This work of salvaging and taking inventory was heartbreaking for Emerson, even more than it was backbreaking, and he soon became physically ill.[15] On 11 August he wrote Furness: ''It is too ridiculous that a fire should make an old scholar sick: but the exposures of that morning and the necessities of the following days which kept me a large part of the time in the blaze of the sun have in every way demoralized me for the present, — incapable of any sane or just action.'' After offering Furness illustrations of his growing forgetfulness, he added, ''These signal proofs of my debility and decay ought to persuade you at your first northern excursion to come and ruminate and renew the failing powers of your still affectionate old Friend.''[16]

Meanwhile, unknown to Emerson, Dr. Le Baron Russell, who for some time had thought Emerson should not feel compelled to lecture, quietly circulated a suggestion that Emerson's friends express their affection. On 13 August, Judge Hoar received from him a check for $10,000 with instructions to deposit it in Emerson's bank account and then tell him about it. When Hoar brought the bankbook and a letter from Russell to Emerson, he led into the matter tactfully. Emerson's friends, he said, had made him treasurer of an association that wanted him to go to England to view the restoration work being done on Warwick Castle and other noted buildings in Britain lately damaged by fire. The association would benefit from the information obtained in carrying out the restoration of a local building recently visited by fire. Hoar then gave him Russell's letter. Only when Emerson read the opening sentence — ''It seems to have been the spontaneous desire of your friends, on hearing of the burning of your house, to be allowed the pleasure of rebuilding it'' — did he see the situation for what it was. Thereupon he soberly invoked the concept of self-reliance only to

have the judge counter with a reminder that "this was the spontaneous act of friends, who wished the privilege of expressing in this
way their respect and affection, and was done only by those who thought
it a privilege to do so." Awed by the sum in the bankbook, Emerson
reserved his decision on whether or not to accept it until he could see
the list of contributors.[17] When the list presently was sent to him and
he saw the names — Hillard, Caroline Tappan, Forbes, Thomas Gold
Appleton, and many others — he was overwhelmed. He wrote to Hoar:

> It cannot be read with dry eyes or pronounced with articulate
> voice. Names of dear and noble friends; names also of high respect
> with me, but on which I had no known claims; names, too, that
> carried me back many years, as they were of friends of friends of
> mine more than of me, and thus I seemed to be drawing on the
> virtues of the departed. Indeed, I ought to be in high health
> to meet such a call on heart and mind, and not the thoughtless
> invalid I happen to be at present.

In the same letter he spoke of himself as being "an imbecile most of
the time, and distracted with the multiplicity of nothings I am pretending to do."[18]

Emerson wrote also to Russell, declaring, "This late calamity, however rude and devastating, soon began to look more wonderful in its
salvages than its ruins." Though protesting that he could "hardly feel
any right to this munificent endowment," he went on to say that it
left "some new aspirations in the old heart toward a better deserving."[19] But the new aspirations were slow in appearing. When Ellen
took him to Waterford, Maine, to get him away from the depressing
reminders of his loss, he passed his time brooding about the disposition
of his manuscripts. He could not rid himself of the thought that he
was coming to the end of his days.

"The best use you can make of it is to go to Egypt with it," Judge
Hoar had said to Emerson when he passed him the fabulous bankbook.
Out of this chance remark, meant to beguile Emerson into accepting
the gift, plans evolved for another European journey that would, in
fact, include a visit to Egypt. The prospect of seeing old friends again,
including Carlyle, was certain to quicken Emerson's spirits. Moreover,
while he was gone, Bush could be restored without any of the burden
of decision-making falling on him. Judge John S. Keyes, whose daughter Annie was about to become engaged to Edward Emerson, volunteered to supervise the work. William Ralph Emerson, a cousin, offered his services as architect. Lidian's advice would be sought at every
turn. This project exactly suited her. For years a lack of funds had
thwarted her ambitions to redecorate and make a few structural changes,

such as creating a bay for the dining room. While "Emerson was set free to travel and recruit his powers," Lidian could stay home and recruit hers.[20] A marvelous opportunity was opening up for Ellen, too, whose life until now had been lived in the shadow of others. She would travel as her father's companion.

Late in August the dispossessed Concordians went for a month to the Forbeses' island "principality" of Naushon to lay final plans for the trip abroad. From there, on 20 September, Emerson wrote Charles Eliot Norton with something of his old assurance: "For my recent disaster — it was of course a rude shock to an old householder who had hoarded all his books & papers & stuffs & trinkets & day-labors & habits in fixed corners, to find them or lose them thrown out on the grass in his door-yard."[21] He spoke of the riches of friendship as well as of the money that had poured in. Even then, both kinds of riches still pursued him. On 21 September he wrote to George Bancroft, thanking him for a gift of $1,000 to the Emerson Voyage and Reconstruction Fund that raised the total to $17,620.[22] In October, Russell sent yet a further check for $1,020. "Are my friends bent on killing me with kindness?" Emerson asked. "It appears that you all will rebuild my house and rejuvenate me in my old days abroad on a young man's excursion."[23] Recalling the help given Chicago, burned the previous November, he wondered if the Emersons had become another Chicago!

After Emerson's death, Russell wrote:

Those who have had the happiness to join in this friendly "conspiracy" may well take pleasure in the thought that what they have done has had the effect to lighten the load of care and anxiety which the calamity of the fire brought with it to Mr. Emerson, and thus perhaps to prolong for some precious years the serene and noble life that was so dear to us all.[24]

This unlooked-for largesse came to Emerson, as well, as a vindication of the way in which he confronted life. Many who came to his support were people who did not share his outlook in many things, including theology, politics, and social issues. His integrity had triumphed over the trials that had beset society in his lifetime. To his fellowman he brought new dignity, and he had helped to make Boston a mecca for those seeking enlightenment. Emerson was too humble to realize it, but they knew the true debt was on their side.

74. Charles Eliot Norton
The Visible God

*I*N April 1872 Carlyle wrote to Emerson that Froude, "the valuablest Friend I now have in England," was going to the United States in October. He asked Emerson to do his "best and wisest towards him."[1] Despite the troubles that had been besetting him, Emerson obliged, helping to arrange Froude's lecture tour in America and traveling to New York for the sole purpose of speaking, on 15 October, at a banquet honoring him.

On 23 October, Emerson and Ellen sailed for England aboard the *Wyoming*. Edward, who was already in England, advised Carlyle of his coming, at the same time explaining that while Emerson was eager to see him, he did not want to see his other British friends until he had given the Mediterranean climate opportunity to mend him in mind and body. At Cheyne Row, where Emerson called on 7 November, Carlyle took him in with a long slow look, then enfolded him in a welcoming embrace. They talked for two or three hours in Carlyle's study and things went much as expected. Emerson spoke of men, now to the fore, whom he admired; Carlyle made mincemeat of some and left the others much diminished. Emerson thought it noteworthy that Carlyle, eight years his senior, still had his memory intact while his own was fast leaving him. He found Carlyle unchanged in other ways, too. To Sam Ward he wrote: "I found in London, the other day, my old Carlyle, whose inimitable soliloquy rather than talking it is a pity you did not permit yourself to hear."[2]

Troubled with a lame foot, Ellen could not go with her father to see Carlyle, so on the ninth Carlyle came to see her at Down Street, where the Emersons had taken quarters lately vacated by the Lowells. They could have spent a further evening together, on the eleventh, when Charles Eliot Norton had the Emersons to dinner, but Norton did not find Carlyle at home when he drove to Cheyne Row to invite him.[3] Emerson apparently made up the loss because Norton noted afterward that he had, during the evening, ''talked admirably, with great discrimination, of Carlyle.'' Since Norton had now drawn close to Carlyle, Emerson's remarks cannot have been antagonistic.

From late November until April, the Emersons traveled on the Continent and in Egypt. One April afternoon, when Norton spent a quiet few hours with Carlyle at Cheyne Row, Carlyle spoke of the difference in outlook separating Emerson and himself:

> ''He seems verra content with life, and takes much satisfaction in the world, especially in your country. One would suppose to hear him that ye had no troubles there, and no share in the darkness that hangs over these old lands. It's a verra strikin' and curious spectacle to behold a man so confidently cheerful as Emerson in these days. Well, it may be as you say. I'm not such a verra bloody-minded old villain after all,'' (here a cordial laugh), ''not quite so horrid an ogre as some good people imagine. But the warld is verra black to me. . . . . There's nothing to hope for from it but confusion.''[4]

William Allingham, the Irish poet, called at Cheyne Row on the afternoon Carlyle intended to bid Emerson a last farewell. Carlyle lingered there unnecessarily long, reaming out an old pipe. When he finally set out, Allingham accompanying him, he chose a roundabout way. After an interval, he consulted his watch, concluded it was too late to achieve his purpose, and turned homeward. To Allingham it seemed as though Carlyle had wanted to avoid that last, sad parting. And indeed he did. He had his dates wrong. Emerson had left London the previous day! But he had reason to be touched with melancholy. That week John Stuart Mill had died at Avignon. Mill had helped facilitate his first meeting with Emerson. Now, it seemed, the two men were being withdrawn simultaneously from his life. And Norton, too, was going. On 8 June, Carlyle wrote in his notebook: ''Emerson, and Norton with family, sailed for Boston from Liverpool, 15th of last month. Kind parting with both, from Norton almost a pathetic, not to meet again.''[5]

In London that spring, when Emerson learned that Norton was ending his long exile abroad, he booked passage for Ellen and himself aboard the same ship, the *Olympus.* As they all sailed down the Mersey on the tug that was meeting the steamer, the weather was closing in, the day getting gloomier by the minute. And Norton's mood kept pace with it. Three months before, at Dresden, his wife had died giving birth to their fifth child. He felt now that the best part of his life was ending and was hardly in a fit state to consort with the prince of optimists. His account of the next ten days, spent chiefly in Emerson's company, shows how Emerson strove to reanimate his spirit.[6]

Although the *Olympus* was carrying more than a thousand passengers, only fifty of these were traveling cabin class. In that small company Norton had Emerson much to himself. He used the opportunity to assess him narrowly.

Norton had begun sidling up to Emerson twenty years earlier, probably, at the outset, as a way of dissociating himself from his father's conservatism. In 1903, when the centenary of Emerson's birth was marked, Norton recalled the surprising beginning of their friendship. He had supposed that Emerson might "incline to hold back from more than merely formal acquaintance" with him because his "father had been conspicuous in opposition to the drift of his teachings and had used language of severe condemnation of them." But Emerson, "too high-minded" for that, had, from their first meeting, treated him "with a simple graciousness and frank confidence" that he had repaid with "affection and reverence."[7]

At the start of his friendship with Emerson, Norton's father died. That seems to have left a vacuum which Emerson filled. Norton found his optimism a true tonic for the age and, more specifically, for himself. When *The Conduct of Life* was published, a few months before the Civil War broke out, he told Clough that, by confirming moral principles based on eternal laws, the book suited precisely the needs of the day.[8] By 1870, however, now into his forties, Norton, without being ready to admit his father had been right in the long run, was ready to suggest that Emerson had been right only in the short run: "No best man with us has done more to influence the nation than Emerson, but the country has in a sense outgrown him. He was the friend and helper of its youth; but for the difficulties and struggles of its manhood we need the wisdom of the reflective and rational understanding, not that of the intuitions."[9]

During the next three years Norton's friendship with Carlyle had deepened, as did his affection for those who spoke for rationalism in England. Their combined efforts wore away the nap of his optimism. Gloomy day or radiant day, Emerson did not need to spend many minutes in Norton's company before realizing that the glow had left his spirit. Nearly fifty years before, on a ten-day voyage, Emerson had sought to implant God in Murat's heart. Now, given a like span of time, he undertook to reignite Norton's faith. But Norton, like his father, was certain that he had the answers, not Emerson. As a result,

he left a unique record that he supposed constituted a true account of
Emerson's inflexibility but that in fact confirmed his own.

Day after day, in chill and gloom, the *Olympus* plowed the Atlantic.
All that gloom lodged in Norton's rational soul. "I had little talk with
anyone but Emerson," he related. And that came when they smoked a
cigar together, sometimes in the course of the day and, finally, at night,
when the women and children had retired, and the two men sat in the
saloon from nine until eleven when the lights were put out.

Emerson's success in adapting to those dreary days bothered Norton. He said: "Emerson was the greatest talker in the ship's company.
He talked with all men, and yet was fresh and zealous for talk at
night." It is a measure of the setness of Norton's mind that he took
Emerson at his word when Emerson told him: "I have never known
what it was to be ill for a whole day." Grudgingly, Norton concluded:
"His temperament is happily mixed; he has had entire health." "Age,"
he decided, "shows in him no apparent weakening of faculties, unless
in occasional failure of memory."[10] Although Emerson's health had
benefited from his tour abroad, the illness that would retire him from
all meaningful activities in the years directly ahead had already laid
its grip on him. To many the change was evident. That Norton suspected nothing further attests to his brooding preoccupation with self.
The price Emerson paid for "entire health," he thought, was a kind
of self-deception: "There is not a touch of vanity or conceit in him;
all sweet and pure and generous. . . . The very sweetness of his being,
at times, obscures his moral, or at least his intellectual perceptions."[11]
Norton seemed to be voicing Carlyle's convictions as his own.

Trying to communicate to the troubled younger man some of the
serenity he himself enjoyed, Emerson systematically laid out his philosophy before him, but Norton would have none of it. He wrote:

> . . . never before in intercourse with him had I been so impressed
> with the limits of his mind. His optimistic philosophy has hard-
> ened into a creed, with the usual effects of a creed in closing the
> avenues of truth. He can accept nothing as fact that tells against
> his dogma. . . . To him this is the best of all possible worlds,
> and the best of all possible times. He refuses to believe in disorder
> or evil. Order is the absolute law; disorder is but a phenomenon;
> good is absolute, evil but good in the making.[12]

Unable to point to anything in Emerson's conduct that affirmed the
bankruptcy of his thought, Norton fell back on the idea that its flaws
became evident when others sought to apply it: "Such inveterate and
persistent optimism, though it may show only its pleasant side in such
a character as Emerson's, is dangerous doctrine for a people. It degen-

erates into fatalistic indifference to moral considerations, and to personal responsibilities.''[13] If all men thus were tasked with the consequences of their thought when misapplied, none would escape censure. Substituting his own rationalism for his father's dogmatism, Norton rendered a sterner verdict on Emerson than Andrews had.

At one point Norton set a snare for Emerson only to be thwarted by Emerson's humility. Norton said: ''He blushed like a youth one day when I spoke to him of his influence on the men of my generation; and of its being one of the chief factors of the intellectual condition of America at the present time.'' Since Norton deplored the intellectual condition of America in that day, he can only have been indulging his cynicism when he said this. He found Emerson's response frustrating: ''He . . . would not admit the idea of his influence, he had done nothing to give direction to the intellectual tendencies of the nation, he had only been in sympathy with what had proved to be the prevailing national currents of thought and feeling.''[14] This was a sound transcendental answer consistent with the thinking of the author of *Representative Men.*

Emerson seemed to have given his views with the therapeutic intent of impelling Norton to elevate his moods: ''The moral element in man is always uppermost, is supreme, is progressive. . . . The order of the external world, the beauty of it, are the proofs that the internal, the spiritual is in accord with the hopes and instincts of man and nature for their perfection.'' He thrust at Norton pithy, epigrammatic phrases:

> Order, goodness, God are the one everlasting, self-existent fact. I measure a man's intellectual sanity by his faith in immortality. Of course a wise man's wish for life is in proportion to his wisdom. . . . It is not credible that a sane man should not wish for life. If you tell me that sorrow has deprived life of its worth and joy to you, that you do not care for more of it, — I must count you diseased, and must send you to the doctor or the mad-house.[15]

Possibly Norton baited him, to see how far he could draw him out on this topic. But here, under the pretext of addressing society at large, Emerson was making a strong personal appeal to Norton to shake off life-threatening moods of depression. Norton's response may even have heightened his concern: ''I found it in vain to suggest instances of misery, of crime, in society, of apparent ruthlessness and disorder in nature, to his view. He would not entertain them. His faith was superior to any exceptions.''[16]

On one of the gloomiest days of the voyage, when the skies were leaden and the ship pitched wildly, Emerson, who had served a lengthy apprenticeship humoring Lidian, sought to give Norton a boyish demonstration of the positive forces watching over the universe. ''How in Heaven's name did Columbus get over!'' Norton had exclaimed. He recounted what followed:

> ''Not so much of a wonder after all,'' said Emerson, ''he had his compass and that was enough for such a soul as his.'' The miracle of the magnet, the witness of the Divine spirit in nature; type of the eternal control of matter by spirit of fidelity to the unseen and the ideal. ''I always carry,'' he added, ''a little compass in my pocket. I like to hold the visible god in my hand.''[17]

In spite of himself, Norton was impressed.

Emerson must have retired to his cabin filled with apprehensions after some of the nighttime sessions with Norton in the forsaken saloon. One wonders what further somber reflections Norton entertained as he paced the darkened deck unattended until midnight drew on. If he thought proof of the fundamental wholesomeness of Emerson's thought was lacking, he had only to consider Emerson's remarks on the man who had appointed himself his nemesis — Andrews Norton:

> Emerson spoke, as he has done in past years to me, with strong feeling of my Father's kindness to him when he came to him desirous to enter the Divinity School, but uncertain whether, owing to weakness of eyes, he would be able to do all that was required of the students. He spoke of the admiration and respect with which all his pupils regarded my Father; of the strong impressions his earnestness, his thoroughness, his sincerity made on them; of the weight and wit of his words. His sayings were treasured. ''We all waited on his lips.''[18]

To this evidence of Emerson's magnanimity, Norton could make no answer. A practical demonstration of the moral force of his ''generous confidence in the universe and in man,'' it routed cold logic.

A further demonstration appears in a disclosure made to Norton as they talked. Norton said: ''He was hardly prepared for the amount of feeling produced by his 'Divinity School Address'. . . ; the thoughts in it were natural to him, and he was intimate with men who sympathized in the main with him, — such as Bartol, Hedge, William Channing, and Ripley.''[19] If this was so, then the rough handling he received from Andrews Norton and those who rallied to Norton's standard must have pained him more than he had previously been willing to concede, though, of course, the enduring pain came in having the doors of the academic world shut against him.

Although Emerson's recent ill health, his consciousness of his waning vigor, and the realization that he had had his final parting with Carlyle and other European friends might have weighed on his spirits, Emerson, maybe in part for Norton's sake, did not give way to them. Only once did he indulge in anything that could be construed as a lamentation and then in a tone that Norton was compelled to concede was "semi-humorous." The day before their arrival, 25 May, was Emerson's seventieth birthday. At breakfast he remarked, "The day is a melancholy anniversary for me. I reckon my seventieth birthday as the close of youth."[20] Before the day was out, Norton paid him tribute by striking off a poem exalting Emerson's enduring youthfulness. And privately in his journal he reiterated this sincere compliment: "His fidelity to his early ideals gives him perennial youth."[21] Norton himself, caught in the trough of middle life, lacking a commitment, uncertain of his future goals, sensing at forty-five that his own youth was spent (Henry James spoke of him as "dissipated"), lacked the strength that fidelity to early ideals could give him. When the *Olympus* arrived in Boston the next day at sunset, Norton departed the ship under cover of darkness. Emerson, however, forestalled his departure to step ashore next day in the brightness of the morning.

Despite his conviction that he had outgrown Emerson, Norton had found Emerson's company on shipboard more bracing than the maritime air. To Lowell he wrote soon afterward: "Emerson . . . made the voyage pleasant to me. . . . He had a spirit of perennial youthfulness. He is the youngest man I know."[22]

When Norton paid his centennial tribute to Emerson in 1903, when he himself was seventy-five, his mind was fixed not on the harm Emerson had done but on his role as a force for good. By then he had edited collections of Emerson's letters, to Carlyle and to Ward, and his spirits had mellowed. He quoted Emerson: "To every serious mind Providence sends from time to time five or six or seven teachers who are of the first importance to him in the lessons they have to impart. The highest of these not so much give particular knowledge as they elevate by sentiment, and by their habitual grandeur of view." Norton then added: "And of these highest inspired men whose acquaintance is beyond price, and who elevate those who come into relations with them by sentiment and habitual grandeur of view, was Emerson himself."[23] He concluded, speaking tenderly of the man who, in ten days' tutelage, undid the worst effects of a three-year indoctrination in British rationalism and Carlylean gloom, and may well have kept him from throwing himself one midnight into the angry Atlantic: "Emerson's fame is secure. . . . In long future time men seeking to elevate and liberate their souls will find help in the words and example in the character of Emerson."[24] Norton had at last survived his guilt and realized that, in finding his role model not in Andrews Norton but in Ralph Waldo Emerson, he had been right after all.

On the morning of 27 May 1873, Edward Emerson joined his father and sister on the deck of the *Olympus*. Before they could disembark, however, they were intercepted by Judge Russell, collector of the Port of Boston, who chatted with them so long they missed the eleven o'clock train to Concord. Inasmuch as the next train did not leave until two-thirty, Emerson decided to pay a visit to James T. Fields. There, at the house on Charles Street, the Emersons were cordially received. Emerson and Fields had much more to talk about than men and letters. During Emerson's absence, the heart of Boston — sixty-four acres — had been consumed by fire, including what remained of the neighborhood of his boyhood and even Trinity Church, where his Haskins grandparents were buried.[25]

Only Edward knew that Judge Hoar had asked Judge Russell to detain Emerson long enough to miss the early train.[26] To pay homage to Emerson on his return and the occasion of his birthday, the town of Concord had prepared a mammoth welcome for him. At a cost of thirty dollars a band had been hired. By his gate workmen had reared a triumphal arch that had taken two days to construct. The word ''WELCOME'' surmounted it. Throughout Concord posters and handbills announcing the reception had been distributed. A procession of citizens and school children would be formed at the railroad station to escort Emerson to his home.

An elaborate set of signals had been devised to let Concord know of Emerson's approach. The bells would ring a dozen times if Emerson was on the noon train, three times if he was on the train due in at half past three. The bells had already sounded to announce a noon arrival when a telegram came saying he would be on the later train. As an extra precaution, John Murray Forbes asked the president of the Fitchburg railroad to have his engineer sound his whistle at Walden. Not only did the engineer oblige, he sounded it all the way in from Walden. By then everyone on the train knew something unusual was in prospect — except possibly Emerson.

The day was warm, the band, equipped with horns of multiregister, played lustily. The townspeople shouted, droves of school children, herded to the scene from schools as far distant as four miles, shouted. The train passengers hung out the windows, adding their three cheers and huzzahs. Lines of carriages were assembled in front of the depot.[27] A few days after Emerson's arrival, John Holmes, who had seen Emerson in Paris a few months earlier and had marked then his failing condition, wrote to Lowell: ''I am told that Mr. Emerson had a reception at the Station in Concord and that he inquired of his daughter what was the meaning of all these people being there.''[28]

The band set off down Main Street. A double row of carriages followed. The Sanborns, with Bronson Alcott and Louisa, were in one. Judge and Mrs. Hoar rode in a second carriage, abreast of them. Then came Judge Keyes, Edward's father-in-law-to-be, and his family. And then Emerson and Ellen in an open barouche, with Ellen standing occasionally to return the greetings of the crowd. She supposed she was the object of their welcome because she had lately been reelected to the school committee. The Forbeses, their children included, had piled into the barouche, too. The wonder would have been if Emerson was *not* confused by what was happening.

The crowd, in carryalls, on horseback, on foot, cutting across the fields, hurried ahead of the barouche and got to Bush first. The school children gave a shrill rendition of ''Home, Sweet Home.'' The barouche passed under the arch and entered the drive. Emerson disembarked at the east door, where Lidian waited to receive him. He could see at a glance that Bush was restored.[29] By the door, the new bay for the dining room jutted out. He went through the house and came out the front door, passing down the path to the gate to acknowledge the multitude of cheering townspeople. He did not feel equal to saying anything. He went back into the house, then reemerged and walked a second time to the gate. He spoke a few words, which Alcott recorded in his journal. Emerson had thanked those present for ''this trick of sympathy to catch an old gentleman returned from his wanderings, being unmistakably the old blood surviving to compliment him.''[30] But he was not sure he had heard correctly. Edward later offered a smoothed-out version: ''My friends! I know that this is not a tribute to an old man and his daughter returned to their house, but to the common blood of us all — one family — in Concord!''[31] But he seems to have said nothing that coherent. He was still asking himself what he asked Ellen as the barouche came along Main Street and the Lexington road, ''What means this gathering? Is it a public day?''

The previous night, Alcott had come to the house with a birthday gift for Emerson, a copy of *Concord Days*, his newest book, warmly inscribed. Alcott preferred this quieter greeting. He knew that the tumult of the reception would embarrass Emerson. Yet when it came to pass, he thought Emerson stood it well.

The drama now was almost over. Concordians knew what restraint and privacy meant. The crowd gave three hearty cheers, then retreated, leaving the Emersons, a houseful of them, to honeymooners' seclusion. In a few days the whole town would be back for an open house, at the invitation of the Emersons, but for now a strenuous day was ended.

On 31 May, to welcome Emerson home, the Saturday Club held the most ambitious dinner in its history. In his journal that night Dana noted the presence there of Longfellow, Agassiz, Hoar, Appleton, Henry James, Sr., Whipple, Fields, Dwight, Charles Francis Adams, Charles W. Eliot, Francis Parkman, Cabot, Wyman, Hedge, Count Corsi, the Italian ambassador, and Robert Dale Owen. Summing it up, Dana said:

> It was really rather a brilliant gathering. Yet, as we sit at a long table, and the room is on the street, and, being warm, the windows open, we have no general conversation. All the talking is in sets, of two to four each. Towards the end of the dinner we change places a little. Emerson looks years younger for his European tour, and is in good spirits. Even his hair has come back, which had nearly left his head last summer. Mrs. Bell was asked what the Sphinx would say to Emerson, and she said, — "You're another."[32]

Space grants beyond his fated road
No inch to the god of day . . .

75. Mortifications and Remorses

*A*T forty-three, Emerson wrote: ''When summer opens, I see how fast it matures, & fear it will be short; but after the heats of July & August, I am reconciled, like one who has had his swing, to the cool of autumn. So will it be with the coming of death.''[1] At that time he had been making arrangements to procure a wheelchair for his mother, who had gone from a life of full vigor to one of limited function. Appalled though he was at the assassination of Lincoln, Emerson found in that event occasion to reflect on the advantages that came with dying before the perfection of one's powers yielded to the encroachments of old age. Not long before that he had entertained similar thoughts with reference to himself:

> Old age brings along with its uglinesses the comfort that you
> will soon be out of it, — which ought to be a substantial relief to
> such discontented pendulums as we are. To be out of the war, out
> of debt, out of the drouth, out of the blues, out of the dentist's
> hands, out of the second thoughts, mortifications, & remorses that
> inflict such twinges & shooting pains, — out of the next winter,
> & the high prices, & company below your ambition, — surely these
> are soothing hints. And harbinger of this, what an alleviator is
> sleep, which muzzles all these dogs for me every day![2]

The year following the Civil War, Emerson wrote in ''Terminus'':

> *It is time to be old,*
> *To take in sail: —*

627

The god of bounds,
Who sets to seas a shore,
Came to me in his fatal rounds,
And said: 'No more!'

He spoke these lines first to his son, Edward, in New York, where they met, paradoxically, as Edward was returning home from a journey and Emerson was setting forth on one. Edward said: "I was startled, for he, looking so healthy, so full of life and young in spirit, was reading his deliberate acknowledgment of failing forces and his trusting and serene acquiescence. I think he smiled as he read."[3] Before many months passed others saw what he had seen already, that his powers indeed were waning.

Conspicuous proof of Emerson's accelerating decline was his gradual abandonment of his journal. Beginning in 1872, the entries grew infrequent. By 1875, save for a few scattered notations, they ceased. By then he had lost interest in writing letters, as well.

John Burroughs, in 1877, detected similar evidences of decay in Emerson's most recent publications: "His corn is no longer in the milk; it has grown hard. . . . He has now ceased to be an expansive, revolutionary force."[4] These later works were, for the most part, assembled by Cabot from pieces Emerson had written earlier. In fact, the foreword he wrote in the summer of 1870 for William Goodwin's edition of Plutarch's *Morals* proved to be his last effort at composition for publication.[5]

As early as 1863, Emerson found that he was forgetting not only the names of friends but the names of things. By the mid-1870's he did not even pretend that this was not happening but made a joke of it. He spoke of his "naughty memory," which gave him but "fitful service." At the Saturday Club he explained to Holmes, "My memory hides itself."[6] Once, unable to think of the word for umbrella, he said, "I can't tell its name, but I can tell its history. Strangers take it away."[7] He might have been playing charades. George W. Smalley, whom he visited in London in 1873, said:

He could not recollect names. . . . He resorted to all kinds of paraphrases and circumlocutions. "One of the men who seemed to me the most sincere and clear-minded I have met was — you know whom I mean, I met him at your house, the biologist, the champion of Darwin — with what lucid energy he talked to us." When I mentioned Huxley's name, Emerson said, "Yes, how could I forget him?" But presently the name had to be given to him again.[8]

The time would come when even cherished names escaped him. When Cabot asked him about his beloved friend, the poet John Sterling, Emerson could not remember ever having heard of him. New names Emerson found it almost impossible to take in. Holmes said that a "natural slight and not unpleasant semicolon pausing of the memory" had always been characteristic of Emerson, and it was this trait that now became acute.[9]

Incidents multiplied. In November 1876 he read a paper at the centennial celebration of the Boston Latin School Association, and commented before he began reading: "I cannot remember anybody's name; not even my recollections of the Latin School. I have therefore guarded against absolute silence by bringing you a few reminiscences which I have written." At length he could not recollect his own name. Conway said that in those last years, when someone asked him how he felt, he answered, "Quite well; I have lost my mental faculties, but am perfectly well."[10]

When, on 6 February 1878 Emerson read his lecture "Education" at the Concord Lyceum, Ellen stood by to prompt him and to dispel such confusions as might arise. Anticipating the spectacle this would create, Emerson said: "A funny occasion it will be — a lecturer who has no idea what he's lecturing about, and an audience who don't know what he *can* mean!"[11]

His decline even put distance between Emerson and his own writings. At seventy-five he told Sanborn, "I have reached an age when I no longer remember what I have written." Rereading his own essays, he said to Ellen, on one occasion, "Why these things are really very good." Yet sometimes he complained about his method of writing much as his critics had complained. After examining some proofs, he said, "I get the impression in reading them that they talk too much about the same thing, but I cannot find out." Perusing *Representative Men,* he remarked, "I was amused in reading the pages; it seemed to me that something was omitted here — and here — and here."[12]

Writing to Lowell in the spring of 1879, Holmes said: "Emerson is afraid to trust himself in society much, on account of the failure of his memory and the great difficulty he finds in getting the words he wants. It is painful to witness his embarrassment at times."[13]

At the centennial observance of Emerson's birth, at Concord in 1903, Norton recalled his last visit with Emerson:

> His powers of recollection were imperfect, but his gracious
> benignity was unchanged. His talk had its old tone, though the
> intermittent thoughts sometimes failed to find perfect expression.
> As I was bidding him good-by at his hospitable door, his daughter,
> who proposed to go with me to the railroad station, urged him to

accompany us. "No," said he, "no, my dear, my good friend
whose name I cannot recall, has had quite enough of me today";
and then turning to me with a smile, as if to apologize for the
seeming lack of courtesy in his inability to recall my name, he said
in words and manner like his old self, "Strange that the kind
Heavens should keep us upon earth after they have destroyed our
connection with things!"[14]

Writing to Carlyle, sometime after this visit, Norton said:

> I have not seen Emerson since the winter, but I heard lately
> that he was physically well. His memory is quite shattered, and at
> times his mind moves as in dreams. I was told of his speaking the
> other day of the pleasure he had once had in a visit from you at
> Concord. The spiritual impression was too strong to be mastered
> by the feeble memory of fact.[15]

When Conway, on a brief visit in 1875, stayed overnight at Bush, he
found it melancholy to observe that Emerson now played the role of
listener exclusively, leaving conversation entirely to others. When he
came again in 1880, he saw that the situation had worsened. On 1 December 1881 Alcott wrote in a journal entry: "I call at Emerson's
seldomer than I would were I sure of his wish to meet his friends
during these days of obliviousness. There is pathos in his present lapse
from his genius. . . . It is an unexpected close of so fair a display of
gifts."[16]

"When one's wits begin to fail," Emerson had observed, "it is time
for the heavens to open and take him away."[17] He thought even suicide might be preferable to living long enough "to mar or undo one's
work."

When Emerson tried to lecture one last time, the effort was not his
but Ellen's. Asked what her father's topic would be, when he read at
the Concord School of Philosophy, Ellen's candid answer was, "I have
not decided."[18] To keep Emerson from harm on his daily walks, she
recruited the support of Concord friends, designating them "the body-
guard," their task being to keep an eye out for him, ready to guide
him home should he become bewildered or lose his way. In his study
now, he would pick up to read whatever lay on his table, reading it
over and over, whispering the words like a tot with his first primer.[19]

Norton found Emerson's state at Longfellow's funeral, on 26 March
1882, a Sunday, grave and disturbing:

> The most striking incident was Emerson's solitary approach to
> the coffin, and his long gaze at the face of the dead. Only the
> family and a few intimate friends went to the grave at Mt.

Auburn. Emerson was there — his memory gone, his mind wavering, but his face pure and noble as ever, though with strange looks
of perplexity wandering over it from time to time. The afternoon
was raw, grey, March-like. Emerson took my arm up the path to
the grave, — and his arm shook as we stood together there. I could
not but think of Longfellow's happier fate.[20]

Supposedly, at this time Emerson said of Longfellow, "That gentleman was a sweet, beautiful soul, but I have entirely forgotten his name."
Conway is the source of the story and he was not present, but it is not
hard to credit.

Much of the burden of caring for Emerson fell to Ellen, for Lidian
now was nearing eighty. On his death, Ellen wrote to Lowell to say
that the family was thankful the end had come.[21] Neither he nor they,
she owned, could have endured going on much longer. In time the
responsibilities Ellen assumed in caring for both her parents took their
toll. At intervals her nerves broke and she had to go away for rest
cures.

Cook and others made much of Emerson's resumption of churchgoing. Cyrus Bartol concluded that Emerson went regularly to meeting in his last days because he "feared the excesses of radicalism."[22]
In view of Emerson's deteriorating mental state that is unlikely. Edward Emerson's explanation that his family regularly attended church
and that his father went along because it offered sociality yet exacted
nothing from him in return seems adequate.[23] When, toward the end
of Emerson's life, Mary Baker Eddy visited him, hoping to convert
him to Christian Science, he was incapable of taking in her arguments.
He had survived all theology.

A month before he died, Emerson attended the centennial celebration of the Concord Social Circle, of which he was the senior member.
He was set at ease only when Judge Hoar advised the twenty-four
assembled members that they could not ask Emerson to speak but should
count themselves fortunate to have him physically present.[24]

Emerson took satisfaction during his last years in knowing that James
Elliot Cabot, upon being approached by the family, had agreed to be
his literary executor and biographer. Franklin Sanborn would have
liked to have been asked, but Emerson mistrusted his scholarship and
his character. Sanborn had once encouraged Ellen to believe that he
was her suitor but then let the pursuit grow cold. Emerson never for-
gave him this injury. Having Cabot as executor rather kept the job in
the family. His father-in-law, the fabled Thomas Handasyd Perkins,
was the granduncle of Edith Emerson's husband, Will Forbes. When
Emerson was told that Cabot had acquiesced, "his heart," Edward
said, "was set entirely at rest."[25]

One curious episode in Emerson's last years may have constituted his last rallying of forces. In the summer of 1878 he accompanied Ellen to a Unitarian convention at Saratoga, New York; with some sketchy directions supplied by Ellen, he went off on his own for several days, in quest of George Tufts, a young mechanic whose intermittent correspondence with him apparently had begun in 1863. Tufts had planned a book, never written — "Theory of the Relation of Human Action to the Economy of Nature" — and his spirited independence caused Emerson to think that he had found in him another of his "men." In December 1863 Emerson had sought to arrange a meeting with Tufts, but Tufts, ashamed of his shabby appearance, had failed to come. Since Tufts never had acted on Emerson's invitations to come to Concord, Emerson now courageously sought him out. But without success. The next year, at Emerson's bidding, Ellen sent Tufts his train fare. Tufts returned the sum and said other reasons kept him away.[26] Emerson's quest ended, but the hope lingered that he would have one further encounter with an inspiring protégé.

After visiting Emerson on his seventy-eighth birthday in 1881, Alcott wrote in his journal: "His chief inquiry, and repeated, was, had I found any new men in those parts. I could only reply, none, in his estimation of newness."[27] While he lived, Emerson never ceased his own personal Grail quest, his search for the complete universal man.

Though defeated every day, yet to victory I am born.

76. The Virginian Immolation

*T*HE story was picked up by newspapers in both the North and South. Emerson had accepted an invitation to address the joint public meeting of the Washington and Jefferson Literary Societies, one of the major events held during Commencement Week at the University of Virginia. A decade had gone by since the Civil War ended, but when an eminent abolitionist agreed to speak in a stronghold of Southern conservatism that was still news.[1]

Emerson had never lectured farther south than Washington. In recent years he had scarcely lectured anywhere. But the gesture the Southerners had made was a warm one. If it could help heal the wounds of alienation, he was glad to come speak to them.

The letter, sent by three law students, advising Emerson that he had been unanimously elected orator for their joint celebration, was sent on 25 November, Thanksgiving Day, 1875. He accepted on the first day of winter.[2] He had already shown he could put past grievances out of his thoughts. After the war he had acted to relieve the distress of his former classmate, Robert Barnwell, a South Carolinian, even though South Carolina had been the object of his maledictions after it had expelled Samuel Hoar over the slavery issue. Emerson was known as a man of peace. Since the twin literary societies had sent generous advance notice of their desire to have him come, he felt sure of the Southerners' cordiality. He would be speaking at Virginia on 28 June 1876, in the centennial year of the republic, a propitious time for a healing gesture.

A healing gesture called for a topic that had no hint of political controversy in it. Emerson chose ''The Natural and Permanent Functions of the Scholar.'' For as far back as ten years he had given versions of this talk elsewhere. He no longer found it easy to work on manuscripts, but, with Ellen's help, he worked on this one. Something of his old spirit took hold and, as had been his practice in the past, he worked on it up to the last minute, even on the night of the twenty-seventh, at Charlottesville, though he had come down with Ellen that day from Philadelphia and that evening had had to make an appearance at the Jefferson Society's celebration at Public Hall. Public Hall was a large rectangular building adjoining Thomas Jefferson's Rotunda, modeled after the Pantheon in Rome. It was a functional edifice, having more than a thousand gas lights and seating more than a thousand people.[3] There Emerson would speak the following night.

On the way south the Emersons had stayed over a day in Philadelphia to visit the Centennial Exhibition at Fairmont Park, as guests of William Furness and Sam Bradford, Emerson's two oldest friends. This was Emerson's last journey as a lecturer. There was something fitting, therefore, in his being able to see dear friends from the starting point of his journey through life, and to view with them the exhibition, which ''dazzled & astounded'' him with its wonders of the coming age. The man who had had the vision to forecast the invention of the phonograph and air warfare owned humbly that he ''had no idea of the glories'' he would find at the exhibition.

Great as the exhibition was, another topic dominated conversation everywhere that week, even in Philadelphia — the ambush and slaughter of General George Custer and two hundred and sixty-four men of the Seventh Regiment under his command, at Little Big Horn, by Sitting Bull's Sioux. To suggest that the two literary societies had schemed to ambush Emerson would be unjust. What they were guilty of was a lack of foresight. The South still smarted from the humiliation that came with defeat in war and the despoliation that took place afterward in the name of Reconstruction. That Emerson should be identified in the *Richmond Enquirer* as ''the gaunt figure of the Abolitionist philosopher of Boston,'' is indication enough of how the average Virginian viewed him. ''The visitors,'' Cabot said, ''were . . . constantly reminded that they were in an oppressed and abused country.''[4]

This rudeness did not originate with those responsible for bringing Emerson to Charlottesville. Upon their arrival, early on the afternoon of the twenty-seventh, the Emersons were received at the railway station by George Frederick Holmes, professor of history and literature at Virginia. By carriage Holmes conveyed them to the campus, at the city's outskirts, and to his home where they were to be his guests, a distinction he was to share with Mrs. Luther Emerson, a cousin's widow.[5] Holmes, at all times, was a gracious and thoughtful host. Professor

Southall, who taught international law at Virginia, was similarly solicitous, as were the three students — W. S. Perry, Alfred P. Thom,
and W. R. McKinney — who sent the original invitation. But neither
students nor faculty members took into sufficient account the irritability of their fellow Southerners at that time nor the frivolous, even
feckless, moods of those who had gathered at Charlottesville for Commencement Week.

The student population at the University of Virginia was all male,
but during Commencement Week a kind of courting ritual superseded
the regular routines. Mothers and sisters swarmed over the campus.
And belles, too, at a ratio of about two per beau — ages mostly seventeen to nineteen. Morning, noon, and night, during the lulls in the
formal program, the students danced. They danced in Washington Hall,
and in the library, cleared for that purpose, to the strains of an orchestra situated in a bandstand in the midst of the quadrangular Lawn;
and at night, in the giddy glow of countless multihued Chinese lan-
terns, they promenaded round and round the arcades that skirted the
lawn. For one and all the academic side of things ceased to matter.
This was hardly the setting into which to introduce any philosopher,
much less a Yankee one who carried the further stigma of being a self-
acknowledged abolitionist. Even had Emerson been in top form, he
would have been battling insurmountable odds. In fact, the previous
year a highly respected Commencement Week speaker, not a Yankee
but a native Virginian, not an abolitionist but an erstwhile secretary
of state for the Confederacy, a former congressman, a former senator,
Robert M. T. Hunt, had been all but shuffled into oblivion by a youthful audience that socialized while he talked, at a pitch that made him
inaudible. The faculty had deplored this and so had serious-minded
students but, with a want of chivalry which contradicts all legends of
Southern gallantry, ascribed the lapse to the distracting charms of
Virginia's belles.[6] The students who invited Emerson and the faculty
that received him knew that all the elements needed for a wholesale
disaster were present. Still, they took no precautions. They had as their
invited guest an elderly and ailing philosopher who also happened to
be the most respected living American, a man who, to come as an emissary of peace among them, had exerted himself beyond his strength.
And they were about to stand by and let him be cruelly humiliated.

On the night of the twenty-eighth, when the hour came for Emerson's lecture, the hot hall was filled to overflowing. The only empty
chairs were those on the platform, awaiting the speaker and his entou-
rage. The band began to play and, in a moment, the marshals came
through the doorway at the far end of the hall. Behind them, in formal
procession, came the professors of the university, the Board of Visitors, guests of distinction, and, at last, the illustrious speaker, Ralph

Waldo Emerson, escorted by the Honorable Benjamin Miles, the presiding officer. Applause rang out when the audience saw Emerson begin his progress down the aisle.

At last the powerful array of notables had filed into their seats on the platform, in front of a huge reproduction of Raphael's *School of Athens*, filling almost the whole of the wall — with what elegant irony Emerson then could not realize.[7] He was to stand at the lectern with this throng behind him, an arrangement he had always deplored. The band fell silent. The university chaplain delivered an invocation. Benjamin Miles stood before the multitude and introduced the speaker. "It was fit that Virginia should hear the sage of the North," he said. His coming was a sign of reunion. With some of this audience that sentiment alone could have been a signal for disorder.

Emerson came forward with his manuscript. A kerosene lamp, kept in readiness for him, was produced and situated so that the light fell on his pages. He began to speak and from the outset it was apparent something was amiss. Ellen's letter home, which for Lidian's sake held back some of the facts, fills in part of the picture: "The uproar of people coming in late and hunting seats continued some ten minutes into the address and I saw with dismay that Father's voice seldom rose clear above it, and all the young & gay . . . concluded they couldn't hear very well and had better enjoy themselves, so the noise rather grew than decreased."[8] Ellen had perceived this visit as the North extending "a right hand of fellowship" to the South and was reluctant to suggest that the proffered hand was struck aside. Yet her account of what next ensued portrays a scene of near-chaos:

Eight front rows; two knots of students, determined to hear, who left their seats and came up the two aisles, and stood; a like knot above on each side hanging over the gallery railings; and as many of the faculty, & "joint-committee-of-the-literary-societies" on the platform as were on a line with Father or before him, heard. Here & there people strained their ears in vain; and the larger part of the audience whispered together, while some talked & laughed aloud all the time. It was too bad.[9]

Emerson put the blame squarely on the audience, but Ellen felt that even if the audience had been quiet, "he could not have reached more than two thirds." But if Emerson was speaking loud enough to reach two-thirds of an audience of more than a thousand and, by Ellen's own reckoning, those in the first eight rows could not hear him, then the audience *was* at fault. Other information we have confirms this. Hoeltje, who tried to make out for the Virginians the best case he could, said:

The murmur rose and swelled until it became apparent that the speaker's voice must presently be wholly drowned in the hubbub. Of course the situation could not be tolerated by those having serious regard either for Emerson or for the University; hence Professor James F. Harrison, a bluff, energetic man of military experience, somewhat of a disciplinarian, rose to request silence and attention. But to no avail. Young Virginia was having a good time, and was not in a mood to be disturbed. Even Professor Charles Scott Venable, affable and popular with the students, could not secure quiet. The merry-making went on.[10]

It is pleasant to think that Emerson's adversary on this occasion was Cupid, that, as a student publication summed it up afterward, "When beauty pleadeth all orators are dumb," but that explanation does not answer the facts. Nor is it quite understandable how several rows full of faculty members and administrators could mutely tolerate so flagrant an insult to a venerable and illustrious visitor. One looks in vain in the annals of American academic life in the nineteenth century for an incident in which an honored guest was so egregiously dishonored.

In September 1882 Ellen prepared for James Elliot Cabot a full account of the visit to Virginia. There she owned that when she wrote to Lidian the day following the address she had "thought it best to make the pleasantest statement I could," so as not to distress her. But the facts had been distressing. Ellen estimated that the clamor was so great that "hardly a hundred people heard him." Even the young men who invited him "did not seem to care about him." She was forced to conclude that what occurred "was intentional hostility to a Northern man." The day following, as they traveled north by train, Ellen had suggested to Emerson that he might have made himself heard had his hosts fed him beforehand instead of leaving him to speak on an empty stomach. Emerson rejected this explanation summarily. "Not at all!" he said, "I was delighted that my voice was so loud. If they would have given me the *least* chance I should have made them hear. They had no manners."[11]

Despite his diminished state, Emerson grandly met this challenge with unerring tact. At the end of half an hour, while yet midway in his address, he caught a dozen or more pages in his hand and spun past them. "I see," he said serenely, "that you understand the drift of my thought; so I will proceed to the next subdivision." And soon he "sought out a suitable passage and swiftly came to a close."[12]

Evidence of calculated hostility was apparent in the newspaper accounts that followed. Two young graduates produced reports for the *Richmond Enquirer*, published on 30 June, that sought to put the university in a good light and the visitor in a bad one. An "immense auditory" had assembled to hear him. He had been received with applause. But he spoke "in a tone so low" that even those who sat within a few feet of him could only occasionally catch a good phrase. Most viciously, it was suggested that:

> Emerson has advertised himself and his "books" in a very characteristic New England style. His visit to the University of Virginia has probably been a profitable one to himself; it has certainly been profitable to no one else. . . . We have paid his expenses, and he has partaken of our Southern hospitality. Now he is about to return to Boston with his address in his carpet-bag, in order to put it "into a book," and receive a more substantial return than expenses and hospitality and applause.[13]

The "carpet-bag" allusion, of course, was singularly snide. No one was less exploitative than Emerson.

Five days later a local Charlottesville paper, the *Jeffersonian Republican,* contributed a further slur. After Emerson spoke, Professor Schele De Vere had made a few brief and witty remarks while presenting an award to a student. This discourse was, said the paper, "a refreshing treat, following as it did Mr. Emerson's; it was a shower of rain after a long, dry summer day."[14] Back at Holmes's house, after the lecture, the professor staged a reception in honor of the Emersons, but if any apologies were made to Emerson then or later, by university officials, by those who arranged the lecture, or even by Holmes himself, they went unrecorded. A request from Alfred Thom for a copy of the lecture for publication seems to have gone unheeded. One of the Richmond reporters professed to be miffed because Emerson had rejected a similar request from him.[15] He quoted Emerson as saying that he hated the press and had been at war with it all his life. In fact, Emerson had long been distressed with newspapers' pirating his speeches or quoting him inaccurately. Long before, at Dartmouth, he had told a student reporter, "I curse the reporters, I curse them."[16] Emerson came away from Virginia with abundant reasons for cursing the press there. Evidence of Emerson's true magnanimity is found in the sole comment he made to Cabot when Cabot tried to draw him out on the ignominious treatment he received from the Virginians: "They are very brave people down there," Emerson said, "and say just what they think."[17]

Those who cared had been courteous and kind to Emerson while he was in Charlottesville, so he did not leave Virginia without some experience of Southern hospitality. And on the journey north, other passengers approached him again and again, people from Alabama, Texas,

Tennessee, and elsewhere, expressing their pleasure at meeting him and asking for a handshake. At Washington, Bret Harte took him under his care, as did the librarian of Congress, giving him a wonderful day. Yet Emerson was mysteriously silent about his Virginian ordeal thereafter. In 1847 he had written in his journal: "The question recurs whether we should descend into the ring. My own very small experience instructs me that the people are to be taken in very small doses." But seven years later Emerson declared: "I am here to represent humanity: it is by no means necessary that I should live, but it is by all means necessary that I should act rightly. If there is danger, I must face it. I tremble. What of that? So did he who said, 'It is my body trembles, out of knowing into what dangers my spirit will carry it.'"[18]

In Virginia Emerson's long contemplation of martyrdom reached its culmination. Not for him was the mob that stripped Garrison and dragged him through the streets of Boston; not for him the blows of the craven bully who left the defenseless Sumner all but lifeless in his Senate seat; not for him the assassin's bullet that felled the century's greatest man of action in America, Abraham Lincoln, in whose fate Emerson saw a new beacon light for mankind. For Emerson — the century's greatest man of ideas in America — destiny had reserved a flagellation of the spirit that would leave no visible marks but would lacerate his lofty soul with wounds no less real than those that maulings, cudgels, and bullets could inflict upon his body. He recognized this ordeal for what it was and accepted it without malice, without reproach. He did not flinch or tremble. For those who sought to demean him he spoke only words of charity and forgiveness, thus fulfilling the mission of peace that brought him to the South, and, at the same time, attesting that truly he did represent humanity.

77. The Concord School
Alcott's Summer University

*I*N the summer of 1840, even while a curious public was scrutinizing the first issue of *The Dial*, letters flew between Emerson and Margaret Fuller as they sought to determine the contents of the next issue, due out in October. Both saw themselves involved beyond their original intentions, yet, not entirely in jest, Emerson now presented to Margaret another proposal that, had it been earnestly pursued, would have made *The Dial* seem at most a minor distraction in their lives. Alcott and he, freely fantasizing, had projected the founding, at Concord, of a liberal university, to be staffed by themselves and such like-minded men as Parker, Ripley, and Hedge. It was to be a winter school, running from October through March. Those who could not pay would not pay. The rich could make up the deficit. To Alcott Emerson consigned psychology, ethics, and the ideal life. For himself he reserved Beaumont and Fletcher, Percy's *Reliques*, rhetoric, belles-lettres. This was, in substance, his old dream, and the inference was that, by creating a college that would "front the world without charter, diploma, corporation, or steward," he might communicate his scorn to colleges that remained rooted in the past.[1] The curriculum of the new college, which would include modern literature and the modern crisis in theology, "would anticipate by years the education of New England."[2] Margaret was asked, "Now do you not wish to come here and join in such a work?" As it happened, she did not. Life was strenuous enough without pursuing these summer will-o'-the-wisps. No more was said and the plan was forgotten.

In 1878, however, the Concord university sprang alive again in the thoughts of Bronson Alcott. Now approaching eighty, Alcott lived with his dreams on more intimate terms than ever. To the annoyance of Louisa (who had subsidized with her labors too many of her father's whims), Franklin Sanborn took over the management of this particular dream for Alcott and called together a faculty for a Concord School of Philosophy and Literature that would meet, not in winter, but for six weeks in summer, beginning on 15 July.

The first sessions of the new school, opened in July 1879, were held in Alcott's old study in Orchard House. Among those recruited to speak, along with the dean of the new school, Alcott himself, were Emerson and Hedge — all three chosen for this faculty nearly forty years before when Emerson had first considered it. Although this powerful idea's time had come at last, had it come in its proper season those involved could have served it better. Emerson, for one, could not do much more now than gaze upon the scene with a look of beatific rapture. Yet the visitors seemed to understand. To come to Concord to see its long-celebrated citizens was like visiting a museum of antiquities. Day after day Elizabeth Peabody sat amid the learned faculty gathered in from other schools then on holiday, refreshing herself with water from the speaker's pitcher and downing peppermints from a pound package till the students actually placed bets among themselves on how many peppermints she would munch to destruction during a given lecture. Although in between times she appeared to doze, she always rallied her forces to leap into the discussion that came when a speaker ended his remarks.

The second year, on receiving a gift from Elizabeth Thompson of New York, Alcott built the Hillside Chapel behind Orchard House.[3] Here the school would hold future sessions.

The Emersons, living a short distance away, welcomed the academic visitors with an occasional tea party. A correspondent for the *Chicago Tribune* reported on one of them in 1880:

> Emerson's house was thrown open last Sunday evening, and parlor and study and hall were filled with friends from the town and the School of Philosophy. Mr. and Mrs. Emerson (whose quaint, sweet face and simple, old-fashioned attire suggested to one lady that "She might have just stepped off the *Mayflower*") bustled around, shaking hands and arranging chairs for the guests. Then Mr. Emerson rapped upon a door-jamb and said: "Some of our friends have something to say to us, and we shall be glad to have them begin." Mr. Channing, Mr. Alcott, Miss Peabody and Dr. Harris did most of the talking. Mrs. Emerson made a single remark, but the host took no part whatever. . . . He feels the weight of years, and though he walks about briskly, his memory is

failing, and he is often thrown into pathetic confusion by his treacherous faculty.[4]

On two occasions Emerson read papers to the Concord School, speaking on memory on 25 July 1879 and, on 2 August 1880, on aristocracy. These he delivered in the vestry of the Trinitarian Congregational Church so that the large numbers wishing to attend could be accommodated. On both occasions Ellen guided him through the bewildering procedure. Attendance at the regular lectures usually came to about forty people. When Emerson spoke, it quadrupled.[5]

For Chicago readers, the *Tribune*'s correspondent recreated one of Emerson's visits as observer to Alcott's spruce and hemlock chapel: "An old man with large eyes, prominent nose, and awkward carriage, may often be seen shyly stealing into the 'School of Philosophy,' just after the beginning of the lecture." Emerson made these furtive entrances, of course, because he did not want to draw attention away from the speaker. The account continued:

> Passing through the aisle on tiptoe, he seats himself in a huge earlap chair at the left of the platform. The lips of the Sphinx are sealed, and their peaceful expression and the far-away look in the eyes would seem to indicate that the discussion going on has not sufficient interest to draw him from the calm joy of reverie. But the way in which he leans forward now and then to catch the tones of an indistinct speaker, and the promptitude with which certain little red spots appear on his cheeks whenever a personal allusion or quotation is made, show that, after all, he is listening with respectful attention.[6]

Emerson's visits to the school actually were less frequent than the *Tribune*'s correspondent wanted his readers to believe — once or twice a summer, perhaps, and then only when the speaker was someone likely to interest him.[7]

Many who attended the school came especially to see Emerson. When it seemed that otherwise they would not see him at all, the bolder among them sought him at Bush. One enrollee, who came to his door in August 1881, left a record of his encounter. The visitor explained that he had called to pay his respects. Emerson thanked him. Small difficulties in articulation were evident as he continued, "I am glad to see you; yet I fear I can do little. I can only disappoint those who come to see me. I find that I am losing myself, and I wander away from the matter that I have in mind." At each attempt to continue, Emerson insisted his mind was not fit for conversation. "I cannot say much," he said, "when I begin to lose myself. And so when my friends come to see me

I run away, instead of going to meet them, that I may not make them suffer.'' When the visitor spoke of an examining committee that Emerson had served on at Harvard, his face became for a moment illumined. Then he recollected his present plight. ''Yes, yes . . . but I see no one now,'' he said, taxed obviously at straying beyond that one safe topic. Realizing the audience was ended, the visitor withdrew.[8]

Lidian, to everyone's surprise, took to the summer school with enthusiasm. An armchair near the platform was reserved for her, and she went daily to both the morning and afternoon sessions, hurrying through breakfast to arrive with the first arrivals and forgoing her afternoon nap.[9] This interest persisted even after Emerson's death. In her eighties she still went to all the lectures. The tea parties had been her idea, too. She conceived of them along the lines of the Alcott ''Conversations'' held at Bush in bygone times, or perhaps in the tradition of her husband's Sunday night causeries. As many as eighty people appeared at Bush for these receptions.[10] Had the School of Philosophy come to pass when the idea was first broached, in 1840, perhaps Lidian would have been offered a diversion that could have routed her melancholy. Yet for her, that option had always existed. Emerson would have entertained much more than he did had Lidian shown herself receptive to company. The truth is, when the Concord School arrived she was ready for it, but not before.

A Concord School in the 1840's may not have been right for Emerson, either. His hardships might have been fewer, but his achievements might have been fewer also. His thwarted vocation as pedagogue cultivated his vocation as essayist. One Alcott was enough for Concord village.

The Concord School was, for the Concord idealists, their last hurrah. For Emerson himself it ended a cycle, providing one of those circular patterns that so much intrigued him. The War of Independence had brought to Concord its first college. Ezra Ripley came to Concord then as a Harvard student and cemented ties that led to his permanent settlement there. Ezra's hospitality drew Emerson to Concord. Emerson's hospitality drew Alcott there. Through Alcott, Concord once more, for an interval, found itself a college town.

In the summer of 1882, less than three months after Emerson's death, on its sixth day in session, 22 July, the Concord School held an ''Emerson Commemoration.'' Sanborn made an introductory address. Bartol, now in his forty-sixth year as pastor of Boston's West Church, spoke on the insular Emerson, a man of ''keen, single perceptions.'' Alcott and Martha Lowe read poems celebrating Emerson, and Joel Benton's paper on Emerson's poetry was read, in Benton's absence, by George Cooke — ''No writer I know of soars so high. . . . What a supreme, audacious splendor!''[11] Dr. W. T. Harris — superintendent of public schools in St. Louis; founder and editor of the *Journal of Speculative Philosophy;* recognized head of the St. Louis Hegelians; and the new owner of Orchard House — examined "Dialectic Unity in Emerson's Prose." Dr. Alexander Wilder considered Emerson's role as philosopher. Ednah Cheney, Julia Ward Howe, and John Albee brought a welcome intimacy to the day by recalling personal encounters with Emerson.[12]

For such a tribute, Hillside Chapel would not suffice. Concord put its town hall at the disposal of those who arranged the commemoration. With affection the townspeople and the school staff decorated the walls and platform, including the speaker's desk, with evergreen boughs. A portrait of Emerson in old age hung on the front of the desk, facing the audience. On the wall behind the speakers, a second portrait, showing Emerson in the full vigor of manhood, was hung. And on a table strewn with evergreen, French's bust of Emerson looked out with serene assurance at those who had assembled. Morning and afternoon sessions were held, thronged by Emerson's friends and neighbors, by the scholars, and by visitors who had come from a distance.

Sanborn scoffed at those who spoke of Emerson's death as "the first great blow" the Concord School received. Even though Alcott had been left crippled by a stroke six months after Emerson died, the school continued for another six years.[13] But in those last years it existed as a memorial to the dreamers whose dream it had been.

The past restore, the day adorn,
And make tomorrow a new morn.

78. Some Final Partings

AT the newly renovated quarters of the Massachusetts Historical Society on Tremont Street, Dr. Samuel Green, the librarian, placed
a small table and two chairs in the Thomas Dowse library room, in
front of several rows of chairs. The day was a Thursday, for two and
a half centuries Boston's special day for sermons, lectures, and Harvard commencements. During the preceding fifty years, Emerson must
have lectured on a thousand Thursdays, one of them being the day
when his "American Scholar" address elevated him to renown. This
day, 10 February 1881, however, differed from all the others. Sitting
behind the table in one of two chairs provided, he was making his last
appearance outside of Concord as a lecturer. Seated next to him, Ellen
selected the pages for him to read and, when necessary, read along
with him.

The manuscript Emerson read from was more than thirty years old.
Yet if he had understood what he was reading he would have believed
it still. The occasion that brought him before his little audience — the
society's total membership was only a hundred — was a commemorative hour arranged by Robert C. Winthrop, the venerable president of
the society, out of respect to the memory of Thomas Carlyle, who had
died in London a week earlier and, on this day, as he had wished, was
being laid to rest with his parents at Ecclefechan, Scotland. As soon
as Carlyle's death was reported, Winthrop had written to Emerson,
asking him to participate in this tribute to the man whose popularity
in America he had done so much to enhance.[1]

Eight years had elapsed since Emerson last saw Carlyle. Nearly as long a time had gone by since any correspondence had passed between them. Before many more months, Emerson, standing in front of Carlyle's framed photograph on his study wall, would say, "That is that man — my man," without being able to recall Carlyle's name.[2] But, at the commemorative hour, he seemed to remember whose death it was that had called him out of seclusion for a public act that could not be refused. The words he read in the Dowse library room he had written in 1848, while a houseguest of the Carlyles at Cheyne Row. They rekindled his awareness, and he delivered his best lines well, not overlooking humor hidden in some of them. As he spoke, his listeners pulled their chairs in closer until they formed a knot of intimacy with him, not because the speaker was inaudible but to share in what was a solemn and special moment.

The manuscript Emerson read from had never been published and would not be in his lifetime. He read, as well, a letter he had written to Carlyle years before, and this, too, invited his listeners into a private world. Men would only later realize how much that was relevant to the history of nineteenth-century thought and letters was preserved in the Carlyle-Emerson correspondence, but enough of a hint was given that day to create high expectations.

Perhaps, as had been true so often in the past, thoughts of Carlyle had swept Emerson's memory back to the joyous moments of his first encounter with the Carlyles at their remote scrabble farm at Craigenputtock. Craigenputtock was now willed by Carlyle to the University of Edinburgh, to found bursaries. And Jane, so beautiful and spirited in that hour, had, in keeping with her wishes, been laid to rest in her father's grave, in the Abbey Church at Haddington. But Ecclefechan, at no great distance from Craigenputtock, must have had, in February, its own wild and lonely splendor. To the Carlyles, Emerson departing from Craigenputtock had seemed an angel vanishing from their midst. Now the Carlyles themselves, Jane and Thomas, were gone forever out of view. But surely, in his inner being, Emerson felt the tug of their continued presence at one with that universal spirit which extends divinity to all.

To many writers Bush meant what Craigenputtock had meant to Emerson, the place to which they had come to be welcomed with warmth and encouragement. For one writer, however, a visit to Bush marked not his first encounter with Emerson, but his last. When Walt Whitman came to Boston in the winter of 1860, Emerson sought him out at his rooming house, strolled with him on Boston Common, and took him to "a bully dinner" — for thus Whitman remembered it — at the American House in Hanover Square. But he did not invite him to Bush because Lidian would not hear of it. When, in 1874, Emerson published his *Parnassus*, a selection of his favorite poems, Whitman found to his dismay that none of his poems had been included. Edith had been her father's helper when he prepared this book and Edith "hated Whitman."[3] Later, when Emerson wanted to invite Whitman to dinner at the Saturday Club, Longfellow and Holmes said they did not care to meet him, so the invitation was never extended. Whitman was finally welcomed under Emerson's roof when Emerson was a scant seven months from the grave. Whether Emerson knew who it was he was welcoming is doubtful. When Annie Gilchrist, Whitman's self-appointed protectress, visited Bush in 1878 and showed Emerson Whitman's picture, he asked her if the subject was an Englishman.[4]

In mid-August 1881 Whitman came to Boston to consult with James Osgood on a new edition of *Leaves of Grass.* On 17 September, with the work well in hand, he accompanied Sanborn to Concord to stay over till Monday, the nineteenth, as Sanborn's guest. Sanborn saw to it that Whitman had the complete Concord tour: the battlefield; the Old Manse; Sleepy Hollow; the graves of Thoreau and Hawthorne; Walden Pond and the hut site, with a chance to place a stone on the cairn raised there by a legion of faceless tourists; and tea and chatter with Louisa May Alcott.[5] But the prospect of seeing Emerson once again was what truly lured Whitman to Concord, and the high point of his visit was the time spent in Emerson's company.[6]

Not until 1 December, when he had been for some time back in Camden, New Jersey, did Whitman compile his thoughts on the Concord encounter. By then whatever disappointment he had felt had been routed and what he recalled was a pastoral idyll:

> I spent such good days at Concord, and with Emerson, seeing
> him under such propitious circumstances, in the calm, peaceful,
> but most radiant twilight of his old age (nothing in the height of
> his literary action and expression so becoming and impressive),
> that I must give a few impromptu notes of it all. So I devote this
> cluster entirely to the man, to the place, the past, and all leading
> up to, and forming, that memorable and peculiar Personality, now
> near his 80th year — as I have just seen him there, in his home,
> silent, sunny, surrounded by a beautiful family.[7]

"Old age," "twilight," "peculiar," "silent" — the choice of words of a man who paved his way with words hints of an uneasiness Whitman did not care to elaborate on.

During his Concord visit, Whitman saw Emerson on two successive days, Saturday, 17 September, and the day following. Only on the second day was he the guest of the Emersons. Saturday evening, Emerson, in the company of the Alcotts, Bronson and Louisa, had passed two hours with him in Sanborn's back parlor. Obviously Whitman had been apprised of Emerson's broken condition because he asked nothing more than to be able to gaze upon Emerson, and this he had been able to do to his heart's content. Of him Whitman said: ''On entering he had spoken very briefly, easily and politely to several of the company, then settled himself in his chair, a trifle pushed back, and, though a listener and apparently an alert one, remained silent through the whole talk and discussion.''[8] Their topic had been Thoreau, some of whose letters were read and, as well, letters that Emerson had received from Horace Greeley, William Henry Channing, and ''one of the best by Margaret Fuller.''

But it was in the chance given to gaze upon the master's face, hours on end, that Whitman found his fullest satisfaction. ''My seat and the relative arrangement were such that, without being rude or anything of the kind,'' Walt gloated, ''I could just look squarely at E[merson]., which I did a good part of the two hours.'' As he gazed Whitman had run up one of his famous inventories: ''A good color in his face, eyes clear, with the well-known expression of sweetness, and the old clear-peering aspect quite the same.'' A cultist cloistered with the object of his veneration could not have experienced higher gratification: ''Never had I a better piece of luck befall me: a long and blessed evening with Emerson, in a way I couldn't have wished better or different.''[9]

On Sunday, at Lidian's invitation, Whitman spent several hours at Bush and had dinner with the Emersons. He liked the ''old-fashioned simplicity'' of the house, its ''plain elegance and fulness, signifying democratic ease.'' Lidian, her former squeamishness vanquished, sat next to Whitman and drew upon her personal recollections to fill him in on Thoreau, for whom he had a great liking. He was glad for the chance to meet Ellen and Edward, and Edward's wife. The Sanborns were there, too, ''and others, relatives and intimates.''[10] Emerson, seen in the context of the world he daily moved in, was a cherished vision, yet no reportable words passed between them.

Whitman's summing up had finally to be based on what he had thought about Emerson all along. There was nothing in the day's events to make the picture fuller:

> How comforting to know of an author who has, through a long life, and in spirit, written as honestly, spontaneously, and innocently, as the sun shines or the wheat grows — the truest, sanest, most moral, sweetest literary man on record — unsoiled by pecuniary or any other warp — ever teaching the law within — ever loyally outcropping his own self only — his own poetic and devout soul![11]

Four months before Emerson's death, Whitman had preached the first of his eulogies.

On his return to Boston on the nineteenth, Whitman learned that President James Garfield, long languishing from an assassin's wound, had died at ten-thirty that night. Garfield and he had been friends. At midnight, once more he addressed his pen to a martyr's remembrance. In the ensuing hours he wrote ''The Sobbing of the Bells,'' for timely inclusion in the new edition of *Leaves of Grass*. In Concord, as elsewhere across the land, the church bells tolled ''the sudden death-news.'' When, seven months later, ''the passionate toll and clang'' again would carry ''that message in the darkness'' to Concord's townspeople, it would be to mark Emerson's passing.

I saw the Days deformed and low,
Short and bent by cold and snow . . .

79. Edward Bok Sees Mr. Emerson

Although in his last years Emerson remained accessible to those determined to see him, none recreated the distressing circumstances of such encounters with the fidelity of Edward Bok, who set down, moment by moment, the painful details of the assault he made on Emerson's privacy on 22 November 1881, when Emerson was close to the end of his life. While Bok, at eighteen, already belonged to that tenacious breed who make demands on celebrities with no thought of the annoyance they are giving, his calculation and resoluteness much surpassed what others of his calling had to offer. Most celebrity-seekers, for example, pursue this sport in a favorable season. Bok, who had already joined the labor force as an office boy, took his vacation in the off-season, correctly surmising that by then all his rivals would have gone to ground. Besides, what reasonable man would turn away Sturdy Dick, cap in hand, standing on his doorstep on a cold November day?

While Bok always took along a copy of Emerson's *Essays* to read while riding back and forth to work on the horse-cars, Emerson was but one of several eminent men he intended to confront on his New England sweep. Phillips Brooks, Wendell Phillips, Charles Francis Adams, Longfellow, Holmes, were others he had marked for visitations.

In his pocket Bok carried his autograph book so that those he cornered could strike off an original quatrain for him or at least an uplifting thought. He wanted letters of introduction, too, for he seems to have visualized his array of celebrities as a row of tenpins, one destined to topple the next into his grasp. Thus he took leave of Phillips Brooks fortified with exactly the advice he needed to get past Ellen Emerson into her father's presence. "And you're going from me now to see Emerson?" Brooks said. He added that he was not at all certain that Bok would see Emerson "at his best." Bok, who knew nothing of Emerson's failing health, did not know what value to assign to that remark. Nonetheless, he took careful note of Brooks's final observation — "To have seen him, even as you may see him, is better, in a way, than not to have seen him at all" — storing it away for future reference.[1]

Thus put on his guard, Bok plotted his Concord strategy with extra caution. Upon arriving in Concord, he went first to Main Street, to the home of the Alcotts, where Louisa gladly received him and hustled him in to give him a seat by the warm fire, perhaps on the very spot where Thoreau's cot stood when, in that room, he last shut his eyes on this world, though Bok probably never gave that a thought. After all, living celebrities were his quarry.

Bok's winsome-lad routine brought big dividends from Louisa. "Why, you good boy," she said, "to come all the way to Concord to see us." As she hustled on coat and hat a few minutes later, to walk across town with Bok in the November chill to Emerson's threshold, maybe it occurred to her that Bok had not come to Concord to see her, after all. But Bok was as beguiling as he was determined, and Louisa saw determination in a young person as a trait that deserved to be rewarded.

Ellen Emerson, over the years, had had abundant practice in shielding her father from the importunate. Had Bok shown up alone that morning she probably would have hustled him on his way. But Louisa was the perfect cicerone. Once again Bok found himself settled before a blazing fire, this time in Emerson's front parlor. The atmosphere cooled, however, as soon as Louisa made clear the purpose of their visit. Ellen was firm; "Father sees no one now." It was time, then, for Bok to play his trump card. He repeated Brooks's words, no doubt assigning to them the authority of Holy Writ. Louisa probably countersigned them with a nod of inducement. What power had these two spinster ladies to resist Bok's boyish eagerness? Ellen rose. "I'll see," she said and bolted off in the direction of Emerson's study, with Louisa tracking her to make sure that her resolve to keep Bok out of Emerson's presence did not rekindle. "Come," said Louisa, reappearing after a short delay, and Bok followed her through the rear access to Emerson's study.

"Father," Ellen said, putting Emerson on notice that he was on display again, quite as though otherwise he might not have realized it. Emerson stood and reached out his hand. His eyes met Bok's but were uncomprehending. Emerson almost always looked past a person, over his shoulder, while he was talking to him. Now he motioned Bok to a chair, but then, strangely, still quick of foot, stepped to the window and, with his back to those in the room, stood whistling to himself at a hushed pitch. Emerson never had liked guests who did not know when it was time to take leave. Possibly he was hoping now, by a feat of philosophical idealism, to dematerialize these intruders and so be left with the only reality that mattered to him now, himself.

Bok awoke at last to the true state of things, especially after Ellen emitted a stifled sob and fled the room. When Bok looked at Louisa, seeking a clue as to what came next, he saw she had put an index finger to her lips, as though hushing a child. He waited. Seconds passed. Emerson turned on his heel, came past him, inclining himself in a courteous bow of respect as to a newcomer, then resumed his chair, with that gesture seemingly obliterating the presence of his two companions.

Louisa tried to break through. Had he read Ruskin's newest book? Emerson took in her suddenly materialized presence, rose, made a second stately bow, and ventured tentatively, "Did you speak to me, madame?" Tears came to Louisa's eyes. She could not trust herself to answer. The redoubtable Bok, stunned though he was, decided the situation called for a man's touch. He was naturally forward and probably merely wanted to accomplish one of the goals of his visit before the situation deteriorated any further. Just as casually as if he was asking for a page from a scratch pad, he asked Emerson to give him one of Carlyle's letters. Emerson's bewilderment was equal to the occasion. With a boyish exuberance the match of Bok's own, he went rummaging in a drawer where he was sure he had a cache of the priceless letters, "Carlyle," he said half aloud, as he rummaged, "yes, he was here this morning. He will be here again tomorrow morning." But nothing of Carlyle's emerged from the drawer. Instead, even as he shuffled papers about, Emerson picked up again with his low whistle. The tablet of his mind was once more a blank page.

Undeterred, Bok struck out in another direction. Would Emerson sign his autograph book? It took a bit of coaching to get Emerson to understand what was meant. Bok rose to the task of tutelage with enthusiasm. He was not going away empty-handed. Emerson asked him what it was he wanted him to put in the album. "Ralph Waldo Emerson, Concord, November 22, 1881," Bok wrote. There was no limit to his willingness to humor the unperceiving seer. Emerson studied the strange message, then copied it with great deliberation, as though it was a mystifying undertaking. The Ralph he took care of with an "R." In an inspired afterthought he slipped a third *o* into Concord, right after the *n* — Conocord!

Emerson's labor accomplished, Bok retrieved his book and tucked it into his pocket only to hear Emerson ask briskly, "You wish me to write my name? With pleasure. Have you a book with you?" Out came the album again and Emerson, in his very prime it seemed, dashed off his name.

Louisa saw there never would be a better chance for them to withdraw in circumstances positive enough to become a cherished memory in the mind of an aspiring boy, especially since he failed to realize he had been privy to that rarest of mortal transfigurations, a vision of Emerson dwelling in the land of the ideal. "So soon?" said Emerson, rising as Louisa rose. "It was very kind of you, Louisa, to run over this morning and bring your young friend." He faced the young friend. "Thank you so much for coming to see me. You must come over again while you are with the Alcotts. Good morning! Isn't it a beautiful day out?" A warm handshake. Eyes alight. His radiant smile. The visit was done.

To sharpen the contrast between Emerson withdrawn and Emerson responsive, Bok perhaps put more verve into Emerson's parting remarks than the facts warranted, but if that is so it merely establishes that Louisa stage-managed their exit in such a way as to let Bok get maximum benefit from it. Even so, she was shaken by the episode. "It is so *sad*, so very sad," she told the enterprising boy, as they walked along the pike road. "The twilight is gently closing in."

Bok left Boston a few days later with autograph letters of John Adams and John Quincy Adams tucked in his luggage. Charles Francis Adams had proved more vulnerable than Emerson. Since such treasures evidently could be had for the asking, why should he not have asked for them? Maybe Bok did not have more than his share of gall. Maybe he just had a goodly share of those vital spirits which Emerson always thought were the glory of boyhood. And maybe they imparted a spark of elation to Emerson as he drifted into his twilight.

Had Bok's visit with Emerson caught Emerson in an unprecedented moment it would be uncivilized to recapitulate it. Taken in conjunction with independent accounts, however, it is apparent that it was all too typical. J. F. Dutton said that when he visited Emerson in 1878, he told Emerson he had seen Herman Grimm in Berlin and that Grimm had inquired after him with particular interest. "Oh, did you?" Emerson said, "And what can you tell me about him? Has he much of a family yet? Is he a success as a professor?" Dutton supplied what information he could. "Give me his name once more," Emerson said, "I wish to ask something of my daughter about him." Dutton repeated Grimm's name. Emerson walked toward the door. Then he came back and said again, "Give me his name once more."[2]

Certainly, painful though it is to see Emerson as he was here, in his broken state, posterity must be grateful to Bok for recreating so scrupulously a representative episode of those days. Phillips Brooks was right — to see Emerson in this way is better than not to have seen him at all. What a pity Bok was not there to record with the same authenticity the occasion of the ''Divinity School Address,'' or the first meeting with Carlyle, or the walk to Harvard with Hawthorne. But, at least, his account makes it clear why Emerson, in old age, sought to hide himself at the approach of visitors.

80. Into the Holy Silence & Eternity

*O*N a bright autumn morning, still in bed and watching the gathering light pour over the earthworks Nature had piled with a regulating hand across from the vale where his house sat, Emerson might have been a bard from Alfred's time, fashioning a lament as only a man can who has been instructed in many sorrows and has come to triumph over them. Writing of that morn of 21 October 1837, he spoke with assurance: "I said when I awoke, After some more sleepings & wakings I shall lie on this mattress sick; then, dead; and through my gay entry they will carry these bones. Where shall I be then? I lifted my head and beheld the spotless orange light of the morning beaming up from the dark hills into the wide Universe."[1]

"I do not fear death," Emerson had written on 19 December 1831, six years before:

> . . . Following my own thought . . . I should lie down in the lap
> of earth as trustingly as ever on my bed. But the terror to
> many persons is in the vague notions of what shall follow death.
> . . . What are your sources of satisfaction? . . . If they are
> contemplation, kind affections, admiration of what is admirable,
> self-command, self improvement, then they survive death & will
> make you as happy then as now.[2]

In the early days of his ministry, Emerson took personal immortality for granted. On several occasions he assured his parishioners that the souls of departed friends did not cease to observe and love them.[3]

At twenty-four he elected for immortality, stating in his journal: "I believe myself immortal. The beam of the balance trembles, to be sure, but settles always on the right side. For otherwise all things look so silly."[4]

Ellen, his first love, went to her grave firm in her belief in personal immortality, and for a time her certitude sustained his. While a belief in immortality persisted, and periodically was reaffirmed by him, for example, in July 1855 — "The blazing evidence of immortality is our dissatisfaction with any other solution" — a belief in personal immortality did not.[5]

By 1841 Emerson had arrived at a clearer statement of what he saw as the alternative to personal immortality: "For this was I born & came into the world to deliver the self of myself to the Universe from the Universe; to do a certain benefit which Nature could not forego, nor I be discharged from rendering, & then immerge again into the holy silence & eternity, out of which as a man I arose." In "Worship" (1860) he would say: "Immortality will come to such as are fit for it, and he who would be a great soul in future, must be a great soul now." Faithfulness to duties enabled one to face death unafraid of what lay beyond.[6]

Emerson assured Fredrika Bremer that "the continuance of our being" was certain. What was uncertain was "in what form or in what manner" this continuation would occur. To a lady in a Chicago audience who put the same question to him, he gave a devastatingly short answer: "Madame, are we swill?" Edward Emerson's request for his father's view of immortality was handled with a dexterity worthy of a Zen master: "I think we may be sure," Emerson told him, "that, whatever may come after death, no one will be disappointed."[7]

In his essay "Immortality," the last one in the last book — *Letters and Social Aims* — published by him in his lifetime, Emerson did not hide behind ambiguities: "I confess that everything connected with our personality fails. Nature never spares the individual."[8] His wider expectation brought with it an assurance that took from death the dread of the unknown.

If immortality was Emerson's frequent theme, death itself was not. He wrote essays on heroism, love, greatness, prudence, friendship, experience, Nature, and a score of other universal themes, but none on death. In "Threnody" and "Dirge" he confronted death, but rarely elsewhere. He left no gathering of notes on the subject. On one of the few occasions when death was his topic, the compensations that come to the bereaved preempted his attention:

The death of a dear friend, wife, brother, lover, . . . commonly operates revolutions in our way of life, terminates an epoch of infancy or of youth which was waiting to be closed, breaks up a wonted occupation, or a household, or style of living, and allows the formation of new ones more friendly to the growth of character.[9]

Death stole upon Emerson as though it did not want to trouble his philosophy. In those last months his mental faculties had been slowly shutting down. While physically he was present at Longfellow's funeral — his last visit away from Concord — he would not have understood had the Fates whispered in his ear that many of those present would gather a month hence for his own funeral. That week Ellen surprised him thrice with the news of Longfellow's death. In those days even the contents of his study seemed unfamiliar to him.

On 15 April 1882 Emerson went down the road to the Concord School to hear Dr. Harris speak on *Sartor Resartus*. He smiled but said nothing and could not have guessed that he himself had brought to America this book that assured Carlyle's American renown.

In New England that year April was harsh. Not put off by rain or unseasonable cold, Emerson took his daily walks. On Sunday, the sixteenth, he was at the First Parish meeting house for both morning and afternoon services. After four he took his walk. Rain was falling, but he did not think to bring his coat. The skies opened in a downpour and he came home soaked. No one realized his plight, and he sat in his wet clothes and took a chill. Next morning when he awoke he was hoarse. In the days immediately following, this hoarseness grew on him. Yet he insisted on holding to a semblance of routines that, in themselves, were a mere semblance of routines he had followed in his active years.[10]

On Patriot's Day Edward looked in on him and found him asleep on the sofa in his study. Physician as well as son, Edward was concerned to find his father feverish, befuddled, and vaguer still in his efforts to find words to express himself. Yet Emerson enjoyed being with Edward and was uncomplaining. Edward knew that he liked to be read to but was equal now only to a simple story line, so he read him Longfellow's "Midnight Ride of Paul Revere."[11] Emerson could not recall having heard the poem before. Neither could he recall Longfellow. From England came the news that Charles Darwin had died, but Edward saw no point in telling him that. He would not have known who Darwin was, either.

The same week his father fell ill, Edward had, for the first time, given a public address, a speech before the Middlesex County Medical Society. Emerson, lucid, would have rejoiced in this event. When Edward told him about it now, he did not understand what his son was talking about.

The next day symptoms of pneumonia were evident. Until then
Emerson still insisted on going out each day for his walk, refusing to
believe anything was wrong. Since lately he flared up when anyone
tried to get him to act contrary to his wishes, the family had not interfered. But that morning, when he came down to breakfast with Ellen, as he came abreast of the rocking horse that stood in the front
entry — the very entry of his death fantasy — "he cried out and staggered as from a blow." He stood stock-still until the spasm passed, yet
could not describe what it was he had experienced. "I hoped it would
not come in this way," he exclaimed. "I would rather — fall down
cellar!"[12]

Still, he did not wish to take to his bed. Edward recalled, "He did
not know how to be sick and desired to be dressed and sit in his study.
. . . I determined that it would not be worth while to trouble and
restrain him as it would a younger person who had more to live for.
He had lived free: his life was essentially spent, and in what must
almost surely be his last illness we would not embitter the occasion by
any restraint that was not absolutely unavoidable." Much of the time
Emerson sat in his study, in a chair pulled up by the fireplace, or
rested on the nearby sofa. Warmth was his sovereign panacea. On 7
February 1839 he had written: "The drunkard retires on a keg &
locks himself up for a three days' debauch. When I am sick I please
myself not less in retiring on a salamander stove, heaping the chamber
with fuel & inundating lungs, liver, head & feet with floods of caloric,
heats on heats."[13]

Conway spoke of Emerson as a "worshipper of health," and believed fear of sickness was the only thing that qualified his optimism.
"I honor health as the first muse," Emerson said on one occasion, and
on another, "Give me health and a day and I will make the pomp of
emperors ridiculous."[14]

Emerson at times contended that men engender the diseases that
beset them: "The disease and deformity around us certify that infrac-
tion of natural, intellectual, and moral laws, and often violation on
violation to breed such compound misery." The positive side of this
thesis engrossed Emerson. "Illness will not visit those who dedicate
themselves to self-command and self-improvement." Conversely, he
believed sickness fostered our worst traits. "It is so vicious, 'Tis a
screen for every fault to hide in; idleness, luxury, meanness, wrath
and the most unmitigated selfishness."[15] (What Lidian, who professed
never to know a well day, thought on reading this passage may well
be imagined.) Emerson's arraignment of the sick did not end with
that bill of particulars. He said as well: "Sickness is a cannibal which
eats up all the life and youth it can lay hold of. . . . We must treat
the sick with . . . firmness, giving them of course every aid, — but
withholding ourselves."[16]

Holmes said that "Emerson was possessed all his life long with the idea of his constitutional infirmity and insufficiency."[17] This Holmes attributed to forebears who had not left the scholar's alcove for generations. "I think," Emerson wrote Carlyle in 1841, after complaining' about his "puny body," that "the branch of the 'tree of life' which headed to a bud in me, curtailed me somehow of a drop or two of sap, and so dwarfed all my florets and drupes."[18] Such passages amused Holmes: "Here was Emerson, a hopelessly confirmed pie-eater, never so far as I remember, complaining of dyspepsia; and there, on the other side, was Carlyle, feeding largely on wholesome oatmeal, groaning with indigestion all his days." Holmes found Emerson's anxieties unjustified: "His presence was fine and impressive, and his muscular strength was enough to make him a rapid and enduring walker."[19]

In those last days, Emerson confronted illness much as he always had. He disapproved of it and did his best to ignore it on the theory that it could not survive inattention.

At mealtime he came to the table, but he ate nothing. Friday night, after dinner, he sat for a while at his study table with a book open before him but read nothing. At length he arose and, spurning assistance, took apart, with his customary fastidiousness, the burnt brands in the fireplace. He went then from window to window, securing in turn each of the four shutters. Lastly, bearing his lamp, he waved aside Ellen's offer of assistance and climbed the stairs to his room. Before he reached the top he stumbled, but recovered himself without letting anyone help him. The shuttered study lay enveloped in darkness. Daylight would look upon it again, but Emerson never would.

On 13 April Alcott had come by to leave a copy of his just-published *Sonnets and Canzonets*. He reported in his journal that Emerson read "several with emphasis and delight." When he stopped in again, on the twenty-second, news of Emerson's illness caught him by surprise — "I have not thought of him as other than well." By the twenty-fourth, Alcott knew Emerson's condition was grave: "Emerson is quite ill, and fears are entertained that his illness may prove fatal."[20]

From the onset of Emerson's illness Lidian had schemed for his comfort. She moved from the master chamber into Edith's room so that he could be ministered to without interference. She sat by his bed and was sure he would grow better. But now that he had to be kept in bed, Edward brought in a trained nurse to attend him and a cousin, Mary Ripley Simmons, to assist as needed. Lidian, hovering over him night and day, was showing the strain.

By mid-week, Emerson's mind was wandering. He supposed he had been taken ill at a friend's house and was, in consequence, a great inconvenience to his host. He wanted to put his clothes on and go home. But every now and again he would recognize Lidian's bed curtains, the room's familiar furnishings, and the pictures on the walls. Most

especially was he reassured when his eyes traveled to the window and
he saw beyond, the house of his late neighbor, Cyrus Stowe. "Why
yes!" he would say, and then, "Here we are in Mamma's room, after
all! I *am* glad." Edward saw that his father was dying. He summoned
loved ones and dear friends to Bush. Edith, who was in the final month
of pregnancy with her eighth child, had come on Sunday with her
husband. At noon on Tuesday her children Ralph and Violet visited
with him, and at noon next day, Cameron and Don climbed up on his
bed to give him a last kiss. "Good boy," he whispered to each of them
as he felt the warmth of their lips.

On Wednesday, 26 April, Alcott made his final visit. April 26 — on
that date Thoreau had first moved into Bush; on that date Emerson
had opened his graduate lecture series at Harvard; and now that day
had come again — his last full day of life. Alcott told of his visit:

> I walk this cloudless morning to Emerson's and am admitted to
> his sick chamber. On being announced by Ellen, he turns his
> kind glance, as none other upon me, and on taking my hand he
> said, "You are quite well?" "Yes," I replied; "and not used to
> find you in bed." Smiling, he seemed confused, and uttered words
> too indistinctly to be discerned. Leaving his bedside and about
> going, he signified his wish to speak further with me, and, return-
> ing to his bed's head, he took my hand affectionately and said in
> strong but broken accents: "You have strong hold on life, and
> maintain it firmly," when his voice faltered and fell into indis-
> tinctness. I came away questioning if this might not be my
> last interview with my long and faithful friend. Though the sun
> shone brightly above, the light that had illumined our friendship
> so long seemed overcast, and I was soon to be left alone.[21]

At times Emerson knew that Lidian was sitting by him on the edge
of his bed, and smiled when he recognized her. Though drifting in and
out of awareness, he found the words to tell her how long and happily
they had lived together — forty-seven years! When the mail brought
new particulars about Edward's speech, Ellen recounted it all to
Emerson twice over. And when she came to his bedside later, he said,
"Tell me about Edward," and she went over the facts a further time.

At night a friend watched by his bedside and afterward reported:

> He kept (when awake) repeating in his sonorous voice, not yet
> weakened, fragments of sentences, almost as if reciting. It seemed
> strange and solemn in the night, alone with him, to hear these
> efforts to deliver something evidently with a thread of fine
> recollection in it; his voice as deep and musical almost as ever.[22]

Thus Emerson, dying, addressed his last audience boldly, independent of a text, his spirit finally free.

The last day of his life was, for Emerson, a celebration of life. A stream of visitors poured into Bush to take leave of him. Sam Staples came, bringing a bottle of fine brandy. Emerson recognized Ellery Channing and invited him to come to dinner as in times past. When Cabot came, he smiled and tried to rise. He said something Cabot could not make out, but at least made his pleasure known. "Elliot Cabot! Praise!" He said something to Lidian, but she could not fathom it. "Oh, that beautiful boy!" This she heard clearly. She believed he meant Waldo and that he looked to be reunited with him in the next world. There was no time Emerson would not have embraced a personal immortality that offered such a hope.

In the afternoon Dr. Charles Pickering Putnam, whom Edward had called in as consultant, came out from Boston. A surge of pain racked Emerson as he was being examined. Putnam gave him ether, putting him under. Others came to see him, Judge Keyes and Charley Emerson, William's son. They stayed below in the parlor. Judge Hoar came back and stood by Emerson's bed, his arm around Lidian, supporting her. Ellen was there, and Mary Simmons. After a time Edward said, "He will breathe once more, perhaps twice." He made it to the second breath. There was a little tremor, and he died. The hour was approaching nine. Edward went downstairs and told Charley and the judge, and they came up and looked at the calm face, in repose finer and stronger than ever. Then all left.

At nine the bell of the church began to toll. It tolled once for each of Emerson's seventy-nine years, and all of the village knew that Concord's greatest man was dead. In Edith's room Lidian sat forlorn and stunned. "I am a widow," she said. She considered the fact further, at last admitting, "I never thought of this."[23]

When she was fifteen, Louisa May Alcott had borrowed from Emerson's bookshelves Goethe's *Correspondence with a Child* and identified so strongly with Bettina that she left wildflowers on Emerson's doorstep and came, when dusk would hide her, to sing Mignon's song, in German, beneath his window, in a voice so tiny he never knew that he was being serenaded. Nearing fifty now, Louisa still saw Emerson as a proper object of veneration. When she heard the bells, she turned to her journal and wrote: "Mr. Emerson died at 9 P.M. suddenly. Our best and greatest American gone. The nearest and dearest Friend father has ever had, and the man who has helped me most by his life, his books, his society. I can never tell all he has been to me. . . . Illustrious and beloved friend, good-by!"[24] In each house in the village there were men and women who paused in their doings to think upon this loss.

By mid-March winter often has fled at Concord. By late April for-sythia flames upon the bough and apple and pear orchards are ready to tumble into bloom. That cold and hostile April was different. The Emersons awoke next morning to find Concord blanketed with new-fallen snow. ''It seemed lovely when we saw it and right,'' Ellen re-membered. The enchantment did not hold. Before noon all traces of it were gone.[25]

At ten, tracking through this fluff of snow, Alcott went to Bush. Dr. Bartol was there on the same errand of sympathy. ''Miss Ellen takes us into the chamber,'' Alcott said. ''He lay sleeping, with but slight change of features from my last sight of him. . . . The change was very little, he was living in the spirit here.''[26]

The news imparted to Concord by the mournful bells now spread across the land, striking everywhere into the hearts of men who could read and think. Many sensed what Richard Garnett later put into words: ''The most shining intellectual glory and the most potent intellectual force of a continent had departed along with him.''[27]

Ellen's whole remembrance of the interval between Emerson's death and burial was of a beautiful, even joyous, time. Lidian wanted to thread black ribbons on her cap in place of the blue ones. Ellen dis-couraged this. ''There is no reason to mourn,'' she insisted. When Fur-ness arrived on Saturday, she greeted him with jubilation. She had been terrified, she told him, at the prospect of her father's life being prolonged. The time was at hand when he would have failed to recog-nize his own children, she said, and that she could scarcely have borne.[28]

Judge Hoar came to the house that evening with the church organ-ist, and a long discussion ensued over which hymns to use at the ser-vice next day. Daniel Chester French came and draped Emerson in a white robe. The black walnut coffin had been placed in the northeast room, behind Emerson's study. In Ellen's eyes, the white-clad figure, framed by black wood, looked ''like a statue.''[29] The only flowers in the room were lilies of the valley, red and white roses, and arbutus, a vase of each, on the fireplace mantel.

Right up to the hour of the funeral, activity in Concord was fever-ish. Through the morning hours on the thirtieth, the Fitchburg rail-road ran special trains, bringing ten carloads of mourners to town. Scores of others converged on Concord, coming in carriages and other conveyances. On Friday the women of the village had organized a committee to make black and white rosettes to be hung over the door-ways of all houses along the route from the depot to the Emerson house, from the house to the church, and from the church to Sleepy Hollow. Concord's public buildings were draped in black, and most homes, even those of the very poor, put out some sign of mourning. Furness was to conduct the private service for the family at Bush, and

James Freeman Clarke, the service at the church. From Cambridge a special train brought President Eliot, and Holmes, Norton, the Jameses, William and Henry, George William Curtis, Professors Peirce, Horsford, and Hills, and Annie Fields. For these visitors pews were held. Although the church could not hold more than a fraction of those who wanted to attend the service, over the weekend the floors were strengthened as well as the underpinnings of the galleries so that the maximum number of people could be let in. Henry James for once was frankly awed by the turnout, acclaiming the funeral in retrospect "a popular manifestation, the most striking I have ever seen provoked by the death of a man of letters."[30]

At 2:30 P.M. at Bush, with Lidian and Ellen sitting beside the coffin and Furness positioned in the hallway outside the door, the private service began. Furness quoted Tennyson's "Deserted Home" and read Longfellow's words: "There is no Death! What seems so is transition / This life of mortal breath / Is but a suburb of the life elysian, / Whose portal we call Death." He said the face they looked upon told of a like quiet of the soul within, and mirrored the peace and purity of that soul while it still tenanted the body.[31]

Outside the house a procession formed to escort the hearse to the church. The pallbearers gathered — Edward; Will Forbes; Will's son Ralph; Elliot Cabot; Professor Thayer; his son William. The members of the Social Circle followed. Behind them came the carriages bearing the new widow and her daughters, other family members, and the notables from Cambridge and Boston.

May Day was in the offing, but April was not relenting. The day was dark and raw, and rain threatened. But the villagers had done their best to adorn the church. Louisa May Alcott had made a lyre of jonquils, which was placed before the pulpit, surrounded with pine and hemlock boughs among where were strewn maple and willow blossoms. White and red geraniums were clustered on either side of the pulpit. And high up on the wall were a laurel wreath and an open book formed of pinks, pansies, and white roses, prepared by the children of the Emerson School. The word FINIS, in blue flowers, was inscribed on one of the pages.[32]

A little before 3:30 P.M., the pallbearers brought the coffin into the church and positioned it in front of the pulpit. The organ intoned "Pleyel's Hymn." Now the coffin was opened and two small bouquets, one of pansies, one of roses, were placed on the lid. Clarke entered the pulpit. Judge Hoar, standing beside the coffin, spoke first. He told those assembled that Emerson's face, at the moment he died, was "as the face of a child and seemed to give a glimpse of the opening heavens." His voice broke. "That impressible nature," he said, "loving and tender and generous, having no repulsion or scorn for anything but meanness and baseness; our friend, brother, father, lover, teacher, inspirer, guide, is gone."[33]

Hymns were sung — "Thy Will Be Done"; "I Will Not Fear the Fate Provided by Thy Love." Furness read from Scripture. Then Clarke spoke: "That power which we knew, that searing intelligence, that soul of fire, that ever-advancing spirit, — *that* cannot have been suddenly annihilated with the decay of these earthly organs. . . . He himself was the best argument for immortality." His voice almost broke as well.

Alcott was ready now with one of his sonnets, struck off for the occasion. His voice did not break.

A Brookline minister, Howard Brown, read the benediction, then followed the steady trooping of those inside the church, and those who had waited outside, past the bier for a last glimpse of the man whose death had attracted worldwide notice. More than an hour passed before the coffin could be closed again and the cortege move off toward Sleepy Hollow.[34] The day was now drifting toward evening.

Emerson had given the dedication speech when Sleepy Hollow was consecrated. Often he had struck out for the Hollow when he sought a haven in Nature. At times he had taken visitors there, strolled there in the company of Cranch, Very, or Margaret Fuller. His grave lots were on the top of the ridge in the highest part of the cemetery, where Hawthorne and Thoreau already lay buried, and Abba Alcott. On the slope of the ridge, on 29 September 1855, he had stood beneath a white pine to give his dedicatory speech. And to the ridge he had brought the bodies of his mother and his "hyacinthine boy." There also Aunt Mary was buried.

The members of the Social Circle flanked the path to make an honor guard for the cortege to pass between. At the grave site the excavated sod lay hidden under pine boughs. The opening in the earth was at the foot of a great white pine. At Newton, almost fifty years before, Emerson had written: "Here sit Mother & I among the pine trees, still almost as we shall lie by & by under them."[35] More boughs lined the grave itself. The services here were conducted by Emerson's cousin Samuel Moody Haskins, rector of St. Mark's Episcopal Church in Brooklyn, tall, rotund, a formidable Dickensian figure. He read the Episcopal commitment service, thus halting the Lord's Prayer at the words "but deliver us from evil," to the discomfiture of some. The casket was lowered and on it Dr. Haskins sprinkled a mixture of sand and dust and ashes, the sand and dust scooped from the path that led to Emerson's front door, the ashes taken from the fireplace in his study.[36] With Emerson there would always be, commingling in time with his own dust, these links with the sanctuary of home.

Lastly, Emerson's grandchildren came forward, and Concord's school children, to drop flowers and sprigs of green into the grave. At that moment, while the mourners were yet assembled, the sun, absent all the day long, broke through the clouds and cascades of light poured over trees and branches and all the world about them.

The year was 1882. Waldo had died forty years before, in 1842. Both father and son had died on the twenty-seventh day of the month, a Thursday, between eight and nine in the evening. Both were buried on the thirtieth day of the month, a Sunday. Seventy-five years before, on Sunday, 26 April, the first of the Emerson brothers, John Clarke, had died. On that same date, forty-six years before, Emerson reached New York with Charles, who had but two weeks more to live. Now the history of that generation of Emersons was rounded out as the last of them was laid in his grave. An elusive immortality had threaded them all on the same string — the boy John Clarke, the young Charles, the boy Waldo, and Emerson who lived always among the young.

When he helped consecrate Sleepy Hollow, Emerson had closed his address with these words: "In this quiet valley, as in the palm of Nature's hand, we shall sleep well, when we have finished our day." On the way back from the cemetery now, Ellen talked to her cousins about the affection her father had had for this resting place. Emerson was at peace but not out of the thoughts of those who reverenced him. One of the mourners sent to Conway, in England, a sprig of the evergreen that bordered Emerson's grave. When Louisa Alcott returned from the cemetery, she sat up till midnight writing a piece on Emerson for the *Youth's Companion* so "that the children may know something of him." It was, she told her journal, "a labor of love." To George Woodberry, a future Emerson biographer, Norton wrote, "There was nothing to lament in the death of Longfellow or of Emerson, except for ourselves. Their loss to us can never be made good."[37]

To Ellen, Lowell wrote from England:

Your father was associated with whatever of my life was capable of sympathy with nobility and beauty of character or the divine simplicity of genius, and no death could so change the earth for me as his. That he walked it was always a consolation and an incentive, but it is something that all who loved him (and I never knew any man so much revered who was also so much loved) should be sure that he will still teach and still inspire us so long as the language lasts to which he added new force and charm.[38]

After long deliberation, the family chose as a marker for Emerson's grave a large rough-hewn boulder of rose quartz from the New Hampshire mountains — "rugged and angular, wholly uncut, just as it was blasted from the ledge," said John Muir when he saw it. On the boulder's far side, unobtrusively facing away from the path, a bronze tablet was set in with lines from ''The Problem'': ''This passive Master lent his hand / To the vast soul that o'er him planned.'' The spontaneity of this unworked mass of quartz draws the visitor to Emerson's gravesite and makes the imagination freshly aware that within each man is vast, unused potential.[39]

A decade after Emerson's death, in the autumn of 1892, a livery stable owner in neighboring Acton boasted that in a month's time he had transported a thousand visitors to Concord to view the graves of Emerson, Thoreau, Hawthorne, and the Alcotts, one hundred and one of these in a single day.[40]

In April 1900, one week before the Patriot's Day observance marking the one hundred and twenty-fifth anniversary of the battle at the North Bridge, the First Church in Concord, from which Emerson was buried, was, in a few hours' time, reduced to cinders by a sudden fire. Out of the ruins the townspeople hauled the bell that Thoreau had rung to summon the villagers to hear Emerson speak on emancipation, and that later announced Emerson's death. Half-melted in the flames, fallen silent for good, it rests on the lawn beside the new meeting house. Here Concordians come together still to worship God and to express thanks for a man who, sojourning for a time in their secluded acres, had, by a life nobly lived and deeds nobly done, given new dignity to the human spirit and new hope to mankind.

ACKNOWLEDGMENTS

CHAPTER NOTES

BIBLIOGRAPHY

INDEX

Acknowledgments

$\mathscr{I}$N PREPARING this biography I have sought help from many sources and incurred many debts. First in distinction is my debt to the Ralph Waldo Emerson Memorial Association for granting me unrestricted access to the Emerson papers at Houghton Library, Harvard University. For various courtesies and insights I am further indebted to several members of the Emerson family — Edith W. Gregg, Ellen Emerson Cotton, Eliot Forbes, Amelia Emerson,* David Emerson, and Margaret Emerson Bancroft.

Concordians who gave me much practical assistance include the Reverend Dana McLean Greeley, pastor of the First Church in Concord; Anne Root McGrath, curator of the Thoreau Lyceum; Malcolm Ferguson, Ruth R. Wheeler,* Thomas Blanding, Marian H. Wheeler, John H. Clymer, Frederick C. Klinck,* Phyllis Cole, Jason Korell, Leroy P. Houck, M.D., Linda Schreiber, and Mary McClintock, Mary Connorton, Mary Grennan, and Mary Lush. I received steady encouragement also from Ann Zwinger, president of the Thoreau Society, and Walter Harding, secretary-treasurer of the society over many years.

Among the scholars who have counseled me and often made available to me the fruits of their own research I mention Perry Miller,* with whom my study of the transcendentalists began, Kenneth W. Cameron, Joel Myerson, Arlin Turner,* Leonard Neufeld, Shoei Ando, Jerome Loving, Margaret Neussendorfer, Edward L. Hirsh,* Louis Marder, Richard Frothingham, Ogura Izumi, Edward Wagenknecht,

---

*Now deceased.

Gay Wilson Allen, Joyce Carol Oates, Raymond Smith, Frederick T. McGill, Michael Meyer, Robin Winks, Lucille Cunningham, Joel Porte, Thomas O'Malley, S.J., Brendan Galvin, James Lowell Bowditch, Marie Ahearn, Geoffrey Proud, David Anderson, and Eleanor M. Tilton.

Boston College has assisted my research with a sabbatical leave and a Faculty Research Grant. Among those of my colleagues who took a concerned interest in my work and expedited its progress are Dean Donald J. White, P. Albert Duhamel, E. Dennis Taylor, Paul C. Doherty, Robert E. Reiter, Raymond Biggar, and John Fitzgerald. I am obligated also to two graduate assistants, Melinda Ponder and Robert J. Tarutis, who met their responsibilities with zeal and enthusiasm. I was ably supported as well by other emerging scholars in our graduate program — Rosalie Ryan, Karen Hedalski, Sherrill Murphy, Joseph L. Rinaldo, and Alan Crowley, and by departmental secretaries Barbara Lloyd and Ann Sibley.

The librarians who have assisted me are legion. I cite Thomas F. O'Connell, university librarian, Boston College; James M. O'Neill, administrative manager, University Libraries, Boston College; Philip McNiff, director of the Boston Public Library; Kathryn Hegarty, curator, Department of Rare Books and Manuscripts, Boston Public Library; Rose Marie Mitten, director of the Concord Free Public Library; Marcia Moss, that library's curator of special collections and a true friend of scholars; Ann P. Lang, reference librarian at the Concord Library; Caroline Preston, the Essex Institute; Elizabeth Dowling, Bedford Public Library; Alan Seaberg, Andover-Harvard Theological Library; Robert Hilton, director, and Margery Howard, reference supervisor, of the Cary Memorial Library, Lexington; Charles E. Mason, Jr., and Cynthia English, the Boston Athenaeum; Dennis Corcoran, director, Marshfield Public Library; Mary Sullivan McMorrow, Cambridge Public Library; Norman Castle, Bapst Library, Boston College; numerous staff members in the public libraries in Arlington, Belmont, Needham, Waltham, and Watertown, Massachusetts; and William H. Bond, former librarian, and Rodney Dennis, curator of manuscripts, Houghton Library, Harvard University.

I am beholden as well to Ives Gammel,* librarian of Boston's Tavern Club, and his successor, Rodney Armstrong (both in that capacity and in his capacity as director of the Athenaeum Library). Taverners whose stimulating questions and insights have spurred my research include Daniel Sargent, Thomas Boylston Adams, Francis D. Moore, M.D., F. Murray Forbes, Jr., Andrew Oliver,* George C. Homans, James Lawrence, Henry Lee, David T. W. McCord, Philip Hofer, David Pickman, Paul Brooks, Stacey Holmes, Grant LaFarge, Sterling Dow,

---

* Now deceased.

and Roger Prouty. My thanks also go to the members of the Saturday Club.

I also made use of the resources of the Massachusetts Historical Society; the Concord Antiquarian Museum; Follen Church, Lexington; the First Parish Church in Duxbury; those of the Norwood Historical Society, made accessible to me by the Society's president, Patricia Fanning; and, as well, those of the Thoreau Society and its Lyceum.

Others who contributed valuable suggestions and information are Margaret Farrar, David McCullough, Edward Rowe Snow,* Myrtle Snow, Barbara Wiener Raisbeck, Robert F. W. Meader, the Reverend Polly Laughland Guild, the Reverend J. Frank Schulman, Jane Langton, Edward R. Horgan, Philip Bridges, John Anderson, Mary Curo, Frank Curo, Julian Demeo, Patrick Keats, Herbert A. Kenny, Irene Keagan, Ernest Starr, Mark Starr, Carroll Dunham, Alice Dunham, Joseph Heaney, Robert Pitha, Doris Pullen, and Elizabeth Erb Ward.

A special word of thanks must go to the Belknap Press of Harvard University Press for permission to quote extensively from the *Journals and Miscellaneous Notebooks of Ralph Waldo Emerson*, edited by William H. Gilman, Alfred R. Ferguson, George P. Clark, Merrell R. Davis, A. W. Plumstead, Harrison Hayford, Ralph H. Orth, J. E. Parsons, Linda Allardt, Susan Sutton Smith, Merton M. Sealts, Jr., David W. Hill, Ruth H. Bennett, Ronald A. Bosco, and Glen M. Johnson, 16 volumes, 1960–1982; to Houghton Mifflin Company for permission to quote from the *Journals of Ralph Waldo Emerson*, edited by Edward Waldo Emerson and Waldo Emerson Forbes (Volume II: copyright 1909 by Edward Waldo Emerson; copyright renewed 1937 by Raymond Emerson; Volume III: copyright 1910 by Edward Waldo Emerson; copyright renewed 1938 by Raymond Emerson and Houghton Mifflin Company; Volume IX: copyright 1913 by Edward Emerson; copyright renewed 1941 by Houghton Mifflin Company; Volume X: copyright 1914 by Edward Emerson; copyright renewed 1942 by Houghton Mifflin Company); to Joel Myerson and the *Harvard Library Bulletin* for permission to quote from "Margaret Fuller's 1842 Journal: At Concord with Emerson" by Joel Myerson (July 1973); to Joel Myerson and Duke University Press for permission to quote from transcripts by Joel Myerson from Miss Francis's copy of Convers Francis's journal in "Convers Francis and Emerson" by Joel Myerson (*American Literature*, Volume 50, Number 1, March 1978, © 1978 by Duke University Press); and to the Ralph Waldo Emerson Memorial Association and the Houghton Library of Harvard University for permission to quote from previously unpublished materials. In

* Now deceased.

all instances the text has been adhered to as given except for dispensing with the apparatus used to record revisions of Emerson's manuscripts in the *Journals and Miscellaneous Notebooks* and for several misspellings, silently emended where found.

The book owes much to my editors at Little, Brown, Ray Roberts and Ann Sleeper, whose judgment and discernment showed me the full potentials of my material, and to Betsy Pitha, who gave symmetry and substance to style and content. My thanks go also to Richard McDonough, Cynthia Reed, and Elisabeth Gleason Humez.

In arriving at a final selection of photographs I am indebted to Marcia Moss, Joe Ofria, and Mary Alycia McAleer.

Finally I must thank my wife, Ruth Delaney McAleer, and my children, Mary Alycia, Saragh, Seana, Jay, Paul, and Andrew, for welcoming Emerson into our home as a guest who stayed for an entire septenniad.

John McAleer

Chapter Notes

Full reference to the sources cited in the notes is in the Bibliography.

1. A UNIVERSAL MAN

1. *JMN*, XIII, 283; Woodbury, 139 *L*, VI, 23.
2. EWE, 156, 153.
3. *Ellen*, II, 224; *L*, III, 221.
4. EWE, 213; *JMN*, XI, 195; *CEC*, 521.
5. *JMN*, VII, 170.
6. EWE, 237.
7. Holmes, 364; Albee, 45; *CEC*, 371; Lowell, 353.
8. Albee, 132, 134, 149–150.
9. Woodbury, 22.
10. Annie Adams Fields, "Glimpses of Emerson," in Bode, 107; *JMN*, VII, 53.
11. *JMN*, XIII, 120.
12. *W*, IV, 226–227; Thayer, 115n.
13. Holmes, 381; Cary, 77; John Burroughs, *Indoor Studies*, 74; Simon

and Parsons, 74; *JMN*, III, 327.
14. *W*, III, 68.
15. *JMN*, V, 229; see also *J*, X, 522.
16. John Burroughs, *Last Harvest*, 38.
17. Woodbury, 75–76.
18. Shepard, 48.
19. *W*, II, 45–46.
20. Lindsay Swift, *Brook Farm: Its Members, Scholars, and Visitors*, 237.
21. Sanborn, 323–324; Frederick T. McGill, Jr., *Channing of Concord: A Life of William Ellery Channing*, II, 186.
22. Blanchard, 185.
23. *W*, III, 94.
24. *JMN*, V, 229.
25. *JMN*, XI, 440–441.

2. BIRTH

1. Cabot, I, 27.
2. Haskins, 80–84.
3. Samuel Adams Drake, *Old Landmarks and Historic Personages of Boston*, 381.
4. Arthur B. Ellis, *History of the First Church in Boston*, 270.
5. *J*, X, 382.
6. Ellis, *History of the First Church*, 270.

7. Arthur Stanwood Pier, *The Story of Harvard*, 55. As "president's freshman" at Harvard in 1817–18, Emerson lived in this house.

8. Ellis, *History of the First Church*, 188–198.

9. Ellis, *History of the First Church*, 307.

3. PARENTAL TIES

1. Haskins, 34.
2. Rusk, 29.
3. Cabot, I, 35.
4. *JMN*, II, 309.
5. John Burroughs, *Last Harvest*, 33.
6. Holmes, 27.
7. Cabot, I, 41.
8. Rusk, 26.
9. Josiah Quincy, *Figures of the Past*, 253.
10. Haskins, 73.
11. Furness, 3.
12. Holmes, 44.
13. Arthur Stanwood Pier, *The Story of Harvard*, 125.
14. Woodberry, 12.
15. Garnett, 28–29.
16. Garnett, 29.
17. And Samuel Lothrop, whom Emerson tutored at Harvard, seeking from the vantage point of maturity to characterize Emerson's manner, said: "He seemed to dwell apart, as if in a tower, from which he looked upon everything from a loophole of his own" (*Some Reminiscences of the Life of Samuel Kirkland Lothrop*, ed. Thornton Kirkland Lothrop, 62); see also Garnett, 28–29.
18. Ireland, *In Memoriam*, 91.
19. Gay, 34.
20. Woodberry, 24.
21. Rusk, 27; Woodberry, 57.
22. EWE, 171.
23. Rusk, 26.
24. *W*, VI, 9; Bremer, *Homes*, II, 563; *The Poems and Prose Remains of Arthur Hugh Clough*, ed. Blanche Clough, I, 183. See also Franklin B. Sanborn, *Ralph Waldo Emerson*, 4.
25. *AJ*, 221; *JMN*, VIII, 230, 380; IX, 267.
26. Albee, 13.
27. William Wynkoop, *Three Children of the Universe: Emerson's View of Shakespeare, Bacon, and Milton*, 184.
28. *The Literary Remains of the Late Henry James*, ed. William James, 293–294.
29. Rusk, 5.
30. Cabot, I, 27.
31. Haskins, 63.
32. Holmes, 13–14.
33. Haskins, 53–54.
34. Phillips Russell, *Emerson: The Wisest American*, 9.
35. Allen, 23–24.
36. Haskins, 31.
37. Haskins, 68–69, 74–75.
38. Haskins, 76.
39. Allen, 10; Rusk, 21.
40. Haskins, 66.
41. *L*, IV, 401; Ward, 81. Ruth Emerson, who died on 16 November 1853, had actually turned eighty-five on 9 November.

4. MARY MOODY EMERSON

1. *W*, VI, 272.
2. Snider, 37.
3. Cabot, I, 30.
4. Franklin B. Sanborn, *Transcendental and Literary New England*, ed. Kenneth W. Cameron, 342–343. This section of the book is a reprint of Sanborn's *The Personality of Emerson* (1903).
5. Sanborn, *Transcendental and Literary New England*, 345.
6. *JMN*, VIII, 135.

7. *W*, X, 407.

8. Swayne, 153; Sanborn, II, 361.

9. Cabot, I, 31.

10. *L*, III, 292–293.

11. *W*, X, 407; *JMN*, XIV, 283–284; *W*, X, 414.

12. Engel, 112; Cary, 20; Cabot, I, 31. See also *JMN*, IV, 53.

13. Swayne, 218–219.

14. Rusk, 24–25.

15. Rusk, 31.

16. Phillips Russell, *Emerson: The Wisest American*, 28.

17. For Mary's attachment to death and her shrouds see Russell, *Emerson*, 29–30, and *W*, X, 432; see also Anna Robeson Burr, ed., *Alice James: Her Brothers — Her Journal*, 13–14.

18. *TJ*, VII, 264.

19. Brown, 38; *TJ*, VII, 265.

20. *JMN*, XIII, 413; Cabot, I, 28; *JMN*, IV, 53; Sanborn, II, 484; *W*, X, 432; EWE, 10. See also Holmes, 18.

21. Russell, *Emerson*, 22.

22. *W*, X, 420.

23. Rusk, 321–322.

24. *L*, II, 397n.

25. *L*, II, 396–397.

5. A BOY'S WAYS

1. *JMN*, III, 15.

2. Gay, 31.

3. Haskins, 55.

4. *L*, II, 45.

5. Furness, Ltr. XXII, 52.

6. EWE, 13.

7. *JMN*, VIII, 30.

8. Rusk, 24.

9. Rusk, 20.

10. Ednah D. Cheney, "Emerson and Boston," in Franklin B. Sanborn, ed., *The Genius and Character of Emerson*, 5–6; Firkins, 10.

11. Franklin B. Sanborn, *Transcendental and Literary New England*, ed. Kenneth W. Cameron, 198.

12. *W*, IX, 359.

13. Nathaniel P. Willis, *Hurry-graphs*, 170.

14. *JMN*, VIII, 258.

15. *L*, II, 255.

16. *JMN*, VIII, 69; Ward, 64. See also *JMN*, VII, 377, where Emerson wrote, "Your life, they say, is but a few spinnings of this top."

17. *JMN*, XVI, 263.

18. *JMN*, V, 367.

19. *J*, X, 229. See also Charles W. Eliot, *A Late Harvest*, 4.

20. *JMN*, IX, 294.

21. Arthur B. Ellis, *History of the First Church in Boston*, 39.

22. *The Diary of William Bentley, D.D.*, IV, 23.

23. *L*, IV, 179.

24. Haskins, 64, 69–75.

6. A SPARTAN YOUTH

1. EWE, 17.

2. Haskins, 55–56.

3. Rusk, 59.

4. Cabot, I, 43; Perry, 33. "The History of Fortus" is in Furness, 177–185.

5. Holmes, 43.

6. *W*, II, 133.

7. *JMN*, XIV, 90.

8. Rusk, 36–37.

9. Franklin B. Sanborn, *Ralph Waldo Emerson*, 8–11.

10. *J*, X, 207–208.

11. Henry Thomas and Dana Lee Thomas, *Living Biographies of Great Philosophers*, 249.

12. *JMN*, IX, 148.

13. *L*, I, 75.

14. Gay, 12.
15. John T. Morse, *Memoir of Colonel Henry Lee*, 335–337, 402.
16. *JMN*, IX, 146–149.
17. *L*, III, 453.
18. EWE, 16.
19. Firkins, 348–349.
20. Edward Everett Hale, *Ralph Waldo Emerson*, 16–17.
21. *W*, VII, 119–121.
22. The Penn annuity was ten pounds per annum, left by Elder James Penn of the First Church in his will of 1671, " 'out of the Rents of his Farm at Pulling Point [present-day Winthrop] for the maintenance of such poor scholar or scholars at the Colledge as they shall see good' " (Samuel Eliot Morison, *Harvard in the Seventeenth Century*, II, 380).

7. HARVARD

1. Samuel Eliot Morison, *Three Centuries of Harvard: 1636–1936*, 200–201.
2. Cabot, I, 48–49.
3. *Some Reminiscences of the Life of Samuel Kirkland Lothrop*, ed. Thornton Kirkland Lothrop, 50–51, 61–67.
4. *L*, I, 82.
5. *JMN*, VIII, 33.
6. *W*, X, 125.
7. Franklin B. Sanborn, *Ralph Waldo Emerson*, 126.
8. *JMN*, II, 4.
9. *JMN*, IV, 110; see also Cabot, I, 54–55.
10. *L*, I, 67.
11. Arthur Stanwood Pier, *The Story of Harvard*, 129.
12. Rusk, 71–72; Allen, 45–46; *W*, I, 119.
13. Pier, *The Story of Harvard*, 136.
14. Pier, *The Story of Harvard*, 137–138.
15. Pier, *The Story of Harvard*, 138; Josiah Quincy, *Figures of the Past*, 36–37.
16. Perry, 34; Frothingham, 23.
17. John T. Morse, Jr., *Life and Letters of Oliver Wendell Holmes*, I, 51.
18. Cabot, I, 67.
19. EWE, 24; Gay, 46; Woodberry, 17.
20. *Abroad*, 62.
21. *JMN*, I, 37.
22. *L*, I, 57.
23. Woodberry, 16.

8. COMMENCEMENT

1. Edward Waldo Emerson, *The Early Years of the Saturday Club*, 183.
2. Josiah Quincy, *Figures of the Past*, 17.
3. Cabot, I, 64.
4. Quincy, *Figures of the Past*, 45.
5. Rusk, 84.
6. Quincy, *Figures of the Past*, 17–18.
7. *JMN*, I, 39.
8. Gay, 48.
9. Rusk, 86.
10. Quincy, *Figures of the Past*, 47.
11. M. A. DeWolfe Howe, ed., *The Articulate Sisters: Passages from Journals and Letters of the Daughters of President Josiah Quincy of Harvard University*, 38–41; Quincy, *Figures of the Past*, 46–47.
12. *L*, I, 101–102.
13. Quincy, *Figures of the Past*, 47.
14. *L*, VI, 77.

9. SCHOOLMASTER

1. *JMN*, I, 46–47.
2. *L*, I, 106.
3. Cabot, I, 70; EWE, 28.
4. Cabot, I, 70–71.
5. Cabot, I, 72–73.
6. *L*, I, 114–115.
7. Wagenknecht, 50.
8. William Sloane Kennedy, ''Clews to Emerson's Mystic Verse,'' *The American Author* (June 1903), 229–230.
9. *L*, I, 133–134.
10. William J. Sowder, *Emerson's Impact on the British Isles and Canada*, 76–78.
11. *JMN*, II, 241.
12. Haskins, 109–110.
13. Charles Francis Adams, *Richard Henry Dana*, I, 5.
14. *L*, II, 348.
15. Holmes, 49–50.
16. Holmes, 50.
17. *J*, II, 244–245.

10. LITERARY AWAKENING

1. *J*, II, 4–5.
2. *L*, I, 55; *JMN*, I, 279; II, 108, 282.
3. *EL*, I, 371–374.
4. Alexander Carlyle, ed., *The Love Letters of Thomas Carlyle and Jane Welsh*, I, 366.
5. Mead, 237; Cary, 90.
6. *JMN*, IX, 376.
7. Ralph Waldo Emerson, ed., *Parnassus*, ix.
8. *W*, IV, 162, 164–166.
9. Cary, 13.
10. Wagenknecht, 109, 182; see also *JMN*, VII, 463.
11. Rusk, 34; *JMN*, VII, 462; *W*, IV, 168.
12. Wagenknecht, 109; *W*, IV, 55; Josephine Miles, *Ralph Waldo Emerson*, 22; *JMN*, IV, 294.
13. *EL*, I, 99ff; *JMN*, II, 222–223, 208, 377.
14. *AJ*, xx.
15. *W*, IV, 168; and see *JMN*, VII, 374; W. L. Ustick, ''Emerson's Debt to Montaigne,'' *Washington University Studies* 9 (1922), 245, 62; Charles Lowell Young, *Emerson's Montaigne*.
16. *W*, VIII, 125.
17. Gay Wilson Allen, *The Solitary Singer: A Critical Biography of Walt Whitman*, 242.
18. *J*, II, 440–441.
19. *W*, IX, 66–67.
20. *W*, XII, 295–296.

11. DIVINITY STUDIES

1. *JMN*, I, 52.
2. *JMN*, II, 237, 238.
3. *JMN*, II, 239–240, 241–242.
4. *L*, I, 143.
5. Cabot, I, 102.
6. *JMN*, II, 332; *W*, I, 91.
7. *JMN*, II, 332.
8. *L*, I, 154–155.
9. *JMN*, III, 44–45. See also C. P. Hotson, ''Sampson Reed, a Teacher of Emerson,'' *New England Quarterly* 2 (April 1929), 249–277.
10. Lathrop, 181.
11. Cabot, I, 259.
12. Hotson, ''Sampson Reed,'' 265.
13. Miller, 204–205.
14. *L*, I, 170.
15. *YES*, 1–12, 215–216.
16. Franklin B. Sanborn, *Ralph Waldo Emerson*, 20.

17. *J*, II, 98n.
18. *YES*, 7; William A. Huggard, *The*

Religious Teachings of Emerson, 130.

12. JOURNEY SOUTH

1. *JMN*, III, 117.
2. *JMN*, III, 77.
3. *L*, I, 193–194.
4. *J*, II, 185.
5. *J*, II, 187–191. Emerson copied Murat's letters in his journal exactly as they were written, retaining Murat's quaint spellings.

6. David Stacton, *The Bonapartes*, 213–214.
7. *JMN*, IV, 242.
8. *L*, III, 311–312.
9. Rusk, 123.
10. *L*, I, 201.
11. *L*, I, 264; Arlin Turner, *Nathaniel Hawthorne: A Biography*, 143.

13. EZRA RIPLEY

1. *W*, X, 388.
2. Ms., 3 July 1828, Houghton Library, Harvard.
3. *JMN*, VIII, 56.
4. *Diaries and Letters of William Emerson: 1743–1776*, ed. Amelia Forbes Emerson, 120.
5. Hawthorne, *Mosses*, X, 11–12.
6. *JMN*, VII, 49.
7. *W*, X, 390; *JMN*, V, 21, 23, 65; . VIII, 60; *W*, X, 386–387.

8. *W*, X, 385–386.
9. Carl Bode, *The American Lyceum: Town Meeting of the Mind*, 31, 46.
10. *L*, II, 21.
11. *JMN*, V, 96.
12. *JMN*, VIII, 53–57.
13. *Lidian*, 90.

14. ELLEN TUCKER

1. Gregg, 168.
2. *JMN*, III, 153.
3. *J*, II, 258.
4. *JMN*, I, 134.
5. *JMN*, II, 238; Samuel McChord Crothers, *Ralph Waldo Emerson: How to Know Him*, 60; *JMN*, II, 241.
6. *J*, II, 123; *JMN*, III, 72, 99.
7. Pommer, 1; *JMN*, III, 149.
8. Pommer, 9; and see Kenneth W. Cameron, "Samuel and Ezra Ripley at Emerson's Ordination," *Emerson Society Quarterly* 48 (3d qu., pt. 2, 1967), 89–91; *JMN*, VIII, 381.
9. Cabot, I, 147–148.
10. *L*, I, 283–284.
11. Gregg, 112.
12. Pommer, 39.

13. *L*, I, 307n.
14. *L*, I, 310.
15. Gregg, 136.
16. Gregg, 135; *L*, I, 316.
17. Gregg, 139.
18. Pommer, 49.
19. *L*, I, 318.
20. *JMN*, III, 227.
21. *YES*, 144.
22. *L*, I, 323.
23. Joel Porte, *Representative Man: Ralph Waldo Emerson in His Time*, 59.
24. *L*, I, 326.
25. Haskins, 112.
26. *JMN*, IV, 7, xv.
27. *JMN*, V, 456; and see II Corinthians 12:7.
28. Gregg, 152.
29. *JMN*, VII, 170.

30. *L*, I, 436.
31. *JMN*, V, 19, 108.
32. *JMN*, VII, 168.
33. *JMN*, VIII, 381.
34. *L*, IV, 33.
35. *L*, IV, 54.
36. Pommer, 96–97.
37. *JMN*, V, 322–323.
38. *JMN*, V, 328–329.
39. A. Bronson Alcott, *Ralph Waldo Emerson: An Estimate of His Genius and Character*, 40–41.

40. *JMN*, VII, 368.
41. *W*, II, 169–170, 173–174.
42. Chapman, 78–83.
43. Cabot, I, 360.
44. *JMN*, VII, 301.
45. *L*, II, 417.
46. *W*, II, 126.
47. *JMN*, VII, 215.
48. "Experience," *W*, III, 48.
49. *JMN*, IX, 236.
50. *Grimm*, 43–44.
51. Holmes, 368.

15. THEOLOGICAL DOUBTS

1. *YES*, 32, 58.
2. *JMN*, IV, 27.
3. *JMN*, III, 318–319.
4. *JMN*, IV, 33; VI, 192, 202.
5. William Emerson, *An Historical Sketch of the First Church in Boston*, 136–138.
6. *Abroad*, 87; and see Frederick B. Tolles, "Emerson and Quakerism," *American Literature* 10 (May 1938), 142–165.
7. *JMN*, III, 153.
8. Cabot, I, 159.
9. Rusk, 160.
10. *LCEN*, I, 509.
11. *Abroad*, 67; Rusk, 161.
12. *YES*, 255.
13. Mary C. Turpie, "A Quaker Source for Emerson's Sermon on the Lord's Supper," *New England Quarterly* 17 (March 1944), 96.
14. Haskins, 48.
15. *W*, XI, 4.
16. Frothingham, 363–380.
17. Rusk, 160.
18. *L*, I, 353n.
19. *JMN*, IV, 28–29.

20. *JMN*, IV, 30.
21. *Abroad*, 138.
22. *W*, XI, 24; and see Dan Vogel, "Orville Dewey on Emerson's 'The Lord's Supper,'" *Emerson Society Quarterly* 31 (2d qu. 1963), 40–42.
23. Barrett Wendell, *A Literary History of America*, 313; Firkins, 36.
24. *W*, XI, 24–25.
25. *W*, XI, 20–21.
26. Charles Feidelson, Jr., *Symbolism and American Literature*, 161.
27. Brown, 31–32; see also EWE, 41.
28. Frothingham, 231–232.
29. Perry, 40.
30. Cabot, I, 158; Mark A. DeWolfe Howe, *John Jay Chapman and His Letters*, 77; *Abroad*, 72–73.
31. Rusk, 167.
32. Rusk, 166.
33. *L*, III, 131; Cyrus Bartol, "Emerson's Religion," in Franklin B. Sanborn, ed., *The Genius and Character of Emerson*, 110.
34. *L*, V, 81–82.

16. SAMUEL TAYLOR COLERIDGE

1. *JMN*, IV, 200.
2. *JMN*, IV, 408.
3. *W*, V, 14.
4. *JMN*, IV, 408.
5. *JMN*, IV, 409.
6. *JMN*, IV, 410.

7. Coleridge, *The Friend*, III (1818), 70–77; *W*, V, 12.
8. *JMN*, IV, 410.
9. *JMN*, IV, 410–411.
10. *JMN*, IV, 411; *W*, V, 10–14.
11. *W*, V, 14.

1 7 . T H O M A S C A R L Y L E

1. James Anthony Froude, *Thomas Carlyle: A History of the First Forty Years of His Life, 1795–1835*, II, 286.
2. *L*, I, 395.
3. *JMN*, IV, 45.
4. *L*, I, 394, 395 ; *JMN*, IV, 219–220.
5. Quoted in Holmes, 78–79.
6. *W*, V, 18.
7. W. S. Tryon, *Parnassus Corner*, 148.
8. Firkins, 411.
9. Cabot, I, 196.
10. Cabot, I, 197.
11. *W*, V, 18.
12. *CEC*, 109.
13. Froude, *Thomas Carlyle*, II, 290–291.
14. *Letters of Thomas Carlyle to John Stuart Mill, John Sterling, and Robert Browning*, ed. Alexander Carlyle, 66–67.
15. Mill to Carlyle, 5 September 1833, quoted in Lawrence and Elizabeth Hansen, *Necessary Evil: The Life of Jane Welsh Carlyle*, 178.
16. Cabot, I, 197 ; CEC, 201.
17. Lawrence and Elizabeth Hansen, *Necessary Evil*, 178.
18. *Abroad*, 77.
19. *CEC*, 101.
20. *JMN*, IV, 82.

1 8 . W I L L I A M W O R D S W O R T H

1. Cabot, I, 198.
2. *W*, V, 24.
3. Ibid.
4. *W*, V, 22.
5. Ibid.
6. *W*, V, 22–23.
7. *JMN*, IV, 225.
8. EWE, 17 ; *JMN*, VIII, 258.
9. Haskins, 123–124.
10. *JMN*, IV, 225.
11. Franklin B. Sanborn, *Ralph Waldo Emerson*, 83–84.
12. *JMN*, IV, 222.
13. *JMN*, IV, 223.
14. *JMN*, IV, 224.
15. Scudder, 30.

1 9 . G L I M P S E S O F T H E U N I V E R S A L

1. *JMN*, I, 51.
2. *JMN*, II, 49–50. See also John Q. Anderson, ''Emerson and the Moral Sentiment,'' *Emerson Society Quarterly* 19 (2d qu. 1960), 13–15.
3. Harold Clarke Goddard, *Studies in New England Transcendentalism*, 46.
4. *JMN*, V, 459.
5. Chapman, 59.
6. *W*, I, 151.
7. *W*, XI, 486.
8. Chapman, 59.
9. *W*, VI, 49.
10. *L*, I, 412–413.
11. *W*, I, 165; and see M. R. Davis, ''Emerson's 'Reason' and the Scottish Philosophers,'' *New England Quarterly* 17 (June 1944), 209–228.
12. A. W. Ward and A. R. Waller, eds., *The Cambridge History of English Literature*, XI, 151–152; Arthur Oucker Lovejoy, *The Reason, the Understanding, and Time*, 8–9.
13. Paul F. Boller, Jr., *American Transcendentalism, 1830–1860: An Intellectual Inquiry*, 180–181.
14. *W*, VIII, 289 ; Snider, 9 ; *Abroad*, 46.
15. Newton Dillaway, *Prophet of America: Emerson and the Problems of Today*, 105.
16. Albee, 122n.
17. *The Dial*, IV:2 (October 1843), 247.
18. *CEC*, 122–123.

19. *L*, I, 450. See also Stephen L. Conroy, "Emerson and Phrenology," *American Quarterly* 16 (Summer 1964), 215–217.
20. *JMN*, VIII, 168.
21. *W*, VI, 169, 177, 179–180.
22. *JMN*, V, 8.
23. EWE, 98.
24. *JMN*, VII, 440–441.
25. EWE, 164.
26. *W*, I, 111–112.

20. THE POET–PHILOSOPHER

1. *J*, II, 101.
2. "The Poet," *W*, III, 5–6.
3. "The Transcendentalist," *W*, I, 338.
4. Paul F. Boller, Jr., *American Transcendentalism, 1830–1860: An Intellectual Inquiry*, 92.
5. *JMN*, V, 37.
6. *JMN*, XII, 198.
7. *CEC*, 317.
8. Townsend Scudder, "Emerson in London and the London Lectures," *American Literature* 8 (March 1936), 34.
9. Stephen E. Whicher, *Freedom and Fate: An Inner Life of Ralph Waldo Emerson*, 50–71.
10. *JMN*, III, 15.
11. *JMN*, II, 240.
12. *TJ*, I, 429–430.
13. Snider, 130–131.
14. Cary, 204.
15. Joel Porte, *Representative Man: Ralph Waldo Emerson in His Time*, 323.
16. Sherman Paul, *The Shores of America: Thoreau's Inward Exploration*, 13–14.
17. *JMN*, VII, 302.
18. "Plato; or, the Philosopher," *W*, IV, 49.
19. "Plato; or, the Philosopher," *W*, IV, 41–42.
20. Holmes, 197. See also Stuart G. Brown, "Emerson's Platonism," *New England Quarterly* 18 (September 1945), 325–345.
21. Lewis Mumford, *The Golden Day: A Study in American Experience and Culture*, 100.
22. "Plato; or, the Philosopher," *W*, IV, 44.
23. Perry, 65.
24. Hopkins, 62, 237.
25. John S. Harrison, *The Teachers of Emerson*, 24.
26. Harrison, *The Teachers of Emerson*, 35; Carpenter, 75.
27. *W*, II, 269.
28. Rod W. Horton and Herbert W. Edwards, *Backgrounds of American Literary Thought*, 114–115.
29. W. T. Harris, "Emerson's Orientalism" in Franklin B. Sanborn, ed., *The Genius and Character of Emerson*, 376.
30. Robert Detweiler, "Emerson and Zen," *American Quarterly* 14 (Fall 1962), 422–438.
31. *W*, II, 3, 45.
32. See *L*, I, l, li, 154–155, 254.
33. René Wellek, "The Minor Transcendentalists and German Philosophy," in Brian M. Barbour, ed., *American Transcendentalism: An Anthology of Criticism*, 117.
34. *JMN*, V, 270–271.
35. *JMN*, V, 271–272.
36. *JMN*, V, 273.
37. *JMN*, V, 272.
38. *JMN*, V, 458.
39. *W*, I, 39.
40. *W*, I, 4.
41. *W*, I, 33–34.
42. *W*, I, 64.
43. *W*, I, 65.
44. *W*, I, 36.
45. "History," *W*, II, 1.
46. "History," *W*, II, 2.
47. "The Over-Soul," *W*, II, 268.
48. "The Over-Soul," *W*, II, 275.
49. "The Over-Soul," *W*, II, 279.
50. "The Over-Soul," *W*, II, 281.
51. *Nature, W*, I, 45.
52. *W*, III, 34.
53. Holmes, 396.
54. Boller, *American Transcendentalism*, 81; and see P. F. Quinn,

"Emerson and Mysticism," *American Literature* 21 (January 1950), 397–414.

55. Wagenknecht, 40.
56. See Lionel Braham, "Emerson and Boehme: A Comparative Study in Mystical Ideas," *Modern Language Quarterly* 20 (March 1959), 31–32; *JMN*, IX, 106–107.
57. *W*, I, 9.
58. Holmes, 398; *JMN*, V, 18–19.

59. *JMN*, II, 238.
60. *J*, II, 170.
61. "Intellect," *W*, II, 328–329.
62. *W*, II, 296.
63. Perry, 60; Harold Bloom, *Figures of Capable Imagination*, 49.
64. Quinn, "Emerson and Mysticism," 414.
65. *JMN*, IX, 106.
66. Braham, "Emerson and Boehme," 34.

21. FATHER TAYLOR: THE SAILORS' POET

1. Justin Kaplan, *Walt Whitman: A Life*, 253; *Collected Writings of Walt Whitman*, ed. Floyd Stovall, II, 549–552.
2. A. B. Muzzey, *Reminiscences and Memorials of Men of the Revolution and Their Families*, 342.
3. *L*, I, 344–345.
4. *JMN*, V, 255.
5. Holmes, 254.
6. *J*, IX, 497–498.
7. Cabot, I, 327–328n.
8. Lindsay Swift, *Brook Farm: Its Members, Scholars, and Visitors*, 241.
9. Brown, 31; Holmes, 56.
10. Franklin B. Sanborn, ed., *The Genius and Character of Emerson*, 17–18; and see Raymond L. Bridgman, ed., *Concord Lectures on Philosophy*, 72–74; Cabot, I, 327–328n.

11. *JMN*, V, 4–5.
12. *L*, I, 430.
13. *JMN*, V, 87.
14. *JMN*, V, 255.
15. Ibid.
16. *JMN*, V, 287.
17. *L*, II, 298; *JMN*, VII, 359.
18. *JMN*, VII, 360.
19. Charles Dickens, *American Notes*, 63–65.
20. *JMN*, IX, 233.
21. *JMN*, IX, 237.
22. *JMN*, XIV, 46; Jonathan Messerli, *Horace Mann*, 157, 234.
23. Julian, I, 214–215.
24. *JMN*, VII, 358; IX, 233–235; Dickens, *American Notes*, 63–64.
25. *JMN*, IX, 234–236.
26. *JMN*, IX, 397.

22. ANCESTRY

1. Woodberry, 3.
2. *JMN*, II, 316; XIII, 443; Edwin Percy Whipple, *Recollections of Eminent Men*, 154.
3. *W*, VI, 9, 10–11.
4. *W*, VI, 181; "Fate," *W*, VI, 10; Holmes, 2.
5. Henry James, "Emerson," in *Partial Portraits*, 440.
6. John Burroughs, *Birds and Poets*, 189–190.

7. Benjamin Kendall Emerson and George A. Gordon, *The Ipswich Emersons: 1636–1900* . . . , 74, 441–442; John J. Currier, *History of Newburyport, Mass., 1764–1909*, II, 578; Charles W. Upham, *Salem Witchcraft*, II, 225–238; Chadwick Hansen, *Witchcraft at Salem*, 150; Sally Smith Booth, *The Witches of Early America*, 58–59. A general amnesty in May 1693

enabled Mary Perkins Bradbury to return to her family. She died on 20 December 1700.

8. Haskins, 32.
9. Haskins, 29.
10. Haskins, 17.
11. Rusk, 42; Haskins, 27.
12. Haskins, 134.
13. Haskins, 24.
14. Haskins, 26. Trinity Church was destroyed in November 1872, in the fire that consumed much of old Boston. The bones of John and Hannah Haskins were reinterred in Dorchester, at Cedar Grove Cemetery.
15. Elizabeth Lowell Everett, *Peter Bulkeley and His Times*, 14–17; Dana McLean Greeley, *Know These Concordians*, 1–4.
16. Townsend Scudder, *Concord: American Town*, 21.

17. Scudder, *Concord: American Town*, 5, 7.
18. Lucy Allen Paton, *Elizabeth Cary Agassiz: A Biography*, 270–271; *Abroad*, 30.
19. Ruth R. Wheeler, *Concord: Climate for Freedom*, 18.
20. Everett, *Peter Bulkeley*, 31.
21. Samuel Eliot Morison, *The Founding of Harvard College*, 290–291.
22. Wheeler, *Concord: Climate for Freedom*, 43; Scudder, *Concord: American Town*, 29.
23. *JMN*, V, 56. Elizabeth's grandmother had been a Waldo, giving Emerson double descent from the Waldo family, since her son Edward, Emerson's great-great-grandfather, took a Waldo for his bride.

23. THE ACTION AT THE NORTH BRIDGE

1. Hawthorne, *Mosses*, X, 17.
2. Ruth R. Wheeler, *Concord: Climate for Freedom*, 70; Townsend Scudder, *Concord: American Town*, 65–68; Swayne, 35; W, XI, 563n.
3. W, XI, 564n.
4. Scudder, *Concord: American Town*, 65–68.
5. Wheeler, *Concord: Climate for Freedom*, 109; *Diaries and Letters of William Emerson: 1743–1776*, ed. Amelia Forbes Emerson, 98.
6. Franklin B. Sanborn, *Transcendental and Literary New England*, ed. Kenneth W. Cameron, 254.
7. Scudder, *Concord: American Town*, 61–68.
8. J, III, 535n.
9. *JMN*, V, 71.
10. *JMN*, V, 70–71.
11. *Diaries and Letters of William Emerson*, 118.
12. W, XI, 77.

13. *Diaries and Letters of William Emerson*, 3.
14. Ibid.; Phillips Russell, *Emerson: The Wisest American*, v.
15. *Diaries and Letters of William Emerson*, 3.
16. *Diaries and Letters of William Emerson*, 42.
17. *Diaries and Letters of William Emerson*, 19.
18. *Diaries and Letters of William Emerson*, 42.
19. Lemuel Shattuck, *A History of the Town of Concord*, 184–186, 187; Rusk, 45.
20. *Diaries and Letters of William Emerson*, 63.
21. *Diaries and Letters of William Emerson*, 73, 133; Shattuck, *History of Concord*, 105–106; Harold Murdock, *The Nineteenth of April, 1775*, 57–58.
22. Murdock, *The Nineteenth of April, 1775*, 57–58.
23. *Diaries and Letters of William Emerson*, 73.

24. Ibid.
25. *Diaries and Letters of William Emerson*, 73–74.
26. *Diaries and Letters of William Emerson*, 74.
27. Hawthorne, *Mosses*, X, 6.
28. Ezra Ripley, *A History of the Fight at Concord on the 19th of April, 1775*, 19.
29. Murdock, *The Nineteenth of April, 1775*, 61.
30. *Diaries and Letters of William Emerson*, 72.
31. *Diaries and Letters of William Emerson*, 75.
32. Wheeler, *Concord: Climate for Freedom*, 132.
33. Scudder, *Concord: American Town*, 84.
34. *Diaries and Letters of William Emerson*, 87.
35. *JMN*, V, 13.
36. *Diaries and Letters of William Emerson*, 115.
37. *Diaries and Letters of William Emerson*, 116.
38. *Diaries and Letters of William Emerson*, 123–125, 134. In 1976, marking the bicentennial of the death of William, members of the Emerson family and other Concordians placed a suitable monument at the Pleasant Street Cemetery, in a dedicatory service conducted by the Reverend Dana McLean Greeley, pastor of Concord's First Church.
39. *JMN*, II, 302.
40. *JMN*, II, 239–240.
41. The quotation is from "Prospects," the sixth of the six lectures called "The Times," delivered in New York City in March 1842; Jeanne Kronman, "Three Unpublished Lectures of Ralph Waldo Emerson," *New England Quarterly* 19 (March 1946), 100.
42. *W*, X, 406.

24. LIDIAN

1. Rusk, 215.
2. *Lidian*, 47.
3. *Lidian*, 47–48.
4. Allen, 239–240.
5. *Lidian*, 48.
6. *L*, I, 436.
7. Cabot, I, 236.
8. *Lidian*, 69, 54.
9. Woodbury, 140.
10. K. W. Dykema, "Why Did Lydia Jackson Become Lidian Emerson?," *American Speech* 17 (December 1942), 285–286.
11. Engel, 59.
12. *L*, I, 434–435.
13. *L*, I, 438.
14. Louise Hall Tharp, *The Peabody Sisters of Salem*, 112.
15. *L*, I, 434.
16. Rusk, 221.
17. *Lidian*, 50–51.
18. *Lidian*, 55.
19. George William Curtis, *Little Journeys to the Houses of Famous American Authors*, 23–24; *JMN*, V, 85.
20. Ruth R. Wheeler, *Concord: Climate for Freedom*, 184; Swayne, 295.
21. *JMN*, XI, xii; V, 241; Engel, 91.
22. *CEC*, 185; Engel, 68.
23. EWE, 112.
24. *JMN*, XV, 287; *J*, X, 170.
25. Until the Civil War years the Emersons referred to their home as Coolidge Castle. Thereafter they called it Bush. Given the precedent offered by the Old Manse, so identified now for all periods of its history though not so designated until Hawthorne took occupancy in 1842, Bush here is referred to throughout as Bush.
26. *W*, IX, 1–2.
27. *Lidian*, 205–206.
28. Sanborn, II, 481.
29. Carpenter, 30–38; *L*, II, 112, 28n; *JMN*, V, 280; *W*, IV, 62.

30. *JMN*, V, 456; *Lidian*, 77.
31. 20 August 1837, *JMN*, V, 371.
32. *JMN*, VIII, 365. In an undated letter Fanny Longfellow told of hearing that "Emerson does not live happily with his wife" (Edward Wagenknecht, *Longfellow*, 237).
33. *L*, III, 181, 226; II, 245, 347; *Lidian*, 108.
34. *L*, IV, 199, 403, 449, 507.
35. *Lidian*, 195.
36. *The Letters and Journals of Waldo Emerson Forbes*, ed. Amelia Forbes Thomas, 303.
37. *Lidian*, 84ff. See also Gay Gaer Luce, *Body Time: Physiological Rhythms and Social Stress*, 258–292.

38. *JMN*, VIII, 11, 242, 289.
39. Howe, 62.
40. Engel, 4.
41. Katherine Burton, *Sorrow Built a Bridge*, 75.
42. Engel, 110; Brown, 34–35.
43. *Lidian*, xiii, 68.
44. *Lidian*, 145.
45. *Lidian*, 162–163.
46. *Lidian*, 70.
47. *Lidian*, 227n.
48. *EL*, I, 162–163. See also R. C. Pettigrew, "Emerson and Milton," *American Literature* 3 (March 1931), 56.
49. *JMN*, VII, 544.
50. 4 February 1841, *JMN*, VII, 420.
51. *JMN*, XI, 213.

25. HARRIET MARTINEAU

1. Harriet Martineau, *Autobiography*, ed. Maria Weston Chapman, I, 375.
2. *JMN*, V, 86.
3. Martineau, *Autobiography*, I, 375.
4. *L*, I, 393.
5. *CEC*, 126.
6. *L*, II, 24.
7. *Lidian*, 62. Eliza Farrar, wife of John Farrar, professor of mathematics at Harvard, was the sister of Emerson's friend Mary Rotch.

8. *L*, II, 24–25.
9. *JMN*, V, 354–355.
10. *CEC*, 181–182.
11. *CEC*, 185.
12. Julian, I, 196–197.
13. Sandford Salyer, *Marmee: The Mother of Little Women*, 58–59.
14. Shepard, 208–209.
15. Harriet Martineau, *Retrospect of Western Travel*, II, 204–205.
16. Martineau, *Retrospect of Western Travel*, II, 205–206.

26. CHARLES CHAUNCY EMERSON

1. *L*, II, 17.
2. *CEC*, 106.
3. *L*, II, 20.
4. *L*, II, 19, note 58.
5. *JMN*, V, 151–152.
6. *CEC*, 147–148.
7. Cabot, I, 272.
8. Townsend Scudder, *Concord: American Town*, 153–154.
9. Lathrop, 16.
10. Oliver Wendell Holmes, *Poems*, 32.
11. Scudder, *Concord: American Town*, 156.
12. EWE, 67.

13. Leonard Neufeldt, "Emerson, Thoreau, and Daniel Webster," *Emerson Society Quarterly* 26 (1st qu. 1980), 45.
14. *Abroad*, 45; Holmes, 21; Edwin Percy Whipple, *Recollections of Eminent Men*, 153.
15. Holmes, 24.
16. *The Dial*, IV:1 (July 1843), 90; III:4 (April 1843), 524.
17. *JMN*, V, 107.
18. *W*, I, 11; Holmes, 98; *W*, I, 46.
19. *Lidian*, 70.

27. *NATURE*

1. *JMN*, IV, 237.
2. *L*, II, 26; *AJ*, 77–78; *L*, II, 32.
3. Richard P. Adams, "Emerson and the Organic Metaphor," *PMLA* 69 (March 1954), 123–126.
4. *W*, I, 27.
5. *W*, I, 49, 56.
6. Albee, 58, 104.

7. Arthur M. Schlesinger, Jr., *Orestes A. Brownson: A Pilgrim's Progress*, 62; Bowen, "Emerson's Nature," *The Christian Examiner* 21 (January 1837), 374; Holmes, 93; Shepard, 78; *CEC*, 149; Holmes, 73.
8. *W*, I, 17.

28. "THE AMERICAN SCHOLAR"

1. C. David Mead, ed., *"The American Scholar" Today*, 5. See also John Erskine, "The American Scholar," *American Scholar* 1 (Winter 1932), 5–15.
2. Holmes, 115.
3. Oliver Wendell Holmes, *Over the Teacups*, 233.
4. Holmes, 115.
5. James Russell Lowell, *My Study Windows*, 197–198.
6. Paul Revere Frothingham, *Edward Everett: Orator and Statesman*, 367–368.
7. Bliss Perry, *The Praise of Folly, and Other Papers*, 93–94.
8. *EL*, I, 381.
9. *JMN*, IV, 297.

10. *W*, VI, 62–63.
11. *JMN*, IV, 335.
12. *The Church Review* 3 (October 1850), 333.
13. *L*, II, 94–95, 153n.
14. *JMN*, V, 373.
15. James Freeman Clarke, *Autobiography, Diary and Correspondence*, ed. E. E. Hale, 120.
16. *JMN*, V, 411.
17. Edward Everett Hale, *Ralph Waldo Emerson*, 49–50.
18. *CEC*, 173–174. See also John E. Hart, "Man Thinking as Hero: Emerson's 'Scholar' Revisited," *Emerson Society Quarterly* 55 (2d qu. 1969), 102–106.

29. THE CHEROKEE EXPULSION

1. *JMN*, V, 475.
2. *L*, I, 317.
3. *L*, I, 346.
4. *JMN*, V, 417.
5. Robert L. Sayre, *Thoreau and the American Indians*, 147.
6. *JMN*, V, 477.
7. *JMN*, V, 479.
8. Gay, 216.
9. All the quotations from the letter are from Cabot, II, 698–702.
10. Snider, 64.
11. The "stink to the world" denunciation, for example, took this

form: "When houses burn or assassins strike men cry Fire & Murder without attempting logic. So we only state the fact that a crime that confounds our wits by its magnitude[,] a crime that really deprives us as well as the Cherokees of a Country for we would not call a conspiracy that shall crush these poor Indians our country any more. You sir would no longer be the president of men[;] we should be brute beasts of hell."

12. *JMN*, XII, 22–23, 25, 30–32.

30. THE ADDRESS AT DIVINITY HALL

1. *JMN*, V, 463, 464. See also Conrad Wright, "Emerson, Barzillai Frost, and the Divinity School Address," *Harvard Theological Review* 49 (January 1956), 19–43.
2. *JMN*, V, 471.
3. *L*, II, 147.
4. *JMN*, VII, 41–42.
5. Allen, 316; William Ellery Channing, *Channing's Works*, ed. George G. Channing, I, 194.
6. *Boston Quarterly Review*, I (April 1838), 8, 129.
7. *Boston Quarterly Review*, I (April 1838), 193, 199. See also Clarence F. Gohdes, *The Periodicals of American Transcendentalism*, 50–51; and Gohdes, "Some Remarks on Emerson's Divinity School Address," *American Literature* 1 (March 1929), 27–31.
8. Arthur M. Schlesinger, Jr., *Orestes A. Brownson: A Pilgrim's Progress*, 131.
9. *Abroad*, 167.
10. Holmes, 116. Holmes reduced it to one comprehensive sentence: "In its simplest and broadest statement this discourse was a plea for the individual consciousness as against all historical creeds, bibles, churches; for the soul as the supreme judge in spiritual matters."
11. Chapman, 21.
12. *CEC*, 191; and see Henry Steele Commager, "Tempest in a Boston Teacup," *New England Quarterly* 6 (December 1923), 651–675.
13. James Russell Lowell, *Uncollected Poems*, ed. Thelma M. Smith, 225. Abner Kneeland (1774–1844), sometime minister and deist, was jailed for sixty days in 1838 in Boston, after a judgment condemning him for blasphemy was upheld by Chief Justice Lemuel Shaw. A petition for pardon was denied. Its one hundred and seventy-five signatories included

Channing, Garrison, Ripley, Alcott, and Emerson.
14. Scudder, *Lowell*, I, 57–60.
15. *L*, II, 159.
16. Martin Duberman, *James Russell Lowell*, 25.
17. Joel Myerson, "Lowell on Emerson: A New Letter from Concord in 1838," *New England Quarterly* 44 (December 1971), 649–652.
18. Scudder, *Lowell*, I, 54; Rusk, 269.
19. Gittleman, 219.
20. Miller, 193–196.
21. *W*, I, 149–150; and see William R. Hutchison, *The Transcendental Ministers: Church Reform in the New England Renaissance*, 70–71.
22. *L*, II, 159.
23. Scudder, *Lowell*, I, 60; *Letters of James Russell Lowell*, ed. Charles Eliot Norton, II, 302.
24. Miller, 193.
25. *JMN*, VII, 110–111.
26. Mead, 98–99.
27. Elizabeth Palmer Peabody, *Reminiscences of William Ellery Channing*, 379.
28. Miller, 198.
29. *JMN*, VII, 60, 65.
30. *JMN*, VII, 139–140.
31. Edwin D. Mead, *Emerson and Parker*, 8.
32. Miller, 198.
33. Miller, 238–239.
34. Miller, 301; James Freeman Clarke, *Autobiography, Diary and Correspondence*, ed. E. E. Hale, 124.
35. *Boston Morning Post*, 31 August 1838. Brownson suggested that Emerson's appeal to the emerging generation came not from his opinions but from his encouragement of free inquiry, something they had sought from their professors in vain. "It is as the advocate of the rights of the mind," Brownson said, "as the defender of personal independence in the spiritual world, not as the Idealist, the Pantheist, or the Atheist,

that he is run after." Norton evidently attributed this letter to the Greenfield editor, George Thomas Davis, but Parker ascribed it to Brownson, who certainly used this argument in his discussion of the address in October in the *Boston Quarterly*. See Hutchison, *The Transcendental Ministers*, 71–72; Schlesinger, *Brownson*, 132.
36. *Boston Quarterly Review*, I (October 1838), 512–514.
37. Cabot, II, 343–344.

31. STORM IN OUR WASHBOWL

1. *CEC*, 196, 200, 215.
2. Rusk, 270.
3. Ibid.
4. Albee, 100–101.
5. *L*, II, 148.
6. Cabot, I, 343; *JMN*, VII, 35; Elizabeth Palmer Peabody, *Reminiscences of William Ellery Channing*, 373. See also Cabot, I, 344, Cooke, 70; Allen, 321.
7. *L*, II, 148–149; James B. Thayer, *Rev. Samuel Ripley of Waltham*, 45.
8. Cabot, II, 689–690.
9. *L*, II, 148–149, 150.
10. Cabot, II, 691–692.
11. Gittleman, 184–192.
12. Miller, 197.
13. *L*, II, 167.
14. Ibid.
15. Ibid.
16. Peabody, *Channing*, 379; Paul F. Boller, Jr., *American Transcendentalism, 1830–1860: An Intellectual Inquiry*, 22.
17. Commager, 67.
18. Miller, 210–212.
19. Miller, 205–209.
20. A. R. Schultz and H. A. Pochmann, "George Ripley: Unitarian, Transcendentalist, or Infidel?," *American Literature* 14 (March 1942), 1–19.
21. *W*, IX, 410n.
22. *W*, I, 423.
23. Henry James, "Emerson," in *Partial Portraits*, 441.
24. Robert Frost, *Complete Poems*, 601; Reginald L. Cook, "Emerson and Frost: A Parallel of Seers," *New England Quarterly* 33 (June 1958), 215.
25. *W*, IX, 14.
26. *W*, II, 205–209; see also Hugh H. Witemeyer, "'Line' and 'Round' in Emerson's 'Uriel,'" *PMLA* 82 (March 1967), 98–103.
27. *W*, IX, 14; see also Charles Malloy, "The Poems of Emerson: 'Uriel,'" *Arena* 32 (September 1904), 278–283.

32. "LITERARY ETHICS"

1. *JMN*, V, 479.
2. *JMN*, V, 481.
3. *L*, II, 145.
4. Holmes, 132.
5. *L*, II, 146.
6. Edward Everett Hale, *Memories of a Hundred Years*, 4; *W*, I, 185–186.
7. Holmes, 133.
8. *CEC*, 199–200.

33. CONVERS FRANCIS

1. All quotations by Francis in this chapter are from Joel Myerson, "Convers Francis and Emerson," *American Literature* 50 (March 1978), 17–36.
2. See also Cabot, I, 338.

3. *L*, II, 71–72.
4. Cooke, 33.
5. *CEC*, 191.
6. Octavius B. Frothingham, *Boston Unitarianism, 1820–1850*, 188.
7. John Weiss, *Discourse Occasioned by the Death of Convers Francis*, 37–39. See also Myerson, "Francis and Emerson," 21.
8. Commager, 77.
9. Ibid.
10. Commager, 24.
11. Miller, 63.
12. Conway, I, 164.
13. Commager, 24.
14. Frothingham, 353–354.
15. Ibid.
16. Commager, 97, 277–278.
17. *JMN*, VII, 86.
18. *JMN*, VII, 84–85.
19. See also *L*, V, 118n.

34. JONES VERY

1. *JMN*, VII, 124.
2. *JMN*, VII, 213.
3. Paul F. Boller, Jr., *American Trancendentalism, 1830–1860: An Intellectual Inquiry*, 30.
4. Upham also had campaigned successfully to deprive Nathaniel Hawthorne of his customs-house job. He stood as model for Judge Pyncheon in *The House of the Seven Gables*. His wife was Ann Holmes, the sister of Oliver Wendell Holmes.
5. EWE, 84–85.
6. Gittleman, 223.
7. Gittleman, 229. In the next generation the Furness name was to be linked with Shakespeare scholarship when William's brilliant son Horace came to renown as editor of the Variorum Shakespeare.
8. Gittleman, 228.
9. *L*, II, 154.
10. *L*, II, 171.
11. *JMN*, VIII, 148.
12. *JMN*, VII, 122; *L*, II, 171.
13. *JMN*, VII, 122.
14. *Lidian*, 78.
15. *JMN*, VII, 127.
16. *JMN*, VII, 123; Carlos Baker, "Emerson and Jones Very," *New England Quarterly* 7 (March 1934), 90–99.
17. *L*, II, 173.
18. *JMN*, VII, 147.
19. *JMN*, VII, 157–158.
20. *JMN*, VII, 123.
21. Gittleman, 262–263.
22. See Gittleman, 168.
23. *AJ*, 113.
24. Gittleman, 268–271.
25. Gittleman, 271–272; Bronson Alcott, Ms. Journal [c. 10 December 1838], XI, 446.
26. *JMN*, VIII, 148; Gittleman, 271.
27. Gittleman, 337.
28. *The Dial*, II:1 (July 1841), 130.
29. *JMN*, VII, 213.
30. *L*, II, 204–205; Gittleman, 345.
31. Lathrop, 29–30.
32. *JMN*, VII, 249.
33. W, II, 202–203.

35. THE EAST VILLAGERS

1. In 1883 the Lyceum building became a branch library for the town of Lexington, which it continues to be in the present day.
2. *CEC*, 171.
3. *YES*, xxxvii; Cooke, 59.
4. *L*, II, 6, 113.
5. *L*, II, 120; Cooke, 59; Carl Bode, *The American Lyceum: Town Meeting of the Mind*, 15.
6. Three votes went to Follen. These were cast by one person who held three pews. The pew-holder said he had nothing against Emerson but thought he should wait.
7. W, IX, 71.

8. *EL*, III, 331–332.
9. *EL*, III, 326.
10. Ibid.; Edward Rowe Snow, *New England Storms and Shipwrecks*, 108–121.
11. Joel Myerson, "Convers Francis and Emerson," *American Literature* 50 (March 1978), 30.

36. CHRISTOPHER PEARSE CRANCH

1. Lindsay Swift, *Brook Farm: Its Members, Scholars, and Visitors*, 15.
2. Paul C. Nagel, *Descent from Glory: Four Generations of the John Adams Family*, 82.
3. Leonora Cranch Scott, *The Life and Letters of Christopher Pearse Cranch*, 59–60.
4. *The Dial*, I:1 (July 1840), 12.
5. Scott, *Cranch*, 59; *L*, II, 259.
6. Scott, *Cranch*, 58–59.
7. Scott, *Cranch*, 4; Hazen C. Carpenter, "Emerson and Christopher Pearse Cranch," *New England Quarterly* 36 (March 1964), 18–20.
8. Scott, *Cranch*, 280–281.
9. Scott, *Cranch*, 9.
10. *L*, II, 450.
11. Scott, *Cranch*, 61–63.
12. *The Western Messenger*, IV (November 1837), 184–188.
13. Scott, *Cranch*, 47.
14. Christopher Pearse Cranch, *Poems* (unpaged).
15. *The Diary of John Quincy Adams*, ed. Allan Nevins, 511.
16. Carpenter, "Emerson and Cranch," 26.
17. *JMN*, VII, 22–23.
18. Scott, *Cranch*, 280–281.
19. *JMN*, IX, 30.
20. *JMN*, VIII, 417.
21. *L*, III, 246; see also Commager, 47–48, and Shepard, 281–283.
22. See Lindsay Swift, *William Lloyd Garrison*, 202–207, 214; John Jay Chapman, *William Lloyd Garrison*, 218–240; Shepard, 282–288. The first session of the Chardon Street Convention was held 17–19 November 1840; the second, 31 March–2 April 1841; the third, 26–28 October 1841.
23. *The Dial*, III:1 (July 1842), 100.
24. *L*, II, 360.
25. *L*, I, 330.
26. *The Dial*, III:1 (July 1842), 101.
27. Wendell Phillips Garrison and Francis Jackson Garrison, *William Lloyd Garrison, 1805–1879: The Story of His Life*, II, 426.
28. *The Dial*, III:1 (July 1842), 101.
29. *Abroad*, 191–192.
30. *The Dial*, III:1 (July 1842), 101–102.
31. Shepard, 284; *The Dial*, III:1 (July 1842), 102.
32. Shepard, 287–288.
33. *The Dial*, III:1 (July 1842), 111–112.
34. *W*, X, 373–377.
35. Carpenter, "Emerson and Cranch," 29.
36. Carpenter, "Emerson and Cranch," 30; Scott, *Cranch*, 61–63.
37. Scott, *Cranch*, 64–65.
38. Carpenter, "Emerson and Cranch," 34; from a hitherto unpublished letter, Massachusetts Historical Society.
39. Carpenter, "Emerson and Cranch," 35.
40. Scott, *Cranch*, 23–24.
41. *The Critic*, n.s. 17 (27 February 1892), 129.
42. Christopher Pearse Cranch, *Ariel and Caliban with Other Poems*, 123–126.
43. Scott, *Cranch*, 50.

37. BROOK FARM

1. *L*, II, 341.
2. *JMN*, VII, 407.
3. *JMN*, VII, 408.
4. *JMN*, VII, 401.
5. *W*, I, 186; *JMN*, VII, 408.
6. *JMN*, VII, 521, 525, 526.
7. *JMN*, VIII, 396.
8. Henry W. Sams, ed., *Autobiography of Brook Farm*, 74. On 8 May 1842, in a letter to Charles Newcomb, Emerson said that Hosmer "should be your foreman at B[rook] F[arm]" (*L*, III, 52).
9. *L*, II, 360.
10. *W*, III, 267.
11. *L*, II, 364.
12. *L*, II, 365.
13. Cabot, II, 437–438.
14. *JMN*, VII, 525.
15. *JMN*, XIII, 120; Joel Porte, *Representative Man: Ralph Waldo Emerson in His Time*, 317.
16. Porte, *Representative Man*, 80; *JMN*, XIII, 249.
17. *JMN*, V, 26; *W*, X, 305; *CEC*, 478.
18. Rusk, 23–24. Writing after Emerson's death on Emerson's religion, his friend Cyrus Bartol said, "Emerson thought Plato with his dialectic had but bit this apple of the world on one side." He does not say whether the image is his or Emerson's. See Franklin B. Sanborn, ed., *The Genius and Character of Emerson*, 145.
19. *W*, IX, 148–158.
20. *JMN*, VII, 524.
21. *W*, IX, 15–19.
22. *L*, II, 368–369.
23. *L*, II, 370, 371.
24. Edith Roelker Curtis, *Season in Utopia: The Story of Brook Farm*, 93.

38. AMOS BRONSON ALCOTT

1. *JMN*, VIII, 215.
2. *JMN*, X, 326.
3. Franklin B. Sanborn, ed., *The Genius and Character of Emerson*, 45.
4. *JMN*, VIII, 212.
5. *JMN*, V, 98.
6. *JMN*, V, 178.
7. *L*, II, 27.
8. *L*, II, 29–30.
9. Blanchard, 111.
10. *L*, II, 76; *JMN*, V, 328.
11. Miller, 168; Shepard, 194–195.
12. Sanborn, II, 339; Swayne, 96.
13. *JMN*, VII, 539.
14. *CEC*, 163, 320; *JMN*, VIII, 211–212.
15. *CEC*, 326; Howe, 75.
16. *CEC*, 331; *AL*, 88.
17. *CEC*, 333, 338.
18. *JMN*, VIII, 300–301.
19. *JMN*, IX, 50.
20. *L*, III, 263.
21. *AL*, 114.
22. *JMN*, XI, 19; XIII, 66.
23. *JMN*, XI, 51; *J*, IX, 401.
24. In July 1848 Emerson wrote: "I am afraid A[lcott] can as little as any man separate his drivelling from his divining" (*JMN*, XI, 130).
25. *L*, IV, 514.
26. *JMN*, XIV, 10.
27. *JMN*, XIV, 82–83, 86–87.
28. *L*, V, 159–160, 166; see also *L*, IV, 511–512.
29. Swayne, 104.

39. MARGARET FULLER

1. *CEC*, 410 and note, 412n. A year after her death Carlyle wrote to Emerson: "Poor Margaret, I often remember her and think how she is asleep now under the surges of the sea" (*CEC*, 469).

2. *Fuller*, I, 102.
3. *JMN*, V, 188.
4. *L*, II, 32.
5. *Fuller*, I, 203.
6. *Fuller*, I, 202–203.
7. *Fuller*, I, 112, 153; *JMN*, V, 407.
8. *Fuller*, I, 95.
9. *JMN*, V, 319.
10. *The Letters of Margaret Fuller*, ed. Robert N. Hudspeth, I, 272. See also Margaret Fuller, *Woman in the Nineteenth Century*, 351.
11. *Fuller*, I, 194–195.
12. *Letters of Margaret Fuller*, I, 283.
13. *Letters of Margaret Fuller*, I, 327.
14. See Carl F. Strauch, "Hatred's Swift Repulsions: Emerson, Margaret Fuller, and Others," *Studies in Romanticism* 7 (Winter 1968), 65–103.
15. *CEC*, 261.
16. *JMN*, VII, 273.
17. *JMN*, XI, 259.
18. Ward, 21.
19. *W*, II, 194, 215. See also John Bard McNulty, "Emerson's Friends and the Essay on Friendship," *New England Quarterly* 19 (September 1946), 390–394.
20. *Fuller*, I, 308–309.
21. *JMN*, VII, 509–510.
22. *L*, II, 324–325.
23. *L*, II, 325.
24. *L*, II, 332.
25. *L*, II, 326–327.
26. *L*, II, 327–328.
27. *L*, II, 336–337, 340n.
28. *JMN*, VII, 400.
29. *L*, II, 342, 344, 349.
30. *Fuller*, I, 228.
31. *L*, II, 352–353.
32. *CEC*, 284.
33. Ellen Wilson, *Margaret Fuller, Bluestocking, Romantic, Revolutionary*, 67; Caroline Healey Dall, *Margaret and Her Friends*, 46; *L*, II, 384.
34. *Letters of Margaret Fuller*, II, 234.
35. *JMN*, VIII, 109.

40. MY GOOD HENRY THOREAU

1. *JMN*, V, 25.
2. *JMN*, V, 453.
3. *L*, II, 154; *JMN*, VII, 230–231; *L*, II, 225.
4. *TJ*, IX, 160.
5. Joel Myerson, "Eight Lowell Letters from Concord in 1838," *Illinois Quarterly* 38 (Winter 1975), 27.
6. Haskins, 121–122.
7. Sanborn, II, 469.
8. Frederick McGill, Jr., *Channing of Concord: A Life of William Ellery Channing*, II, 181.
9. Henry Seidel Canby, *Thoreau*, 192.
10. *EWE*, 115; Franklin B. Sanborn, *The Life of Henry David Thoreau*, 360. Writing in the *North American Review* (64 [April 1847], 414–415), under the heading "Nine New Poets," Francis Bowen said of Channing's poetry, "His poetry is a feeble and diluted copy of Mr. Emerson's."
11. *Abroad*, 282–283.
12. *JMN*, VIII, 96; and see *JMN*, XIII, 66.
13. Canby, *Thoreau*, 92; Joel Porte, *Representative Man: Ralph Waldo Emerson in His Time*, 309–310.
14. *JMN*, XIII, 27–28; X, 344.
15. *L*, II, 393–394.
16. *TJ*, I, 253.
17. *L*, II, 402.
18. *JMN*, VII, 463. Emerson thought well enough of this passage to transfer it later into "The Poet": *W*, III, 9–10.
19. Hawthorne, *American Notebooks*, VIII, 371.
20. *TJ*, I, 429–430.
21. *JMN*, VIII, 257; *TC*, 88.
22. *W*, I, 266.
23. *W*, X, 606, 607; and see *J*, VII, 336–337n.
24. *TC*, 78.
25. *TC*, 86.
26. *L*, III, 172.

27. *TC*, 103.
28. *TC*, 119–120, 124.
29. *JMN*, IX, 103.
30. *TC*, 161. See also Walter Harding, *The Days of Henry Thoreau*, 180.
31. A provision later rescinded.
32. Furness, Ltr. XXV, 60.
33. *CEC*, 422, 457.
34. *TC*, 189.
35. Canby, *Thoreau*, 160–163. Alexander Forbes made his comment to David Pickman.
36. Sanborn, II, 344–350.
37. *TJ*, II, 109.
38. *JMN*, XI, 404, 400.
39. *TJ*, III, 167–168. See also Franklin B. Sanborn, *Transcendental and Literary New England*, ed. Kenneth W. Cameron, 208.
40. *TJ*, III, 141–142.
41. *TJ*, III, 216, 256. See also J. B. Moore, "Thoreau Rejects Emerson," *American Literature* 4 (November 1932), 241–256.
42. Sanborn, II, 350–351.
43. *TJ*, V, 188; III, 399.
44. Albee, 18–19.
45. *JMN*, XIII, 66.
46. *JMN*, XIII, 183.
47. *L*, IV, 459.
48. *TJ*, VI, 199–200.
49. *J*, IX, 15–16.
50. *JMN*, XIV, 76.
51. D. Edgell, "A Note on a Transcendental Friendship," *New England Quarterly* 24 (December 1951), 529.
52. Ibid.
53. *TJ*, VIII, 231.
54. *TJ*, IX, 249–250, 265, 272, 276.
55. Franklin B. Sanborn, *Henry D. Thoreau*, 313.
56. Fields, 70.
57. *W*, X, 456, 479.
58. *W*, X, 478, 454–455.
59. *W*, X, 484–485.
60. *JMN*, XV, 261–262.
61. *JMN*, XV, 268.
62. *JMN*, XV, 352–353.
63. John Burroughs, *Last Harvest*, 20.
64. Sanborn, *Henry D. Thoreau*, 306.
65. Fields, 68–69.
66. George Hendrick, ed., *Remembrances of Concord and the Thoreaus*, xix.
67. Howe, 89.

41. THE WATERVILLE ORATION

1. Waterville changed its name to Colby in 1867.
2. *L*, II, 388, 390, 392, 396.
3. *JMN*, VII, 431.
4. See Scudder, *Lowell*, I, 78–79, and William M. Bergan, *Old Nantasket*, 24.
5. *L*, II, 416.
6. *L*, II, 419, 423.
7. *L*, II, 422, 421.
8. *L*, IV, 179. There may be some significance in Emerson's observation that from 1790 to 1820, an interval that encompasses the period in which his father flourished, "There was not a book, a speech, a conversation or a thought" in the whole Commonwealth of Massachusetts (Conrad Wright, *The Beginnings of Unitarianism in America*, 246). Kenneth W. Cameron, remarking Emerson's failure to prepare a memorial of his father and his apparent destruction of William's sermons, conjectures that this behavior amounted to an "unconscious repudiation" of William. The sermons may have perished in the fire that ravaged Bush in 1872, however; and we must also remember that he prepared no memorial of his mother. See Kenneth W. Cameron, "Early Background for Emerson's 'The Problem,' " *Emerson Society Quarterly* 27 (2d qu. 1962), 37–46.
9. *L*, II, 432.
10. *L*, II, 431.
11. *W*, I, 207.
12. *W*, I, 206.
13. *L*, II, 423.

14. *W*, I, 223.
15. *L*, II, 420, 431, 433.
16. *L*, II, 419, 421, 427–428.
17. *L*, II, 423, 428.
18. *W*, I, 205.
19. *W*, II, 191–192.
20. *L*, II, 431.
21. Ward, 35–36; *W*, III, 46.
22. *L*, II, 435.
23. *CEC*, 304.
24. *L*, II, 439–440.
25. Edwin Percy Whipple, *Recollections of Eminent Men*, 146–147.
26. *L*, II, 440; and see Arthur J. Roberts, ''Emerson's Visits to Waterville College,'' annotated by Carl J. Weber, *The Colby Mercury* 5, (1 April 1934), 41–45.
27. *CEC*, 312; *New Letters of James Russell Lowell*, ed. Mark A. DeWolfe Howe, 5; Whipple, *Recollections of Eminent Men*, 145–146.
28. This and the following quotations from ''The Method of Nature'' are taken from the text in *CW*, 120–137.
29. *L*, II, 439–440.
30. *L*, II, 459n.
31. Holmes, 141. Holmes transcribed the word *multiform* as *manifold*.
32. Firkins, 168.
33. *W*, I, 436. See also David Robinson, '' 'The Method of Nature' and Emerson's Period of Crisis,'' in Joel Myerson, ed., *Emerson Centenary Essays*, 74–92.

42. WALDO

1. *Louisa May Alcott, Her Life, Letters, and Journals*, ed. Ednah D. Cheney, 299–300, 324; Shepard, 509.
2. Social Circle of Concord, *The Centenary of the Birth of Ralph Waldo Emerson*, 87; Swayne, 78–85; *L*, II, 8.
3. *JMN*, VIII, 163–164.
4. *Abroad*, 141.
5. EWE, 167.
6. *CEC*, 261; *L*, III, 8.
7. *JMN*, V, 234, 293.
8. *Abroad*, 15.
9. *L*, V, 481.
10. Cabot, II, 481.
11. *JMN*, VII, 228.
12. Franklin B. Sanborn, *Transcendental and Literary New England*, ed. Kenneth W. Cameron, 188.
13. Snider, 279.
14. Jonathan Bishop, *Emerson on the Soul*, 188.
15. *JMN*, VIII, 163–164.
16. *JMN*, VIII, 165; *TC*, 63.
17. *L*, III, 9–10.
18. Cabot, II, 484; *L*, III, 9; *JMN*, VIII, 165.
19. *L*, III, 9.
20. *JMN*, VIII, 205.
21. *CEC*, 317.
22. *JMN*, VII, 358. See *J*, V, 403, for Edward Emerson's annotation.
23. *Lidian*, 78–79, 229; *JMN*, VII, 343, 541; VIII, 164–166; ''Lecture on the Times,'' *W*, I, 284.
24. *Lidian*, 70.
25. Wagenknecht, 156.
26. *L*, III, 5.
27. *L*, III, 11; *JMN*, VIII, 201.
28. *L*, III, 67, 61, 66, 55–56; Lindsay Swift, *Brook Farm: Its Members, Scholars, and Visitors*, 199.
29. *JMN*, VIII, 178–179.
30. *The Dial*, III:1 (July 1842), 116.
31. *CEC*, 318.
32. *L*, III, 238–239.
33. Holmes, 178; Cabot, II, 483–484.
34. Alfred Noyes, *Pageant of Letters*, 234–235.
35. *L*, III, 7.
36. *W*, IX, 148–158; and see B. Bernard Cohen, '' 'Threnody': Emerson's Struggle with Grief,'' *Indiana University Folio* 14 (1948), 13–15.
37. *W*, III, 48–49.
38. Furness, Ltr. LXXIV, 149.
39. *W*, I, 76.
40. *W*, I, 199; III, 178.
41. Hopkins, 2–3.

43. HENRY JAMES

1. Cabot, I, 358.
2. Ralph Barton Perry, *The Thought and Character of William James,* I, 62.
3. Perry, *William James,* I, 39–40.
4. Perry, *William James,* I, 40.
5. *L,* III, 23.
6. *L,* III, 30.
7. Perry, *William James,* I, 42.
8. William T. Stafford, ''Emerson and the James Family,'' *American Literature* 24 (January 1953), 443.
9. Perry, *William James,* I, 51, 352.
10. *TC,* 110; Austin Warren, *The Elder Henry James,* 182–183.
11. Henry James, *Notes of a Son and Brother,* 191.
12. *JMN,* XI, 248; Edward Waldo Emerson, *The Early Years of the*
Saturday Club, 325; Perry, *William James,* I, 58.
13. Perry, *William James,* I, 80.
14. Anna Robeson Burr, ed., *Alice James: Her Brothers — Her Journal,* 13; Emerson, *Early Years of the Saturday Club,* 328–329; Jean Strouse, *Alice James: A Biography,* 68.
15. *Alice James,* 3–5; James, *Notes of a Son and Brother,* 222.
16. Perry, *William James,* I, 96–97.
17. Henry James, Sr., ''Emerson,'' *The Atlantic Monthly* 94 (December 1904), 744.
18. Howe, 79, 84.
19. The following quotations are from *The Literary Remains of the Late Henry James,* ed. William James, 293–302.

44. HAWTHORNE AND HOSMER

1. Arlin Turner, *Nathaniel Hawthorne,* 148.
2. Lloyd Morris, *The Rebellious Puritan: Portrait of Mr. Hawthorne,* 162.
3. *JMN,* VII, 491.
4. *W,* XII, 474; Edith Roelker Curtis, *Season in Utopia: The Story of Brook Farm,* 93.
5. *The Dial,* III:1 (July 1842), 123–126; *W,* XII, 358–359.
6. *W,* XII, 364, 474; EWE, 136.
7. Henry David Thoreau, *Walden,* 197; Swayne, 212.
8. *JMN,* V, 452.
9. Julian, I, 290–291.
10. *JMN,* VIII, 195, 256.
11. Hawthorne, *Mosses,* X, 31.
12. Newton Arvin, ed., *The Heart of Hawthorne's Journals,* 99. See also Robert Cantwell, *Nathaniel Hawthorne: The American Years,* 355.
13. Turner, *Nathaniel Hawthorne,* 147; Lewis Mumford, *Herman Melville,* 95.
14. EWE, 130.
15. Hawthorne, *American Notebooks,* VIII, 337.

45. MARGARET FULLER

1. *L,* III, 79–80.
2. All the quotations in this chapter from Margaret Fuller, unless otherwise noted, are from Joel Myerson, ''Margaret Fuller's 1842 Journal: At Concord with Emerson,'' *Harvard Library Bulletin* 21 (July 1973), 320–340.
3. *JMN,* VIII, 195–196.
4. *Fuller,* II, 67–69.
5. Because Emerson was sensitive to cold Lidian had made him a sweeping study-gown, with a broad velvet collar. Actually, it was dark purple. He called it his ''gaberlunzie,'' and, before 1852, when a furnace was installed at Bush, always wore it in raw weather. See *J,* VI, 288–289n.
6. *JMN,* VII, 27.

7. Seven and a half miles long and a mile and a half wide, Naushon is the largest of the Elizabeth Islands. Owned then by Bowdoin College, it was sold in 1843 to John Murray Forbes and his uncle William Swain. Emerson was a frequent visitor there after his daughter Edith married John Forbes's son William in 1865. It remains in the hands of their descendants.
8. Blanchard, 160–162.
9. Miller, 402; Eugenia Kaledin, *The Education of Mrs. Henry Adams*, 19–31. Ellen had good reason to envy Emerson his emotional placidity. The Sturgises were highstrung. A third Sturgis sister, Susan Bigelow, killed herself in Clover's presence with a dose of arsenic when Clover was ten. Both Clover and her sister, Ellen, took their own lives. Their brother, Ned, Ellen Hooper's remaining child, died in a mental institution in 1901.
10. *L*, III, 89n.
11. *JMN*, VIII, 368–369.
12. *JMN*, VII, 463.
13. *JMN*, XI, 256–258; and see Harry R. Warfel, "Margaret Fuller and Ralph Waldo Emerson," *PMLA* 50 (June 1935), 576–594.
14. *JMN*, XI, 431–432.
15. *JMN*, XIII, 139.
16. Julian, 259–262.
17. *Fuller*, I, 213.
18. Blanchard, 339–340.
19. *AJ*, 410.
20. Thomas Wentworth Higginson, *Margaret Fuller Ossoli*, 300.
21. Chapman, 70–73.

46. NATHANIEL HAWTHORNE

1. *JMN*, XV, 60.
2. Ibid.
3. Hawthorne, *American Notebooks*, VIII, 362.
4. Ibid.
5. Lloyd Morris, *The Rebellious Puritan: Portrait of Mr. Hawthorne*, 167.
6. Robert Cantwell, *Nathaniel Hawthorne: The American Years*, 359.
7. Hawthorne, *American Notebooks*, VIII, 362.
8. Ward, Ltr. XXII, 53.
9. Hawthorne, *American Notebooks*, VIII, 362.
10. *JMN*, VIII, 272–273.
11. Hawthorne, *American Notebooks*, VIII, 171.
12. Julian, I, 255–256.
13. *JMN*, VIII, 273.
14. Lathrop, 59.
15. *JMN*, VIII, 273.
16. Chiang Yee, *The Silent Traveller in Boston*, 172.
17. Swayne, 116.
18. Rusk, 449.
19. *JMN*, IV, 4; *J*, IX, 232; *W*, III, 28.
20. *JMN*, VIII, 274.
21. Julian, I, 420.
22. Edward R. Horgan, *The Shaker Holy Land: A Community Portrait*, 78–84.
23. Lathrop, 51.
24. Newton Arvin, ed., *The Heart of Hawthorne's Journals*, 113.
25. Cantwell, *Hawthorne*, 370.
26. Newton Dillaway, *Prophet of America: Emerson and the Problems of Today*, 23–24; *JMN*, VIII, 271–276; E. L. Carey, "Hawthorne and Emerson," *Critic* 45 (July 1904), 25–27.
27. George William Curtis, *Literary and Social Essays*, 44.
28. Lathrop, 29.
29. *JMN*, VII, 21, 242.
30. Julian, I, 270–271; Hawthorne, *Mosses*, X, 31.
31. *JMN*, VII, 465.
32. Edwin Percy Whipple, *Recollections of Eminent Men*, 149.
33. Woodbury, 55–57.
34. Woodbury, 64
35. Annie Adams Fields, "Glimpses of Emerson," in Bode, 103.
36. James T. Fields, *Yesterdays with Authors*, 107–108.

37. *JMN*, XI, 440; Cabot, I, 377; Sanborn, II, 533.

38. Lathrop, 456.
39. Howe, 105.

47. A LOOK AT EMERSON

1. Cabot, II, 678–679; *Ellen*, II, 347.
2. *Grimm*, 63.
3. Cabot, II, 679.
4. Cabot, II, 678.
5. *Abroad*, 328.
6. *The Memoirs of Julian Hawthorne*, ed. Edith G. Hawthorne, 94–95.
7. Rusk, 446–447.
8. Edward Wagenknecht, ed., *Mrs. Longfellow: Selected Letters and Journal of Fanny Appleton Longfellow (1817–1861)*, 127.
9. John Townsend Trowbridge, *My Own Story: With Recollections of Noted Persons*, 347.
10. Iris Origo, "The Carlyles and the Ashburtons," *Cornhill Magazine* 164 (Autumn 1950), 461; Holmes, 360. See also *Ellen*, II, 307.
11. John Burroughs, *Birds and Poets*, 185; Holmes, 360; *Lidian*, 43.
12. *Ellen*, II, 67.
13. *The Poems and Prose Remains of Arthur Hugh Clough*, ed. Blanche Clough, I, 133; Holmes, 359–361.
14. Lathrop, 414.
15. Holmes, 361; Wagenknecht, 20; *Scottish Review* 5 (January 1857), 18; Emma Lazarus, "Emerson's Personality," *Century Magazine*, n.s. 2 (1882), 545–546; Cabot, II, 620.
16. Woodbury, 122; Newton Dillaway, "Emerson's Remarkable Face," *Christian Science Monthly* 38 (3 January 1946), 8.
17. *Fuller*, I, 202; Howe, 98; Holmes, 364; Thayer, 49.
18. John W. Chadwick, "Emerson," *Arena* 15 (1895), 12–16; Rusk, 343; Holmes, 360; *Grimm*, 10.
19. Lathrop, 412–414.
20. Holmes, 238–239.
21. Hawthorne, *Mosses*, X, 31.
22. W, III, 345; Perry, 1. In "My Double and How He Undid Me," Edward Everett Hale said: "Greenough once told me, that, in studying for the statue of Franklin, he found that the left side of the great man's face was philosophic and reflective, and the right side funny and smiling. If you will go and look at the bronze statue, you will find he has repeated this observation there for posterity. The eastern profile is the portrait of the statesman Franklin, the western of poor Richard." Hale, *If, Yes, and Perhaps*, 173–174.
23. Cabot, II, 678; Burroughs, *Birds and Poets*, 190.

48. THOMAS CARLYLE

1. *L*, V, 23.
2. *L*, IV, 94.
3. Mead, 212.
4. *JMN*, V, 111–112.
5. *JMN*, V, 459; VIII, 187.
6. *CEC*, 201.
7. *Letters and Memorials of Jane Welsh Carlyle*, ed. Thomas Carlyle, I, 182–183.
8. *Jane Welsh Carlyle: A New Selection of Her Letters*, ed. Trudy Bliss, 140–141.
9. *CEC*, 426.
10. *CEC*, 430–431.
11. *CEC*, 431.
12. *Letters and Memorials of Jane Welsh Carlyle*, I, 305.
13. *Letters and Memorials of Jane Welsh Carlyle*, II, 49.
14. *JMN*, X, 540–541.

15. *JMN*, X, 179.
16. *JMN*, X, 541.
17. Scudder, 153. "Ettercap" is a Scottish term for a fierce, aggressive spider.
18. *L*, III, 424.
19. James Anthony Froude, *Carlyle's Life in London*, I, 422.
20. *CEC*, 440.
21. *Letters and Memorials of Jane Welsh Carlyle*, I, 244–245.
22. Mead, 216.
23. *New Letters and Memorials of Jane Welsh Carlyle*, ed. Alexander Carlyle, I, 210; Iris Origo, "The Carlyles and the Ashburtons," *Cornhill Magazine* 164 (Autumn 1950), 461.
24. *CEC*, 35.
25. Andrew J. Symington, *Some Personal Reminiscences of Carlyle*, 52; Origo, "The Carlyles and the Ashburtons," 461–462.
26. *JMN*, X, 541.
27. Harris, 108.
28. Gavan Duffy, *Conversations with Carlyle*, 94.
29. January Searle [George Searle Phillips], *Emerson: His Life and Writings*, 47.
30. *W*, V, 279.
31. *L*, IV, 97; *JMN*, X, 273–274, 528–529.
32. *L*, IV, 96.
33. *Thomas Carlyle: Letters to His Wife*, ed. Trudy Bliss, 246.
34. *W*, V, 274–275.
35. *W*, V, 275–276.
36. *W*, V, 287.
37. Mead, 194–195.
38. *Jane Welsh Carlyle: A New Selection of Her Letters*, 188.
39. *JMN*, X, 431.
40. *JMN*, X, 334.
41. *JMN*, X, 432.
42. *W*, V, 277.
43. *W*, V, 289.
44. *W*, V, 276.
45. *W*, V, 273.
46. *W*, V, 279.
47. Froude, *Carlyle's Life in London*, I, 270. Anthony à Wood's *Athenae Oxonienses* was later donated by Emerson to Harvard College Library when Carlyle made his gift to Harvard of his collection of books on Cromwell and Frederick the Great.
48. Scudder, 152–153.
49. Mead, 195.
50. *Letters of Jane Welsh Carlyle to Joseph Neuberg*, ed. Townsend Scudder, III, 1–48.
51. Caroline Fox, *Memories of Old Friends*, 240, 168–169.
52. Scudder, 147–148, from a review by G. S. Venables of Froude's *Thomas Carlyle: The History of His Life in London* in *Fortnightly Review* (November 1884).
53. Harris, 108.
54. Gordon S. Haight, ed., *The George Eliot Letters*, I, 372.
55. Sanborn, II, 304.
56. W. S. Tryon, *Parnassus Corner*, 148.
57. Charles Francis Adams, *Richard Henry Dana*, II, 349.
58. *CEC*, 443, 454.
59. *CEC*, 459. See also Frank T. Thompson, "Emerson and Carlyle," *Studies in Philology* 24 (July 1927), 438–453.
60. Scudder, 171.
61. *CEC*, 463.
62. *L*, IV, 236.
63. *CEC*, 462.
64. *CEC*, 517–518.
65. *CEC*, 548.
66. "Ralph Waldo Emerson," *Times Literary Supplement*, 29 May 1903.
67. *LCEN*, I, 338–341; *CEC*, 558–568.
68. Wagenknecht, 130.

49. PERSONS OF MARK AND GENIUS

1. The accounts are January Searle [George Searle Phillips], *Emerson: His Life and Writings;* Alexander Ireland, ed., *Ralph Waldo Emerson: His Life, Genius, and Writings;* Francis Espinasse, *Lit-*

erary Recollections and Sketches.
Ellen Emerson said of her father's visitors at Bush, ''Aunt Lizzy [Elizabeth Hoar] called them 'Waldo's menagerie' '' (*Lidian*, 80).

2. Searle, *Emerson*, 44–45; *L*, III, 447.
3. *L*, IV, 15n.
4. Searle, *Emerson*, 44.
5. Ibid.
6. Searle, *Emerson*, 45.
7. Searle, *Emerson*, 43–44.
8. Searle, *Emerson*, 45.
9. *L*, III, 455.
10. Searle, *Emerson*, 42–43.
11. Ireland, *Emerson*, 162–165.
12. Ireland, *Emerson*, 165.
13. Ibid.
14. *JMN*, X, 534.
15. *Fuller*, II, 173.
16. William Bell Scott, *Memoir of David Scott*, 293; *L*, IV, 21.
17. *L*, IV, 18.
18. *L*, IV, 19.
19. *JMN*, X, 535.
20. *JMN*, X, 536.
21. *L*, IV, 20.
22. Franklin Sanborn, *Transcendental and Literary New England*, ed. Kenneth W. Cameron, 183; see, however, *Abroad*, 328–329.
23. *L*, IV, 40.
24. Scott, *Memoir of David Scott*, 299; *L*, IV, 20.
25. *L*, IV, 100.
26. *L*, VI, 86–87.
27. Social Circle of Concord, *The Centenary of the Birth of Ralph Waldo Emerson*, 126–127.

50. INTO THE LAKE DISTRICT

1. Cooke, 117.
2. *CEC*, 439.
3. Harriet Martineau, *Autobiography*, ed. Maria Weston Chapman, I, 549; Cooke, 117.
4. *JMN*, X, 558.
5. *JMN*, X, 559.
6. *JMN*, X, 559–560.
7. *W*, V, 294–296; *CEC*, 439.
8. *W*, V, 297–298. See also J. B. Moore, ''Emerson on Wordsworth,'' *PMLA* 41 (March 1926), 179–192.

51. SCOTT, DICKENS, AND OTHERS

1. *W*, XI, 466; see also *L*, VI, 171; Wagenknecht, 90.
2. *L*, I, 198.
3. *JMN*, I, 42; *L*, I, 134; *JMN*, VII, 418.
4. *JMN*, III, 150–151.
5. *EL*, I, 375–376.
6. Joel Myerson, ''Convers Francis and Emerson,'' *American Literature* 50 (March 1978), 26. See also J. T. Flanagan, ''Emerson as a Critic of Fiction,'' *Philological Quarterly* 15 (January 1936), 30–45.
7. *JMN*, IV, 177; VII, 418.
8. *L*, IV, 343, 302–303.
9. *JMN*, XV, 146.
10. *JMN*, XI, 239, 246.
11. *JMN*, V, 483. See also Woodberry, 54.
12. *JMN*, VII, 244–245.
13. *JMN*, VIII, 222–223.
14. Wagenknecht, 89.
15. *W*, V, 310; see also *JMN*, X, 504–505.
16. *L*, IV, 66; *JMN*, X, 550–551, 333. Since Dickens's oldest son was then twelve, obviously he was twitting Emerson.
17. Edgar Johnson, *Charles Dickens: His Tragedy and Triumph*, II, 1078; Howe, 141; *L*, V, 542.
18. Howe, 157–158; and see Fields, 74; *L*, V, 542–543.

19. Howe, 157.
20. Louise Hastings, "Emerson in Cincinnati," *New England Quar-* *terly* 11 (September 1938), 445; W, X, 52–54.

52. GEORGE ELIOT AND HER CIRCLE

1. Conway, II, 156.
2. *Abroad*, 337–338.
3. Conway, II, 157.
4. Carpenter, 2, 11–12. See also Perry, 77–78; Chapman, 46.
5. Carpenter, 25.
6. Chapman, 46.
7. *JMN*, XIV, 166.
8. Conway, II, 157, 158; Rusk, 355; Scudder, 112.
9. *Abroad*, 339; Conway, II, 156.
10. *Abroad*, 336.
11. Rusk, 474.

53. ARTHUR HUGH CLOUGH

1. Edward Everett Hale, *James Russell Lowell and His Friends*, 136–137.
2. *Clough*, Ltr. 6; John Insley Osborne, *Arthur Hugh Clough*, 66, 177; Scudder, 70–71; Rusk, 357.
3. *Clough*, vi.
4. *Clough*, Ltr. 1.
5. *L*, IV, 47.
6. *Clough*, Ltr. 34.
7. Scudder, 70.
8. *The Poems and Prose Remains of Arthur Hugh Clough*, ed. Blanche Clough, I, 133.
9. *L*, IV, 48.
10. *L*, IV, 77; *JMN*, X, 329; Rusk, 347.
11. Osborne, *Clough*, 9, 19–20, 99, 18, 58–59.
12. *JMN*, X, 321–322.
13. *Clough*, Ltr. 7, Ltr. 8.
14. *Clough*, Ltr. 8.
15. *Clough*, Ltr. 10.
16. *Clough*, Ltr. 13.
17. *Clough*, Ltr. 14n.
18. *Abroad*, 253.
19. Ibid.
20. Osborne, *Clough*, 167; Rusk, 387.
21. *Abroad*, 252.
22. *Abroad*, 253.
23. Lathrop, 456–457.
24. *Clough*, Ltr. 14n.
25. Scudder, 160–161; Conway, II, 74.
26. *Abroad*, 253–254.
27. Scudder, *Lowell*, I, 246–247.
28. *LLJ*, II, 231.
29. W. S. Tryon, *Parnassus Corner*, 153–154.
30. Conway, I, 156.
31. *LCEN*, I, 88.
32. Hubert H. Hoeltje, *Inward Sky: The Mind and Heart of Nathaniel Hawthorne*, 379.
33. *Clough*, Ltr. 19n.
34. *Clough*, Ltr. 20.
35. Scudder, 162–163.
36. *Clough*, Ltr. 20.
37. *CEC*, 492.
38. *CEC*, 495–496.
39. *CEC*, 491–492.
40. *Clough*, Ltr. 22, Ltr. 29.
41. Scudder, 163.
42. Osborne, *Clough*, 170.
43. *Clough*, Ltr. 20; Osborne, *Clough*, 156.
44. Osborne, *Clough*, 156.
45. *Clough*, Ltr. 34, Ltr. 36.

54. FREDRIKA BREMER

1. Allen, 532.
2. Bremer, *Homes*, I, 30.
3. Bremer, *Homes*, I, 122.
4. Bremer, *Homes*, I, 72–73.
5. Bremer, *Homes*, I, 73.
6. Bremer, *Homes*, I, 117.

7. Bremer, *Homes*, I, 118.
8. Ibid.
9. Bremer, *Homes*, I, 121; Edwin Percy Whipple, *Recollections of Eminent Men*, 135–136. Fredrika's visit coincided with the murder, at Harvard Medical College, of Dr. George Parkman by Professor John Webster. "People now talk about scarcely anything else," Fredrika said, but she did not draw out Emerson on the subject; see Bode, 13–14.
10. Bremer, *Homes*, I, 121–122.
11. Bremer, *Homes*, I, 232.
12. Bremer, *Homes*, I, 176.
13. Bremer, *Homes*, I, 234.
14. Bremer, *Homes*, I, 232–233.
15. Bremer, *Homes*, I, 153.
16. Ibid.
17. *Lidian*, 237.
18. Bremer, *Homes*, I, 153.
19. Bremer, *Homes*, I, 156, 161.
20. Bremer, *Homes*, I, 154.
21. Bremer, *Homes*, I, 166.
22. Bremer, *Homes*, I, 169.
23. Bremer, *Homes*, I, 156.
24. Bremer, *Homes*, I, 221–222.
25. Bremer, *Homes*, I, 224.
26. Quoted in *L*, IV, 184n.
27. Bremer, *Homes*, II, 562–563.
28. Bremer, *Homes*, II, 563.
29. Bremer, *Homes*, II, 565.
30. Ibid.
31. Bremer, *Homes*, I, 154. And see Karl A. Olsson, "Fredrika Bremer and Ralph Waldo Emerson," *Swedish Pioneer Historical Journal* 2 (August 1951), 39–52.

55. THE SPEAKER

1. *J*, III, 260–261n. See also *JMN*, IV, 264.
2. Chapman, 33.
3. *AJ*, 338.
4. Perry, 89; Woodberry, 75; Richard F. Adams, "Emerson and the Organic Metaphor," *PMLA* 69 (March 1954), 121; *L*, V, 183. See also EWE, 128.
5. Cabot, I, 150.
6. Holmes, 314; Joel Porte, *Representative Man: Ralph Waldo Emerson in His Time*, 75.
7. Henry A. Beers, *Four Americans*, 80; Henry Seidel Canby, *Classic Americans*, 165.
8. John Burroughs, *Birds and Poets*, 191; Burroughs, *Literary Values and Other Papers*, 192.
9. Barrett Wendell, "Ralph Waldo Emerson," in Milton R. Konvitz, ed., *The Recognition of Ralph Waldo Emerson*, 119.
10. *CEC*, 321; *JMN*, X, 28.
11. *Cincinnati Gazette*, 27 January 1857; *L*, II, 323n; David Mead, *Yankee Eloquence in the Middle West: The Ohio Lyceum, 1850–1880*, 43.
12. *W*, VIII, 88. The lady who made the remark was Cornelia Frances, younger sister of John Murray Forbes.
13. Henry James, *Partial Portraits*, 10.
14. Fields, 92.
15. Alexander Ireland, ed., *Ralph Waldo Emerson: His Life, Genius, and Writings*, 116. Published in 1882, this is an enlarged edition of Ireland's *In Memoriam: Ralph Waldo Emerson*, also published in 1882.
16. Ireland, *In Memoriam*, 22–23.
17. Henry James, Sr., "Emerson," *The Atlantic Monthly* 94 (December 1904), 741.
18. *Grimm*, 49–51.
19. Garnett, 170; Rusk, 419; Albee, 21; Edward Waldo Emerson, *The Early Years of the Saturday Club*, 477.
20. Franklin B. Sanborn, ed., *The Genius and Character of Emerson*, 1–2n.
21. Martha Dickinson Bianchi, ed., *Emily Dickinson Face to Face*, 152.
22. Edwin Percy Whipple, *Recollections of Eminent Men*, 131–132.

23. *AJ*, 338; Ireland, *In Memoriam*, 23; Maud Howe Elliott, *Three Generations*, 137; Woodberry, quoting Willis, 78; Lowell, 359.
24. *L*, V, 131n; Woodbury, 123–124; John Townsend Trowbridge, *My Own Story: With Recollections of Noted Persons*, 348.
25. Ireland, *In Memoriam*, 17.

26. *Abroad*, 226; Louise Hastings, "Emerson in Cincinnati," *New England Quarterly* 11 (September 1938), 467.
27. Frank Preston Stearns, *Sketches from Concord and Appledore*, 104–105; Trowbridge, *My Own Story*, 348; Lowell, 359.

56. EMERSON AS LECTURER

1. *CEC*, 462.
2. *L*, IV, 224.
3. *L*, IV, 201.
4. *L*, IV, 428.
5. *L*, IV, 207n.
6. Louise Hastings, "Emerson in Cincinnati," *New England Quarterly* 11 (September 1938), 444.
7. *L*, IV, 245–246.
8. *L*, III, 24. See also Cabot, II, 475.
9. *JMN*, XV, 457.
10. *L*, IV, 342.
11. *CEC*, 498–499.
12. *JMN*, XIV, 25; *J*, X, 223; *L*, V, 4.
13. *L*, V, 6.
14. *JMN*, XIV, 27–28.
15. *L*, V, 4.
16. *L*, V, 304.
17. Ibid.
18. *L*, V, 197; *J*, X, 183; *L*, V, 406–407.
19. Hastings, "Emerson in Cincinnati," 461–462.
20. *JMN*, XIII, 313; *Rock Island Daily Argus*, 19 January 1866.
21. Eleanor Bryce Scott, "Emerson Wins the Nine Hundred Dollars," *American Literature* 17 (March 1945), 84.
22. *JMN*, X, 18.
23. *Diary and Letters of Rutherford Birchard Hayes*, ed. Charles R. Williams, I, 301; and see L. N. Richardson, "What Rutherford B. Hayes Liked in Emerson," *American Literature* 17 (March 1945), 22–32.
24. Hayes, *Diary and Letters*, IV, 576–577; V, 9.
25. Conway, I, 283–284; *W*, IX, 163–181.
26. *L*, III, 18.
27. Hayes, *Diary and Letters*, I, 303–305.
28. *JMN*, V, 218.
29. *L*, II, 266.
30. *W*, X, 342–343.
31. *L*, IV, 211.
32. *L*, IV, 208–217.
33. *L*, IV, 209.
34. *JMN*, XI, 86.

57. HORATIO GREENOUGH

1. *L*, I, 380.
2. *L*, I, 381–382.
3. *L*, IV, 271–272.
4. *L*, III, 120–121.
5. *L*, IV, 271–272.
6. *JMN*, XIII, 85.
7. Nathalia Wright, "Ralph Waldo Emerson to Horatio Greenough," *Harvard Library Bulletin* 12 (Winter 1958), 112.
8. *LLJ*, I, 215.
9. Nathalia Wright, *Horatio Greenough: The First American Sculptor*, 290.
10. John Forster, *The Works and Life of Walter Savage Landor*, II, 266.
11. *JMN*, XIII, 84.
12. *JMN*, XVI, 112.
13. Wright, *Horatio Greenough*, 296–297; *AJ*, 263; ms. letter, Richard

Henry Dana, Jr., 20 December 1852, Houghton Library, Harvard.
14. *CEC*, 486.
15. Wright, "Emerson to Greenough," 113.
16. Wright, "Emerson to Greenough," 115–116.
17. Ms., "Art and Nature," 1, Houghton Library, Harvard; *J*, X, 357. See also Charles R. Metzger, *Emerson and Greenough: Transcendental Pioneers of an American Esthetic.*

58. DANIEL WEBSTER

1. *JMN*, VIII, 111.
2. Irving H. Bartlett, *Daniel Webster*, 8; *L*, I, 123–124; *W*, IX, 398; *CEC*, 245–246.
3. *JMN*, VIII, 102.
4. *CEC*, 246.
5. *JMN*, VII, 323.
6. *JMN*, VIII, 325.
7. *JMN*, IX, 249.
8. Franklin B. Sanborn, *Henry D. Thoreau*, 89–95.
9. *Lidian*, 30, 91; Franklin B. Sanborn, *The Personality of Emerson*, 19.
10. *JMN*, VIII, 357–361.
11. *JMN*, IX, 17.
12. Bartlett, *Daniel Webster*, 293.
13. Walter Harding, *The Days of Henry Thoreau*, 175.
14. *W*, XI, 129.
15. Ward, 57.
16. Sanborn, *Henry D. Thoreau*, 95.
17. *JMN*, IX, 380.
18. *JMN*, IX, 444–445.
19. Ralph Waldo Emerson, *Uncollected Writings: Essays, Addresses, Poems, Reviews and Letters*, 195–196.
20. *JMN*, XI, 152.

59. SOCIAL REFORM

1. *JMN*, III, 127.
2. *The Western Messenger*, II, 387.
3. *W*, I, 100; *JMN*, VII, 361; *W*, II, 161.
4. *W*, I, 268–269, 272.
5. *The Harbinger*, V, 192.
6. *The Harbinger*, VII, 6.
7. Charles W. Eliot, *Four American Leaders*, 78–79.
8. Chapman, 48–57; Quentin Anderson, *The Imperial Self: An Essay in American Literary and Cultural History*, 3–58.
9. *W*, II, 261. See also Percy H. Boynton, "Emerson's Feeling toward Reform," *New Republic* 1 (30 January 1915), 16–18.
10. *CEC*, 373; *JMN*, IX, 180.
11. *W*, VI, 249, 121.
12. *W*, IX, 114–118; EWE, 159.
13. *W*, I, 348–351.
14. *W*, I, 390. See also M. M. Moody, "The Evolution of Emerson as an Abolitionist," *American Literature* 17 (March 1945), 1–21.
15. *The Dial*, I:4 (April 1841), 523.
16. *JMN*, V, 445.
17. Cabot, II, 426–427.
18. *W*, I, 214–216; see Chapter 41.
19. *W*, I, 277–278.
20. *W*, II, 51.
21. Holmes, 141–142; *W*, I, 350. See also R. G. Silver, "Emerson as Abolitionist," *New England Quarterly* 6 (March 1933), 154–158.
22. *JMN*, VIII, 149–150, 356, 372.
23. *L*, IV, 230.
24. *JMN*, XIV, 14; *W*, XI, 424; *L*, VI, 77–78.
25. Snider, 346.
26. EWE, 87.
27. *W*, XI, 259.
28. Simon and Parsons, 145.

60. THE COMPLETEST MAN

1. Samuel W. McCall, *Daniel Webster*, 104–105.
2. *JMN*, XI, 249.
3. *JMN*, XI, xv–xvi.
4. *JMN*, XI, 346, 351, 361, 385, 412.
5. Chapman, 52–53.
6. Ibid.
7. Franklin B. Sanborn, *Henry D. Thoreau*, 94.
8. *JMN*, XIII, 111–112.
9. *Abroad*, 306.
10. *W*, XI, 217.
11. *L*, IX, 484.
12. *LLJ*, 56.
13. Perry, 107.
14. *W*, XI, 219, 223.
15. Firkins, 137.
16. *JMN*, XV, 76.
17. Townsend Scudder, *Concord: American Town*, 201.
18. *CEC*, 470.
19. Edwin Percy Whipple, *Recollections of Eminent Men*, 140–141.
20. *The Liberator*, 23 May 1851, quoted in Rusk, 367.
21. Cabot, II, 586.
22. Whipple, *Recollections of Eminent Men*, 141–142.
23. Whipple, *Recollections of Eminent Men*, 142.
24. Phyllis Cole, "Emerson, England, and Fate," in David Levin, ed., *Emerson: Prophecy, Metamorphosis and Influence*, 93.
25. This and the following quotations from the speech are from Cabot, II, 578–582.
26. Quoted by Cabot, II, 587.

61. MARTYRDOM

1. *JMN*, XIII, 80.
2. *EWE*, 82. Emerson's forebear, Edward Bulkeley, father of Peter Bulkeley, wrote a supplement to Fox's *Book of Martyrs*.
3. Samuel W. McCall, *Daniel Webster*, 103. See also Leonard Neufeldt, *The House of Emerson*, 101–121.
4. *YES*, 14.
5. *JMN*, IV, 315–316.
6. *W*, I, 20–21.
7. *W*, II, 425–426.
8. *W*, II, 262.
9. *JMN*, V, 437: "The brave Lovejoy has given his breast to the bullet for his part, and has died when it was better not to live. . . . I sternly rejoice that one was bound to die for humanity & the rights of free speech & opinion."
10. *L*, II, 347.
11. *W*, III, 114; II, 120.
12. *JMN*, XI, 347.
13. *JMN*, XIV, 95–96.
14. *JMN*, XIV, 333; *AJ*, 320; Rusk, 402; *The Liberator*, 29:45 (11 November 1859), 178; Cooke, 140–141.
15. *Abroad*, 310–311.
16. David Mead, *Yankee Eloquence in the Middle West: The Ohio Lyceum, 1850–1880*, 49.
17. Cabot, II, 597.
18. Ibid.
19. Mead, *Yankee Eloquence*, 49–50.
20. J. J. McDonald, "Emerson and John Brown," *New England Quarterly* 44 (Summer 1971), 387n; *The Atlantic Monthly* 10 (July 1862), 54.
21. Arlin Turner, *Nathaniel Hawthorne*, 368.
22. Lawrence Lader, *The Bold Brahmins*, 252–253.
23. *JMN*, XIV, 353.
24. *JMN*, XIV, 355–356.
25. *JMN*, XVI, 111.
26. Julia Ward Howe, *Reminiscences: 1819–1899*, 155–156.
27. *J*, IX, 305, 306.
28. McDonald, "Emerson and John Brown," 396n.
29. Holmes, 420–421.

62. MONCURE DANIEL CONWAY

1. *L*, IV, 321–322.
2. Haskins, 83–84.
3. *L*, IV, 398.
4. *L*, IV, 322.
5. Lathrop, 191. Sophia Hawthorne characterized the summer house as "Gothic."
6. *Abroad*, 7 ; Conway, I, 135.
7. Conway, I, 109.
8. *Abroad*, 5.
9. Conway, I, 101.
10. *Abroad*, 6–7 ; Conway, I, 109–110.
11. *Abroad*, 7.
12. Conway, I, 136.
13. Conway, I, 137.
14. *L*, III, 117 ; Cabot, II, 472.
15. Conway, I, 138.
16. Kenneth Murdock, *Literature and Theology in Colonial New England*, 11–15.
17. Conway, I, 138.
18. Ibid.
19. Conway, I, 138–139.

63. A HARVARD INCURSION

1. Conway, I, 141.
2. Conway, I, 147.
3. Conway, I, 148.
4. Conway, I, 172, 145.
5. Conway, I, 168.
6. *W*, VIII, 368–369.
7. *LLJ*, II, 243.
8. *LCEN*, I, 109.
9. Conway, I, 164–169.
10. Conway, I, 171.
11. *Abroad*, 368.
12. *Abroad*, 15–16.
13. *Abroad*, 380–381.
14. Conway, II, 407–413.
15. Charles Eliot Norton, ed., *The Correspondence of Thomas Carlyle and Ralph Waldo Emerson 1834–1872*, I, iv.
16. *Lidian*, xxix. See also EWE, 189.

64. PIGEON COVE AND THE ADIRONDAC CLUB

1. *L*, V, 24–26. Now known as the Ralph Waldo Emerson Inn, the Pigeon Cove House still welcomes guests. The management identifies Room 109 as Emerson's room. For a time Emerson's words, inscribed on a bronze plaque, were on view on Andrew's Point, Pigeon Cove. Fear of vandalism has led to the removal of the plaque to the Old Castle for safekeeping.
2. EWE, 234–235 ; *JMN*, XIV, 100–101.
3. *W*, IX, 242–243.
4. Holmes, 222 ; Edward Waldo Emerson, *The Early Years of the Saturday Club*, 5–20, 54–61 ; Martin Duberman, *James Russell Lowell*, 184–190 ; Charles Francis Adams, *Richard Henry Dana*, 162–169.
5. *JMN*, XIII, 34–35n, 105, 55–56.
6. *LLJ*, II, 363 ; Emerson, *The Early Years of the Saturday Club*, 171.
7. *TJ*, XI, 77.
8. Moorfield Storey and Edward Waldo Emerson, *Ebenezer Rockwood Hoar: A Memoir*, 144–148.
9. *TJ*, XI, 120.
10. Storey and Emerson, *Ebenezer Rockwood Hoar*, 148.
11. Storey and Emerson, *Ebenezer Rockwood Hoar*, 145.
12. This cable was not the enduring triumph it was at first believed to be. In October its electrical insulation broke down and it was rendered useless. Eight more years

passed before a serviceable cable was laid. See Kenneth W. Cameron, "Emerson, Thoreau, and the Atlantic Cable," *Emerson Soci-* *ety Quarterly* 26 (1st qu. 1962), 45–87.
13. *W,* IX, 182–194.

· 65. THE POET'S EAR

1. *JMN,* XV, 68; X, 260.
2. *The Dial,* I:2 (October 1840), 149; *L,* IV, 84.
3. *JMN,* VII, 152.
4. *JMN,* VII, 137–138; quoted in Norman Foerster, *American Criticism: A Study of Literary Theory from Poe to the Present,* 100; EWE, 173.
5. Holmes, 361.
6. Engel, 26.
7. *JMN,* VII, 9–10.
8. EWE, 165.
9. Firkins, 262, 276–278; *W,* IX, 174;
Kathryn A. McEuen, "Emerson's Rhymes," *American Literature* 20 (March 1948), 31–42.
10. Wagenknecht, 104–105; Hyatt H. Waggoner, *Emerson as Poet,* 75.
11. EWE, 173.
12. Firkins, 289.
13. *JMN,* IX, 227.
14. Firkins, 232–233.
15. *W,* VIII, 49.
16. Brandes, in Cary, 192; *W,* IV, 195–196. See also Charmenz Lenhart, *Musical Influence on American Poetry,* 110–112.

66. THE BURNS CENTENNIAL

1. *JMN,* VIII, 46.
2. *JMN,* XII, 204; XIV, 179.
3. Franklin B. Sanborn, *The Personality of Emerson,* 121.
4. Mead, 233–234.
5. Lowell, 359–360.
6. Edward Waldo Emerson, *The Early Years of the Saturday Club,* 197.
7. Quotations from the speech are from *W,* XI, 437–443.
8. Cooke, 180; *L,* VI, 270.

67. WILLIAM DEAN HOWELLS

1. Moncure D. Conway, *Life of Nathaniel Hawthorne,* 202.
2. Kenneth Lynn, *William Dean Howells: An American Life,* 97–100; Walter Harding, *The Days of Henry Thoreau,* 433–434; William Dean Howells, *Literary Friends and Acquaintances,* 60–65.
3. Howells, *Literary Friends and Acquaintances,* 61.
4. *JMN,* XI, 32; EWE, 160; *Lidian,* 80.
5. Howells, *Literary Friends and Acquaintances,* 63.
6. *JMN,* IX, 376.
7. Kenneth W. Cameron, *Transcendental Log,* 275; Clyde Kenneth Hyder, *Swinburne's Literary Career and Fame,* 178–179, 304n; *Abroad,* 380. When Conway asked about the remark, Emerson said, "Its publication was one of the damnable things."
8. Howells, *Literary Friends and Acquaintances,* 64.
9. Howells, *Literary Friends and Acquaintances,* 137; *L,* VI, 255.
10. *JMN,* VII, 306.

68. CIVIL WAR YEARS

1. Newton Dillaway, *Prophet of America: Emerson and the Problems of Today*, 18.
2. Cabot, II, 605.
3. *JMN*, XV, 187.
4. Ibid.
5. Forbes, Edith Emerson's future father-in-law, had been a presidential elector in 1860.
6. *JMN*, XV, 194, 292, 297, 218.
7. *W*, XI, 317–318.
8. Miller, 410–411.
9. William R. Hutchison, *The Transcendental Ministers: Church Reform in the New England Renais-*
sance, 181–182; Justin Winsor, *The Memorial History of Boston,* IV, 436.
10. George Willis Cooke, *John Sullivan Dwight*, 190.
11. Carl F. Strauch, ''The Background for Emerson's 'Boston Hymn,' '' *American Literature* 14 (March 1942), 36–47.
12. Cooke, *John Sullivan Dwight*, 191.
13. Fields, 95.
14. *W*, IX, 201–204.
15. *Abroad*, 47.
16. Rusk, 418.
17. *W*, XI, 329–338.

69. CHARLES WOODBURY

1. Woodbury, 6.
2. *J*, X, 117.
3. Woodbury, 15.
4. Woodbury, 15–16.
5. Woodbury, 139.
6. *J*, X, 118.
7. *L*, VI, 434.
8. Woodbury, 16.
9. *JMN*, XVI, 79.
10. Woodbury, 95–96.
11. Woodbury, 126.
12. Woodbury, 127.
13. Woodbury, 123.
14. Woodbury, 124.
15. Woodbury, 129.
16. Woodbury, 127, 132.
17. Woodbury, 132–133.
18. Woodbury, 162.
19. Woodbury, 160.
20. Woodbury, 154.
21. Woodbury, 23.
22. Woodbury, 42.
23. Woodbury, 62.
24. Woodbury, 142–143.
25. Woodbury, 146–147.

70. FALTERING POWERS

1. *Letters of James Russell Lowell,* ed. Charles Eliot Norton, I, 393.
2. Fields, 94.
3. Ibid.
4. Lowell, 353.
5. John Olin Eidson, ''Two Unpublished Letters of Emerson,'' *American Literature* 21 (November 1949), 335–338.
6. *L*, VI, 195.
7. Ibid.
8. *J*, X, 379.
9. *L*, VI, 196.
10. *L*, VI, 194; Fields, 104–105.
11. Oral Sumner Coad, ''An Unpublished Lecture by Ralph Waldo Emerson,'' *American Literature* 14 (January 1943), 421–426.
12. Clara Barrus, *Whitman and Burroughs: Comrades*, 65–66; see also Clara Barrus, *The Life and Letters of John Burroughs*, I, 155–156.
13. Ireland, *In Memoriam*, 105–107.
14. Fields, 104.
15. Fields, 104–105.
16. *L*, VI, 304.

71. UNIVERSITY LECTURER

1. Henry James, *Charles W. Eliot*, I, 230–231.
2. John Spencer Clark, *The Life and Letters of John Fiske*, I, 228.
3. Ibid.
4. James, *Charles W. Eliot*, I, 200.
5. James, *Charles W. Eliot*, I, 349.
6. James, *Charles W. Eliot*, I, 43–44.
7. James, *Charles W. Eliot*, I, 349.
8. Simon and Parsons, 38; Hazen C. Carpenter, ''Emerson, Eliot, and the Elective System,'' *New England Quarterly* 24 (March 1951), 13–34.
9. James, *Charles W. Eliot*, II, 198.
10. Clark, *John Fiske*, I, 213–214.
11. EWE, 183.
12. Josephine Miles, *Ralph Waldo Emerson*, 30.
13. Ms., Peabody notebook on philosophy, Houghton Library, Harvard.
14. Cabot, II, 643.
15. *CEC*, 570.
16. *CEC*, 578.
17. James, *Charles W. Eliot*, I, 251.
18. John T. Morse, *Memoir of Colonel Henry Lee*, 143.
19. Edward Waldo Emerson, *The Early Years of the Saturday Club*, 63.

72. JOHN MUIR

1. *Letters and Recollections of John Murray Forbes*, ed. Sarah Forbes Hughes, II, 174.
2. Thayer, 1; *L*, VI, 149–153.
3. *W*, IX, 251–252.
4. *CEC*, 580.
5. Thayer, 97.
6. *CEC*, 580.
7. *CEC*, 582.
8. Holmes, 264.
9. C. A. Murdock, ''Emerson in California,'' *Pacific Unitarian* 11 (May 1903), 263–268; Holmes, 267.
10. Holmes, 264.
11. Thayer, 74.
12. Linnie Marsh Wolfe, *Son of the Wilderness: The Life of John Muir*, 145.
13. Stephen Fox, *John Muir and His Legacy: The American Conservation Movement*, 5; *L*, VI, 154–155.
14. Thayer, 90.
15. Fox, *John Muir*, 5; Edwin Way Teale, ed., *The Wilderness World of John Muir*, 163.
16. Linnie Marsh Wolfe, ed., *John of the Mountains: The Unpublished Journals of John Muir*, 436.
17. *JMN*, X, 188.
18. *Muir*, I, 255.
19. Teale, *Wilderness World*, 163; Thayer, 64.
20. John Muir, *Our National Parks*, 149–150; Teale, *Wilderness World*, 164.
21. *Muir*, I, 256.
22. *Muir*, I, 257.
23. *Muir*, I, 262.
24. *Muir*, I, 257.
25. Ibid.
26. *Muir*, I, 258.
27. Ibid.
28. *Muir*, I, 259, 260.
29. *L*, VI, 202n.
30. *Muir*, I, 258–260.
31. *L*, VI, 202.
32. *L*, VI, 155.
33. *L*, VI, 156.
34. Fox, *John Muir*, 6.
35. *Muir*, II, 267.
36. *Ellen*, II, 56–57.
37. *Muir*, II, 409–415.
38. Fox, *John Muir*, 126.
39. *JMN*, X, 230.
40. Thayer, 61–62.
41. Thayer, 61, 95.
42. Cabot, II, 648.

7 3 . B U S H A B L A Z E

1. *Lidian*, 159.
2. Pommer, v.
3. *Abroad*, 142.
4. *L*, VI, 214.
5. *J*, X, 386; *Lidian*, 159.
6. *Lidian*, 160.
7. *Abroad*, 378.
8. *J*, X, 391; *Abroad*, 379.
9. *Lidian*, 160.
10. Howe, 88.
11. *JMN*, XVI, 304.
12. Ferris Greenslet, *The Lowells and Their Seven Worlds*, 216n.
13. *JMN*, XVI, 302–305.
14. Regis Michaud, *Emerson: The Enraptured Yankee*, 438.
15. *Lidian*, 160; see also Townsend Scudder, *Concord: American Town*, 268.
16. Furness, Ltr. LXXVIII, 155; EWE, 186.
17. *Lidian*, 160.
18. Cabot, II, 708–709.
19. Cabot, II, 706–708.
20. *L*, V, 49n.
21. *L*, VI, 219.
22. *L*, VI, 220.
23. Cabot, II, 707.
24. Cabot, II, 704.

7 4 . C H A R L E S E L I O T N O R T O N

1. *CEC*, 589.
2. Ms. owned by Harvard College Library, quoted in *CEC*, 464 n3.
3. *LCEN*, I, 424; *L*, VI, 226–227.
4. *LCEN*, I, 484–485.
5. *LCEN*, I, 501.
6. Norton's account is included in *LCEN*.
7. Social Circle of Concord, *The Centenary of the Birth of Ralph Waldo Emerson*, 53.
8. Rusk, 405.
9. Alfred Kazin, *On Native Grounds*, 18n.
10. *LCEN*, I, 504, 512.
11. *LCEN*, I, 510–511.
12. *LCEN*, I, 503–504.
13. *LCEN*, I, 506–507.
14. *LCEN*, I, 511.
15. *LCEN*, I, 505–506.
16. *LCEN*, I, 506.
17. *LCEN*, I, 512–513.
18. *LCEN*, I, 513.
19. *LCEN*, I, 510.
20. *LCEN*, I, 511.
21. *LCEN*, I, 512.
22. *LCEN*, II, 12; and see Kermit Vanderbilt, *Charles Eliot Norton: Apostle of Culture in a Democracy*, 114–116.
23. Social Circle of Concord, *The Emerson Centenary*, 46.
24. Social Circle of Concord, *The Emerson Centenary*, 57–58.
25. Mary Caroline Crawford, *Romantic Days in Old Boston*, 354–361; John Holmes, *Letters of John Holmes to James Russell Lowell and Others*, ed. William Roscoe Thayer, 104n. The fire was believed to have started on Chauncy Place itself.
26. *Lidian*, 161–162.
27. *Lidian*, 162.
28. *Letters of John Holmes*, 128.
29. Ireland, *In Memoriam*, 31–32.
30. *AJ*, 433.
31. Social Circle of Concord, *The Emerson Centenary*, 120.
32. Charles Francis Adams, *Richard Henry Dana*, II, 359–360. "Mrs. Bell" is undoubtedly Helen Choate (Mrs. Joseph) Bell. She had been a guest at Bush.

75. MORTIFICATIONS AND REMORSES

1. *JMN*, IX, 393.
2. *JMN*, XV, 428.
3. EWE, 183; *W*, IX, 251–252.
4. John Burroughs, *Birds and Poets*, 182.
5. Cabot, II, 652.
6. Holmes, 346.
7. Brown, 43.
8. George W. Smalley, *Anglo-Saxon Memories*, 62.
9. Cabot, II, 672; Holmes, 364.
10. Phillips Russell, *Emerson: The Wisest American*, 294; *Abroad*, 379.
11. *Ellen*, II, 286.
12. Franklin Sanborn, *Transcendental and Literary New England*, ed. Kenneth W. Cameron, 113; August Derleth, *Emerson, Our Contemporary*, 153.
13. John T. Morse, *Life and Letters of Oliver Wendell Holmes*, II, 122.
14. Social Circle of Concord, *The Centenary of the Birth of Ralph Waldo Emerson*, 57.
15. *LCEN*, II, 112.
16. *AJ*, 528–529.
17. Garnett, 185.
18. Kenneth W. Cameron, *Transcendental Log*, 334.
19. Holmes, 348.
20. *LCEN*, II, 132.
21. *Abroad*, 382; *Ellen*, II, 24.
22. Cyrus Bartol, "The Nature of Knowledge — Emerson's Way," in Raymond L. Bridgman, ed., *Concord Lectures on Philosophy*, 56.
23. EWE, 190.
24. Townsend Scudder, *Concord: American Town*, 285.
25. EWE, 188.
26. Rusk, 499–500; Garnett, 185; *L*, V, 341–342; VI, 321.
27. *AJ*, 524.

76. THE VIRGINIAN IMMOLATION

1. *W*, X, 563n.
2. Hubert H. Hoeltje, "Emerson in Virginia," *New England Quarterly* 5 (October 1932), 754.
3. "The Rotunda . . . stands majestically at the head of the rectangular Lawn, a lovely stretch of green bordered by towering trees. Greco-Roman pavilions and colonnades, with variances inspired by the great Italian architect Palladio, furnish an enchanting ensemble" (Virginius Dabney, *Mr. Jefferson's University: A History*, 1). Public Hall, a nineteenth-century addition to the Rotunda, was destroyed by fire in 1895.
4. Cabot, II, 674.
5. D. M. R. Culbreth, *The University of Virginia*, 323, 412.
6. Hoeltje, "Emerson in Virginia," 766–767.
7. Hoeltje, "Emerson in Virginia," 759.
8. *Ellen*, II, 210–211.
9. *Ellen*, II, 212.
10. Hoeltje, "Emerson in Virginia," 762.
11. *Ellen*, II, 663–669.
12. Hoeltje, "Emerson in Virginia," 762; Cabot, II, 674.
13. *L*, VI, 295n.
14. Hoeltje, "Emerson in Virginia," 762–763.
15. Hoeltje, "Emerson in Virginia," 764.
16. Sanborn, II, 263.
17. Cabot, II, 674–675.
18. *JMN*, X, 31–32; XIII, 327.

77. THE CONCORD SCHOOL

1. Cabot, II, 410.
2. *L,* II, 323–324.
3. Sanborn, II, 489.
4. Ireland, *In Memoriam,* 110.
5. Austin Warren, "The Concord School of Philosophy," *New England Quarterly* 2 (April 1929), 202.
6. Ireland, *In Memoriam,* 109.
7. Henry A. Beers, *Four Americans,* 71–72.
8. Ireland, *In Memoriam,* 111.
9. Warren, "The Concord School," 223.
10. *Ellen,* xviii, 181–183, 251.
11. Raymond L. Bridgman, ed., *Concord Lectures on Philosophy,* 62.
12. *Concord Lectures,* 62–63, 66–69, 72–74. Orchard House was sold to Dr. Harris soon after Bronson Alcott was felled by a stroke on 24 October 1882; see *Louisa May Alcott: Her Life, Letters, and Journals,* ed. Ednah D. Cheney, 347.
13. Warren, "The Concord School," 227–233.

78. SOME FINAL PARTINGS

1. Mead, 157–161. Mead based his report on the account given by Dr. George E. Ellis in *Scribner's Magazine* (May 1881). Ellis was vice-president of the Massachusetts Historical Society and succeeded Winthrop as president.
2. EWE, 194.
3. Emerson also omitted his own poems from *Parnassus.*
4. Justin Kaplan, *Walt Whitman: A Life,* 354.
5. Sanborn, *The Personality of Emerson,* 128.
6. Gay Wilson Allen, *The Solitary Singer: A Critical Biography of Walt Whitman,* 494–495.
7. Ireland, *In Memoriam,* 113.
8. Ireland, *In Memoriam,* 114.
9. Ibid.
10. Ireland, *In Memoriam,* 114–115.
11. Ireland, *In Memoriam,* 115.

79. EDWARD BOK SEES MR. EMERSON

1. The details of Bok's visit and the relevant quotes are from Edward Bok, *The Americanization of Edward Bok,* 54–60.
2. Kenneth W. Cameron, *Transcendental Log,* 320.

80. INTO THE HOLY SILENCE & ETERNITY

1. *JMN,* V, 408.
2. *JMN,* III, 312–313.
3. *YES,* 245n.
4. *J,* II, 211.
5. *JMN,* XIV, 17.
6. *JMN,* VII, 435; *W,* VI, 238.
7. Wagenknecht, 216–217.
8. *W,* VIII, 342–343.
9. *W,* II, 126.
10. *Lidian,* 187; EWE, 193.
11. EWE, 193–194.
12. *Lidian,* 187. Ellen explained: "Now he could only speak ordinary English a part of the time, often made up words. So there was no way to learn just what was the matter."
13. *JMN,* VII, 165; EWE, 194.

14. *Abroad*, 242 ; *W, I*, 17.
15. EWE, 212.
16. *W, VI*, 263.
17. Holmes, 362.
18. *CEC*, 303–304.
19. Holmes, 269–270, 363.
20. *AJ*, 533.
21. Ibid.
22. Cabot, II, 683.
23. *Lidian*, 188.
24. *Louisa May Alcott: Her Life, Letters, and Journals*, ed. Ednah D. Cheney, 345.
25. *Lidian*, 187–189. See also EWE, 193–195 ; Holmes, 349 ; Rusk, 507–508.
26. *AJ*, 534.
27. Garnett, 186.
28. Furness, xv–xvi.

29. *Lidian*, 189.
30. F. O. Matthiessen, *The James Family*, 447.
31. Ireland, *In Memoriam*, 42.
32. *Abroad*, 9.
33. Ireland, *In Memoriam*, 44.
34. Holmes, 349–356.
35. *L*, I, 412.
36. Haskins, 134–136.
37. *W, XI*, 434 ; Alcott, *Life, Letters, and Journals*, 345 ; *LCEN*, II, 133.
38. *New Letters of James Russell Lowell*, ed. Mark A. DeWolfe Howe, 267.
39. *Muir*, II, 267 ; *W, IX*, 6–9.
40. George Hendrick, ed., *Remembrances of Concord and the Thoreaus*, 104.

Bibliography

ABBREVIATIONS FOR PRIMARY SOURCES

AJ *The Journals of Bronson Alcott*, ed. Odell Shepard, Boston, 1938.

AL *The Letters of Bronson Alcott*, ed. Richard L. Herrnstadt, Ames, Iowa, 1969.

CEC *The Correspondence of Emerson and Carlyle*, ed. Joseph Slater, New York, 1964.

CW *The Collected Works of Ralph Waldo Emerson*, ed. Robert E. Spiller and Alfred R. Ferguson; volume I: *Nature, Addresses, and Lectures*, Cambridge, Mass., 1971.

EL *The Early Lectures of Ralph Waldo Emerson*, ed. Stephen E. Whicher, Robert E. Spiller, and Wallace E. Williams, 3 vols., Cambridge, Mass., 1959, 1964, 1972.

J *The Journals of Ralph Waldo Emerson*, ed. Edward Waldo Emerson and Waldo Emerson Forbes, 10 vols., Boston and New York, 1909–1914.

JMN *The Journals and Miscellaneous Notebooks of Ralph Waldo Emerson*, ed. William H. Gilman, Alfred R. Ferguson, George P. Clark, Merrell R. Davis, A. W. Plumstead, Harrison Hayford, Ralph H. Orth, J. E. Parsons, Linda Allardt, Susan Sutton Smith, Merton M. Sealts, Jr., David W. Hill, Ruth H. Bennett, Ronald A. Bosco, and Glen M. Johnson, 16 vols., Cambridge, Mass., 1960–1982.

L *The Letters of Ralph Waldo Emerson*, ed. Ralph L. Rusk, 6 vols., New York, 1939.

LCEN *Letters of Charles Eliot Norton*, ed. Sara Norton and M. A. DeWolfe Howe, 2 vols., Boston and New York, 1913.

LLJ *Life of Henry Wadsworth Longfellow: With Extracts from His Journals and Correspondence*, ed. Samuel Longfellow, 2 vols., Boston, 1886.

TC *The Correspondence of Henry David Thoreau*, ed. Walter Harding and Carl Bode, New York, 1958.

TJ   *The Journal of Henry D. Thoreau*, ed. Bradford Torrey and Francis
           H. Allen, 20 vols., Boston, 1906.
W   *The Complete Works of Ralph Waldo Emerson*, Centenary Edi-
           tion, ed. Edward Waldo Emerson, 12 vols., Boston and New York,
           1903–1904.
YES   *Young Emerson Speaks: Unpublished Discourses on Many Sub-
           jects*, ed. Arthur Cushman McGiffert, Jr., Boston, 1938.

ABBREVIATIONS FOR SECONDARY SOURCES

Abroad   Moncure Daniel Conway, *Emerson at Home and Abroad*,
                  Boston, 1882.
Albee   John Albee, *Remembrances of Emerson*, New York, 1900.
Allen   Gay Wilson Allen, *Waldo Emerson*, New York, 1981.
Blanchard   Paula Blanchard, *Margaret Fuller: From Transcenden-
                  talism to Revolution*, New York, 1978.
Bode   Carl Bode, ed., *Ralph Waldo Emerson: A Profile*, New
                  York, 1969.
Bremer, *Homes*   Fredrika Bremer, *The Homes of the New World:
                  Impressions of America*, 2 vols., New York, 1853.
Brown   Mary Hosmer Brown, *Memories of Concord*, Boston, 1926.
Cabot   James Elliot Cabot, *A Memoir of Ralph Waldo Emerson*,
                  2 vols., Boston, 1887.
Carpenter   Frederic Ives Carpenter, *Emerson and Asia*, Cambridge,
                  Mass., 1930.
Cary   Elisabeth Luther Cary, *Emerson: Poet and Thinker*, New
                  York, 1904.
Chapman   John Jay Chapman, *Emerson and Other Essays*, New
                  York, 1898.
Clough   *Emerson-Clough Letters*, ed. Howard F. Lowry and Ralph
                  L. Rusk, Hamden, Conn., 1968.
Commager   Henry Steele Commager, *Theodore Parker: Yankee Cru-
                  sader*, Boston, 1936.
Conway   Moncure Daniel Conway, *Autobiography, Memories and
                  Experiences*, 2 vols., Boston, 1904.
Cooke   George Willis Cooke, *Ralph Waldo Emerson: His Life,
                  Writings, and Philosophy*, Boston, 1882.
Ellen   *The Letters of Ellen Tucker Emerson*, ed. Edith E. W.
                  Gregg, 2 vols., Kent, Ohio, 1982.
Engel   Mary Miller Engel, *I Remember the Emersons*, Los An-
                  geles, 1941.
EWE   Edward Waldo Emerson, *Emerson in Concord*, Boston and
                  New York, 1890.
Fields   Annie Adams Fields, *Authors and Friends*, Boston, 1897.
Firkins   O. W. Firkins, *Ralph Waldo Emerson*, Boston, 1915.
Frothingham   Octavius Brooks Frothingham, *Transcendentalism in New
                  England*, New York, 1876.
Fuller   *Memoirs of Margaret Fuller Ossoli*, ed. Ralph Waldo
                  Emerson, William Henry Channing, and James Freeman
                  Clarke, 2 vols., Boston, 1852.
Furness   *Records of a Lifelong Friendship, 1807–1882: Ralph*

	Waldo Emerson and William Henry Furness, ed. Horace Howard Furness, Boston, 1910.
Garnett	Richard Garnett, *Life of Ralph Waldo Emerson,* London, 1888.
Gay	Robert M. Gay, *Ralph Waldo Emerson: A Study of the Poet as Seer,* New York, 1928.
Gittleman	Edwin Gittleman, *Jones Very: The Effective Years 1833–1840,* New York, 1967.
Gregg	Edith E. W. Gregg, ed., *One First Love: The Letters of Ellen Louisa Tucker to Ralph Waldo Emerson,* Cambridge, Mass., 1962.
Grimm	*Correspondence between Ralph Waldo Emerson and Herman Grimm,* ed. Frederick William Holls, Boston, 1903.
Harris	Kenneth Marc Harris, *Carlyle and Emerson: Their Long Debate,* Cambridge, Mass., 1978.
Haskins	David Greene Haskins, *Ralph Waldo Emerson: His Maternal Ancestors with Some Reminiscences of Him,* Boston, 1887.
Hawthorne, *American Notebooks*	*The American Notebooks,* vol. VIII (1972) in *The Works of Nathaniel Hawthorne,* Centenary Edition, ed. William Charvat, Roy Harvey Pearse, and Claude M. Simpson, 14 vols., Columbus, Ohio, 1962–1980.
Hawthorne, *Mosses*	*Mosses from an Old Manse,* vol. X (1974) in *The Works of Nathaniel Hawthorne,* Centenary Edition, ed. William Charvat, Roy Harvey Pearse, and Claude M. Simpson, 14 vols., Columbus, Ohio, 1962–1980.
Holmes	Oliver Wendell Holmes, *Ralph Waldo Emerson,* Boston, 1885.
Hopkins	Vivian C. Hopkins, *Spires of Form: A Study of Emerson's Aesthetic Theory,* Cambridge, Mass., 1951.
Howe	Mark A. DeWolfe Howe, *Memories of a Hostess,* Boston, 1922.
Ireland, *In Memoriam*	Alexander Ireland, ed., *In Memoriam: Ralph Waldo Emerson,* London, 1882.
Julian	Julian Hawthorne, *Nathaniel Hawthorne and His Wife,* 2 vols., Boston, 1884.
Lidian	Ellen Tucker Emerson, *The Life of Lidian Jackson Emerson,* ed. Delores Bird Carpenter, Boston, 1980.
Lathrop	Rose Hawthorne Lathrop, *Memories of Hawthorne,* Boston and New York, 1897.
Lowell	James Russell Lowell, *Literary Essays,* Boston and New York, 1892.
Mead	Edwin D. Mead, *The Influence of Emerson,* Boston, 1903.
Miller	Perry G. E. Miller, *The Transcendentalists: An Anthology,* Cambridge, Mass., 1950.
Muir	*The Life and Letters of John Muir,* ed. W. F. Badè, 2 vols., Boston, 1924.
Perry	Bliss Perry, *Emerson Today,* Princeton, 1931.
Pommer	Henry F. Pommer, *Emerson's First Marriage,* Carbondale, Ill., 1967.
Rusk	Ralph L. Rusk, *The Life of Ralph Waldo Emerson,* New York, 1949.

Sanborn	Franklin B. Sanborn, *Recollections of Seventy Years*, 2 vols., Boston, 1909.
Scudder, *Lowell*	Horace E. Scudder, *James Russell Lowell: A Biography*, Boston and New York, 1901.
Scudder	Townsend Scudder, *The Lonely Wayfaring Man: Emerson and Some Englishmen*, London, 1936.
Shepard	Odell Shepard, *Pedlar's Progress: The Life of Bronson Alcott*, Boston, 1937.
Simon and Parsons	Myron Simon and Thornton H. Parsons, eds., *Transcendentalism and Its Legacy*, Ann Arbor, 1967.
Snider	Denton J. Snider, *A Biography of Ralph Waldo Emerson: Set Forth as His Life Essay*, St. Louis, 1921.
Strauch	Carl Ferdinand Strauch, ed., *Characteristics of Emerson, Transcendental Poet: A Symposium*, Hartford, 1975.
Swayne	Josephine Latham Swayne, ed., *The Story of Concord*, Boston, 1906.
Thayer	James B. Thayer, *A Western Journey with Mr. Emerson*, Boston, 1884.
Wagenknecht	Edward Wagenknecht, *Ralph Waldo Emerson: Portrait of a Balanced Soul*, New York, 1974.
Ward	*Letters from Ralph Waldo Emerson to a Friend 1838–1853* [Samuel Ward], ed. Charles Eliot Norton, Boston, 1899.
Woodberry	George Edward Woodberry, *Ralph Waldo Emerson*, New York, 1907.
Woodbury	Charles J. Woodbury, Jr., *Talks with Ralph Waldo Emerson*, New York, 1890.

ARTICLES

Adams, Richard P., "Emerson and the Organic Metaphor," *PMLA* 69 (March 1954), 117–130.

Anderson, John Q., "Emerson and the Moral Sentiment," *Emerson Society Quarterly* 19 (2d qu. 1960), 13–15.

Baker, Carlos, "Emerson and Jones Very," *New England Quarterly* 7 (March 1934), 90–99.

Bowen, Francis, "Emerson's Nature," *The Christian Examiner* 21 (January 1837).

———, "Nine New Poets," *North American Review* 64 (April 1847), 414–415.

Boynton, Percy H., "Emerson's Feeling toward Reform," *New Republic* 1 (30 January 1915), 16–18.

Braham, Lionel, "Emerson and Boehme: A Comparative Study in Mystical Ideas," *Modern Language Quarterly* 20 (March 1959), 31–35.

Brewer, Priscilla J., "Emerson, Lane and the Shakers: A Case of Converging Ideologies," *New England Quarterly* 55 (June 1982), 254–275.

Brown, Stuart G., "Emerson's Platonism," *New England Quarterly* 18 (September 1945), 325–345.

Cameron, Kenneth W., "Early Background for Emerson's 'The Problem,'" *Emerson Society Quarterly* 27 (2d qu. 1962), 37–46.

———, "Emerson, Thoreau, and the Atlantic Cable," *Emerson Society Quarterly* 26 (1st qu. 1962), 45–87.

———, "Samuel and Ezra Ripley at Emerson's Ordination," *Emerson Society Quarterly* 48 (3d qu., pt. 2, 1967), 92–93.

Carey, E. L., "Hawthorne and Emerson," *Critic* 45 (July 1904), 25–27.

Carpenter, Hazen C., "Emerson and Christopher Pearse Cranch," *New England Quarterly* 36 (March 1964), 18–42.

———, "Emerson, Eliot, and the Elective System," *New England Quarterly* 24 (March 1951), 13–34.

Chadwick, John W., "Emerson," *Arena* 15 (1895), 12–16.

Coad, Oral Sumner, "An Unpublished Lecture by Ralph Waldo Emerson," *American Literature* 14 (January 1943), 421–426.

Cohen, B. Bernard, " 'Threnody': Emerson's Struggle with Grief," *Indiana University Folio* 14 (1948), 13–15.

Commager, Henry Steele, "Tempest in a Boston Teacup," *New England Quarterly* 6 (December 1923), 651–675.

Conroy, Stephen L., "Emerson and Phrenology," *American Quarterly* 16 (Summer 1964), 215–217.

Cook, Reginald L., "Emerson and Frost: A Parallel of Seers," *New England Quarterly* 33 (June 1958), 209–217.

Cranch, Christopher Pearse, "Emerson's Limitations as a Poet," *Critic* n.s. 17 (27 February 1892).

Davis, M. R., "Emerson's 'Reason' and the Scottish Philosophers," *New England Quarterly* 17 (June 1944), 209–228.

Detweiler, Robert, "Emerson and Zen," *American Quarterly* 14 (Fall 1962), 422–438.

Dillaway, Newton, "Emerson's Remarkable Face," *Christian Science Monthly* 38 (3 January 1946), 8.

Dykema, K. W., "Why Did Lydia Jackson Become Lidian Emerson?," *American Speech* 17 (December 1942), 285–286.

Edgell, D., "A Note on a Transcendental Friendship," *New England Quarterly* 24 (December 1951), 528–532.

Eidson, John Olin, "Two Unpublished Letters of Emerson," *American Literature* 21 (November 1949), 335–338.

Erskine, John, "The American Scholar," *American Scholar* 1 (Winter 1932), 5–15.

Flanagan, J. T., "Emerson as a Critic of Fiction," *Philological Quarterly* 15 (January 1936), 243–261.

Gohdes, Clarence F., "Some Remarks on Emerson's Divinity School Address, *American Literature* 1 (March 1929), 27–31.

Hart, John E., "Man Thinking as Hero: Emerson's 'Scholar' Revisited," *Emerson Society Quarterly* 55 (2d. qu. 1969), 102–106.

Hastings, Louise, "Emerson in Cincinnati," *New England Quarterly* 11 (September 1938), 443–469.

Hoeltje, Hubert H., "Emerson in Virginia," *New England Quarterly* 5 (October 1932), 753–768.

Hotson, Clarence P., "Sampson Reed, a Teacher of Emerson," *New England Quarterly* 2 (April 1929), 249–277.

James, Henry, Sr., "Emerson," *The Atlantic Monthly* 94 (December 1904), 740–745.

Kennedy, William Sloane, "Clews to Emerson's Mystic Verse," *The American Author* (June 1903).

Kronman, Jeanne, "Three Unpublished Lectures of Ralph Waldo Emerson," *New England Quarterly* 19 (March 1946), 98–110.

Lazarus, Emma, "Emerson's Personality," *Century Magazine* n.s. 2 (1882), 545–546.

McDonald, J. J., "Emerson and John Brown," *New England Quarterly* 44 (Summer 1971), 377–396.

McEuen, Kathryn A., "Emerson's Rhymes," *American Literature* 20 (March 1948), 31–42.

McNulty, John Bard, "Emerson's Friends and the Essay on Friendship," *New England Quarterly* 19 (September 1946), 390–394.

Malloy, Charles, "The Poems of Emerson: 'Uriel,'" *Arena* 32 (September 1904), 278–283.

Marble, A. R., "Emerson as a Public Speaker," *The Dial* 34 (16 May 1903), 327–329.

Moody, M. M., "The Evolution of Emerson as an Abolitionist," *American Literature* 17 (March 1945), 1–21.

Moore, J. B., "Emerson on Wordsworth," *PMLA* 41 (March 1926), 179–192.

———, "Thoreau Rejects Emerson," *American Literature* 4 (November 1932), 241–256.

Murdock, C. A., "Emerson in California," *Pacific Unitarian* 11 (May 1903), 263–268.

Myerson, Joel, "A Calendar of Transcendental Club Meetings," *American Literature* 44 (May 1972), 197–207.

———, "A History of the Transcendental Club," *Emerson Society Quarterly* 23 (1st qu. 1977), 27–35.

———, "Convers Francis and Emerson," *American Literature* 50 (March 1978), 17–36.

———, "Eight Lowell Letters from Concord in 1838," *Illinois Quarterly* 38 (Winter 1975), 20–42.

———, "Lowell on Emerson: A New Letter from Concord in 1838," *New England Quarterly* 44 (December 1971), 649–652.

———, "Margaret Fuller's 1842 Journal: At Concord with Emerson," *Harvard Library Bulletin* 21 (July 1973), 320–340.

Neufeldt, Leonard, "Emerson, Thoreau, and Daniel Webster," *Emerson Society Quarterly* 26 (1st qu. 1980), 26–37.

Olsson, Karl A., "Fredrika Bremer and Ralph Waldo Emerson," *Swedish Pioneer Historical Journal* 2 (August 1951), 39–52.

Origo, Iris, "The Carlyles and the Ashburtons," *Cornhill Magazine* 164 (Autumn 1950), 441–483.

Pettigrew, R. C., "Emerson and Milton," *American Literature* 3 (March 1931), 45–59.

Quinn, P. F., "Emerson and Mysticism," *American Literature* 21 (January 1950), 397–414.

Richardson, L. N., "What Rutherford B. Hayes Liked in Emerson," *American Literature* 17 (March 1945), 22–32.

Roberts, Arthur J., "Emerson's Visits to Waterville College"; annotated by Carl J. Webber, *The Colby Mercury* 5 (1 April 1934), 41–45.

Schultz, A. R., and H. A. Pochmann, "George Ripley: Unitarian, Transcendentalist, or Infidel?," *American Literature* 14 (March 1942), 1–19.

Scott, Eleanor Bryce, "Emerson Wins the Nine Hundred Dollars," *American Literature* 17 (March 1945), 78–85.

Scudder, Townsend, "Emerson in London and the London Lectures," *American Literature* 8 (March 1936), 22–36.

Silver, Mildred, "Emerson and the Idea of Progress," *American Literature* 12 (March 1940), 1–19.

Silver, R. G., "Emerson as Abolitionist," *New England Quarterly* 6 (March 1933), 154–158.

Sloan, J. M., "Carlyle and Emerson," *Living Age* 309 (21 May 1921), 486–489.

Stafford, William T., "Emerson and the James Family," *American Literature* 24 (January 1953), 433–461.

Strauch, Carl F., "Hatred's Swift Repulsions: Emerson, Margaret Fuller, and Others," *Studies in Romanticism* 7 (Winter 1968), 65–103.

———, "The Background for Emerson's 'Boston Hymn,' " *American Literature* 14 (March 1942), 36–47.

Thompson, Frank T., "Emerson and Carlyle," *Studies in Philology* 24 (July 1927), 151–157.

Tilton, Eleanor M., "Emerson's Latest Lecture Schedule — 1837–1838 — Revised," *Harvard Library Bulletin* 21 (October 1973), 382–399.

Tolles, Frederick B., "Emerson and Quakerism," *American Literature* 10 (May 1938), 142–165.

Turpie, Mary C., "A Quaker Source for Emerson's Sermon on the Lord's Supper," *New England Quarterly* 17 (March 1944), 95–101.

Ustick, W. L., "Emerson's Debt to Montaigne," *Washington University Studies* 9 (1922), 245–262.

Venables, G. S., "Froude's *Thomas Carlyle: The History of His Life in London*," *Fortnightly Review* (November 1884).

Vogel, Dan, "Orville Dewey on Emerson's 'The Lord's Supper,' " *Emerson Society Quarterly* 31 (2d qu. 1963), 40–42.

Warfel, Harry R., "Margaret Fuller and Ralph Waldo Emerson," *PMLA* 50 (June 1935), 576–594.

Warren, Austin, "The Concord School of Philosophy," *New England Quarterly* 2 (April 1929), 199–233.

Wellek, René, "Emerson on German Philosophy," *New England Quarterly* 16 (March 1943), 41–62.

White, William, "Two Unpublished Emerson Letters," *American Literature* 31 (November 1959), 334–336.

Witemeyer, Hugh H., " 'Line' and 'Round' in Emerson's 'Uriel,' " *PMLA* 82 (March 1967), 98–103.

Wright, Conrad, "Emerson, Barzillai Frost, and the Divinity School Address," *Harvard Theological Review* 49 (January 1956), 19–43.

Wright, Nathalia, "Ralph Waldo Emerson to Horatio Greenough," *Harvard Library Bulletin* 12 (Winter 1958), 91–116.

BOOKS

Adams, Charles Francis, *Richard Henry Dana*, Boston, 1890.

Adams, John Quincy, *The Diary of John Quincy Adams*, ed. Allan Nevins, New York, 1928.

Alcott, Amos Bronson, *Ralph Waldo Emerson: An Estimate of His Character and Genius*, Boston, 1882.

Alcott, Louisa May, *Louisa May Alcott: Her Life, Letters, and Journals*, ed. Ednah D. Cheney, Boston, 1895.

Allen, Gay Wilson, *The Solitary Singer: A Critical Biography of Walt Whitman*, New York, 1955.

Anderson, John Q., *The Liberating Gods: Emerson on Poets and Poetry*, Coral Gables, Fla., 1971.

Anderson, Quentin, *The Imperial Self: An Essay in American Literary and Cultural History*, New York, 1971.

Arvin, Newton, ed., *The Heart of Hawthorne's Journals*, Boston, 1929.

Barbour, Brian M., ed., *American Transcendentalism: An Anthology of Criticism*, Notre Dame, Ind., 1973.

Barrus, Clare, *The Life and Letters of John Burroughs*, Boston, 1925.

———, *Whitman and Burroughs: Comrades*, Boston, 1931.

Bartlett, George B., *Concord: Historic, Literary, and Picturesque*, Boston, 1885.

Bartlett, Irving H., *Daniel Webster*, New York, 1978.

Bartlett, William I., *Jones Very: Emerson's "Brave Saint,"* Durham, N.C., 1942.

Beers, Henry A., *Four Leaders*, New York, 1919.

Bentley, William, *The Diary of William Bentley, D.D.*, 4 vols., rpt. Gloucester, Mass., 1962.

Bergan, William M., *Old Nantasket*, North Quincy, Mass., 1972.

Berry, Edmund Grindlay, *Emerson's Plutarch*, Cambridge, Mass., 1961.

Bianchi, Martha Dickinson, ed., *Emily Dickinson Face to Face*, Boston, 1932.

Bishop, Jonathan, *Emerson on the Soul*, Cambridge, Mass., 1964.

Bloom, Harold, *Figures of Capable Imagination*, New York, 1976.

Blunt, Reginald, *The Carlyles' Chelsea Home*, London, 1895.

Bode, Carl, *The American Lyceum: Town Meeting of the Mind*, Carbondale, Ill., 1968.

Bok, Edward, *The Americanization of Edward Bok*, New York, 1922.

Boller, Paul F., Jr., *American Transcendentalism, 1830–1860: An Intellectual Inquiry*, New York, 1974.

Booth, Sally Smith, *The Witches of Early America*, New York, 1975.

Bremer, Fredrika, *America of the Fifties: Letters of Fredrika Bremer*, New York, 1924.

Bridgman, Raymond L., ed., *Concord Lectures on Philosophy*, Cambridge, Mass., 1883.

Buell, Lawrence, *Literary Transcendentalism: Style and Vision in the American Renaissance*, Ithaca, N.Y., 1973.

Burr, Anna Robeson, ed., *Alice James: Her Brothers — Her Journal*, New York, 1934.

Burroughs, John, *Birds and Poets*, Boston, 1877, 1904.

———, *Indoor Studies*, Boston, 1896.

———, *Last Harvest*, Boston, 1922.

———, *Literary Values and Other Papers*, Boston, 1902.

Burton, Katherine, *Sorrow Built a Bridge*, New York, 1954.

Cameron, Kenneth W., *Emerson among His Contemporaries*, Hartford, Conn., 1967.

———, *Emerson the Essayist*, Hartford, Conn., 1945.

———, *Emerson's Workshop*, Hartford, Conn., 1964.

———, *Ralph Waldo Emerson's Reading*, Hartford, Conn., 1941.

———, *Transcendental Log*, Hartford, Conn., 1973.

———, *Transcendental Reading Patterns*, Hartford, Conn., 1970.

Canby, Henry Seidel, *Classic Americans*, New York, 1931.

———, *Thoreau*, Boston, 1939.

Cantwell, Robert, *Nathaniel Hawthorne: The American Years*, New York, 1948.

Carlson, Eric W., and J. Lasley Dameron, eds., *Emerson's Relevance Today*, Hartford, Conn., 1971.

Carlyle, Alexander, ed., *The Love Letters of Thomas Carlyle and Jane Welsh*, 2 vols., London, 1909.

Carlyle, Jane Welsh, *Jane Welsh Carlyle: A New Selection of Her Letters*, ed. Trudy Bliss, New York, 1950.

———, *Letters and Memorials of Jane Welsh Carlyle*, ed. Thomas Carlyle, 2 vols., London, 1903.

————, *Letters of Jane Welsh Carlyle to Joseph Neuberg*, ed. Townsend Scudder, 3 vols., New York, 1931.

————, *New Letters and Memorials*, ed. Alexander Carlyle, 2 vols., London, 1903.

Carlyle, Thomas, *Letters of Thomas Carlyle to John Stuart Mill, John Sterling, and Robert Browning*, ed. Alexander Carlyle, London, 1923.

————, *Letters to His Wife*, ed. Trudy Bliss, London, 1953.

Carpenter, Frederic Ives, *Emerson Handbook*, New York, 1967.

Chadwick, John White, *Theodore Parker: Preacher and Reformer*, Boston, 1901.

Channing, William Ellery, *Channing's Works*, ed. George G. Channing, Boston, 1849.

Chapman, John Jay, *William Lloyd Garrison*, New York, 1913.

Charvat, William, *Emerson's American Lecture Engagements: A Chronological List*, New York, 1961.

Chevigny, Bell Gale, *The Woman and the Myth: Margaret Fuller's Life and Writings*, Old Westbury, N.Y., 1976.

Chipperfield, Faith, *In Quest of Love: The Life and Death of Margaret Fuller*, New York, 1957.

Christy, Arthur, *The Orient in American Transcendentalism: A Study of Emerson, Thoreau, and Alcott*, New York, 1932.

Chubb, Edwin Watts, *Stories of Authors, British and American*, New York, 1926.

Clark, John Spencer, *The Life and Letters of John Fiske*, 2 vols., Boston, 1917.

Clarke, James Freeman, *Autobiography, Diary and Correspondence*, ed. E. E. Hale, Boston, 1891.

Clough, Arthur Hugh, *The Poems and Prose Remains of Arthur Hugh Clough*, ed. Blanche Clough, 2 vols., London, 1869.

Codman, John Thomas, *Brook Farm: Historic and Personal Memoirs*, Boston, 1894.

Collis, Jack Stewart, *The Carlyles*, New York, 1971.

Conway, Moncure D., *Life of Nathaniel Hawthorne*, London, 1895.

Cooke, George Willis, *An Historical and Biographical Introduction to Accompany the Dial*, 2 vols., New York, 1961.

————, *John Sullivan Dwight*, Boston, 1898.

————, *Memorabilia of the Transcendentalists in New England*, Hartford, Conn., 1973.

————, *The Poets of Transcendentalism*, Boston, 1903.

Copleston, Frederick, *A History of Philosophy*, 9 vols., Westminster, Md., 1946–1975.

Cranch, Christopher Pearse, *Ariel and Caliban with Other Poems*, Boston, 1887.

————, *Poems*, Philadelphia, 1844.

Crawford, Mary Caroline, *Famous Families of Massachusetts*, 2 vols., Boston, 1930.

————, *Romantic Days in Old Boston*, Boston, 1910.

Cross, W. W., *George Eliot's Life*, London, 1885.

Crothers, Samuel McChord, *Ralph Waldo Emerson: How to Know Him*, Indianapolis, 1921.

Culbreth, D. M. R., *The University of Virginia*, New York, 1908.

Currier, John J., *History of Newburyport, Mass., 1764–1909*, 2 vols., Newburyport, Mass., 1909.

Curtis, Edith Roelker, *Season in Utopia: The Story of Brook Farm*, New York, 1961.

Curtis, George William, *Literary and Social Essays*, New York, 1894.

———, *Little Journeys to the Houses of Famous American Authors*, New York, 1896.

Dabney, Virginius, *Mr. Jefferson's University: A History*, Charlottesville, Va., 1981.

Dall, Caroline Healey, *Margaret and Her Friends*, Boston, 1895.

Deiss, Joseph Jay, *The Roman Years of Margaret Fuller*, New York, 1969.

Derleth, August, *Emerson, Our Contemporary*, New York, 1970.

Dial, The, ed. Margaret Fuller, R. W. Emerson, & H. D. Thoreau, rpt. 4 vols., New York, 1961.

Dickens, Charles, *American Notes*, New York, n.d.

Dillaway, Newton, *Prophet of America: Emerson and the Problems of Today*, Boston, 1936.

Drake, Samuel Adams, *Old Landmarks and Historic Personages of Boston*, Boston, 1906.

Duberman, Martin, *James Russell Lowell*, Boston, 1960.

Duffy, Gavan, *Conversations with Carlyle*, London, 1892.

Duncan, Jeffrey L., *The Power and Form of Emerson's Thought*, Charlottesville, Va., 1973.

Eidson, John Olin, *Charles Stearns Wheeler: Friend of Emerson*, Athens, Ga., 1951.

Eliot, Charles W., *A Late Harvest*, Boston, 1924.

———, *Four American Leaders*, Boston, 1906.

Elliott, Maud Howe, *Three Generations*, Boston, 1923.

Ellis, Arthur B., *History of the First Church in Boston*, Boston, 1881.

Emerson, Benjamin Kendall, and George A. Gordon, *The Ipswich Emersons, A.D. 1636–1900 — A Genealogy of the Descendants of Thomas Emerson of Ipswich, Mass.*, Boston, 1900.

Emerson, Edward Waldo, *Henry Thoreau as Remembered by a Young Friend*, Boston, 1917.

———, *The Early Years of the Saturday Club: 1855–1870*, Boston, 1918.

———, *The Life and Letters of Charles Russell Lowell*, Boston, 1907.

Emerson, Ralph Waldo, *Uncollected Writings: Essays, Addresses, Poems, Reviews and Letters*, New York, 1912.

———, ed., *Parnassus*, Boston, 1875.

Emerson, William, *Diaries and Letters of William Emerson: 1743–1776*, ed. Amelia Forbes Emerson, Concord, 1972.

Emerson, William (1769–1811), *An Historical Sketch of the First Church in Boston*, Boston, 1812.

Emmons, H. H., ed., *Light of Emerson*, Cleveland, Ohio, 1930.

Espinasse, Francis, *Literary Recollections and Sketches*, London, 1893.

Everett, Elizabeth Lowell, *Peter Bulkeley and His Times*, Leominster, Mass., 1935.

Falk, Robert, ed., *Literature and Ideas in America: Essays in Memory of Harry Hayden Clark*, Columbus, Ohio, 1975.

Feidelson, Charles, Jr., *Symbolism and American Literature*, Chicago, 1953.

Fields, James T., *Yesterdays with Authors*, Boston, 1872.

Foerster, Norman, *American Criticism: A Study of Literary Theory from Poe to the Present*, Boston, 1928.

Forbes, John Murray, *Letters and Recollections of John Murray Forbes*, ed. Sarah Forbes Hughes, 2 vols., Boston, 1899.

Forbes, Waldo Emerson, *The Letters and Journals of Waldo Emerson Forbes*, ed. Amelia Forbes Thomas, Philadelphia, 1977.

Forster, John, *The Works and Life of Walter Savage Landor,* 2 vols., London, 1876.

Fox, Caroline, *Memories of Old Friends,* London, 1882.

Fox, Stephen, *John Muir and His Legacy: The American Conservation Movement,* Boston, 1981.

Freese, J. W., *Historic Houses and Spots in Cambridge, Mass., and Near-by Towns,* Boston, 1897.

Frost, Robert, *Complete Poems,* New York, 1949.

Frothingham, Octavius Brooks, *Boston Unitarianism, 1820–1850,* New York, 1890.

———, *George Ripley,* Boston, 1882.

Frothingham, Paul Revere, *Edward Everett: Orator and Statesman,* Boston, 1925.

Froude, James Anthony, *Carlyle's Life in London,* London, 1884.

———, *Life of Carlyle,* ed. John Clubbe, Columbus, Ohio, 1879.

———, *Thomas Carlyle: A History of the First Forty Years of His Life, 1795–1835,* 2 vols., London, 1872.

Fuller, Margaret, *The Letters of Margaret Fuller,* ed. Robert N. Hudspeth, 2 vols., Ithaca, N.Y., 1983.

———, *Woman in the Nineteenth Century,* ed. Arthur B. Fuller, Boston, 1874.

Garnett, Richard, *Life of Thomas Carlyle,* London, 1887.

Garrison, Wendell Phillips and Francis Jackson Garrison, *William Lloyd Garrison, 1805–1879: The Story of His Life, Told by His Children,* 4 vols., New York, 1886–1889.

Goddard, Harold Clarke, *Studies in New England Transcendentalism,* New York, 1908.

Gohdes, Clarence F., *The Periodicals of American Transcendentalism,* Durham, N.C., 1931.

Greeley, Dana McLean, *Know These Concordians,* Concord, Mass., 1975.

Greenslet, Ferris, *The Lowells and Their Seven Worlds,* Boston, 1946.

Guernsey, Alfred H., *Ralph Waldo Emerson: Philosopher and Poet,* Appleton, Wis., 1881.

Haight, Gordon S., ed., *The George Eliot Letters,* 7 vols., New Haven, 1954–1955.

Hale, Edward Everett, *If, Yes, and Perhaps,* rpt. New York, 1969.

———, *James Russell Lowell and His Friends,* Boston, 1899.

———, *Memories of a Hundred Years,* New York, 1904.

———, *Ralph Waldo Emerson,* Boston, 1902.

Hansen, Chadwick, *Witchcraft at Salem,* New York, 1969.

Hansen, Lawrence and Elizabeth, *Necessary Evil: The Life of Jane Welsh Carlyle,* New York, 1952.

Harding, Walter, *Emerson's Library,* Charlottesville, Va., 1967.

———, *The Days of Henry Thoreau,* New York, 1965.

Harrison, John S., *The Teachers of Emerson,* New York, 1910.

Hawthorne, Julian, *The Memoirs of Julian Hawthorne,* ed. Edith G. Hawthorne, 2 vols., New York, 1938.

Hayes, Rutherford B., *Diary and Letters of Rutherford Birchard Hayes,* ed. Charles R. Williams, Columbus, Ohio, 1922.

Hendrick, George, ed., *Remembrances of Concord and the Thoreaus,* Urbana, Ill., 1977.

Higginson, Thomas Wentworth, *Cheerful Yesterdays,* Boston, 1898.

———, *Margaret Fuller Ossoli,* Boston, 1884.

———, *Short Studies of American Authors,* Boston, 1879.

Hoeltje, Hubert H., *Inward Sky: The Mind and Heart of Nathaniel Haw-thorne*, Durham, N.C., 1962.

———, *Sheltering Tree: A Story of the Friendship of Ralph Waldo Emerson and Amos Bronson Alcott*, Port Washington, N.Y., 1943.

Holloway, Mark, *Heavens on Earth: Utopian Communities in America, 1680–1880*, New York, 1966.

Holmes, John, *Letters of John Holmes to James Russell Lowell and Others*, ed. William Roscoe Thayer, Boston, 1917.

Holmes, Oliver Wendell, *Over the Teacups*, Boston, 1891.

———, *Poems*, London, 1846.

Horgan, Edward R., *The Shaker Holy Land: A Community Portrait*, Harvard, Mass., 1982.

Horton, Rod W., and Herbert W. Edwards, *Backgrounds of American Literary Thought*, New York, 1952.

Howard, Leon, *Victorian Knight Errant*, Berkeley, Calif., 1952.

Howe, Julia Ward, *Reminiscences: 1819–1899*, Boston, 1900.

Howe, M. A. DeWolfe, *John Jay Chapman and His Letters*, Boston, 1937.

———, ed., *The Articulate Sisters: Passages from Journals and Letters of the Daughters of President Josiah Quincy of Harvard University*, Cambridge, Mass., 1946.

Howells, William Dean, *Literary Friends and Acquaintances*, New York, 1900.

Huggard, William A., *The Religious Teachings of Emerson*, New York, 1972.

Hutchison, William R., *The Transcendental Ministers: Church Reform in the New England Renaissance*, New Haven, 1959.

Hyder, Clyde Kenneth, *Swinburne's Literary Career and Fame*, Durham, N.C., 1933.

Ireland, Alexander, ed., *Ralph Waldo Emerson: His Life, Genius, and Writings*, London, 1882.

Irie, Yukio, *Emerson and Quakerism*, Tokyo, 1967.

Jackson, Holbrook, *Dreamers of Dreams: The Rise and Fall of Nineteenth Century Idealism*, New York, n.d.

James, Henry, *Charles W. Eliot: President of Harvard 1869–1909*, 2 vols., New York, 1930.

James, Henry, Jr., *Notes of a Son and Brother*, London, 1914.

———, *Partial Portraits*, London, 1888.

James, Henry, Sr., *The Literary Remains of the Late Henry James*, ed. and intro. by William James, Boston, 1885.

Johnson, Edgar, *Charles Dickens: His Tragedy and Triumph*, 2 vols., New York, 1952.

Kaledin, Eugenia, *The Education of Mrs. Henry Adams*, Philadelphia, 1981.

Kaplan, Justin, *Walt Whitman: A Life*, New York, 1980.

Kazin, Alfred, *On Native Grounds*, New York, 1942.

Konvitz, Milton R., ed., *The Recognition of Ralph Waldo Emerson*, Ann Arbor, Mich., 1972.

Lader, Lawrence, *The Bold Brahmins*, New York, 1961.

Lenhart, Charmenz, *Musical Influence on American Poetry*, Atlanta, 1956.

Levin, David, ed., *Emerson: Prophecy, Metamorphosis and Influence*, New York, 1975.

Lothrop, Samuel Kirkland, *Some Reminiscences of the Life of Samuel Kirkland Lothrop*, ed. Thornton Kirkland Lothrop, Cambridge, Mass., 1888.

Lovejoy, Arthur Oucker, *The Reason, the Understanding, and Time*, Baltimore, 1961.

Loving, Jerome, *Walt Whitman's Champion: William Douglas O'Connor*, College Station, Tex., 1978.

Lowell, James Russell, *Letters of James Russell Lowell,* ed. Charles Eliot Norton, 2 vols., Boston, 1904.
———, *My Study Windows,* Boston, 1871.
———, *New Letters of James Russell Lowell,* ed. Mark A. DeWolfe Howe, New York, 1932.
———, *Poetical Works,* Boston, 1890.
———, *Uncollected Poems,* ed. Thelma M. Smith, Philadelphia, 1950.
Luce, Gay Gaer, *Body Time: Physiological Rhythms and Social Stress,* New York, 1971.
Lyon, Kenneth, *William Dean Howells: An American Life,* New York, 1971.
McCall, Samuel W., *Daniel Webster,* Boston, 1902.
McGill, Frederick, Jr., *Channing of Concord: A Life of William Ellery Channing, II,* New Brunswick, N.J., 1967.
McKinsey, Elizabeth R., *The Western Experiment: New England Transcendentalism in the Ohio Valley,* Cambridge, Mass., 1973.
Martineau, Harriet, *Autobiography,* ed. Maria Weston Chapman, London, 1877.
———, *Retrospect of Western Travel,* 2 vols., London, 1838.
Matthiessen, F. O., *The James Family,* New York, 1947.
Mead, C. David, ed., *"The American Scholar" Today,* New York, 1970.
Mead, David, *Yankee Eloquence in the Middle West: The Ohio Lyceum, 1850–1880,* East Lansing, Mich., 1951.
Mead, Edwin D., *Emerson and Parker,* Boston, 1910.
Meltzer, Milton, and Walter Harding, eds., *A Thoreau Profile,* Concord, Mass., 1962.
Messerli, Jonathan, *Horace Mann,* New York, 1972.
Metzger, Charles R., *Emerson and Greenough: Transcendental Pioneers of an American Esthetic,* Berkeley, Calif., 1954.
Michaud, Regis, *Emerson: The Enraptured Yankee,* New York, 1930.
Miles, Josephine, *Ralph Waldo Emerson,* Minneapolis, 1964.
Miller, F. DeWolfe, *Christopher Pearse Cranch: And His Caricatures of New England Transcendentalism,* Cambridge, Mass., 1951.
Morison, Samuel Eliot, *Harvard in the Seventeenth Century,* 2 vols., Cambridge, Mass., 1936.
———, *The Founding of Harvard College,* Cambridge, Mass., 1935.
———, *Three Centuries of Harvard: 1636–1936,* Cambridge, Mass., 1936.
Morris, Lloyd, *The Rebellious Puritan: Portrait of Mr. Hawthorne,* New York, 1927.
Morse, John T., *Life and Letters of Oliver Wendell Holmes,* 2 vols., Boston, 1896.
———, *Memoir of Colonel Henry Lee,* Boston, 1905.
Muir, John, *Our National Parks,* Boston, 1901.
Mumford, Lewis, *Herman Melville,* New York, 1929.
———, *The Golden Day: A Study in American Experience and Culture,* New York, 1926.
Munroe, Alfred, *Concord Sketches,* Concord, Mass., 1903.
Murdock, Harold, *The Nineteenth of April, 1775,* Boston, 1923.
Murdock, Kenneth, *Literature and Theology in Colonial New England,* Cambridge, Mass., 1949.
Muzzey, A. B., *Reminiscences and Memorials of Men of the Revolution and Their Families,* Boston, 1883.
Myerson, Joel, *The New England Transcendentalists and The Dial: A History of the Magazine and its Contributors,* Rutherford, N.J., 1980.
———, ed., *Emerson Centenary Essays,* Carbondale and Edwardsville, Ill., 1982.

————, ed., *Studies in the American Renaissance*, Boston, 1979.

Nagel, Paul C., *Descent from Glory: Four Generations of the John Adams Family*, New York, 1983.

Neufeldt, Leonard, *The House of Emerson*, Lincoln, Neb., 1982.

————, ed., *Ralph Waldo Emerson: New Appraisals: A Symposium*, Hartford, Conn., 1973.

Nicoloff, Philip L., *Emerson on Race and History*, New York, 1961.

Norton, Charles Eliot, ed., *The Correspondence of Thomas Carlyle and Ralph Waldo Emerson 1834–1872*, 2 vols., Boston, 1883–1884.

Noyes, Alfred, *Pageant of Letters*, New York, 1940.

Noyes, Sybil, Charles Thornton Libby, and Walter Goodwin Davis, *Genealogical Dictionary of Maine and New Hampshire*, Baltimore, 1972.

Osborne, John Insley, *Arthur Hugh Clough*, Boston, 1920.

Paton, Lucy Allen, *Elizabeth Cary Agassiz: A Biography*, Boston, 1919.

Paul, Sherman, *Emerson's Angle of Vision: Man and Nature in American Experience*, Cambridge, Mass., 1952.

————, *The Shores of America: Thoreau's Inward Exploration*, Urbana, Ill., 1958.

Peabody, Elizabeth Palmer, *Reminiscences of William Ellery Channing*, Boston, 1880.

Perry, Bliss, *The Praise of Folly, and Other Papers*, Boston, 1923.

Perry, Ralph Barton, *The Thought and Character of William James*, 2 vols., Boston, 1935.

Pier, Arthur Stanwood, *The Story of Harvard*, Boston, 1913.

Porte, Joel, *Emerson and Thoreau: Transcendentalists in Conflict*, Middletown, Conn., 1966.

————, *Representative Man: Ralph Waldo Emerson in His Time*, New York, 1979.

Porter, David, *Emerson and Literary Change*, Cambridge, Mass., 1978.

Quincy, Josiah, *Figures of the Past*, Boston, 1926.

Rantoul, Robert S., *Personal Recollections*, Cambridge, Mass., 1916.

Reaver, J. Russell, *Emerson as Mythmaker*, Gainesville, Fla., 1954.

Ripley, Ezra, *A History of the Fight at Concord on the 19th of April, 1775*, Concord, Mass., 1827.

Robinson, David, *Apostle of Culture: Emerson as Preacher and Lecturer*, Philadelphia, 1982.

Rossiter, William S., *Days and Ways in Old Boston*, Boston, 1915.

Rountree, Thomas J., *Critics on Emerson*, Coral Gables, Fla., 1973.

Russell, Phillips, *Emerson: The Wisest American*, New York, 1929.

Salyer, Sandford, *Marmee: The Mother of Little Women*, Norman, Okla., 1949.

Sams, Henry W., ed., *Autobiography of Brook Farm*, Englewood Cliffs, N.J., 1958.

Sanborn, Franklin Benjamin, *Henry D. Thoreau*, Boston, 1882.

————, *Ralph Waldo Emerson*, Boston, 1901.

————, *The Life of Henry David Thoreau*, Boston, 1917.

————, *The Personality of Emerson*, Boston, 1903.

————, *Transcendental and Literary New England*, ed. Kenneth W. Cameron, Hartford, Conn., 1975.

————, ed., *The Genius and Character of Emerson: Lectures at the Concord School of Philosophy*, Boston, 1885.

Sayre, Robert L., *Thoreau and the American Indians*, Princeton, 1977.

Schlesinger, Arthur M., Jr., *Orestes A. Brownson: A Pilgrim's Progress*, Boston, 1939.

Scott, Leonora Cranch, *The Life and Letters of Christopher Pearse Cranch*, Boston, 1917.

Scott, William B., *Memoir of David Scott*, Edinburgh, 1850.

Scudder, Townsend, *Concord: American Town*, Boston, 1947.

Sealts, Merton M., Jr., and Alfred R. Ferguson, eds., *Emerson's Nature — Origin, Growth, Meaning*, New York, 1969.

Searle, January [Phillips, George Searle], *Emerson: His Life and Writings*, London, 1855.

Shackleton, Robert, *The Book of Boston*, Philadelphia, 1916.

Shattuck, Lemuel, *A History of the Town of Concord*, Boston, 1835, rpt. Clinton, Mass., 1971.

Shepard, William, ed., *Pen Pictures of Modern Authors*, New York, 1882.

Shurtleff, Nathaniel B., *A Topographical and Historical Description of Boston*, Boston, 1891.

Smalley, George W., *Anglo-Saxon Memories*, New York, 1911.

Snow, Edward Rowe, *New England Storms and Shipwrecks*, Boston, 1943.

Social Circle of Concord, *The Centenary of the Birth of Ralph Waldo Emerson*, Concord, Mass., 1903.

Sowder, William J., *Emerson's Impact on the British Isles and Canada*, Charlottesville, Va., 1966.

Stacton, David, *The Bonapartes*, New York, 1966.

Starkey, Marion L., *The Devil in Massachusetts: A Modern Enquiry into the Salem Witch Trials*, New York, 1961.

Stearns, Frank Preston, *Sketches from Concord and Appledore*, New York, 1895.

Stern, Madeleine B., *The Life of Margaret Fuller*, New York, 1942.

Stillman, William J., *The Autobiography of a Journalist*, Boston, 1901.

Storey, Moorfield, and Edward Waldo Emerson, *Ebenezer Rockwood Hoar: A Memoir*, Boston, 1911.

Strouse, Jean, *Alice James: A Biography*, Boston, 1980.

Swift, Lindsay, *Brook Farm: Its Members, Scholars, and Visitors*, Boston, 1900.

———, *William Lloyd Garrison*, Philadelphia, 1911.

Symington, Andrew J., *Some Personal Reminiscences of Carlyle*, Paisley, Scotland, 1886.

Teale, Edwin Way, ed., *The Wilderness World of John Muir*, Boston, 1954.

Tharp, Louise Hall, *The Peabody Sisters of Salem*, Boston, 1950.

Thayer, James B., *Rev. Samuel Ripley of Waltham*, Cambridge, Mass., 1897.

Thomas, Henry and Dana Lee Thomas, *Living Biographies of Great Philosophers*, New York, 1941.

Thoreau, Henry David, *Walden*, rpt. Boston, 1964.

Ticknor, Caroline, ed., *Classic Concord*, Boston, 1926.

Tilton, Eleanor M., *Amiable Autocrat: A Biography of Dr. Oliver Wendell Holmes*, New York, 1947.

Tolman, George, *Mary Moody Emerson*, privately printed, 1929.

Trowbridge, John Townsend, *My Own Story: With Recollections of Noted Persons*, Boston, 1903.

Tryon, W. S., *Parnassus Corner: A Life of James T. Fields, Publisher to the Victorians*, Boston, 1963.

Turner, Arlin, *Nathaniel Hawthorne: A Biography*, New York, 1980.

Upham, Charles W., *Salem Witchcraft*, 2 vols., Boston, 1867.

Vanderbilt, Kermit, *Charles Eliot Norton: Apostle of Culture in a Democracy*, Cambridge, Mass., 1959.

Wade, Mason, *Margaret Fuller: Whetstone of Genius*, New York, 1940.

Wagenknecht, Edward, *Longfellow*, New York, 1955.
———, ed., *Mrs. Longfellow: Selected Letters and Journal of Fanny Appleton Longfellow (1817–1861)*, New York, 1956.
Waggoner, Hyatt H., *Emerson as Poet*, Princeton, N.J., 1974.
Ward, A. W., and A. R. Waller, eds., *The Cambridge History of English Literature*, 14 vols., Cambridge, 1914.
Warren, Austin, *The Elder Henry James*, New York, 1934.
Weiss, John, *Discourse Occasioned by the Death of Convers Francis*, Cambridge, Mass., 1863.
———, *Life and Correspondence of Theodore Parker*, New York, 1863.
Wendell, Barrett, *A Literary History of America*, New York, 1900.
Wheeler, Ruth R., *Concord: Climate for Freedom*, Concord, Mass., 1967.
Whicher, Stephen, *Freedom and Fate: An Inner Life of Ralph Waldo Emerson*, Philadelphia, 1953.
Whipple, Edwin Percy, *Recollections of Eminent Men*, Boston, 1887.
Whiting, Lilian, *Boston Days*, Boston, 1902.
Whitman, Walt, *Collected Writings of Walt Whitman*, ed. Floyd Stovall, New York, 1892.
Willis, Nathaniel P. *Hurry-graphs; or, Sketches of Scenery, Celebrities and Society, Taken from Life*, New York, 1851.
Wilson, Ellen, *Margaret Fuller, Bluestocking, Romantic, Revolutionary*, New York, 1977.
Winsor, Justin, *The Memorial History of Boston*, 4 vols., Boston, 1880–1881.
Wolfe, Linnie Marsh, *Son of the Wilderness: The Life of John Muir*, New York, 1945.
———, ed., *John of the Mountains: The Unpublished Journals of John Muir*, Boston, 1938.
Wright, Conrad, *The Beginnings of Unitarianism in America*, Boston, 1955.
Wright, Nathalia, *Horatio Greenough: The First American Sculptor*, Philadelphia, 1963.
Wynkoop, William, *Three Children of the Universe: Emerson's View of Shakespeare, Bacon, and Milton*, London, 1966.
Yee, Chiang, *The Silent Traveller in Boston*, New York, 1959.
Yoder, R. A., *Emerson and the Orphic Poet in America*, Berkeley, Calif., 1978.
Young, Charles Lowell, *Emerson's Montaigne*, New York, 1941.

Index

ESSAYS AND LECTURES *(continued)*
"Heroism," 531; "Historical Discourse at Concord," 244; "History," 161; "Holiness," 272; "Hospitality, Homes," 585; "Human Culture," 5, 276; "Immortality," 500, 599; "Lecture on the Times," 377, 385, 515, 518; "Literary Ethics," 151, 259, 267–270; "Love," 113; "Man the Reformer," 367, 516; "The Man with the Hoe," 279; "Memory," 305; "The Method of Nature," 357–369, 518; "Modern Aspects of Letters," 236, 457; "The Natural and Permanent Function of the Scholar," 634; "Nature and Art," 583; "The Natural History of the Intellect," 592; "New England Reformers," 310, 516; "The Over-Soul," 160, 161, 167; "The Poet," 166, 415; "Poetry," 545; "Poetry and Imagination," 546, 559, 586; "Power," 236; "The Present Age," 297; "The Progress of Culture," 582; "Reforms," 294; "Resources,"599;"Schools in American Literature," 237; "Self-Possession," 279; "Self-Reliance," 9, 161, 518; "Social Aims," 576; "Society in America," 599; "The Spirit of the Times," 377, 385, 484; "Spiritual Laws," 514; "The Uses of Natural History," 171; "Works and Days," xiii, 498; "Worship," 506, 589, 656; "The Young American," 516

SERMONS

"A Feast of Remembrance," 117; "The Genuine Man," 125; "The Lord's Supper," 117–127, 312; "On Showing Piety at Home," 530; "Pray without Ceasing," 86–87, 88, 92; "Summer," 228; "The Uses of Unhappiness," 92

POEMS

"The Adirondacs," 555; "The Boston Hymn," 559, 574; "Dirge," 656; "Good-bye, Proud World!" 69, 210; "Grace," 38; "The History of

Fortus," 43–44; "The Humblebee," 9, 62; "Indian Superstitions," 558; "Initial, Daemonic, and Celestial Love," 114, 516; "May-Day," 501; "Monadnoc," 78; "The Pilgrims," 573; "The Problem," 190, 292, 293, 666; "Quatrains," 547; "The Romany Girl," 559; "The Sacred Dance," 547; "Seashore," 550–552; "Terminus," 598, 627; "Threnody," 304, 313, 372, 380–381, 383, 656; "Uriel," 265–266; "Voluntaries," 4; "Woodnotes," 62, 604; "The World-Soul," 314

Emerson, Rebecca (aunt), 197, 417
Emerson, Rebecca Waldo (great-great grandmother), 12
Emerson, Robert Bulkeley (brother), 23, 63, 64, 83, 93, 96, 106, 108, 351
Emerson, Ruth Haskins (mother), 12, 15, 16, 19, 21, 22, 23–24, 26, 27, 31, 41–42, 45, 48, 49, 60, 63, 68, 80, 84, 93, 95, 96, 105, 115, 152, 182, 201, 207, 268, 351, 359–360, 376, 402, 403, 406, 510, 536–537, 664
Emerson, Susan Haven, 212, 273, 340, 342, 502
Emerson, Thomas (great-great-great-great grandfather), 122, 273
Emerson, Waldo (son), 36, 100, 109, 115–116, 157, 210, 211, 227, 313, 361, 362, 370–383, 398, 405, 458, 661, 664, 665
Emerson, William (grandfather), 17, 29–30, 65, 72, 81, 95, 179, 189, 191–198, 228, 240, 420, 518–519
Emerson, William (father), 11, 12–26 *passim,* 26, 31, 35, 37, 40–45 *passim,* 48, 81, 86, 95, 119, 182, 183, 188, 299, 360, 362, 614, 693
Emerson, William (brother), 16, 19, 21, 24, 26, 27, 29, 40, 41, 47, 49, 51, 53, 56, 57, 59, 66, 67, 70, 80, 83, 84, 90, 92, 93, 96, 106, 108, 110, 118, 119, 121, 124, 208, 212, 222, 228, 229, 258, 273, 280, 311, 317, 320–321, 339, 340, 342, 361, 372, 377, 428, 495, 504, 524, 537
Emerson, William (nephew), 340, 344
Emerson, William Ralph, 615
Engel, Mary Miller, 557